Science Fiction
and Fantasy Authors

L. W. Currey

With the editorial assistance
of David G. Hartwell

April 13, 1980
For Charlie!
Bibliographical
minutae for a
fellow collector.
From Lloyd

Science Fiction and Fantasy Authors

A Bibliography of First Printings of Their Fiction and Selected Nonfiction

G. K. Hall & Co.   Boston, Massachusetts

Library of Congress Cataloging in Publication Data
Currey, L W
  Science fiction and fantasy authors.

  1. Science fiction, American—Bibliography—
First editions. 2. Science fiction, English—
Bibliography—First editions. 3. Fantastic fiction,
American—Bibliography—First editions. 4. Fantastic
fiction, English—Bibliography—First editions.
I. Hartwell, David G. II. Title.
Z1231.F5C87   [PS374.S35]   016.823′0876   79-18217
ISBN 0-8161-8242-6

This publication is printed on permanent/durable acid-free paper
MANUFACTURED IN THE UNITED STATES OF AMERICA

FOR ALIDA

Contents

x   Contents

Pseudonyms

Adams, Chuck   Edwin Charles Tubb

Akers, Alan Burt   Henry Kenneth Bulmer

Anthony, Piers   Piers Anthony Dillingham Jacob

Archer, Ron   Theodore Edward White

Aston, James   Terence Hanbury White

Atheling, William, Jr.   James Benjamin Blish

Avery, Richard   Edmund Cooper

Barclay, Bill   Michael John Moorcock

Barry, Mike   Barry N. Malzberg

Bass, T. J.   Thomas J. Bassler

Beynon, John   John Wyndham Parkes Lucas Beynon Harris

Binder, Eando   Otto Oscar Binder

Blake, Ken   Henry Kenneth Bulmer

Bliss, Reginald   Herbert George Wells

Bok, Hannes   Wayne Woodard

Boyd, John   Boyd Bradfield Upchurch

Bradbury, Edward P   Michael John Moorcock

Butler, Nathan   Gerald Allan Sohl

Carnac, Levin   George Chetwynd Griffith-Jones

Cary, Judy   Edwin Charles Tubb

Chapman, Lee   Marion Eleanor Zimmer Bradley

Charteris, Leslie   Harry Maxwell Harrison

Cherryh, C. J.   Carolyn Janice Cherry

Christopher, John   Christopher Samuel Youd

Clarkson, J. F.   Edwin Charles Tubb

Clement, Hal   Harry Clement Stubbs

Coleridge, John   Otto Oscar Binder

Colvin, James   Michael John Moorcock

Compton, Guy   David Guy Compton

Corley, Ernest   Henry Kenneth Bulmer

Cowper, Richard   John Middleton Murry

Curtis, Wade   Jerry Pournelle

Demijohn, Thom   Thomas Michael Disch and John T. Sladek

Dexter, John   Marion Eleanor Zimmer Bradley

Di Natale, Francine   Barry N. Malzberg

Dumas, Claudine   Barry N. Malzberg

Edwards, Norman   Theodore Edward White

Eisner, Simon   Cyril M. Kornbluth

Ewing, Frederick R.   Theodore Hamilton Sturgeon and Jean Sheperd

Fairman, Paul W.   Lester del Rey

Falk, Lee   Ronald Joseph Goulart

Farley, Ralph Milne   Roger Sherman Hoar

Farrow, James S.   Edwin Charles Tubb

Fenner, James R.   Edwin Charles Tubb

Field, Gans T.   Manly Wade Wellman

Finney, Jack   Walter Braden Finney

Fletcher, George U.   Fletcher Pratt

Ford, Hilary   Christopher Samuel Youd

Forrest, Felix C.   Paul Myron Anthony Linebarger

Fowler, Sydney   Sydney Fowler Wright

Frazier, Arthur   Henry Kenneth Bulmer

French, Paul   Isaac Asimov

Gardner, Miriam   Marion Eleanor Zimmer Bradley

Gerrold, David   Jerrold David Friedman

Gilmore, Anthony   Harry Bates

Godfrey, William   Christopher Samuel Youd

Gordon, Rex   Stanley Bennett Hough

Graaf, Peter   Christopher Samuel Youd

Graham, Charles S.   Edwin Charles Tubb

Graham, Robert   Joseph W. Haldeman

Grandrith, Lord   Philip Jose Farmer

Graves, Valerie   Marion Eleanor Zimmer Bradley

Grendon, Stephen   August Derleth

Grey, Charles   Edwin Charles Tubb

Gridban, Volsted   Edwin Charles Tubb

Grinnell, David   Donald Allen Wollheim

Hardy, Adam   Henry Kenneth Bulmer

Hargrave, Leonie   Thomas Michael Disch

Harris, Johnson   John Wyndham Parkes Lucas Beynon Harris

Harris, Roger   Michael John Moorcock

Harrison, Bruce   Edgar Pangborn

Held, Peter   John Holbrook Vance

Homesley, Leatrice   Philip Gordon Wylie

Hull, E. Mayne   Alfred Elton van Vogt

Hunt, Gill   John Kilian Houston Brunner

Hunt, Gill   Edwin Charles Tubb

Ives, Morgan   Marion Eleanor Zimmer Bradley

Jackson, E. F.   Edwin Charles Tubb

Johnson, M. L.   Barry N. Malzberg

Johnson, Mel   Barry N. Malzberg

Jorgenson, Ivar   Robert Silverberg

Judd, Cyril   Cyril M. Kornbluth and Judith Merril

Kent, Philip   Henry Kenneth Bulmer

Kern, Gregory   Edwin Charles Tubb

Knox, Calvin M.   Robert Silverberg

Knye, Cassandra   Thomas Michael Disch and John T. Sladek

Knye, Cassandra   John T. Sladek

Lang, King   Edwin Charles Tubb

Langart, Darrel T.   Gordon Randall Philip David Garrett

Langholm, Neil   Henry Kenneth Bulmer

Lantry, Mike   Edwin Charles Tubb

Lasly, Walt   Frederik Pohl

Lawrence, P.   Edwin Charles Tubb

Lawson, Chet   Edwin Charles Tubb

Le Baron, Anthony   John Keith Laumer

Lee, Howard   Ronald Joseph Goulart

Lee, Howard   Barry N. Malzberg

Leinster, Murray   William Fitzgerald Jenkins

Long, Lyda Belknap   Frank Belknap Long

Lucas, George   Alan Dean Foster

Luther, Ray   Robert Arthur Ley

Lynch, Frances   David Guy Compton

McCann, Edson   Lester del Rey and Frederik Pohl

McIntosh, J. T.   James Murdoch Macgregor

M'Intosh, J. T.   James Murdoch Macgregor

Maddox, Carl   Edwin Charles Tubb

Maine, Charles Eric   David McIlwain

Maras, Karl   Henry Kenneth Bulmer

Margulies, Leo   Sam Moskowitz

Mason, Lee W.   Barry N. Malzberg

Merchant, Paul   Harlan Jay Ellison

Milligan, William   William Milligan Sloane III

Morich, Stanton   George Chetwynd Griffith-Jones

Murry, Colin   John Middleton Murry

Murry, Colin Middleton   John Middleton Murry

Nichols, Peter   Christopher Samuel Youd

Norman, John   John Frederick Lange, Jr.

North, Andrew   Andre Norton

Norvil, Manning   Henry Kenneth Bulmer

O'Donnell, K. M.   Barry N. Malzberg

Osborne, David   Robert Silverberg

Padgett, Lewis   Henry Kuttner

Padgett, Lewis   Henry Kuttner and Catherine Lucile Moore

Park, Jordan   Cyril M. Kornbluth

Park, Jordan   Cyril M. Kornbluth and Frederik Pohl

Parkes, Lucas   John Wyndham Parkes Lucas Beynon Harris

Phillips, Mark   Gordon Randall Philip David Garrett

Pike, Charles R.   Henry Kenneth Bulmer

Powers, M. L.   Edwin Charles Tubb

Queen, Ellery   Avram Davidson

Queen, Ellery   Theodore Hamilton Sturgeon

Queen, Ellery   John Holbrook Vance

Quiller, Andrew   Henry Kenneth Bulmer

Randall, Robert   Gordon Randall Philip David Garrett and Robert Silverberg

Rankine, John   Douglas Rankine Mason

Rayner, Richard   David McIlwain

Reid, Desmond   Michael John Moorcock

Reynolds, Mack   Dallas McCord Reynolds

Reynolds, Maxine   Dallas McCord Reynolds

Robeson, Kenneth   Ronald Joseph Goulart

Robinson, Spider   Paul Robinson

Rye, Anthony   Christopher Samuel Youd

St. John, Philip   Lester del Rey

Sanders, George   Leigh Brackett

Sellings, Arthur   Robert Arthur Ley

Serling, Rod   Gordon Rupert Dickson

Shaw, Brian   Edwin Charles Tubb

Shaw, Frank S.   Ronald Joseph Goulart

Shawn, Frank S.   Ronald Joseph Goulart

Sheldon, Roy   Edwin Charles Tubb

Silva, Joseph   Ronald Joseph Goulart

Silver, Richard   Henry Kenneth Bulmer

Smith, Carmichael   Paul Myron Anthony Linebarger

Smith, Cordwainer   Paul Myron Anthony Linebarger

Stacy, Donald   Frederick Pohl

Stanley, Bennett   Stanley Bennett Hough

Steffanson, Con   Ronald Joseph Goulart

Sterling, Brett   Edmond Moore Hamilton

Stevens, Francis   Gertrude (Barrows) Bennett

Stevens, John   Edwin Charles Tubb

Stewart, Will   Jack (John Stewart) Williamson

Sullivan, Sean Mei   Gerald Allan Sohl

Taine, John   Eric Temple Bell

Tenn, William   Philip J. Klass

Thomson, Edward   Edwin Charles Tubb

Tiptree, James, Jr.   Alice Sheldon

Trout, Kilgore   Philip José Farmer

Turek, Ian Francis   Otto Oscar Binder

Turek, Ione Frances   Otto Oscar Binder

van Lhin, Erik   Lester del Rey

Vance, Jack   John Holbrook Vance

Wade, Alan   John Holbrook Vance

Watkins, Gerrold   Barry N. Malzberg

Watson, John H., M. D.   Philip José Farmer

Weston, Allen   Andre Norton and Grace Allen Hogarth

Wingrave, Anthony   Sydney Fowler Wright

Woodcott, Keith   John Kilian Houston Brunner

Wright, Kenneth	Lester del Rey
Wyndham, John	John Wyndham Parkes Lucas Beynon Harris
Youd, Samuel	Christopher Samuel Youd
Young, Collier	Robert Albert Bloch
Zetford, Tully	Henry Kenneth Bulmer

Introduction

What purpose is served by the collection of rare books is no more
to be argued here than why is golf or music. First editions are
collected to the interest and edification of an increasing number of
persons, and these lists are for the service of those people and of
dealers who supply the wants of collectors.—Merle Johnson,
American First Editions *(1929)*

There has long been a need for an extensive bibliographic checklist of major and/or important writers in the fantasy and science fiction genres. Currently there is strong growth of interest in these areas among both academics and private collectors. Interest in these genres is wide spread and is comparable to a similar phenomenon which occured in the 1930's—the emergence of collector interest in detective fiction.

Both scholars and collectors have faced a major obstacle in their quest for bibliographic details pertaining to fantasy and science fiction books. Previously published bibliographies and checklists were often incomplete and inaccurate, and, at present, most are outdated as well. These earlier works were prepared in part from secondary sources and often the books listed had not actually been examined by compilers. Most recent bibliographic work in these genres has been severely limited in scope. The pioneer general checklists—Everett F. Bleiler (editor), *The Checklist of Fantastic Literature: A Bibliography of Fantasy, Weird, and Science Fiction Books Published in the English Language* (Chicago: Shasta Publishers, 1948),[1] Bradford M. Day, *The Supplemental Checklist of Fantastic Literature* (Denver, New York: Science-Fiction & Fantasy Publications, 1963), and Bradford M. Day, *The Checklist of Fantastic Literature in Paperbound Books* (Denver, New York: Science-Fiction & Fantasy Publications, 1965)—were followed by an avalanche of single-author checklists, specialty press and single-publisher checklists, and subgenre checklists (utopian fiction, the interplanetary novel, the tale of the future and others).

To date, only two general research tools in fantasy and science fiction author bibliography have been published. The first, R. Reginald (pseudonym of M. R. Burgess), *Stella Nova: The Contemporary Science Fiction Authors* (Los Angeles: Unicorn & Son, 1970), remains a comprehensive reference work for contemporary science fiction authors. While useful, it does have faults. The 483 authors covered had to be actively publishing during the period 1960–1968. As a result, some major twentieth-century science fiction authors are excluded. Also the author checklists are recorded in the compiler's peculiar bibliographic shorthand—difficult for one familiar with the material to interpret and virtually impossible for use by others, save for constant referral to the list of unique abbreviations.[2] The second and the more comprehensive general science fiction and fantasy author bibliography is Donald H. Tuck, *The Encyclopedia of Science Fiction and Fantasy Through 1968* (Chicago: Advent, 1974–1978), of which two of the projected three volumes have been published. The culmination of more than twenty years of research, this work is, in fact, the third edition of Tuck's *A Handbook of Science Fiction and Fantasy.*[3] Tuck stresses in his introduction that the encyclopedia compliments the 1948 Bleiler *Checklist*, and "can be considered as a sort of continuation to that book." The two published volumes comprise biographical sketches and briefly annotated author checklists. The bibliographies are incomplete and occasionally inaccurate. Additionally, the author checklists are carried only to 1968, resulting in a decade-long gap in the listings of contemporary writers.

Neither the general science fiction and fantasy bibliographies described above nor the more specialized single-author or subject checklists have addressed the problem of identifying and describing first editions.

Scope and Coverage

Each book entry in *Science Fiction and Fantasy Authors: A Bibliography of First Printings of Their Fiction and Selected Nonfiction* includes sufficient data to identify the first printing of the book, as well as subsequent printings and editions of interest to researchers and collectors. The author checklists were compiled over a five-year period beginning in 1975. Both scope and format evolved during that time, and the work was subject to constant modification. For most of the subject authors, no adequate bibliography or checklist was available, and a substantial amount of original research was required to prepare their checklists. None of these lists is intended to replace a comprehensive author checklist or descriptive bibliography. However, where possible, considerable effort was made to supplement or correct previously published bibliographical data when these bibliographies were found to be outdated or inaccurate. Over ninety-eight percent of the listed titles have been examined by the compiler, including all known printings and states and issues within the first printing, as well as binding and dust jacket variants. Entries for the few items not seen are preceded by an asterisk. Although titles so marked are potential ghost entries, they have been included when reliable information has been obtained from secondary sources. This procedure has laid to rest a high percentage of phantom titles listed in earlier bibliographies and corrected much previously published misinformation. Some of the lists are more detailed than others, and a few can only be regarded as a foundation upon which a more substantial checklist can be constructed. Nevertheless, partial information is preferable to no information. By publishing what is known, the compiler hopes to stimulate further bibliographical inquiry.

These author checklists are designed to provide two primary services: (1) to present for each subject author a complete record of all fiction and selected nonfiction published in book, pamphlet, or broadside format through 31 December 1977; and (2) to present descriptions which will enable the reader to identify both first printings and any other significant printings and editions. To aid researchers and collectors, in addition to a description of the first printing of the first edition, a description of the first hardcover printing of any book preceded by a paperback printing (or printings) has been provided. Moreover, later printings or editions with title changes or revised texts, as well as reprint collections with rearranged contents, abridgements, or enlargements are included. These supplementary entries follow the main entry under the heading "ALSO," or in the case of title changes are positioned in their appropriate alphabetical location within the author checklist. Most double-novel reprint collections are omitted. These include new combinations of Ace Doubles, Science Fiction Book Club combinations of Burrough's Mars series (*Swords of Mars and Synthetic Men of Mars, Thuvia, Maid of Mars and The Chessman of Mars*, and others), and various combinations of H. G. Wells's novels issued in London by The Literary Press and Odhams (later reissued by Collins). The first English-language printing is given preference even if a foreign-language printing was issued earlier (as was *Orphans of the Sky* by Robert A. Heinlein). Earlier printings in the English language published outside the United States and the United Kingdom are excluded (*The Sign of the Burning Hart* by David Keller for example).

Each author checklist provides a core list of book fiction, including prose dramatic works. Where applicable, additional sections include: (1) edited books of fiction; (2) translated books of fiction; (3) associational fiction (books by others based on the subject author's fictional work); (4) nonfiction relating to science fiction and fantasy, autobiography, interviews, letters, and journals (other nonfiction, poetry, and verse plays are excluded); and (5) biographical, bibliographical, and critical works concerning the subject author. Periodical literature is excluded in all sections. Wherever possible, significant reference material published through June 1979 has been included. In every case when a complete bibliography exists, it is listed. References for C. S. Lewis, J. R. R. Tolkien, and H. G. Wells have been selected from a large body of bibliographical, biographical, and critical material. However, additional sources for secondary material are cited for these authors.

Arrangement

The subject authors are arranged alphabetically. A separate alphabetical pseudonym index following the table of contents provides access to those authors known under their literary pen names. Each author checklist is arranged alphabetically by title with title changes cross-indexed within each checklist. Traditionally, the most favored method of arranging a literary bibliography has been a chronological sequence from the author's earliest to most recent publications. In the early stages of compilation a chronological arrangement was contemplated and preliminary lists for bibliographically complex authors (Ray Bradbury, Robert E. Howard, H. P. Lovecraft and H. G. Wells) were compiled. However, the resultant morass of retitled, combined, rearranged, abridged or enlarged editions, plus the need for hundreds of cross-references, led to adoption of the less favored but more servicable alphabetical arrangement.

Each entry provides the following data: (1) title; (2) place of publication, publisher, and date of publication; (3) binding; (4) transcription of publisher's statement of printing (where present). In addition, where applicable, printings, states, and issues are recorded, as are binding and dust jacket variants. Book stock number and price are provided for all mass-market paperback titles. Titles forming part of a numbered series are indicated. Miscellaneous notes provide additional information on printing, binding, or distribution for many entries.

Terms of description

TITLE: The title of an entry is that which is found on the title page of a book or at the head of a broadside, postcard, or other ephemeral piece. If there is no title page, the cover title or caption title is cited. In a few instances, a title has been supplied, indicated by enclosure within brackets. Subtitles are generally omitted.

PLACE OF PUBLICATION, PUBLISHER, DATE: If the place of publication, publisher, or date of publication appears on the face of the same sheet as the title, each is shown without brackets. If not, it is shown within brackets, regardless of the source of the supplied information.

BINDING: If no binding style is recorded, it is full cloth. Full cloth bindings are described where necessary to distinguish variants within a single printing. All other styles of binding are indicated. "Boards" describes a pasteboard binding material which is not covered by cloth. "Wrappers" describes a flexible binding material other than pasteboard or cloth covered boards. The binding of mass-market paperbacks is described as wrappers. If the wrappers are of the same paper stock as the text, they are termed self-wrappers. "Broadside" refers to an unfolded sheet printed on one side only. If an unfolded sheet is printed on both sides, it is termed a single sheet printed on both sides.

FORMAT: The process by which books, pamphlets, and ephemeral material are duplicated by mimeograph, hectograph, or a similar quick method of producing mechanically reproduced sheets is identified.

DUST JACKETS: Most modern hardcover books were published with dust jackets. The presence of a dust jacket is not indicated unless a printing has been observed with variant dust jackets. Dust jacket variants are described when known. If a modern book is known to have been published without a dust jacket, this fact is so indicated.

IDENTIFICATION OF PRINTING AND EDITION: The four basic terms of bibliographical description are edition, printing (or impression), state, and issue.

> *Edition:* An edition consists of all the copies printed from one
> setting of type (or plates made from that typesetting or by offset).
> One edition may include many printings.

> *Printing:* A printing consists of all the copies printed at one time
> from the same press run. A printing may include states and issues.
> The term impression is synonymous with printing.

> *State:* States occur only within single printings and are created by
> an alteration to some copies of a printing not affecting the condi-
> tions of publication. These variant forms of typesettings or makeup
> of one or more sheets of the printing are the result of any alteration
> (a) made during the impression of the sheets, (b) made after
> impression but before publication, or (c) made after initial publica-
> tion, providing the alterations are attempts to create a form of
> "ideal copy" envisaged at the time of publication.

> *Issue:* Issues occur only within single printings and are created by
> an alteration to some copies of a printing affecting the conditions of
> publication or sale. This special form of the original sheets of
> printing is the result of post-publication-date alterations made in-
> tentionally on order of the publisher or issuer and constitute a
> definite effort to improve or change the import of a portion of the
> sheets within a printing.

Properly used, the terms edition, printing, state, and issue refer only to the imprinted sheets of the book and should not be applied to binding variants. However, the term issue has also been used in this bibliography to distinguish different binding forms which clearly represent the publisher's or issuer's alteration of conditions of publication or sale within a single printing. Such issues generally occur as the result of the creation of deluxe or special copies from a portion of the trade printing.

When present, the statement of printing on the copyright page is transcribed. Unless otherwise noted, reference to the copyright page means title page verso. Many books and pamphlets, especially those printed in the United Kingdom or privately issued, do not carry a copyright statement on this page. Thus, employment of the phrase "no statement of printing on copyright page" for a work lacking a notice of copyright on the title page verso indicates that a statement of printing is not present there or elsewhere in the volume. If a statement of printing is not found on the copyright page, but is present elsewhere in the volume, it is recorded for example as *"first published in Great Britain, 1954* on page [2]," or *"first published in 1976* on page [48]." When present, publisher's statement of printing, other than "first edition" and "first printing" is transcribed in whole, or in part where it is not particularly informative. Omitted information is indicated by the employment of ellipses. Generally, the typography of the publisher's printing statement has not been duplicated. Thus, such typography as "FIRST PRINTING–1976" is reproduced in italics as *"First printing–1976,"* and "FIRST PRINTING, MAY 1979 / 1 2 3 4 5 6 7 8 9" is recorded as *"First printing, May 1979 / 1 2 3 4 5 6 7 8 9."* If the publisher's printing statement employs both upper- and lower-case letters, their setting is generally followed.

PRIORITY OF ISSUE: Where known, the chronological priority of multiple states or issues is indicated by the phrase "priority as listed." Simultaneous states or issues are indicated by the phrase "no priority." If the sequence of state or issue has not been determined, the phrase "no priority established" is employed. All states or issues within a printing are described when known.

MASS-MARKET PAPERBACK BOOK STOCK NUMBER AND PRICE: Paperback book stock number and price (when present) are transcribed from the front, rear, or spine of the wrapper. The price printed on the wrapper is recorded following the book stock number transcription and is placed within parentheses. Some mass-market paperbacks lack a printed price. If known, the price is supplied within parentheses, regardless of the source of the parenthetical information.

NUMBERED SERIES: Numbered series are distinguished from excluded serial publications by their lack of regular publishing schedule and, in most cases, lack of availability by subscription. A numbered series or group title of which an entry is a part is always given. Among the numbered series included are *Avon Fantasy Reader* (edited by Donald A. Wollheim), *Galaxy Science Fiction Novels, Science Fiction Classics, Science Fiction Stories,* and anthology series such as *New Dimensions* (edited by Robert Silverberg), and *Quark* (edited by Samuel R. Delany and Marilyn Hacker).

SERIAL PUBLICATIONS: Serial publications, which include professional and amateur periodicals and journals, are defined as works issued by subscription or as the organ of a professional or amateur organization and for which the publisher's intent was to issue them at regular intervals. Both numbered and unnumbered serials, including special issues, are generally excluded. Excluded are such titles as "The Scientists Revolt" by Edgar Rice Burroughs, issued as *The Burroughs Bulletin* no. 40 and E. C. Tubb's "Alien Impact," which comprised the whole issue of *Authentic* no. 21. *American Science Fiction* (later *American Science Fiction Magazine*), published monthly in Australia between May 1952 and September 1955 is also excluded. However, a few titles of exceptional interest which are serials have been included.

ANTHOLOGY APPEARANCES: Contributions to books other than those written or edited by the subject author are generally excluded. Some two and three author collections of original fiction are included. Examples include Ace and Belmont double novels and a few of the titles issued in Great Britain during the mid-1940's by Utopian Publications, Ltd.

This compilation has no bibliographical antecedents in the science fiction and fantasy genres, or for that matter, within the entire field of modern popular fiction. It was compiled to meet the need for a one-volume bibliography which would provide up-to-date, comprehensive, and accurate checklists of book fiction by 215 authors identified with the science fiction and fantasy genres from the late nineteenth century to the present. From late Victorian writers such as H. G. Wells, George Griffith, Fred T. Jane, and Garrett P. Serviss, the bibliography progresses through the authors of the Gernsback era, the "golden age" of the late 1930's and early 1940's, the post-war boom of the 1950's, the "new wave" of the 1960's, to the emerging new writers of the 1970's.

The choice of subject authors was not the result of arbitrary selection. Every name represents a writer whose works influenced the science fiction and fantasy field or whose works today are being read and/or collected. Subject authors include major writers of established reputation like Wells, Clarke, Bradbury, Heinlein, Tolkien, and C. S. Lewis; writers important in the historical development of the genres like Cummings, Burroughs, England, Lindsay, Hodgson, and E. E. Smith; and the moderns—young writers like Gardner Dozois, George Alec Effinger, Stephen King, C. J. Cherry, and George R. R. Martin. Also included are some pulp fictioneers as well as representative editors and anthologists. Out of this crucible came the subject authors who influenced (or are influencing) the course of science and fantasy fiction. A balanced and representative selection of active writers was sought, but some who deserve inclusion have been omitted. The compiler has no window into the future, and author selections were not made in the spirit of prophecy. Twenty years from now some of the names appearing herein will be neglected as the result of the inevitable change in reader and collector interest. Other names will endure to provide a sense of wonder for generations to come.

This book is intended for the collector, bookseller, and scholar who wish to identify first and significant later printings and editions by the subject authors. Loosely modeled on the classic *American First Editions* (first published in 1929 under the editorial direction of Merle Johnson, with three revised editions following, the last appearing in 1942 with Jacob Blanck as editor), *Science Fiction and Fantasy Authors* was developed to serve the same need to which Johnson's compilation was addressed. Addenda and corrigenda are invited and recommendations for additional author lists are welcome. The need for a second edition, revised and enlarged, is anticipated and, in fact, welcomed.

L. W. CURREY
Elizabethtown, New York

Notes

1. Revised edition published as *The Checklist of Science-Fiction and Supernatural Fiction* (Glen Rock, New Jersey: Firebell Books, 1978).

2. Reginald has completed a similar, but greatly expanded, conpilation which is scheduled for publication by Gale Research company in late 1979.

3. Donald H. Tuck, *A Handbook of Science Fiction and Fantasy* (Hobart, Tasmania: Tuck, 1954); 2nd ed. (Hobart, Tasmania: Tuck, 1959), 2 vols.

Acknowledgements

This bibliography could not have been completed without the effort and continuing support of Gerry de la Ree of Saddle River, New Jersey, and David G. Hartwell of Pleasantville, New York—two long-time friends and colleagues who provided full access to their extensive private collections of fantasy and science fiction and their vast personal knowledge of these genres. Research facilities crucial to the creation of comprehensive checklists were provided by Ms. Doris Mehegan (Spaced Out Library, Totonto Public Libraries) and Messrs. Malcolm Edwards and David Pringle (Science Fiction Foundation, North East London Polytechnic) who provided good counsel as well as good fellowship.

I am also indebted to Miss Binnie S. Braunstein (University of Maryland, Baltimore County) for aid in tracking down fugitive titles through the OCLC data system; Charles N. Brown (Locus Publications), who graciously responded to hours of bibliographical queries; Frank Pipes, who hosted my week-long sojourn in Washington; William Matheson (Head, Rare Book Division, Library of Congress) who guided me through the labyrinth of the library; Miss E. M. Plincke (Curator, H. G. Wells Collection, Bromley Central Library); Donn Albright, who answered endless questions pertaining to Ray Bradbury; Michael Moorcock, John Clute, and Peter Nicholls for their London hospitality; Margaret and Brian Aldiss, who provided an Oxford connection; Eric Korn for sharing his bibliographical knowledge of H. G. Wells; George Locke who displayed his collection, his knowledge, and his hospitality; Mike Burgess (alias R. Reginald) for midnight telephone conferences; Sam Moskowitz, who responded graciously to numerous bibliographical queries; Bruce Francis, who shared his Theordore Sturgeon collection; Roy A. Squires, who provided necessary bibliographical minutae as well as a great Mexican dinner; Roger Schlobin, who shared his Andre Norton research; Kevin B. Hancer, who helped with ERB; Peter B. Howard (Serendipity Books) for posing a number of difficult questions; Harvey J. Satty, who helped with Olaf Stapledon; David Y. Hughes, who supplied crucial material on Wells; Melissa and Mark Hime, who responded to endless queries about J. R. R. Tolkien; and Mike Ashley for information on E. C. Tubb.

Thanks are also due to C. W. Brooks, Jr., Robert E. Briney, Donald M. Grant, Henry H. Heins, Vernell Coriell, Giancarlo Cavagna, Marshall Tymn, Stuart W. Wells, III, Neil Barron, Richard Fawcett, William R. Cagle, Mark T. Hurst, Richard Landon, Leslie Kay Swigart, Norman L. Hills, Richard Spelman, Glenn Lord, George T. Hamilton, Daniel Gobbett, Bruce Kahn, Frank M. Halpern, Jeffrey H. Levin, David A. McClintock, John H. Stanley, David G. Gibson and Ted Ball (Fantasy Centre), S. T. Joshi, Stuart Teitler (Kaleidoscope Books), Stuart David Schiff, Dirk W. Mosig, Marc A. Michaud (Necronomicon Press), Mary C. Pangborn, Muriel Becker, John R. Hale, Bob Roehm, J. Grant Thiessen, Harrison T. Watson, Jr., Tim Underwood, Asa Pieratt, Max Abrams, Christine and Robert Liska (Colophon Book Store), Bill Leone, Jr., Tom Whitmore, Donald H. Tuck, Stephen R. Landan, Richard Frahm, Virginia Kidd, James W. Bittner, Stephen W. Bridge, John E. Stith, Brian N. Lockhart, Michael Anft, Tom Martin, James R. Ward, Ralph B. Sipper (Joseph the Provider—Books), Larry Rothstein, Steven T. Miller, Stephen F. Scott, Mike Parsons, J. Andrew Cutten, and Judith Blish.

Many subject authors commented upon, corrected, or enlarged draft checklists of their fiction. My thanks to all who responded. I am especially indebted to Robert Bloch, Nelson Bond, John Brunner, H. K. Bulmer, Lin Carter, Arthur C. Clarke, Catherine C. and L. Sprague deCamp, Samuel R. Delany, Gordon R. Dickson, Thomas M. Disch, Harlan Ellison, Ron Goulart, Piers Anthony Jacob, Richard A. Lupoff, Barry N. Malzberg, Frederick Pohl, Robert Silverberg, E. C. Tubb, Manly Wade Wellman, Jack Williamson, Donald A. Wollhein, and C. S. Youd.

All of these kind people helped to correct errors and expand the checklists. I alone am responsible for any remaining errors and omissions. The advice and continuing support of Tom Beeler, Publisher of G. K. Hall & Co., provided the impetus needed to finish the book. The editorial assistance of Deborah Pokos and Paul Wright is gratefully acknowledged. Mere words can hardly express my gratitude for the constant encouragement and aid provided by my secretary, Carolyn Karcher. The usual secretarial acknowledgement is not proper here. While I moonlighted on the bibliography, she held our antiquarian book business together. The project could not have advanced without her capable efforts. To my wife, I present an author's ultimate token of gratitude, the dedication of this, my first book, along with a promise to quit spending so many nights at the office.

Science Fiction
and Fantasy Authors

Brian Wilson Aldiss
(b. 1925)

AN AGE. *London: Faber and Faber,* [*1967*].
First published in mcmlxvii on copyright page. Issued later in the U.S. as CRYPTOZOIC!

THE AIRS OF EARTH. *London: Faber and Faber,* [*1963*].
First published in mcmlxiii on copyright page. Published later in the U.S. with textual differences as STARSWARM.

BAREFOOT IN THE HEAD. *London: Faber and Faber,* [*1969*].
First published in 1969 on copyright page.

BEST SCIENCE FICTION STORIES. . . . *London: Faber and Faber,* [*1965*].
First published in mcmlxv on copyright page. Issued later in the U.S. as WHO CAN REPLACE A MAN?

BEST SCIENCE FICTION STORIES. . . . *London: Faber and Faber,* [*1971*].
New and revised edition 1971 on copyright page. Differs considerably from the 1965 collection; drops six stories, "Psyclops," "Dumb Show," "The New Father Christmas," "Ahead," "Basis for Negotiation," and "A Kind of Artistry" and adds eight, "Shards," "Girl and Robot With Flowers," "The Moment of Eclipse," "Swastika!," "Sober Noises of Morning in a Marginal Land," "Judas Danced," "Still Trajectories," and "Another Little Boy."

THE BOOK OF BRIAN ALDISS. *New York: DAW Books, Inc.,* [*1972*].
Wrappers. *First Printing, 1972* on copyright page. *DAW: sf Books No. 29 UQ 1029* (95¢). Issued later in Great Britain as THE COMIC INFERNO.

BOW DOWN TO NUL. *New York: Ace Books, Inc.,* [*1960*].
Wrappers. No statement of printing on copyright page. *Ace D–443* (35¢). Bound with THE DARK DESTROYERS by Manly Wade Wellman. Issued later in Great Britain as THE INTERPRETER.

A BRIAN ALDISS OMNIBUS. *London: Sidgwick & Jackson,* [*1969*].
Boards. No statement of printing on copyright page. All material reprinted from earlier books.

BRIAN ALDISS OMNIBUS (2). *London: Sidgwick & Jackson,* [*1971*].
Boards. No statement of printing on copyright page. Collects SPACE, TIME AND NATHANIEL, NON-STOP, and THE MALE RESPONSE.

THE BRIGHTFOUNT DIARIES. *London: Faber and Faber Ltd,* [*1955*].
First published in mcmlv on copyright page.

BROTHERS OF THE HEAD. [*London*]: *Pierrot Publishing Limited,* [*1977*].
Two issues, no priority: (A) Boards; (B) Wrappers. *First published in Great Britain in 1977/PIERROT PUBLISHING LIMITED/First published in the United States of America in 1977/PIERROT/TWO CONTINENTS* . . . on copyright page. Note: Hardcover issue was not distributed in the U.S.

THE CANOPY OF TIME. *London: Faber and Faber,* [*1959*].
Boards. *First published in mcmlix* on copyright page. An abridgment with connecting material issued later in the U.S. as GALAXIES LIKE GRAINS OF SAND.

THE COMIC INFERNO. [*London*]: *New English Library*, [*1973*].
Wrappers. *First NEL paperback edition October 1973* on copyright page. *New English Library 016366* (40p). Published earlier in the U.S. as THE BOOK OF BRIAN ALDISS.

CRYPTOZOIC! *Garden City: Doubleday & Company, Inc., 1968.*
First Edition in the United States of America on copyright page. Issued earlier in Great Britain as AN AGE.

THE DARK LIGHT YEARS. *London: Faber and Faber*, [*1964*].
First published in mcmlxiv on copyright page.

EARTHWORKS. *London: Faber and Faber*, [*1965*].
First published in mcmlxv on copyright page.

ALSO: *Garden City: Doubleday & Company, Inc., 1966. First Edition in the United States of America* on copyright page. Minor textual changes.

THE EIGHTY-MINUTE HOUR. *Garden City: Doubleday & Company, Inc., 1974.*
First edition so stated on copyright page.

ALSO: *London: Jonathan Cape*, [*1974*]. Boards. *First published 1974* on copyright page. A few textual changes.

EQUATOR. *London: Brown, Watson Limited*, [*1958*].
Wrappers. *First U.K. publication in book form* on copyright page. *Digit R695* (2'6). Includes "Segregation," pp. 105–57. Issued earlier in the U.S. as VANGUARD FROM ALPHA.

EXCOMMUNICATION. [*London: Post Card Partnership, 1975.*]
Postcard. 10.5 X 15 cm. No statement of printing. Note: Recto prints a short, short story, "Excommunication," by Aldiss. Verso carries publisher's imprint and copyright notice.

FRANKENSTEIN UNBOUND. *London: Jonathan Cape*, [*1973*].
Boards. *First published 1973* on copyright page.

GALAXIES LIKE GRAINS OF SAND. [*New York*]: *Published by The New American Library*, [*1960*].
Wrappers. *First printing, July, 1960* on copyright page. *Signet Books S1815* (35¢). An abridgment of an earlier edition issued in Great Britain as THE CANOPY OF TIME.

ALSO: *Boston: Gregg Press, 1977. First Printing, June 1977* on copyright page. First hardcover edition. Note: Not issued in dust jacket.

GREYBEARD. *New York: Harcourt, Brace & World, Inc.*, [*1964*].
First edition so stated on copyright page.

THE HAND-REARED BOY. *London: Weidenfeld and Nicolson*, [*1970*].
Boards. *First published January 1970* on copyright page. Note: Later copies have the statement *Reprinted before publication* on copyright page.

HOTHOUSE. *London: Faber and Faber*, [*1962*].
First published in mcmlxii on copyright page. Issued earlier the same year in the U.S. in a shorter version as THE LONG AFTERNOON OF EARTH.

INTANGIBLES INC. *London: Faber and Faber*, [*1969*].
First published in 1969 on copyright page. Issued later in the U.S. with slightly altered contents as NEANDERTHAL PLANET.

THE INTERPRETER.*London: Brown, Watson Limited*, [*1961*].
   Wrappers. No statement of printing on copyright page. *Digit Books R506* (2'6). Issued
   earlier in the U.S. as BOW DOWN TO NUL.

LAST ORDERS AND OTHER STORIES.*London: Jonathan Cape*, [*1977*].
   Boards. *First published 1977* on copyright page.

THE LONG AFTERNOON OF EARTH. [*New York*]: *Published by The New American Library*,
   [*1962*].
   Wrappers. *First printing, January, 1962* on copyright page. *Signet Books D2018* (50¢).
   Issued later the same year in Great Britain in a version extended by some 8000 words as
   HOTHOUSE.

THE MALACIA TAPESTRY.*London: Jonathan Cape*, [*1976*].
   Boards. *First published 1976* on copyright page.

THE MALE RESPONSE.*New York: Galaxy Publishing Corp.*, [*1961*].
   Wrappers. No statement of printing on copyright page. *Beacon Book No. 305* (35¢).

   ALSO:*London: Dennis Dobson*, [*1963*]. Boards. *First published in Great Britain in 1963*
   on copyright page. First hardcover edition.

THE MOMENT OF ECLIPSE.*London: Faber and Faber*, [*1970*].
   First published in 1970 on copyright page.

NEANDERTHAL PLANET. [*New York*]: *Avon*, [*1970*].
   Wrappers. *First Avon Printing, January, 1970* on copyright page. *Avon V2322* (75¢).
   Issued earlier in Great Britain with slightly altered contents as INTANGIBLES INC.

   ALSO:*New York: Avon*, [*1970*]. Boards. Two printings, priority as listed: (A) Code *23 L* on
   page 187; (B) Code *01 M* on page 187. No statement of printing on copyright page. First
   hardcover edition. Note: Issued by the Science Fiction Book Club.

NO TIME LIKE TOMORROW. [*New York*]: *Published by The New American Library*, [*1959*].
   Wrappers. *First printing, July, 1959* on copyright page. *Signet Books S1683* (35¢). Six of
   the stories collected earlier in SPACE, TIME AND NATHANIEL.

NON-STOP.*London: Faber and Faber*, [*1958*].
   Two printings, priority as listed: (A) Red boards, spine lettered in gold; signatures sewn in
   gatherings of 8s; credits on [A²] verso list two titles, SPACE, TIME AND NATHANIEL and THE
   BRIGHTFOUNT DIARIES; (B) Brown cloth, spine lettered in gold; signatures perfect bound in
   gatherings of 16s; credits on [A²] verso list eight titles commencing with HOTHOUSE.*First
   published in mcmlviii* on copyright page. Issued later in the U.S. with textual differences as
   STARSHIP.

THE PRIMAL URGE.*New York: Ballantine Books*, [*1961*].
   Wrappers. No statement of printing on copyright page. *A Ballantine Science Fiction Novel
   F 555* (50¢).

REPORT ON PROBABILITY A.*London: Faber and Faber*, [*1968*].
   First published mcmlxviii on copyright page.

THE SALIVA TREE AND OTHER STRANGE GROWTHS.*London: Faber and Faber* [*1966*].
   Two bindings, priority as listed: (A) Dark green cloth, spine lettered in gold; (B) Dark
   green boards, spine lettered in gold. *First published in mcmlxvi* on copyright page.

A SOLDIER ERECT.*London: Weidenfeld and Nicolson*, [*1971*].
   Boards. No statement of printing on copyright page.

SPACE, TIME AND NATHANIEL. *London: Faber and Faber*, [*1957*].
   First published in mcmlvii on copyright page. Six of these stories later collected in NO TIME
   LIKE TOMORROW.

STARSHIP. *New York: Criterion Books*, [*1959*].
   Boards. No statement of printing on copyright page. Issued earlier in Great Britain with
   textual differences as NON-STOP.

STARSWARM. [*New York*]: *Published by The New American Library*, [*1964*].
   Wrappers. *First printing, January, 1964* on copyright page. *Signet Books D2411* (50¢).
   Published earlier in Great Britain with textual differences as THE AIRS OF EARTH.

VANGUARD FROM ALPHA. *New York: Ace Books, Inc.*, [*1959*].
   Wrappers. No statement of printing on copyright page. *Ace Double Novel Books D-369*
   (35¢). Bound with THE CHANGELING WORLDS by Kenneth Bulmer. Published later in Great
   Britain as EQUATOR. The latter includes ''Segregation,'' not printed in the Ace edition.

WHO CAN REPLACE A MAN? *New York: Harcourt, Brace & World, Inc.*, [*1966*].
   First American edition 1966 on copyright page. Issued earlier in Great Britain as BEST
   SCIENCE FICTION STORIES OF BRIAN W. ALDISS.

Edited Fiction

All About Venus. [*New York*]: *A Dell Book*, [*1968*].
   Wrappers. *First printing— October 1968* on copyright page. *Dell 0085* (60¢). Edited, with
   foreword, introductions, and notes, by Aldiss. With HARRY HARRISON. A much enlarged
   edition issued later the same month in Great Britain as *Farewell, Fantastic Venus!*

The Astounding • Analog Reader. *Garden City: Doubleday & Company, Inc., 1972-1973*.
   First edition so stated on copyright pages. Two volumes. Edited, with introductions, by
   Aldiss. With HARRY HARRISON.

Best Fantasy Stories. *London: Faber and Faber*, [*1962*].
   First published in mcmlxii on copyright page. Edited, with introduction and short story
   ''Intangibles Inc.,'' by Aldiss.

Best SF: 1967. [*New York*]: *Published by Berkley Publishing Corporation*, [*1968*].
   Wrappers. *March, 1968* on copyright page. *Berkley S1529* (75¢). Edited, with afterword,
   by Aldiss. With HARRY HARRISON. Issued the same month in Great Britain as *The Year's
   Best Science Fiction No. 1.*

Best SF: 1968. *New York: G. P. Putnam's Sons*, [*1969*].
   No statement of printing on copyright page. Edited, with afterword and short story ''The
   Serpent of Kundalini,'' by Aldiss. With HARRY HARRISON. Issued earlier in Great Britain
   without the Aldiss story as *The Year's Best Science Fiction No. 2.*

Best SF: 1969. *New York: G. P. Putnam's Sons*, [*1970*].
   Boards. No statement of printing on copyright page. Edited, with afterword and short story
   ''Working in the Spaceship Yards,'' by Aldiss. With HARRY HARRISON. Issued earlier in
   Great Britain as *The Year's Best Science Fiction No. 3.*

Best SF: 1970. *New York: G. P. Putnam's Sons*, [*1971*].
   No statement of printing on copyright page. Edited, with afterword, by Aldiss. With
   HARRY HARRISON. Issued earlier in Great Britain as *The Year's Best Science Fiction
   No. 4.*

Best SF: 1971. *New York: G. P. Putnam's Sons, [1972]*.
No statement of printing on copyright page. Edited, with afterword and short story "The Hunter at his Ease," by Aldiss. With HARRY HARRISON. Published in Great Britain the same month, possibly simultaneously, as *The Year's Best Science Fiction No. 5*.

Best SF: 1972. *New York: G. P. Putnam's Sons, [1973]*.
No statement of printing on copyright page. Edited, with afterword and short story "As For Our Fatal Continuity . . . ," by Aldiss. With HARRY HARRISON. Issued later in Great Britain as *The Year's Best Science Fiction No. 6*.

Best SF:73. *[New York]: Published by Berkley Publishing Corporation, [1974]*.
Wrappers. *June, 1974* on copyright page. *A Berkley Medallion Book 425–02581–095* (95¢). Edited, with afterword and short story "Serpent Burning on an Altar," by Aldiss. With HARRY HARRISON. Issued later in Great Britain with abridgment as *The Year's Best Science Fiction No. 7*.
ALSO: *New York: G. P. Putnam's Sons, [1974]*. Boards. No statement of printing on copyright page. First hardcover edition.

Best SF1974. *Indianapolis/New York: The Bobbs-Merrill Company, Inc., [1975]*.
Boards with cloth shelf back. First printing so stated on copyright page. Edited, with afterword and short story "Listen With Big Brother," by Aldiss. With HARRY HARRISON. Issued later in Great Britain without poem "Eyes of a Woman — From a Portrait by Picasso" by Lisa Conesa as *The Year's Best Science Fiction No. 8*.

Best SF:75. The Ninth Annual. *Indianapolis/New York: The Bobbs-Merrill Company, Inc., [1976]*.
Boards with cloth shelf back. First printing so stated on copyright page. Edited, with afterword, by Aldiss. With HARRY HARRISON. Issued earlier in Great Britain as *The Year's Best Science Fiction No. 9*.

Decade the 1940s. *[London]: M[acmillan London Limited, 1975]*.
Boards. *First published 1975 . . .* on copyright page. Edited, with introduction, by Aldiss. With HARRY HARRISON.

Decade the 1950s. *[London]: M[acmillan London Limited, 1976]*.
Boards. *First published 1976 . . .* on copyright page. Edited by Aldiss. With HARRY HARRISON.

Decade the 1960s. *[London]: M[acmillan, 1977]*.
Boards. *First published 1977 . . .* on copyright page. Edited, with introduction and short story "The Village Swindler," by Aldiss. With HARRY HARRISON.

Evil Earths. *London: Weidenfeld & Nicolson, [1975]*.
Boards. *First published in hard cover by Weidenfeld and Nicolson* on copyright page. Edited, with introduction, notes, and short story "Heresies of the Huge God," by Aldiss.

Farewell, Fantastic Venus! *[London]: Macdonald Science Fiction, [1968]*.
Boards. *First published in Great Britain in 1968* on copyright page. Edited, with foreword, introductions, and notes, by Aldiss. With HARRY HARRISON. Issued earlier the same month in the U.S. in a much abridged version as *All About Venus*.

Galactic Empires. *London: Weidenfeld and Nicolson, [1976]*.
Boards. Two volumes. *First published in hardcover by Weidenfeld and Nicolson* on copyright pages. Edited, with introduction and notes, by Aldiss.

Introducing SF. *London: Faber and Faber*, [*1964*].
First published in mcmlxiv on copyright page. Edited, with introduction and short story "Gesture of Farewell," by Aldiss.

Last and First Men . . . , [by] Olaf Stapledon. [*Harmondsworth*]: *Penguin Books*, [*1963*].
Wrappers. *Reprinted in Penguin Books 1963* on copyright page. *Penguin Science Fiction 1875* (3'6). Edited, with introduction, by Aldiss. Note: First edition to bear the Aldiss introduction.

More Penguin Science Fiction. [*Harmondsworth*]: *Penguin Books*, [*1963*].
Wrappers. *First published 1963* on copyright page. *Penguin Science Fiction 1963* (3/6). Edited, with introduction, by Aldiss.

Nebula Award Stories Two. *Garden City: Doubleday and Company, Inc., 1967*.
First edition so stated on copyright page. Edited, with introduction, afterword, and short story "Man in His Time," by Aldiss. With HARRY HARRISON.

Penguin Science Fiction. [*Harmondsworth*]: *Penguin Books*, [*1961*]:
Wrappers. *First published 1961* on copyright page. *Penguin Books 1638* (3'6). Edited, with introduction and short story "Poor Little Warrior!" by Aldiss.

The Penguin Science Fiction Omnibus. [*Harmondsworth*]: *Penguin Books*, [*1973*].
Wrappers. *Published in one volume 1973* on copyright page. *Penguin 3145* (60p). Reprint, save for new introduction by Aldiss. Collects *Penguin Science Fiction*, *More Penguin Science Fiction*, and *Yet More Penguin Science Fiction*.

Space Odysseys. [*London*]: *Futura Publications Limited*, [*1974*].
Wrappers. *First published in Great Britain in 1974/by Weidenfeld & Nicholson* [sic]/*Orbit Edition first published in 1974/by Futura Publications Limited* on copyright page. *Orbit Science Fiction 0 8600 78167* (75p). Edited, with introduction and notes, by Aldiss. Note: Publisher's printing history is incorrect. The Orbit edition was published in December 1974 and precedes the Weidenfeld and Nicolson edition published in March 1975.

ALSO:*London: Weidenfeld and Nicolson*, [*1975*]. Boards. *First published in hard cover by Weidenfeld & Nicolson* . . . on copyright page. First hardcover edition.

Space Opera. [*London*]: *Futura Publications Limited*, [*1974*].
Wrappers. *First published in Great Britain in 1974/by Weidenfeld and Nicolson/First Futura Publications edition 1974* on copyright page. *Futura Science Fiction 0 8600 7058 1* (50p). Edited, with introduction, notes, and afterword, by Aldiss. Publisher's printing history is incorrect, according to *Whitaker's Cumulative Book List*, which records the Orbit edition as published in August 1974, followed by the Weidenfeld and Nicolson edition published in November 1974.

ALSO:*London: Weidenfeld and Nicolson*, [*1974*]. Boards. No statement of printing on copyright page. First hardcover edition.

The Year's Best Science Fiction. [*London*]: *Severn House*, [*1977*].
Boards. *The first British hardcover edition published in 1977* . . . on copyright page. Edited, with afterword, by Aldiss. With HARRY HARRISON. Issued earlier as *The Year's Best Science Fiction No. 2*.

The Year's Best Science Fiction No. 1. *London: Sphere Books Limited*, [*1968*].
Wrappers. *First published in Great Britain 1968* . . . on copyright page. *Sphere Science Fiction 43311* (5/0). Edited, with afterword, by Aldiss. With HARRY HARRISON. Issued the same month in the U.S. as *Best SF: 1967*.

The Year's Best Science Fiction No. 2. *London: Sphere Books Limited*, [*1969*].
Wrappers. *First published in Great Britain in 1969* . . . on copyright page. *Sphere 43354*

(5/–). Edited, with afterword, by Aldiss. With HARRY HARRISON. Does not print "The Serpent of Kundalini" by Aldiss but does include "Like Young" by Theodore Sturgeon. Issued later in Great Britain as *The Year's Best Science Fiction.* Issued later in the U.S. with the Aldiss story and without the Sturgeon story as *Best SF: 1968.*

The Year's Best Science Fiction No. 3. *London: Sphere Books Limited,* [*1970*]. Wrappers. *First published in Great Britain in 1970* . . . on copyright page. *Sphere Science Fiction 43419* (30p). Edited, with afterword and short story "Working in the Spaceship Yards," by Aldiss. With HARRY HARRISON. Issued later in the U.S. as *Best SF: 1969.*

The Year's Best Science Fiction No. 4. *London: Sphere Books Limited,* [*1971*]. Wrappers. *First published in Great Britain in 1971* on copyright page. *Science Fiction Sphere 43435* (30p). Edited, with afterword, by Aldiss. With HARRY HARRISON. Issued later in the U.S. as *Best SF: 1970.*

The Year's Best Science Fiction No. 5. *London: Sphere Books Limited,* [*1972*]. Wrappers. *First published in Great Britain in 1972* on copyright page. *Sphere Science Fiction 43443* (35p). Edited, with afterword and short story "The Hunter at his Ease," by Aldiss. With HARRY HARRISON. Published in the U.S. the same month, possibly simultaneously, as *Best SF: 1971.*

The Year's Best Science Fiction No. 6. *London: Sphere Books Limited,* [*1973*]. Wrappers. *First published in Great Britain in 1973* . . . on copyright page. *Sphere Science Fiction 0 7221 4355 9* (35p). Edited, with afterword and short story "As For Our Fatal Continuity . . . ," by Aldiss. With HARRY HARRISON. Note: Reprinted in November 1973 with cover title reading *The Year's Best S.F. 1972.* Issued earlier in the U.S. as *Best SF: 1972.*

The Year's Best Science Fiction No. 7. *London: Sphere Books Limited,* [*1975*]. Wrappers. *First published in Great Britain* . . . *1975* on copyright page. *Sphere Science Fiction 0 7221 4361 3* (55p). Edited, with short story "Serpent Burning on an Altar," by Aldiss. With HARRY HARRISON. This abridged edition omits the five poems, four stories, and afterword by Aldiss following "La Befana" by Gene Wolfe. Complete text issued earlier in the U.S. as *Best SF 73.*

The Year's Best Science Fiction No. 8. *London: Sphere Books Limited,* [*1976*]. Wrappers. *First published in Great Britain* . . . *1976* . . . on copyright page. *Sphere 0 7221 4398 2* (65p). Edited, with afterword and short story "Listen With Big Brother," by Aldiss. With HARRY HARRISON. Deletes poem by Lisa Conesa. Issued earlier in the U.S. as *Best SF 1974.*

The Year's Best Science Fiction No. 9. [*London*]: *Futura Publications Limited,* [*1976*]. Wrappers. *First published in Great Britain in 1976* . . . on copyright page. *Orbit Science Fiction 0 8600 7894 9* (65p). Edited, with afterword, by Aldiss. With HARRY HARRISON. Issued later in the U.S. as *Best SF: 75. The Ninth Annual.*

ALSO: *London: Weidenfeld and Nicolson,* [*1976*]. Boards. No statement of printing on copyright page. First British hardcover edition.

Yet more Penguin Science Fiction. [*Harmondsworth*]: *Penguin Books,* [*1964*]. Wrappers. *First published 1964* on copyright page. *Penguin Science Fiction 2189* (3'6). Edited, with introduction, by Aldiss.

Nonfiction (Dealing with the Fantasy Genre only)

Billion Year Spree: The History of Science Fiction. *London: Weidenfeld & Nicolson,* [*1973*]. Boards. No statement of printing on copyright page. Note: Features eight pages of illustrations not included in later U.S. edition published by Doubleday & Company, Inc.

Science Fiction Art. [*London*]: *New English Library*, [*1975*].
>   Wrappers. *First published in 1975* . . . on copyright page. Notes: (1) Advertised in *The Bookseller*, 4 October 1975 as "just published." (2) Simultaneous with U.S. edition published by Crown Publishers, Inc.

The Shape of Further Things: Speculations on Change. *London: Faber & Faber*, [*1970*].
>   *First published in 1970* on copyright page.

Edited Nonfiction (Dealing with the Fantasy Genre only)

Hell's Cartographers. [*London*]: *Weidenfeld and Nicolson*, [*1975*].
>   Boards. *First published by Weidenfeld and Nicolson* . . . on copyright page. Edited, with introduction and contribution "Magic and Bare Boards," by Aldiss. With HARRY HARRISON.

Reference

Aldiss Unbound: The Science Fiction of Brian W. Aldiss, [by] Richard Mathews. *San Bernardino, California: R. Reginald The Borgo Press, MCMLXXVII*.
>   Wrappers. *First Edition* ——— *October, 1977* on copyright page. *The Milford Series Popular Writers of Today Volume Nine* at head of title.

Item Eighty-Three: Brian W. Aldiss, a Bibliography 1954–1972. Compiled by Margaret Aldiss. [*Oxford: The Bocardo Press, 1973.*]
>   Wrappers. Two issues, no priority: (A) 200 numbered copies signed by compiler and subject; (B) Trade issue. No statement of printing. Cover title. Note: An expanded version of an earlier work printed in 1962 as *Item Forty-Three: Brian W. Aldiss, a Bibliography 1954–1962* in an edition of 500 copies.

Poul William Anderson
(b. 1926)

AFTER DOOMSDAY. *New York: Ballantine Books*, [*1962*].
Wrappers. No statement of printing on copyright page. *Ballantine Books 579* (35¢).

ALSO: *London: Victor Gollancz Ltd, 1963*. Boards. No statement of printing on copyright page. First hardcover edition.

AGENT OF THE TERRAN EMPIRE. *Philadelphia and New York: Chilton Books*, [*1965*].
First edition so stated on copyright page.

THE BEST OF POUL ANDERSON. *New York: Published by Pocket Books*, [*1976*].
Wrappers. *August, 1976* on copyright page. *Pocket Books 80671* ($1.95).

BEYOND THE BEYOND. [*New York*]: *Published by The New American Library*, [*1969*].
Wrappers. *First printing, August, 1969* on copyright page. *Signet Science Fiction T3947* (75¢).

ALSO: *New York: New American Library*, [*1969*]. Boards. Two printings, priority as listed: (A) Code *19 L* on page 275; (B) Code *42 L* on page 275. First hardcover edition. Note: Issued by the Science Fiction Book Club.

ALSO: *London: Victor Gollancz Ltd, 1970*. Boards. No statement of printing on copyright page. Deletes "Day of Burning."

THE BOOK OF POUL ANDERSON. *New York: DAW Books, Inc.*, [*1975*].
Wrappers. *First printing, June 1975/1 2 3 4 5 6 7 8 9* on copyright page. *DAW: sf Books No. 153 UW1176* ($1.50). Reissue of THE MANY WORLDS OF POUL ANDERSON.

BRAIN WAVE. *New York: Ballantine Books*, [*1954*].
Wrappers. No statement of printing on copyright page. *Ballantine Books 80* (35¢).

ALSO: *Melbourne :: London :: Toronto: William Heinemann Ltd*, [*1955*]. Boards. No statement of printing on copyright page. First hardcover edition.

THE BROKEN SWORD. *New York: Abelard-Schuman*, [*1954*].
Boards. No statement of printing on copyright page.

ALSO: *New York: Ballantine Books*, [*1971*]. Wrappers. *First Printing: January, 1971* on copyright page. *Ballantine Books 02107–X–095* (95¢). Revised text.

ALSO: [*Tisbury, Wiltshire*]: *Compton Russell*, [*1974*]. Boards. *This Library Edition published in Great Britain 1974* . . . on copyright page. First hardcover edition of revised text. Note: Issued in an imprinted plastic dust jacket.

THE BYWORLDER. [*New York*]: *New American Library*, [*1971*].
Wrappers. *First Printing, September, 1971* on copyright page. *Signet Science Fiction T4780* (75¢).

ALSO: *London: Victor Gollancz Ltd, 1972*. Boards. No statement of printing on copyright page. First hardcover edition.

A CIRCUS OF HELLS. [*New York*]: *New American Library*, [*1970*].
Wrappers. *First Printing, May, 1970* on copyright page. *A Signet Science Fiction T4250* (75¢).

THE CORRIDORS OF TIME. *Garden City: Doubleday & Company, Inc., 1965.*
First edition so stated on copyright page.

THE DANCER FROM ATLANTIS. *Garden City: Nelson Doubleday, Inc., [1971].*
Boards. Seven printings, priority as listed with the exception of the first two, both printed in the same week. Copies exhibiting both codes were distributed in August 1971, the month of publication : (A) Code *29 M* on page 179; (B) Code *B29* on page 182; (C) Code *48M* on page 179; (D) Code *21N* on page 179; (E) Code *D41* on page 181; (F) Code *E36* on page 181; (G) Code *G3* on page 181. No statement of printing on copyright page. Note: Issued by the Science Fiction Book Club.

THE DAY OF THEIR RETURN. *Garden City: Nelson Doubleday, Inc., [1974].*
Boards. Three printings, priority as listed: (A) No printing code; (B) Code *E24* on page 181; (C) Code *F48* on page 181. No statement of printing on copyright page. Note: Issued by the Science Fiction Book Club.

EARTHMAN, GO HOME! *New York: Ace Books, Inc., [1961].*
Wrappers. No statement of printing on copyright page. *Ace Double Novel Books D-479* (35¢). Bound with TO THE TOMBAUGH STATION by Wilson Tucker. Collected later in FLANDRY OF TERRA.

EARTHMAN'S BURDEN. *New York: Gnome Press Inc., [1957].*
Two bindings, probable priority as listed: (A) Pale blue boards printed in dark blue: (B) Gray cloth printed in red. First edition so stated on copyright page. With GORDON R. DICKSON.

THE ENEMY STARS. *Philadelphia and New York: J. B. Lippincott Company, 1959.*
Boards. First edition so stated on copyright page.

ENSIGN FLANDRY. *Philadelphia and New York: Chilton Books, [1966].*
First edition so stated on copyright page.

FIRE TIME. *Garden City: Doubleday & Company, Inc., 1974.*
Boards. First edition so stated on copyright page.

FLANDRY OF TERRA. *Philadelphia and New York: Chilton Books, [1965].*
First edition so stated on copyright page. ''The Game of Glory'' appears for the first time in book form while the others, ''A Message in Secret'' and ''A Plague of Masters,'' appeared in book form as MAYDAY ORBIT and EARTHMAN, GO HOME! respectively.

THE FOX, THE DOG, AND THE GRIFFIN A FOLK TALE ADAPTED FROM THE DANISH OF C. MOLBECH. *Garden City: Doubleday & Company, Inc., [1966].*
First edition so stated on copyright page.

THE GOLDEN SLAVE. *New York: Avon Book Division, [1960].*
Wrappers. No statement of printing on copyright page. *Avon T-388* (35¢).

GUARDIANS OF TIME. *New York: Ballantine Books, [1960].*
Wrappers. No statement of printing on copyright page. *Ballantine Books 422K* (35¢).

ALSO: *London: Victor Gollancz Ltd, 1961.* Boards. No statement of printing on copyright page. First hardcover edition.

THE HIGH CRUSADE. *Garden City: Doubleday & Company, Inc., 1960.*
First edition so stated on copyright page.

HOMEBREW. *Cambridge, Massachusetts: The NESFA Press, 1976.*
Two issues, no priority: (A) Three-quarter leather and marbled boards. 17 copies lettered

A—Q signed by the author. "Finebound" issue. (B) 500 numbered copies signed by the author. No statement of printing on copyright page. Contains three short stories, "House Rule," "A Philosophical Dialogue," and "Lost Secrets Revealed," plus other material.

HOMEWARD AND BEYOND. *Garden City: Doubleday & Company, Inc., 1975.*
Boards. First edition so stated on copyright page.

THE HORN OF TIME. *[New York]: Published by The New American Library, [1968].*
Wrappers. *First printing, January, 1968* on copyright page. *Signet Science Fiction P3349* (60¢).

HROLF KRAKI'S SAGA. *New York: Ballantine Books, [1973].*
Wrappers. *First Printing: October, 1973* on copyright page. *Ballantine Books 23562* ($1.25).

INHERITORS OF EARTH. *Radnor, Pennsylvania: Chilton Book Company, [1974].*
Boards. First edition so stated on copyright page. With GORDON EKLUND.

A KNIGHT OF GHOSTS AND SHADOWS. *Garden City: Nelson Doubleday, Inc., [1975].*
Boards. Code *12R* on page 179. No statement of printing on copyright page. Note: Issued by the Science Fiction Book Club.

LET THE SPACEMEN BEWARE! *New York: Ace Books, Inc., [1963].*
Wrappers. No statement of printing on copyright page. *Ace Double F–209* (40¢). Bound with THE WIZARD OF STARSHIP POSEIDON by Kenneth Bulmer.

ALSO: *London: Dennis Dobson, [1969].* Boards. *First published in Great Britain in 1969* on copyright page. First hardcover edition.

THE LONG WAY HOME. *[Frogmore]: Panther, [1975].*
Wrappers. *First Published in Great Britain in 1975 . . .* on copyright page. *Panther Science Fiction 586 04284 9* (50p). Reissue with textual changes of NO WORLD OF THEIR OWN.

THE MAKESHIFT ROCKET. *New York: Ace Books, Inc., [1962].*
Wrappers. No statement of printing on copyright page. *Ace Double F–139* (40¢). Bound with UN-MAN AND OTHER NOVELLAS by Anderson.

ALSO: *London: Dennis Dobson, [1969].* Boards. *First published in Great Britain 1969* on copyright page. First hardcover edition.

THE MANY WORLDS OF POUL ANDERSON. *Radnor, Pennsylvania: Chilton Book Company, [1974].*
First edition so stated on copyright page. Reissued as THE BOOK OF POUL ANDERSON.

MAYDAY ORBIT. *New York: Ace Books, Inc., [1961].*
Wrappers. No statement of printing on copyright page. *Ace Double Novel Books F–104* (40¢). Bound with NO MAN'S WORLD by Kenneth Bulmer. Collected later in FLANDRY OF TERRA.

A MIDSUMMER TEMPEST. *Garden City: Doubleday & Company, Inc., 1974.*
First edition so stated on copyright page.

MIRKHEIM. *New York: Published by Berkley Publishing Corporation, [1977].*
No statement of printing on copyright page.

MURDER BOUND. *New York: The Macmillan Company, 1962.*
Boards. First printing so stated on copyright page.

MURDER IN BLACK LETTER. *New York: The Macmillan Company, 1960.*
Boards. First printing so stated on copyright page.

NO WORLD OF THEIR OWN. *New York: Ace Books, Inc.,* [*1955*].
Wrappers. No statement of printing on copyright page. *Ace Double Novel Books D–110*
(35¢). Bound with THE 1,000 YEAR PLAN by Isaac Asimov. Reissued as THE LONG WAY
HOME. *Done 1st SINGLE ACE D 550*

OPERATION CHAOS. *Garden City: Doubleday & Company, Inc., 1971.*
First edition so stated on copyright page.

ORBIT UNLIMITED. *New York: Pyramid Books,* [*1961*].
Wrappers. *First printing: May 1961* on copyright page. *Pyramid G615* (35¢).

ALSO:*London: Sidgwick & Jackson,* [*1974*]. Boards. *First published in Great Britain in
1974* on copyright page. First hardcover edition.

THE PEOPLE OF THE WIND. [*New York*]: *New American Library,* [*1973*].
Wrappers. *First printing, May 1973* on copyright page. *Signet 451–Q5479–095* (95¢).

ALSO:*Boston: Gregg Press, 1977. First Printing, June 1977* on copyright page. First
hardcover edition.

PERISH BY THE SWORD. *New York: The Macmillan Company, 1959.*
Boards. First printing so stated on copyright page.

PLANET OF NO RETURN. *New York: Ace Books,* [*1957*].
Wrappers. No statement of printing on copyright page. *Ace Double Novel Books D–199*
(35¢). Bound with STAR GUARD by Andre Norton.

ALSO:*London: Dennis Dobson,* [*1966*]. Boards. *First published in Great Britain in 1966*
on copyright page. First hardcover edition.

THE QUEEN OF AIR AND DARKNESS AND OTHER STORIES. [*New York*]: *New American
Library,* [*1973*].
Wrappers. *First printing, December, 1973/1 2 3 4 5 6 7 8 9* on copyright page. *Signet
Q5713* (95¢).

THE REBEL WORLDS. [*New York*]: *Published by The New American Library,* [*1969*].
Wrappers. *First printing, October, 1969* on copyright page. *A Signet Science Fiction
T4041* (75¢).

ROGUE SWORD. *New York: Avon Book Division,* [*1960*].
Wrappers. No statement of printing on copyright page. *Avon T–472* (35¢).

SATAN'S WORLD. *Garden City: Doubleday & Company, Inc. 1969.*
First edition so stated on copyright page.

SEVEN CONQUESTS. [*New York*]: *The Macmillan Company Collier-Macmillan Ltd., London,*
[*1969*].
First printing so stated on copyright page.

SHIELD. [*New York*]: *Published by Berkley Publishing Corporation,* [*1963*].
Wrappers. *April, 1963* on copyright page. *Berkley Medallion F743* (50¢).

ALSO:*London: Dennis Dobson,* [*1965*]. Boards. *First published in Great Britain in 1965*
on copyright page. First hardcover edition.

THE SNOWS OF GANYMEDE. *New York: Ace Books, Inc.*, [*1958*].
Wrappers. No statement of printing on copyright page. *Ace Double Novel Books D–303* (35¢). Bound with WAR OF THE WING-MEN by Anderson.

THE STAR FOX. *Garden City: Doubleday & Company, Inc.*, *1965*.
First edition so stated on copyright page.

STAR PRINCE CHARLIE. *New York: G. P. Putnam's Sons*, [*1975*].
No statement of printing on copyright page. Two dust jacket states, priority as listed: (A) *Anderson/Dickson* on dust jacket spine panel with slash between authors' names barely discernible; (B) Slash is apparent. With GORDON R. DICKSON.

ALSO: [*New York*]: *Published by Berkley Publishing Corporation*, [*1977*].
Wrappers. *January, 1977* on copyright page. *A Berkley Medallion Book 0–425–03078–4* ($1.25). Text copy edited.

STAR WAYS. *New York: Avalon Books*, [*1956*].
No statement of printing on copyright page.

STRANGERS FROM EARTH. *New York: Ballantine Books*, [*1961*].
Wrappers. No statement of printing on copyright page. *Ballantine Books 483 K* (35¢).

TALES OF THE FLYING MOUNTAINS. [*New York*]: *The Macmillan Company*, [*1970*].
First printing so stated on copyright page.

TAU ZERO. *Garden City: Doubleday & Company, Inc.*, *1970*.
First edition so stated on copyright page.

THERE WILL BE TIME. *Garden City: Nelson Doubleday, Inc.*, [*1972*].
Boards. Three printings, priority as listed: (A) Code *31N* on page 177; (B) Code *23P* on page 177; (C) Code *29Q* on page 177. No statement of printing on copyright page. Note: Issued by the Science Fiction Book Club.

THREE HEARTS AND THREE LIONS. *Garden City: Doubleday & Company, Inc.*, *1961*.
First edition so stated on copyright page.

THREE WORLDS TO CONQUER. *New York: Pyramid Books*, [*1964*].
Wrappers. *First printing April 1964* on copyright page. *Pyramid Books R–994* (50¢).

TIME AND STARS. *Garden City: Doubleday & Company, Inc.*, *1964*.
First edition so stated on copyright page.

ALSO: *London: Victor Gollancz Ltd, 1964*. Boards. No statement of printing on copyright page. Drops ''Eve Times Four.''

TRADER TO THE STARS. *Garden City: Doubleday & Company, Inc.*, *1964*.
First edition so stated on copyright page.

THE TROUBLE TWISTERS. *Garden City: Doubleday & Company, Inc.*, *1966*.
First edition so stated on copyright page.

TWILIGHT WORLD. *New York: A Torquil Book Distributed by Dodd, Mead & Company*, [*1961*].
Boards. Two issues, priority not established but probably simultaneous: (A) Price *$2.95* appears in upper right corner of front dust jacket flap. Trade issue. (B) No price, *BOOK CLUB/EDITION* in lower right corner of front dust jacket flap. Book club issue. Code *B-49* on page 181 of both issues. Note: Both issues were produced from the same print run and released in February 1961.

UN-MAN AND OTHER NOVELLAS. *New York: Ace Books, Inc.*, [*1962*].
Wrappers. No statement of printing on copyright page. *Ace Double F–139* (40¢). Bound with THE MAKESHIFT ROCKET by Anderson.

ALSO: *London: Dennis Dobson*, [*1972*]. Boards. *First published in Great Britain in 1972* on copyright page. First hardcover edition.

VAULT OF THE AGES. *Philadelphia Toronto: The John C. Winston Company*, [*1952*].
First edition so stated on copyright page.

VIRGIN PLANET. *New York: Avalon Books*, [*1959*].
No statement of printing on copyright page.

WAR OF THE WING-MEN. *New York: Ace Books, Inc.*, [*1958*].
Wrappers. No statement of printing on copyright page. *Ace Double Novel Books D–303* (35¢). Bound with THE SNOWS OF GANYMEDE by Anderson.

ALSO: *Boston: Gregg Press, 1976. First Printing, June 1976* on copyright page. First hardcover edition. Note: Not issued in dust jacket.

THE WAR OF TWO WORLDS. *New York: Ace Books, Inc.*, [*1959*].
Wrappers. No statement of printing on copyright page. *Ace Double Novel Books D–335* (35¢). Bound with THRESHOLD OF ETERNITY by John Brunner.

ALSO: *London: Dennis Dobson*, [*1970*]. Boards. *First published in Great Britain in 1970* on copyright page. First hardcover edition.

WE CLAIM THESE STARS. *New York: Ace Books, Inc.*, [*1959*].
Wrappers. No statement of printing on copyright page. *Ace Double Novel Books D–407* (35¢). Bound with THE PLANET KILLERS by Robert Silverberg.

ALSO: *London: Dennis Dobson*, [*1976*]. Boards. *First published in Great Britain in 1976* on copyright page. First hardcover edition.

THE WINTER OF THE WORLD. *Garden City: Nelson Doubleday, Inc.*, [*1976*].
Boards. Four printings, priority as listed: (A) Code *F 51* on page 181; (B) Code *G 16* on page 181; (C) Code *H 01* on page 181; (D) No printing code (sequence not determined but probably later). No statement of printing on copyright page. Note: Issued by the Science Fiction Book Club.

WORLD WITHOUT STARS. *New York: Ace Books, Inc.*, [*1966*].
Wrappers. No statement of printing on copyright page. *Ace Books F–425* (40¢).

ALSO: *London: Dennis Dobson*, [*1975*]. Boards. *First published in Great Britain in 1975* on copyright page. First hardcover edition.

THE WORLDS OF POUL ANDERSON. *New York: Ace Books*, [*1974*].
Wrappers. No statement of printing on copyright page. *Ace 91055* ($1.25). Reprint. Collects PLANET OF NO RETURN, THE WAR OF TWO WORLDS, and WORLD WITHOUT STARS.

Edited Fiction

Nebula Award Stories Four. *Garden City: Doubleday & Company, Inc.*, 1969.
First edition so stated on copyright page. Edited, with introduction and foreword, by Anderson.

West By One and By One: An Anthology of Irregular Writings by The Scowrers and Molly Maguires of San Francisco and The Trained Cormorants of Los Angeles County. *San Francisco: Privately Printed, 1965.*

   No statement of printing on copyright page. Edited anonymously, with contribution "In the Island of Uffa," by Anderson.

Reference

Against Time's Arrow: The High Crusade of Poul Anderson, by Sandra Miesel. *San Bernardino, California: R. Reginald The Borgo Press. MCMLXXVIII.*

   Wrappers. *First Edition ———December, 1978* on copyright page. *The Milford Series Popular Writers of Today Volume Eighteen* at head of title.

Isaac Asimov

(b. 1920)

ASIMOV'S MYSTERIES.*Garden City: Doubleday & Company, Inc., 1968*.
First edition so stated on copyright page.

AUTHORIZED MURDER.*London: Victor Gollancz Ltd, 1976*.
Boards. No statement of printing on copyright page. Issued earlier in the U.S. as MURDER AT THE ABA.

THE BEST OF ISAAC ASIMOV.*London: Sidgwick & Jackson, [1973]*.
Boards. *First published in Great Britain in 1973* on copyright page.

ALSO:*Garden City: Doubleday & Company, Inc., 1974*. First edition so stated on copyright page. Deletes bibliography compiled by Gerald Bishop and portion of introduction.

THE BEST NEW THING.*New York and Cleveland: The World Publishing Company, 1971*.
Boards. *First printing–1971* on copyright page.

THE BICENTENNIAL MAN AND OTHER STORIES.*Garden City: Doubleday & Company, Inc., 1976*.
Boards. First edition so stated on copyright page.

BUY JUPITER AND OTHER STORIES.*Garden City: Doubleday & Company, Inc., 1975*.
Boards. First edition so stated on copyright page.

THE CAVES OF STEEL.*Garden City: Doubleday & Company, Inc., 1954*.
Boards. First edition so stated on copyright page.

THE CURRENTS OF SPACE.*Garden City: Doubleday & Company, Inc., 1952*.
Boards. First edition so stated on copyright page.

DAVID STARR SPACE RANGER.*Garden City: Doubleday & Company, Inc., 1952*.
Boards. First edition so stated on copyright page.*Paul French, pseudonym*. Collected later in AN ISAAC ASIMOV DOUBLE.

THE DEATH DEALERS.*New York: Avon Publications, Inc., [1958]*.
Wrappers. No statement of printing on copyright page.*Avon T–287* (35¢). Reissued as A WHIFF OF DEATH.

"THE DREAM" "BENJAMIN'S DREAM" and "BENJAMIN'S BICENTENNIAL BLAST" THREE SHORT STORIES....*New York: Privately Printed, Nineteen Hundred Seventy-Six*.
Boards. No statement of printing.

THE EARLY ASIMOV.*Garden City: Doubleday & Company, Inc., 1972*.
First edition so stated on copyright page.

EARTH IS ROOM ENOUGH.*Garden City: Doubleday & Company, Inc., 1957*.
First edition so stated on copyright page.

EIGHT STORIES FROM THE REST OF THE ROBOTS.*New York: Pyramid Books, [1966]*.
Wrappers. *Pyramid edition, January 1966* on copyright page. *Pyramid Books R–1283* (50¢). Reprint. Abridged collection.

THE END OF ETERNITY.*Garden City: Doubleday & Company, Inc., 1955.*
First edition so stated on copyright page.

FANTASTIC VOYAGE.*Boston: Houghton Mifflin Company, 1966.*
First printing so stated on copyright page.

FOUNDATION.*New York: Gnome Press Publishers, [1951].*
Two bindings, priority as listed: (A) Cloth; sheets measure 20.3 x 13.5 cm; sheets bulk 1.9 cm across the top; (B) Boards; sheets measure 20.3 x 12.5 cm; sheets bulk 1.4 cm across the top. First edition so stated on copyright page. Reissued with abridged text as THE 1,000 YEAR PLAN.

FOUNDATION AND EMPIRE.*New York: Gnome Press Publishers, [1952].*
Three bindings, priority as listed: (A) Red boards lettered in black; publisher's imprint on spine measures 2.2 cm across. (B) Red boards lettered in black; publisher's imprint on spine measures 2.8 cm across. (C) Green boards lettered in black; publisher's imprint on spine measures 2.8 cm across. Two issues (printings?), priority as listed: (1) Sheets bulk 1.8 cm across the top. (2) Sheets bulk 2.3 cm across the top. Two states of the dust jacket. priority as listed: (A) Printed in four colors; 26 titles listed on rear panel. (B) Printed in blue and black only; 32 titles listed on rear panel. First edition so stated on copyright page. Reissued as THE MAN WHO UPSET THE UNIVERSE.

THE FOUNDATION TRILOGY.*[Garden City: Doubleday & Company, Inc., 1963.]*
Boards. Full printing details not determined; earliest printing code and total number of printings not established. Note: A copy without a printing code has been observed and it may represent the earliest printing if no copy bearing an "E" (the letter indicating 1963) can be located. Located printings are as follows, sequence of first listed not established, others later: (A) No code; (B) Code *19G* on page 221; (C) Code *34G* on page 221; (D) Code *44M* on page 221. No statement of printing on copyright page. Reprint. Collects FOUNDATION, FOUNDATION AND EMPIRE, and SECOND FOUNDATION. Note: Issued by the Science Fiction Book Club. Issued later in Great Britain as AN ISAAC ASIMOV OMNIBUS.

THE GODS THEMSELVES.*Garden City: Doubleday & Company, Inc., 1972.*
First edition so stated on copyright page.

GOOD TASTE: A STORY. . . . *[Topeka, Kansas: Apocalypse Press, 1977.]*
Wrappers. 1012 copies printed. Three issues, no priority: (A) 12 proof copies (not seen); (B) 500 numbered copies signed by the author; (C) 500 numbered copies with author's signature in facsimile. No statement of printing on copyright page.

HAVE YOU SEEN THESE? *Boston: The NESFA Press, 1974.*
First edition so stated on copyright page. 500 numbered copies only, signed by the author.

THE HEAVENLY HOST.*New York: Walker and Company, [1975].*
Boards. *First published . . . 1975 . . .* on copyright page. Code *10 9 8 7 6 5 4 3 2 1* on copyright page.

I, ROBOT.*New York: Gnome Press, Inc. Publishers, [1950].*
Two bindings, priority as listed: (A) Cloth; (B) Wrappers. First edition so stated on copyright page.

ALSO:*London: Brown, Watson Limited, [1958].*
Wrappers. No statement of printing on copyright page. *Digit Books D164* (2'–). Abridged reprint. Collects seven of the nine stories.

AN ISAAC ASIMOV DOUBLE.*[London]: New English Library, [1972].*
Boards. No statement of printing on copyright page. Save for author's note, a reprint. Collects DAVID STARR, SPACE RANGER and THE PIRATES OF THE ASTEROIDS.

AN ISAAC ASIMOV OMNIBUS. *London: Sidgwick & Jackson*, [*1966*].
  Boards. No statement of printing on copyright page. Reprint. Collects FOUNDATION, FOUNDATION AND EMPIRE, and SECOND FOUNDATION. Issued earlier in the U.S. as THE FOUNDATION TRILOGY.

AN ISAAC ASIMOV SECOND OMNIBUS. *London: Sidgwick & Jackson*, [*1969*].
  Boards. *First published in Great Britain 1969* on copyright page. Reprint. Collects THE CURRENTS OF SPACE, PEBBLE IN THE SKY, and THE STARS, LIKE DUST. Issued earlier in the U.S. as TRIANGLE.

THE KEY WORD AND OTHER MYSTERIES. *New York: Walker and Company*, [*1977*].
  Two bindings, no priority: (A) Trade binding (advertised by the publisher but not seen); (B) Reinforced blue cloth. Library binding. Code *10 9 8 7 6 5 4 3 2 1* on copyright page.

LIAR! [*Cambridge: Published by the Syndics of the Cambridge University Press, 1977.*]
  Wrappers. *This edition first published 1977* on inside rear cover. Revised and simplified text. A different version appeared earlier in I, ROBOT.

LITTLE LOST ROBOT. [*Cambridge: Published by the Syndics of the Cambridge University Press, 1977.*]
  Wrappers. *This edition first published 1977* on inside rear cover. Revised and simplified text. A different version appeared earlier in I, ROBOT.

LUCKY STARR AND THE BIG SUN OF MERCURY. *Garden City: Doubleday & Company, Inc., 1956.*
  Boards. First edition so stated on copyright page. *Paul French, pseudonym.* Collected later in A SECOND ISAAC ASIMOV DOUBLE.

LUCKY STARR AND THE MOONS OF JUPITER. *Garden City: Doubleday & Company, Inc., 1957.*
  Boards. First edition so stated on copyright page. *Paul French, pseudonym.* Collected later in THE THIRD ISAAC ASIMOV DOUBLE.

LUCKY STARR AND THE OCEANS OF VENUS. *Garden City: Doubleday & Company, Inc., 1954.*
  Boards. First edition so stated on copyright page. *Paul French, pseudonym.* Collected later in A SECOND ISAAC ASIMOV DOUBLE.

LUCKY STARR AND THE PIRATES OF THE ASTEROIDS. *Garden City: Doubleday & Company, Inc., 1953.*
  Boards. First edition so stated on copryright page. *Paul French, pseudonym.* Collected later in AN ISAAC ASIMOV DOUBLE.

LUCKY STARR AND THE RINGS OF SATURN. *Garden City: Doubleday & Company, Inc., 1958.*
  Boards. First edition so stated on copyright page. *Paul French, pseudonym.* Collected later in THE THIRD ISAAC ASIMOV DOUBLE.

THE MAN WHO UPSET THE UNIVERSE. *New York: Ace Books, Inc.,* [*1955*].
  Wrappers. No statement of printing on copyright page. *Ace Double Size Novel D–125* (35¢). Reissue of FOUNDATION AND EMPIRE.

THE MARTIAN WAY. *Garden City: Doubleday & Company, Inc., 1955.*
  Boards. First edition so stated on copyright page. Note: All examined copies have *AZIMOV* for *ASIMOV* on spine.

MORE TALES OF THE BLACK WIDOWERS. *Garden City: Published for the Crime Club by Doubleday & Company, Inc., 1976.*
  Boards. First edition so stated on copyright page.

MURDER AT THE ABA.*Garden City: Doubleday & Company, Inc., 1976.*
Boards with cloth shelf back. First edition so stated on copyright page. Issued later in Great Britain as AUTHORIZED MURDER.

THE NAKED SUN.*Garden City: Doubleday & Company, Inc., 1957.*
First edition so stated on copyright page.

NIGHTFALL AND OTHER STORIES.*Garden City: Doubleday & Company, Inc., 1969.*
First edition so stated on copyright page.

NINE TOMORROWS.*Garden City: Doubleday & Company, Inc., 1959.*
First edition so stated on copyright page.

ONLY A TRILLION.*London New York: Abelard-Schuman, 1957.*
No statement of printing on copyright page. Essays plus three satires.

OPUS 100.*Boston: Houghton Mifflin Company, 1969.*
First Printing w on copyright page. Fiction and nonfiction, most reprinted from earlier works.

PEBBLE IN THE SKY.*Garden City: Doubleday & Company, Inc., 1950.*
First edition so stated on copyright page.

THE REBELLIOUS STARS.*New York: Ace Books, Inc., [1954].*
Wrappers. No statement of printing on copyright page. *Ace Double Novel Books D-84* (35¢). Bound with AN EARTH GONE MAD by Roger Dee. Reissue with unauthorized cuts of THE STARS, LIKE DUST.

THE REST OF THE ROBOTS.*Garden City: Doubleday & Company, Inc., 1964.*
First edition so stated on copyright page.

THE ROBOT NOVELS.*Garden City: Doubleday & Company, Inc., [1971].*
Boards. Code *12 M* on page 401. No statement of printing on copyright page. Reprint. Collects THE CAVES OF STEEL and THE NAKED SUN. Note: Issued by the Science Fiction Book Club.

SECOND FOUNDATION.*[New York]: Gnome Press, Inc., [1953].*
Four bindings, priority as listed: (A) Blue boards lettered in brown; (B) Green boards lettered in black; (C) Gray cloth lettered in red; (D) Boards with cloth shelf back; *DOUBLEDAY/SCIENCE/FICTION* at base of spine. First edition so stated on copyright page.

A SECOND ISAAC ASIMOV DOUBLE.*[London]: New English Library, [1973].*
Boards. No statement of printing on copyright page. Reprint. Collects LUCKY STARR AND THE BIG SUN OF MERCURY and LUCKY STARR AND THE OCEANS OF VENUS.

THE STARS, LIKE DUST.*Garden City: Doubleday & Company, Inc., 1951.*
First edition so stated on copyright page. Issued later with unauthorized cuts as THE REBELLIOUS STARS.

TALES OF THE BLACK WIDOWERS.*Garden City: Doubleday & Company, Inc., 1974.*
First edition so stated on copyright page.

THE THIRD ISAAC ASIMOV DOUBLE.*[London]: New English Library, [1973].*
Boards. No statement of printing on copyright page. Reprint. Collects LUCKY STARR AND THE RINGS OF SATURN and LUCKY STARR AND THE MOONS OF JUPITER.

THE 1,000 YEAR PLAN. *New York: Ace Books*, [*1955*].
Wrappers. No statement of printing on copyright page. *Ace Double Novel Books D–110* (35¢). Bound with NO WORLD OF THEIR OWN by Poul Anderson. Reissue of FOUNDATION with abridged text.

THROUGH A GLASS, CLEARLY. [*London*]: *A Four Square Book*, [*1967*].
Wrappers. *This collection first published in Great Britain . . . in April 1967* on copyright page. *Four Square Science Fiction 1866* (3/6).

ALSO: [*Hornchurch, Essex*]: *Ian Henry Publications, 1977*. Boards. *This hardback edition, 1977* on copyright page. First hardcover edition.

TRIANGLE. *Garden City: Doubleday & Company, Inc., 1961*.
Two issues, priority as listed: (A) Boards; No price on front dust jacket flap; *BOOK CLUB/EDITION* in lower right corner of front dust jacket flap. Book club issue. (B) Cloth; *$4.95* in upper right corner of front dust jacket flap. Trade issue. Code *C13* on page 516 of both issues. No statement of printing on copyright page. Note: Both produced from the same print run, but the book club issue was released as a May 1961 selection while the trade issue was published 2 June. Reprint. Collects THE CURRENTS OF SPACE, PEBBLE IN THE SKY, and THE STARS, LIKE DUST. Issued later in Great Britain as A SECOND ISAAC ASIMOV OMNIBUS.

A WHIFF OF DEATH. *New York: Walker and Company*, [*1968*].
Boards. No statement of printing on copyright page. First hardcover edition. Issued earlier as THE DEATH DEALERS.

Edited Fiction

Before the Golden Age. *Garden City: Doubleday & Company, Inc., 1974*.
First edition so stated on copyright page. Edited, with introductions and short story "Big Game," by Asimov.

Fifty Short Science Fiction Tales. *New York: Collier Books*, [*1963*].
Wrappers. *First Collier Books Edition 1962* on copyright page. *AS295V* (95¢). Edited, with introduction, by Asimov.

The Hugo Winners. *Garden City: Doubleday & Company, Inc., 1962*.
First edition so stated on copyright page. Edited, with introduction and notes, by Asimov.

The Hugo Winners. *Garden City: Doubleday & Company, Inc., 1971*.
First edition so stated on copyright page. Edited, with introduction and notes, by Asimov. *Volume Two* at head of title.

The Hugo Winners. *Garden City: Doubleday & Company, Inc., 1977*.
Boards with cloth shelf back. First edition so stated on copyright page. Edited, with introduction, notes, and afterword, by Asimov. *Volume Three* at head of title.

More Soviet Science Fiction. *New York: Collier Books*, [*1962*].
Wrappers. *First Collier Books Edition 1962* on copyright page. *AS 295V* (95¢). Edited, with introduction, by Asimov.

Nebula Award Stories Eight. *New York Evanston San Francisco London: Harper & Row, Publishers*, [*1973*].
Cloth and boards. First edition so stated on copyright page. Edited, with introduction, by Asimov.

Soviet Science Fiction. *New York: Collier Books*, [*1962*].
  Wrappers. *First Collier Books Edition 1962* on copyright page. *AS279V* (95¢). Edited,
  with introduction, by Asimov.

Tomorrow's Children. *Garden City: Doubleday & Company, Inc.*, [*1966*].
  First edition so stated on copyright page. Edited, with introduction by Asimov.

Where Do We Go From Here? *Garden City: Doubleday & Company, Inc., 1971*.
  First edition so stated on copyright page. Edited, with introduction and short story "Pâté de
  Foie Gras," by Asimov.

Reference

Asimov Analyzed, [by] Neil Goble. *Baltimore: Mirage, 1972*.
  No statement of printing on copyright page. Approximately 1500 copies printed.

Asimov's Foundation Trilogy and Other Works: Notes . . . , by L. David Allen. *Lincoln,
Nebraska: Cliffs Notes*, [*1977*].
  Wrappers. No statement of printing on copyright page.

Isaac Asimov, edited by Joseph D. Olander and Martin Harry Greenberg. *New York:
Taplinger Publishing Company*, [*1977*].
  Two bindings, no priority: (A) Boards with cloth shelf back; (B) Wrappers. First edition so
  stated on copyright page.

Isaac Asimov: A Checklist . . . , by Marjorie M. Miller. [*Kent, Ohio*]: *The Kent State
University Press*, [*1972*].
  First edition so stated on copyright page.

The Science Fiction of Isaac Asimov, by Joseph F. Patrouch, Jr. *Garden City: Doubleday &
Company, Inc., 1974*.
  Boards. First edition so stated on copyright page.

James Graham Ballard
(b. 1930)

THE ATROCITY EXHIBITION. *London: Jonathan Cape*, [*1970*].
Boards. *First published in Great Britain 1970* on copyright page.

ALSO:*Garden City: Doubleday & Company, Inc., 1970. First edition in the United States of America* on copyright page. First publication of "The New Science Fiction," a transcript of a conversation between Ballard and George MacBeth. Some minor textual changes (cf. section "Notes Towards a Mental Breakdown"). This edition was suppressed and never issued; only a few copies survive. First published U.S. edition issued later as LOVE & NAPALM: EXPORT U.S.A.

THE BEST OF J.G. BALLARD. [*London*]: *Futura Publications Limited*, [*1977*].
Wrappers. *First published in Great Britain 1977 . . .* on copyright page. *Orbit 0 8600 79430* (£1.25).

BILLENIUM. [*New York*]: *Published by Berkley Publishing Corp.*, [*1962*].
Wrappers. No statement of printing on copyright page. *Berkley Medallion F667* (50¢).

THE BURNING WORLD. [*New York*]: *Published by Berkley Publishing Corporation*, [*1964*].
Wrappers. *August, 1964* on copyright page. *Berkley Medallion F961* (50¢). Expanded version issued later as THE DROUGHT.

BY DAY FANTASTIC BIRDS FLEW THROUGH THE PETRIFIED FOREST. . . .*Brighton: Eosgraphics for Firebird Visions Ltd, 1967*.
Broadside. Two issues, no priority: (A) 50 numbered copies signed by Ballard; (B) Unsigned trade issue. Text from THE CRYSTAL WORLD. Illustration by Ivan Tyrrell.

CHRONOPOLIS AND OTHER STORIES. *New York: G. P. Putnam's Sons*, [*1971*].
No statement of printing on copyright page.

CONCRETE ISLAND. *London: Jonathan Cape*, [*1974*].
Boards. *First published 1974* on copyright page.

CRASH. *London: Jonathan Cape*, [*1973*].
Boards. *First published 1973* on copyright page.

THE CRYSTAL WORLD. *London: Jonathan Cape*, [*1966*].
Boards. *First published 1966* on copyright page.

THE DAY OF FOREVER. *London: A Panther Book*, [*1967*].
Wrappers. *This collection first published by Panther Books Limited 1967* on copyright page. *Panther Science Fiction 2307* (3/6).

ALSO: [*London*]: *A Panther Book*, [*1971*]. Wrappers. *Reprinted 1971* on copyright page. *Panther 586 023070* (25p). Deletes "The Assassination of John F. Kennedy Considered as a Downhill Motor Race" and adds "The Killing Ground."

THE DISASTER AREA. *London: Jonathan Cape*, [*1967*].
Boards. *First published 1967* on copyright page.

THE DROUGHT. *London: Jonathan Cape*, [*1965*].
Boards. *First published 1965* on copyright page. Expanded version of THE BURNING WORLD.

THE DROWNED WORLD. *[New York]: Published by Berkley Publishing Corp.*, *[1962]*.
Wrappers. No statement of printing on copyright page. *Berkley Medallion F655* (50¢).
Collected later in THE DROWNED WORLD AND THE WIND FROM NOWHERE.

ALSO:*London: Victor Gollancz Ltd, 1962 [i.e., January 1963]*. Boards. No statement of printing on copyright page. First hardcover edition. ·

THE DROWNED WORLD AND THE WIND FROM NOWHERE.*Garden City: Doubleday & Company, Inc., 1965*.
First edition so stated on copyright page. Reprint. Collects THE DROWNED WORLD and THE WIND FROM NOWHERE. Note: First hardcover publication of THE WIND FROM NOWHERE.

THE FOUR-DIMENSIONAL NIGHTMARE.*London: Victor Gollancz Ltd., 1963*.
Boards. No statement of printing on copyright page.

ALSO:*London: Victor Gollancz Ltd, 1974*. Boards. No statement of printing on copyright page. Reissue with two stories from original edition dropped and two added from other previously published collections.

HIGH-RISE.*London: Jonathan Cape, [1975]*.
Boards. *First published 1975* on copyright page.

THE IMPOSSIBLE MAN AND OTHER STORIES. *[New York]: Published by Berkley Publishing Corporation, [1966]*.
Wrappers. *April, 1966* on copyright page. *Berkley Medallion F1204* (50¢).

LOVE AND NAPALM: EXPORT U.S.A.*New York: Grove Press, Inc., [1972]*.
First American Edition/First Printing on copyright page. First published U.S. edition; follows the text published earlier in Great Britain as THE ATROCITY EXHIBITION. Preface by William S. Burroughs appears for the first time.

LOW-FLYING AIRCRAFT AND OTHER STORIES.*London: Jonathan Cape, [1976]*.
Boards. *First published 1976* on copyright page.

THE OVERLOADED MAN.*[London]: A Panther Book, [1967]*.
Wrappers. *This collection first published by Panther Books Limited 1967* on copyright page. *Panther Books 2336* (3/6).

PASSPORT TO ETERNITY. *[New York]: Published by Berkley Publishing Corporation, [1963]*.
Wrappers. *September, 1963* on copyright page. *Berkley Medallion F823* (50¢).

TERMINAL BEACH. *[New York]: Published by Berkley Publishing Corporation, [1964]*.
Wrappers.*June, 1964* on copyright page.*Berkley Medallion F928* (50¢).

ALSO:*London: Victor Gollancz Ltd, 1964*. Boards. No statement of printing on copyright page. First hardcover edition. Contents differ from Berkley version.

VERMILION SANDS. *[New York]: Published by Berkley Publishing Corporation, [1971]*.
Wrappers.*April, 1971* on copyright page.*A Berkley Medallion Book S1980* (75¢).

ALSO:*London: Jonathan Cape, [1973]*. Boards. *First published in Great Britain 1973* on copyright page. First hardcover edition. Adds "The Singing Statues."

THE VOICES OF TIME AND OTHER STORIES. *[New York]: Published by Berkley Publishing Corporation, [1962]*.
Wrappers.*February, 1962* on copyright page.*Berkley Medallion F607* (50¢).

WHY I WANT TO FUCK RONALD REAGAN.*[Brighton]: Unicorn Bookshop, 1968*.
Wrappers. Stapled. 250 copies printed. Two issues, no priority: (A) 50 numbered copies signed by the author; (B) 200 unnumbered trade copies. First printing so stated on colophon page. Later collected in THE ATROCITY EXHIBITION.

THE WIND FROM NOWHERE. [*New York*]: *Published by Berkley Publishing Corporation,* [*1962*].
> Wrappers. *January, 1962* on copyright page. *Berkley Medallion F600* (50¢). Collected later in THE DROWNED WORLD AND THE WIND FROM NOWHERE.

Reference

J. G. Ballard: A Bibliography, compiled by James Goddard. *Milford on Sea, Lymington, Hants.: Prepared and produced by James Goddard. . . . A Cypher Press Publication, 1970.*
> Wrappers. Offset, stapled. No statement of printing on copyright page. Cover title.

J. G. Ballard: The First Twenty Years, edited and compiled by James Goddard & David Pringle . . . . [*Hayes, Middlesex*]: *Bran's Head Books Ltd*, [*1976*].
> Two bindings, no priority: (A) Boards; (B) Wrappers. *First Published by Bran's Head Books Ltd . . .* on copyright page. Note: Includes material by and about Ballard as well as a bibliography of his writings.

Thomas J. Bassler
(b. 1932)

THE GODWHALE. *New York: Ballantine Books*, [*1974*].
  Wrappers. *First Printing: January, 1974* on copyright page. *Ballantine Books 23712*
(\$1.25). *T. J. Bass, pseudonym.*

   ALSO: *London: Eyre Methuen*, [*1975*]. Boards. *First published in Great Britain 1975* on
copyright page. First hardcover edition.

HALF PAST HUMAN. *New York: Ballantine Books*, [*1971*].
  Wrappers. *First Printing: July, 1971* on copyright page. *Ballantine Books Science Fiction
02306-4-095* (95¢). *T. J. Bass, pseudonym.*

Harry Bates
(b. 1900)

SPACE HAWK. *New York: Greenberg: Publisher*, [*1952*].
  Boards. No statement of printing on copyright page. With DESMOND W. HALL. *Anthony Gilmore, pseudonym*.

Barrington J. Bayley
(b. 1937)

ANNIHILATION FACTOR. *New York: Ace Books*, [*1972*].
  Wrappers. No statement of printing on copyright page. *Ace Double 33710* (95¢). Bound with HIGHWOOD by Neal Barrett, Jr.

COLLISION COURSE. *New York: DAW Books, Inc.*, [*1973*].
  Wrappers. *First printing* [through] *Tenth printing* set on ten lines must appear below art credit in addition to *First printing, February 1973* on copyright page. *DAW: sf Books No. 43 UQ1043* (95¢). Issued later in Great Britain as COLLISION WITH CHRONOS.

COLLISION WITH CHRONOS. *London: Allison & Busby*, [*1977*].
  Boards. *First published in Great Britain 1977* . . . on copyright page. Issued earlier in the U.S. as COLLISION COURSE.

EMPIRE OF TWO WORLDS. *New York: Ace Books*, [*1972*].
  Wrappers. No statement of printing on copyright page. *Ace Book 20565* (75¢).

  ALSO: *London: Robert Hale & Company*, [*1974*]. Boards. *First published in Great Britain 1974* on copyright page. First hardcover edition.

THE FALL OF CHRONOPOLIS. *New York: DAW Books, Inc.*, [*1974*].
  Wrappers. *First printing, June 1974/1 2 3 4 5 6 7 8 9* on copyright page. *DAW: sf Books No. 105 UQ1114* (95¢).

THE GARMENTS OF CAEAN. *Garden City: Doubleday & Company, Inc.*, 1976.
  Boards. First edition so stated on copyright page.

THE GRAND WHEEL. *New York: DAW Books, Inc.*, [*1977*].
  Wrappers. *First printing, August 1977/1 2 3 4 5 6 7 8 9* on copyright page. *DAW: sf Books No. 255 UW1318* ($1.50).

SOUL OF THE ROBOT. *Garden City: Doubleday & Company, Inc.*, 1974.
  First edition so stated on copyright page.

  ALSO: THE SOUL OF THE ROBOT. *London: Allison & Busby*, [*1976*]. Boards. *First published in Great Britain by Allison & Busby Limited* . . . on copyright page. Minor textual revisions.

THE STAR VIRUS. *New York: Ace Publishing Corporation*, [*1970*].
  Wrappers. No statement of printing on copyright page. *Ace Double 78400* (75¢). Bound with MASK OF CHAOS by John Jakes.

Peter Soyer Beagle
(b. 1939)

A FINE AND PRIVATE PLACE. *New York: The Viking Press, Mcmlx.*
Boards with cloth shelf back. *First published in 1960* on copyright page.

THE LAST UNICORN. *New York: The Viking Press,* [*1968*].
Boards with cloth shelf back. *First published in 1968* . . . on copyright page.

LILA THE WEREWOLF. *Santa Barbara: Capra Press, 1974.*
Two issues, no priority: (A) Boards, 75 numbered copies signed by the author; (B) Wrappers. Note: First printing bears $1.95 price on rear cover; second printing carries $2.50 price. No statement of printing on copyright page.

Eric Temple Bell
(1883–1960)

BEFORE THE DAWN.*Baltimore: The Williams & Wilkins Company, 1934.*
Published June, 1934 on copyright page.*John Taine, pseudonym.*

THE COSMIC GEOIDS AND ONE OTHER.*Los Angeles: Fantasy Publishing Co., Inc., 1949.*
First edition so stated on copyright page.*John Taine, pseudonym.*

THE CRYSTAL HORDE.*Reading, Pennsylvania: Fantasy Press, 1952.*
  Two issues, no priority: (A) 300 copies with numbered leaf signed by the author inserted;
  (B) Trade issue. First edition so stated on copyright page.*John Taine, pseudonym.*
  Collected later with SEEDS OF LIFE as WHITE LILY.

THE FORBIDDEN GARDEN.*Reading, Pennsylvania: Fantasy Press, 1947.*
  Two issues, no priority: (A) 500 copies with numbered leaf signed by the author inserted;
  (B) Trade issue. First edition so stated on copyright page.*John Taine, pseudonym.*

G. O. G. 666.*Reading, Pennsylvania: Fantasy Press, Inc., [1954].*
  Two issues, no priority: (A) 300 copies with numbered leaf signed by the author inserted;
  (B) Trade issue. First edition so stated on copyright page.*John Taine, pseudonym.*

THE GOLD TOOTH.*New York: E. P. Dutton & Company, [1927].*
  No statement of printing on copyright page.*John Taine, pseudonym.*

THE GREATEST ADVENTURE.*New York: E. P. Dutton & Company, Inc., [1929].*
  First edition so stated on copyright page.*John Taine, pseudonym.*

GREEN FIRE.*New York: E. P. Dutton & Company, [1928].*
  No statement of printing on copyright page.*John Taine, pseudonym.*

THE IRON STAR.*New York: E. P. Dutton & Co., Inc., [1930].*
  Two bindings, priority as listed: (A) Purple cloth lettered in gold; (B) Brown cloth
  lettered in dark brown. First edition so stated on copyright page.*John Taine, pseudonym.*

THE PURPLE SAPPHIRE.*New York: E. P. Dutton & Company, [1924].*
  No statement of printing on copyright page.*John Taine, pseudonym.*

QUAYLE'S INVENTION.*New York: E. P. Dutton & Company, [1927].*
  No statement of printing on copyright page.*John Taine, pseudonym.*

SEEDS OF LIFE.*Reading, Pennsylvania: Fantasy Press, 1951.*
  Two issues, no priority: (A) 300 copies with numbered leaf signed by the author inserted;
  (B) Trade issue. First edition so stated on copyright page.*John Taine, pseudonym.*

SEEDS OF LIFE AND WHITE LILY.*New York: Dover Publications, Inc., [1966].*
  Wrappers. *First published in 1966* on copyright page. Reissue of SEEDS OF LIFE and WHITE
  LILY (the latter first published as a book under the title THE CRYSTAL HORDE).*John Taine,
  pseudonym.*

THE TIME STREAM. *[Providence, Rhode Island]: Buffalo Book Company and G. H. E.,*
[1946].
  No statement of printing on copyright page.*John Taine, pseudonym.*

THE TIME STREAM, THE GREATEST ADVENTURE [and] THE PURPLE SAPPHIRE: THREE SCIENCE FICTION NOVELS . . . . *New York: Dover Publications, Inc., [1964]*.
   Wrappers. *This Dover edition, first published in 1964* . . . on copyright page. *Dover T1180* ($2.00). Reprint. Collects THE TIME STREAM, THE GREATEST ADVENTURE, and THE PURPLE SAPPHIRE. Note: Publisher's statement on copyright page indicates these novels were "slightly edited" for this edition. *John Taine, pseudonym*.

Associational

Green Fire: A Melodrama of 1990 in Three Acts, by Glenn Hughes. *New York: Samuel French, Inc., cop. 1932*.
   Wrappers. Two states noted, priority not established but presumed as listed: (A) *PRICE 75 ¢* rubber-stamped on front wrapper (not seen); (B) *PRICE 85 ¢* rubber-stamped on front wrapper. No statement of printing. Note: Based on GREEN FIRE by Bell.

Gregory Benford
(b. 1941)

DEEPER THAN THE DARKNESS. *New York: Ace Publishing Corporation*, [*1970*].
   Wrappers. No statement of printing on copyright page. *Ace Book 14215* (60¢).

IF THE STARS ARE GODS. *New York: Published by Berkley Publishing Corporation*, [*1977*].
   No statement of printing on copyright page. With GORDON EKLUND.

IN THE OCEAN OF NIGHT. *New York: The Dial Press/James Wade*, [*1977*].
   Boards. First printing so stated on copyright page.

JUPITER PROJECT. *Nashville/New York: Thomas Nelson Inc., Publishers*, [*1975*].
   Boards. First edition so stated on copyright page.

Gertrude (Barrows) Bennett
(1884–1939?)

THE CITADEL OF FEAR. *New York: Paperback Library*, [*1970*].
Wrappers. *First Printing: August, 1970* on copyright page. *Paperback Library Fantasy Novel 65–401* (95¢). *Francis Stevens, pseudonym*.

CLAIMED. *New York: Avalon Books*, [*1966*].
No statement of printing on copyright page. *Francis Stevens, pseudonym*.

THE HEADS OF CERBERUS. *Reading, Penna.: Polaris Press, 1952*.
Two bindings, no priority: (A) Cloth with leather shelf back. 10 numbered copies. (B) Full cloth. 1490 numbered copies. First edition so stated on page [8]. *Francis Stevens, pseudonym*. Note: All copies boxed but some issued without dust jacket.

Alfred Bester

(b. 1913)

AN ALFRED BESTER OMNIBUS.*London: Sidgwick & Jackson*, [*1967*].
Boards. No statement of printing on copyright page. Reprint. Collects THE DEMOLISHED MAN, TIGER! TIGER!, and THE DARK SIDE OF EARTH. Note: Only hardcover publication of THE DARK SIDE OF EARTH.

THE COMPUTER CONNECTION.*New York: Berkley Publishing Corporation*, [*1975*].
Boards. No statement of printing on copyright page. Issued later in Great Britain as EXTRO.

THE DARK SIDE OF EARTH.[*New York*]: *Published by The New American Library*, [*1964*].
Wrappers. *First printing, May, 1964* on copyright page. *Signet Books D2474* (50¢).
Collected later in AN ALFRED BESTER OMNIBUS.

THE DEMOLISHED MAN.*Chicago: Shasta Publishers*, [*1953*].
Boards with cloth shelf back. First edition so stated on copyright page. Collected later in AN ALFRED BESTER OMNIBUS.

EXTRO.*London: Eyre Methuen*, [*1975*].
Boards. *First published in Great Britain 1975* . . . on copyright page. Issued earlier in the U.S. as THE COMPUTER CONNECTION.

THE LIGHT FANTASTIC.*New York: Published by Berkley Publishing Corporation*, [*1976*].
Boards. No statement of printing on copyright page. Collected later in STARLIGHT: THE GREAT SHORT FICTION OF ALFRED BESTER.

THE RAT RACE.*New York: Berkley Publishing Corp.*, [*1956*].
Wrappers. *February, 1956* on copyright page. *Berkley Books G–19* (35¢). Reissue of "WHO HE?"

STAR LIGHT, STAR BRIGHT.*New York: Published by Berkley Publishing Corporation*, [*1976*].
No statement of printing on copyright page. Collected later in STARLIGHT: THE GREAT SHORT FICTION OF ALFRED BESTER.

STARBURST.[*New York*]: *Published by The New American Library*, [*1958*].
Wrappers. *First printing, May, 1958* on copyright page. *Signet Books S1524* (35¢).

STARLIGHT: THE GREAT SHORT FICTION OF ALFRED BESTER.*Garden City: Nelson Double-day, Inc.*, [*1976*].
Boards. No statement of printing on copyright page. Code *G 47* on page 408. Reprint. Collects THE LIGHT FANTASTIC and STAR LIGHT, STAR BRIGHT. Note: Issued by the Science Fiction Book Club.

THE STARS MY DESTINATION.[*New York*]: *Published by the New American Library*, [*1957*].
Wrappers. *First Printing, March, 1957* on copyright page. *Signet Books S1389* (35¢).
Revised text of TIGER! TIGER!

ALSO: *Boston: Gregg Press, 1975*. No statement of printing on copyright page. First hardcover edition of the revised text. Note: Not issued in dust jacket.

TIGER! TIGER!*London: Sidgwick and Jackson*, [*1956*].
Boards. No statement of printing on copyright page. Collected later in AN ALFRED BESTER OMNIBUS. Issued later in the U.S. with textual changes as THE STARS MY DESTINATION.

"WHO HE?" *New York: The Dial Press, 1953.*
    Boards with cloth shelf back. No statement of printing on copyright page. Reissued as THE
    RAT RACE.

Reference

Experiment Perilous: Three Essays on Science Fiction, [edited by Andrew Porter].
[New York]: Algol Press, [1976].
    Wrappers. No statement of printing on copyright page. Contains ''Writing and *The
    Demolished Man*'' by Bester.

Hell's Cartographers, edited by Brian W. Aldiss [and] Harry Harrison. *[London]: Weidenfeld
and Nicolson, [1975]*.
    Boards. No statement of printing on copyright page. Contains ''My Affair With Science
    Fiction'' by Bester.

Lloyd Biggle, Jr.
(b. 1923)

ALL THE COLORS OF DARKNESS. *Garden City: Doubleday & Company, Inc., 1963.*
First edition so stated on copyright page.

THE ANGRY ESPERS. *New York: Ace Books, Inc., [1961].*
Wrappers. No statement of printing on copyright page. *Ace Double Novel Books D-485* (35¢). Bound with THE PUZZLE PLANET by Robert A. W. Lowndes.

ALSO: *London: Robert Hale, [1968].* Boards. *First published in Great Britain 1968* on copyright page. First hardcover edition.

THE FURY OUT OF TIME. *Garden City: Doubleday & Company, Inc., 1965.*
First edition so stated on copyright page.

A GALAXY OF STRANGERS. *Garden City: Doubleday & Company, Inc., 1976.*
Boards. First edition so stated on copyright page.

THE LIGHT THAT NEVER WAS. *Garden City: Doubleday & Company, Inc., 1972.*
First edition so stated on copyright page.

THE METALLIC MUSE. *Garden City: Doubleday & Company, Inc., 1972.*
First edition so stated on copyright page.

MONUMENT. *Garden City: Doubleday & Company, Inc., 1974.*
First edition so stated on copyright page.

OUT OF THE SILENT SKY. *New York: Belmont Tower Books, [1977].*
Wrappers. No statement of printing on copyright page. *BT 51122* ($1.50). Issued earlier as THE RULE OF THE DOOR AND OTHER FANCIFUL REGULATIONS. Note: Cover title reads *The Silent Sky.*

THE RULE OF THE DOOR AND OTHER FANCIFUL REGULATIONS. *Garden City: Doubleday & Company, Inc., 1967.*
First edition so stated on copyright page. Reissued as OUT OF THE SILENT SKY.

SILENCE IS DEADLY. *Garden City: Doubleday & Company, Inc., 1977.*
Boards. First edition so stated on copyright page.

THE STILL SMALL VOICE OF TRUMPETS. *Garden City: Doubleday & Company, Inc., 1968.*
First edition so stated on copyright page.

THIS DARKENING UNIVERSE. *Garden City: Doubleday & Company, Inc., 1975.*
Boards. First edition so stated on copyright page.

WATCHERS OF THE DARK. *Garden City: Doubleday & Company, Inc., 1966.*
First edition so stated on copyright page.

THE WORLD MENDERS. *Garden City: Doubleday & Company, Inc., 1971.*
First edition so stated on copyright page.

Edited Fiction

Nebula Award Stories 7. *London: Victor Gollancz Limited, 1972.*
    Boards. No statement of printing on copyright page. Edited, with introduction and notes,
    by Biggle.

    ALSO:*New York Evanston San Francisco London: Harper & Row, Publishers, [1973].*
    Cloth and boards. First edition so stated on copyright page. Adds a section of obituaries
    headed "In Memoriam."

Miscellaneous

The Double: Bill Symposium: Being 94 Replies to "A Questionnaire for Professional
Science Fiction Writers and Editors" as Created by Lloyd Biggle, Jr. *[Akron, Ohio]:
D:B Press, 1969.*
    Wrappers. First edition so stated on copyright page. 500 copies only. Offset. Edited by
    William L. Bowers and William C. Mallardi.

Otto Oscar Binder

(1911–1974)

ADAM LINK IN THE PAST. *[Sydney: Whitman Press], n.d. [but 1950]*.
  Wrappers. No statement of printing. Caption title. *Eando Binder, pseudonym*.

ADAM LINK — ROBOT. *New York: Paperback Library, Inc., [1965]*.
  Wrappers. *First Printing: September, 1965* on copyright page. *Paperback Library 52–847* (50¢). *Eando Binder, pseudonym*.

ANTON YORK, IMMORTAL. *New York: Belmont Books, [1965]*.
  Wrappers. *May 1965* on copyright page. *Belmont Science Fiction B50–627* (50¢). *Eando Binder, pseudonym*.

THE AVENGERS BATTLE THE EARTH-WRECKER. *Toronto New York London: Bantam Books, [1967]*.
  Wrappers. *Published June 1967* on copyright page. *A Bantam Book F3569* (50¢). *Eando Binder, pseudonym*.

THE CANCER MACHINE. *Millheim, Penna.: The Bizarre Series, [1940]*.
  Wrappers. No statement of printing. Issued as *Bizarre Number 3*. *Eando Binder, pseudonym*.

THE DOUBLE MAN. *New York: Curtis Books, [1971]*.
  Wrappers. No statement of printing on copyright page. *Curtis Books 502–07167–075* (75¢). *Eando Binder, pseudonym*.

DRACULA. *New York: Ballantine Books, [1966]*.
  Wrappers. No statement of printing on copyright page. *Ballantine Books U2271* (50¢). With CRAIG TENNIS. Notes: (1) Stoker's novel adapted to comic book format. (2) Text of this adaptation credited to Binder and Tennis on copyright page.

ENSLAVED BRAINS. *New York: Avalon Books, [1965]*.
  No statement of printing on copyright page. *Eando Binder, pseudonym*. With EARL ANDREW BINDER.

FIVE STEPS TO TOMORROW. *New York: Curtis Books, [1970]*.
  Wrappers. No statement of printing on copyright page. *Curtis Books 502–07106–075* (75¢). *Eando Binder, pseudonym*.

THE FORGOTTEN COLONY. *New York: Popular Library, [1972]*.
  Wrappers. No statement of printing on copyright page. *Popular Library 445–00394–095* (95¢).

THE FRONTIER'S SECRET. *New York: Popular Library, [1973]*.
  Wrappers. No statement of printing on copyright page. *Popular Library 445–00501–095* (95¢). *Ian Francis Turek, pseudonym*.

GET OFF MY WORLD. *New York: Curtis Books, [1971]*.
  Wrappers. No statement of printing on copyright page. *Curtis Books 502–07121-075* (75¢). *Eando Binder, pseudonym*.

THE HOSPITAL HORROR. *New York: Popular Library*, *[1973]*.
Wrappers. No statement of printing on copyright page. *Popular Library 445–01593–075* (75¢).

THE IMPOSSIBLE WORLD. *New York: Curtis Books*, *[1970]*.
Wrappers. No statement of printing on copyright page. *Curtis Books 502–07113–075* (75¢). *Eando Binder, pseudonym.*

LORDS OF CREATION. *Philadelphia: The Prime Press*, *[1949]*.
Two issues, no priority: (A) 112 copies on special paper bound with all edges untrimmed in dark blue cloth. Label affixed to front free endpaper numbered and signed by Otto Binder. This issue has no dust jacket but was issued in a card box. Note: Some of these special copies have been noted without the limitation label. (B) Trade issue bound in purple cloth with all edges trimmed. First edition so stated on copyright page. *Eando Binder, pseudonym.*

MARTIAN MARTYRS. *New York: Columbia Publications, Inc.*, *n.d.*
Wrappers. No statement of printing. Cover title. Issued as *Science Fiction Classics No. 1*. *John Coleridge, pseudonym.* With EARL ANDREW BINDER. Note: Printed after March 1940.

MENACE OF THE SAUCERS. *New York: Belmont Books*, *[1969]*.
Wrappers. *October 1969* on copyright page. *Belmont B60–1050* (60¢). *Eando Binder, pseudonym.*

THE MIND FROM OUTER SPACE. *New York: Curtis Books*, *[1972]*.
Wrappers. No statement of printing on copyright page. *Curtis Books 502–07188–075* (75¢). *Eando Binder, pseudonym.*

THE MYSTERIOUS ISLAND. *West Haven, Connecticut: Pendulum Press, Inc.*, *[1974]*.
Two issues, no priority: (A) Boards; (B) Wrappers. *Now Age Books 64–1387* ($1.25). No statement of printing on copyright page. Notes: (1) Jules Verne's novel adapted to comic book format. (2) Text of this adaptation credited to Binder on page [6].

THE NEW LIFE. *New York: Columbia Publications, Inc.*, *n.d.*
Wrappers. No statement of printing. Cover title. Issued as *Science Fiction Classics No. 4*. *John Coleridge, pseudonym.* With EARL ANDREW BINDER. Note: Printed after March 1940.

NIGHT OF THE SAUCERS. *New York: Belmont Books*, *[1971]*.
Wrappers. *April 1971* on copyright page. *Belmont B75–2116* (75¢). *Eando Binder, pseudonym.*

PUZZLE OF THE SPACE PYRAMIDS. *New York: Curtis Books*, *[1971]*.
Wrappers. No statement of printing on copyright page. *Curtis Books 502–07134–075* (75¢). *Eando Binder, pseudonym.*

SECRET OF THE RED SPOT. *New York: Curtis Books*, *[1971]*.
Wrappers. No statement of printing on copyright page. *Curtis Books 502–07163–075* (75¢). *Eando Binder, pseudonym.*

TERROR IN THE BAY. *New York: Curtis Books*, *[1971]*.
Wrappers. No statement of printing on copyright page. *Curtis Books 502–07181–075* (75¢). *Ione Frances Turek, pseudonym.*

THE THREE ETERNALS. *[Sydney: Whitman Press]*, *n.d.* *[but 1949]*.
Wrappers. No statement of printing. Caption title. *Eando Binder, pseudonym.*

WHERE ETERNITY ENDS. *[Sydney: Whitman Press]*, *n.d.* *[but 1950]*.
Wrappers. No statement of printing. Caption title. *Eando Binder, pseudonym.*

Michael Bishop

(b. 1945)

AND STRANGE AT ECBATAN THE TREES. *New York, Hagerstown, San Francisco, London: Harper & Row, Publishers*, [*1976*].
Boards with cloth shelf back. First edition so stated on copyright page. Reissued as BENEATH THE SHATTERED MOONS.

BENEATH THE SHATTERED MOONS. *New York: DAW Books, Inc.*, [*1977*].
Wrappers. *First DAW printing, June 1977/1 2 3 4 5 6 7 8 9* on copyright page. *DAW: sf Books No. 246 UW1305* ($1.50). Reprint of AND STRANGE AT ECBATAN THE TREES.

A FUNERAL FOR THE EYES OF FIRE. *New York: Ballantine Books*, [*1975*].
Wrappers. *First Printing: February, 1975* on copyright page. *Ballantine Books SF 24350* ($1.50).

A LITTLE KNOWLEDGE. *New York: Published by Berkley Publishing Corporation*, [*1977*].
No statement of printing on copyright page.

STOLEN FACES. *New York, Hagerstown, San Francisco, London: Harper & Row, Publishers*, [*1977*].
Boards with cloth shelf back. First edition so stated on copyright page.

James Benjamin Blish
(1921–1975)

. . . AND ALL THE STARS A STAGE. *Garden City: Doubleday & Company, Inc., 1971.*
Boards. First edition so stated on copyright page.

ANYWHEN. *Garden City: Doubleday & Company, Inc., 1970.*
First edition so stated on copyright page.

ALSO: *London: Faber and Faber, [1971].* Boards. *First published in England in 1971* on copyright page. Preface slightly revised; adds ''Skysign.''

BEST SCIENCE FICTION STORIES OF JAMES BLISH. *London: Faber and Faber Ltd, [1965].*
First published in mcmlxv on copyright page.

ALSO: *London: Faber and Faber Ltd, [1973].* Boards. *This revised edition 1973* on copyright page. Deletes one story collected in the earlier edition and adds two. Reissued as THE TESTAMENT OF ANDROS.

BLACK EASTER. *Garden City: Doubleday & Company, Inc., 1968.*
Two (three?) printings, priority as listed: (A) Code *J21* on page 165; (B) Code *J26* on page 165 (not seen); (C) Code *J32* on page 165. Note: Contrary to this publisher's normal practice, no statement of printing appears on copyright page. British edition issued by Faber and Faber states *published in England in 1968* on copyright page. According to *Whitaker's Five-Year Cumulative Book List 1968–1972*, this edition was published in February 1969.

A CASE OF CONSCIENCE. *New York: Ballantine Books, [1958].*
Wrappers. No statement of printing on copyright page. *Ballantine Books 256* (35¢).

ALSO: *London: Faber and Faber Limited, [1959].* Boards. *First published in mcmlix* on copyright page. First hardcover edition.

CITIES IN FLIGHT. *[New York]: Avon, [1970].*
Wrappers. *First Avon Printing, February, 1970* on copyright page. *Avon W187* ($1.25). Reprint. Contains THEY SHALL HAVE STARS, A LIFE FOR THE STARS, EARTHMAN, COME HOME, and THE TRIUMPH OF TIME.

ALSO: *Garden City: Nelson Doubleday, Inc., [1973].* Boards. Two printings, priority as listed: (A) Code *03O* on page [595]; (B) Code *04O* on page [595]. No statement of printing on copyright page. First hardcover edition. Note: Issued by the Science Fiction Book Club.

A CLASH OF CYMBALS. *London: Faber & Faber, [1959].*
First published in mcmlix on copyright page. Issued earlier in the U.S. as THE TRIUMPH OF TIME.

ALSO: *London: Faber & Faber, [1965]. Second impression mcmlxv* on copyright page. Adds ''Author's Note.''

THE DAY AFTER JUDGMENT. *Garden City: Doubleday & Company, Inc., 1971.*
Note: Contrary to this publisher's normal practice, no statement of printing appears on copyright page. Code *L47* on page 166.

DOCTOR MIRABILIS. *London: Faber and Faber, [1964].*
First published in mcmlxiv on copyright page.

ALSO: *New York: Dodd, Mead & Company, [1971].* Boards with cloth shelf back. No statement of printing on copyright page. Textual changes. Note: This edition preceded by a mimeographed printing limited to 250 copies circulated in 1968 for protection of copyright, with text following Faber and Faber edition. Copies were sent as a supplement to *Kalki*, the journal of the James Branch Society, with the remainder for sale.

THE DUPLICATED MAN.*New York: Avalon Books*, [*1959*].
No statement of printing on copyright page. With ROBERT LOWNDES.

EARTHMAN, COME HOME.*New York: G. P. Putnam's Sons*, [*1955*].
Boards. No statement of printing on copyright page.

ALSO:*New York: Avon Publications, Inc.*, [*1958*]. Wrappers. No statement of printing on copyright page.*Avon T–225* (35¢). Abridged text.

ESPER.*New York: Avon Publications, Inc.*, [*1958*].
Wrappers. No statement of printing on copyright page.*Avon T–268* (35¢). Reissue of JACK OF EAGLES.

FALLEN STAR.*London: Faber and Faber*, [*1957*].
First published in England in mcmlvii on copyright page. Issued earlier in the U.S. as THE FROZEN YEAR.

THE FROZEN YEAR.*New York: Ballantine Books*, [*1957*].
Two issues, priority as listed: (A) Wrappers.*Ballantine Books 197* (35¢). Published 19 March 1957. (B) Cloth. Published 22 April 1957. No statement of printing on copyright page. Issued later in Great Britain as FALLEN STAR.

GALACTIC CLUSTER.[*New York*]:*Published by The New American Library*, [*1959*].
Wrappers.*First printing, October, 1959* on copyright page.*Signet Books S1719* (35¢).

ALSO:*London: Faber and Faber*, [*1960*]. Boards.*First published in mcmlx* on copyright page. Drops three stories collected in the U.S. edition and adds "Beanstalk."

JACK OF EAGLES.*New York: New York: Greenberg: Publisher*, [*1952*].
Boards. No statement of printing on copyright page. Reissued as ESPER.

ALSO:*New York: Galaxy Publishing Corp.*, [*1953*]. Wrappers. No statement of printing on copyright page. Issued as *Galaxy Science Fiction Novel No. 19* (35¢). Abridged text.

A LIFE FOR THE STARS.*New York G. P. Putnam's Sons*, [*1962*].
No statement of printing on copyright page.

MIDSUMMER CENTURY.*Garden City: Doubleday & Company, Inc.*, *1972*.
First edition so stated on copyright page.

ALSO:*New York: DAW Books, Inc.*, [*1974*]. Wrappers.*First Printing, February 1974/1 2 3 4 5 6 7 8 9* on copyright page.*DAW: sf Books No. 89 UQ 1094* (95¢). Adds two stories, "Skysign" and "A Style in Treason."

MISSION TO THE HEART STARS.*New York: G. P. Putnam's Sons*, [*1965*].
No statement of printing on copyright page.

ALSO:*London: Faber & Faber*, [*1965*].*First published in mcmlxv* on copyright page. Note: Published simultaneously in U.S. and Great Britain on 11 November 1965.

THE NIGHT SHAPES.*New York: Ballantine Books*, [*1962*].
Wrappers. No statement of printing on copyright page.*Ballantine Books F–647* (50¢).

THE QUINCUNX OF TIME.[*New York*]:*A Dell Book*, [*1973*].
Wrappers.*First printing —October 1973* on copyright page.*Dell 7244* (95¢).

ALSO:*London: Faber and Faber*, [*1975*]. Boards.*First published in England 1975* on copyright page. First hardcover edition.

THE SEEDLING STARS. *N.Y.: Gnome Press, Publishers, [1957]*.
Four bindings. Priority of first three not established, fourth is a later state: (A) Green boards, spine lettered in brown; (B) Red boards, spine lettered in black; (C) Gray boards, spine lettered in red; (D) Gray cloth, spine lettered in red. First edition so stated on copyright page.

SO CLOSE TO HOME.*New York: Ballantine Books, [1961]*.
Wrappers. No statement of printing on copyright page. *Ballantine Books 465K* (35¢).

SPOCK MUST DIE!*Toronto New York London: Bantam Books, [1970]*.
Wrappers.*Published February 1970* on copyright page.*A Bantam Book H5515* (60¢).

THE STAR DWELLERS.*New York: G. P. Putnam's Sons, [1961]*.
No statement of printing on copyright page.

STAR TREK.*Toronto New York London: Bantam Books, [1967]*.
Wrappers.*Published January 1967* on copyright page.*A Bantam Fifty F3459 (50¢)*.
Collected later in THE STAR TREK READER II.

ALSO:*London New York Sydney Toronto: White Lion Publishers, [1974]*. Boards.*White Lion edition, 1974* on copyright page. First hardcover edition.

STAR TREK 2.*Toronto New York London: Bantam Books, [1968]*.
Wrappers.*Published February 1968* on copyright page.*A Bantam Book F3439* (50¢).
Collected later in THE STAR TREK READER.

ALSO:*London, New York, Sydney and Toronto: White Lion Publishers Limited, [1975]*.
Boards.*White Lion Edition, 1975* on copyright page. First hardcover edition.

STAR TREK 3.*Toronto New York London: Bantam Books, [1969]*.
Wrappers.*Published April 1969* on copyright page.*A Bantam Book F4371* (50¢). Collected later in THE STAR TRECK READER.

ALSO:*London, New York, Sydney and Toronto: White Lion Publishers Limited, [1975]*. Boards.
First British Hardcover Edition . . . 1975 on copyright page. Note: Title reads *Startrek* [sic] *3*.
First hardcover edition.

STAR TREK 4. *Toronto New York London: Bantam Books, [1971]*.
Wrappers.*Published July 1971* on copyright page.*A Bantam Book S7009* (75¢). Collected later in THE STAR TREK READER II.

ALSO:*[London]: Severn House, [1977]*. Boards.*This first hardcover publication published 1977 . . .* on copyright page. First hardcover edition.

STAR TREK 5.*Toronto New York London: Bantam Books, [1972]*.
Wrappers.*Published February 1972* on copyright page.*A Bantam Book S7300* (75¢).
Collected later in THE STAR TREK READER III.

ALSO:*[London]: Severn House, [1977]*. Boards.*This first hardcover publication published 1977 . . .* on copyright page. First hardcover edition.

STAR TREK 6.*Toronto New York London: Bantam Books, [1972]*.
Wrappers.*Published April 1972* on copyright page.*A Bantam Book S7364* (75¢). Collected later in THE STAR TREK READER III.

STAR TREK 7.*Toronto New York London: Bantam Books, [1972]*.
Wrappers.*Published July 1972* on copyright page.*A Bantam Book S7480* (75¢). Collected later in THE STAR TREK READER III.

STAR TREK 8. *Toronto/New York/London: Bantam Pathfinder Editions*, [*1972*].
Wrappers. *Published November 1972* on copyright page. *A Bantam Book SP7550* (75¢).
Collected later in THE STAR TREK READER.

STAR TREK 9. *Toronto/New York/London: Bantam Pathfinder Editions*, [*1973*].
Wrappers. *Published August 1973* on copyright page. *A Bantam Book SP7808* (75¢).
Collected later in THE STAR TREK READER II.

STAR TREK 10. *Toronto/New York/London: Bantam Pathfinder Editions*, [*1974*].
Wrappers. *Published February 1974* on copyright page. *A Bantam Book SP8401* (75¢).

STAR TREK 11. *Toronto New York London: Bantam Books*, [*1975*].
Wrappers. *Published April 1975* on copyright page. *A Bantam Book Q8717* ($1.25).

STAR TREK 12. *Toronto • New York • London: Bantam Books*, [*1977*].
Wrappers. *Published November 1977* on copyright page. *A Bantam Book 11382–8* ($1.75).
Note: Two of the five adaptations were completed by JUDITH A. LAWRENCE (Mrs. James
Blish).

THE STAR TREK READER. *New York: E. P. Dutton & Co., Inc.*, [*1976*].
Boards with cloth shelf back. First edition so stated on copyright page. Reprint. Collects
STAR TREK 2, STAR TREK 3, and STAR TREK 8. First hardcover appearance of STAR TREK 8.

THE STAR TREK READER II. *New York: E. P. Dutton*, [*1977*].
Boards with cloth shelf back. First edition so stated on copyright page. Reprint. Collects
STAR TREK 1, STAR TREK 4, and STAR TREK 9. First hardcover appearance of STAR TREK 9.

THE STAR TREK READER III. *New York: E. P. Dutton*, [*1977*].
Boards with cloth shelf back. First edition so stated on copyright page. Reprint. Collects
STAR TREK 5, STAR TREK 6, and STAR TREK 7. First hardcover appearance of STAR TREK 6 and
STAR TREK 7.

THE TESTAMENT OF ANDROS. [*London*]: *Arrow Books*, [*1977*].
Wrappers. *Arrow edition 1977* on copyright page. *Arrow 0 09 914840 4* (60p). Reprint.
Issued earlier as BEST SCIENCE FICTION STORIES OF JAMES BLISH, revised edition 1973.

THEY SHALL HAVE STARS. *London: Faber and Faber Ltd*, [*1956*].
First published in mcmlvi on copyright page. Issued later in the U.S. as YEAR 2018! with
textual differences.

ALSO: *London: Faber and Faber Ltd*, [*1965*]. *First published in mcmlvi . . . Second
Impression mcmlxv* on copyright page. Adds ''Author's Note'' dated ''New York 1964''
and ''Chronology.''

TITAN'S DAUGHTER. [*New York*]: *Published by The Berkley Publishing Corporation* [*1961*].
Wrappers. *March, 1961* on copyright page. *Berkley Medallion G507* (35¢). Note: Expanded from the novelette ''Beanstalk,'' a.k.a. ''Giants in the Earth.''

ALSO: *London, New York, Sydney and Toronto: White Lion Publishers Limited*, [*1975*].
Boards. *White Lion Edition, 1975* on copyright page. First hardcover edition.

A TORRENT OF FACES. *Garden City: Doubleday & Company, Inc.*, *1967*.
First edition so stated on copyright page. With NORMAN L. KNIGHT.

THE TRIUMPH OF TIME. *New York: Avon Publications, Inc.*, [*1958*].
Wrappers. No statement of printing on copyright page. *Avon T-279* (35¢). Issued later in
Great Britain as A CLASH OF CYMBALS.

THE VANISHED JET. *New York: Weybright and Talley*, [*1968*].
No statement of printing on copyright page.   *LVB, BVMMV*

VOR. *New York: Avon Publications, Inc.*, [*1958*].
Wrappers. No statement of printing on copyright page. *Avon T-238* (35¢).

THE WARRIORS OF DAY. *New York: Galaxy Publishing Corp.*, [*1953*].
Wrappers. No statement of printing on copyright page. Issued as *Galaxy Science Fiction Novel No. 16* (35¢).

WELCOME TO MARS. *London: Faber and Faber*, [*1967*].
First published in mcmlxvii on copyright page.

YEAR 2018! *New York: Avon Publications, Inc.*, [*1957*].
Wrappers. No statement of printing on copyright page. *Avon T-193* (35¢). Revised version of THEY SHALL HAVE STARS.

Edited Fiction

Nebula Award Stories Five. *Garden City: Doubleday & Company, Inc.*, *1970*.
First edition so stated on copyright page. Edited, with introduction, by Blish.

New Dreams This Morning. *New York: Ballantine Books*, [*1966*].
Wrappers. First Printing: October, 1966 on copyright page. *Ballantine Science Fiction U2331* (50¢). Edited, with preface and two stories, "A Work of Art" and "The Dark Night of the Soul," by Blish.

Thirteen O'Clock . . . , [by] C. M. Kornbluth. [*New York*]: *A Dell Book*, [*1970*].
Wrappers. *First printing — December 1970* on copyright page. *Dell 8731* (75¢). Edited, with preface, by Blish.

ALSO: *London: Robert Hale & Company, 1972*. Boards. *First published in Great Britain 1972* on copyright page. First hardcover edition.

Nonfiction (Dealing with the Fantasy Genre only)

The Issue at Hand. *Chicago: Advent: Publishers, 1964*.
First edition so stated on copyright page. *William Atheling, Jr., pseudonym.*

More Issues at Hand. *Chicago: Advent: Publishers, Inc., 1970*.
First edition so stated on copyright page. *William Atheling, Jr., pseudonym.*

Reference

James Blish: A Bibliography 1940-1976, compiled by Judith A. Blish. *Harpsden, Henley-on-Thames: Judith A. Blish*, [*1976*].
Self wrappers. No statement of printing.

Robert Albert Bloch
(b. 1917)

AMERICAN GOTHIC. *New York: Simon and Schuster*, [*1974*].
Boards. Code *1 2 3 4 5 6 7 8 9 10* on copyright page.

ATOMS AND EVIL. *Greenwich, Conn.: Fawcett Publications, Inc.*, [*1962*].
Wrappers. *First Gold Medal printing August 1962* on copyright page. *Gold Medal s1231* (35¢).

ALSO: *London: Robert Hale & Company*, [*1976*]. Boards. *This edition 1976* on copyright page. First hardcover edition.

THE BEST OF ROBERT BLOCH. *New York: Ballantine Books*, [*1977*].
Wrappers. *First Edition: November 1977* on copyright page. *Ballantine 25757* ($1.95).

BLOCH AND BRADBURY. [*New York*]: *A Tower Book*, [*1969*].
Wrappers. No statement of printing on copyright page. *Tower 43–246* (60¢). With RAY BRADBURY. Issued later in Great Britain as FEVER DREAM AND OTHER FANTASIES. Note: Reprinted in 1972 by Peacock Press of Chicago with additional material by others.

BLOOD RUNS COLD. *New York: Simon and Schuster*, *1961*.
Boards. First printing so stated on copyright page.

BOGEY MEN. *New York: Pyramid Books*, [*1963*].
Wrappers. *First printing, March 1963* on copyright page. *Pyramid Books F–839* (40¢).

CHAMBER OF HORRORS. *New York: Award Books*, [*1966*].
Wrappers. *First printing 1966* on copyright page. *Award Books A187X* (60¢).

COLD CHILLS. *Garden City: Doubleday & Company, Inc.*, *1977*.
Boards. First edition so stated on copyright page.

THE COUCH. *Greenwich, Conn.: Fawcett Publications, Inc.*, [*1962*].
Wrappers. *First printing February 1962* on copyright page. *Gold Medal s1192* (35¢).

THE DEAD BEAT. *New York: Simon and Schuster*, *1960*.
Boards. First printing so stated on copyright page.

DRAGONS AND NIGHTMARES. *Baltimore: Mirage*, *1968*.
No statement of printing on copyright page. 1000 numbered copies.

FEAR TODAY, GONE TOMORROW. *New York: Award Books/London: Tandem Books*, [*1971*].
Wrappers. No statement of printing on copyright page. *Award Books A811S* (75¢).

FEVER DREAM AND OTHER FANTASIES. *London: Sphere Books Limited*, [*1970*].
Wrappers. *First published in Great Britain in 1970 . . .* on copyright page. *Sphere 17140* (25p). With RAY BRADBURY. Issued earlier in the U.S. as BLOCH AND BRADBURY.

FIREBUG. *Evanston, Illinois: Regency Books*, [*1961*].
Wrappers. *Published June 1961* on copyright page. *RB 101* (50¢).

HORROR-7. *New York: Belmont Books*, [*1963*].
Wrappers. *First printing February 1963* on copyright page. *Belmont 90-275* (40¢). Re-

print. Stories collected from THE OPENER OF THE WAY and PLEASANT DREAMS —
NIGHTMARES. Issued later in Great Britain as TORTURE GARDEN.

THE HOUSE OF THE HATCHET AND OTHER TALES OF HORROR. *London: Tandem Books
Limited, [1965].*
  Wrappers. *First Tandem Edition 1965* on copyright page. *Tandem Books T 19* (3'6). Issued
  earlier in the U.S. as YOURS TRULY, JACK THE RIPPER.

IT'S ALL IN YOUR MIND. *New York: Curtis Books, [1971].*
  Wrappers. No statement of printing on copyright page. *Curtis Books 502–07147–075*
  (75¢).

THE KIDNAPER. *New York: Lion Books, Inc., [1954].*
  Wrappers. *Lion edition published January, 1954* on copyright page. *Lion Book 185* (25¢).

THE KING OF TERRORS. *New York: The Mysterious Press, 1977.*
  Two issues, no priority: (A) 250 numbered copies signed by the anthor, in cloth slipcase;
  (B) Trade issue. First edition so stated on copyright page.

LADIES' DAY [and] THIS CROWDED EARTH. *New York: Belmont Books, [1968].*
  Wrappers. *August 1968* on copyright page. *A Belmont Double B60–080* (60¢).

THE LAUGHTER OF A GHOUL [and] WHAT EVERY YOUNG GHOUL SHOULD KNOW. [*West Warwick, R.I.*]: *Necronomicon Press, [1977].*
  Wrappers. *This edition, the first, of Robert/Bloch's two stories, is limited to a/numbered
  printing of 500 copies* on page [8]. Cover title. Offset from typewritten copy. Issued as *F &
  SF Fragments 2.*

THE LIVING DEMONS. *New York: Belmont Books, [1967].*
  Wrappers. *September 1967* on copyright page. *Belmont B50-787* (50¢).

MORE NIGHTMARES. *New York: Belmont Books, [1962].*
  Wrappers. *First printing February 1962* on copyright page. *Belmont L92–530* (50¢).
  Reprint. All stories collected earlier in THE OPENER OF THE WAY and PLEASANT DREAMS —
  NIGHTMARES.

NIGHTMARES. [*New York*]: *Belmont Books, [1961].*
  Wrappers. *Belmont Books Edition 1961* on copyright page. *Belmont Books 233* (35¢).
  Reprint. All stories collected earlier in PLEASANT DREAMS—NIGHTMARES.

NIGHT-WORLD. *New York: Simon and Schuster, [1972].*
  Boards. First printing so stated on copyright page.

THE OPENER OF THE WAY. *Sauk City: Arkham House, 1945.*
  No statement of printing on copyright page.

PLEASANT DREAMS — NIGHTMARES. *Sauk City: Arkham: House: Publishers, 1960.*
  No statement of printing on copyright page.

PSYCHO. *New York: Simon and Schuster, 1959.*
  Boards. First printing so stated on copyright page.

THE SCARF. *New York: The Dial Press, 1947.*
  Boards. No statement of printing on copyright page. Reprinted as THE SCARF OF PASSION.
    ALSO: *Greenwich, Conn.: Fawcett Publications, Inc., [1966].* Wrappers. No statement of
  printing on copyright page. *A Fawcett Gold Medal Book d1727* (50¢). Textual revisions.

THE SCARF OF PASSION. *New York: Avon Publishing Co., Inc.*, [*1949*].
Wrappers. No statement of printing on copyright page. *Avon 211* (25¢). Reissue of THE
SCARF.

SEA KISSED. [*London: Utopian Publications Ltd.*], *n.d.* [*1945*].
Self wrappers. Two printings, priority as listed: (A) 39 pages. Collects four short stories by
Bloch. *Printed in Great Britain* on page 39. (B) 36 pages. Adds "Goper's Head" by
Benson Herbert. *Printed in Eire* on page 36. No statement of printing. Cover title. Note:
According to Walter Gillings in *Vision of Tomorrow*, July 1970, this booklet was first
printed in February 1945, preceding THE OPENER OF THE WAY published later the same
year. Also see George Locke, ed., *Ferret Fantasy Christmas Annual for 1973* (London:
Ferret Fantasy, 1974), p. 5.

SHOOTING STAR. *New York: Ace Books, Inc.*, [*1958*].
Wrappers. No statement of printing on copyright page. *Ace Double Novel Books D–265*
(35¢). Bound with TERROR IN THE NIGHT by Bloch.

THE SKULL OF THE MARQUIS DE SADE AND OTHER STORIES. *New York: Pyramid Books*,
[*1965*].
Wrappers. *First printing, October 1965* on copyright page. *Pyramid Books R–1247* (50¢).

ALSO: *London: Robert Hale & Company*, [*1975*]. Boards. *First published in Great Britain
1975* on copyright page. First hardcover edition.

SNEAK PREVIEW. *New York: Paperback Library*, [*1971*].
Wrappers. *First Printing: August, 1971* on copyright page. *A Paperback Library Science
Fiction Novel 64–660* (75¢).

SPIDERWEB. *New York: Ace Books, Inc.*, [*1954*].
Wrappers. No statement of printing on copyright page. *Ace Double Novel Books D–59*
(35¢). Bound with THE CORPSE IN MY BED by David Alexander.

THE STAR STALKER. *New York: Pyramid Books*, [*1968*].
Wrappers. *First printing September, 1968* on copyright page. *Pyramid T–1869* (75¢).

TALES IN A JUGULAR VEIN. *New York: Pyramid Books*, [*1965*].
Wrappers. *First printing, February 1965* on copyright page. *Pyramid Books R–1139*
(50¢).

TERROR. *New York: Belmont Books*, [*1962*].
Wrappers. *First Printing May 1962* on copyright page. *Belmont L92–537* (50¢).

TERROR IN THE NIGHT AND OTHER STORIES. *New York: Ace Books, Inc.*, [*1958*],
Wrappers. No statement of printing on copyright page. *Ace Double Novel Books D–265*
(35¢). Bound with SHOOTING STAR by Bloch.

THIS CROWDED EARTH. See LADIES' DAY.

THE TODD DOSSIER. [New York]: *Delacorte Press*, [*1969*].
First printing so stated on copyright page. *Collier Young, pseudonym*. Note: In a letter to
the compiler Bloch comments, "Since I had no contractual protection, it was bylined 'by
Collier Young.' He didn't write a line — I did it all, from a film treatment by Joan Didion
& her husband John Dunne — also robbed of credit!"

THE WILL TO KILL. *New York: Ace Books, Inc.*, [*1954*].
Wrappers. No statement of printing on copyright page. *Ace Books S–67* (25¢).

YOURS TRULY, JACK THE RIPPER. *New York: Belmont Books, [1962]*.
Wrappers. *First printing January 1962* on copyright page. *Belmont L92–527* (50¢). Reprint. All stories collected earlier in THE OPENER OF THE WAY and PLEASANT DREAMS—NIGHTMARES. Reissued as THE HOUSE OF THE HATCHET AND OTHER TALES OF HORROR.

Associational

The Night Walker, by Sidney Stuart. *New York: Award Books, [1964]*.
Wrappers. *First printing December, 1964* on copyright page. *Award Books K A124F* (50¢). Note: This novel by Stuart is based on a screenplay by Bloch. Introduction by Bloch.

Asylum, by William Johnston. *Toronto New York London: Bantam Books, [1972]*.
Wrappers. *Published December 1972* on copyright page. *A Bantam Book N7672* (95¢). Note: This novel by Johnston is based on a screenplay by Bloch.

Nonfiction (Dealing with the Fantasy Genre only):

The Eighth Stage of Fandom: Selections From 25 Years of Fan Writing. *Chicago: Advent: Publishers, 1962.*
725 copies printed. Three issues, no priority: (A) Buckram. 125 numbered and signed copies of which numbers 26–125, termed the "Collector's Edition," were for sale at the 20th World Science Fiction Convention, Chicago 1962. (B) Gray cloth. 200 copies. (C) Wrappers. 400 copies. First edition so stated on copyright page.

Reference

Robert Bloch: Bibliography, compiled by Graham M. Hall. [*Tewkesbury, Gloucestershire: Published by Graham M. Hall, 1965.*]
Wrappers. No statement of printing. Mimeographed, stapled. Cover title.

Nelson Slade Bond

(b. 1908)

ANIMAL FARM: A FABLE IN TWO ACTS. *New York Hollywood London Toronto: Samuel French, Inc., [1964]*.
  Wrappers. At least two printings, priority as listed: (A) Outer rear wrapper headed *RECENT MUSICALS*; inner front wrapper headed *RECENT ACQUISITIONS*; (B) Outer rear wrapper headed *RECENT ACQUISITIONS*; inner front wrapper headed *RECENT MUSICALS*. No statement of printing on copyright page. Note: Adapted from the satire ANIMAL FARM by George Orwell.

EXILES OF TIME. *Philadelphia: Prime Press, 1949*.
  Two issues, no priority: (A) Black cloth, spine lettered in gold. 112 numbered copies signed by the author. Enclosed in paper slipcase, issued without dust jacket. Limited issue. (B) Gray cloth, spine lettered in gold, issued with dust jacket. Trade issue. First edition so stated on copyright page.

MR MERGENTHWIRKER'S LOBBLIES A FANTASTIC COMEDY IN THREE ACTS. *New York Hollywood London Toronto: Samuel French, Inc., [1957]*.
  Wrappers. No statement of printing on copyright page.

MR. MERGENTHWIRKER'S LOBBLIES AND OTHER FANTASTIC TALES. *New York: Coward-McCann, Inc., [1946]*.
  No statement of printing on copyright page.

NIGHTMARES AND DAYDREAMS. *Sauk City: Arkham House, 1968*.
  First edition so stated on copyright page.

NO TIME LIKE THE FUTURE. *New York: Avon Publications, Inc., [1954]*.
  Wrappers. No statement of printing on copyright page. *Avon T–80 (35¢)*.

THE REMARKABLE EXPLOITS OF LANCELOT BIGGS: SPACEMAN. *Garden City: Doubleday & Company, Inc., 1950*.
  Two issues, no priority: (A) Black cloth with facsimile of Bond's signature in gold in lower right corner of front cover, gray cloth spine lettered in black. Four numbered copies signed by the author. Special copies prepared for the author (not seen; information supplied by Nelson Bond). (B) Dark blue cloth, spine lettered in white. Trade issue. First edition so stated on copyright page.

STATE OF MIND A COMEDY IN THREE ACTS. *New York Hollywood London Toronto: Samuel French, Inc., [1957]*.
  Wrappers. No statement of printing on copyright page.

THE THIRTY-FIRST OF FEBRUARY. *New York: Gnome Press, [1949]*.
  Two issues, no priority: (A) Crimson and black cloth lettered in gold. 112 numbered copies signed by the author. Enclosed in paper slipcase, issued without dust jacket. Limited issue. (B) Magenta cloth lettered in black. Trade issue. First edition so stated on copyright page. Note: Reprinted circa 1952 in paper wrappers for distribution to U.S. military personnel. Although a later printing, the first edition statement is retained on the copyright page.

Benjamin William Bova

(b. 1932)

AS ON A DARKLING PLAIN. *New York: Walker and Company,* [*1972*].
  Boards. *First published in the United States of America in 1972* on copyright page.

CITY OF DARKNESS. *New York: Charles Scribner's Sons,* [*1976*].
  Code *1 3 5 7 9 11 13 15 17 19 V/C 20 18 16 14 12 10 8 6 4 2* on copyright page.

THE DUELING MACHINE. *New York–Chicago–San Francisco: Holt, Rinehart and Winston,*
  [*1969*].
  Bindings, no priority: (A) Cloth; (B) Boards. First edition so stated on copyright page.

END OF EXILE. *New York: E. P. Dutton & Co., Inc.,* [*1975*].
  First edition so stated on copyright page.

ESCAPE! *New York/Chicago/San Francisco: Holt, Rinehart and Winston,* [*1970*].
  Bindings, no priority: (A) Cloth; (B) Boards. First edition so stated on copyright page.

EXILED FROM EARTH. *New York: E.P. Dutton & Co., Inc.,* [*1971*].
  First edition so stated on copyright page.

FLIGHT OF EXILES. *New York: E. P. Dutton & Co., Inc.,* [*1972*].
  First edition so stated on copyright page.

FORWARD IN TIME. *New York: Walker and Company,* [*1973*].
  Boards. *First publishd* [sic] *in the United States of America in 1973* on copyright page.

GREMLINS, GO HOME! *New York: St. Martin's Press,* [*1974*].
  Boards. No statement of printing on copyright page. With GORDON R. DICKSON.

MILLENNIUM. *New York: Random House,* [*1976*].
  Boards. First edition so stated on copyright page.

THE MULTIPLE MAN. *Indianapolis/New York: The Bobbs-Merrill Company, Inc.,* [*1976*].
  Boards. First printing so stated on copyright page.

OUT OF THE SUN. *New York Chicago San Francisco: Holt, Rinehart and Winston,* [*1968*].
  Two bindings, no priority: (A) Cloth; (B) Boards. First edition so stated on copyright page.

THE STAR CONQUERORS. *Philadelphia Toronto: The John C. Winston Company,* [*1959*].
  First edition so stated on copyright page.

STAR WATCHMAN. *New York/Chicago/San Francisco: Holt, Rinehart and Winston,* [*1964*].
  Two bindings, no priority: (A) Cloth; (B) Boards. First edition so stated on copyright page.

THE STARCROSSED. *Radnor, Pennsylvania: Chilton Book Company,* [*1975*].
  Boards. First edition so stated on copyright page.

THX 1138. *New York: Paperback Library,* [*1971*].
  Wrappers. *First Printing: April, 1971* on copyright page. *Paperback Library 64–624*
  (75¢).

THE WEATHERMAKERS. *New York Chicago San Francisco: Holt, Rinehart and Winston,* [*1967*].
> Bindings, no priority: (A) Cloth; (B) Boards. First edition so stated on copyright page.

WHEN THE SKY BURNED. *New York: Walker and Company,* [*1973*].
> Boards. *First published in the United States of America in 1973* on copyright page.

THE WINDS OF ALTAIR. *New York: E. P. Dutton & Co., Inc.,* [*1973*].
> First edition so stated on copyright page.

Edited Fiction

Aliens. [*London*]: *Futura Publications Ltd,* [*1977*].
> Wrappers. *First published in Great Britain . . . 1977* on copyright page. *Orbit Science Fiction 0 8600 7958 9* (70p). Edited, with introduction, by Bova.

Analog Annual. *New York: Pyramid Books,* [*1976*].
> Wrappers. *April 1976* on copyright page. *Pyramid A4016* ($1.50). Edited, with introduction, by Bova.

Analog 9. *Garden City: Doubleday & Company, Inc., 1973.*
> First edition so stated on copyright page. Edited, with introduction, by Bova.

Exiles. [*London*]: *Futura Publications Limited,* [*1977*].
> Wrappers. *First published in Great Britain . . . 1977* on copyright page. *Orbit Science Fiction 0 8600 7959 7* (70p). Edited, with introduction, by Bova.

The Many Worlds of Science Fiction. *New York: E. P. Dutton & Co., Inc.,* [*1971*].
> First edition so stated on copyright page. Edited, with introduction, by Bova.

The Science Fiction Hall of Fame. *Garden City: Doubleday & Company, Inc.,* [*1973*].
> First edition so stated on copyright pages. Two volumes. Edited, with introduction (duplicated in each volume), by Bova.

Nonfiction (Dealing with the Fantasy Genre only)

Notes to a Science Fiction Writer. *New York: Charles Scribner's Sons,* [*1975*].
> Code *1 3 5 7 9 11 13 15 17 19 v/c 20 18 16 14 12 10 8 6 4 2* on copyright page. Four of Bova's stories are used as examples: ''Fifteen Miles,'' ''Men of Good Will,'' ''Stars, Won't You Hide Me?'' and ''The Shining Ones.''

Through Eyes of Wonder. [*Reading, Massachusetts*]: *Addison-Wesley,* [*1975*].
> Boards. First printing so stated on copyright page.

Viewpoint. *Cambridge, Massachusetts: The NESFA Press, 1977.*
> Two issues, no priority: (A) Three-quarter leather and marbled boards. 15 copies lettered A–O signed by the author. ''Finebound'' issue. (B) Cloth. 800 numbered copies signed by the author. No statement of printing on copyright page.

Leigh Brackett (Hamilton)
(1915–1978)

ALPHA CENTAURI — OR DIE! *New York: Ace Books, Inc.,* [*1963*].
Wrappers. No statement of printing on copyright page. *Ace Double F–187* (40¢). Bound with LEGEND OF LOST EARTH by G. McDonald Wallis.

THE BEST OF LEIGH BRACKETT. *Garden City: Nelson Doubleday, Inc.,* [*1977*].
Boards. No statement of printing on copyright page. Code *S24* on page [367]. Note: Issued by the Science Fiction Book Club.

THE BIG JUMP. *New York: Ace Books, Inc.,* [*1955*].
Wrappers. No statement of printing on copyright page. *Ace Double Novel Books D–103* (35¢). Bound with SOLAR LOTTERY by Philip K. Dick.

THE BOOK OF SKAITH. *Garden City: Nelson Doubleday, Inc.,* [*1976*].
Boards. No statement of printing on copyright page. Code *R39* on page 468. Reprint. Collects THE GINGER STAR, THE HOUNDS OF SKAITH, and THE REAVERS OF SKAITH. First hardcover edition for all titles. Note: Issued by the Science Fiction Book Club.

THE COMING OF THE TERRANS. *New York: Ace Books, Inc.,* [*1967*].
Wrappers. No statement of printing on copyright page. *Ace Book G–669* (50¢).

AN EYE FOR AN EYE. *Garden City: Doubleday & Company, Inc.,* 1957.
Boards. First edition so stated on copyright page.

FEAR NO EVIL. *London: Transworld Publishers,* [*1960*].
Wrappers. *Corgi Edition published 1960* on copyright page. *Corgi Books SC902* (2'6). Reissue of THE TIGER AMONG US.

FOLLOW THE FREE WIND. *Garden City: Doubleday & Company, Inc.,* 1963.
First edition so stated on copyright page.

THE GALACTIC BREED. *New York: Ace Books, Inc.,* [*1955*].
Wrappers. No statement of printing on copyright page. *Ace Double Novel Books D–99* (35¢). Bound with CONQUEST OF THE SPACE SEA by Robert Moore Williams. Note: This edition of THE STARMEN has been altered by the publisher and cut by approximately 20,000 words.

THE GINGER STAR. *New York: Ballantine Books,* [*1974*].
Wrappers. *First Printing: May, 1974* on copyright page. *Ballantine Science Fiction 23963* ($1.25). Collected later in THE BOOK OF SKAITH.

THE HALFLING AND OTHER STORIES. *New York: Ace Books,* [*1973*].
Wrappers. *First Ace Printing: September 1973* on copyright page. *An Ace Book 31590* ($1.25).

THE HOUNDS OF SKAITH. *New York: Ballantine Books,* [*1974*].
Wrappers. *First Printing: October, 1974* on copyright page. *Ballantine Science Fiction 24230* ($1.25). Collected later in THE BOOK OF SKAITH.

THE LONG TOMORROW. *Garden City: Doubleday & Company, Inc.,* 1955.
Boards. First edition so stated on copyright page.

THE NEMESIS FROM TERRA. *New York: Ace Books, Inc.*, [*1961*].
Wrappers. No statement of printing on copyright page. *Ace Double Novel F–123* (40¢).
Bound with COLLISION COURSE by Robert Silverberg. Issued earlier as SHADOW OVER
MARS.

NO GOOD FROM A CORPSE. *New York: Coward-McCann, Inc.*, [*1944*].
No statement of printing on copyright page.

PEOPLE OF THE TALISMAN. *New York: Ace Books, Inc.*, [*1964*].
Wrappers. No statement of printing on copyright page. *Ace Double M–101* (45¢). Bound
with THE SECRET OF SINHARAT by Brackett.

THE REAVERS OF SKAITH. *New York: Ballantine Books*, [*1976*].
Wrappers. *First Edition: August, 1976* on copyright page. *Ballantine Books SF 24438*
($1.50). At the head of title: *Stark #3*. Collected later in THE BOOK OF SKAITH.

RIO BRAVO. *New York: Bantam Books*, [*1959*].
Wrappers. *Published January 1959* on copyright page. *A Bantam Western 1893* (25¢).
Note: Novelization of a movie script by Leigh Brackett and Jules Furthman.

THE SECRET OF SINHARAT. *New York: Ace Books, Inc.*, [*1964*].
Wrappers. No statement of printing on copyright page. *Ace Double M–101* (45¢). Bound
with PEOPLE OF THE TALISMAN by Brackett.

SHADOW OVER MARS. *Manchester: World Distributors Manchester Ltd., Sydney Pemberton
Publisher*, [*1951*].
Wrappers. No statement of printing on copyright page. *A World Fantasy Classic* (1'6).
Reissued as THE NEMESIS FROM TERRA.

SILENT PARTNER. *New York: G. P. Putnam's Sons*, [*1969*].
No statement of printing on copyright page.

THE STARMEN. *New York: Gnome Press, Inc.*, [*1952*].
Boards. First edition so stated on copyright page. Reissued with abridgment and editorial
changes as THE GALACTIC BREED. The 1952 Gnome Press text was reprinted as THE
STARMEN OF LLYRDIS.

THE STARMEN OF LLYRDIS. *New York: Ballantine Books*, [*1976*].
Wrappers. *First Printing: January, 1976* on copyright page. *Ballantine Books SF Classic
24668* ($1.50). Reissue of THE STARMEN.

STRANGER AT HOME. *New York: Simon and Schuster, 1946*.
Boards. No statement of printing on copyright page. *George Sanders, pseudonym*. Note:
This novel was ghost-written for George Sanders, an actor whose roles included ''The
Saint.'' See Robert E. Briney, ''In Memoriam: Leigh Brackett,'' *The Armchair Detective*,
11 (July 1978), p. 259.

THE SWORD OF RHIANNON. *New York: Ace Books, Inc.*, [*1953*].
Wrappers. No statement of printing on copyright page. *Ace Double Novel Books D–36*
(35¢). Bound with CONAN THE CONQUEROR by Robert E. Howard.

ALSO: *London New York: T. V. Boardman & Company Limited*, [*1955*]. Boards. *First
published in Great Britain, 1955* on copyright page. First hardcover edition.

THE TIGER AMONG US. *Garden City: Doubleday & Company, Inc., 1957*.
Boards. First edition so stated on copyright page. Reissued as 13 WEST STREET and in Great
Britain as FEAR NO EVIL.

13 WEST STREET. *New York: Bantam Books,* [*1962*].
  Wrappers. *Bantam edition published May 1962* on copyright page. *A Bantam Book J2323* (40¢). Issued earlier as THE TIGER AMONG US.

Associational

*Follow the Free Wind, by Leigh Brackett. Adapted by Laurence Swinburne. *New York: McGraw-Hill Book Company,* [*1970*].
  Wrappers. In the *Reading Shelf II* series. Note: Brackett's novel, FOLLOW THE FREE WIND, adapted for young readers.

Edited Fiction

The Best of Edmond Hamilton. *Garden City: Nelson Doubleday, Inc.,* [*1977*].
  Boards. No statement of printing on copyright page. Code *H 10* on page 333. Edited, with introduction, by Brackett. Note: Issued by the Science Fiction Book Club.

The Best of Planet Stories #1. *New York: Ballantine Books,* [*1975*].
  Wrappers. *First Printing: January, 1975* on copyright page. *Ballantine Science Fiction 24334* ($1.25). Edited, with introduction and short story "Lorelei of the Red Mist" (in collaboration with Ray Bradbury), by Brackett.

Raymond Douglas Bradbury

(b. 1920)

THE ANTHEM SPRINTERS. *New York: The Dial Press, 1963*.
Two simultaneous bindings, but paperbound copies were probably available a few weeks prior to hardbound copies: (A) Wrappers. *Apollo Editions A–75* ($1.95); (B) Cloth. No statement of printing on copyright page.

THE AUTUMN PEOPLE. *New York: Ballantine Books, [1965]*.
Wrappers. *First Ballantine Printing October 1965* on copyright page. *Ballantine Books U2141* (50¢). Stories adapted to comic book format. Foreword and ''The Screaming Woman'' appear for the first time in book form.

BLOCH AND BRADBURY. *[New York]: A Tower Book, [1969]*.
Wrappers. No statement of printing on copyright page. *Tower 43–246* (60¢). With ROBERT BLOCH. ''The Watchers'' appears for the first time in a Bradbury collection, with four other stories reprinted from earlier books. Issued later in Great Britain as FEVER DREAM AND OTHER FANTASIES. Note: Reprinted in 1972 by Peacock Press of Chicago with additional material by others.

DANDELION WINE. *Garden City: Doubleday & Company, Inc., 1957*.
First edition so stated on copyright page.

ALSO: *New York: Alfred A. Knopf, 1975*. No statement of printing on copyright page. New introduction by Bradbury.

DARK CARNIVAL. *Sauk City: Arkham House, 1947*.
No statement of printing on copyright page.

ALSO: *London: Hamish Hamilton, [1948]*. Boards. *First published in Great Britain, 1948* on copyright page. Abridged reprint. Collects twenty of the twenty-seven stories.

THE DAY IT RAINED FOREVER. *London: Rupert Hart-Davis, 1959*.
Two bindings, priority as listed: (A) Olive green boards (not seen, reported by Donn Albright); (B) Blue boards. No statement of printing on copyright page. Collects stories from A MEDICINE FOR MELANCHOLY with the following changes: deletes four stories, ''A Medicine for Melancholy,'' ''The First Night of Lent,'' ''All Summer in a Day,'' and ''The Great Collision of Monday Last'' and adds ''Referent,'' ''Almost the End of the World,'' ''Here There Be Tygers,'' ''Perchance to Dream,'' and ''And the Rock Cried Out.''

THE DAY IT RAINED FOREVER A COMEDY IN ONE ACT. *New York Hollywood Toronto: Samuel French, Inc., [1966]*.
Wrappers. No statement of printing on copyright page. Note: *PRICE, 75 CENTS* at base of front wrapper. Copies distributed later have price $1.00 and still later $1.25 rubber-stamped on front wrapper.

FAHRENHEIT 451. *New York: Ballantine Books, Inc., [1953]*.
Five bindings. No sequence for hardcover copies determined but all are preceded by those in wrappers: (A) Wrappers. *Ballantine Books 41* (35¢), (B) Red cloth lettered in gold. Note: According to Bradbury 50 copies for his personal use were so bound, (C) Red boards lettered in gold, (D) Red boards lettered in yellow, (E) Johns-Manville Quinterra, an asbestos material. Note: this issue, limited to 200 numbered copies signed by the author,

was issued without dust jacket. No statement of printing on copyright page. In addition to the title novel, collects ''The Playground'' and ''And the Rock Cried Out.''

ALSO:*London: Rupert Hart-Davis, 1954.* Boards. No statement of printing on copyright page. First British edition. Features the title novel only.

ALSO:*New York: Simon and Schuster,* [*1967*]. Boards. First printing so stated on copyright page. Text follows 1953 Ballantine edition. New introduction by Bradbury.

FEVER DREAM AND OTHER FANTASIES.*London: Sphere Books Limited,* [*1970*]. Wrappers. *First published in Great Britain in 1970 . . .* on copyright page. *Sphere 17140* (25p). With ROBERT BLOCH. Issued earlier in the U.S. as BLOCH AND BRADBURY.

THE GOLDEN APPLES OF THE SUN.*Garden City: Doubleday & Company, Inc., 1953.* Boards. First edition so stated on copyright page. Later combined with A MEDICINE FOR MELANCHOLY as TWICE TWENTY TWO.

ALSO:*London: Rupert Hart-Davis, 1953.* Boards. No statement of printing on copyright page. Deletes two stories, ''The Big Black and White Game'' and ''The Great Fire.''

THE HALLOWEEN TREE.*New York: Alfred A. Knopf, 1972.* Two bindings, no priority: (A) Black cloth stamped in orange and white; (B) White cloth stamped in black, orange, and brown reproducing dust jacket design. Note: Issued without dust jacket. First edition so stated on copyright page.

ALSO:*London: Hart-Davis, MacGibbon,* [*1973*]. *First published in Great Britain* on copyright page. Note: Printed from same plates as U.S. edition but drops two leaves, page [*147*], ''About the Author and Illustrator,'' and page [*149*] ''A Note on the Type.''

I SING THE BODY ELECTRIC!*New York: Alfred A. Knopf, 1969.* First edition so stated on copyright page. Note: Lines 18 and 19 transposed on page 231. Error persists in the second printing, the British edition (printed from the U.S. plates), and possibly unobserved later printings.

THE ILLUSTRATED MAN.*Garden City: Doubleday & Company, Inc., 1951.* First edition so stated on copyright page.

ALSO:*London: Rupert Hart-Davis, 1952.* Boards. No statement of printing on copyright page. Includes two stories not in the U.S. edition, ''Usher II'' and ''The Playground'' and deletes four, ''The Rocket Man,'' ''The Fire Balloons,'' ''The Exiles,'' and ''The Concrete Mixer.''

LONG AFTER MIDNIGHT. *New York: Alfred A. Knopf, 1976.* Boards with cloth shelf back. First edition so stated on copyright page. Note: Two states of the proof copies bound in wrappers and issued to reviewers. Earliest has ''I Rocket'' which Bradbury insisted be replaced. Later copies substitute ''The Better Part of Wisdom.'' Published version includes the latter story.

THE MACHINERIES OF JOY.*New York: Simon and Schuster, 1964.* Boards with cloth shelf back. First printing so stated on copyright page.

ALSO:*London: Rupert Hart-Davis, 1964.* Boards. No statement of printing on copyright page. Deletes ''Almost the End of the World,'' included earlier in THE DAY IT RAINED FOREVER.

THE MARTIAN CHRONICLES.*Garden City: Doubleday & Company, Inc., 1950.* First edition so stated on copyright page.

ALSO:*London: Rupert Hart-Davis, 1951.* Boards. No statement of printing on copyright page. Retitled THE SILVER LOCUSTS. Adds ''The Fire Balloons'' and deletes ''Usher II.''

ALSO:[*London*]: *The Science Fiction Book Club*, [*1953*]. Boards. *This edition . . . was produced in 1953 . . .* on copyright page. Carries the U.S. title, drops "Usher II" and adds "The Fire Balloons" and "The Wilderness." Note: Issued by the British Science Fiction Book Club.

ALSO:*New York: Time Incorporated*, [*1963*]. Wrappers. No statement of printing on copyright page. First printing of the complete text. Includes the 1950 Doubleday text, "The Fire Balloons," and "The Wilderness."

ALSO: *Garden City: Doubleday & Company, Inc.*, [*1973*]. No statement of printing on copyright page. First hardcover edition of the complete text. Includes biographical sketch and bibliography of Bradbury by William F. Nolan.

A MEDICINE FOR MELANCHOLY. *Garden City: Doubleday & Company, Inc.*, *1959.*
First edition so stated on copyright page. A number of these stories were reprinted in THE DAY IT RAINED FOREVER.

THE OCTOBER COUNTRY. *New York: Ballantine Books*, [*1955*].
Three bindings, no priority established: (A) Red cloth lettered in gold. Note: According to Bradbury 50 copies for the author's use were so bound (not seen, reported by Donn Albright), (B) Dull red cloth lettered in black. Two states, probable priority as listed: (1) ꓭB monogram on spine is printed upside down; (2) ꓭB monogram is correctly printed. (C) Red boards lettered in black. No statement of printing on copyright page. Note: Four stories appear for the first time in book form, "The Dwarf," "The Watchful Poker Chip of H. Matisse," "Touched With Fire," and "The Wonderful Death of Dudley Stone." Remainder are reprinted — most with revisions — from DARK CARNIVAL.

ALSO:*New York: Ballantine Books*, [*1956*]. Wrappers. No statement of printing on copyright page. *Ballantine Books F139* (50¢). Adds prefatory note by the author.

ALSO:*London: Ace Books Limited*, [*1961*]. Wrappers. *First Ace Books edition 1961* on copyright page. *Ace Books H422* (2/6). Contents differ. Twelve of the thirteen stories are from THE OCTOBER COUNTRY. "The Traveller" is reprinted from DARK CARNIVAL and did not appear in earlier U.S. or British editions of THE OCTOBER COUNTRY.

THE PEDESTRIAN. [*Glendale, California: Roy A. Squires, 1964.*]
Wrappers. No statement of printing on copyright page. 280 copies only. Reprint. Collected earlier in THE GOLDEN APPLES OF THE SUN.

THE PEDESTRIAN A FANTASY IN ONE ACT. *New York Hollywood London Toronto: Samuel French, Inc.*, [*1966*].
Wrappers. No statement of printing on copyright page. Note: *PRICE, 75 CENTS* at base of front wrapper. Copies distributed later have *$1.00* price and still later *$1.25* rubber-stamped on front wrapper.

PILLAR OF FIRE AND OTHER PLAYS. . . . *Toronto New York London: Bantam Books*, [*1975*].
Wrappers. *November 1975* on copyright page. *Bantam Drama N2173* (95¢).

R IS FOR ROCKET. *Garden City: Doubleday & Company, Inc.*, [*1962*].
Boards. First edition so stated on copyright page. All but two stories, "R is For Rocket" and "Frost and Fire," reprinted from earlier books.

RAY BRADBURY. *London Harrap*, [*1975*].
Flexible cloth wrappers. *First published in Great Britain in 1975 . . .* on copyright page. Reprint collection. Edited, with introduction and notes, by Anthony Adams. Note: *Whitaker's Cumulative Book List* enters this volume as *Short Stories*. This title appears nowhere in the book.

S IS FOR SPACE. *Garden City: Doubleday & Company, Inc., 1966.*
First edition so stated on copyright page. All but four stories, "Chrysalis," "Pillar of Fire," "Time in Thy Flight," and "The Screaming Woman" (the latter published in a different format earlier in THE AUTUMN PEOPLE), reprinted from earlier books.

Here reprint

THE SILVER LOCUSTS. See THE MARTIAN CHRONICLES.

THE SMALL ASSASSIN. *London: The New English Library Limited, [1962].*
Wrappers. *First Ace Books edition 1962* on copyright page. *Ace H521* (2/6). Reprint. All stories appeared earlier in the U.S. edition of DARK CARNIVAL.

SOMETHING WICKED THIS WAY COMES. *New York: Simon and Schuster, 1962.*
First printing so stated on copyright page.

SUN AND SHADOW. *Berkeley: [The Quenian Press], 1957.*
Wrappers. 90 copies only. Two states, sequence unknown: (A) Text ends on page 19, copyright notice on page [20], colophon on page [21]; (B) Text ends on page 19, page [20] is blank, colophon on page [21], copyright notice on page [22] (not seen; reported by Donn Albright). No statement of printing on colophon leaf. Reprint. Collected earlier in THE GOLDEN APPLES OF THE SUN. Note: Printed by Kenneth J. Carpenter for members of the Roxburghe Club of San Francisco and other friends.

SWITCH ON THE NIGHT. *[New York]: Pantheon Books, [1955].*
Boards. No statement of printing. Earliest printing bears the following statement on title page: *Text copyright 1955 by Ray Bradbury/Illustrations copyright 1955 by Pantheon Books, Inc./Library of Congress Card No. 55-5545/Printed in the United States of America/by Graphic Offset Company, New York, N.Y.* Note: A later printing bears a similar statement on verso of title page but gives the publisher as *Pantheon Books, a Division of Random House, Inc.* These copies are bound in washable white cloth printed in black, yellow, and olive green. Still later printings lack the dedication to Bradbury's daughters and list new Library of Congress serial numbers for library and trade bindings on rear cover.

THAT GHOST, THAT BRIDE OF TIME EXCERPTS FROM A PLAY-IN-PROGRESS. . . . *[Glendale, California: Roy A. Squires, March 1976.]*
Wrappers. No statement of printing on copyright page. 400 copies printed. The first 150 bear the statement *Subscriber's Copy* and the author's signature on page [21].

TOMORROW MIDNIGHT. *New York: Ballantine Books, [1966].*
Wrappers. *First Ballantine Printing June 1966* on copyright page. *A Ballantine Book U2142* (50¢). Stories adapted to comic book format. Introduction and two stories, "Punishment Without Crime" and "I, Rocket," appear for the first time.

TWICE TWENTY TWO. *Garden City: Doubleday & Company, Inc., 1966.*
No statement of printing on copyright page. Code *47G* on page 405. Note: Later printings delete date from title page. Reprint. Combines THE GOLDEN APPLES OF THE SUN and A MEDICINE FOR MELANCHOLY.

Comb of H 1966 stated SFBC

THE VINTAGE BRADBURY. *New York: Vintage Books, [1965].*
Two bindings, no priority: (A) Orange buckram stamped in gold and black; (B) Wrappers. *Vintage Book V–294* ($1.45). *First Vintage edition, September, 1965* on copyright page. All but one story reprinted from earlier books.

wraps

THE WONDERFUL ICE CREAM SUIT AND OTHER PLAYS. *Toronto/New York/London: Bantam Pathfinder Editions, [1972].*
Wrappers. *Published April 1972* on copyright page. *Bantam Pathfinder Edition SP7297* (75¢).

ALSO:*London: Hart-Davis, MacGibbon, [1973]*. Boards. *First published in Great Britain 1973* on copyright page. First hardcover edition.

Edited Fiction

The Circus of Dr. Lao and Other Improbable Stories. *New York: Bantam Books, [1956]*. Wrappers. *Published, October, 1956* on copyright page. *A Bantam Giant A1519* (35¢). Edited, with introduction, by Bradbury.

Timeless Stories for Today and Tomorrow. *New York: Bantam Books, [1952]*. Wrappers. First edition so stated on copyright page. *A Bantam Giant A944* (35¢). Edited, with introduction and short story "The Pedestrian," by Bradbury.

Reference

The Bradbury Chronicles, [by] George Edgar Slusser. *San Bernardino, California: R. Reginald The Borgo Press, MCMLXXVII*. Wrappers. *First Edition — April, 1977* on copyright page. *The Milford Popular Writers of Today, Volume Four* at head of title.

Bradbury's Works . . . , by Audrey Smoak Manning. *Lincoln, Nebraska: Cliffs Notes, [1977]*. Wrappers. No statement of printing on copyright page.

The Drama of Ray Bradbury, by Ben F. Indick. *[Baltimore: T. K. Graphics, 1977.]* Wrappers. No statement of printing on copyright page.

The Ray Bradbury Companion . . ., by William F. Nolan. *Detroit: A Bruccoli Clark Book Published by Gale Research, 1975*. No statement of printing on copyright page. Primarily a comprehensive checklist of writings by and about Bradbury with facsimiles from his unpublished and uncollected work in all media.

Marion Eleanor Zimmer Bradley (Breen)

(b. 1930)

*ANYTHING GOES.*Sydney, Australia: Stag Publishing Co.*, [*1964*].
   Wrappers. *Morgan Ives, pseudonym.* Abridged reprint of SPARE HER HEAVEN.

THE BLOODY SUN.*New York: Ace Books, Inc.*, [*1964*].
   Wrappers. No statement of printing on copyright page. *Ace Book F–303* (40¢).

BLUEBEARD'S DAUGHTER. *New York: Lancer Books*, [*1968*].
   Wrappers. *A Lancer Book • 1968* on copyright page. *Lancer Books 73–739* (60¢).

THE BRASS DRAGON.*New York: An Ace Book*, [*1969*].
   Wrappers. No statement of printing on copyright page. *Ace Double 37250* (60¢). Bound with IPOMOEA by John Rackham.

CAN ELLEN BE SAVED?*New York: Grosset & Dunlap Publishers*, [*1975*].
   Wrappers. No statement of printing on copyright page. *Tempo Books 7444* ($1.25). Note. Novelization of a teleplay by Emmett Roberts.

CASTLE TERROR. *New York: Lancer Books*, [*1965*].
   Wrappers. *A Lancer Original • 1965* on copyright page. *Lancer Books 72–983* (50¢).

THE COLORS OF SPACE.*Derby, Connecticut: Monarch Books, Inc.*, [*1963*].
   Wrappers.*Published in August, 1963* on copyright page. *Monarch Books 368* (35¢).

THE DARK INTRUDER & OTHER STORIES.*New York: Ace Books, Inc.*, [*1964*].
   Wrappers. No statement of printing on copyright page.*Ace Double F–273* (40¢). Bound with FALCONS OF NARABEDLA by Bradley.

DARK SATANIC.[*New York*]: *Published by Berkley Publishing Corporation*, [*1972*].
   Wrappers. *September, 1972* on copyright page.*A Berkley Medallion Book S2231* (75¢).

DARKOVER LANDFALL.*New York: DAW Books, Inc.*, [*1972*].
   Wrappers. *First printing, December 1972* on copyright page. *DAW: sf Books No. 36 UQ1036* (95¢).

THE DOOR THROUGH SPACE.*New York: Ace Books, Inc.*, [*1961*].
   Wrappers. No statement of printing on copyright page.*Ace Double Novel F–117* (40¢). Bound with RENDEZVOUS ON A LOST WORLD by A. Bertram Chandler.

DRUMS OF DARKNESS.*New York: Ballantine Books*, [*1976*].
   Wrappers. *First Edition: August, 1976* on copyright page. *Ballantine Gothic 25108* ($1.25).

ENDLESS VOYAGE.*New York: Ace Books*, [*1975*].
   Wrappers. No statement of printing on copyright page. *Ace 20660* ($1.25).

FALCONS OF NARABEDLA.*New York: Ace Books, Inc.*, [*1964*].
   Wrappers. No statement of printing on copyright page. *Ace Double F–273* (40¢). Bound with THE DARK INTRUDER & OTHER STORIES by Bradley.

THE FORBIDDEN TOWER. *New York: DAW Books, Inc.,* [*1977*].
Wrappers. *First printing, September 1977/1 2 3 4 5 6 7 8 9* on copyright page. *DAW: sf Books No. 256 UJ1323* ($1.95).   *Greece 1979*

THE HERITAGE OF HASTUR. *New York: DAW Books, Inc.,* [*1975*].
Wrappers. *First printing, August 1975/1 2 3 4 5 6 7 8 9* on copyright page. *DAW: sf Books No. 160 UW1189* ($1.50).

ALSO: *Boston: Gregg Press, 1977. First Printing, June 1977* on copyright page. First hardcover edition. Note: Not issued in dust jacket.

HUNTERS OF THE RED MOON. *New York: DAW Books, Inc.,* [*1973*].
Wrappers. *First Printing, September 1973/1 2 3 4 5 6 7 8 9* on copyright page. *DAW: sf Books No. 71 UQ1071* (95¢).

*I AM A LESBIAN. *Derby, Connecticut: Monarch Books, Inc.,* [*1962*].
Wrappers. *A Monarch Human Behavior Book MB529. Lee Chapman, pseudonym.*

IN THE STEPS OF THE MASTER. *New York: Grosset & Dunlap, Inc. A National General Company Publishers,* [*1973*].
Wrappers. No statement of printing on copyright page. *Tempo Books 5595* (95¢). *The Sixth Sense #2* at head of title. Note: A novel based on the Universal Television series *The Sixth Sense* created by Anthony Lawrence.

THE JEWEL OF ARWEN. [*Baltimore: T–K Graphics, 1974.*]
Wrappers. No statement of printing.

*KNIVES OF DESIRE. *San Diego: Corinth Publications,* [*1966*].
Wrappers. In the *Evening Readers* series. *Morgan Ives, pseudonym.*

*MY SISTER, MY LOVE. *Derby, Connecticut: Monarch Books, Inc.,* [*1963*].
Wrappers. *Monarch Books 352. Miriam Gardner, pseudonym.*

*NO ADAM FOR EVE. *San Diego: Corinth Publications,* [*1966*].
Wrappers. In the *Evening Readers* series. *John Dexter, pseudonym.*

THE PARTING OF ARWEN. [*Baltimore: T–K Graphics, 1974.*]
Wrappers. No statement of printing on copyright page. Cover title.

THE PLANET SAVERS. *New York: Ace Books, Inc.,* [*1962*].
Wrappers. No statement of printing on copyright page. *Ace Double F–153* (40¢). Bound with THE SWORD OF ALDONES by Bradley.
Greece 1979
ALSO: *New York: Ace Books,* [*1976*]. Wrappers. No statement of printing on copyright page. *Ace 67020* ($1.50). Adds "The Waterfall."

SEVEN FROM THE STARS. *New York: Ace Books, Inc.,* [*1962*].
Wrappers. No statement of printing on copyright page. *Ace Double Novel F–127* (40¢). Bound with WORLDS OF THE IMPERIUM by Keith Laumer.

THE SHATTERED CHAIN. *New York: DAW Books, Inc.,* [*1976*].
Wrappers. *First printing, April 1976/1 2 3 4 5 6 7 8 9* on copyright page. *DAW: sf Books No. 191 UW1229* ($1.50).
– Crtbcc

SOUVENIR OF MONIQUE. *New York: Ace Books, Inc.,* [*1967*].
Wrappers. No statement of printing on copyright page. *Ace Book G–616* (50¢).

SPARE HER HEAVEN. *Derby, Connecticut: Monarch Books, Inc., [1963]*.
Wrappers. *Published in March, 1963* on copyright page. *Monarch Books 335* (40¢).
Morgan Ives, pseudonym. Later abridged as ANYTHING GOES.

THE SPELL SWORD. *New York: DAW Books, Inc., [1974]*.
Wrappers. *First printing, September 1974/1 2 3 4 5 6 7 8 9* on copyright page. *DAW: sf
Books No. 119 UQ1131* (95¢).

STAR OF DANGER. *New York: Ace Books, Inc., [1965]*.
Wrappers. No statement of printing on copyright page. *Ace Book F–350* (40¢).

*THE STRANGE WOMEN. *Derby, Connecticut: Monarch Books, Inc., [1962]*.
Wrappers. *Monarch Books 249. Miriam Gardner, pseudonym.*

THE SWORD OF ALDONES. *New York: Ace Books, Inc., [1962]*.
Wrappers. No statement of printing on copyright page. *Ace Double F–153* (40¢). Bound
with THE PLANET SAVERS by Bradley.

ALSO: *Boston: Gregg Press, 1977. First Printing, June 1977* on copyright page. First
hardcover edition. Note: Not issued in dust jacket.

*TWILIGHT LOVERS. *Derby, Connecticut: Monarch Books, Inc., [1964]*.
Wrappers. *Monarch Books 418. Miriam Gardner, pseudonym.*

THE WINDS OF DARKOVER. *New York: An Ace Book, [1970]*.
Wrappers. No statement of printing on copyright page. *Ace Double 89250* (75¢). Bound
with THE ANYTHING TREE by John Rackham.

*WITCH HILL. *[Los Angeles]: Greenleaf Publishers, [1972]*.
Wrappers. *Valerie Graves, pseudonym.*

THE WORLD WRECKERS. *New York: Ace Books, [1971]*.
Wrappers. No statement of printing on copyright page. *Ace Book 91170* (75¢).

Nonfiction (Dealing with the Fantasy Genre only)

Experiment Perilous: Three Essays on Science Fiction, [edited by Andrew Porter].
[New York]: Algol Press, [1976].
Wrappers. No statement of printing on copyright page. Contains "Experiment Perilous:
The Art and Science of Anguish in Science Fiction" by Bradley.

The Necessity for Beauty: Robert W. Chambers & the Romantic Tradition. *[Baltimore: T–K
Graphics, 1974.]*
Wrappers. No statement of printing on copyright page.

Of Men, Halflings and Hero Worship. *Rochester, Texas: Published for the . . . 95th mailing
of the Fantasy Amateur Press Association . . ., May 1961.*
Wrappers. No statement of printing. Mimeographed, stapled. Issued as *Astra's Tower
Special Leaflet #5.* The author recorded the following details of publication for this edition
in her introduction to the 1973 T K Graphics edition: "It seemed sufficient to mimeograph
eighty copies, running sixty-eight of them through the mailings of the FAPA (Fantasy
Amateur Press Association) and sending the remaining few to friends and relatives."

ALSO: Men, Halflings & Hero Worship. *[Baltimore]: T K Graphics, [1973]*. Wrappers. No
statement of printing on copyright page. Adds author's "Introduction."

Reference

The Gemini Problem: A Study in Darkover, by Walter Breen. [*Berkeley: Walter Breen, February 1973.*]
  Wrappers. No statement of printing on copyright page. Mimeographed, stapled. Caption title. 200 copies printed, some of which were numbered. Issued as "*Allerlei* Special Leaflet #1."

The Darkover Dilemma, by S. Wise. [*Baltimore: T–K Graphics, 1976.*]
  Wrappers. No statement of printing on copyright page.

Joseph Payne Brennan
(b. 1918)

THE CASEBOOK OF LUCIUS LEFFING. *New Haven: Macabre House, 1973.*
    No statement of printing on copyright page.

THE CHRONICLES OF LUCIUS LEFFING. *West Kingston, Rhode Island: Donald M. Grant, Publisher, 1977.*
    First edition so stated on copyright page.

THE DARK RETURNERS. *New Haven, Connecticut: Macabre House, 1959.*
    Boards. No statement of printing on copyright page. 150 numbered copies only.

NINE HORRORS AND A DREAM. *Sauk City: Arkham House, 1958.*
    No statement of printing on copyright page.

SCREAM AT MIDNIGHT. *New Haven, Connecticut: Macabre House, 1963.*
    No statement of printing on copyright page. 250 copies printed.

STORIES OF DARKNESS AND DREAD. *Sauk City: Arkham House, 1973.*
    No statement of printing on copyright page.

Nonfiction (Dealing with the Fantasy Genre only)

H. P. Lovecraft: A Bibliography. *Washington: Biblio Press, [1952].*
    Self wrappers. *Revised edition* on copyright page. A revised version of *A Select Bibliography of H. P. Lovecraft.*

H. P. Lovecraft: An Evaluation. [*New Haven, Connecticut: Macabre House, 1955.*]
    Wrappers. Multilithographed. Cover title. No statement of printing. 75 numbered copies only.

A Select Bibliography of H. P. Lovecraft. *N p.: [The Author, 1952].*
    Self wrappers. No statement of printing. Privately printed in a small edition and circulated by Brennan. Later revised as *H. P. Lovecraft: A Bibliography.*

Fredric William Brown
(1906–1972)

ANGELS AND SPACESHIPS.*New York: E. P. Dutton & Company, Inc., 1954*.
Boards. First edition so stated on copyright page. Reissued as STAR SHINE.

THE BEST OF FREDRIC BROWN.*Garden City: Nelson Doubleday, Inc., [1976]*.
Boards. No statement of printing on copyright page. Code *G 50* on page 278. Note: Issued by the Science Fiction Book Club.

THE BLOODY MOONLIGHT.*New York: E. P. Dutton & Company, Inc., 1949*.
Boards. First edition so stated on copyright page. Issued later in Great Britain as MURDER IN MOONLIGHT.

THE CASE OF THE DANCING SANDWICHES.*New York: Published by Dell Publishing Company, Inc., [1951]*.
Wrappers. No statement of printing on copyright page. *Dell Book 33* (10¢).

COMPLIMENTS OF A FIEND.*New York: E. P. Dutton & Company, Inc., 1950*.
Boards. First edition so stated on copyright page.

DAYMARES.*New York: Lancer Books, [1968]*.
Wrappers. *A Lancer Book • 1968* on copyright page. *Lancer Books 73–727* (60¢).

THE DEAD RINGER.*New York: E. P. Dutton & Company, Inc., 1948*.
Boards. First edition so stated on copyright page.

DEATH HAS MANY DOORS.*New York: E. P. Dutton & Company, Incorporated, MCMLI*.
Boards. First edition so stated on copyright page.

THE DEEP END.*New York: E. P. Dutton & Company, Inc., 1952*.
Boards. First edition so stated on copyright page.

THE FABULOUS CLIPJOINT.*New York: E. P. Dutton & Company, Inc., 1947*.
First edition so stated on copyright page.

THE FAR CRY.*New York: E. P. Dutton & Co., Inc., 1951*.
Boards. First edition so stated on copyright page.

THE FIVE-DAY NIGHTMARE.*New York: E. P. Dutton & Co., Inc., 1962*.
Boards. First edition so stated on copyright page.

HERE COMES A CANDLE.*New York: E. P. Dutton & Co., Inc., 1950*.
First edition so stated on copyright page.

HIS NAME WAS DEATH.*New York: E. P. Dutton & Company, Inc., 1954*.
Boards. First edition so stated on copyright page.

HONEYMOON IN HELL. *[New York]: Bantam Books, Inc., [1958]*.
Wrappers. *Published August 1958* on copyright page. *Bantam Books A1812* (35¢).

KNOCK THREE-ONE-TWO.*New York: E. P. Dutton & Co., Inc., 1959*.
Boards. First edition so stated on copyright page.

THE LATE LAMENTED. *New York: E. P. Dutton & Company, Inc., 1959.*
Boards. First edition so stated on copyright page.

THE LENIENT BEAST. *New York: E. P. Dutton & Company, Inc., 1956.*
Boards. First edition so stated on copyright page.

THE LIGHTS IN THE SKY ARE STARS. *New York: E. P. Dutton & Company, Inc., 1953.*
Boards. First edition so stated on copyright page. Issued later in Great Britain as PROJECT JUPITER.

MADBALL. [*New York*]: *A Dell First Edition,* [*1953*].
Wrappers. No statement of printing on copyright page. *Dell First Edition 2 E* (25¢).

MARTIANS, GO HOME. *New York: E. P. Dutton & Company, Inc., 1955.*
Boards. First edition so stated on copyright page.

THE MIND THING. [*New York*]: *Bantam Books,* [*1961*].
Wrappers. *Published January 1961* on copyright page. *A Bantam Book A2187* (35¢).

MITKEY ASTROMOUSE. [*New York*]: *Harlin Quist, Incorporated,* [*1971*].
Two bindings, no priority: (A) Cloth; (B) Boards. Notes: (1) Published simultaneously in Great Britain by Quist Publishing Limited. (2) Adapted by Brown from THE STARMOUSE PART I by Ann Sperber.

MOSTLY MURDER. *New York: E P Dutton & Co Inc, 1-9-5-3.*
Boards. First edition so stated on copyright page.

MRS. MURPHY'S UNDERPANTS. *New York: E. P. Dutton & Co., Inc., 1963.*
First edition so stated on copyright page.

MURDER CAN BE FUN. *New York: E. P. Dutton & Company, Inc., 1948.*
Boards. First edition so stated on copyright page. Reissued as A PLOT FOR MURDER.

MURDER IN MOONLIGHT. *London* ★ *New York: T. V. Boardman and Company Limited,* [*1950*].
First published in Great Britain, 1950 on copyright page. Issued earlier in the U.S. as THE BLOODY MOONLIGHT.

THE MURDERERS. *New York: E. P. Dutton & Co., Inc., 1961.*
Boards. First edition so stated on copyright page.

NIGHT OF THE JABBERWOCK. *New York: E. P. Dutton & Co., Inc. Publishers, 1951.*
Boards. First edition so stated on copyright page.

NIGHTMARES AND GEEZENSTACKS. *New York: Bantam Books,* [*1961*].
Wrappers. *Published July 1961* on copyright page. *A Bantam Book J2296* (40¢). Three of the stories in collaboration with MACK REYNOLDS.

THE OFFICE. *New York: E. P. Dutton & Company, Inc., 1958.*
Boards. First edition so stated on copyright page.

ONE FOR THE ROAD. *New York: E. P. Dutton & Co., Inc., 1958.*
Boards. First edition so stated on copyright page.

PARADOX LOST. *New York: Random House,* [*1973*].
First edition so stated on copyright page.

A PLOT FOR MURDER. *New York: Bantam Books*, [*1949*].
   Wrappers. *Bantam edition Published November 1949* on copyright page. *A Bantam Book 735* (25¢). Reissue of MURDER CAN BE FUN.

PROJECT JUPITER. *London New York: T. V. Boardman & Company, Limited*, [*1954*].
   First published in Great Britain 1954 on copyright page. Issued earlier in the U.S. as THE LIGHTS IN THE SKY ARE STARS.

ROGUE IN SPACE. *New York: E. P. Dutton & Company, Inc.*, *1957*.
   Boards. First edition so stated on copyright page.

THE SCREAMING MIMI. *New York: E. P. Dutton & Company, Inc.*, *1949*.
   Boards. First edition so stated on copyright page.

THE SHAGGY DOG AND OTHER MURDERS. *New York: E. P. Dutton & Co., Inc.*, *1963*.
   Boards. First edition so stated on copyright page.

SPACE ON MY HANDS. *Chicago: Shasta Publishers*, [*1951*].
   First edition so stated on copyright page.

STAR SHINE. *New York: Bantam Books*, [*1956*].
   Wrappers. *February 1956* on copyright page. *Bantam Books 1423* (25¢). Reissue of ANGELS AND SPACESHIPS.

WE ALL KILLED GRANDMA. *New York: E. P. Dutton & Co., Inc.*, *1952*.
   Boards. First edition so stated on copyright page.

THE WENCH IS DEAD. *New York: E. P. Dutton & Company, Inc.*, *1955*.
   Boards. First edition so stated on copyright page.

WHAT MAD UNIVERSE. *New York: E. P. Dutton & Co., Inc.*, *1949*.
   Boards. First edition so stated on copyright page.

Edited Fiction

Science-Fiction Carnival. *Chicago: Shasta Publishers*, [*1953*].
   Boards with cloth shelf back. First edition so stated on copyright page. Edited, with introduction, notes, and short story "Paradox Lost," by Brown. With MACK REYNOLDS.

   ALSO: *New York: Bantam Books*, [*1957*]. Wrappers. *Bantam edition published June 1957* on copyright page. *Bantam Books A1615* (35¢). Abridged reprint. Collects eleven of the thirteen stories.

Rosel George Brown
(1926–1967)

EARTHBLOOD. *Garden City: Doubleday & Company, Inc., 1966.*
First edition so stated on copyright page. With KEITH LAUMER.

GALACTIC SIBYL SUE BLUE. [*New York*]: *Published by Berkley Publishing Corporation,* [*1968*].
Wrappers. *January, 1968* on copyright page. *Berkley X 1503* (60¢). Issued earlier as SIBYL SUE BLUE.

A HANDFUL OF TIME. *New York: Ballantine Books,* [*1963*].
Wrappers. No statement of printing on copyright page. *Ballantine Book F 703* (50¢).

SIBYL SUE BLUE. *Garden City: Doubleday & Company, Inc., 1966.*
First edition so stated on copyright page. Reissued as GALACTIC SIBYL SUE BLUE.

THE WATERS OF CENTAURUS. *Garden City: Doubleday & Company, Inc., 1970.*
First edition so stated on copyright page.

John Kilian Houston Brunner
(b. 1934)

AGE OF MIRACLES.*London: Sidgwick & Jackson*, [*1973*].
Boards. *First published in Great Britain in 1973* on copyright page. A revision of THE DAY OF THE STAR CITIES. Note: Possibly preceded by the Ace Books printing also issued in May 1973.

THE ALTAR ON ASCONEL. *New York: Ace Books, Inc.*, [*1965*].
Wrappers. No statement of printing on copyright page. *Ace Double M–123* (45¢). Bound with ANDROID AVENGER by Ted White. Later collected in INTERSTELLAR EMPIRE.

THE ASTRONAUTS MUST NOT LAND.*New York: Ace Books, Inc.*, [*1963*].
Wrappers. No statement of printing on copyright page.*Ace Double F–227* (40¢). Bound with THE SPACE-TIME JUGGLER by Brunner. Later revised as MORE THINGS IN HEAVEN.

THE ATLANTIC ABOMINATION. *New York: Ace Books, Inc.*, [*1960*].
Wrappers. No statement of printing on copyright page. *Ace Double Novel Books D–465* (35¢). Bound with THE MARTIAN MISSILE by David Grinnell.

THE AVENGERS OF CARRIG. [*New York*]: *A Dell Book*, [*1969*].
Wrappers. *First printing —October 1969* on copyright page. *Dell 0356* (50¢). Revised and expanded version of SECRET AGENT OF TERRA.

BEDLAM PLANET.*New York: Ace Books, Inc.*, [*1968*].
Wrappers. No statement of printing on copyright page.*An Ace Book G–709* (50¢).

ALSO:*London: Sidgwick & Jackson*, [*1973*]. Boards.*First published in Great Britain in 1973* on copyright page. First hardcover edition.

BLACK IS THE COLOR.*New York: Pyramid Books*, [*1969*].
Wrappers. *First printing, February 1969* on copyright page.*Pyramid Books X–1955* (60¢).

BLACKLASH.*New York: Pyramid Books*, [*1969*].
Wrappers. *First printing, November 1969* on copyright page.*Pyramid Spy Thriller T2107* (75¢). Issued earlier in Great Britain as A PLAGUE ON BOTH YOUR CAUSES.

THE BOOK OF JOHN BRUNNER.*New York: DAW Books, Inc.*, [*1976*].
Wrappers. *First printing, January 1976/1 2 3 4 5 6 7 8 9* on copyright page.*DAW: sf Books No. 177 UY1213* ($1.25).

BORN UNDER MARS.*New York: Ace Books, Inc.*, [*1967*].
Wrappers. No statement of printing on copyright page.*An Ace Book G–664* (50¢).

THE BRINK.*London: Victor Gollancz Ltd*, 1959.
Boards. No statement of printing on copyright page.

CASTAWAYS' WORLD.*New York: Ace Books, Inc.*, [*1963*].
Wrappers. No statement of printing on copyright page.*Ace Double F–242* (40¢). Bound with THE RITES OF OHE by Brunner. Later revised as POLYMATH.

CATCH A FALLING STAR. *New York: Ace Books, Inc.*, [*1968*].
Wrappers. No statement of printing on copyright page.*Ace Book G–761* (50¢). Expanded version of THE 100TH MILLENNIUM.

THE CRUTCH OF MEMORY.*London: Barrie and Rockliff*, [*1964*].
Boards. *First published 1964* . . . on copyright page.

THE DAY OF THE STAR CITIES.*New York: Ace Books, Inc.*, [*1965*].
Wrappers. No statement of printing on copyright page. *Ace Book F–361* (40¢). Later
revised as AGE OF MIRACLES.

THE DEVIL'S WORK.*New York: W. W. Norton & Company, Inc.*, [*1970*].
First edition so stated on copyright page.

DOUBLE, DOUBLE.*New York: Ballantine Books*, [*1969*].
Wrappers. *First Printing: January, 1969* on copyright page. *A Ballantine Science Fiction
Original 72019* (75¢).

ALSO:*London: Sidgwick & Jackson* [*1971*]. Boards. *First published in Great Britain in
1971* on copyright page. First hardcover edition.

THE DRAMATURGES OF YAN.*New York: Ace Books*, [*1972*].
Wrappers. No statement of printing on copyright page. *Ace Book 16668* (75¢).

THE DREAMING EARTH.*New York: Pyramid Books*, [*1963*].
Wrappers. *First printing, February 1963* on copyright page. *Pyramid Books F–829* (40¢).

ALSO:*London: Sidgwick & Jackson*, [*1972*]. Boards. *First published in Great Britain 1972*
on copyright page. First hardcover edition.

ECHO IN THE SKULL.*New York: Ace Books, Inc.*, [*1959*].
Wrappers. No statement of printing on copyright page. *Ace Double Novel Books D–385*
(35¢). Bound with ROCKET TO LIMBO by Alan E. Nourse. Later revised as GIVE WARNING
TO THE WORLD.

ENDLESS SHADOW.*New York: Ace Books, Inc.*, [*1964*].
Wrappers. No statement of printing on copyright page. *Ace Double F–299* (40¢). Bound
with THE ARSENAL OF MIRACLES by Gardner F. Fox.

ENIGMA FROM TANTALUS.*New York: Ace Books, Inc.*, [*1965*].
Wrappers. No statement of printing on copyright page. *Ace Double M–115* (45¢). Bound
with THE REPAIRMEN OF CYCLOPS by Brunner.

ENTRY TO ELSEWHEN.*New York: DAW Books, Inc.*, [*1972*].
Wrappers. *First printing 1972* on copyright page. *DAW: sf Books No. 26 UQ1026* (95¢).
Note: Later printings have a number sequence following the first printing statement on the
copyright page.

THE EVIL THAT MEN DO.*New York: Belmont Books*, [*1969*].
Wrappers. *May 1969* on copyright page. *Belmont B60–1010* (60¢). Bound with THE PUR-
LOINED PLANET by Lin Carter.

FATHER OF LIES.*New York: Belmont Books*, [*1968*].
Wrappers. *October 1968* on copyright page. *A Belmont Double B60–081* (60¢). Bound
with MIRROR IMAGE by Bruce Duncan.

FROM THIS DAY FORWARD.*Garden City: Doubleday & Company, Inc.*, 1972.
First edition so stated on copyright page.

GALACTIC STORM.*London: Printed in Great Britain and Published by Curtis Warren
Limited*, [*1952*].
Wrappers. No statement of printing on copyright page. *Curtis Books Science Fiction* (1'6).
Gill Hunt, pseudonym.

THE GAUDY SHADOWS.*London: Constable*, [*1970*].
   Boards.*First published 1970* on copyright page.

GIVE WARNING TO THE WORLD.*New York: DAW Books, Inc.*, [*1974*].
   Wrappers.*First printing, July 1974/1 2 3 4 5 6 7 8 9* on copyright page. *DAW: sf Books No. 112 UQ1122* (95¢). Revised version of ECHO IN THE SKULL.

GOOD MEN DO NOTHING. [*London*]: *Hodder and Stoughton*, [*1970*].
   Boards. No statement of printing on copyright page.

HONKY IN THE WOODPILE.*London: Constable*, [*1971*].
   Boards.*First published 1971* on copyright page.

THE 100TH MILLENNIUM.*New York: Ace Books, Inc.*, [*1959*].
   Wrappers. No statement of printing on copyright page.*Ace Double Novel Books D-362* (35¢). Bound with EDGE OF TIME by David Grinnell. Later enlarged as CATCH A FALLING STAR.

I SPEAK FOR EARTH.*New York: Ace Books, Inc.*, [*1961*].
   Wrappers. No statement of printing on copyright page.*Ace Double Novel Books D-497* (35¢).*Keith Woodcott, pseudonym.* Bound with WANDL THE INVADER by Ray Cummings.

INTERSTELLAR EMPIRE.*New York: DAW Books, Inc.*, [*1976*].
   Wrappers.*First Printing, September 1976/1 2 3 4 5 6 7 8 9* on copyright page. *DAW: sf Books No. 208 UW1252* ($1.50).

INTO THE SLAVE NEBULA. *New York: Lancer Books*, [*1968*].
   Wrappers. *A Lancer Book · 1968* on copyright page. *Lancer Books 73-797* (60¢). Revised version of SLAVERS OF SPACE.

THE JAGGED ORBIT.*New York: Ace Books, Inc.*, [*1969*].
   Wrappers. No statement of printing on copyright page.*An Ace Science Fiction Special 38120* (95¢).

   ALSO:*New York: Ace Books Inc.*, [*1969*]. Boards. No statement of printing on copyright page. Code *40 K* on page 339. First hardcover edition. Note: Issued by the Science Fiction Book Club.

THE LADDER IN THE SKY.*New York: Ace Books, Inc.*, [*1962*].
   Wrappers. No statement of printing on copyright page.*Ace Double F–141* (40¢).*Keith Woodcott, pseudonym.* Bound with THE DARKNESS BEFORE TOMORROW by Robert Moore Williams.

LISTEN! THE STARS!*New York: Ace Books, Inc.*, [*1963*].
   Wrappers. No statement of printing on copyright page.*Ace Double F–215* (40¢). Bound with THE REBELLERS by Jane Roberts. Expanded as THE STARDROPPERS.

THE LONG RESULT.*London: Faber and Faber*, [*1965*].
   First published in mcmlxv on copyright page.

THE MARTIAN SPHINX.*New York: Ace Books, Inc.*, [*1965*].
   Wrappers. No statement of printing on copyright page.*Ace Book F–320* (40¢).*Keith Woodcott, pseudonym.*

MEETING AT INFINITY.*New York: Ace Books, Inc.*, [*1961*].
   Wrappers. No statement of printing on copyright page.*Ace Double Novel Books D-507* (35¢). Bound with BEYOND THE SILVER SKY by Kenneth Bulmer.

MORE THINGS IN HEAVEN. [*New York*]: *A Dell Book*, [*1973*].
Wrappers. *First printing–November 1973* on copyright page. *Dell 5824* (95¢). Revised version of THE ASTRONAUTS MUST NOT LAND.

NO FUTURE IN IT. *London: Victor Gollancz Ltd, 1962*.
Boards. No statement of printing on copyright page.

NO OTHER GODS BUT ME. *London: Compact Books*, [*1966*] .
Wrappers. No statement of printing on copyright page. *Compact SF F317* (3/6).

NOT BEFORE TIME. [*London*]: *The New English Library*, [*1968*].
Wrappers. *First NEL edition April 1968* on copyright page. *Four Square Science Fiction 2138* (3/6). Note: Some stories appeared earlier in the U.S. edition of OUT OF MY MIND.

NOW THEN. [*London*]: *A Mayflower-Dell Paperback*, [*1965*].
Wrappers. *October 1965* on copyright page. *Mayflower Dell 6500* (3/6).

OUT OF MY MIND. *New York: Ballantine Books*, [*1967*].
Wrappers. *First edition: February, 1967* on copyright page. *A Ballantine Science Fiction Original U5064* (60¢).

ALSO: [*London*]: *The New English Library*, [*1968*]. Wrappers. *This collection first published in Great Britain . . . January 1968* on copyright page. *Four Square Science Fiction 2102* (3/6). Contents differ.

A PLAGUE ON BOTH YOUR CAUSES. [*London*]: *Hodder and Stoughton*, [*1969*].
Boards. *First printed 1969* on copyright page. Issued later in the U.S. as BLACKLASH.

A PLANET OF YOUR OWN. *New York: Ace Books, Inc.*, [*1966*].
Wrappers. No statement of printing on copyright page. *Ace Double G–592* (50¢). Bound with THE BEASTS OF KOHL by John Rackham.

POLYMATH. *New York: DAW Books, Inc.*, [*1974*].
Wrappers. *First printing, January 1974/1 2 3 4 5 6 7 8 9* on copyright page. *DAW: sf Books No. 85 UQ1089* (95¢). Revised version of CASTAWAYS' WORLD.

THE PRODUCTIONS OF TIME. [*New York*]: *Published by The New American Library*, [*1967*].
Wrappers. *First printing, February, 1967* on copyright page. *A Signet Book P3113* (60¢). Note: Brunner states that this edition was badly edited without his approval.

ALSO: [*Harmondsworth*]: *Penguin Books*, [*1970*]. Wrappers. *Published in Penguin Books 1970* on copyright page. *Penguin Science Fiction 14003141 3* (25p). Authorized text.

THE PSIONIC MENACE. *New York: Ace Books, Inc.*, [*1963*].
Wrappers. No statement of printing on copyright page. *Ace Double F–199* (40¢). *Keith Woodcott, pseudonym.* Bound with CAPTIVES OF THE FLAME by Samuel R. Delany.

QUICKSAND. *Garden City: Doubleday & Company, Inc.*, *1967*.
First edition so stated on copyright page.

THE REPAIRMEN OF CYCLOPS. *New York: Ace Books, Inc.*, [*1965*].
Wrappers. No statement of printing on copyright page. *Ace Double M–115* (45¢). Bound with ENIGMA FROM TANTALUS by Brunner.

THE RITES OF OHE. *New York: Ace Books, Inc.*, [*1963*].
Wrappers. No statement of printing on copyright page. *Ace Double F-242* (40¢). Bound with CASTAWAYS' WORLD by Brunner.

SANCTUARY IN THE SKY.*New York: Ace Books, Inc.*, [*1960*].
Wrappers. No statement of printing on copyright page. *Ace Double Novel Books D–471* (35¢). Bound with THE SECRET MARTIANS by Jack Sharkey.

SECRET AGENT OF TERRA.*New York: Ace Books, Inc.*, [*1962*].
Wrappers. No statement of printing on copyright page. *Ace Double F–133* (40¢). Bound with THE RIM OF SPACE by A. Bertram Chandler. Later revised as THE AVENGERS OF CARRIG.

THE SHEEP LOOK UP.*New York, Evanston, San Francisco, London: Harper & Row, Publishers*, [*1972*].
Cloth and boards. First edition so stated on copyright page.

THE SHOCKWAVE RIDER.*New York, Evanston, San Francisco, London: Harper & Row, Publishers*, [*1975*].
Boards with cloth shelf back. First edition so stated on copyright page. Unauthorized editorial changes in text.

ALSO:*New York: Ballantine Books*, [*1976*]. Wrappers. *First Ballantine Books Edition: March, 1976* on copyright page. *Ballantine Books SF 24853* ($1.50). Follows author's original text.

THE SKYNAPPERS.*New York: Ace Books, Inc.*, [*1960*].
Wrappers. No statement of printing on copyright page. *Ace Double Novel Books D–457* (35¢). Bound with VULCAN'S HAMMER by Philip K. Dick.

SLAVERS OF SPACE.*New York: Ace Books, Inc.*, [*1960*].
Wrappers. No statement of printing on copyright page. *Ace Double Novel Books D–421* (35¢). Bound with DR. FUTURITY by Philip K. Dick. Later revised as INTO THE SLAVE NEBULA.

THE SPACE-TIME JUGGLER.*New York: Ace Books, Inc.*, [*1963*].
Wrappers. No statement of printing on copyright page. *Ace Double F–227* (40¢). Bound with THE ASTRONAUTS MUST NOT LAND by Brunner. Collected later in INTERSTELLAR EMPIRE as ''The Wanton of Argus.''

THE SQUARES OF THE CITY.*New York: Ballantine Books*, [*1965*].
Wrappers. *First Printing: December, 1965* on copyright page. *A Ballantine Science Fiction Original U6035* (75¢).

STAND ON ZANZIBAR.*Garden City: Doubleday & Company, Inc.*, *1968*.
First edition so stated on copyright page.

THE STARDROPPERS.*New York: DAW Books, Inc.*, [*1972*].
Wrappers. *First printing 1972* on copyright page. *DAW: sf Books No. 23 UQ1023* (95¢). Expanded version of LISTEN! THE STARS!

THE STONE THAT NEVER CAME DOWN.*Garden City: Doubleday & Company, Inc.*, *1973*.
First edition so stated on copyright page.

THE SUPER BARBARIANS.*New York: Ace Books*, [*1962*].
Wrappers. No statement of printing on copyright page. *Ace Book D–547* (35¢).

TELEPATHIST.*London: Faber and Faber*, [*1965*].
First published in mcmlxv on copyright page. Issued earlier in the U.S. as THE WHOLE MAN.

THRESHOLD OF ETERNITY. *New York: Ace Books, Inc.*, [*1959*].
Wrappers. No statement of printing on copyright page. *Ace Double Novel Books D–335* (35¢). Bound with THE WAR OF TWO WORLDS by Poul Anderson.

TIME-JUMP. [*New York*]: *A Dell Book*, [*1973*].
Wrappers. *First printing —December 1973* on copyright page. *Dell 8917* (95¢).

TIMES WITHOUT NUMBER. *New York: Ace Books, Inc.*, [*1962*].
Wrappers. No statement of printing on copyright page. *Ace Double F–161* (40¢). Bound with DESTINY'S ORBIT by David Grinnell.

ALSO: *New York: Ace Publishing Corporation*, [*1969*]. Wrappers. No statement of printing on copyright page. *Ace Book 81270* (60¢). Revised and expanded edition.

ALSO: [*Morley*]: *The Elmfield Press*, [*1974*]. Boards. No statement of printing on copyright page. First hardcover edition. Follows the 1969 Ace text.

TIMESCOOP. [*New York*]: *A Dell Book*, [*1969*].
Wrappers. *First printing —July 1969* on copyright page. *Dell 8916* (50¢).

ALSO: *London: Sidgwick & Jackson*, [*1972*]. Boards. *First published in Great Britain 1972* on copyright page. First hardcover edition.

TO CONQUER CHAOS. *New York: Ace Books, Inc.*, [*1964*].
Wrappers. No statement of printing on copyright page. *Ace Book F–277* (40¢).

TOTAL ECLIPSE. *Garden City: Doubleday & Company, Inc.*, *1974*.
First edition so stated on copyright page.

THE TRAVELER IN BLACK. *New York: Ace Books*, [*1971*].
Wrappers. No statement of printing on copyright page. *Ace Book 82210* (75¢).

WEAR THE BUTCHERS' MEDAL. *New York: Pocket Books, Inc.*, [*1965*].
Wrappers. *First printing . . . May, 1965* on copyright page. *Pocket Books 50129* (50¢).

WEB OF EVERYWHERE. *Toronto New York London: Bantam Books*, [*1974*].
Wrappers. *Published June 1974* on copyright page. *Bantam Science Fiction Q8398* ($1.25).

THE WHOLE MAN. *New York: Ballantine Books*, [*1964*].
Wrappers. *First printing . . . August, 1964* on copyright page. *An Original Ballantine Science Fiction Novel U2219* (50¢). Issued later in Great Britain as TELEPATHIST.

ALSO: *New York: Walker and Company*, [*1969*]. Boards. *Published in the United States of America in 1969* on copyright page. First U.S. hardcover edition.

THE WORLD SWAPPERS. *New York: Ace Books, Inc.*, [*1959*].
Wrappers. No statement of printing on copyright page. *Ace Double Novel Books D–391* (35¢). Bound with SIEGE OF THE UNSEEN by A. E. van Vogt.

THE WRONG END OF TIME. *Garden City: Doubleday & Company, Inc.*, *1971*.
First edition so stated on copyright page.

Translated Fiction

The Overlords of War, [by] Gerard Klein. *Garden City: Doubleday & Company, Inc.*, [*1973*].
No statement of printing on copyright page. Translated by Brunner.

Edited Fiction

The Best of Philip K. Dick. *New York: Ballantine Books*, [*1977*].
  Wrappers. *First Edition: March 1977* on copyright page. *Ballantine 25359* ($1.95).
  Edited, with introduction, by Brunner.

Reference

About John Brunner. [*London: Goodwin Press Limited, 1973.*]
  Single sheet, 25.5 x 38 cm, printed on both sides, folded into 12 panels. Issued by Brunner
  Fact & Fiction Ltd. Promotional brochure including biographical and bibliographical data,
  excerpts from reviewers' comments on Brunner's work, and other material.

The Happening Worlds of John Brunner . . . , edited by Joe De Bolt. *Port Washington,*
N.Y. • London: Kennikat Press, 1975.
  No statement of printing on copyright page. Contains a ''Response'' by Brunner; also an
  extensive bibliography of writings by and about Brunner in books and periodicals.

Edward Bryant
(b. 1945)

AMONG THE DEAD. *New York: The Macmillan Company,* [*1973*].
First printing so stated on copyright page.

CINNABAR. *New York: Macmillan Publishing Co., Inc.,* [*1976*].
Boards with cloth shelf back. *First printing 1976* on copyright page.

PHOENIX WITHOUT ASHES. *Greenwich, Connecticut: Fawcett Publications, Inc.,* [*1975*].
Wrappers. *First printing: February 1975/1 2 3 4 5 6 7 8 9 10* on copyright page. *Fawcett Gold Medal M3188* (95¢). With HARLAN ELLISON.

Edited Fiction

2076: The American Tricentennial. *New York: Pyramid Books,* [*1977*].
Wrappers. Two states, priority as listed: (A) Title of Peter Dillingham's poem "X–2076" missing on pages 195 and 197; (B) Title present on pages 195 and 197. (Note: This point not observed by the compiler; information supplied by Edward Bryant.) *April 1977* on copyright page. *Pyramid Y4203* ($1.95). Edited, with foreword and notes, by Bryant. With JO ANN HARPER.

Algirdas (Algis) Jonas Budrys
(b. 1931)

THE AMSIRS AND THE IRON THORN. *Greenwich, Conn.: Fawcett Publications, Inc., [1967].*
Wrappers. No statement of printing on copyright page. *A Fawcett Gold Medal Book d1852* (50¢). Issued later in Great Britain as THE IRON THORN.

BUDRYS' INFERNO. *[New York]: Published by Berkley Publishing Corporation, [1963].*
Wrappers. *July, 1963* on copyright page. *Berkley Medallion F799* (50¢). Issued later in Great Britain as THE FURIOUS FUTURE.

THE FALLING TORCH. *New York: Pyramid Books, [1959].*
Wrappers. *First printing, June 1959* on copyright page. *Pyramid G416* (35¢).

FALSE NIGHT. *New York: Lion Books, Inc., [1954].*
Wrappers. *Lion edition published December, 1954* on copyright page. *Lion Book 230* (25¢). Note: Seriously abridged by the publisher; full text published later as SOME WILL NOT DIE.

THE FURIOUS FUTURE. *London: Victor Gollancz Ltd, 1964.*
Boards. No statement of printing on copyright page. Issued earlier in the U.S. as BUDRYS' INFERNO.

THE IRON THORN. *London: Victor Gollancz Ltd, 1968.*
Boards. No statement of printing on copyright page. Issued earlier in the U.S. as THE AMSIRS AND THE IRON THORN.

MAN OF EARTH. *New York: Ballantine Books, [1958].*
Wrappers. No statement of printing on copyright page. *Ballantine Books 243* (35¢).

MICHAELMAS. *New York: Published by Berkley Publishing Corporation, [1977].*
No statement of printing on copyright page.

ROGUE MOON. *Greenwich, Conn.: Fawcett Publications, Inc., [1960].*
Wrappers. *First Printing, November 1960* on copyright page. *Gold Medal s1057* (35¢).

ALSO: *Boston: Gregg Press, 1977. First Printing, June 1977* on copyright page. New introduction by the author. First hardcover edition. Note: Not issued in dust jacket.

SOME WILL NOT DIE. *Evanston, Ill.: Regency Books, [1961].*
Wrappers. *A Regency Book Published November, 1961* on copyright page. *Regency RB 110* (50¢). Rewritten and enlarged version of FALSE NIGHT.

THE UNEXPECTED DIMENSION. *New York: Ballantine Books, [1960].*
Wrappers. No statement of printing on copyright page. *Ballantine Book 388 K* (35¢).

ALSO: *London: Victor Gollancz Ltd, 1962.* Boards. No statement of printing on copyright page. First hardcover edition.

WHO? *New York: Pyramid Books, [1958].*
Wrappers. *Pyramid Books Edition 1958* on copyright page. *Pyramid Books G339* (35¢).

ALSO: *London: Victor Gollancz Ltd, 1962.* Boards. No statement of printing on copyright page. First hardcover edition.

Henry Kenneth Bulmer

(b. 1921)

ARENA OF ANTARES. *New York: DAW Books, Inc.*, *[1974]*.
Wrappers. *First printing, December 1974/1 2 3 4 5 6 7 8 9* on copyright page. *DAW: sf Books No. 129 UY1145* ($1.25). *Alan Burt Akers, pseudonym.*

ARMADA OF ANTARES. *New York: DAW Books, Inc.*, *[1976]*.
Wrappers. *First printing, April 1976/1 2 3 4 5 6 7 8 9* on copyright page. *DAW: sf Books No. 189 UY1227* ($1.25). *Alan Burt Akers, pseudonym.*

AVENGER OF ANTARES. *New York: DAW Books, Inc.*, *[1975]*.
Wrappers. *First printing, December 1975/1 2 3 4 5 6 7 8 9* on copyright page. *DAW: sf Books No. 173 UY1208* ($1.25). *Alan Burt Akers, pseudonym.*

AN AXE IN MIKLAGARD. *[London]: New English Library*, *[1975]*.
Wrappers. *First NEL paperback edition March 1975* on copyright page. *New English Library 022749* (35p). *Arthur Frazier, pseudonym. Wolfshead* at head of title.

BATTLE SMOKE. *[London]: New English Library*, *[1974]*.
Wrappers. *First NEL paperback edition September 1974* on copyright page. *New English Library 019675* (30p). *Adam Hardy, pseudonym. Fox* at head of title.

BEHOLD THE STARS. *New York: Ace Books, Inc.*, *[1965]*.
Wrappers. No statement of printing on copyright page. *Ace Double M–131* (45¢). Bound with PLANETARY AGENT X by Mack Reynolds.

BEYOND THE SILVER SKY. *New York: Ace Books, Inc.*, *[1961]*.
Wrappers. No statement of printing on copyright page. *Ace Double Novel Books D-507* (35¢) Bound with MEETING AT INFINITY by John Brunner.

BLADESMAN OF ANTARES. *New York: DAW Books, Inc.*, *[1975]*.
Wrappers. *First printing, August 1975/1 2 3 4 5 6 7 8 9* on copyright page. *DAW: sf Books No. 159 UY1188* ($1.25). *Alan Burt Akers, pseudonym.*

BLAZON. *New York: Curtis Books*, *[1970]*.
Wrappers. No statement of printing on copyright page. *Curtis Books 123–07099–075* (75¢). The complete text of QUENCH THE BURNING STARS.

BLOOD BEACH. *[London]: New English Library*, *[1975]*.
Wrappers. *First NEL paperback edition November 1975* on copyright page. *New English Library 24946* (35p). *Adam Hardy, pseudonym.*

BLOOD FOR BREAKFAST. *[London]: New English Library*, *[1974]*.
Wrappers. *First NEL paperback edition February 1974* on copyright page, *New English Library 017192* (30p). *Adam Hardy, pseudonym. Fox 6* at head of title.

BLOOD SACRIFICE. *London: Sphere Books Limited*, *[1975]*.
Wrappers. *First published in Great Britain . . . 1975* on copyright page. *Sphere 0 7221 5390 2* (45p). *Neil Langholm, pseudonym. The Vikings* at head of title.

BOARDERS AWAY! *[London]: New English Library*, *[1975]*.
Wrappers. *First NEL paperback edition April 1975* on copyright page. *New English Library 21300* (35p). *Adam Hardy, pseudonym.*

THE BOOSTED MAN. *[London]: New English Library*, *[1974]*.
  Wrappers. *First NEL paperback edition June 1974* on copyright page. *New English Library 018393* (30p). *Tully Zetford, pseudonym. Hook* at head of title.

BY PIRATE'S BLOOD. *New York: Pinnacle Books*, *[1975]*.
  Wrappers. *First Printing, May 1975* on copyright page. *P523–220631–6* ($1.25). *Richard Silver, pseudonym. Captain Shark* at head of title.

CHALLENGE. *London: Curtis Books*, *[1954]*.
  Wrappers. *November 1954* on copyright page. *Curtis Books 141* (1'6).

THE CHANGELING WORLDS. *New York: Ace Books, Inc.*, *[1959]*.
  Wrappers. No statement of printing on copyright page. *Ace Double-Size Books D–369* (35¢). Bound with VANGUARD FROM ALPHA by Brian W. Aldiss.

THE CHARIOTS OF RA. *New York: Ace Books*, *[1972]*.
  Wrappers. *First Ace printing July 1972* on copyright page. *Ace Double 10293* (95¢). Bound with EARTH-STRINGS by John Rackham.

CITY UNDER THE SEA. *New York: Ace Books, Inc.*, *[1957]*.
  Wrappers. No statement of printing on copyright page. *Ace Double Novel Books D–255* (35¢). Bound with STAR WAYS by Poul Anderson.

  ALSO: *London: Robert Hale*, *[1969]*. Boards. *This edition 1969* on copyright page. First hardcover edition.

CLOSE QUARTERS. *[London]: New English Library*, *[1977]*.
  Wrappers. *First NEL paperback edition March 1977* on copyright page. *New English Library 28925* (50p). *Adam Hardy, pseudonym.*

COURT MARTIAL. *[London]: New English Library*, *[1974]*.
  Wrappers. *First NEL paperback edition April 1974* on copyright page. *New English Library 017842* (30p). *Adam Hardy, pseudonym.*

CUT AND THRUST. *[London]: New English Library*, *[1974]*.
  Wrappers. *First NEL paperback edition November 1974* on copyright page. *New English Library 450 02016 9* (30p). *Adam Hardy, pseudonym.*

CYBERNETIC CONTROLLER. *London: Hamilton & Co. (Stafford), Ltd.*, *[1952]*.
  Wrappers. No statement of printing on copyright page. *Panther Books* (1'6). With A. V. CLARKE.

CYCLE OF NEMESIS. *New York: Ace Books, Inc.*, *[1967]*.
  Wrappers. No statement of printing on copyright page. *Ace Book G–680* (50¢).

THE DARK RETURN. *London: Sphere Books Limited*, *[1975]*.
  Wrappers. *First published in Great Britain . . . 1975* on copyright page. *Sphere Fiction Adventure 0 7221 5391 0* (50p). *Neil Langholm, pseudonym. The Vikings* at head of title.

DEFIANCE. *London: Brown, Watson Limited*, *[1963]*.
  Wrappers. No statement of printing on copyright page. *Digit Books R666* (2'6).

THE DEMONS. *London: Compact Books*, *[1965]*.
  Wrappers. No statement of printing on copyright page. *Compact SF F277* (3/6). Issued earlier in the U. S. as DEMONS' WORLD.

DEMONS' WORLD. *New York: Ace Books, Inc.*, *[1964]*.
  Wrappers. No statement of printing on copyright page. *Ace Double F–289* (40¢). Bound with I WANT THE STARS by Tom Purdom. Issued later in Great Britain as THE DEMONS.

THE DOOMSDAY MEN. *Garden City: Doubleday & Company, Inc., 1968.*
First edition so stated on copyright page.

DREAM CHARIOTS. *New York: DAW Books, Inc., [1977].*
Wrappers. *First printing, October 1977/1 2 3 4 5 6 7 8 9* on copyright page. *DAW: sf Books No. 260 UW1328* ($1.50). *Manning Norvil, pseudonym.*

THE EARTH GODS ARE COMING. *New York: Ace Books, Inc., [1960].*
Wrappers. No statement of printing on copyright page. *Ace Double Novel Books D-453* (35¢). Bound with THE GAMES OF NEITH by Margaret St. Clair. Issued later in Great Britain as OF EARTH FORETOLD.

EARTH'S LONG SHADOW. *London: Brown, Watson Ltd., [1962].*
Wrappers. *First world publication in book form* on copyright page. *Digit Books R572* (2'6). Issued earlier in the U.S. as NO MAN'S WORLD. Note: British edition includes short story "Strange Highway" not in U.S. edition.

THE ELECTRIC SWORD-SWALLOWERS. *New York: Ace Books, [1971].*
Wrappers. No statement of printing on copyright page. *Ace Double 05595* (75¢). Bound with BEYOND CAPELLA by John Rackham.

EMPIRE OF CHAOS. *London: Panther Books are printed in Great Britain and Published by Hamilton & Co. (Stafford) Ltd., [1953].*
Two bindings, no priority: (A) Cloth; (B) Wrappers. *Panther Books 69* (1/6). No statement of printing on copyright page.

ENCOUNTER IN SPACE. *London: Panther Books, [1952].*
Wrappers. No statement of printing on copyright page. *Panther Books 29* (1'6).

THE FATAL FIRE. *London: Brown, Watson Limited, [1960].*
Wrappers. *First world publication in book form* on copyright page. *Digit Books R597* (2'6).

ALSO: *London: Robert Hale, [1969].* Boards. *This edition 1969* on copyright page. First hardcover edition.

FIRESHIP. *[London]: New English Library, [1975].*
Wrappers. *First NEL paperback edition August 1975* on copyright page. *New English Library 23125* (35p). *Adam Hardy, pseudonym.*

A FLAME IN THE FENS. *[London]: New English Library, [1974].*
Wrappers. *First NEL paperback edition July 1974* on copyright page. *New English Library 018261* (30p). *Arthur Frazier, pseudonym. Wolfshead* at head of title.

FLIERS OF ANTARES. *New York: DAW Books, Inc., [1975].*
Wrappers. *First printing, April 1975/1 2 3 4 5 6 7 8 9* on copyright page. *DAW: sf Books No. 145 UY1165* ($1.25). *Alan Burt Akers, pseudonym.*

A FOX DOUBLE. *[London]: New English Library, [1973].*
Boards. *These two novels first published in one volume in 1973 . . .* on copyright page. Reprint. Collects PRESS GANG and PRIZE MONEY. *Adam Hardy, pseudonym.*

FOX DOUBLE NO. 2. *[London]: New English Library, [1974].*
Boards. *First NEL hardcover edition 1974* on copyright page. Reprint. Collects THE SIEGE and TREASURE. *Adam Hardy, pseudonym.*

GALACTIC INTRIGUE. *London: Panther Books are Printed in Great Britain and Published by Hamilton & Co. (Stafford) Ltd., [1953].*

Two bindings, no priority: (A) Cloth; (B) Wrappers. *Panther Books No. 60* (1'6). No statement of printing on copyright page.

HOME IS THE MARTIAN. [*London: C. Arthur Pearson Ltd., 1954.*]
Wrappers. Caption title. No statement of printing. *Tit-Bits Science Fiction Library* (9d). *Philip Kent, pseudonym.*

THE HUNTERS OF JUNDAGAI. *New York: Ace Books, [1971].*
Wrappers. No statement of printing on copyright page. *Ace Double 68310* (75¢). Bound with PROJECT JOVE by John Glasby.

THE INSANE CITY. *New York: Curtis Books, [1971].*
Wrappers. No statement of printing on copyright page. *Curtis Books 502–07122–075* (75¢).

JAWS OF DEATH. *New York: Pinnacle Books, [1975].*
Wrappers. *First printing, December 1975* on copyright page. *Pinnacle Books Fiction Adventure 523–220783–5* ($1.25). *Richard Silver, pseudonym. Captain Shark* at head of title.

KANDAR. *New York: Paperback Library, [1969].*
Wrappers. *First Printing: May, 1969* on copyright page. *Paperback Library 62–120* (50¢).

THE KEY TO IRUNIUM. *New York: Ace Books, Inc., [1967].*
Wrappers. No statement of printing on copyright page. *Ace Double H–20* (60¢). Bound with THE WANDERING TELLURIAN by Alan Schwartz.

THE KEY TO VENUDINE. *New York: Ace Books, Inc., [1968].*
Wrappers. No statement of printing on copyright page. *Ace Double H–65* (60¢). Bound with MERCENARY FROM TOMORROW by Mack Reynolds.

THE KING'S DEATH. [*London*]: *New English Library, [1973].*
Wrappers. *First NEL paperback edition September 1973* on copyright page, *New English Library 015807* (30p). *Arthur Frazier, pseudonym. Wolfshead* at head of title.

KROZAIR OF KREGEN. *New York: DAW Books, Inc., [1977].*
Wrappers. *First printing, April 1977/1 2 3 4 5 6 7 8 9* on copyright page. *DAW: sf Books No. 237 UW1288* ($1.50). *Alan Burt Akers, pseudonym.*

LAND BEYOND THE MAP. *New York: Ace Books, Inc., [1965].*
Wrappers. No statement of printing on copyright page. *Ace Double M–111* (45¢). Bound with FUGITIVE OF THE STARS by Edmond Hamilton.

*THE LAND OF MIST. *London: Mayflower, [1976].*
Wrappers. *Andrew Quiller, pseudonym. The Eagles* at head of title.

A LIGHT IN THE WEST. [*London*]: *New English Library, [1973].*
Wrappers. *First NEL paperback edition January 1974* on copyright page. *New English Library 017370* (30p). *Arthur Frazier, pseudonym. Wolfshead* at head of title.

MANHOUNDS OF ANTARES. *New York: DAW Books, Inc., [1974].*
Wrappers. *First printing, August 1974/1 2 3 4 5 6 7 8 9* on copyright page. *DAW: sf Books No. 113 UY1124* ($1.25). *Alan Burt Akers, pseudonym.*

THE MILLION YEAR HUNT. *New York: Ace Books, Inc., [1964].*
Wrappers. No statement of printing on copyright page. *Ace Double F–285* (40¢). Bound with SHIPS TO THE STARS by Fritz Leiber.

MISSION TO THE STARS. [*London: C. Arthur Pearson, Ltd., 1953.*]
   Wrappers. Caption title. No statement of printing. *Tit-Bits Science Fiction Library* (9d).
   Philip Kent, pseudonym.

NO MAN'S WORLD. *New York: Ace Books, Inc., [1961].*
   Wrappers. No statement of printing on copyright page. *Ace Double Novel Books F-104*
   (40¢). Bound with MAYDAY ORBIT by Poul Anderson. Issued later in Great Britain as
   EARTH'S LONG SHADOW.

OATH OF BLOOD. [*London*]: *New English Library, [1973].*
   Wrappers. *First NEL paperback edition September 1973* on copyright page. *New English
   Library 015793* (30p). *Arthur Frazier, pseudonym. Wolfshead* at head of title.

OF EARTH FORETOLD. *London: Brown, Watson Limited, [1960].*
   Wrappers. No statement of printing on copyright page. *Digit Books R539* (2'6). Issued
   earlier in the U. S. as THE EARTH GODS ARE COMING. Note: British edition includes short
   story "The Aztec Plan" not in the U. S. edition.

ON THE SYMB-SOCKET CIRCUIT. *New York: Ace Books, [1972].*
   Wrappers. No statement of printing on copyright page. *Ace Book SF 63165* (75¢).

THE PATIENT DARK. *London: Robert Hale, [1969].*
   Boards. *This edition 1969* on copyright page. Revised version of THE SECRET OF ZI.

PERIL FROM SPACE. *London: Comyns (Publishers) Ltd., [1954].*
   Wrappers. No statement of printing on copyright page. *Comyns Science Fiction Novels*
   (1'6). *Karl Maras, pseudonym.*

POWDER MONKEY. [*London*]: *New English Library, [1973].*
   Wrappers. *First NEL paperback edition November 1973* on copyright page. *New English
   Library 016218* (30p). *Adam Hardy, pseudonym.*

PRESS GANG. [*London*]: *New English Library, [1973].*
   Wrappers. *First NEL paperback edition January 1973* on copyright page. *New English
   Library 013553* (30p). *Adam Hardy, pseudonym.* Collected later in A FOX DOUBLE.

PRETENDERS. [*London*]: *New English Library/Times Mirror/in Association with TV Times,
   [1972].*
   Wrappers. *First NEL Edition March 1972* on copyright page. *TV Times/New English
   Library 012514* (25p).

PRINCE OF SCORPIO. *New York: DAW Books, Inc., [1974].*
   Wrappers. *First Printing, April 1974/1 2 3 4 5 6 7 8 9* on copyright page. *DAW: sf Books
   No. 97 UY1104* ($1.25). *Alan Burt Akers, pseudonym.*

PRIZE MONEY. [*London*]: *New English Library, [1973].*
   Wrappers. *First NEL paperback edition January 1973* on copyright page. *New English
   Library 013561* (30p). *Adam Hardy, pseudonym.* Collected later in A FOX DOUBLE.

QUENCH THE BURNING STARS. *London: Robert Hale, [1970].*
   Boards. *First published in Great Britain 1970* on copyright page. Abridged. Full text
   published as BLAZON.

RENEGADE OF KREGEN. *New York: DAW Books, Inc., [1976].*
   Wrappers. *First printing, December 1976/1 2 3 4 5 6 7 8 9* on copyright page. *DAW: sf
   Books No. 221 UY1271* ($1.25). *Alan Burt Akers, pseudonym.*

ROLLER COASTER WORLD. *New York: Ace Books*, [*1972*].
  Wrappers. *First Ace printing July 1972* on copyright page. *Ace Book SF 73438* (75¢).

SEA FLAME. [*London*]: *New English Library*, [*1976*].
  Wrappers. *First NEL paperback edition July 1976* on copyright page. *New English
  Library 27651* (40p). *Adam Hardy, pseudonym.*

*SEA OF SWORDS. *London: Mayflower Books*, [*1977*].
  Wrappers. *Andrew Quiller, pseudonym. The Eagles* at head of title.

THE SECRET OF ZI. *New York: Ace Books, Inc.*, [*1958*].
  Wrappers. No statement of printing on copyright page. *Ace Double Novel Books D–331*
  (35¢). Bound with BEYOND THE VANISHING POINT by Ray Cummings. Later revised as THE
  PATIENT DARK.

SECRET SCORPIO. *New York: DAW Books, Inc.*, [*1977*].
  Wrappers. *First printing, December 1977/1 2 3 4 5 6 7 8 9* on copyright page. *DAW: sf Books
  No. 269 UW1344* ($1.50). *Alan Burt Akers, pseudonym.*

THE SHIPS OF DUROSTORUM. *New York: An Ace Book*, [*1970*].
  Wrappers. No statement of printing on copyright page. *Ace Double 76096* (75¢). Bound
  with ALTON'S UNGUESSABLE by Jeff Sutton.

THE SIEGE. [*London*]: *New English Library*, [*1973*].
  Wrappers. *First NEL paperback edition April 1973* on copyright page. *New English
  Library 014355* (30p). *Adam Hardy, pseudonym.* Collected later in FOX DOUBLE NO. 2.

SLAVES OF THE SPECTRUM. [*London: C. Arthur Pearson Ltd., 1954.*]
  Wrappers. No statement of printing. Caption title. *Tit-Bits Science-Fiction Library* (9d).
  Philip Kent, pseudonym.

SPACE SALVAGE. *London: Panther Books Printed in Holland and Published by Hamilton &
Co. (Stafford) Limited*, [*1953*].
  Wrappers. No statement of printing on copyright page. *Panther Books 37* (1'6).

SPACE TREASON. *London: Printed in Great Britain and Published by Hamilton & Co. (Staf-
ford) Limited*, [*1952*].
  Wrappers. No statement of printing on copyright page. *Panther Books* (1'6). With A. V.
  CLARKE.

STAINED-GLASS WORLD. [*London*]: *New English Library*, [*1976*].
  Wrappers. *July 1976* on copyright page. *New English Library 450 02763 5* (50p). Reissue
  of THE ULCER CULTURE.

STAR CITY. [*London*]: *New English Library*, [*1974*].
  Wrappers. *First NEL paperback edition October 1974* on copyright page. *New English
  Library 019632* (30p). *Tully Zetford, pseudonym.*

STAR TROVE. *London: Robert Hale*, [*1970*].
  Boards. *First published in Great Britain 1970* on copyright page.

THE STAR VENTURERS. *New York: Ace Books*, [*1969*].
  Wrappers. No statement of printing on copyright page. *Ace Double 22600* (60¢). Bound
  with THE FALL OF THE DREAM MACHINE by Dean R. Koontz.

THE STARS ARE OURS. *London: Panther Books are Printed in Great Britain and Published by
Hamilton & Co. (Stafford) Ltd.*, [*1953*].

Two bindings, no priority: (A) Cloth; (B) Wrappers. *Panther Books 48* (1/6). No statement of printing on copyright page.

SUN IN THE NIGHT. *London: Sphere Books Limited*, [*1975*].
Wrappers. *First published in Great Britain . . . 1975* on copyright page. *Sphere Fiction/Adventure 0 7221 5392 9 (45p). Neil Langholm, pseudonym. The Vikings* at head of title.

THE SUNS OF SCORPIO. *New York: DAW Books, Inc.*, [*1973*].
Wrappers. *First printing, April 1973/1 2 3 4 5 6 7 8 9* on copyright page. *DAW: sf Books No. 49 UQ1049 (95¢). Alan Burt Akers, pseudonym.*

SWORDS OF THE BARBARIANS. [*London*]: *New English Library*, [*1970*].
Wrappers. *November 1970* on copyright page. *NEL 2857 (25p).*

SWORDSHIPS OF SCORPIO. *New York: DAW Books, Inc.*, [*1973*].
Wrappers. *First printing, December 1973/1 2 3 4 5 6 7 8 9* on copyright page. *DAW: sf Books No. 81 UQ1085 (95¢). Alan Burt Akers, pseudonym.*

THE TIDES OF KREGEN. *New York: DAW Books, Inc.*, [*1976*].
Wrappers. *First printing, August 1976/1 2 3 4 5 6 7 8 9* on copyright page. *DAW: sf Books No. 204 UY1247 ($1.25). Alan Burt Akers, pseudonym.*

TO OUTRUN DOOMSDAY. *New York: Ace Books, Inc.*, [*1967*].
Wrappers. No statement of printing on copyright page. *Ace Book G-625 (50¢).*

TRAIL OF BLOOD. *London: Sphere Books Limited*, [*1976*].
Wrappers. *First published in Great Britain . . . 1976* on copyright page. *Sphere 0 7221 4995 6 (50p). Neil Langholm, pseudonym. The Vikings* at head of title.

TRANSIT TO SCORPIO. *New York: DAW Books, Inc.*, [*1972*].
Wrappers. *First printing, December 1972* on copyright page. *DAW: sf Books No. 33 UQ1033 (95¢). Alan Burt Akers, pseudonym.*

TREASURE. [*London*]: *New English Library*, [*1973*].
Wrappers. *First NEL paperback edition July 1973* on copyright page. *New English Library 015246 (30p). Adam Hardy, pseudonym. Fox 4* at head of title. Collected later in FOX DOUBLE NO. 2.

THE ULCER CULTURE. [*London*]: *Macdonald Science Fiction*, [*1969*].
Boards. *First published in Great Britain in 1969* on copyright page. Reissued as STAINED-GLASS WORLD.

VASSALS OF VENUS. [*London: C. Arthur Pearson Ltd.*, *1953.*]
Wrappers. Caption title. No statement of printing. *Tit-Bits Science Fiction Library (9d). Philip Kent, pseudonym.*

VIKING SLAUGHTER. [*London*]: *New English Library*, [*1974*].
Wrappers. *First NEL paperback edition May 1974* on copyright page. *New English Library 450 01805 9 (30p). Arthur Frazier, pseudonym. Wolfshead* at head of title.

VIRILITY GENE. [*London*]: *New English Library*, [*1975*].
Wrappers. *First NEL paperback edition May 1975* on copyright page. *New English Library 021971 (35p). Tully Zetford, pseudonym. Hook* at head of title.

WARRIOR OF SCORPIO. *New York: DAW Books, Inc.*, [*1973*].
Wrappers. *First printing, August 1973/1 2 3 4 5 6 7 8 9* on copyright page. *DAW: sf Books No. 65 UQ1065 (95¢). Alan Burt Akers, pseudonym.*

WHIRLPOOL OF STARS. [*London*]: *New English Library*, [*1974*].
Wrappers. *First NEL paperback edition May 1974* on copyright page. *New English Library 018385* (30p). *Tully Zetford, pseudonym. Hook* at head of title.

WHITE-OUT. [*London*]: *Jarrolds*, [*1960*].
Boards. *First published 1960* on copyright page. *Ernest Corley, pseudonym.*

THE WIND OF LIBERTY. *London: Brown, Watson Ltd.*, [*1962*].
Wrappers. No statement of printing on copyright page. *Digit Books R607* (2'6).

THE WIZARD OF STARSHIP POSEIDON. *New York: Ace Books, Inc.*, [*1963*].
Wrappers. No statement of printing on copyright page. *Ace Double F–209* (40¢). Bound with LET THE SPACEMEN BEWARE! by Poul Anderson.

THE WIZARDS OF SENCHURIA. *New York: An Ace Book*, [*1969*].
Wrappers. No statement of printing on copyright page. *Ace Double 12140* (75¢). Bound with CRADLE OF THE SUN by Brian M. Stableford.

WORLD AFLAME. *London: Panther Books*, [*1954*].
Two bindings, no priority: (A) Cloth; (B) Wrappers. *Panther Books 159* (1'6). No statement of printing on copyright page.

WORLDS FOR THE TAKING. *New York: Ace Books, Inc.*, [*1966*].
Wrappers. No statement of printing on copyright page. *Ace Book F–396* (40¢).

ZHORANI. *London: Comyns (Publishers) Ltd.*, [*1953*].
Wrappers. No statement of printing on copyright page. *Karl Maras, pseudonym.*

Edited Fiction

New Writings in SF (22). *London: Sidgwick & Jackson*, [*1973*].
Boards. *First published in Great Britain . . . in 1973* on copyright page. Edited, with foreword, by Bulmer.

New Writings in SF (23). *London: Sidgwick & Jackson*, [*1973*].
Boards. *First published in Great Britain . . . in 1973* on copyright page. Edited, with foreword, by Bulmer.

New Writings in SF (24). *London: Sidgwick & Jackson*, [*1974*].
Boards. No statement of printing on copyright page. Edited, with foreword and notes, by Bulmer.

New Writings in SF (25). *London: Sidgwick & Jackson*, [*1975*].
Boards. *First published in Great Britain . . . in 1975* on copyright page. Edited, with introduction, by Bulmer.

New Writings in SF (26). *London: Sidgwick & Jackson*, [*1975*].
Boards. No statement of printing on copyright page. Edited, with foreword, by Bulmer.

New Writings in SF (27). *London: Sidgwick & Jackson*, [*1975*].
Boards. *First published in Great Britain . . . in 1975 . . .* on copyright page. Edited, with foreword, by Bulmer.

New Writings in SF (28). *London: Sidgwick & Jackson*, [*1976*].
Boards. *First published in Great Britain in 1976* on copyright page. Edited, with foreword and notes, by Bulmer.

New Writings in SF (29). *London: Sidgwick & Jackson,* [*1976*].
  Boards. *First published in Great Britain in 1976* on copyright page. Edited, with foreword,
  by Bulmer.

Edgar Rice Burroughs
(1875–1950)

APACHE DEVIL. *Tarzana: Edgar Rice Burroughs, Inc. Publishers*, [*1933*].
No statement of printing on copyright page.

AT THE EARTH'S CORE. *Chicago: A.C. McClurg & Co., 1922.*
Published July, 1922 on copyright page. *M.A. DONOHUE & CO.; PRINTERS AND
BINDERS, CHICAGO* at base of copyright page.

AT THE EARTH'S CORE, PELLUCIDAR [and] TANAR OF PELLUCIDAR: THREE SCIENCE FICTION
NOVELS. . . . *New York: Dover Publications, Inc.*, [*1963*].
Wrappers. *This Dover edition, first published in 1963* . . . on copyright page. *Dover
T1051* ($2.00). Reprint. Collects AT THE EARTH'S CORE, PELLUCIDAR, and TANAR OF
PELLUCIDAR.

BACK TO THE STONE AGE. *Tarzana: Edgar Rice Burroughs, Inc. Publishers*, [*1937*].
First edition so stated on copyright page.

THE BANDIT OF HELL'S BEND. *Chicago: A. C. McClurg & Co., 1925.*
Published June, 1925 on copyright page. *M. A. DONOHUE & CO., PRINTERS AND
BINDERS, CHICAGO* at base of copyright page.

THE BEASTS OF TARZAN. *Chicago: A. C. McClurg & Co., 1916.*
Published March, 1916 on copyright page. *W.F. HALL PRINTING COMPANY,
CHICAGO* at base of copyright page.

BEYOND THE FARTHEST STAR. *New York: Ace Books, Inc.*, [*1964*].
Wrappers. No statement of printing on copyright page. *Ace Science Fiction Classic F-282*
(40¢). Collected in TALES OF THREE PLANETS.

BEYOND THIRTY. *N.p., n.d.*
Wrappers. No statement of printing. Offset from typewritten copy. 300 copies published
anonymously without authorization circa 1955 by Lloyd A. Eshbach. Note: Henry Hardy
Heins reports "a still earlier anonymously produced hectographed-type booklet of 102
pages, dated Feb. 1953" (not seen). Collected later in BEYOND THIRTY AND THE MAN-
EATER. Reissued as THE LOST CONTINENT.

BEYOND THIRTY AND THE MAN-EATER. *South Ozone Park, New York: Science-Fiction &
Fantasy Publications, 1957.*
First edition so stated on copyright page. Reprint. Collects BEYOND THIRTY and THE
MAN-EATER.

CARSON OF VENUS. *Tarzana: Edgar Rice Burroughs, Inc. Publishers*, [*1939*].
First edition so stated on copyright page.

THE CAVE GIRL. *Chicago: A. C. McClurg & Co., 1925.*
Two bindings, priority as listed: (A) *A. C. McCLURG/& CO.* on spine; (B) *GROSSET/&
DUNLAP* on spine. *Published March, 1925* on copyright page. *M. A. DONOHUE &
CO., PRINTERS AND BINDERS, CHICAGO* at base of copyright page.

THE CHESSMEN OF MARS. *Chicago: A. C. McClurg & Co., 1922.*
Published November, 1922 on copyright page. *M. A. DONOHUE & CO., PRINTERS
AND BINDERS, CHICAGO* at base of copyright page.

THE DEPUTY SHERIFF OF COMANCHE COUNTY. *Tarzana: Edgar Rice Burroughs, Inc. Publishers, [1940]*.
First edition so stated on copyright page.

THE EFFICIENCY EXPERT. *Kansas City, Missouri: House of Greystoke, 1966*.
Wrappers. *Authorized first edition* on copyright page.

ESCAPE ON VENUS. *Tarzana: Edgar Rice Burroughs, Inc. Publishers, [1946]*.
First edition so stated on copyright page.

THE ETERNAL LOVER. *Chicago: A.C. McClurg & Co., 1925*.
Published October, 1925 on copyright page. *M. A. DONOHUE & CO., PRINTERS AND BINDERS, CHICAGO* on copyright page. Reissued as THE ETERNAL SAVAGE.

THE ETERNAL SAVAGE. *New York: Ace Books, Inc., [1963]*.
Wrappers. No statement of printing on copyright page. *Ace Science Fiction Classic F–234* (40¢). Reissue of THE ETERNAL LOVER.

A FIGHTING MAN OF MARS. *New York: Metropolitan Books, Inc. Publishers, [1931]*.
No statement of printing on copyright page.

* THE GIRL FROM FARRIS'S. *Tacoma, Washington: The Wilma Company, 1959*.
250 copies printed. Three bindings, priority as listed: (A) Rust marbled boards, blue cloth tape spine. 150 copies. (B) Black leatherette. 20 copies. (C) Wrappers. 80 copies. Information supplied by Kevin B. Hancer, who also reports that "at a later date, a reprint was made from copy #186 in the enlarged size of 4 ½ X 5 ½ inches. These were in wrappers also, and at least ten copies were so produced."

THE GIRL FROM HOLLYWOOD. *New York: The Macaulay Company, [1923]*.
Three bindings, sequence for the first two probably as listed, the last definitely later:
(A) Coarse mesh weave red cloth lettered in yellow-green; (B) Pebbled red cloth lettered in yellow-green; (C) Tight mesh weave red cloth lettered in black. Three printings, probable sequence for the first two as listed, the last definitely later: (A) Signatures: (1) triple sewn; (2) quadruple sewn; the frontispiece caption reads, "The Director's eyes snapped. . . . 'Only a camera man/and myself are here' he said"; (B) Signatures triple sewn; the frontispiece caption reads "The Director's eyes snapped. . . . 'Only a camera man/and myself are here' "; first line of type on caption measures 9.3 cm; (C) Signatures quadruple sewn; frontispiece caption as per B, but first line measures 8.8 cm. No statement of printing on copyright page. Note: Positive identification of the first printing has not been documented. Heins in *A Golden Anniversary Bibliography of Edgar Rice Burroughs* (1964) designates copies with the frontispiece caption lacking "he said" and bound in red pebbled cloth lettered in yellow-green as the first printing. Recent research suggests that the red mesh weave binding lettered in yellow-green with the caption including "he said" is the first printing. An obvious later printing (binding C, printing C) lacks "he said" in the caption.

THE GODS OF MARS. *Chicago: A. C. McClurg & Co., 1918*.
Published September, 1918 on copyright page. *W. F. HALL PRINTING COMPANY, CHICAGO* at base of copyright page.

I AM A BARBARIAN. *Tarzana: Edgar Rice Burroughs, Inc., [1967]*.
First edition so stated on copyright page.

JOHN CARTER OF MARS. *Racine, Wisconsin: Whitman Publishing Company, [1940]*.
Boards. No statement of printing on copyright page. *The Better Little Book 1402*. Note: "Written largely (and perhaps totally) by John Coleman Burroughs, who also did the art for it as well."—Kevin B. Hancer. See next entry for revised and expanded text.

JOHN CARTER OF MARS. *New York: Canaveral Press, 1964.*
Two (four?) bindings, priority as listed: (A) Binding title incorrectly reads *John Carter and the Giant of Mars*. Two variants: (1) Light blue-gray cloth; (2) Blue cloth. (B) Binding title reads *John Carter of Mars*. Two variants: (1) Light blue-gray cloth; (2) Blue cloth. First edition so stated on copyright page. Note: Collects "John Carter and the Giant of Mars" (*Amazing*, January 1941) and "Skeleton Men of Jupiter" (*Amazing*, February 1943). "John Carter and the Giant of Mars" is an enlargement of the 1940 Racine version. According to Kevin B. Hancer, "In 1941, with *Amazing* requesting a new Mars story, ERB and JCB collaborated to add 5,000–6,000 words with some revising." This text was used for Canaveral and subsequent editions.

JUNGLE GIRL. *Tarzana: Edgar Rice Burroughs, Inc. Publishers*, [*1932*].
No statement of printing on copyright page. Reissued as THE LAND OF HIDDEN MEN.

JUNGLE TALES OF TARZAN. *Chicago: A. C. McClurg & Co., 1919.*
Two bindings, priority as listed: (A) Orange cloth, spine imprint in three lines: *A. C./McCLURG/& CO.*; (B) Orange cloth, spine imprint in two lines: *A. C. McCLURG/& CO.* Later McClurg printings were bound in green cloth. No statement of printing on copyright page. *W. F. HALL PRINTING COMPANY, CHICAGO* at base of copyright page.

THE LAD AND THE LION. *Tarzana: Edgar Rice Burroughs, Inc. Publishers*, [*1938*].
First edition so stated on copyright page.

THE LAND OF HIDDEN MEN. *New York: Ace Books, Inc.*, [*1963*].
Wrappers. No statement of printing on copyright page. *Ace Science Fiction Classic F–232* (40¢). Reissue of JUNGLE GIRL.

LAND OF TERROR. *Tarzana: Edgar Rice Burroughs, Inc. Publishers*, [*1944*].
First edition so stated on copyright page.

THE LAND THAT TIME FORGOT. *Chicago: A. C. McClurg & Co., 1924.*
Published June, 1924 on copyright page. *M. A. DONOHUE & CO., PRINTERS AND BINDERS, CHICAGO* at base of copyright page. Note: Text of the 1918 magazine version of this novel was issued in 1963 by Ace Books in three volumes as THE LAND THAT TIME FORGOT, THE PEOPLE THAT TIME FORGOT, and OUT OF TIME'S ABYSS.

THE LAND THAT TIME FORGOT. *New York: Ace Books, Inc.*, [*1963*].
Wrappers. No statement of printing on copyright page. *Ace Science Fiction Classic F–213* (40¢). Note: Follows text of the version appearing in *Blue Book Magazine*, August 1918.

LLANA OF GATHOL. *Tarzana: Edgar Rice Burroughs, Inc.*, [*1948*].
First edition so stated on copyright page.

THE LOST CONTINENT. *New York: Ace Books, Inc.*, [*1963*].
Wrappers. No statement of printing on copyright page. *Ace Science Fiction Classic F–235* (40¢). Reissue of BEYOND THIRTY.

LOST ON VENUS. *Tarzana: Edgar Rice Burroughs, Inc. Publishers*, [*1935*].
First edition so stated on copyright page.

THE MAD KING. *Chicago: A. C. McClurg & Co., 1926.*
Published August, 1926 on copyright page.

THE MAN-EATER. *N.p., n.d.*
Wrappers. No statement of printing. Offset from typewritten copy. 300 copies published anonymously without authorization circa 1955 by Lloyd A. Eshbach. Collected later in BEYOND THIRTY AND THE MAN-EATER.

ALSO: THE MAN EATER (BEN, KING OF BEASTS). *North Hollywood, California: Fantasy House, 1974*. Wrappers. First edition so stated on title page. *Fantasy Reader 5* ($1.00). Cuts in text.

THE MAN WITHOUT A SOUL. *London: Methuen & Co. Ltd., [1922]*.
First published in Great Britain in 1922 on copyright page. Reprint. Collected earlier as second part of the U. S. edition of THE MUCKER.

THE MASTER MIND OF MARS. *Chicago: A. C. McClurg & Co., 1928*.
No statement of printing on copyright page. McClurg acorn device on copyright page.

THE MONSTER MEN. *Chicago: A. C. McClurg & Co., 1929*.
No statement of printing on copyright page. McClurg acorn device on copyright page.

THE MOON MAID. *Chicago: A. C. McClurg & Co., 1926*.
Published February, 1926 on copyright page. Reissued as THE MOON MEN by Canaveral Press in 1962. Note: Text of the 1925 magazine version of this novel was issued in 1962 by Ace Books in two volumes as THE MOON MAID and THE MOON MEN.

THE MOON MAID. *New York: Ace Books, Inc., [1962]*.
Wrappers. No statement of printing on copyright page. *Ace Science Fiction Classic F–157* (40¢). Note: Follows text of the original version appearing in *Argosy All-Story Weekly*, 5 May–2 June 1923.

THE MOON MEN. *New York: Canaveral Press, 1962*.
No statement of printing on copyright page. Reissue of the McClurg text of THE MOON MAID.

THE MOON MEN. *New York: Ace Books, Inc., [1962]*.
Wrappers. No statement of printing on copyright page. *Ace Science Fiction Classic F–159* (40¢). Note: Follows text of the original versions appearing as "The Moon Men" in *Argosy All-Story Weekly* (21 February–14 March 1925) and "The Red Hawk" in *Argosy All-Story Weekly* (5–19 September 1925).

THE MUCKER. *London: Methuen & Co. Ltd., [1921]*.
First Published in Great Britain in 1921 on copyright page. Note: Part one only. This edition was published 6 October 1921 and precedes U. S. publication of the complete text issued 31 October 1921. The second part was published in Great Britain as THE MAN WITHOUT A SOUL in 1922.

THE MUCKER. *Chicago: A. C. McClurg & Co., 1921*.
Published October, 1921 on copyright page. Note: First book appearance of the complete text. This novel was published in two volumes in Great Britain as THE MUCKER and THE MAN WITHOUT A SOUL in 1921 and 1922 respectively. Reissued in 1974 by Ace Books in two volumes utilizing the original magazine serial titles, THE MUCKER and THE RETURN OF THE MUCKER.

THE OAKDALE AFFAIR/THE RIDER. *Tarzana: Edgar Rice Burroughs, Inc. Publishers, [1937]*.
First edition so stated on copyright page.

THE OAKDALE AFFAIR. *New York: Ace Books, [1974]*.
Wrappers. No statement of printing on copyright page. *Ace 60563* ($1.25). Reprint. Note: Restores the final 173 lines of the novel as published in *The Blue Book*, March 1918 which were inadvertently dropped from the 1937 Burroughs edition of THE OAKDALE AFFAIR/THE RIDER.

OUT OF TIME'S ABYSS. *New York: Ace Books, Inc., [1963].*
Wrappers. No statement of printing on copyright page. *Ace Science Fiction Classic F–233* (40¢). The third part of THE LAND THAT TIME FORGOT. Note: Follows text of the original version in *Blue Book Magazine*, December 1918.

THE OUTLAW OF TORN. *Chicago: A. C. McClurg & Co., 1927.*
No statement of printing on copyright page. McClurg acorn device on copyright page. Note: Second printing bears statement *First Edition Printed February 1927/First Reprinting, March 1927* on copyright page.

PELLUCIDAR. *Chicago: A. C. McClurg & Co., 1923.*
Published September, 1923 on copyright page.

THE PEOPLE THAT TIME FORGOT. *New York: Ace Books, Inc., [1963].*
Wrappers. No statement of printing on copyright page. *Ace Science Fiction Classic F–220* (40¢). Second part of THE LAND THAT TIME FORGOT. Note: Follows text of the original version in *Blue Book Magazine*, October 1918.

PIRATES OF VENUS. *Tarzana: Edgar Rice Burroughs, Inc. Publishers, [1934].*
First edition so stated on copyright page.

A PRINCESS OF MARS. *Chicago: A. C. McClurg & Co., 1917.*
Published October, 1917 on copyright page. *W. F. HALL PRINTING COMPANY, CHICAGO* at base of copyright page.

THE RETURN OF TARZAN. *Chicago: A. C. McClurg & Co., 1915.*
Published March, 1915 on copyright page. *W. F. HALL PRINTING COMPANY, CHICAGO* at base of copyright page.

THE RETURN OF THE MUCKER. *New York: Ace Books, [1974].*
Wrappers. No statement of printing on copyright page. *Ace 71815* (95¢). Reprint of second part of the McClurg edition of THE MUCKER.

THE RIDER. *New York: Ace Books, [1974].*
Wrappers. No statement of printing on copyright page. *Ace 72280* ($1.25). Reprint. Collected earlier in THE OAKDALE AFFAIR/THE RIDER.

SAVAGE PELLUCIDAR. *New York: Canaveral Press, 1963.*
No statement of printing on copyright page.

THE SON OF TARZAN. *Chicago: A. C. McClurg & Co., 1917.*
Published March, 1917 on copyright page. Note: The earliest printing has *W. F. HALL PRINTING COMPANY, CHICAGO* at base of copyright page and lacks the leaf bearing the dedication to Hulbert Burroughs.

SWORDS OF MARS. *Tarzana: Edgar Rice Burroughs, Inc. Publishers, [1936].*
First edition so stated on copyright page.

SYNTHETIC MEN OF MARS. *Tarzana: Edgar Rice Burroughs, Inc., Publishers, [1940].*
First edition so stated on copyright page.

TALES OF THREE PLANETS. *New York: Canaveral Press, 1964.*
First edition so stated on copyright page.

TANAR OF PELLUCIDAR. *New York: Metropolitan Books Publishers, [1930].*
No statement of printing on copyright page.

TARZAN AND THE ANT MEN. *Chicago: A. C. McClurg & Co., 1924.*
Two bindings, priority as listed: (A) *A. C. McCLURG/& CO.* on spine; (B) *GROSSET/& DUNLAP* on spine. *Published September, 1924* on copyright page.

ALSO: *London: Methuen & Co., Ltd., [1925]. First Published in Great Britain in 1925* on copyright page. Notes: (1) Follows the original version serialized in *Argosy All-Story Weekly*, 2 February–15 March 1924. (2) *Ant Men* is hyphenated in the British title.

TARZAN AND THE CASTAWAYS. *New York: Canaveral Press, Inc., 1965 [i.e., 1964].*
First edition so stated on copyright page. Note: Some later copies (distributed after 1 January 1965) have cancel sticker affixed to copyright page bearing corrected date "© 1964." About 400 copies were distributed in December 1964 without the sticker.

TARZAN AND THE CITY OF GOLD. *Tarzana: Edgar Rice Burroughs, Inc. Publishers, [1933].*
First edition so stated on copyright page.

TARZAN AND THE FORBIDDEN CITY. *Tarzana: Edgar Rice Burroughs, Inc. Publishers, [1938].*
First edition so stated on copyright page.

TARZAN AND "THE FOREIGN LEGION." *Tarzana: Edgar Rice Burroughs, Inc. Publishers, [1947].*
First edition so stated on copyright page.

TARZAN AND THE GOLDEN LION. *Chicago: A. C. McClurg & Co., 1923.*
Published March, 1923 on copyright page. *M. A. DONOHUE & CO., PRINTERS AND BINDERS, CHICAGO* at base of copyright page.

TARZAN AND THE JEWELS OF OPAR. *Chicago: A. C. McClurg & Co., 1918.*
Published, April, 1918 on copyright page. *W. F. HALL PRINTING COMPANY, CHICAGO* at base of copyright page.

TARZAN AND THE LEOPARD MEN. *Tarzana: Edgar Rice Burroughs, Inc. Publishers, [1935].*
First edition so stated on copyright page.

TARZAN AND THE LION MAN. *Tarzana: Edgar Rice Burroughs, Inc. Publishers. [1934].*
First edition so stated on copyright page.

TARZAN AND THE LOST EMPIRE. *New York: Metropolitan Books Publishers. [1929].*
Two bindings, priority as listed: (A) Orange cloth lettered in black. *METROPOLITAN* at base of spine. (B) Red cloth lettered in black. *GROSSET/&DUNLAP* at base of spine. No statement of printing on copyright page.

TARZAN AND THE MADMAN. *New York: Canaveral Press, 1964.*
First edition so stated on copyright page.

TARZAN AND THE TARZAN TWINS. *New York: Canaveral Press, 1963.*
No statement of printing on copyright page. Reprint. Collects TARZAN AND THE TARZAN TWINS WITH JAD-BAL-JA, THE GOLDEN LION and THE TARZAN TWINS. Text of the first is slightly edited.

TARZAN AND THE TARZAN TWINS WITH JAD-BAL-JA, THE GOLDEN LION. *Racine, Wisconsin: Whitman Publishing Company, [1936].*
Boards. Three bindings, priority as listed: (A) Spine reads down, *TARZAN* [small circular picture of Tarzan]/*EDGAR/RICE/BURROUGHS/4056*; (B) Blank spine save for series number; (C) Solid black spine. No statement of printing on copyright page. *The Big Big Book 4056* (29¢). Note: Issued without dust jacket. Collected later in TARZAN AND THE TARZAN TWINS.

TARZAN AT THE EARTH'S CORE. *New York: Metropolitan Books, Inc. Publishers,* [*1930*].
Two bindings, priority as listed: (A) Green cloth lettered in black. *METROPOLITAN* at
base of spine. (B) Red cloth lettered in black. *GROSSET/& DUNLAP* at base of spine. No
statement of printing on copyright page.

TARZAN LORD OF THE JUNGLE. *Chicago: A. C. McClurg & Co., 1928.*
No statement of printing on copyright page. McClurg acorn device on copyright page.

TARZAN OF THE APES. *Chicago: A. C. McClurg & Co., 1914.*
Bindings, priority as listed: (A) Red cloth; *A. C. McCLURG/& CO.* at base of spine.
(B) Later bindings, priority as listed: (1) Red cloth; *A.* [acorn device] *C./McCLURG/& CO.*
at base of spine; (2) Green cloth; Orange cloth. Two printings (states?), priority as listed:
(A) *W. F. Hall Printing Co./Chicago* set in two lines of Old English type on copyright page;
(B) *W. F. HALL PRINTING COMPANY, CHICAGO* set in one line of plain Gothic type
on copyright page. Notes: (1) Copy of binding A, printing A was presented by ERB to his
wife. (2) Copies with printer's slug set in two lines of Old English type have been noted in
bindings with and without acorn device on the spine. (3) Later copies with printer's slug set
in one line of plain Gothic type have been observed in red, green, and orange cloth.

TARZAN THE INVINCIBLE. *Tarzana: Edgar Rice Burroughs, Inc. Publishers,* [*1931*].
No statement of printing on copyright page.

TARZAN THE MAGNIFICENT. *Tarzana: Edgar Rice Burroughs, Inc. Publishers,* [*1939*].
First edition so stated on copyright page.

TARZAN THE TERRIBLE. *Chicago: A. C. McClurg & Co., 1921.*
Published June, 1921 on copyright page. *M. A. DONOHUE & CO., PRINTERS AND
BINDERS, CHICAGO* at base of copyright page.

TARZAN THE UNTAMED. *Chicago: A. C. McClurg & Co., 1920.*
Published April, 1920 on copyright page. *M. A. DONOHUE & CO., PRINTERS AND
BINDERS, CHICAGO* at base of copyright page.

TARZAN TRIUMPHANT. *Tarzana: Edgar Rice Burroughs, Inc. Publishers,* [*1932*].
No statement of printing on copyright page.

THE TARZAN TWINS. *New York Boston: Published by The P. F. Volland Company,* [*1927*].
Pictorial boards with cloth shelf back. First edition so stated on copyright page. Note:
Issued in cardboard box without dust jacket. According to Kevin B. Hancer, "The first
edition was issued in a box, all others were issued in dust jackets and instructions were
given retailers/jobbers to replace the remaining boxes with extra dust jackets supplied for
that purpose. (Established through research of Volland correspondence.)"

TARZAN'S QUEST. *Tarzana: Edgar Rice Burroughs, Inc Publishers,* [*1936*].
First edition so stated on copyright page.

THREE MARTIAN NOVELS. *New York: Dover Publications,* [*1962*].
Wrappers. *This new Dover edition, first published in 1962 . . .* on copyright page. *Dover
T39* ($1.75). Reprint. Collects THUVIA, MAID OF MARS, THE CHESSMEN OF MARS, and THE
MASTER MIND OF MARS.

THREE SCIENCE FICTION NOVELS. See AT THE EARTH'S CORE, PELLUCIDAR, [and] TANAR OF
PELLUCIDAR.

THUVIA MAID OF MARS. *Chicago: A. C. McClurg & Co., 1920.*
Published October, 1920 on copyright page. *M.A. DONOHUE & CO., PRINTERS AND
BINDERS, CHICAGO* at base of copyright page.

THE WAR CHIEF. *Chicago: A. C. McClurg & Co., 1927.*
No statement of printing on copyright page. McClurg acorn device on copyright page.

THE WARLORD OF MARS. *Chicago: A. C. McClurg & Co., 1919.*
Two printings, priority as listed: (A) *W. F. HALL PRINTING COMPANY, CHICAGO* appears at base of copyright page. Publisher's imprint at base of spine set in three lines: *A. C./McCLURG/& CO.* (B) Printer's slug does not appear on copyright page. Publisher's imprint at base of spine set in two lines: *A. C. McCLURG/& CO. Published September, 1919* on copyright page.

THE WIZARD OF VENUS. *New York: Ace Publishing Corporation, [1970].*
Wrappers. No statement of printing on copyright page. *Ace Book 90190* (60¢). "Pirate Blood" appears for the first time. "The Wizard of Venus" was collected earlier in TALES OF THREE PLANETS. Note: First printing has no sketch by Roy G. Krenkel, Jr. on title page.

Reference

Barsoom: Edgar Rice Burroughs and the Martian Vision, by Richard A. Lupoff. *Baltimore: The Mirage Press, Ltd., 1976.*
Boards. *First printing: October 1, 1976* on page [162].

The Big Swingers, [by] Robert W. Fenton. *Englewood Cliffs, N.J.: Prentice-Hall, Inc., [1967].*
No statement of printing on copyright page.

Burroughs' Science Fiction, by Robert R. Kudlay and Joan Leiby. With an Analytical Subject and Name Index. . . . *Geneseo, New York: School of Library and Information Science, State University College of Arts and Science, 1973.*
Wrappers. No statement of printing on copyright page. *Geneseo Studies in Library and Information Science No. 5* at head of title.

Edgar Rice Burroughs: The Man Who Created Tarzan, [by] Irwin Porges. *Provo, Utah: Brigham Young University Press, [1975].*
Cloth with imitation leather shelf back. *First edition, first printing* on copyright page.

Edgar Rice Burroughs: Master of Adventure, by Richard A. Lupoff. *New York: Canaveral Press, 1965.*
Two issues, priority not determined but probably simultaneous: (A) Boards with cloth shelf back. No statement of printing. Trade issue. (B) Pebbled cloth. 150 numbered copies and a few out-of-series copies signed by the author. The following statement is printed on the front pastedown: *First Edition/Limited to 150 numbered copies/on Number Seventy, plate finish opaque paper. /Signed by the Author./This copy is No*[holograph number or "out of series" notation]/[signature]. Limited issue.

ALSO: *New York: Ace Books, Inc., [1968].* Wrappers. No statement of printing on copyright page. *Ace Book N–6* (95¢). Revised and enlarged edition.

ALSO: *New York: Ace Books, [1975].* Wrappers. No statement of printing on copyright page. *Ace 18771* ($1.25). Adds author's "Introduction to the Centennial Edition."

A Golden Anniversary Bibliography of Edgar Rice Burroughs, compiled by Henry Hardy Heins. *Albany: [Henry Hardy Heins], 1962.*
148 copies. Two bindings, no priority: (A) 98 copies; distributed as loose sheets and paper covers punched for three-ring binders; (B) 50 copies; wrappers with white plastic spine for presentation and libraries. No statement of printing on copyright page.

ALSO: *West Kingston, Rhode Island: Published by Donald M. Grant, 1964. Complete Edition, Revised: June 1964* on copyright page. 1000 copies printed.

A Guide to Barsoom . . ., compiled by John Flint Roy. *New York: Ballantine Books, [1976]*.
    Wrappers. *First edition: October 1976* on copyright page. *Ballantine Books SF 24722*
    ($1.75).

The Literature of Burroughsiana . . ., by John Harwood. *Baton Rouge, La.: Editor and
    Publisher Camille Cazedessus, Jr., 1963*.
    Wrappers. First edition so stated on copyright page.

The Reader's Guide to Barsoom and Amtor, by David G. Van Arnam and others, [edited by
    Richard A. Lupoff]. *[New York: Richard Lupoff, 1963.]*
    Issued as loose sheets, offset. 500 copies printed. Two states, no priority: (A) *The/first
    printing is limited to 200 copies,/numbered and signed* on verso of title leaf; (B) Printing
    statement removed from verso of title leaf.

Francis Marion Busby

(b. 1921)

CAGE A MAN. *Garden City: Nelson Doubleday, Inc., [1973].*
Boards. No statement of printing on copyright page. Code *D 33* on page 149. Note: Issued by the Science Fiction Book Club.

THE LONG VIEW. *New York: Published by Berkley Publishing Corporation, [1976].*
No statement of printing on copyright page. Later collected in RISSA KERGUELEN (1977).

THE PROUD ENEMY. *[New York]: Published by Berkley Publishing Corporation, [1975].*
Wrappers. *June, 1975* on copyright page. *A Berkley Medallion Book N2846* (95¢).

RISSA KERGUELEN. *New York: Published by Berkley Publishing Corporation, [1976].*
No statement of printing on copyright page.

RISSA KERGUELEN. *[New York]: Published by Berkley Publishing Corporation, [1977].*
Wrappers. *June, 1977* on copyright page. *A Berkley Medallion Book 0-425-03411-9* ($1.95). Reprint. Collects RISSA KERGUELEN and THE LONG VIEW.

John Wood Campbell, Jr.

(1910–1971)

THE BEST OF JOHN W. CAMPBELL. *London: Sidgwick & Jackson, [1973]*.
Boards. *First published in Great Britain in 1973* on copyright page. Note: Contents differ from following entry.

THE BEST OF JOHN W. CAMPBELL. *Garden City: Nelson Doubleday, Inc., [1976]*.
Boards. Two printings, priority as listed: (A) Code *G13* at base of page 306; (B) Code *H23* at base of page 306. No statement of printing on copyright page. Notes: (1) Issued by the Science Fiction Book Club. (2) Contents differ from preceding entry.

THE BLACK STAR PASSES. *Reading, Pennsylvania: Fantasy Press, [1953]*.
Three bindings, priority as listed: (A) Purple cloth, spine lettered in gold; (B) Blue cloth, spine lettered in gold (title only is printed on spine); (C) Blue-gray cloth, spine lettered in black. Two issues, no priority: (A) 500 copies with numbered leaf signed by the author inserted; (B) Trade issue. First edition so stated on copyright page. Collected later in JOHN W. CAMPBELL ANTHOLOGY.

CLOAK OF AESIR. *[Chicago]: Shasta Publishers, [1952]*.
First edition so stated on copyright page.

EMPIRE. *New York: World Editions, Inc., [1951]*.
Wrappers. No statement of printing on copyright page. *Galaxy Science Fiction Novel No. 7 (35¢)*. Byline of CLIFFORD D. SIMAK on title page. Note: The original version of EMPIRE was written by Campbell as a teenager. Unable to find a publisher for it, he turned it over to Simak and asked that he rewrite it for *Astounding*. According to Simak, "EMPIRE was essentially a rewrite of John's plot. I may have taken a few of the ideas and action, but I didn't use any of his words. And I certainly tried to humanize his characters" (quote via Muriel Becker). Simak's version was rejected by Campbell and ultimately appeared as a Galaxy Novel.

THE INCREDIBLE PLANET. *Reading, Pennsylvania: Fantasy Press, 1949*.
Two issues, no priority: (A) 500 copies with numbered leaf inserted of which 250 are signed by the author; (B) Trade issue. First edition so stated on copyright page.

INVADERS FROM THE INFINITE. *Hicksville, New York: Gnome Press, Inc., [1961]*.
Two issues, priority as listed: (A) Gnome Press imprint as above. Two bindings, priority as listed: (1) Blue boards, spine lettered in yellow; (2) Gray cloth, spine lettered in red. Trade issue. Note: Fewer than 1000 copies printed, some of which may never have been bound. (B) Imprint on title page reads: *Reading, Penna.: Fantasy Press, [1961]*. Boards. 112 signed copies only. Limited issue. Notes: (1) Carries the standard Fantasy Press limitation notice (erroneous in this case) . . . *limited to 3000 copies/of which 300 are numbered and autographed*. (2) Issued without dust jacket. First edition so stated on copyright page. Collected later in JOHN W. CAMPBELL ANTHOLOGY.

ISLANDS OF SPACE. *Reading, Pennsylvania: Fantasy Press, [1956]*.
Two bindings, priority as listed: (A) Blue cloth, spine lettered in gold; (B) Blue-gray cloth, spine lettered in black. Two issues, no priority: (A) 50 copies with numbered leaf signed by the author inserted. Note: Carries the standard Fantasy Press limitation notice (erroneous in this case) . . . *limited to 3000 copies,/of which 500 are numbered and autographed*. According to the publisher's mimeographed statement inserted in some copies of the trade

issue "Mr. Campbell would not sign more than fifty copies, hence only the first fifty copies ordered are autographed and numbered." Limited issue. (B) Trade issue. First edition so stated on copyright page. Collected later in JOHN W. CAMPBELL ANTHOLOGY.

JOHN W. CAMPBELL ANTHOLOGY. *Garden City: Doubleday & Company, Inc., 1973.*
First edition so stated on copyright page. Reprint. Collects THE BLACK STAR PASSES, ISLANDS OF SPACE, and INVADERS FROM THE INFINITE.

THE MIGHTIEST MACHINE. *Providence, R.I.: Hadley Publishing Company, [1947].*
No statement of printing on copyright page. Notes: (1) Copies have been noted in black, blue, and red cloth bindings with no evident priority of issue. (2) Later copies were issued in an F.F.F. dust jacket.

THE MOON IS HELL! *Reading, Pennsylvania: Fantasy Press, 1951.*
Three bindings, first two probably simultaneous, third later: (A) Purple cloth, spine lettered in gold (all numbered and signed copies are so bound); (B) Blue cloth, spine lettered in gold; (C) Wrappers (reported but not seen). Two issues, no priority: (A) 500 copies with numbered leaf signed by the author inserted. Limited issue. (B) Trade issue. First edition so stated on copyright page.

THE PLANETEERS. *New York: Ace Books, Inc., [1966].*
Wrappers. No statement of printing on copyright page. *Ace Double G–585 (50¢).* Bound with THE ULTIMATE WEAPON by Campbell.

THE SPACE BEYOND. *New York: Pyramid Books, [1976].*
Wrappers. *June 1976* on copyright page. *Pyramid Science Fiction M3742 ($1.75).*

THE THING. *London: Tandem Books Limited, [1966].*
Wrappers. No statement of printing on copyright page. *A Tandem Book T75 (3/6).* Reprint of WHO GOES THERE? Note: Wrapper title reads *THE THING FROM OUTER SPACE.*

THE THING AND OTHER STORIES. *[London]: Fantasy Books, [1952].*
Wrappers. A *Cherry Tree Novel/Published by Kemsley Newspapers Limited . . .* on copyright page. *Cherry Tree Book No. 408 (1/6).* Reprint of WHO GOES THERE?

THE ULTIMATE WEAPON. *New York: Ace Books, Inc., [1966].*
Wrappers. No statement of printing on copyright page. *Ace Double G-585 (50¢).* Bound with THE PLANETEERS by Campbell.

WHO GOES THERE? *Chicago: Shasta Publishers, 1948.*
First edition so stated on copyright page. Issued later in Great Britain as THE THING and THE THING AND OTHER STORIES.

WHO GOES THERE? *[New York]: A Dell Book, [1955].*
Wrappers. No statement of printing on copyright page. *Dell Book D150 (35¢).* Reprint. Stories selected from WHO GOES THERE? and CLOAK OF AESIR. Note: Wrapper title reads *WHO GOES THERE? AND OTHER STORIES.*

Associational

A One-Act Play: John W. Campbell Jr.'s Forgetfulness, adapted by Wayne Gordon. *Elgin, Illinois: Performance Publishing, [1973].*
Wrappers. No statement of printing on copyright page. Adapted by Gordon from "Forgetfulness" by Campbell.

Edited Fiction

Analog Anthology. *London: Dennis Dobson*, [*1965*].
Boards. No statement of printing on copyright page. Reprint. Collects *Prologue to Analog*, *Analog I*, and *Analog II*. Edited by Campbell.

Analog I. *Garden City: Doubleday & Company, Inc., 1963*.
First edition so stated on copyright page. Edited, with introduction, by Campbell.

Analog II. *Garden City: Doubleday & Company, Inc., 1964*.
First edition so stated on copyright page. Edited, with preface, by Campbell.

Analog 3. *Garden City: Doubleday & Company, Inc., 1965*.
First edition so stated on copyright page. Edited, with an introduction, by Campbell.
Reissued as *A World By the Tale*.

Analog 4. *Garden City: Doubleday & Company, Inc., 1966*.
First edition so stated on copyright page. Edited, with an introduction, by Campbell.
Reissued as *The Permanent Implosion*.

Analog 5. *Garden City: Doubleday & Company, Inc., 1967*.
First edition so stated on copyright page. Edited, with introduction, by Campbell. Reissued as *Countercommandment*.

Analog 6. *Garden City: Doubleday & Company, Inc., 1968*.
First edition so stated on copyright page. Edited, with introduction, by Campbell.

Analog 7. *Garden City: Doubleday & Company, Inc., 1969*.
First edition so stated on copyright page. Edited by Campbell.

Analog 8. *Garden City: Doubleday & Company, Inc., 1971*.
First edition so stated on copyright page. Edited by Campbell.

The Astounding Science Fiction Anthology. *New York: Simon and Schuster*, [*1952*].
First printing so stated copyright page. Edited, with introduction, by Campbell.

ALSO: *New York: Berkley Publishing Corp.*, [*1956*]. Wrappers. No statement of printing on copyright page. *Berkley Books G–41* (35¢). Abridged collection. Prints eight of the twenty-three stories. Reissued as *Selections From The Astounding Science Fiction Anthology*.

Astounding Tales of Space and Time. *New York: Berkley Publishing Corp.*, [*1957*].
Wrappers. No statement of printing on copyright page. *Berkley Books G-47* (35¢). Reprint. Collects seven stories from *The Astounding Science Fiction Anthology*.

Countercommandment and Other Stories. *New York: Curtis Books*, [*1970*].
Wrappers. No statement of printing on copyright page. *Curtis Books 123–07067–075* (75¢). Reissue of *Analog 5*.

The First Astounding Science Fiction Anthology. [*London*]: *Grayson & Grayson Ltd*, [*1954*].
Boards. *First published in Great Britain 1954* on copyright page. Reprint. Collects seven stories from *The Astounding Science Fiction Anthology*.

From Unknown Worlds. *New York: Street & Smith Publications, Inc., 1948*.
Wrappers. No statement of printing. Edited, with foreword, by Campbell.

ALSO:*London: Atlas Publishing & Distributing Co. Ltd., 1952*. Two bindings, no priority: (A) Boards; (B) Wrappers. *Reprinted in Great Britain 1952* on copyright page. Copies of the British printing in boards constitute the first hardcover edition.

The Permanent Implosion. *New York: Curtis Books*, [*1970*].
   Wrappers. No statement of printing on copyright page. *Curtis Books 123–07064–075* (75¢). Reissue of *Analog 4*.

Prologue to Analog. *Garden City: Doubleday & Company, Inc., 1962*
   First edition so stated on copyright page. Edited, with introduction, by Campbell.

The Second Astounding Science Fiction Anthology. [*London*]: *Grayson & Grayson Ltd.,* [*1954*].
   Boards. *First published in Great Britain 1954* on copyright page. Reprint. Collects eight stories from *The Astounding Science Fiction Anthology*.

Selections From the Astounding Science Fiction Anthology. [*New York*]: *Published by Berkley Publishing Corporation*, [*1967*].
   Wrappers. *3rd Printing, December, 1967* on copyright page. *Berkley X1490* (60¢). Reprint of the 1956 Berkley edition of *The Astounding Science Fiction Anthology*.

A World By the Tale. *New York: Curtis Books*, [*1970*].
   Wrappers. No statement of printing on copyright page. *Curtis Books 123-07060-075* (75¢). Reissue of *Analog 3*.

Nonfiction (Dealing with the Fantasy Genre only)

Collected Editorials From Analog. *Garden City: Doubleday & Company, Inc., 1966*.
   First edition so stated on copyright page. Introduction and selection by Harry Harrison.

Reference

John W. Campbell: An Australian Tribute, edited by John Bangsund. *Canberra: Published by Ronald E. Graham & John Bangsund, 1972*.
   Wrappers. First edition so stated on copyright page. 300 copies printed. Includes the text of three Campbell letters and checklist of his fiction by Donald H. Tuck.

Linwood Vrooman Carter

(b. 1930)

AS THE GREEN STAR RISES. *New York: DAW Books, Inc.*, [1975].
Wrappers. *First printing, February 1975/1 2 3 4 5 6 7 8 9* on copyright page. *DAW: sf Books No. 138 UY1156* ($1.25).

THE BARBARIAN OF WORLD'S END. *New York: DAW Books, Inc.*, [1977].
Wrappers. *First printing, May 1977/1 2 3 4 5 6 7 8 9* on copyright page. *DAW: sf Books No. 243 UW1300* ($1.50).

BEYOND THE GATES OF DREAM. *New York: Belmont Books*, [1969].
Wrappers. *A Belmont Book–August 1969* on copyright page. *Belmont B60–1032* (60¢).

BLACK LEGION OF CALLISTO. [*New York*]: *A Dell Book*, [1972].
Wrappers. *First printing–December 1972* on copyright page. *Dell 0925* (95¢).

THE BLACK STAR. [*New York*]: *A Dell Book*, [1973].
Wrappers. *First printing–May 1973* on copyright page. *Dell 0932* (95¢).

BY THE LIGHT OF THE GREEN STAR. *New York: DAW Books, Inc.*, [1974].
Wrappers. *First printing, July 1974/1 2 3 4 5 6 7 8 9* on copyright page. *DAW: sf Books No. 110 UQ1120* (95¢).

THE CITY OUTSIDE THE WORLD. [*New York*]: *Berkley Publishing Corporation*, [1977].
Wrappers. *October, 1977* on copyright page. *A Berkley Medallion Book 0-425–03549–2* ($1.50).

CONAN. *New York: Lancer Books*, [1967].
Wrappers. *A Lancer Book • 1967* on copyright page. *Lancer Books 73–685* (60¢). With L. SPRAGUE DE CAMP and ROBERT E. HOWARD.

CONAN OF AQUILONIA. [*New York*]: *Prestige Books Inc., Publishers*, [1977].
Wrappers. No statement of printing on copyright page. *Ace Books 11682–5* ($1.95). With L. SPRAGUE DE CAMP.

CONAN OF CIMMERIA. *New York: Lancer Books*, [1969].
Wrappers. *A Lancer Book • 1969* on copyright page. *Lancer Books 75–072* (95¢). With L. SPRAGUE DE CAMP and ROBERT E. HOWARD.

CONAN OF THE ISLES. *New York: Lancer Books*, [1968].
Wrappers. *A Lancer Book • 1968* on copyright page. *Lancer Books 73-800* (60¢). With L. SPRAGUE DE CAMP.

CONAN THE BUCCANEER. *New York: Lancer Books*, [1971].
Wrappers. No statement of printing on copyright page. *Lancer Books 75181–095* (95¢). With L. SPRAGUE DE CAMP. Note: The first printing has all edges stained purple and the first title listed on page [192] is *CONAN THE WARRIOR*.

CONAN THE WANDERER. *New York: Lancer Books*, [1968].
Wrappers. *A Lancer Book • 1968* on copyright page. *Lancer Books 74–976* (95¢). With L. SPRAGUE DE CAMP and ROBERT E. HOWARD. Note: Advertisement on page [223] lists six

Conan titles. A later printing with the same book stock number bears the statement *A Lancer Book* on the copyright page, but drops the date following and lists ten Conan titles on page [223].

DESTINATION: SATURN. *New York: Avalon Books*, [*1967*].
No statement of printing on copyright page. With DONALD A. WOLLHEIM writing as *David Grinnell, pseudonym.*

THE ENCHANTRESS OF WORLD'S END. *New York: DAW Books, Inc.*, [*1975*].
Wrappers. *First printing, May 1975/1 2 3 4 5 6 7 8 9* on copyright page. *DAW: sf Books No. 150 UY1172* ($1.25).

THE FLAME OF IRIDAR. *New York: Belmont Books*, [*1967*].
Wrappers. *A Belmont Book—May 1967* on copyright page. *Belmont Double Science Fiction B50–759* (50¢). Bound with PERIL OF THE STARMEN by Kris Neville.

GIANT OF WORLD'S END. *New York: Belmont Books*, [*1969*].
Wrappers. *February 1969* on copyright page. *Belmont B50–853* (50¢).

THE IMMORTAL OF WORLD'S END. *New York: DAW Books, Inc.*, [*1976*].
Wrappers. *First printing, September 1976/1 2 3 4 5 6 7 8 9* on copyright page. *DAW: sf Books No. 210 UY1254* ($1.25).

IN THE GREEN STAR'S GLOW. *New York: DAW Books, Inc.*, [*1976*].
Wrappers. *First printing, January 1976/1 2 3 4 5 6 7 8 9* on copyright page. *DAW: sf Books No. 180 UY1216* ($1.25).

INVISIBLE DEATH. *Garden City: Doubleday & Company, Inc.*, *1975*.
Boards. First edition so stated on copyright page. *Zarkon, Lord of the Unknown* at head of title.

JANDAR OF CALLISTO. [*New York*]: *A Dell Book*, [*1972*].
Wrappers. *First printing–December 1972* on copyright page. *Dell 4182* (95¢).

KING KULL. *New York: Lancer Books*, [*1967*].
Wrappers. *A Lancer Book • 1967* on copyright page. *Lancer Books 73–650* (60¢). With ROBERT E. HOWARD.

LANKAR OF CALLISTO. [*New York*]: *A Dell Book*, [*1975*].
Wrappers. *First printing–June 1975* on copyright page. *Dell 4648* (95¢).

LOST WORLD OF TIME. [*New York*]: *Published by The New American Library*, [*1969*].
Wrappers. *First printing, November, 1969* on copyright page. *A Signet Science Fiction P4068* (60¢).

MAD EMPRESS OF CALLISTO. [*New York*]: *A Dell Book*, [*1975*].
Wrappers. *First printing–February 1975* on copyright page. *Dell 6143* (95¢).

THE MAN WHO LOVED MARS. *Greenwich, Conn.: Fawcett Publications, Inc.*, [*1973*].
Wrappers. *March 1973* on copyright page. *Fawcett Gold Medal T2690* (75¢).

ALSO: *London and New York: White Lion Publishers*, [*1973*]. Boards. *First British Hardcover Edition published . . . 1973* on copyright page. First hardcover edition.

THE MAN WITHOUT A PLANET. *New York: Ace Books, Inc.*, [*1966*].
Wrappers. No statement of printing on copyright page. *Ace Double G–606* (50¢). Bound with TIME TO LIVE by John Rackham.

MIDDLE EARTH THE WORLD OF TOLKIEN ILLUSTRATED BY DAVID WENZEL. TEXT BY LIN
CARTER. *New York: Centaur Books, Inc.*, [*1977*].
   Wrappers. First edition so stated on copyright page.

MIND WIZARDS OF CALLISTO. [*New York*]: *A Dell Book*, [*1975*].
   Wrappers. *First printing–March 1975* on copyright page. *Dell 5600* (95¢).

THE NEMESIS OF EVIL. *Garden City: Doubleday & Company, Inc.*, *1975*.
   Boards. First edition so stated on copyright page. *Zarkon, Lord of the Unknown* at head of
   title.

OUTWORLDER. *New York: Lancer Books*, [*1971*].
   Wrappers. No statement of printing on copyright page. *Lancer Books 74722–075* (75¢).

THE PURLOINED PLANET. *New York: Belmont Books*, [*1969*].
   Wrappers. *May 1969* on copyright page. *Belmont B60-1010* (60¢). Bound with THE EVIL
   THAT MEN DO by John Brunner.

THE QUEST OF KADJI. *New York: Belmont Books*, [*1971*].
   Wrappers. *July 1971* on copyright page. *Belmont B95–2146* (95¢).

SKY PIRATES OF CALLISTO. [*New York*]: *A Dell Book*, [*1973*].
   Wrappers. *First printing–January 1973* on copyright page. *Dell 8050* (95¢).

THE STAR MAGICIANS. *New York: Ace Books, Inc.*, [*1966*].
   Wrappers. No statement of printing on copyright page. *Ace Double G588* (50¢). Bound
   with THE OFF-WORLDERS by John Baxter.

STAR ROGUE. *New York: Lancer Books*, [*1970*].
   Wrappers. No statement of printing on copyright page. *Lancer Books 74649–075* (75¢).

THE THIEF OF THOTH. *New York: Belmont Books*, [*1968*].
   Wrappers. *January 1968* on copyright page. *Belmont Double B50–809* (50¢). Bound with
   . . . AND OTHERS SHALL BE BORN by Frank Belknap Long.

THONGOR AGAINST THE GODS. *New York: Paperback Library, Inc.*, [*1967*].
   Wrappers. *First Printing: November, 1967* on copyright page. *A Paperback Library Science Fiction Novel 52–586* (50¢).

THONGOR AND THE DRAGON CITY. [*New York*]: *Published by Berkley Publishing
Corporation*, [*1970*].
   Wrappers. *February 1970* on copyright page. *A Berkley Medallion Book X1799* (60¢).
   Revised and expanded version of THONGOR OF LEMURIA.

THONGOR AND THE WIZARD OF LEMURIA. *New York: Published by Berkley Publishing
Corporation*, [*1969*].
   Wrappers. *December, 1969* on copyright page. *A Berkley Medallion Book X1777* (60¢).
   Revised and expanded version of THE WIZARD OF LEMURIA.

THONGOR AT THE END OF TIME. *New York: Paperback Library, Inc.*, [*1968*].
   Wrappers. *First Printing: October, 1968* on copyright page. *Paperback Library 53–780*
   (60¢).

THONGOR FIGHTS THE PIRATES OF TARAKUS. [*New York*]: *Published by Berkley Publishing
Corporation*, [*1970*].
   Wrappers. *July, 1970* on copyright page. *A Berkley Medallion Book X1861* (60¢).

THONGOR IN THE CITY OF MAGICIANS. *New York: Paperback Library, Inc.,* [*1968*].
Wrappers. *First Printing: April, 1968* on copyright page. *Paperback Library 53–665*
(60¢).

THONGOR OF LEMURIA. *New York: Ace Books, Inc.,* [*1966*].
Wrappers. No statement of printing on copyright page. *Ace Book F–383* (40¢). Revised
and expanded as THONGOR AND THE DRAGON CITY.

TIME WAR. [*New York*]: *A Dell Book,* [*1974*].
Wrappers. *First printing—November 1974* on copyright page. *Dell 8625* (95¢).

TOWER OF THE EDGE OF TIME. *New York: Belmont Books,* [*1968*].
Wrappers. *January 1968* on copyright page. *Belmont Science-Fantasy B50–804* (50¢).

TOWER OF THE MEDUSA. *New York: An Ace Book,* [*1969*].
Wrappers. No statement of printing on copyright page. *Ace Double 42900* (75¢). Bound
with KAR KABALLA by George H. Smith.

UNDER THE GREEN STAR. *New York: DAW Books, Inc.,* [*1972*].
Wrappers. *First Printing 1972* on copyright page. *DAW: sf Books No. 30 UQ1030* (95¢).

THE VALLEY WHERE TIME STOOD STILL. *Garden City: Doubleday & Company, Inc., 1974.*
Boards. First edition so stated on copyright page.

THE VOLCANO OGRE. *Garden City: Doubleday & Company, Inc., 1976.*
Boards. First edition so stated on copyright page. *Zarkon, Lord of the Unknown* at head of
title.

THE WARRIOR OF WORLD'S END. *New York: DAW Books, Inc.,* [*1974*].
Wrappers. *First printing, November 1974 / 1 2 3 4 5 6 7 8 9* on copyright page. *DAW: sf
Books No. 125 UQ1140* (95¢).

WHEN THE GREEN STAR CALLS. *New York: DAW Books, Inc.,* [*1973*].
Wrappers. *First printing, July 1973 / 1 2 3 4 5 6 7 8 9* on copyright page. *DAW: sf Books
No. 62 UQ1062* (95¢).

THE WIZARD OF LEMURIA. *New York: Ace Books, Inc.,* [*1965*].
Wrappers. No statement of printing on copyright page. *Ace Book F–326* (40¢). Revised
and expanded as THONGOR AND THE WIZARD OF LEMURIA.

YLANA OF CALLISTO. [*New York*]: *A Dell Book,* [*1977*].
Wrappers. *First printing—October 1977* on copyright page. *Dell SF 14244* ($1.50).

Edited Fiction

At the Edge of the World, [by] Lord Dunsany. *New York: Ballantine Books,* [*1970*].
Wrappers. *First Edition: March, 1970* on copyright page. *Ballantine Books 01879–6–095*
(95¢). Edited, with introduction and notes, by Carter.

Beyond the Fields We Know, [by] Lord Dunsany. *New York: Ballantine Books,* [*1972*].
Wrappers. *First Printing: May, 1972* on copyright page. *Ballantine Books Adult Fantasy
02599–7–125* ($1.25). Edited, with introduction and notes, by Carter.

Discoveries in Fantasy. *New York: Ballantine Books,* [*1972*].
Wrappers. *First Printing, March 1972* on copyright page. *Ballantine Books 02546–6–125*
($1.25). Edited, with introduction and notes, by Carter.

The Doom That Came to Sarnath, [by] H. P. Lovecraft. *New York: Ballantine Books,* [*1971*].
>   Wrappers. *First Printing: February, 1971* on copyright page. *Ballantine Books 02146–0–095* (95¢). Edited, with introduction and notes, by Carter.

Dragons, Elves, and Heroes. *New York: Ballantine Books,* [*1969*].
>   Wrappers. *First Printing: October, 1969* on copyright page. *Ballantine Books 01731* (95¢). Edited, with introduction, notes, and a translation, by Carter.

The Dream-Quest of Unknown Kadath, [by] H. P. Lovecraft. *New York: Ballantine Books,* [*1970*].
>   Wrappers. *First Printing: May, 1970* on copyright page. *Ballantine Books 01923–7–095* (95¢). Edited, with introduction and postscript, by Carter.

Evenor, [by] George MacDonald. *New York: Ballantine Books,* [*1972*].
>   Wrappers. *First Printing: November, 1972* on copyright page. *Ballantine Books 02874–0–125* ($1.25). Edited, with introduction and notes, by Carter.

Flashing Swords! #1. *Garden City: Nelson Doubleday, Inc.,* [*1973*].
>   Boards. No statement of printing on copyright page. Code *D 11* on page 173. Edited, with introduction, notes, and novelette "The Higher Heresies of Oolimar," by Carter. Note: Issued by the Science Fiction Book Club.

Flashing Swords! #2. *Garden City: Nelson Doubleday, Inc.,* [*1973*].
>   Boards. No statement of printing on copyright page. Two printings, priority as listed: (A) Code *D39* on page 192; (B) Code *E39* on page 192. Edited, with introduction and notes, by Carter. Note: Issued by the Science Fiction Book Club.

Flashing Swords! #3. Warriors and Wizards. [*New York*]: *A Dell Book,* [*1976*].
>   Wrappers. *First printing —August 1976* on copyright page. *Dell 2579* ($1.25). Edited, with introduction, notes, and novelette "The Curious Custom of the Turjan Seraad," by Carter.

Flashing Swords! #4. Barbarians and Black Magicians. *Garden City: Nelson Doubleday, Inc.,* [*1977*].
>   Boards. No statement of printing on copyright page. Code *H 19* on page 182. Edited, with introduction and notes, by Carter. Note: Issued by the Science Fiction Book Club.

Golden Cities, Far. *New York: Ballantine Books,* [*1970*].
>   Wrappers. *First Printing: October, 1970* on copyright page. *Ballantine Books 02045–6–095* (95¢). Edited, with introduction, notes, and a translation, by Carter.

Great Short Novels of Adult Fantasy. *New York: Ballantine Books,* [*1972*].
>   Wrappers. *First Printing: September, 1972* on copyright page. *Ballantine Books 027789–2–125* ($1.25). Edited, with introduction and notes, by Carter.

Great Short Novels of Adult Fantasy, Volume II. *New York: Ballantine Books,* [*1973*].
>   Wrappers. *First Printing: March, 1973* on copyright page. *Ballantine Books 03162–8–125* ($1.25). Edited, with introduction and notes, by Carter.

Hyperborea, [by] Clark Ashton Smith. *New York: Ballantine Books,* [*1971*].
>   Wrappers. *First Printing: April, 1971* on copyright page. *Ballantine Books 02206–8–095* (95¢). Edited, with introduction and notes, by Carter.

Kingdoms of Sorcery. *Garden City: Doubleday & Company, Inc.,* 1976.
>   Boards. First edition so stated on copyright page. Edited, with introduction, notes and novelette "The Twelve Wizards of Ong," by Carter.

The Magic of Atlantis. *New York: Lancer Books*, [*1970*].
   Wrappers. No statement of printing on copyright page. *Lancer Books 74699–075* (75¢).
   Edited, with introduction and short story "The Seal of Zaon Sathla," by Carter.

New Worlds for Old. *New York: Ballantine Books*, [*1971*].
   Wrappers. *First Printing: September, 1971* on copyright page. *Ballantine Books
   02365–X–125* ($1.25). Edited, with introduction, notes, and short stories, "Zingazar" and
   "The Sword of Power," by Carter.

Over the Hills and Far Away, [by] Lord Dunsany. *New York: Ballantine Books*, [*1974*].
   Wrappers. *First Printing: April, 1974* on copyright page. *Ballantine 23886* ($1.25).
   Edited, with introduction and notes, by Carter.

Poseidonis, [by] Clark Ashton Smith. *New York: Ballantine Books*, [*1973*].
   Wrappers. *First Printing: July, 1973* on copyright page. *Ballantine Books 03353–1–125*
   ($1.25). Edited, with introduction and notes, by Carter.

Realms of Wizardry. *Garden City: Doubleday & Company, Inc.*, 1976.
   Boards. First edition so stated on copyright page. Edited, with introduction and notes, by
   Carter.

The Spawn of Cthulhu. *New York: Ballantine Books*, [*1971*].
   Wrappers. *First Printing: October, 1971* on copyright page. *Ballantine Books
   02394–3–095* (95¢). Edited, with introduction, notes, and sonnet sequence "Litany to
   Hastur," by Carter.

Xiccarph, [by] Clark Ashton Smith. *New York: Ballantine Books*, [*1972*].
   Wrappers. *First Printing: February, 1972* on copyright page. *Ballantine Books
   02501–6–125* ($1.25). Edited, with introduction and notes, by Carter.

The Year's Best Fantasy Stories. *New York: DAW Books, Inc.*, [*1975*].
   Wrappers. *First printing, October 1975/1 2 3 4 5 6 7 8 9* on copyright page. *DAW: sf Books
   No. 166 UY1199* ($1.25). Edited, with introduction, notes, appendix, and short story
   "Black Hawk of Valkarth," by Carter.

The Year's Best Fantasy Stories: 2. *New York: DAW Books, Inc.*, [*1976*].
   Wrappers. *First printing, August 1976/1 2 3 4 5 6 7 8 9* on copyright page. *DAW: sf Books
   No. 205 UY1248* ($1.25). Edited, with introduction, appendix, notes, short story "The
   City in the Jewel," and collaboration "The Scroll of Morloc" (with Clark Ashton Smith),
   by Carter.

The Year's Best Fantasy Stories: 3. *New York: DAW Books, Inc.*, [*1977*].
   Wrappers. *First printing, November 1977/1 2 3 4 5 6 7 8 9* on copyright page. *DAW: sf
   Books No. 267 UW1338* ($1.50). Edited, with introduction, notes, appendix, and short
   story "Black Moonlight," by Carter.

The Young Magicians. *New York: Ballantine Books*, [*1969*].
   Wrappers. *First printing: October, 1969* on copyright page. *Ballantine Books 01730* (95¢).
   Edited, with introduction, notes, and two short stories, "The Whelming of Oom" and
   "Azlon," by Carter.

Zothique, [by] Clark Ashton Smith. *New York: Ballantine Books*, [*1970*].
   Wrappers. *First Printing: June 1970* on copyright page. *Ballantine Books 01938–5–095*
   (95¢). Edited, with introduction and epilogue, by Carter.

Nonfiction (Dealing with the Fantasy Genre only)

Imaginary Worlds: The Art of Fantasy. *New York: Ballantine Books*, [*1973*].
Wrappers. *First Printing: June 1973* on copyright page. *Ballantine Books 03309–4–125*
($1.25).

Lovecraft: A Look Behind the "Cthulhu Mythos." *New York: Ballantine Books*, [*1972*].
Wrappers. *First Printing: February, 1972* on copyright page. Ballantine Books
02427–3–095 (95¢).

Tolkien: A Look Behind "The Lord of the Rings." *New York: Ballantine Books*, [*1969*].
Wrappers. *First Printing: March, 1969* on copyright page. *A Ballantine Book 01550*
(95¢).

Arthur Bertram Chandler

(b. 1912)

THE ALTERNATE MARTIANS. *New York: Ace Books, Inc.,* [*1965*].
Wrappers. No statement of printing on copyright page. *Ace Double M–129* (45¢). Bound
with EMPRESS OF OUTER SPACE by Chandler.

ALTERNATE ORBITS. *New York: Ace Books,* [*1971*].
Wrappers. No statement of printing on copyright page. *Ace Double 13783* (75¢). Bound
with THE DARK DIMENSIONS by Chandler.

BEYOND THE GALACTIC RIM. *New York: Ace Books, Inc.,* [*1963*].
Wrappers. No statement of printing on copyright page. *Ace Double F–237* (40¢). Bound
with THE SHIP FROM OUTSIDE by Chandler.

THE BIG BLACK MARK. *New York: DAW Books, Inc.,* [*1975*].
Wrappers. *First printing, February 1975/1 2 3 4 5 6 7 8 9* on copyright page. *DAW: sf
Books No. 139 UY1157* ($1.25).

THE BITTER PILL. [*Melbourne*]: *Wren* [*Publishing Pty Ltd, 1974*].
Boards. *First published 1974* on copyright page.

BRING BACK YESTERDAY. *New York: Ace Books, Inc.,* [*1961*].
Wrappers. No statement of printing on copyright page. *Ace Double Novel Books D–517*
(35¢). Bound with THE TROUBLE WITH TYCHO by Clifford Simak.

THE BROKEN CYCLE. *London: Robert Hale & Company,* [*1975*].
Boards. *First published in Great Britain 1975* on copyright page.

CATCH THE STAR WINDS. *New York: Lancer Books,* [*1969*].
Wrappers. *A Lancer Book • 1969* on copyright page. *Lancer Books 74–533* (75¢).

THE COILS OF TIME. *New York: Ace Books, Inc.,* [*1964*].
Wrappers. No statement of printing on copyright page. *Ace Double M–107* (45¢). Bound
with INTO THE ALTERNATE UNIVERSE by Chandler.

CONTRABAND FROM OTHERSPACE. *New York: Ace Books, Inc.,* [*1967*].
Wrappers. No statement of printing on copyright page. *Ace Double G–609* (50¢). Bound
with REALITY FORBIDDEN by Philip E. High.

THE DARK DIMENSIONS. *New York: Ace Books,* [*1971*].
Wrappers. No statement of printing on copyright page. *Ace Double 13783* (75¢). Bound
with ALTERNATE ORBITS by Chandler.

THE DEEP REACHES OF SPACE. *London: Herbert Jenkins,* [*1964*].
Boards. *First published . . . 1964* on copyright page.

EMPRESS OF OUTER SPACE. *New York: Ace Books, Inc.,* [*1965*].
Wrappers. No statement of printing on copyright page. *Ace Double M–129* (45¢). Bound
with THE ALTERNATE MARTIANS by Chandler.

FALSE FATHERLAND. *London • Melbourne • Sydney: Horwitz Publications,* [*1968*].
Wrappers. *First published in New Zealand and simultaneously in Australia 1968* on
copyright page. *PB374* (65¢). Issued later in the U.S. as SPARTAN PLANET.

THE FAR TRAVELLER. *London: Robert Hale*, [*1977*].
Boards. *First published in Great Britain 1977* on copyright page.

THE GATEWAY TO NEVER. *New York: Ace Books*, [*1972*].
Wrappers. No statement of printing on copyright page. *Ace Double 37062* (95¢). Bound
with THE INHERITORS by Chandler.

GLORY PLANET. *New York: Avalon Books*, [*1964*].
No statement of printing on copyright page.

THE HAMELIN PLAGUE. *Derby, Connecticut: Monarch Books, Inc.*, [*1963*].
Wrappers. *Published in November, 1963* on copyright page. *Monarch Books 390* (35¢).

THE HARD WAY UP. *New York: Ace Books*, [*1972*].
Wrappers. *First Ace printing: October, 1972* on copyright page. *Ace Double 31755* (95¢).
Bound with THE VEILED WORLD by Robert Lory.

THE INHERITORS. *New York: Ace Books*, [*1972*].
Wrappers. No statement of printing on copyright page. *Ace Double 37062* (95¢). Bound
with THE GATEWAY TO NEVER by Chandler.

INTO THE ALTERNATE UNIVERSE. *New York: Ace Books, Inc.*, [*1964*].
Wrappers. No statement of printing on copyright page. *Ace Double M–107* (45¢). Bound
with THE COILS OF TIME by Chandler.

NEBULA ALERT. *New York: Ace Books, Inc.*, [*1967*].
Wrappers. No statement of printing on copyright page. *Ace Double G–632* (50¢). Bound
with THE RIVAL RIGELIANS by Mack Reynolds.

RENDEZVOUS ON A LOST WORLD. *New York: Ace Books, Inc.*, [*1961*].
Wrappers. No statement of printing on copyright page. *Ace Double Novel F–117* (40¢).
Bound with THE DOOR THROUGH SPACE by Marion Zimmer Bradley.

THE RIM GODS. *New York: Ace Books, Inc.*, [*1969*].
Wrappers. No statement of printing on copyright page. *Ace Double 72400* (60¢). Bound
with THE HIGH HEX by Laurence M. Janifer and S. J. Treibich.

THE RIM OF SPACE. *New York: Avalon Books*, [*1961*].
No statement of printing on copyright page.

THE ROAD TO THE RIM. *New York: Ace Books, Inc.*, [*1967*].
Wrappers. No statement of printing on copyright page. *Ace Double H–29* (60¢). Bound
with THE LOST MILLENNIUM by Walt and Leigh Richmond.

THE SEA BEASTS. *New York: Curtis Books*, [*1971*].
Wrappers. No statement of printing on copyright page. *Curtis Books 502–07135–075*
(75¢).

THE SHIP FROM OUTSIDE. *New York: Ace Books, Inc.*, [*1963*].
Wrappers. No statement of printing on copyright page. *Ace Double F–237* (40¢). Bound
with BEYOND THE GALACTIC RIM by Chandler.

SPACE MERCENARIES. *New York: Ace Books, Inc.*, [*1965*].
Wrappers. No statement of printing on copyright page. *Ace Double M–133* (45¢). Bound
with THE CAVES OF MARS by Emil Petaja.

SPARTAN PLANET. [*New York*]: *A Dell Book*, [*1969*].
Wrappers. *First printing—April 1969* on copyright page. *Dell 8174* (50¢). Issued earlier in
Australia as FALSE FATHERLAND.

SILNED OK

STAR COURIER. *New York: DAW Books, Inc., [1977].*
Wrappers. *First DAW printing, March 1977/1 2 3 4 5 6 7 8 9* on copyright page. *DAW: sf Books No. 234 UY1292* ($1.25).

ALSO:*London: Robert Hale, [1977].* Boards. *First published in Great Britain 1977* on copyright page. First hardcover edition.

TO PRIME THE PUMP. *New York: Curtis Books, [1971].*
Wrappers. No statement of printing on copyright page. *Curtis Books 502–07116–075* (70¢).

SILNED OK

THE WAY BACK. *London: Robert Hale & Company, [1976].*
Boards. *First published in Great Britain 1976* on copyright page.

SILNED OK ⊘ TO KEEP THE SHIP — DAW 1978

Suzy McKee Charnas
(b. 1939)

WALK TO THE END OF THE WORLD. *New York: Ballantine Books,* [*1974*].
Wrappers. *First Printing: February, 1974* on copyright page. *Ballantine 23788* ($1.25).

MOTHERLINES

Carolyn Janice Cherry

(b. 1942)

BROTHERS OF EARTH. *Garden City: Nelson Doubleday, Inc.*, [1976].
Boards. No statement of printing on copyright page. Code *G21* on page 245. *C. J. Cherryh, pseudonym*. Note: Issued by the Science Fiction Book Club.

GATE OF IVREL. *New York: DAW Books, Inc.*, [1976].
Wrappers. *First printing, March 1976/1 2 3 4 5 6 7 8 9* on copyright page. *DAW: sf Books No. 188 UY1226* ($1.25). *C. J. Cherryh, pseudonym*.

HUNTER OF WORLDS. *Garden City: Nelson Doubleday, Inc.*, [1977].
Boards. No statement of printing on copyright page. Code *H 06* on page 213. *C. J. Cherryh, pseudonym*. Note: Issued by the Science Fiction Book Club.

Arthur Charles Clarke
(b. 1917)

ACROSS THE SEA OF STARS. *New York: Harcourt, Brace and Company*, [*1959*].
First edition so stated on copyright page. Reprint. Collects CHILDHOOD'S END, EARTH-
LIGHT, and eighteen stories selected from EXPEDITION TO EARTH, TALES FROM THE WHITE
HART, and REACH FOR TOMORROW.

AGAINST THE FALL OF NIGHT. [*New York*]: *Gnome Press, Inc.*, [*1953*].
Boards. First edition so stated on copyright page. Later revised and expanded as THE CITY
AND THE STARS.

AN ARTHUR C. CLARKE SECOND OMNIBUS.*London: Sidgwick & Jackson*, [*1968*].
Boards. No statement of printing on copyright page. Reprint. Collects A FALL OF MOON
DUST, EARTHLIGHT, and SANDS OF MARS.

AN ARTHUR CLARKE OMNIBUS. *London: Sidgwick & Jackson*, [*1965*].
Boards. No statement of printing on copyright page. Reprint. Collects CHILDHOOD'S END,
PRELUDE TO SPACE, and EXPEDITION TO EARTH.

THE BEST OF ARTHUR C. CLARKE.*London: Sidgwick & Jackson*, [*1973*].
Boards. *First published in Great Britain in 1973* on copyright page.

CHILDHOOD'S END.*New York: Ballantine Books*, [*1953*].
Two issues, no priority: (A) Cloth; (B) Wrappers. *Ballantine Books 33* (35¢). No statement
of printing on copyright page.

THE CITY AND THE STARS.*New York: Harcourt, Brace and Company*, [*1956*].
Boards. First edition so stated on copyright page. Revised and expanded version of
AGAINST THE FALL OF NIGHT.

THE DEEP RANGE.*New York: Harcourt, Brace and Company*, [*1957*].
Boards. First edition so stated on copyright page.

DOLPHIN ISLAND.*New York/Chicago/San Francisco: Holt, Rinehart and Winston*, [*1963*].
Two bindings, no priority: (A) Boards. Trade binding. (B) Pictorial cloth reproducing the
dust jacket design. Library binding (not seen). First edition so stated on copyright page.

EARTHLIGHT.*New York: Ballantine Books*, [*1955*].
Two issues, no priority: (A) Cloth; (B) Wrappers. *Ballantine Books 97* (35¢). No statement
of printing on copyright page.

ALSO:*New York: Harcourt Brace Jovanovich, Inc.*, *1972*. First printing has HBJ monogram and code *BCDE* on copyright page. New preface by the author.

EXPEDITION TO EARTH.*New York: Ballantine Books*, [*1953*].
Two issues, no priority: (A) Boards; (B) Wrappers. *Ballantine Books 52* (35¢). No statement of printing on copyright page.

ALSO:*London: Sidgwick and Jackson*, [*1954*]. Boards. *First published 1954* on copyright
page. Same contents as U.S. edition but three story title changes, "Exile of the Eons"
retitled "Nemesis," "Expedition to Earth," retitled "Encounter in the Dawn," and "History Lesson," retitled "Expedition to Earth."

ALSO:*New York: Harcourt, Brace & World, Inc.*, [*1970*]. Cloth-backed boards. No
statement of printing on copyright page. New preface by the author.

Signed A FALL OF MOONDUST. *New York: Harcourt, Brace & World, Inc.*, [*1961*].
First edition so stated on copyright page.

Signed FROM THE OCEAN, FROM THE STARS. *New York: Harcourt, Brace & World, Inc.*, [*1962*].
First edition so stated on copyright page. Reprint. Collects THE CITY AND THE STARS, THE DEEP RANGE, and THE OTHER SIDE OF THE SKY.

Signed / o/w worn GLIDE PATH. *New York: Harcourt, Brace & World, Inc.*, [*1963*].
First edition so stated on copyright page.

IMPERIAL EARTH. *London: Victor Gollancz Ltd, 1975.*
Boards. No statement of printing on copyright page.

Signed ALSO:*New York and London: Harcourt Brace Jovanovich*, [*1976.*]. Boards with cloth shelf back. *First edition/B C D E* on copyright page. Adds five chapters (approximately 10,000 words).

Signed / extra d/w ISLANDS IN THE SKY. *Philadelphia Toronto: The John C. Winston Company*, [*1952*].
First edition so stated on copyright page.

ALSO:*London: Sidgwick and Jackson Limited*, [*1952*]. No statement of printing on copyright page. Drops preface "Cities in Space."

Signed THE LION OF COMARRE & AGAINST THE FALL OF NIGHT. *New York: Harcourt, Brace & World, Inc.*, [*1968*].
First edition so stated on copyright page. First book publication for "The Lion of Comarre."

Have Gregg 14 6 THE LOST WORLDS OF 2001. [*New York*]: *New American Library*, [*1972*].
Wrappers. *First printing, January, 1972* on copyright page. *Signet Y4949* ($1.25). Notes: (1) Later printings retain the first printing slug but add a row of numbers below. (2) In addition to the narrative concerning creation of the film *2001: A Space Odyssey*, this work includes the original fictional treatment, including alternate endings, preceding the final draft of the novel.

ALSO:*London: Sidgwick & Jackson*, [*1972*]. Boards. *First published in Great Britain in 1972* on copyright page. First hardcover edition.

MASTER OF SPACE. *New York: Lancer Books*, [*1961*].
Wrappers. *Lancer Books edition published in 1961* on copyright page. *Lancer Books 72–610* (50¢). Reissue of PRELUDE TO SPACE. New foreword by the author.

Signed THE NINE BILLION NAMES OF GOD. *New York: Harcourt, Brace & World, Inc.*, [*1967*].
First edition so stated on copyright page.

OF TIME AND STARS. *London: Victor Gollancz Ltd, 1972.*
Boards. No statement of printing on copyright page. All stories reprinted from earlier collections. New preface by the author.

Signed, THE OTHER SIDE OF THE SKY. *New York: Harcourt, Brace and Company*, [*1958*].
Boards with cloth shelf back. First edition so stated on copyright page.

Worn d/w PRELUDE TO MARS. *New York: Harcourt, Brace & World, Inc.*, [*1965*].
First edition so stated on copyright page. Reprint. Collects PRELUDE TO SPACE, THE SANDS OF MARS, and sixteen stories selected from TALES FROM THE WHITE HART, EXPEDITION TO EARTH, and REACH FOR TOMORROW.

OK PRELUDE TO SPACE. *New York: World Editions, Inc.*, [*1951*].
Wrappers. No statement of printing on copyright page. *Galaxy Science Fiction Novel No. 3* (25¢).

ALSO: *London: Sidgwick and Jackson Limited, [1953]. First published in 1953* on copyright page. Textual revisions.

ALSO: *[New York]: Gnome Press, [1954]*. Three bindings, priority not established for first two, last is a later state: (A) Blue boards, spine lettered in yellow; (B) Black boards, spine lettered in red; (C) Gray cloth, spine lettered in red. First edition so stated on copyright page. Minor textual changes.

ALSO: *New York: Harcourt, Brace & World, Inc., [1970]*. No statement of printing on copyright page. Adds ''Post-Apollo Preface'' by the author. Reissued as MASTER OF SPACE and later as THE SPACE DREAMERS.

REACH FOR TOMORROW. *New York: Ballantine Books, [1956]*.
Two issues, no priority: (A) Cloth; (B) Wrappers. *Ballantine Books 135* (35¢). No statement of printing on copyright page.

*ALSO: *New York: Harcourt, Brace & World, Inc., [1970]*. New introduction by the author.

RENDEZVOUS WITH RAMA. *London: Victor Gollancz Ltd, 1973*.
Boards. No statement of printing on copyright page.

THE SANDS OF MARS. *London: Sidgwick and Jackson Limited, [1951]*.
Boards. *First published in 1951* on copyright page.
ALSO: *New York: Harcourt, Brace & World, Inc., [1967]*. No statement of printing on copyright page. New foreword by Clarke.

THE SPACE DREAMERS. *New York: Lancer Books, [1969]*.
Wrappers. *Second edition May 1969* on copyright page. *Lancer Books 74–524* (75¢). Reissue of PRELUDE TO SPACE. Note: First printing under this title.

TALES FROM THE WHITE HART. *New York: Ballantine Books, [1957]*.
Wrappers. No statement of printing on copyright page. *Ballantine Books 186* (35¢).

ALSO: *New York: Harcourt, Brace & World, Inc., [1970]*. No statement of printing on copyright page. New preface by the author. First hardcover edition.

TALES OF TEN WORLDS. *New York: Harcourt, Brace & World, Inc., [1962]*.
First edition so stated on copyright page.

2001 A SPACE ODYSSEY. *[New York]: The New American Library, [1968]*.
Boards. First printing so stated on copyright page.

THE WIND FROM THE SUN. *New York: Harcourt Brace Jovanovich, Inc., [1972]*.
First edition so stated on copyright page. Also code letters *BCDEF* on copyright page.

Edited Fiction

Time Probe. *New York: Delacorte Press, [1966]*.
First printing so stated on copyright page. Compiled, with introduction and short story ''Take a Deep Breath,'' by Clarke.

Autobiography

The View From Serendip. *New York: Random House, [1977]*.
Boards with cloth shelf back. *2 4 6 8 9 7 5 3/First Edition* on copyright page. Autobiography and miscellany.

Reference

Arthur C. Clarke, [by] Eric S. Rabkin. *West Linn, Oregon: Starmont House,* [*1979*].
   Wrappers. No statement of printing on copyright page. *Starmont Reader's Guide 1.*

Arthur C. Clarke, edited by Joseph D. Olander and Martin Harry Greenberg. *New York:*
Taplinger Publishing Company, [*1977*].
   Two bindings, no priority: (A) Boards with cloth shelf back; (B) Wrappers. First edition so
stated on copyright page.

The Space Odysseys of Arthur C. Clarke, [by] George Edgar Slusser. *San Bernardino,*
California: R. Reginald The Borgo Press, MCMLXXVIII.
   Wrappers. *First Edition———July, 1978* on copyright page. *The Milford Series Popular*
Writers of Today Volume Eight at head of title.

Mark Clifton
(1906–1963)

EIGHT KEYS TO EDEN. *Garden City: Doubleday & Company, Inc., 1960.*
First edition so stated on copyright page.

THE FOREVER MACHINE. *New York: Galaxy Publishing Corp., [1958].*
Wrappers. No statement of printing on copyright page. *Galaxy Novel No. 35* (35¢). With
FRANK RILEY. Reissue of THEY'D RATHER BE RIGHT.

THEY'D RATHER BE RIGHT. *New York: Gnome Press, Inc., Publishers, 1957.*
Boards. First edition so stated on copyright page. With FRANK RILEY. Reissued as THE
FOREVER MACHINE.

WHEN THEY COME FROM SPACE. *Garden City: Doubleday & Company, Inc., 1962.*
First edition so stated on copyright page.

Stanton Arthur Coblentz
(b. 1896)

AFTER 12,000 YEARS. *Los Angeles: Fantasy Publishing Co., Inc., 1950.*
No statement of printing on copyright page.

THE ANIMAL PEOPLE. *New York: Belmont Books, [1970].*
Wrappers. *August 1970* on copyright page. *Belmont B75–2038* (75¢). Reissue of THE
CRIMSON CAPSULE.

THE BLUE BARBARIANS. *New York: Avalon Books, [1958].*
No statement of printing on copyright page.

THE CRIMSON CAPSULE. *New York: Avalon Books, [1967].*
No statement of printing on copyright page. Reissued as THE ANIMAL PEOPLE.

THE DAY THE WORLD STOPPED. *New York: Avalon Books, [1968].*
No statement of printing on copyright page.

HIDDEN WORLD. *New York: Avalon Books, [1957].*
No statement of printing on copyright page. Reissued as IN CAVERNS BELOW.

IN CAVERNS BELOW. *[New York & London: Garland Publishing, Inc., 1975.]*
No statement of printing on copyright page. Reissue of HIDDEN WORLD.

INTO PLUTONIAN DEPTHS. *New York: Avon Publishing Co., Inc., [1950].*
Wrappers. No statement of printing on copyright page. *Avon Fantasy Novels 281* (25¢).

THE ISLAND PEOPLE. *New York: Belmont Books, [1971].*
Wrappers. *November 1971* on copyright page. *Belmont B75–2180* (75¢).

THE LAST OF THE GREAT RACE. *[New York]: Arcadia House, [1964].*
No statement of printing on copyright page.

THE LIZARD LORDS. *New York: Avalon Books, [1964].*
No statement of printing on copyright page.

LORD OF TRANERICA. *New York: Avalon Books, [1966].*
No statement of printing on copyright page.

THE LOST COMET. *[New York]: Arcadia House, [1964].*
No statement of printing on copyright page.

THE MOON PEOPLE. *New York: Avalon Books, [1964].*
No statement of printing on copyright page.

NEXT DOOR TO THE SUN. *New York: Avalon Books, [1960].*
No statement of printing on copyright page.

THE PLANET OF YOUTH. *Los Angeles: Fantasy Publishing Company, Inc., [1952].*
Two bindings, priority as listed: (A) Boards; (B) Wrappers. No statement of printing on
copyright page.

THE RUNAWAY WORLD. *New York: Avalon Books*, [*1961*].
No statement of printing on copyright page.

THE SUNKEN WORLD. *Los Angeles: Fantasy Publishing Co., Inc., 1948*.
First edition so stated on copyright page.

UNDER THE TRIPLE SUNS. *Reading, Pennsylvania; Fantasy Press, Inc.*, [*1955*].
Two issues, no priority: (A) 300 copies with numbered leaf signed by the author inserted.
Limited issue. (B) Trade issue. First edition so stated on copyright page.

WHEN THE BIRDS FLY SOUTH. *Mill Valley, Calif. New York, N.Y.: The Wings Press, 1945*.
No statement of printing on copyright page.

THE WONDER STICK. *New York: Cosmopolitan Book Corporation, MCMXXIX*.
No statement of printing on copyright page.

YOUTH MADNESS. [*London: Utopian Publications Ltd.*], *n.d.* [*ca. 1944–1945*].
Wrappers. No statement of printing. Cover title. Issued as *American Fiction No. 8* (One
Shilling Net). *Printed in Great Britain* on page 36.

Theodore Rose Cogswell
(b. 1918)

SPOCK, MESSIAH! *Toronto New York London: Bantam Books*, [*1976*].
  Wrappers. *September 1976* on copyright page. *Bantam Science Fiction 10159-5* ($1.75).
  With CHARLES A. SPANO, JR.

THE THIRD EYE. *New York: Belmont Books*, [*1968*].
  Wrappers. *September 1968* on copyright page. *Belmont Science Fiction B50-840* (50¢).

THE WALL AROUND THE WORLD. *New York: Pyramid Books*, [*1962*].
  Wrappers. *February 1962* on copyright page. *Pyramid Books F-703* (40¢).

John Henry Noyes Collier
(b. 1901)

THE BEST OF JOHN COLLIER. *New York: Published by Pocket Books, [1975]*.
Wrappers. *Pocket Book edition published September, 1975* on copyright page. *Pocket Books Fiction 80076* ($1.95). Abridged reissue of THE JOHN COLLIER READER.

DEFY THE FOUL FIEND OR THE MISADVENTURES OF A HEART. *London: Macmillan and Co., Limited, 1934*.
No statement of printing on copyright page. *— HAVE 1ST AMERICAN KNOPF 1934*

THE DEVIL AND ALL. *[London]: Nonesuch Press, 1934*.
No statement of printing on copyright page. 1000 numbered copies signed by the author.

FANCIES AND GOODNIGHTS. *Garden City: Doubleday & Company, Inc., 1951*.
First edition so stated on copyright page. Abridged as OF DEMONS AND DARKNESS.

FULL CIRCLE. *New York: D. Appleton & Company, 1933*.
No statement of printing on copyright page. First printing has code *(1)* at base of text on page [291]. Issued earlier in Great Britain as TOM'S A-COLD.

GREEN THOUGHTS. *London: William Jackson (Books) Ltd, 1932*.
No statement of printing on copyright page. 550 numbered copies signed by the author.

GREEN THOUGHTS AND OTHER STRANGE TALES. *New York: Editions for the Armed Services, Inc., [1945]*.
Wrappers. No statement of printing on copyright page. *Armed Services Edition 871*.
Reprint collection. All stories appeared previously in THE TOUCH OF NUTMEG.

HIS MONKEY WIFE OR, MARRIED TO A CHIMP. *London: Peter Davies, 1930*.
Published in November, 1930 on copyright page. *— HAVE AMERICAN APPLETON 1931*

THE JOHN COLLIER READER. *New York: Alfred A. Knopf, 1972*.
First edition so stated on copyright page. Four stories appear for the first time. *n/w*

NO TRAVELLER RETURNS. *London: The White Owl Press, 1931*.
No statement of printing on copyright page. 210 numbered copies signed by the author.
Two issues, no priority: (A) 25 copies on iridescent Japanese vellum; (B) 185 copies on hand-made paper.

OF DEMONS AND DARKNESS. *[London]: Corgi Books, [1965]*.
Wrappers. *First publication in this form/in Great Britain/ . . ./Corgi Edition published 1965* on copyright page. *A Corgi Book FS7126* (5/–). This abridged edition contains the first thirty-seven stories appearing earlier in FANCIES AND GOODNIGHTS.

PICTURES IN THE FIRE. *London: Rupert Hart-Davis, 1958*.
Boards. No statement of printing on copyright page.

PRESENTING MOONSHINE. *New York: The Viking Press, 1941*. *n/w*
Published in January 1941 on copyright page.

TOM'S A-COLD. *London: Macmillan and Co., Limited, 1933*.
No statement of printing on copyright page. Issued later in the U.S. as FULL CIRCLE.

THE TOUCH OF NUTMEG AND MORE UNLIKELY STORIES. *New York: The Press of The Readers Club*, [*1943*].
 No statement of printing on copyright page.

VARIATION ON A THEME. *London: Grayson & Grayson, 1935.*
 No statement of printing on copyright page. 285 numbered copies signed by the author.

*WET SATURDAY: A PLAY ADAPTED FROM THE NEW YORKER SHORT STORY. *Boston: One Act*,
 [*1941?*].
 Wrappers. Price 50¢.

WITCH'S MONEY. *New York: The Viking Press Publishers, 1940.*
 Published . . . in December 1940 on copyright page. 350 copies signed by the author.
 Note: Privately distributed to friends of the author and the publisher.

David Guy Compton
(b. 1930)

AND MURDER CAME TOO. *London: John Long*, [*1966*].
   Boards. *First published 1966* on copyright page. Published under the byline GUY
   COMPTON.

✓ CHRONOCULES. *New York: Ace Books*, [*1970*].
   Wrappers. No statement of printing on copyright page. *An Ace Science Fiction Special
   10480* (75¢). Published later in Great Britain as HOT WIRELESS SETS, ASPRIN TABLETS, THE
   SANDPAPER SIDES OF USED MATCHBOXES & SOMETHING THAT MIGHT HAVE BEEN CASTOR
   OIL.

✓ THE CONTINUOUS KATHERINE MORTENHOE. *London: Victor Gollancz Ltd*, *1974*.
   Boards. No statement of printing on copyright page. Issued the same month in the U.S. as
   THE UNSLEEPING EYE.

DEAD ON CUE. *London: John Long*, [*1964*].
   Boards. *First published 1964* on copyright page. Published under the byline GUY
   COMPTON.

DISGUISE FOR A DEAD GENTLEMAN. *London: John Long*, [*1964*].
   Boards. *First published 1964* on copyright page. Published under the byline GUY
   COMPTON.

THE ELECTRIC CROCODILE. [*London*]: *Hodder and Stoughton*, [*1970*].
   Boards. *First printed 1970* on copyright page. Issued earlier in the U.S. as THE STEEL
   CROCODILE.

FAREWELL, EARTH'S BLISS. [*London*]: *Hodder and Stoughton*, [*1966*].
   Boards. *First Printed 1966* on copyright page.

   ✓ ALSO: *New York: Ace Books*, [*1971*]. Wrappers. No statement of printing on copyright
   page. *Ace Book 22830* (75¢). Revised text.

THE FINE AND HANDSOME CAPTAIN. *New York: St. Martin's Press*, [*1975*].
   Boards. No statement of printing on copyright page. *Frances Lynch, pseudonym*.

HIGH TIDE FOR HANGING. *London: John Long*, [*1965*].
   Boards. *First published 1965* on copyright page. Published under the byline GUY
   COMPTON.

HOT WIRELESS SETS, ASPRIN TABLETS, THE SANDPAPER SIDES OF USED MATCHBOXES &
SOMETHING THAT MIGHT HAVE BEEN CASTOR OIL. *London: Michael Joseph*, [*1971*].
   Boards. *First published in Great Britain . . . 1971* on copyright page. Issued earlier in the
   U.S. as CHRONOCULES.

MEDIUM FOR MURDER. *London: John Long*, [*1963*].
   Boards. *First published 1963* on copyright page. Published under the byline GUY
   COMPTON.

✓ THE MISSIONARIES. *New York: Ace Books*, [*1972*].
   Wrappers. No statement of printing on copyright page. *Ace Book SF 53570* (75¢).

   ALSO: *London: Robert Hale & Company*, [*1975*]. Boards. *First published in Great Britain
   1975* on copyright page. First hardcover edition.

THE PALACE. [*London*]: *Hodder and Stoughton*, [*1969*].
Boards. *First printed 1969* on copyright page.

[handwritten: First Printed 1961] THE QUALITY OF MERCY. [*London*]: *Hodder and Stoughton*, [*1965*].
Boards. *First published 1965* on copyright page.

✓ ALSO: *New York: Ace Publishing Corporation*, [*1970*]. Wrappers. No statement of printing on copyright page. *Ace Book 69540* (75¢). Revised text.

✓ THE SILENT MULTITUDE. *New York: Ace Publishing Corporation*, [*1966*].
Wrappers. No statement of printing on copyright page. *An Ace Science Fiction Special 76385* (75¢).

✓ ALSO: [*London*]: *Hodder and Stoughton*, [*1967*]. Boards. *First printed 1967* on copyright page. First hardcover edition.

THE STEEL CROCODILE. *New York: Ace Publishing Corporation*, [*1970*].
Wrappers. No statement of printing on copyright page. *An Ace Science Fiction Special 78575* (75¢). Issued later in Great Britain as THE ELECTRIC CROCODILE.
[handwritten: → Green]

STRANGER AT THE WEDDING. *New York: St. Martin's Press*, [*1976*].
Boards. No statement of printing on copyright page. *Frances Lynch, pseudonym*.

SYNTHAJOY. [*London*]: *Hodder and Stoughton*, [*1968*].
Boards. *First printed 1968* on copyright page.

TOO MANY MURDERERS. *London: John Long*, [*1962*].
Boards. *First published 1962* on copyright page. Published under the byline GUY COMPTON.

*TWICE TEN THOUSAND MILES. [*London*]: *Souvenir Press*, [*1974*].
Frances Lynch, pseudonym.

THE UNSLEEPING EYE. *New York: DAW Books, Inc.*, [*1974*].
Wrappers. *First printing, May 1974/1 2 3 4 5 6 7 8 9* on copyright page. *DAW: sf Books No. 102 UY1110* ($1.25). Issued the same month in Great Britain as THE CONTINUOUS KATHERINE MORTENHOE.

Michael Greatrey Coney
(b. 1932)

BRONTOMEK!*London: Victor Gollancz Ltd, 1976*.
   Boards. No statement of printing on copyright page.

CHARISMA.*London: Victor Gollancz Ltd, 1975*.
   Boards. No statement of printing on copyright page.

FRIENDS COME IN BOXES.*New York: DAW Books, Inc.*, [*1973*].
   Wrappers. *First printing, May 1973/1 2 3 4 5 6 7 8 9* on copyright page. *DAW: sf Books No. 56 UQ1056* (95¢).

   ALSO:*London: Victor Gollancz, 1974*. Boards. No statement of printing on copyright page First hardcover edition. Textual revisions.

THE GIRL WITH A SYMPHONY IN HER FINGERS. [*Morley*]: *The Elmfield Press*, [*1975*].
   Boards. *Published 1975* on copyright page. Issued earlier in the U.S. as THE JAWS THAT BITE, THE CLAWS THAT CATCH.

HELLO SUMMER, GOODBYE. *London: Victor Gollancz Ltd, 1975*.
   Boards. No statement of printing on copyright page. Issued later in the U.S. as RAX.

THE HERO OF DOWNWAYS.*New York: DAW Books, Inc.*, [*1973*].
   Wrappers. *First Printing, September 1973/1 2 3 4 5 6 7 8 9* on copyright page. *DAW: sf Books No. 70* (95¢).

THE JAWS THAT BITE, THE CLAWS THAT CATCH.*New York: DAW Books, Inc.*, [*1975*].
   Wrappers.*First Printing, March 1975/1 2 3 4 5 6 7 8 9* on copyright page. *DAW: sf Books No. 144 UY1163* ($1.25). Issued later in Great Britain as THE GIRL WITH A SYMPHONY IN HER FINGERS.

MIRROR IMAGE.*New York: DAW Books, Inc.*, [*1972*].
   Wrappers.*First Printing, 1972* on copyright page. *DAW: sf Books No. 31 UQ1031* (95¢).

   ALSO:*London: Victor Gollancz Ltd, 1973*. Boards. No statement of printing on copyright page. First hardcover edition.

MONITOR FOUND IN ORBIT.*New York: DAW Books, Inc.*, [*1974*].
   Wrappers.*First printing, September 1974/1 2 3 4 5 6 7 8 9* on copyright page. *DAW: sf Books No. 120 UQ1132* (95¢).

RAX.*New York: DAW Books, Inc.*, [*1975*].
   Wrappers.*First printing, November 1975/1 2 3 4 5 6 7 8 9* on copyright page. *DAW: sf Books No. 170 UY1205* ($1.25). Issued earlier in Great Britain as HELLO SUMMER, GOOD-BYE.

SYZYGY.*New York: Ballantine Books*, [*1973*].
   Wrappers. *First Printing: January, 1973* on copyright page.*Ballantine Books Science Fiction 03056-7-125* ($1.25).

   ALSO: [*Morley*]: *The Elmfield Press*, [*1973*]. Boards.*Published 1973* on copyright page. First hardcover edition.

WINTER'S CHILDREN.*London: Victor Gollancz Ltd, 1974*.
   Boards. No statement of printing on copyright page.

Edmund Cooper
(b. 1926)

ALL FOOL'S DAY. [*London*]: *Hodder and Stoughton*, [*1966*].
Boards. *First printed 1966* on copyright page.

THE CLOUD WALKER. *London Sydney Auckland Toronto: Hodder and Stoughton*, [*1973*].
Boards. *First printed 1973* on copyright page.

DEADLY IMAGE. *New York: Ballantine Books*, [*1958*].
Wrappers. No statement of printing on copyright page. *Ballantine Books 260* (35¢). Issued later in Great Britain as THE UNCERTAIN MIDNIGHT.

THE DEATHWORMS OF KRATOS. *London: Hodder Paperbacks Ltd.*, [*1975*].
Wrappers. *First published in this edition by Coronet Books 1975* on copyright page. *Coronet Science Fiction 19472 3* (35p). *Richard Avery, pseudonym.*

ALSO: [*London*]: *Severn House*, [*1977*]. Boards. *This first U.K. hardback edition published 1977 . . .* on copyright page. *The Expendables: Volume One* at head of title. First hardcover edition. Note: This edition credits the novel to Cooper.

A FAR SUNSET. [*London*]: *Hodder and Stoughton*, [*1967*].
Boards. *First printed 1967* on copyright page.

FIVE TO TWELVE. [*London*]: *Hodder and Stoughton*, [*1968*].
Boards. *First printed 1968* on copyright page.

GENDER GENOCIDE. *New York: Ace Books*, [*1972*].
Wrappers. No statement of printing on copyright page. *Ace SF 27905* (95¢). Issued earlier in Great Britain as WHO NEEDS MEN?

KRONK. *New York: G. P. Putnam's Sons*, [*1971*].
No statement of printing on copyright page. Issued earlier in Great Britain as SON OF KRONK.

THE LAST CONTINENT. [*New York*]: *A Dell Book*, [*1969*].
Wrappers. *First Printing —September 1969* on copyright page. *Dell 4655* (60¢).

ALSO: [*London*]: *Hodder and Stoughton*, [*1970*]. Boards. *First printed 1970* on copyright page. First hardcover edition.

NEWS FROM ELSEWHERE. [*London*]: *A Mayflower Paperback*, [*1968*].
Wrappers. *Published as a Mayflower Paperback 1968* on copyright page. *Mayflower 6304–8* (3/6).

THE OVERMAN CULTURE. *London Sydney Auckland Toronto: Hodder and Stoughton*, [*1971*].
Boards. *First printed 1971* on copyright page.

PRISONER OF FIRE. *London Sydney Auckland Toronto: Hodder and Stoughton*, [*1974*].
Boards. *First printed 1974* on copyright page.

THE RINGS OF TANTALUS. [*London*]: *Hodder and Stoughton*, [*1975*].
Wrappers. *First published in this edition by Coronet Books 1975* on copyright page. *Coronet Science Fiction 19889 3* (40p). *Richard Avery, pseudonym.*

ALSO: [*London*]*: Severn House*, [*1977*]. Boards. *This first hardback edition published in 1977 . . .* on copyright page. *The Expendables: Volume Two* at head of title. First hardcover edition. Note: This edition credits the novel to Cooper.

SEA-HORSE IN THE SKY. [*London*]*: Hodder and Stoughton*, [*1969*].
  Boards. *First printed 1969* on copyright page.

SEED OF LIGHT. *London: Hutchinson*, [*1959*].
  Boards. *First published 1959* on copyright page.

THE SLAVES OF HEAVEN. *New York: G. P. Putnam's Sons*, [*1974*].
  No statement of printing on copyright page.

SON OF KRONK. [*London*]*: Hodder and Stoughton*, [*1970*].
  Boards. *First printed 1970* on copyright page. Issued later in the U.S. as KRONK.

THE SQUARE ROOT OF TOMORROW. *London: Robert Hale*, [*1970*].
  Boards. *First published in Great Britain 1970* on copyright page.

THE TENTH PLANET. *London Sydney Auckland Toronto: Hodder and Stoughton*, [*1973*].
  Boards. *First printed 1973* on copyright page. Note: Both the Hodder and Stoughton and the U.S. edition published by G. P. Putnam's Sons were issued the same month, the latter on 20 November. Priority, if any, not established.

TOMORROW CAME. [*London*]*: A Panther Book*, [*1963*].
  Wrappers. *First published . . . May 1963* on copyright page. *Panther Books 1511* (2'6).

TOMORROW'S GIFT. *New York: Ballantine Books*, [*1958*].
  Wrappers. No statement of printing on copyright page. *Ballantine Books 297K* (35¢).

TRANSIT. *London: Faber and Faber*, [*1964*].
  First published in mcmlxiv on copyright page.

UNBORN TOMORROW. *London: Robert Hale*, [*1971*].
  Boards. *First published in Great Britain 1971* on copyright page.

THE UNCERTAIN MIDNIGHT. *London: Hutchinson*, [*1958*].
  Boards. *First published 1958* on copyright page. Issued earlier in the U. S. as DEADLY IMAGE.

THE VENOM OF ARGUS. [*London*]*: Hodder and Stoughton*, [*1976*].
  Wrappers. *First published in this edition by Coronet Books 1976* on copyright page. *Coronet Science Fiction 19918 0* (60p). *Richard Avery, pseudonym. The Expendables* at head of title.

VOICES IN THE DARK. *London: Brown, Watson Ltd*, [*1960*].
  Wrappers. *First world publication* on copyright page. *Digit Books D349* (2'–). Note: A later printing (published 31 January 1963) has *Digit Book R663* (2'6) on the cover.

THE WAR GAMES OF ZELOS. [*London*]*: Hodder and Stoughton*, [*1975*].
  Wrappers. *First published by Coronet Books in 1975* on copyright page. *Coronet Science Fiction 19875 3* (50p). *Richard Avery, pseudonym.*

WHO NEEDS MEN? *London Sydney Auckland Toronto: Hodder and Stoughton*, [*1972*].
  Boards. *First printed 1972* on copyright page. Issued later in the U.S. as GENDER GENOCIDE.

WISH GOES TO SLUMBER LAND. *London: Hutchinson*, [*1960*].
  Boards with cloth shelf back. No statement of printing on copyright page.

Raymond King Cummings

(1887–1957)

BEYOND THE STARS. *New York: Ace Books Inc.*, [*1963*].
Wrappers. No statement of printing on copyright page. *Ace Science Fiction Classic F–248* (40¢).

BEYOND THE VANISHING POINT. *New York: Ace Books, Inc.*, [*1958*].
Wrappers. No statement of printing on copyright page. *Ace Double Novel Books D–331* (35¢). Bound with THE SECRET OF ZI by Kenneth Bulmer.

A BRAND NEW WORLD. *New York: Ace Books, Inc.*, [*1964*].
Wrappers. No statement of printing on copyright page. *Ace Book F–313* (40¢).

BRIGANDS OF THE MOON. *Chicago: A. C. McClurg & Co., Publishers, 1931*.
No statement of printing on copyright page. McClurg acorn device on copyright page.

THE EXILE OF TIME. *New York: Avalon Books*, [*1964*].
No statement of printing on copyright page.

EXPLORERS INTO INFINITY. *New York: Avalon Books*, [*1965*].
No statement of printing on copyright page.

THE GIRL IN THE GOLDEN ATOM. *London: Methuen & Co., Ltd.*, [*1922*].
First Published in 1922 on copyright page.

ALSO: *New York and London: Harper & Brothers, 1923*. Two bindings, priority as listed: (A) Light yellow-brown cloth, lettered in black; (B) Purple cloth, lettered in yellow. No statement of printing, but code letters *I–X*, appear on the copyright page. Text differs from that of the Methuen edition.

THE INSECT INVASION. *New York: Avalon Books*, [*1967*].
No statement of printing on copyright page.

THE MAN ON THE METEOR. [*London: Gerald G. Swan Ltd.*], n.d. [ca. 1952].
Wrappers. No statement of printing. Cover title. Note: Issued without title page.

THE MAN WHO MASTERED TIME. *Chicago: A. C. McClurg & Co., 1929*.
No statement of printing on copyright page. McClurg acorn device on copyright page.

THE PRINCESS OF THE ATOM. *New York: Avon Publishing Corp.*, [*1950*].
Wrappers. *Avon Reprint Edition* on copyright page. *Avon Fantasy Novels No. 1* (25¢).

ALSO: *London New York: T. V. Boardman and Company Limited*, [*1951*]. *First printed in Great Britain 1951* on copyright page. First hardcover edition.

THE SEA GIRL. *Chicago: A. C. McClurg & Co., 1930*.
No statement of printing on copyright page. McClurg acorn device on copyright page.

THE SHADOW GIRL. *London: Gerald G. Swan*, [*1946*].
First published 1946 on copyright page.

TAMA OF THE LIGHT COUNTRY. *New York: Ace Books, Inc.*, [*1965*].
Wrappers. No statement of printing on copyright page. *Ace Science Fiction Classic F–363* (40¢).

TAMA, PRINCESS OF MERCURY. *New York: Ace Books, Inc.*, [*1966*].
  Wrappers. No statement of printing on copyright page. *Ace Science Fiction Classic F-406* (40¢).

TARRANO THE CONQUEROR. *Chicago: A. C. McClurg & Co.*, *1930*.
  No statement of printing on copyright page. McClurg acorn device on copyright page.

WANDL THE INVADER. *New York: Ace Books, Inc.*, [*1961*].
  Wrappers. No statement of printing on copyright page. *Ace Double Novel Books D-497* (35¢). Bound with I SPEAK FOR EARTH by Keith Woodcott.

Avram Davidson

(b. 1923)

AND ON THE EIGHTH DAY. *New York: Random House*, [*1964*].
  Boards. First printing so stated on copyright page. *Ellery Queen, pseudonym.*

CLASH OF STAR-KINGS. *New York: Ace Books, Inc.*, [*1966*].
  Wrappers. No statement of printing on copyright page. *Ace Double G–576* (50¢). Bound with DANGER FROM VEGA by John Rackham.

THE ENEMY OF MY ENEMY. [*New York*]: *Published by Berkley Publishing Corporation*, [*1966*].
  Wrappers. *December, 1966* on copyright page. *Berkley Medallion X1341* (60¢).

THE ENQUIRIES OF DOCTOR ESZTERHAZY. [*New York*]: *Warner Books*, [*1975*].
  Wrappers. *First Printing: December, 1975* on copyright page. *Warner Books 76–981* ($1.25).

THE FOURTH SIDE OF THE TRIANGLE. *New York: Random House*, [*1965*].
  First printing so stated on copyright page. *Ellery Queen, pseudonym.*

THE ISLAND UNDER THE EARTH. *New York: Ace Publishing Corporation*, [*1969*].
  Wrappers. No statement of printing on copyright page. *An Ace Science Fiction Special 37425* (75¢).

JOYLEG. *New York: Pyramid Boods*, [*1962*].
  Wrappers. *First printing, December 1962* on copyright page. *Pyramid Books F–805* (40¢). With WARD MOORE.

  ALSO: *New York: Walker and Company*, [*1971*]. Boards. *First published in the United States of America in 1971* on copyright page. First hardcover edition.

THE KAR-CHEE REIGN. *New York: Ace Books, Inc.*, [*1966*].
  Wrappers. No statement of printing on copyright page. *Ace Double G–574* (50¢). Bound with ROCANNON'S WORLD by Ursula K. Le Guin.

MASTERS OF THE MAZE. *New York: Pyramid Books*, [*1965*].
  Wrappers. *First printing, July 1965* on copyright page. *Pyramid Books R–1208* (50¢).

  ALSO: *London and New York: White Lion Publishers*, [*1974*]. Boards. *This White Lion edition, 1974* on copyright page. First hardcover edition.

MUTINY IN SPACE. *New York: Pyramid Books*, [*1964*].
  Wrappers. *Published September 1964* on copyright page. *Pyramid Books R–1069* (50¢).

  ALSO: *London and New York: White Lion Publishers*, [*1973*]. Boards. *This White Lion edition, 1973* on copyright page. First hardcover edition.

OR ALL THE SEAS WITH OYSTERS. [*New York*]: *Published by Berkley Publishing Corporation*, [*1962*].
  Wrappers. No statement of printing on copyright page. *Berkley Medallion F639* (50¢).

  ALSO: *London, New York, Sydney and Toronto: White Lion Publishers Limited*, [*1976*]. Boards. *White Lion edition 1976* on copyright page. First hardcover edition.

PEREGRINE PRIMUS. *New York: Walker and Company,* [*1971*].
  Boards. *First published in the United States of America in 1971* on copyright page.

THE PHOENIX AND THE MIRROR. *Garden City: Doubleday & Company, Inc., 1969.*
  First edition so stated on copyright page.

ROGUE DRAGON. *New York: Ace Books, Inc.,* [*1965*].
  Wrappers. No statement of printing on copyright page. *Ace Book F–353* (40¢).

RORK! [*New York*]: *Published by Berkley Publishing Corporation,* [*1965*].
  Wrappers. *October, 1965* on copyright page. *Berkley Medallion F1146* (50¢).

  ALSO: *London: Rapp & Whiting,* [*1968*]. Boards. *First published in Great Britain 1968* on
  copyright page. First hardcover edition.

STRANGE SEAS AND SHORES. *Garden City: Doubleday & Company, Inc., 1971.*
  First edition so stated on copyright page.

URSUS OF ULTIMA THULE. [*New York*]: *Avon,* [*1973*].
  Wrappers. *First Avon Printing, December, 1973* on copyright page. *Avon Science Fiction
  17657* (95¢).

WHAT STRANGE STARS AND SKIES. *New York: Ace Books, Inc.,* [*1965*].
  Wrappers. No statement of printing on copyright page. *Ace Book F–330* (40¢).

Edited Fiction

The Best from Fantasy and Science Fiction Twelfth Series. *Garden City: Doubleday &
Company, Inc., 1963.*
  First edition so stated on copyright page. Edited, with introduction and short story ''The
  Singular Events which Occurred in the Hovel on the Alley Off of Eye Street,'' by David-
  son.

The Best from Fantasy and Science Fiction Thirteenth Series. *Garden City: Doubleday &
Company, Inc., 1964.*
  First edition so stated on copyright page. Edited, with introduction, notes, and short story
  ''What Strange Stars and Skies,'' by Davidson.

The Best from Fantasy and Science Fiction Fourteenth Series. *Garden City: Doubleday &
Company, Inc., 1965.*
  First edition so stated on copyright page. Edited, with notes and short story ''Sacheverell,''
  by Davidson.

Lyon Sprague de Camp
(b. 1907)

THE ARROWS OF HERCULES. *Garden City: Doubleday & Company, Inc., 1965.*
First edition so stated on copyright page.

THE BRONZE GOD OF RHODES. *Garden City: Doubleday & Company, Inc., 1960.*
First edition so stated on copyright page.

THE CARNELIAN CUBE. *New York: Gnome Press, 1948.*
First edition so stated on copyright page. With FLETCHER PRATT.

THE CASTLE OF IRON. *New York: Gnome Press,* [1950].
Boards. First edition so stated on copyright page. With FLETCHER PRATT.

[handwritten annotation: 1st BINDING HAS GNOME PRESS "in 1 line on spine 2nd has two lines]

THE CLOCKS OF IRAZ. *New York: Pyramid Books,* [1971].
Wrappers. *First printing, November 1971* on copyright page. *Pyramid T2584* (75¢).

THE COMPLEAT ENCHANTER. *Garden City: Nelson Doubleday, Inc.,* [1975].
Boards. No statement of printing on copyright page. Code *44 R* on page 337. Reprint.
Collects THE INCOMPLETE ENCHANTER and THE CASTLE OF IRON. With FLETCHER PRATT.
Note: Issued by the Science Fiction Book Club.

CONAN. *New York: Lancer Books,* [1967].
Wrappers. *A Lancer Book • 1967* on copyright page. *Lancer Books 73–685* (60¢). With
LIN CARTER and ROBERT E. HOWARD.

CONAN OF AQUILONIA. [*New York*]: *Prestige Books Inc., Publishers,* [1977].
Wrappers. No statement of printing on copyright page. *Ace Books 11682–5* ($1.95). With
LIN CARTER.

CONAN OF CIMMERIA. *New York: Lancer Books,* [1969].
Wrappers. *A Lancer Book • 1969* on copyright page. *Lancer Books 75–072* (95¢). With
LIN CARTER and ROBERT E. HOWARD.

CONAN OF THE ISLES. *New York: Lancer Books,* [1968].
Wrappers. *A Lancer Book • 1968* on copyright page. *Lancer Books 73–800* (60¢). With LIN
CARTER.

CONAN THE ADVENTURER. See Edited Fiction.

CONAN THE AVENGER. *New York: Lancer Books,* [1968].
Wrappers. *A Lancer Book • 1968* on copyright page. *Lancer Books 73–780* (60¢). With BJORN
NYBERG. Reissue of THE RETURN OF CONAN with a new introduction by de Camp.

CONAN THE BUCCANEER. *New York: Lancer Books,* [1971].
Wrappers. No statement of printing on copyright page. *Lancer Books 75181–095* (95¢).
With LIN CARTER. Note: First printing has all edges stained purple and first title listed on
page [192] is *CONAN THE WARRIOR.*

CONAN THE CONQUEROR. See Edited Fiction.

CONAN THE FREEBOOTER. *New York: Lancer Books*, [*1968*].
  Wrappers. *A Lancer Book • 1968* on copyright page. *Lancer Books 74–963* (75¢). With
  ROBERT E. HOWARD.

CONAN THE USURPER. See Edited Fiction.

CONAN THE WANDERER. *New York: Lancer Books*, [*1968*].
  Wrappers. *A Lancer Book • 1968* on copyright page. *Lancer Books 74–976* (95¢). With
  LIN CARTER and ROBERT E. HOWARD. Note: Ad on page [223] lists six Conan titles. A later
  printing with the same stock number has been noted with *A Lancer Book* but no date
  following on the copyright page and the ad on page [223] listing ten Conan titles.

CONAN THE WARRIOR. See Edited Fiction.

THE CONTINENT MAKERS. *New York: Twayne Publishers Inc.*, [*1953*].
  Noted in the following bindings, priority not established: (A) Tan cloth lettered in red; (B)
  Blue boards lettered in white; (C) Brown boards lettered in blue. No statement of printing
  on copyright page.

COSMIC MANHUNT. *New York: Ace Books, Inc.*, [*1954*].
  Wrappers. No statement of printing on copyright page. *Ace Double Novel Books D–61*
  (35¢). Bound with RING AROUND THE SUN by Clifford D. Simak. Issued later in Great
  Britain as A PLANET CALLED KRISHNA. Reprinted with textual differences as THE QUEEN OF
  ZAMBA.

DIVIDE AND RULE. *Reading, Pennsylvania: Fantasy Press, 1948*.
  Two issues, no priority: (A) 500 copies with numbered leaf signed by the author inserted.
  Limited issue. (B) Trade issue. First edition so stated on copyright page.

THE DRAGON OF THE ISHTAR GATE. *Garden City: Doubleday & Company, Inc., 1961*.
  First edition so stated on copyright page.

AN ELEPHANT FOR ARISTOTLE. *Garden City: Doubleday & Company, Inc., 1958*.
  First edition so stated on copyright page.

THE FALLIBLE FIEND. [*New York*]: *New American Library*, [*1973*].
  Wrappers. *First printing, February, 1973* on copyright page. *Signet Science Fiction Q5370*
  (95¢).

  ALSO: [*London*]: *Remploy*, [*1974*]. Boards. *This Remploy Reprint Edition 1974* on
  copyright page. First hardcover edition.

[FANTASY TWIN.] See THE UNDESIRED PRINCESS.

THE FLOATING CONTINENT. *London: Compact* [*Books, 1966*].
  Wrappers. No statement of printing on copyright page. *Compact SF F321* (3/6). Issued earlier
  in the U.S. as THE SEARCH FOR ZEI.

GENUS HOMO. *Reading, Pennsylvania: Fantasy Press, 1950*.
  Two bindings, priority as listed: (A) Green cloth, spine lettered in gold; (B) Blue boards,
  spine lettered in black. Two issues, no priority: (A) 500 copies with numbered leaf signed
  by the authors inserted. Limited issue. (B) Trade issue. First edition so stated on copyright
  page. With P. SCHUYLER MILLER.

THE GLORY THAT WAS. *New York: Avalon Books*, [*1960*].
  No statement of printing on copyright page.

THE GOBLIN TOWER. *New York: Pyramid Books*, [*1968*].
Wrappers. *First printing December, 1968* on copyright page. *Pyramid T–1927* (75¢).

THE GOLDEN WIND. *Garden City: Doubleday & Company, Inc.*, *1969*.
First edition so stated on copyright page.

A GUN FOR DINOSAUR. *Garden City: Doubleday & Company, Inc.*, *1963*.
Boards with cloth shelf back. First edition so stated on copyright page.

THE HAND OF ZEI. *New York: Avalon Books*, [*1963*].
No statement of printing on copyright page.

THE HOSTAGE OF ZIR. *New York: Published by Berkley Publishing Corporation*, [*1977*].
No statement of printing on copyright page.

THE INCOMPLETE ENCHANTER. *New York: Henry Holt and Company*, [*1941*].
No statement of printing on copyright page. With FLETCHER PRATT.

LAND OF UNREASON. *New York: Henry Holt and Company*, [*1942*].
No statement of printing on copyright page. With FLETCHER PRATT.

LEST DARKNESS FALL. *New York: Henry Holt and Company*, [*1941*].
No statement of printing on copyright page.

A PLANET CALLED KRISHNA. *London: Compact Books*, [*1966*].
Wrappers. No statement of printing on copyright page. *Compact SF F311* (3/6). Issued earlier in the U.S. as COSMIC MANHUNT. Reprinted with textual differences as THE QUEEN OF ZAMBA.

THE QUEEN OF ZAMBA. *New York: Davis Publications, Inc.*, [*1977*].
Wrappers. No statement of printing on copyright page. *A Dale Book 0–89559–006–9* ($1.50). Collects ''The Queen of Zamba'' and ''Perpetual Motion.'' Notes: (1) ''The Queen of Zamba'' originally appeared as a serial in *Astounding Science Fiction* in 1949. It appeared in book form as COSMIC MANHUNT and later as A PLANET CALLED KRISHNA with alterations made at the suggestion of editor Donald A. Wollheim. This printing follows the original magazine text with minor changes by de Camp. (2) ''Perpetual Motion'' was collected earlier in THE CONTINENT MAKERS.

THE RELUCTANT SHAMAN AND OTHER FANTASTIC TALES. *New York: Pyramid Books;* [*1970*].
Wrappers. *First printing, November 1970* on copyright page. *Pyramid T2347* (75¢).

THE RETURN OF CONAN. *New York: Gnome Press, Inc., Publishers, 1957.*
Boards. First printing so stated on copyright page. With BJÖRN NYBERG. Reissued as CONAN THE AVENGER.

ROGUE QUEEN. *Garden City: Doubleday & Company, Inc., 1951.*
First edition so stated on copyright page.

SCRIBBLINGS. *Boston: The NESFA Press, 1972.*
First edition so stated on copyright page. 500 numbered copies. Collects four short stories and other material.

THE SEARCH FOR ZEI. *New York: Avalon Books*, [*1962*].
No statement of printing on copyright page. Issued later in Great Britain as THE FLOATING CONTINENT.

SOLOMON'S STONE. *New York: Avalon Books,* [*1957*].
No statement of printing on copyright page.

SPRAGUE DE CAMP'S NEW ANTHOLOGY OF SCIENCE FICTION. *London: Panther Books Hamilton & Co., (Stafford) Ltd.,* [*1953*].
Two bindings, no priority: (A) Cloth; (B) Wrappers. *Panther Books 92* (1'6). No statement of printing on copyright page.

TALES FROM GAVAGAN'S BAR. *N[ew] Y[ork]: Twayne Publishers,* [*1953*].
No statement of printing on copyright page. With FLETCHER PRATT.

TALES OF CONAN. *New York: Gnome Press, Inc., Publishers,* [*1955*].
Five bindings, earliest as listed, but sequence for remainder not established: (A) Red boards lettered in black; (B) Green (boards?) lettered in black (not seen); (C) Black boards lettered in red; (D) Gray boards lettered in red; (E) Gray cloth lettered in red. First edition so stated on copyright page. With ROBERT E. HOWARD.

THE TOWER OF ZANID. *New York: Avalon Books,* [*1958*].
No statement of printing on copyright page.

THE TRITONIAN RING. *New York: Twayne Publishers Inc.,* [*1953*].
No statement of printing on copyright page.

THE UNDESIRED PRINCESS. *Los Angeles: Fantasy Publishing Company, Inc., 1951.*
Three bindings, priority as listed: (A) Cloth; (B) Boards with *Gnome Press* imprint at base of spine; (C) Wrappers. First edition so stated on copyright page. Note: Sheets of this book were later combined with those of THE DARK OTHER by Stanley G. Weinbaum and issued in 1953 as [FANTASY TWIN]. According to Owings and Chalker in *The Index to the Science-Fantasy Publishers,* approximately 500 copies were so bound.

THE VIRGIN & THE WHEELS. *New York: Popular Library,* [*1976*].
Wrappers. *April, 1976* on copyright page. *Popular Library Science Fiction 445–00362–125* ($1.25). First book appearance of "The Virgin of Zesh."

WALL OF SERPENTS. *New York: Avalon Books,* [*1960*].
No statement of printing on copyright page. With FLETCHER PRATT.

THE WHEELS OF IF. *Chicago: Shasta Publishers, 1948.*
First edition so stated on copyright page.

Edited Fiction

Conan the Adventurer, [by] Robert E. Howard. *New York: Lancer Books,* [*1966*].
Wrappers. *A Lancer Book • 1966* on copyright page. *Lancer Books 73–526* (60¢). Edited, with introduction and story completion "Drums of Tombalku," by de Camp.

Conan the Conqueror, [by] Robert E. Howard. *New York: Lancer Books,* [*1967*].
Wrappers. *A Lancer Book • 1967* on copyright page. *Lancer Books 73–572* (60¢). Edited, with textual changes and introduction, by de Camp.

Conan the Usurper, [by] Robert E. Howard. *New York: Lancer Books,* [*1967*].
Wrappers. *A Lancer Book • 1967* on copyright page. *Lancer Books 73–599* (60¢). Edited, with introduction, revisions, and story completion "Wolves Beyond the Border," by de Camp.

Conan the Warrior, [by] Robert E. Howard. *New York: Lancer Books, [1967]*.
  Wrappers. *A Lancer Book • 1967* on copyright page. *Lancer Books 73–549* (60¢). Edited, with introduction, by de Camp.

The Fantastic Swordsmen. *New York: Pyramid Books, [1967]*.
  Wrappers. *First printing May, 1967* on copyright page. *Pyramid R–1621* (50¢). Edited, with introduction, by de Camp. Includes short story "Drums of Tombalku" by de Camp and Robert E. Howard.

The Spell of Seven. *New York: Pyramid Books, [1965]*.
  Wrappers. *First printing, June 1965* on copyright page. *Pyramid Books. R-1192* (50¢). Edited, with introduction, notes, and short story "The Hungry Hercynian," by de Camp.

Swords and Sorcery. *New York: Pyramid Books, [1963]*.
  Wrappers. *First printing, December 1963* on copyright page. *Pyramid Books R–950* (50¢). Selected, with an introduction, by de Camp.

Tales Beyond Time. *New York: Lothrop, Lee & Shepard Company, [1973]*.
  1 2 3 4 5 77 76 75 74 73 on copyright page. Compiled by de Camp. With CATHERINE CROOK DE CAMP.

3000 Years of Fantasy and Science Fiction. *New York: Lothrop, Lee & Shepard Company, [1972]*.
  Boards. *1 2 3 4 5 76 75 74 73 72* on copyright page. Edited, with introduction and short story "A Gun for Dinosaur," by de Camp. With CATHERINE CROOK DE CAMP.

Warlocks and Warriors. *New York: G. P. Putnam's Sons, [1970]*.
  Boards. No statement of printing on copyright page. Edited, with introduction, by de Camp.

The Wolf Leader, [by] Alexander Dumas. *Philadelphia: Prime Press, 1950*.
  Published Fall, 1950 on copyright page. Edited by de Camp.

Nonfiction (Dealing with the Fantasy Genre only)

Blond Barbarians and Noble Savages. *[Baltimore: T–K Graphics, 1975.]*
  Wrappers. No statement of printing on copyright page.

The Conan Reader. *Baltimore: Mirage, 1968*.
  No statement of printing on copyright page. 1500 copies printed.

Literary Swordsmen and Sorcerers: The Makers of Heroic Fantasy. *Sauk City: Arkham House, [1976]*.
  No statement of printing on copyright page.

Lovecraft a Biography. *Garden City: Doubleday & Company, Inc., 1975*.
  Boards. First edition so stated on copyright page.

The Miscast Barbarian: A Biography of Robert E. Howard (1906–1936). *Saddle River, N.J.: Published by Gerry de la Ree, 1975*.
  Two bindings, no priority: (A) 130 numbered copies in cloth. Not issued with dust jacket. (B) 900 numbered copies in wrappers. No statement of printing. Note: A second printing of 512 copies can be identified by the absence of a limitation statement on the outside rear cover.

Science-Fiction Handbook: The Writing of Imaginative Fiction. *New York: Hermitage House, 1953.*

> Boards with cloth shelf back. First edition so stated on copyright page.

> ALSO: Science Fiction Handbook, Revised. *Philadelphia: Owlswick Press, 1975.* Revised edition. With CATHERINE CROOK DE CAMP.

Edited Nonfiction (Dealing with the Fantasy Genre only)

The Conan Grimore. *Baltimore: The Mirage Press, 1972.*

> Two printings, priority as listed: (A) Dust jacket of white stock printed in gray. 1500 copies printed. (B) Dust jacket of white stock printed in blue. 500 copies printed. No statement of printing on copyright page. Edited, with contributions, by de Camp. With GEORGE H. SCITHERS. Note: Second printing is not so marked.

The Conan Swordbook. *Baltimore: The Mirage Press, 1969.*

> No statement of printing on copyright page. Approximately 1500 copies printed. Edited, with contributions, by de Camp. With GEORGE H. SCITHERS.

To Quebec and the Stars, [by] H. P. Lovecraft. *West Kingston, Rhode Island: Donald M. Grant, Publisher, 1976.*

> First edition so stated on copyright page. Edited, with introduction and notes, by de Camp.

Miriam Allen deFord (Shipley)
(1888–1975)

ELSEWHERE, ELSEWHEN, ELSEHOW. *New York: Walker & Company,* [*1971*].
   Boards. *First published in the United States of America in 1971* on copyright page.

SHAKEN WITH THE WIND. *Garden City: Doubleday, Doran and Company, Inc., 1942.*
   First edition so stated on copyright page.

THE THEME IS MURDER. *London New York Toronto: Abelard-Schuman,* [*1967*].
   Boards. No statement of printing on copyright page.

XENOGENESIS. *New York: Ballantine Books,* [*1969*].
   Wrappers. *First Printing: March, 1969* on copyright page. *A Ballantine Science Fiction 01546 (75¢).*

Edited Fiction

Space, Time & Crime. *New York: Paperback Library, Inc.,* [*1964*].
   Wrappers. *First Printing: November, 1964* on copyright page. *Paperback Library 52–502 (50¢).* Edited, with introduction and short story "Rope's End," by deFord.

Samuel Ray Delany, Jr.

(b. 1942)

BABEL-17. *New York: Ace Books, Inc.*, [*1966*].
Wrappers. No statement of printing on copyright page. *Ace Book F–388* (40¢).

ALSO: *London: Victor Gollancz Ltd, 1967.* Boards. No statement of printing on copyright page. First hardcover edition.

ALSO: *London: Sphere Books Ltd,* [*1969*]. Wrappers. *First Sphere Books edition, 1969* on copyright page. *Sphere Science Fiction 28887* (5/0). Revised text.

ALSO: *Boston: Gregg Press, 1976. First Printing, June 1976* on copyright page. First hardcover edition of the revised text. Notes: (1) Photographically reproduced from a copy of the 1969 Sphere Books edition, the only complete text and the one preferred by the author. (2) Not issued in dust jacket.

THE BALLAD OF BETA-2. *New York: Ace Books, Inc.*, [*1965*].
Wrappers. No statement of printing on copyright page. *Ace Double M–121* (45¢). Bound with ALPHA YES, TERRA NO! by Emil Petaja.

ALSO: *Boston: Gregg Press, 1977. First Printing, December 1977* on copyright page. First hardcover edition. Notes: (1) Photographically reproduced from a copy of the 1971 Ace Books printing *(Ace Books 04722)* with a few textual corrections. (2) Not issued in dust jacket.

CAPTIVES OF THE FLAME. *New York: Ace Books, Inc.*, [*1963*].
Wrappers. No statement of printing on copyright page. *Ace Double F–199* (40¢). Bound with THE PSIONIC MENACE by Keith Woodcott. Enlarged as OUT OF THE DEAD CITY. Collected later in THE FALL OF THE TOWERS.

CITY OF A THOUSAND SUNS. *New York: Ace Books, Inc.*, [*1965*].
Wrappers. No statement of printing on copyright page. *Ace Book F–322* (40¢).

ALSO: *London: Sphere Books Ltd.*, [*1969*]. Wrappers. *First published in Great Britain in 1969* on copyright page. *Sphere Science Fiction 28851* (5/–). Revised text. Collected later in THE FALL OF THE TOWERS.

DHALGREN. *Toronto New York London: Bantam Books*, [*1975*].
Wrappers. *January 1975* on copyright page. *Bantam Science Fiction Y8554* ($1.95).

*ALSO: *Toronto New York London: Bantam Books*, [?]. Wrappers. Sixth printing. Approximately 65 textual corrections.

ALSO: *Boston: Gregg Press, 1977. First Printing, December, 1977* on copyright page. Numerous textual corrections appear for the first time. First hardcover edition. Note: Not issued in dust jacket.

DRIFTGLASS. *Garden City: Nelson Doubleday, Inc.*, [*1971*].
Boards. No statement of printing on copyright page. Code *24M* on page 273. Notes: (1) Author's name misspelled "Delaney" on title page. (2) Issued by the Science Fiction Book Club.

THE EINSTEIN INTERSECTION. *New York: Ace Books, Inc.*, [*1967*].
Wrappers. No statement of printing on copyright page. *Ace Book F–427* (40¢). Note: All U.S. editions lack one chapter.

ALSO:*London: Victor Gollancz Ltd, 1968*. Boards. No statement of printing on copyright page. First hardcover edition.

EMPIRE STAR.*New York: Ace Books, Inc.*, [*1966*].
Wrappers. No statement of printing on copyright page.*Ace Double M–139* (45¢). Bound with THE TREE LORD OF IMETEN by Tom Purdom.

ALSO:*Boston: Gregg Press, 1977. First Printing, December 1977* on copyright page. First separate hardcover edition. Notes: (1) Text is photographically reproduced, with corrections, from the 1971 *Ace Science Fiction Reader* edited by Donald A. Wollheim. (2) Not issued in dust jacket.

THE FALL OF THE TOWERS.*New York: Ace Books*, [*1970*].
Wrappers. No statement of printing on copyright page.*Ace Book 22640* (95¢). Collects CAPTIVES OF THE FLAME (later OUT OF THE DEAD CITY), THE TOWERS OF TORON, and CITY OF A THOUSAND SUNS. Revised texts. Adds "Author's Note on the Revision of this Edition."

ALSO:*Boston: Gregg Press, 1977. First Printing, June 1977* on copyright page. First hardcover edition. Note: Not issued in dust jacket.

THE JEWELS OF APTOR.*New York: Ace Books, Inc.*, [*1962*].
Wrappers. No statement of printing on copyright page.*Ace Double F–173* (40¢). Bound with SECOND ENDING by James White.

ALSO:*New York: Ace Books, Inc.*, [*1968*]. Wrappers. No statement of printing on copyright page.*An Ace Book G–706* (50¢). Revised and enlarged text.

ALSO:*London: Victor Gollancz Ltd, 1968*. Boards. No statement of printing on copyright page. Text follows 1968 Ace edition. First hardcover edition.

ALSO:*London: Sphere Books Ltd*, [*1971*]. Wrappers.*First Sphere Books edition 1971* on copyright page.*Sphere Science Fiction 28894* (25p). Additional textual revisions.

ALSO:*Boston: Gregg Press, 1976. First Printing, June 1976* on copyright page. First hardcover edition of this text. Notes: (1) Photographically reproduced from the 1971 Sphere Books edition, the complete text preferred by Delany. (2) Not issued in dust jacket.

NOVA.*Garden City: Doubleday & Company, Inc., 1968*.
First edition so stated on copyright page. Note: Half page of text missing on page 242.

ALSO:*Garden City: Doubleday & Company, Inc*, [*1969*]. Boards. No statement of printing on copyright page. Code *11 K* on page [283]. Incorporates textual corrections. Note: Issued by the Science Fiction Book Club.

OUT OF THE DEAD CITY.*London: Sphere Books Ltd*, [*1968*].
Wrappers.*First published in Great Britain in 1968 . . .* on copyright page.*Sphere Science Fiction 28835* (5/0). Revised version of CAPTIVES OF THE FLAME. Collected later in THE FALL OF THE TOWERS.

THE TIDES OF LUST.*New York: Lancer Books*, [*1973*].
Wrappers. Two bindings, no priority established: (A) With Lancer horse head silhouette at base of spine; (B) No horse head at base of spine. No statement of printing on copyright page.*Lancer Books 71344–150* ($1.50).

THE TOWERS OF TORON.*New York: Ace Books, Inc.*, [*1964*].
Wrappers. No statement of printing on copyright page.*Ace Double F–261* (40¢). Bound with THE LUNAR EYE by Robert Moore Williams.

ALSO:*London: Sphere Books Ltd.*, [*1968*]. Wrappers.*First published in Great Britain in 1968 . . .* on copyright page.*Sphere Science Fiction 28843* (5/–). Revised text. Collected later in THE FALL OF THE TOWERS.

TRITON. *Toronto New York London: Bantam Books*, [*1976*].
Wrappers. *Published February 1976* on copyright page. *Bantam Science Fiction Y2567* ($1.95).

ALSO: *Boston: Gregg Press, 1977. First Printing, June 1977* on copyright page. First hardcover edition. Notes: (1) Photographically reproduced from the *2nd printing* of the Bantam Books edition. (2) Not issued in dust jacket.

Edited Fiction

Quark/1. *New York: Paperback Library*, [*1970*].
Wrappers. *First Printing: November, 1970* on copyright page. *A Paperback Library Original Review 66–480* ($1.25). Edited, with editorial, by Delany with MARILYN HACKER.

Quark/2. *New York: Paperback Library*, [*1971*].
Wrappers. *First Printing: February, 1971* on copyright page. *A Paperback Library Original Review 66–530* ($1.25). Edited, with introduction, by Delany with MARILYN HACKER.

Quark/3. *New York: Paperback Library*, [*1971*].
Wrappers. *First Printing: May, 1971* on copyright page. *A Paperback Library Original Review 66–593* ($1.25). Edited, with foreword, by Delany with MARILYN HACKER.

Quark/4. *New York: Paperback Library*, [*1971*].
Wrappers. *First Printing: August, 1971* on copyright page. *A Paperback Library Original Review 66–658* ($1.25). Edited, with introduction, by Delany with MARILYN HACKER.

Nonfiction (Dealing with the Fantasy Genre only)

The Jewel-Hinged Jaw: Notes on the Language of Science Fiction. *Elizabethtown, New York: Dragon Press, 1977.*
1108 copies printed. Three issues, no priority: (A) 4 copies lettered A–D, signed by the author and illustrator Richard Powers. Reserved for the use of author and publisher. (B) 110 numbered copies signed by the author. Limited issue. (C) 994 trade copies. First edition so stated on copyright page. Note: Not issued in dust jacket.

Reference

The Delany Intersection: Samuel R. Delany Considered as a Writer of Semi-Precious Words, [by] George Edgar Slusser. *San Bernardino, California: R. Reginald The Borgo Press, MCMLXXVII.*
Wrappers. *First Edition———December, 1977* on copyright page. *The Milford Series Popular Writers of Today Volume Ten* at head of title.

Lester del Rey

(b. 1915)

". . . AND SOME WERE HUMAN." *Philadelphia: Prime Press, 1948.*
Two issues, priority as listed: (A) Integral hand-lettered title page dated 1948; (B) Typeset title page dated 1949 is a cancel. No statement of printing on copyright page. Later abridged as TALES OF SOARING SCIENCE FICTION FROM ". . . AND SOME WERE HUMAN."

ATTACK FROM ATLANTIS. *Philadelphia Toronto: The John C. Winston Company,* [*1953*].
First edition so stated on copyright page.

BADGE OF INFAMY. *London: Dennis Dobson,* [*1976*].
Boards. *First published in Great Britain in 1976* on copyright page. For prior U.S. book publication see TWO COMPLETE NOVELS.

BATTLE ON MERCURY. *Philadelphia Toronto: The John C. Winston Company,* [*1953*].
First edition so stated on copyright page. *Erik van Lhin, pseudonym.*

THE CAVE OF SPEARS. *New York: Alfred A. Knopf, 1957.*
First edition so stated on copyright page.

DAY OF THE GIANTS. *New York: Avalon Books,* [*1959*].
No statement of printing on copyright page. Note: Author's name misspelled "del Ray" on dust jacket.

EARLY DEL REY. *Garden City: Doubleday & Company, Inc., 1975.*
Boards. First edition so stated on copyright page.

THE ELEVENTH COMMANDMENT. *Evanston: Regency Books,* [*1962*].
Wrappers. *Published January, 1962* on copyright page. *RB 113* (50¢).

ALSO: *New York: Ballantine Books,* [*1970*]. Wrappers. *First Printing: November, 1970* on copyright page. *Ballantine Books Science Fiction 02068–5–095* (95¢). Revised text.

GODS AND GOLEMS. *New York: Ballantine Books,* [*1973*].
Wrappers. *First Printing: February, 1973* on copyright page. *Ballantine Books Science Fiction 03087–7–125* ($1.25). Note: Author's name misspelled "del Ray" on title page.

THE INFINITE WORLDS OF MAYBE. *New York, Chicago, San Francisco: Holt, Rinehart and Winston,* [*1966*].
Two bindings, no priority: (A) Black boards lettered in purple. Trade binding; (B) Pictorial cloth reproducing dust jacket design. Library binding. First edition so stated on copyright page.

THE MAN WITHOUT A PLANET. *New York: Lancer Books,* [*1969*].
Wrappers. No statement of printing on copyright page. *Lancer Books 74–538* (75¢). Reissue of SIEGE PERILOUS.

MAROONED ON MARS. *Philadelphia Toronto: The John C. Winston Company,* [*1952*].
First edition so stated on copyright page.

MISSION TO THE MOON. *Philadelphia Toronto: The John C. Winston Company,* [*1956*].
First edition so stated on copyright page.

MOON OF MUTINY. *New York: Holt, Rinehart and Winston*, [*1961*].
First edition so stated on copyright page.

MORTALS AND MONSTERS. *New York: Ballantine Books*, [*1965*].
Wrappers. No statement of printing on copyright page. *A Ballantine Science Fiction Original U2236 (50¢)*.

THE MYSTERIOUS PLANET. *Philadelphia • Toronto: The John C. Winston Company*, [*1953*].
First edition so stated on copyright page. *Kenneth Wright, pseudonym*.

NERVES. *New York: Ballantine Books*, [*1956*].
Two issues, no priority: (A) Cloth; (B) Wrappers. *Ballantine Books 151* (35¢). No statement of printing on copyright page.

OUTPOST OF JUPITER. *New York/Chicago/San Francisco: Holt, Rinehart and Winston*,
[*1963*].
Two bindings, no priority: (A) Boards. Trade binding. (B) Pictorial cloth reproducing dust jacket design. Library binding. First edition so stated on copyright page.

PIRATE FLAG FOR MONTEREY. THE STORY OF THE SACK OF MONTEREY.
Philadelphia • Toronto: The John C. Winston Company, [*1952*].
Boards with cloth shelf back. First edition so stated on copyright page.

POLICE YOUR PLANET. *New York: Avalon Books*, [*1956*].
No statement of printing on copyright page. *Eric van Lhin, pseudonym*.

ALSO: *New York: Ballantine Books*, [*1975*]. Wrappers. *First Printing: May, 1975* on copyright page. *Ballantine Books SF 24465* ($1.50). Revised and enlarged text.

PREFERRED RISK. *New York: Simon and Schuster, 1955*.
Boards with cloth shelf back. First printing so stated on copyright page. *Edson McCann, pseudonym*. With FREDERIK POHL.

PRISONERS OF SPACE. *Philadelphia: The Westminster Press*, [*1968*].
No statement of printing on copyright page. Note: Although published under del Rey's byline, this work was actually written by PAUL W. FAIRMAN.

PSTALEMATE. *New York: G. P. Putnam's Sons*, [*1971*].
No statement of printing on copyright page.

ROBOTS AND CHANGELINGS. *New York: Ballantine Books*, [*1958*].
Wrappers. No statement of printing on copyright page. *Ballantine Books 246* (35¢).

ROCKET FROM INFINITY. *New York/Chicago/San Francisco: Holt, Rinehart and Winston*,
[*1966*].
Two bindings, no priority: (A) Boards. Trade binding. (B) Pictorial cloth reproducing dust jacket design. Library binding. First edition so stated on copyright page.

ROCKET JOCKEY. *Philadelphia Toronto: The John C. Winston Company*, [*1952*].
First edition so stated on copyright page. *Philip St. John, pseudonym*. Issued later in Great Britain as ROCKET PILOT.

*ROCKET PILOT. *London: Hutchinson*, [*1955*].
Philip St. John, pseudonym. Issued earlier in the U.S. as ROCKET JOCKEY.

ROCKETS TO NOWHERE. *Phildelphia Toronto: The John C. Winston Company*, [*1954*].
First edition so stated on copyright page. *Philip St. John, pseudonym*.

THE RUNAWAY ROBOT. *Philadelphia: The Westminster Press,* [*1965*].
No statement of printing on copyright page. Although published under del Rey's byline, this work was actually written by PAUL W. FAIRMAN.

THE SCHEME OF THINGS. *New York: Belmont Books,* [*1966*].
Wrappers. *July 1966* on copyright page. *Belmont Science Fiction B50–682* (50¢). Note: Published under del Rey's byline, this novel was outlined by del Rey but written by PAUL W. FAIRMAN.

SIEGE PERILOUS. *New York: A Lancer Book,* [*1966*].
Wrappers. *A Lancer Book • 1966* on copyright page. *Lancer Books 73–468* (60¢). Reissued as THE MAN WITHOUT A PLANET. Note: Although published under del Rey's byline, this work was actually written by PAUL W. FAIRMAN.

THE SKY IS FALLING. See TWO COMPLETE NOVELS.

STEP TO THE STARS. *Philadelphia Toronto: The John C. Winston Company,* [*1954*].
First edition so stated on copyright page.

TALES OF SOARING SCIENCE FANTASY FROM ". . . AND SOME WERE HUMAN." *New York: Ballantine Books,* [*1961*].
Wrappers. No statement of printing on copyright page. *Ballantine Books 552* (35¢). An abridged reprint of ". . . AND SOME WERE HUMAN."

TWO COMPLETE NOVELS. [*New York*]: *Published by Galaxy Publishing Co.,* [*1963*].
Wrappers. No statement of printing on copyright page. *Galaxy Magabook No. 1* (50¢). Prints "The Sky is Falling" and "Badge of Infamy."

TUNNEL THROUGH TIME. *Philadelphia: The Westminster Press,* [*1966*].
No statement of printing on copyright page. Note: Although published under del Rey's byline, this work was actually written by PAUL W. FAIRMAN.

Associational

A One-Act Play: Lester del Rey's For I Am a Jealous People, adapted by John Jakes. [*Elgin, Illinois*]: *Performance Publishing,* [*1972*].
Wrappers. No statement of printing on copyright page. Adapted by Jakes from "For I Am a Jealous People" by del Rey.

Edited Fiction

The Best of John W. Campbell. *Garden City: Nelson Doubleday, Inc.,* [*1976*].
Boards. Two printings, priority as listed: (A) Code *G13* on page 306; (B) Code *H23* on page 306. No statement of printing on copyright page. Edited, with introduction, by del Rey. Note: Issued by the Science Fiction Book Club.

The Best of C. L. Moore. *Garden City: Nelson Doubleday, Inc.,* [*1975*].
Boards. No statement of printing on copyright page. Code *42 R* on page 307. Edited, with introduction, by del Rey. Note: Issued by the Science Fiction Book Club.

The Best of Robert Bloch. *New York: Ballantine Books,* [*1977*].
Wrappers. *First Edition: November 1977* on copyright page. *Ballantine 25757* ($1.95). Edited, with introduction, by del Rey.

Best Science Fiction Stories of the Year. *New York: E. P. Dutton & Co., Inc., 1972.*
First edition so stated on copyright page. Edited, with foreword and afterword, by del Rey.

Best Science Fiction Stories of the Year: Second Annual Collection. *New York: E. P. Dutton & Co., Inc., 1973.*
First edition so stated on copyright page. Edited, with foreword, afterword, and notes, by del Rey.

Best Science Fiction Stories of the Year: Third Annual Collection. *New York: E. P. Dutton & Co., Inc., 1974.*
First edition so stated on copyright page. Edited, with foreword, afterword, and notes, by del Rey.

Best Science Fiction Stories of the Year: Fourth Annual Collection. *New York: E. P. Dutton & Co., Inc., 1975.*
Boards with cloth shelf back. First edition so stated on copyright page. Edited, with foreword and afterword, by del Rey.

Best Science Fiction Stories of the Year: Fifth Annual Collection. *New York: E. P. Dutton & Co., Inc., [1976].*
First edition so stated on copyright page. Edited, with foreword and afterword, by del Rey.

ALSO: *London: Kaye & Ward, [1977].* Boards. *First published in Great Britain . . . 1977* on copyright page. Drops afterword "The Science Fiction Yearbook."

The Year After Tomorrow. *Philadelphia • Toronto: The John C. Winston Company, [1954].*
Three bindings, no priority established: (A) Green cloth; (B) Gray cloth; (C) Tan boards. First edition so stated on copyright page. Edited, with foreword and two short stories, "The Luck of Ignatz" and "Kindness," by del Rey. With CECILE MATSCHAT and CARL CARMER.

Nonfiction (Dealing with the Fantasy Genre only)

Fantastic Science-Fiction Art 1926–1954. *New York: Ballantine Books, [1975].*
Wrappers. *First Printing: September, 1975* on copyright page. *Ballantine Books 24731* ($5.95). Compiled, with introduction, by del Rey.

August William Derleth
(1909–1971)

THE ADVENTURE OF THE ORIENT EXPRESS. *New York: The Candlelight Press, 1965.*
Wrappers. *First Edition/First Printing, April 1965* on copyright page. Note: Offset from typewritten copy.

THE ADVENTURE OF THE UNIQUE DICKENSIANS. *Sauk City: Mycroft & Moran, 1968.*
Wrappers. No statement of printing on copyright page. Later collected in THE CHRONICLES OF SOLAR PONS. Note: 35 copies were later bound in black cloth by Gerry de la Ree of Saddle River, N.J. Each bears a paper label affixed to the front paste-down noting limitation and copy number.

THE ADVENTURES OF SOLAR PONS. *[London]: Robson Books, [1975].*
Boards. *First published in Great Britain in 1975 . . .* on copyright page. Issued earlier in the U.S. as "IN RE: SHERLOCK HOLMES" THE ADVENTURES OF SOLAR PONS.

ANY DAY NOW. *Chicago: Normandie House, 1938.*
First edition so stated on copyright page.

ATMOSPHERE OF HOUSES. *Muscatine, Iowa: The Prairie Press, 1939.*
No statement of printing on copyright page. 290 copies printed. Later collected in EVENING IN SPRING.

THE BEAST IN HOLGER'S WOODS. *New York: Thomas Y. Crowell Company, [1968].*
Code *1 2 3 4 5 6 7 8 9 10* on copyright page.

BRIGHT JOURNEY. *New York: Charles Scribner's Sons, 1940.*
First printing has Scribner seal and *A* on copyright page.

THE CAPTIVE ISLAND. *New York: Duell, Sloan and Pearce, [1952].*
First edition so stated on copyright page.

THE CASEBOOK OF SOLAR PONS. *Sauk City: Mycroft & Moran: Publishers, 1965.*
No statement of printing on copyright page.

THE CHRONICLES OF SOLAR PONS. *Sauk City: Mycroft & Moran: Publishers, 1973.*
No statement of printing on copyright page.

COLONEL MARKESAN AND LESS PLEASANT PEOPLE. *Sauk City: Arkham House: Publishers, [1966].*
No statement of printing on copyright page. With MARK SCHORER.

COLUMBUS AND THE NEW WORLD. *New York: Farrar, Straus and Cudahy/London: Burns and Oates, [1957].*
First Printing, 1957 on copyright page. Note: Juvenile history with fictionalized dialogue.

COUNTRY GROWTH. *New York: Charles Scribner's Sons, 1940.*
First printing has Scribner seal and *A* on copyright page.

THE COUNTRY OF THE HAWK. *New York: Aladdin Books, 1952.*
First edition so stated on copyright page.

DEATH BY DESIGN. [*New York*]: *Arcadia House*, [*1953*].
No statement of printing on copyright page.

*DEATH STALKS THE WAKELY FAMILY. *London: Newnes*, [*1937*].
Issued earlier in the U.S. as MURDER STALKS THE WAKELY FAMILY.

DWELLERS IN DARKNESS. *Sauk City: Arkham House*, *1976*.
No statement of printing on copyright page.

EMPIRE OF FUR. *New York: Aladdin Books*, *1953*.
First edition so stated on copyright page.

EVENING IN SPRING. *New York: Charles Scribner's Sons*, *1941*.
First printing has Scribner seal and *A* on copyright page.

FATHER MARQUETTE AND THE GREAT RIVERS. *New York: Vision Books Farrar, Straus & Cudahy*, [*1955*].
First printing, 1955 on copyright page. Note: Juvenile history with fictionalized dialogue.

FELL PURPOSE. [*New York*]: *Arcadia House*, [*1953*].
No statement of printing on copyright page.

THE GHOST OF BLACK HAWK ISLAND. *New York: Duell, Sloan and Pearce*, [*1961*].
First edition so stated on copyright page.

HARRIGAN'S FILE. *Sauk City: Arkham House*, *1975*.
No statement of printing on copyright page.

THE HILLS STAND WATCH. *New York: Duell, Sloan and Pearce*, [*1960*].
First edition so stated on copyright page.

A HOUSE ABOVE CUZCO. *New York: The Candlelight Press*, *1969*.
Boards with cloth shelf back. No statement of printing on copyright page.

THE HOUSE BY THE RIVER. *New York: Duell, Sloan and Pearce*, [*1965*].
First edition so stated on copyright page.

THE HOUSE OF MOONLIGHT. *Iowa City: The Prairie Press*, [*1953*].
Boards with cloth shelf back. No statement printing on copyright page. 550 copies printed. Later collected in WISCONSIN IN THEIR BONES.

THE HOUSE ON THE MOUND. *New York: Duell, Sloan and Pearce*, [*1958*].
First edition so stated on copyright page.

"IN RE: SHERLOCK HOLMES" THE ADVENTURES OF SOLAR PONS. *Sauk City: Mycroft and Moran*, *1945*.
No statement of printing on copyright page. Reissued as REGARDING SHERLOCK HOLMES and later as THE ADVENTURES OF SOLAR PONS.

THE IRREGULARS STRIKE AGAIN. *New York: Duell, Sloan and Pearce*, [*1964*].
First edition so stated on copyright page.

LAND OF GRAY GOLD. *New York: Aladdin Books*, *1954*.
First edition so stated on copyright page.

LAND OF SKY-BLUE WATERS. *New York: Aladdin Books*, *1955*.
First edition so stated on copyright page. Note: Juvenile history with fictionalized dialogue.

LONESOME PLACES. *Sauk City: Arkham House*, [*1962*].
  No statement of printing on copyright page.

THE LURKER AT THE THRESHOLD. *Sauk City: Arkham House, 1945*.
  No statement of printing on copyright page. With H.P. LOVECRAFT.

THE MAN ON ALL FOURS. *New York: Loring & Mussey*, [*1934*].
  No statement of printing on copyright page.

THE MASK OF CTHULHU. *Sauk City: Arkham House: Publishers, 1958*.
  No statement of printing on copyright page.

THE MEMOIRS OF SOLAR PONS. *Sauk City: Mycroft & Moran: Publishers, 1951*.
  No statement of printing on copyright page.

THE MILL CREEK IRREGULARS. *New York; Duell, Sloan and Pearce*, [*1959*].
  First edition so stated on copyright page.

MISCHIEF IN THE LANE. *New York: Charles Scribner's Sons, 1944*.
  Boards. First printing has Scribner seal and *A* on copyright page.

MR. FAIRLIE'S FINAL JOURNEY. *Sauk City: Mycroft & Moran: Publishers, 1968*.
  No statement of printing on copyright page.

MR. GEORGE AND OTHER ODD PERSONS. *Sauk City: Arkham House, 1963*.
  No statement of printing on copyright page. *Stephen Grendon, pseudonym*. Issued later in
  Great Britain as WHEN GRAVEYARDS YAWN.

THE MOON TENDERS. *New York: Duell, Sloan and Pearce*, [*1958*].
  First edition so stated on copyright page.

MURDER STALKS THE WAKELY FAMILY. *New York: Loring & Mussey*, [*1934*].
  No statement of printing on copyright page. Issued later in Great Britain as DEATH STALKS
  THE WAKELY FAMILY.

THE NARRACONG RIDDLE. *New York: Charles Scribner's Sons, 1940*.
  First printing has Scribner seal and *A* on copyright page.

NO FUTURE FOR LUANA. *New York: Charles Scribner's Sons, 1945*.
  Boards. First printing has Scribner seal and *A* on copyright page.

NOT LONG FOR THIS WORLD. *Sauk City: Arkham House: Publishers, 1948*.
  No statement of printing on copyright page. Later abridged as TALES FROM NOT LONG FOR
  THIS WORLD.

OLIVER, THE WAYWARD OWL. *Sauk City: Stanton & Lee, Publishers, 1945*.
  Boards. No statement of printing on copyright page.

THE PINKERTONS RIDE AGAIN. *New York: Duell, Sloan and Pearce*, [*1960*].
  First edition so stated on copyright page.

PLACE OF HAWKS. *New York: Loring & Mussey Publishers*, [*1935*].
  No statement of printing on copyright page. Later collected in WISCONSIN EARTH.

A PRAED STREET DOSSIER. *Sauk City: Mycroft & Moran: Publishers, 1968*.
  No statement of printing on copyright page. One story is a collaboration with MACK
  REYNOLDS.

PRAED STREET PAPERS. *New York: The Candlelight Press, 1965.*
Wrappers. *First Edition, First Printing, May 1965* on copyright page. Note: Offset from typewritten copy.

THE PRINCE GOES WEST. *New York: Meredith Press, [1968].*
Boards with cloth shelf back. First edition so stated on copyright page.

REGARDING SHERLOCK HOLMES: THE ADVENTURES OF SOLAR PONS. *New York: Pinnacle Books, [1974].*
Wrappers. *First printing November 1974* on copyright page. *Pinnacle Fiction Mystery 0–523–00477–X* ($1.25). Reissue of "IN RE: SHERLOCK HOLMES" THE ADVENTURES OF SOLAR PONS.

THE REMINISCENCES OF SOLAR PONS. *Sauk City: Mycroft & Moran: Publishers, 1961.*
No statement of printing on copyright page.

RESTLESS IS THE RIVER. *New York: Charles Scribner's Sons, 1939.*
First printing has Scribner seal and *A* on copyright page.

THE RETURN OF SOLAR PONS. *Sauk City: Mycroft & Moran: Publishers, 1958.*
No statement of printing on copyright page.

SAC PRAIRIE PEOPLE. *Sauk City: Stanton & Lee: Publishers, 1948.*
No statement of printing on copyright page.

ST. IGNATIUS AND THE COMPANY OF JESUS. *New York: Vision Books Farrar, Straus & Cudahy/London: Burns & Oates, [1965].*
First printing, 1956 on copyright page. Note: Juvenile history with fictionalized dialogue.

SENTENCE DEFERRED. *New York: Charles Scribner's Sons, 1939.*
First printing has Scribner seal and *A* on copyright page.

THE SEVEN WHO WAITED. *New York: Charles Scribner's Sons, 1943.*
First printing has Scribner seal and *A* on copyright page.

THE SHADOW IN THE GLASS. *New York: Duell, Sloan and Pearce, [1963].*
First edition so stated on copyright page.

SHADOW OF NIGHT. *New York: Charles Scribner's Sons, 1943.*
First printing has Scribner seal and *A* on copyright page.

THE SHADOW OUT OF TIME. *London: Victor Gollancz Ltd, 1968.*
Boards. No statement of printing on copyright page. Reprint. All material collected from earlier books. With H. P. LOVECRAFT. Note: A number of these stories were completed by Derleth from Lovecraft's notes.

THE SHIELD OF THE VALIANT. *New York: Charles Scribner's Sons, 1945.*
First printing has Scribner seal and *A* on copyright page.

THE SHUTTERED ROOM AND OTHER PIECES. See Edited Fiction.

THE SHUTTERED ROOM AND OTHER TALES OF HORROR. *London: A Panther Book, [1970].*
Wrappers. *Panther Books edition published 1970* on copyright page. *Panther 586 033998* (30p). With H. P. LOVECRAFT. Abridged reprint. Collects ten stories from THE SHADOW OUT OF TIME AND OTHER TALES OF HORROR.

THE SHUTTERED ROOM AND OTHER TALES OF TERROR. *New York: Beagle Books*, [*1971*].
Wrappers. *First printing: April 1971* on copyright page. *A Beagle Horror Anthology 95068*
(95¢). With H. P. LOVECRAFT. Reprint collection. Contents differ from 1959 Arkham
House and 1970 Panther Books collections.

SIGN OF FEAR. *New York: Loring & Mussey, Publishers*, [*1935*].
No statement of printing on copyright page.

SOMEONE IN THE DARK. [*Sauk City*]*: Arkham House, 1941*.
Two printings, priority as listed: (A) Sheets bulk 1.6 cm across; height of page is 17.2 cm;
no headbands; (B) Sheets bulk 1.8 cm across; height of page is 17.6 cm; has headbands. No
statement of printing on copyright page. Note: According to Derleth, the photo-offset
second printing was unauthorized and limited to 200 copies.

SOMETHING NEAR. *Sauk City: Arkham House, 1945*.
No statement of printing on copyright page.

STILL IS THE SUMMER NIGHT. *New York: Charles Scribner's Sons, 1937*.
First printing has Scribner seal and *A* on copyright page. Note: Some copies have a printed
sticker affixed to the title page reading, *This is a/publication of/Arkham House:*
Publishers/Sauk City,/Wisconsin.

THE SURVIVOR AND OTHERS. *Sauk City: Arkham House: Publishers, 1957*.
No statement of printing on copyright page. With H. P. LOVECRAFT.

SWEET GENEVIEVE. *New York: Charles Scribner's Sons, 1942*.
First printing has Scribner seal and *A* on copyright page.

SWEET LAND OF MICHIGAN. *New York: Duell, Sloan and Pearce*, [*1962*].
First edition so stated on copyright page.

TALES FROM NOT LONG FOR THIS WORLD. *New York: Ballantine Books*, [*1961*].
Wrappers. No statement of printing on copyright page. *Ballantine Books 542* (35¢).
Abridged collection. Prints twenty-two of the thirty-three stories collected earlier in NOT
LONG FOR THIS WORLD.

THE TENT SHOW SUMMER. [*New York*]*: Duell, Sloan and Pearce*, [*1963*].
First edition so stated on copyright page.

THREE PROBLEMS FOR SOLAR PONS. *Sauk City: Mycroft & Moran: Publishers, 1952*.
No statement of printing on copyright page. 996 copies printed. Stories later collected in
THE RETURN OF SOLAR PONS.

THE THREE STRAW MEN. *New York: Candlelight Press, 1970*.
Boards. *First edition/First printing: November, 1970* on copyright page.

THREE WHO DIED. *New York: Loring & Mussey Publishers*, [*1935*].
No statement of printing on copyright page.

THE TRAIL OF CTHULHU. *Sauk City: Arkham House: Publishers, 1962*.
No statement of printing on copyright page.

THE WATCHER ON THE HEIGHTS. *New York: Duell, Sloan and Pearce*, [*1966*].
First edition so stated on copyright page.

THE WATCHERS OUT OF TIME AND OTHERS. *Sauk City: Arkham House: Publishers, 1974*.
No statement of printing on copyright page. Reprint, save for "The Watchers Out of
Time." With H. P. LOVECRAFT.

WHEN GRAVEYARDS YAWN. *London: Tandem Books Limited*, [*1965*].
Wrappers. *First Tandem Edition 1965* on copyright page. *Tandem Books T30* (3'6). Reissue of MR. GEORGE AND OTHER ODD PERSONS.

WILBUR, THE TRUSTING WHIPPOORWILL. *Sauk City: Stanton & Lee, 1959*.
Boards. No statement of printing on copyright page.

THE WIND LEANS WEST. *New York: The Candlelight Press, 1969*.
No statement of printing on copyright page.

WIND OVER WISCONSIN. *New York: Charles Scribner's Sons, 1938*.
First printing has Scribner seal and *A* on copyright page.

WISCONSIN EARTH. *Sauk City: Stanton & Lee: Publishers, 1948*.
No statement of printing on copyright page. Reprint. Collects SHADOW OF NIGHT, PLACE OF HAWKS, and VILLAGE YEAR: A SAC PRAIRIE JOURNAL.

WISCONSIN IN THEIR BONES. *New York: Duell, Sloan and Pearce*, [*1961*].
No statement of printing on copyright page.

Edited Fiction

Titles listed in this section include only those books acknowledging Derleth as editor on the title page. Numerous works issued under the Arkham House and Mycroft and Moran imprints were edited and in many cases compiled by Derleth. In addition, he was H. P. Lovecraft's literary executor, and beginning in 1939 with THE OUTSIDER AND OTHERS he edited, often with revisions or completions, Lovecraft's writings. For additional edited works and compilations see *100 Books by August Derleth* or the article on Derleth in *Contemporary Novelists*, James Vinson, ed. (New York: St. Martin's Press, 1972), pp. 342–47.

Beachheads in Space. [*New York*]: *Pellegrini & Cudahy*, [*1952*].
No statement of printing on copyright page. Edited, with introduction, by Derleth.

ALSO: *London: Weidenfeld & Nicolson*, [*1954*] Boards. *First published in Great Britain 1954* on copyright page. Abridged reprint. Collects seven of the fourteen stories.

ALSO: *New York: Berkley Publishing Corp.*, [*1957*]. Wrappers. No statement of printing on copyright page. *Berkley Books G–77* (35¢). Abridged reprint. Collects seven of the fourteen stories.

ALSO: [*London*]: *A Four Square Book*, [*1964*]. Wrappers. *First Four Square Edition 1964* on copyright page. *Four Square 1073* (3'6). Abridged reprint. Collects seven of the fourteen stories.

Beyond Time & Space. *New York: Pellegrini & Cudahy, 1950*.
Boards with cloth shelf back. No statement of printing on copyright page. Edited, with introduction, by Derleth.

ALSO: *New York: Berkley Publishing Corp.*, [*1958*]. Wrappers. No statement of printing on copyright page. *Berkley Books G–104* (35¢). Abridged reprint. Collects eight of the thirty-two stories.

Dark Mind, Dark Heart. *Sauk City: Arkham House: Publishers, 1962*.
No statement of printing on copyright page. Edited, with foreword, by Derleth.

Dark Things. *Sauk City: Arkham House: Publishers, 1971*.
No statement of printing on copyright page. Edited by Derleth.

Far Boundaries. *New York: Pellegrini & Cudahy, Publishers,* [*1951*].
Boards. No statement of printing on copyright page. Edited, with introduction, by Derleth.

From Other Worlds. [*London*]: *A Four Square Book,* [*1964*].
Wrappers. *First Four Square edition 1964* on copyright page. *A Four Square Book 1107* (3'6). Abridged reprint. Collects seven of the fourteen stories from *Beachheads in Space.*

New Worlds for Old. [*London*]: *A Four Square Book,* [*1963*].
Wrappers. *First Four Square edition 1963* on copyright page. *A Four Square Book 842* (2'6). Abridged reprint. Collects nine of the nineteen stories from *Worlds of Tomorrow.*

The Night Side. *New York Toronto: Rinehart & Company, Inc.,* [*1947*].
First printing has publisher's monogram on copyright page. Edited, with foreword and short story "The Extra Passenger," by Derleth.

ALSO: [*London*]: *A Four Square Book,* [*1966*]. Wrappers. *First Four Square edition November 1966* on copyright page. *Four Square Horror 1657 (5/–)*. Abridged reprint. Collects nineteen of the twenty-three stories.

Night's Yawning Peal. [*Sauk City*]: *Arkham House: Publishers, 1952.*
Two printings, priority as listed: (A) Signatures sewn in gatherings of 8 leaves, price in upper right corner of front dust jacket flap is *$3.00;* (B) Signatures sewn in gatherings of 16 leaves, *SECOND PRINTING* in upper left corner, and price *$3.50* in upper right corner of front dust jacket flap. No statement of printing on copyright page. Edited, with foreword and two stories, "Mr. George" and "The Lonesome Place," by Derleth.

ALSO: [*New York*]: *New American Library,* [*1974*]. Wrappers. *First Printing, August, 1974/1 2 3 4 5 6 7 8 9* on copyright page. *Signet 451–Y6025* ($1.25). Abridged reprint. Collects eight of the fifteen stories.

The Other Side of the Moon. *New York: Pellegrini & Cudahy,* [*1949*].
No statement of printing on copyright page. Edited, with introduction, by Derleth.

ALSO: [*London*]: *Grayson & Grayson,* [*1956*]. Boards. *First published in Great Britain in 1956 . . .* on copyright page. Abridged reprint. Collects eleven of the twenty stories.

ALSO: [*New York*]: *Published by Berkley Publishing Corp.,* [*1959*]. Wrappers. No statement of printing on copyright page. *Berkley Books G249* (35¢). Abridged reprint. Collects ten of the twenty stories.

ALSO: [*London*]: *A Panther Book,* [*1963*]. Wrappers. *Panther edition published July 1963* on copyright page. *Panther Books 1541* (2'6). Abridged reprint. Collects ten of the twenty stories.

ALSO: [*London*]: *A Mayflower-Dell Paperback,* [*1966*]. Wrappers. *First publication in Great Britain of this edition. Published . . . December 1966* on copyright page. *Mayflower Dell 6740* (3/6). Abridged reprint. Collects ten of the twenty stories.

The Outer Reaches. [*New York*]: *Pellegrini & Cudahy, Publishers,* [*1951*].
No statement of printing on copyright page. Edited, with foreword, by Derleth.

ALSO: *New York: Berkley Publishing Corp.,* [*1958*]. Wrappers. No statement of printing on copyright page. *Berkley Books G–116* (35¢). Abridged reprint. Collects ten of the seventeen stories.

ALSO: *London: World Distributors,* [*1963*]. Wrappers. *This Consul edition . . . published in England, 1963 . . .* on copyright page. *Consul Books Selected Science Fiction 1268* (2'6). Abridged reprint. Collects eight of the seventeen stories.

Over the Edge. *Sauk City: Arkham House: Publishers, 1964*.
No statement of printing on copyright page. Edited, with foreword and short story "The Patchwork Quilt," by Derleth.

Portals of Tomorrow. *New York Toronto: Rinehart and Company, Inc., [1954]*.
Boards with cloth shelf back. First printing has publisher's monogram on copyright page. Edited, with introduction, by Derleth.

The Shuttered Room and Other Pieces, by H. P. Lovecraft & Divers Hands. *Sauk City: Arkham House: Publishers, 1959*.
No statement of printing on copyright page. Edited, with foreword, two short story completions, "The Shuttered Room" and "The Fisherman of Falcon Point," and other material, by Derleth.

Sleep No More. *New York Toronto: Farrar & Rinehart, Inc., [1944]*.
First printing has publisher's monogram on copyright page. Edited, with foreword and short story "A Gentleman from Prague," by Derleth. Later abridged as *Stories From Sleep No More*.

ALSO: [*London*]: A Panther Book [*1964*]. Wrappers. *First published in Great Britain . . . December 1964* on copyright page. *Panther 1770* (3'6). Abridged reprint. Collects twelve of the twenty stories.

The Sleeping & the Dead. *Chicago: Pellegrini & Cudahy, [1947]*.
No statement of printing on copyright page. Edited, with introduction and short story "Glory Hand," by Derleth.

ALSO: [*London*]: *A Four Square Book, [1963]*. Wrappers. *First Four Square edition 1963* on copyright page. *A Four Square Book 943* (3'6). Abridged reprint. Collects fifteen of the thirty stories.

Stories From Sleep No More. *Toronto New York London: Bantam Books, [1967]*.
Wrappers. *Published February 1967* on copyright page. *Bantam Supernatural Horror H3425* (60¢). Abridged reprint. Collects ten of the twenty stories from *Sleep No More*. *Nine Nerve-Shattering Tales of Unrelenting Terror!* at head of title.

Strange Ports of Call. *New York: Pellegrini & Cudahy, [1948]*.
Boards with cloth shelf back. No statement of printing on copyright page. Edited, with introduction, by Derleth.

ALSO: *New York: Berkley Publishing Corp., [1958]*. Wrappers. *June, 1958* on copyright page. *Berkley Books G–131* (35¢). Abridged reprint. Collects ten of the twenty stories.

Tales of the Cthulhu Mythos. *Sauk City: Arkham House: Publishers, 1969*.
No statement of printing on copyright page. Edited, with introduction and two stories, "The Dweller in Darkness" and "Beyond the Threshold," by Derleth.

The Time of Infinity. *London: World Distributors, [1963]*.
Wrappers. *This Consul edition, complete and unabridged, published in England, 1963 . . .* on copyright page. *Consul Books Selected Science Fiction 1268* (2'6). Abridged reprint. Collects nine of the seventeen stories from *The Outer Reaches*.

Time to Come. *New York: Farrar, Straus and Young, [1954]*.
Boards with cloth shelf back. *First printing 1954* on copyright page. Edited, with foreword, by Derleth.

ALSO: [*New York*]: *Published by Berkley Publishing Corp., [1958]*.
Wrappers. *December, 1958* on copyright page. *Berkley Books G–189* (35¢). Abridged reprint. Collects ten of the twelve stories.

Travellers by Night. *Sauk City: Arkham House: Publishers, 1967*.
  No statement of printing on copyright page. Edited by Derleth.

The Unquiet Grave. [*London*]: *A Four Square Book*, [*1964*].
  Wrappers. *First Four Square edition 1964* on copyright page. *Four Square 982* (3'6).
  Abridged reprint. Collects fifteen of the thirty stories from *The Sleeping & the Dead*.

When Evil Wakes. [*London*]: *Souvenir Press*, [*1963*].
  Boards. *First published 1963* on copyright page. Edited, with introduction and short story
  "The Tsanta in the Parlour," by Derleth.

Who Knocks? *New York Toronto: Rinehart & Company, Inc.*, [*1946*].
  First printing has publisher's monogram on copyright page. Edited, with foreword and
  short story "Alannah," by Derleth.

  ALSO: [*London*]: *A Panther Book*, [*1964*]. Wrappers. *First published in Great Britain . . .
  December 1964* on copyright page. *Panther 1769* (3'6). Abridged reprint. Collects twelve
  of the twenty stories.

A Wisconsin Harvest. *Sauk City: Stanton & Lee: Publishers, 1966*.
  No statement of printing on copyright page. Edited, with introduction, by Derleth.

Worlds of Tomorrow. [*New York*]: *Pellegrini & Cudahy, 1953*.
  No statement of printing on copyright page. Edited, with foreword and short story
  "McIlvaine's Star," by Derleth.

  ALSO: *London: Weidenfeld & Nicolson*, [*1954*]. Boards. *First published in Great Britain
  1954* on copyright page. Abridged reprint. Collects fifteen of the nineteen stories.

  ALSO: [*New York*]: *Published by Berkley Publishing Corp.*, [*1958*].
  Wrappers. *October, 1958* on copyright page. *Berkley Books G–163* (35¢). Abridged
  reprint. Collects ten of the nineteen stories.

  ALSO: [*London*]: *A Four Square Book*, [*1963*]. Wrappers. *First Four Square edition 1963*
  on copyright page. *A Four Square Book 794* (2'6). Abridged reprint. Collects ten of the
  nineteen stories.

Nonfiction (Dealing with the Fantasy Genre only)

Arkham House: the First 20 Years 1939–1959. *Sauk City: Arkham House: Publishers, 1959*.
  Two issues, no priority: (A) Boards; (B) Wrappers. No statement of printing on copyright
  page. Later enlarged as *Thirty Years of Arkham House 1939–1969*.

H. P. L.: A Memoir. *New York: Ben Abramson, Publisher, 1945*.
  No statement of printing on copyright page.

Some Notes on H. P. Lovecraft. [*Sauk City*]: *Arkham House: Publishers, 1959*.
  Wrappers. No statement of printing on copyright page.

Thirty Years of Arkham House 1939–1969. A History and Bibliography. *Sauk City: Arkham
House: Publishers, 1970*.
  No statement of printing on copyright page.

Writing Fiction. *Boston: The Writer, Inc. Publishers*, [*1946*].
  No statement of printing on copyright page. Includes "The Imaginative Story," pp.
  96–159.

Edited Nonfiction (Dealing with the Fantasy Genre only)

Selected Letters 1911–1924, [by] H. P. Lovecraft. *Sauk City: Arkham House: Publishers, 1965.*
  No statement of printing on copyright page. Edited, with preface, by Derleth. With DONALD WANDREI.

Selected Letters 1925–1929, [by] H. P. Lovecraft. *Sauk City: Arkham House: Publishers, 1968.*
  No statement of printing on copyright page. Edited, with preface, by Derleth. With DONALD WANDREI.

Selected Letters 1929–1931, [by] H. P. Lovecraft. *Sauk City: Arkham House: Publishers, 1971.*
  No statement of printing on copyright page. Edited, with preface, by Derleth. With DONALD WANDREI.

Selected Letters 1932–1934, [by] H. P. Lovecraft. *Sauk City: Arkham House: Publishers, Inc., 1976.*
  No statement of printing on copyright page. Edited by Derleth with JAMES TURNER.

Selected Letters 1934–1937, [by] H. P. Lovecraft. *Sauk City: Arkham House Publishers, Inc., 1976.*
  No statement of printing on copyright page. Edited by Derleth with JAMES TURNER.

Reference

August Derleth, Thirty Years of Writing 1926–1956, [compiled by August Derleth]. *[Sauk City: Arkham House: Publishers], n.d. [but 1957].*
  Wrappers. No statement of printing.

100 Books by August Derleth. *Sauk City: Arkham House: Publishers, 1962.*
  Two issues, no priority: (A) Boards; (B) Wrappers. No statement of printing on copyright page.

Philip Kindred Dick
(b. 1928)

THE BEST OF PHILIP K. DICK. *New York: Ballantine Books, [1977].*
Wrappers. *First Edition: March 1977* on copyright page. *Ballantine 25359* ($1.95).

THE BOOK OF PHILIP K. DICK. *New York: DAW Books, Inc., [1973].*
Wrappers. *First printing, February 1973* on copyright page. Also, *First Printing* [through]
Tenth Printing set in ten lines following the dedication on copyright page. *DAW: sf Books
No. 44 UQ1044* (95¢). Reissued as THE TURNING WHEEL AND OTHER STORIES.

CLANS OF THE ALPHANE MOON. *New York: Ace Books, Inc., [1964].*
Wrappers. No statement of printing on copyright page. *Ace Book F–309* (40¢).

CONFESSIONS OF A CRAP ARTIST. *New York: Entwhistle Books, 1975.*
Two bindings, priority as listed: (A) Red cloth. 500 copies; (B) Wrappers. 500 copies.
Three issues, no priority for the first two, the last bound later: (A) Cloth; 90 numbered
copies signed by the author; (B) Cloth; 410 unsigned trade copies; (C) Wrappers. All issues
occur in two states: (A) *First edition: 500 copies, cloth bound* on copyright page; (B) This
statement not present on copyright page. Notes: (1) 1000 sets of sheets were printed. The
press was stopped at 500 copies and the first edition statement was removed. Both states
were mixed by the printer and the three issues were prepared using sheets with and without
the statement. Of the 500 hardbound copies, 90 were selected at random and a signed issue
was prepared. (2) Hardbound copies were issued without dust jacket.

THE COSMIC PUPPETS. *New York: Ace Books, [1957].*
Wrappers. No statement of printing on copyright page. *Ace Double Novel Books D–249*
(35¢). Bound with SARGASSO OF SPACE by Andrew North.

COUNTER-CLOCK WORLD. *[New York]: Published by Berkley Publishing Corporation,*
[1967].
Wrappers. *February, 1967* on copyright page. *Berkley X1372* (60¢).

ALSO: *London, Sydney and Toronto: White Lion Publishers Limited, [1977].* Boards. *First*
published in Great Britain . . . 1977 on copyright page. First hardcover edition.

THE CRACK IN SPACE. *New York: Ace Books, Inc., [1966].*
Wrappers. No statement of printing on copyright page. *Ace Book F–377* (40¢). Later
collected in A PHILIP K. DICK OMNIBUS.

DEUS IRAE. *Garden City: Doubleday & Company, Inc., 1976.*
Boards. First edition so stated on copyright page. With ROGER ZELAZNY.

DO ANDROIDS DREAM OF ELECTRIC SHEEP? *Garden City: Doubleday & Company, Inc.,*
1968.
First edition so stated on copyright page.

DR. BLOODMONEY OR HOW WE GOT ALONG AFTER THE BOMB. *New York: Ace Books, Inc.,*
[1965].
Wrappers. No statement of printing on copyright page. *Ace Book F–337* (40¢).

ALSO: *Boston: Gregg Press, 1977. First Printing, June 1977* on copyright page. First
hardcover edition. Notes: (1) Photographically reproduced from the 1965 Ace Books
edition. (2) Not issued in dust jacket.

DR. FUTURITY. *New York: Ace Books, Inc.*, *[1960]*.
Wrappers. No statement of printing on copyright page. *Ace Double Novel Books D–421* (35¢). Bound with SLAVERS OF SPACE by John Brunner. Later collected in A PHILIP K. DICK OMNIBUS.

EYE IN THE SKY. *New York: Ace Books*, *[1957]*.
Wrappers. No statement of printing on copyright page. *Ace Double-Size Books D–211* (35¢).

FLOW MY TEARS, THE POLICEMAN SAID. *Garden City: Doubleday & Company, Inc.*, *1974*.
First edition so stated on copyright page.

GALACTIC POT-HEALER. *[New York]: Published by Berkley Publishing Corporation*, *[1969]*.
Wrappers. *June, 1969* on copyright page. *A Berkley Medallion Book X1705* (60¢).

ALSO: *New York: Berkley Publishing Corporation*, *[1970]*. Boards. No statement of printing on copyright page. Code *08L* on page 145. First hardcover edition. Note: Issued by the Science Fiction Book Club.

THE GAME-PLAYERS OF TITAN. *New York: Ace Books, Inc.*, *[1963]*.
Wrappers. No statement of printing on copyright page. *Ace Book F–251* (40¢).

ALSO: *London, New York, Sydney and Toronto: White Lion Publishers Limited*, *[1974]*. Boards. *White Lion edition, 1974* on copyright page. First hardcover edition.

THE GANYMEDE TAKEOVER. *New York: Ace Books, Inc.*, *[1967]*.
Wrappers. No statement of printing on copyright page. *Ace Book G–637* (50¢). With RAY NELSON.

A HANDFUL OF DARKNESS. *London Melbourne Sydney Auckland Bombay Cape Town New York Toronto: Rich and Cowan*, *[1955]*.
Two bindings, priority as listed: (A) Blue boards lettered in silver; (B) Orange boards lettered in black. *First published — 1955* on copyright page. Note: A later dust jacket listing Dick's WORLD OF CHANCE has been observed on both bindings.

THE MAN IN THE HIGH CASTLE. *New York: G. P. Putnam's Sons*, *[1962]*.
No statement of printing on copyright page. Code *D36* at base of page 239.

THE MAN WHO JAPED. *New York: Ace Books*, *[1956]*.
Wrappers. No statement of printing on copyright page. *Ace Double Novel Books D–193* (35¢). Bound with THE SPACE-BORN by E. C. Tubb.

MARTIAN TIME-SLIP. *New York: Ballantine Books*, *[1964]*.
Wrappers. No statement of printing on copyright page. *An Original Ballantine Science Fiction Novel U2191* (50¢).

ALSO: *[London]: New English Library*, *[1976]*. Boards. *This edition first published in Great Britain . . . in 1976* on copyright page. First hardcover edition.

A MAZE OF DEATH. *Garden City: Doubleday & Company, Inc.*, *1970*.
First edition so stated on copyright page.

NOW WAIT FOR LAST YEAR. *Garden City: Doubleday & Company, Inc.*, *1966*.
First edition so stated on copyright page.

OUR FRIENDS FROM FROLIX 8. *New York: Ace Publishing Corporation*, *[1970]*.
Wrappers. No statement of printing on copyright page. *Ace Book 64400* (60¢).

ALSO:*New York: Ace Books*, [*1971*]. Boards. No statement of printing on copyright page. Code *B3* on page 184. First hardcover edition. Note: Issued by the Science Fiction Book Club.

THE PENULTIMATE TRUTH.*New York: Belmont Books*, [*1964*].
Wrappers. *September 1964* on copyright page. *Belmont 92–603* (50¢).

ALSO:*London: Jonathan Cape*, [*1967*]. Boards. *First published in Great Britain 1967* on copyright page. First hardcover edition.

A PHILIP K. DICK OMNIBUS.*London: Sidgwick & Jackson*, [*1970*].
Boards. No statement of printing on copyright page. Reprint. Collects THE CRACK IN SPACE, THE UNTELEPORTED MAN, and DR. FUTURITY. Note: First hardcover publication for all titles.

THE PRESERVING MACHINE.*New York: Ace Publishing Corporation*, [*1969*].
Wrappers. No statement of printing on copyright page. *An Ace Science Fiction Special 67800* (95¢).

ALSO:*New York: Ace Books, Inc.*, [*1970*]. Boards. No statement of printing on copyright page. Code *48K* on page 309. First hardcover edition. Note: Issued by the Science Fiction Book Club.

ALSO:*London: Victor Gollancz Ltd, 1971*. Boards. No statement of printing on copyright page. Drops one story, "What the Dead Men Say."

A SCANNER DARKLY.*Garden City: Doubleday & Company, Inc.*, *1977*.
Boards. First edition so stated on copyright page.

THE SIMULACRA.*New York: Ace Books, Inc.*, [*1964*].
Wrappers. No statement of printing on copyright page. *Ace Book F–301* (40¢).

ALSO:*London: Eyre Methuen*, [*1977*]. Boards. *First published in Great Britain 1977 . . .* on copyright page. First hardcover edition.

SOLAR LOTTERY.*New York: Ace Books, Inc.*, [*1955*].
Wrappers. No statement of printing on copyright page. *Ace Double Novel Books D–103* (35¢). Bound with THE BIG JUMP by Leigh Brackett. Issued later in Great Britain with unauthorized editorial changes as WORLD OF CHANCE.

ALSO:*Boston: Gregg Press, 1976. First Printing, June 1976* on copyright page. First U.S. hardcover edition. Notes: (1) Photographically reproduced from the 1955 Ace Books edition. (2) Not issued in dust jacket.

THE THREE STIGMATA OF PALMER ELDRITCH.*Garden City: Doubleday & Company, Inc.*, *1965*.
First edition so stated on copyright page.

TIME OUT OF JOINT.*Philadelphia New York: J. B. Lippincott Company*, [*1959*].
Boards. First edition so stated on copyright page.

THE TURNING WHEEL AND OTHER STORIES. [*London*]: *Coronet Books*, [*1977*].
Wrappers. *Coronet Edition 1977* on copyright page. *Coronet 21829 0* (80p). Issued earlier in the U.S. as THE BOOK OF PHILIP K. DICK.

UBIK.*Garden City: Doubleday & Company, Inc.*, *1969*.
First edition so stated on copyright page.

THE UNTELEPORTED MAN.*New York: Ace Books, Inc.*, [*1966*].
Wrappers. No statement of printing on copyright page. *Ace Double G–602* (50¢). Bound with THE MIND MONSTERS by Howard L. Cory. Later collected in A PHILIP K. DICK OMNIBUS.

THE VARIABLE MAN AND OTHER STORIES.*New York: Ace Books, Inc.*, [*1957*].
Wrappers. No statement of printing on copyright page. *Ace Double-Size Books D–261* (35¢).

VULCAN'S HAMMER.*New York: Ace Books, Inc.*, [*1960*].
Wrappers. No statement of printing on copyright page. *Ace Double Novel Books D–457* (35¢). Bound with THE SKYNAPPERS by John Brunner.

WE CAN BUILD YOU.*New York: DAW Books, Inc.*, [*1972*].
Wrappers. No statement of printing on copyright page. *DAW: sf Books No. 14 UQ1014* (95¢). Note: Later printings state *First printing, July 1972* and carry the publisher's printing code on the copyright page.

THE WORLD JONES MADE.*New York: Ace Books*, [*1956*].
Wrappers. No statement of printing on copyright page. *Ace Double Novel Books D–150* (35¢). Bound with AGENT OF THE UNKNOWN by Margaret St. Clair.

ALSO:*London: Sidgwick & Jackson*, [*1968*]. Boards. *This edition published 1968* on copyright page. First hardcover edition.

WORLD OF CHANCE.*London Melbourne Sydney Auckland Bombay Johannesburg New York Toronto: Rich and Cowan*, [*1956*].
Boards. *First published 1956* on copyright page. Unauthorized editorial changes. Issued earlier in the U.S. with author's preferred text as SOLAR LOTTERY.

THE ZAP GUN.*New York: Pyramid Books*, [*1967*].
Wrappers. *First printing January, 1967* on copyright page. *Pyramid Science Fiction R–1569* (50¢).

Reference

Philip K. Dick & the Umbrella of Light, [by] Angus Taylor. [*Baltimore: T. K. Graphics, 1975.*]
Wrappers. No statement of printing on copyright page. Cover title. At head of title: *sf author studies 1*.

Philip K. Dick: Electric Shepherd, edited by Bruce Gillespie. *Melbourne, Australia: Norstrilia Press*, [*1975*].
Wrappers. *First published 1975 . . .* on copyright page. *Best of SF Commentary Number 1* at head of title. Note: Includes two letters by Dick as well as the text of a lecture, "The Android and the Human."

Gordon Rupert Dickson
(b. 1923)

ALIEN ART. *New York: E. P. Dutton & Co., Inc.,* [*1973*].
First edition so stated on copyright page.

ALIEN FROM ARCTURUS. *New York: Ace Books, Inc.,* [*1956*].
Wrappers. No statement of printing on copyright page. *Ace Double Novel Books D–139* (35¢). Bound with ATOM CURTAIN by Nick Boddie Williams.

THE ALIEN WAY. *Toronto New York London: Bantam Books,* [*1965*].
Wrappers. *Published February 1965* on copyright page. *A Bantam Fifty F2941* (50¢).

ANCIENT, MY ENEMY. *Garden City: Doubleday & Company, Inc., 1974.*
First edition so stated on copyright page.

THE BOOK OF GORDON DICKSON. *New York: DAW Books, Inc.,* [*1973*].
Wrappers. *First printing, May 1973/1 2 3 4 5 6 7 8 9* on copyright page. *DAW: sf Books No. 55 UQ1055* (95¢). Reprint of DANGER—HUMAN.

DANGER—HUMAN. *Garden City: Doubleday & Company, Inc., 1970.*
First edition so stated on copyright page. Reissued as THE BOOK OF GORDON DICKSON.

DELUSION WORLD. *New York: Ace Books, Inc.,* [*1961*].
Wrappers. No statement of printing on copyright page. *Ace Double Novel F–119* (40¢). Bound with SPACIAL DELIVERY by Dickson.

DORSAI! *New York: DAW Books, Inc.,* [*1976*].
Wrappers. *First printing, February 1976/1 2 3 4 5 6 7 8 9* on copyright page. *DAW: sf Books No. 181 UW1218* ($1.50). Revised and expanded version of THE GENETIC GENERAL. Note: This edition preceded by the Science Fiction Book Club printing of the expanded version in THREE TO DORSAI!

THE DRAGON AND THE GEORGE. *Garden City: Nelson Doubleday, Inc.,* [*1976*].
Boards. Two printings, priority as listed: (A) Code *G24* on page 243; (B) Code *G38* on page 243. No statement of printing on copyright page. Note: Issued by the Science Fiction Book Club.

EARTHMAN'S BURDEN. *New York: Gnome Press Inc.,* [*1957*].
Two bindings, probable priority as listed: (A) Pale blue boards lettered in dark blue; (B) Gray cloth lettered in red. First edition so stated on copyright page. With POUL ANDERSON.

THE GENETIC GENERAL. *New York: Ace Books, Inc.,* [*1960*].
Wrappers. No statement of printing on copyright page. *Ace Double Novel Books D-449* (35¢). Bound with TIME TO TELEPORT by Dickson. Later expanded as DORSAI!

GREMLINS, GO HOME! *New York: St. Martin's Press,* [*1974*].
Boards. No statement of printing on copyright page. With BEN BOVA.

HOUR OF THE HORDE. *New York: G. P. Putnam's Sons,* [*1970*].
No statement of printing on copyright page.

THE LIFESHIP. *New York, Hagerstown, San Francisco, London: Harper & Row, Publishers,* [*1976*].
> Boards with cloth shelf back. First edition so stated on copyright page. With HARRY HARRISON.

MANKIND ON THE RUN. *New York: Ace Books,* [*1956*].
> Wrappers. No statement of printing on copyright page. *Ace Double Novel Books D–164* (35¢). Bound with THE CROSSROADS OF TIME by Andre Norton.

MISSION TO UNIVERSE. [*New York*]: *Published by Berkley Publishing Corporation,* [*1965*].
> Wrappers. *October, 1965* on copyright page. *Berkley Medallion F1147* (50¢).

> ALSO: *New York: Ballantine Books,* [*1977*]. Wrappers. *First Edition: March 1977* on copyright page. *Ballantine 25703* ($1.50). Revised and expanded text.

MUTANTS. [*New York*]: *The Macmillan Company,* [*1970*].
> First printing so stated on copyright page. Note: Some copies have a small acknowledgments slip laid in.

NAKED TO THE STARS. *New York: Pyramid Books,* [*1961*].
> Wrappers. *First printing: December 1961* on copyright page. *Pyramid Books F–682* (40¢).

NECROMANCER. *Garden City: Doubleday & Company, Inc., 1962.*
> Boards. First edition so stated on copyright page. Reissued as NO ROOM FOR MAN.

NO ROOM FOR MAN. [*New York*]: *A Macfadden Book,* [*1963*].
> Wrappers. *A Macfadden Book . . . 1963* on copyright page. *Macfadden Books 50–179* (50¢). Reissue of NECROMANCER.

NONE BUT MAN. *Garden City: Doubleday & Company, Inc., 1969.*
> First edition so stated on copyright page.

THE OUTPOSTER. *Philadelphia and New York: J. B. Lippincott Company,* [*1972*].
> First edition so stated on copyright page.

PLANET RUN. *Garden City: Doubleday & Company, Inc., 1967.*
> First edition so stated on copyright page. With KEITH LAUMER.

THE PRITCHER MASS. *Garden City: Doubleday & Company, Inc., 1972.*
> First edition so stated on copyright page.

THE R-MASTER. *Philadelphia: J. B. Lippincott Company,* [*1973*].
> First edition so stated on copyright page. Note: This novel was originally announced as MIND MASTER.

SECRET UNDER ANTARCTICA. *New York Chicago San Francisco: Holt Rinehart and Winston,* [*1963*].
> Two bindings, no priority: (A) Boards. Trade binding. (B) Pictorial cloth reproducing dust jacket design. Library binding. First edition so stated on copyright page.

SECRET UNDER THE CARIBBEAN. *New York • Chicago • San Francisco: Holt, Rinehart and Winston,* [*1964*].
> Two bindings, no priority: (A) Boards. Trade binding. (B) Pictorial cloth reproducing dust jacket design. Library binding. First edition so stated on copyright page.

SECRET UNDER THE SEA. *New York: Holt, Rinehart and Winston,* [*1960*].
> First edition so stated on copyright page.

SLEEPWALKER'S WORLD. *Philadelphia and New York: J. B. Lippincott Company*, [*1971*].
   Boards with cloth shelf back. First edition so stated on copyright page.

SOLDIER, ASK NOT. [*New York*]: *A Dell Book*, [*1967*].
   Wrappers. *First Dell Printing —July, 1967* on copyright page.
   Dell 8090 (60¢).

THE SPACE SWIMMERS. [*New York*]: *Published by Berkley Publishing Corporation*, [*1967*].
   Wrappers. *February, 1967* on copyright page. *Berkley X1371* (60¢).

   ALSO: *London: Sidgwick & Jackson*, [*1968*]. Boards. *This edition published 1968* on
   copyright page. First hardcover edition.

SPACE WINNERS. *New York Chicago San Francisco: Holt Rinehart and Winston*, [*1965*].
   Two bindings, no priority: (A) Boards. Trade binding. (B) Pictorial cloth reproducing dust
   jacket design. Library binding. First edition so stated on copyright page.

SPACEPAW. *New York: G. P. Putnam's Sons*, [*1969*].
   No statement of printing on copyright page.

SPACIAL DELIVERY. *New York: Ace Books, Inc.*, [*1961*].
   Wrappers. No statement of printing on copyright page. *Ace Double Novel F–119* (40¢).
   Bound with DELUSION WORLD by Dickson.

STAR PRINCE CHARLIE. *New York: G. P. Putnam's Sons*, [*1975*].
   No statement of printing on copyright page. Two dust jacket states, priority as listed: (A)
   Anderson/Dickson on dust jacket spine panel with slash between authors' names barely
   discernible; (B) Slash is apparent. With POUL ANDERSON.

   ALSO: [*New York*]: *Published by Berkley Publishing Corporation*, [*1977*]. Wrappers.
   January, 1977 on copyright page. *A Berkley Medallion Book 0–425–03078–4* ($1.25).
   Text copy edited.

THE STAR ROAD. *Garden City: Doubleday & Company, Inc.*, *1973*.
   First edition so stated on copyright page.

THE TACTICS OF MISTAKE. *Garden City: Doubleday & Company, Inc.*, *1971*.
   First edition so stated on copyright page.

THREE TO DORSAI! *Garden City: Nelson Doubleday, Inc.*, [*1975*].
   Boards. Three printings, priority as listed: (A) Code *39R* on page 532; (B) Code *S10* on
   page 532; (C) Code *S19* on page 532. No statement of printing on copyright page. Collects
   NECROMANCER, TACTICS OF MISTAKE, and DORSAI! (published earlier in abridged version
   as THE GENETIC GENERAL). New introduction by the author. Note: Issued by the Science
   Fiction Book Club.

TIME TO TELEPORT. *New York: Ace Books, Inc.*, [*1960*].
   Wrappers. No statement of printing on copyright page. *Ace Double Novel Books D–449*
   (35¢). Bound with THE GENETIC GENERAL by Dickson.

TIMESTORM. *New York: St. Martin's Press*, [*1977*].
   Boards. No statement of printing on copyright page. Note: Correct title of this novel is
   TIME STORM; set on the title page as *TIMESTORM*.

WOLFLING [*New York*]: *A Dell Book*, [*1969*].
   Wrappers. *First printing, May 1969* on copyright page. *Dell 9633* (50¢).

Edited Fiction

Combat SF. *Garden City: Doubleday & Company, Inc., 1975 .*
  Boards. First edition so stated on copyright page. Edited, with introduction and short story
  ''Ricochet on Miza,'' by Dickson.

Rod Serling's Devils and Demons. *Toronto New York London: Bantam Books,* [*1967*].
  Wrappers. *Published February 1967* on copyright page. *Bantam Supernatural Horror
  H3324* (60¢). *Rod Serling, pseudonym.* Ghost-edited by Dickson.

Rod Serling's Triple W: Witches, Warlocks and Werewolves. *New York: Bantam Books,*
  [*1963*].
  Wrappers. *Published May 1963* on copyright page. *A Bantam Book J2623* (40¢). *Rod
  Serling, pseudonym.* Ghost-edited, with short story ''The Amulet,'' by Dickson.

Thomas Michael Disch

(b.1940)

BLACK ALICE.*Garden City: Doubleday & Company, Inc., 1968*.
First edition so stated on copyright page.*Thom Demijohn, pseudonym*. With JOHN SLADEK.

CAMP CONCENTRATION. *London: Rupert Hart-Davis, 1968*.
Boards.*First published 1968* on copyright page. Note: All examined copies have title leaf mounted on a stub.

CLARA REEVE.*New York: Alfred A. Knopf, 1975*.
Boards with cloth shelf back. First edition so stated on copyright page.*Leonie Hargrave, pseudonym*.

THE EARLY SCIENCE FICTION STORIES OF THOMAS M. DISCH.*Boston: Gregg Press, 1977*.
First Printing, June 1977 on copyright page. Note: Not issued in dust jacket.

ECHO ROUND HIS BONES. *[New York]: Published by Berkley Publishing Corporation, [1967]*.
Wrappers.*January, 1967* on copyright page.*Berkley Medallion X1349* (60¢).

ALSO:*London: Rupert Hart-Davis, 1969*. Boards.*First published 1969* on copyright page.
First hardcover edition.

FUN WITH YOUR NEW HEAD. *Garden City: Doubleday & Company, Inc., 1971*.
First edition in the United States of America on copyright page. Issued earlier in Great Britain as UNDER COMPULSION.

THE GENOCIDES. *[New York]: Published by Berkley Publishing Corporation, [1965]*.
Wrappers.*December, 1965* on copyright page.*Berkley Medallion F1170* (50¢).

ALSO:*London: Ronald Whiting & Wheaton, [1967]*. Boards.*First published in Great Britain 1967* on copyright page. First hardcover edition.

GETTING INTO DEATH. *London: Hart-Davis, MacGibbon, [1973]*.
Boards. *First published in Great Britain 1973* on copyright page. Contents differ from U.S. edition.

ALSO:*New York: Alfred A. Knopf, 1976*. Boards with cloth shelf back. First edition so stated on copyright page. Contents differ from British edition.

THE HOUSE THAT FEAR BUILT. *New York: Paperback Library, Inc., [1966]*.
Wrappers.*First Printing: March, 1966* on copyright page.*A Paperback Library Gothic 52–923* (50¢).*Cassandra Knye, pseudonym*. With JOHN SLADEK.

MANKIND UNDER THE LEASH.*New York: Ace Books, Inc., [1968]*.
Wrappers. No statement of printing on copyright page.*Ace Double G–597* (50¢). Bound with PLANET OF EXILE by Ursula K. Le Guin.

ONE HUNDRED AND TWO H BOMBS.*London: Compact Books, [1966]*.
Wrappers. No statement of printing on copyright page.*Compact SF F327* (3/6). Reissued later with seven new stories as WHITE FANG GOES DINGO.

ALSO: *[New York]: Published by Berkley Publishing Corporation, [1971]*.
Wrappers.*August, 1971* on copyright page.*A Berkley Medallion Book S2044* (75¢).
Contents differ slightly from British edition. Drops ''White Fang Goes Dingo'' and ''Leader of the Revolution'' and adds ''The Points on the Demographic Curve'' and ''5 Eggs.''

THE PRISONER.*New York: Ace Publishing Corporation*, [*1969*].
Wrappers. No statement of printing on copyright page. *Ace Book 67900* (60¢).

334.*London: MacGibbon & Kee*, [*1972*].
Boards. *First published in Great Britain 1972* on copyright page.

UNDER COMPULSION.*London: Rupert Hart-Davis, 1968*.
Boards. *First published 1968* on copyright page. Issued later in the U.S. as FUN WITH YOUR NEW HEAD.

WHITE FANG GOES DINGO AND OTHER FUNNY S.F. STORIES. [*London*]: *Arrow Books*, [*1971*].
Wrappers. *This edition, containing additional stories, first published . . . 1971* on copyright page. *Arrow Books SF 484* (6s/30p). Enlarged edition of ONE HUNDRED AND TWO H BOMBS with seven stories added.

Edited Fiction

Bad Moon Rising. *New York, Evanston, San Francisco, London: Harper & Row, Publishers*, [*1973*].
First edition so stated on copyright page. Edited, with introduction and short story "Everyday Life in the Later Roman Empire," by Disch.

New Constellations. *New York, Hagerstown, San Francisco, London: Harper & Row, Publishers*, [*1976*].
Boards with cloth shelf back. First edition so stated on copyright page. Edited, with introduction and short story in collaboration with John T. Sladek, "Mystery Diet of the Gods: A Revelation," by Disch. With CHARLES NAYLOR.

The New Improved Sun. *New York • Evanston • San Francisco • London: Harper & Row, Publishers*, [*1975*].
Boards with cloth shelf back. *First U.S. Edition* on copyright page. Edited, with introduction and satire "Pyramids For Minnesota: A Serious Proposal," by Disch.

The Ruins of Earth. *New York: G. P. Putnam's Sons*, [*1971*].
No statement of printing on copyright page. Edited, with introduction, by Disch.

Strangeness: A Collection of Curious Tales. *New York: Charles Scribner's Sons*, [*1977*].
Boards. Code *1 3 5 7 9 11 13 15 17 19 V/C 20 18 16 14 12 10 8 6 4 2* on copyright page. Edited, with introduction and short story "The Roaches," by Disch. With CHARLES NAYLOR.

Stephen R. Donaldson
(b. 1947)

THE ILLEARTH WAR. *New York: Holt, Rinehart and Winston, [1977].*
   Boards with cloth shelf back. First printing has code *1 3 5 7 9 10 8 6 4 2* on copyright page. *The Chronicles of Thomas Covenant the Unbeliever* at head of title.

LORD FOUL'S BANE. *Garden City: Nelson Doubleday, Inc., [1977].*
   Boards. No statement of printing on copyright page. Code *H 21* on page 403. Note: Issued by the Science Fiction Book Club.

THE POWER THAT PRESERVES. *New York: Holt, Rinehart and Winston, [1977].*
   Boards with cloth shelf back. First printing has code *1 3 5 7 9 10 8 6 4 2* on copyright page. *The Chronicles of Thomas Covenant the Unbeliever* at head of title.

Gardner R. Dozois
(b. 1947)

NIGHTMARE BLUE. [*New York*]: *Published by Berkley Publishing Corporation,* [*1975*].
Wrappers. *October, 1975* on copyright page. *A Berkley Medallion Book N2819* (95¢).
With GEORGE ALEC EFFINGER.

THE VISIBLE MAN. [*New York*]: *Published by Berkley Publishing Corporation,* [*1977*].
Wrappers. *December, 1977* on copyright page. *A Berkley Medallion Book 0-425-03595-6*
($1.75).

Edited Fiction

Another World. *Chicago: Follett Publishing Company,* [*1977*].
Two binding states, no priority: (A) Red boards, spine lettered in gold. Trade binding. (B)
Pictorial boards reproducing dust jacket design. Library binding. Code
123456789/828180797877 on copyright page. Edited, with introduction and commentary,
by Dozois.

Best Science Fiction Stories of the Year: Sixth Annual Collection. *New York: E. P. Dutton,*
[*1977*].
First edition so stated on copyright page. Edited, with introduction, by Dozois.

A Day in the Life. *New York Evanston San Francisco London: Harper & Row Publishers,*
[*1972*].
First edition so stated on copyright page. Edited, with introduction, by Dozois.

Future Power. [*New York: Random House, 1976.*]
Boards with cloth shelf back. First edition so stated on copyright page. Edited, with
introduction and notes, by Dozois. With JACK DANN.

Nonfiction (Dealing with the Fantasy Genre only)

The Fiction of James Tiptree, Jr., [by] Gardner Dozois. [*New York*]: *Algol Press,* [*1977*].
Wrappers. *This edition is printed in a limited edition of 1,000 copies* on copyright page.
Note: The essay was originally published as an introduction to the Gregg Press edition of
10,000 LIGHT YEARS FROM HOME by James Tiptree, Jr.

Edward John Moreton Drax Plunkett, 18th Baron Dunsany

(1878–1957)

ALEXANDER & THREE SMALL PLAYS. *London & New York: G. P. Putnam's Sons*, [*1925*].
First published October 1925 on copyright page. 250 numbered copies only.

THE AMUSEMENTS OF KHAN KHARUDA. *London & New York: G. P. Putnam's Sons*, [*1925*].
Wrappers. *First printed separately, November 1925* on copyright page. Reprint. Collected
earlier the same month in ALEXANDER & THREE SMALL PLAYS.

AT THE EDGE OF THE WORLD. *New York: Ballantine Books*, [*1970*].
Wrappers. *First Edition: March, 1970* on copyright page. *Ballantine Books 01879-6-095*
(95¢). All material reprinted from earlier books.

BEYOND THE FIELDS WE KNOW. *New York: Ballantine Books*, [*1972*].
Wrappers. *First Printing: May, 1972* on copyright page. *Ballantine Books Adult Fantasy
02599-7-125* ($1.25). All material reprinted from earlier books.

THE BLESSING OF PAN. *London & New York: G. P. Putnam's Sons*, [*1927*].
First published September 1927 on copyright page.

THE BOOK OF WONDER. *London: William Heinemann, 1912*.
Boards with cloth shelf back. No statement of printing on copyright page.

CARCASSONE. *Boston: John W. Luce & Company, n.d.* [*1916?*].
Wrappers. No statement of printing on copyright page. *LIMITED EDITION/
REPRINTED FOR/MISS VIRGINIA BERRY* on title page. Reprint. Collected earlier
in A DREAMER'S TALES.

THE CHARWOMAN'S SHADOW. *London & New York: G. P. Putnam's Sons*, [*1926*].
First published March 1926 on copyright page.

CHEEZO. *London & New York: G. P. Putnam's Sons, n.d.*
Wrappers. No statement of printing on copyright page. Reprint. Collected earlier in PLAYS
OF NEAR & FAR.

THE CHRONICLES OF RODRIGUEZ. *London & New York: G. P. Putnam's Sons*, [*1922*].
Two issues, no priority: (A) Brown cloth with paper vellum shelf back, leather spine label.
500 numbered copies signed by Dunsany and illustrator Sidney H. Sime. Limited issue. (B)
Blue cloth. Trade issue. *First printed February, 1922* on copyright page. Issued later in the
U.S. as DON RODRIGUEZ. CHRONICLES OF SHADOW VALLEY.

THE COMPROMISE OF THE KING OF THE GOLDEN ISLES. *London & New York: G. P. Putnam's
Sons, n.d.* [*but 1923*].
Wrappers. No statement of printing on copyright page. Reprint. Collected earlier in PLAYS
OF NEAR & FAR.

ALSO: *New York: Grolier Club, 1924*. Boards with cloth shelf back. No statement of
printing on copyright page. 300 numbered copies. First separate hardcover edition.

THE CURSE OF THE WISE WOMAN.*London: William Heinemann Ltd, [1933].*
First published 1933 on copyright page.

DON RODRIGUEZ. CHRONICLES OF SHADOW VALLEY.*New York and London: G. P. Putnam's Sons, 1922.*
No statement of printing on copyright page. Issued earlier in Great Britain as THE CHRONICLES OF RODRIGUEZ.

A DREAMER'S TALES. *London: George Allen & Sons, 1910.*
Three bindings, priority as listed: (A) Top edge gilt, fore and bottom edge rough cut; *GEORGE ALLEN/& SONS* stamped on spine in type with serifs. (B) Top edge gilt, fore and bottom edge untrimmed; *GEORGE ALLEN/& SONS* stamped at base of spine in *sans-serif* type. (C) Top edge plain, all edges trimmed; *GEORGE ALLEN* at base of spine. Remainder binding. Two states, probable priority as listed: (A) Title leaf integral with [*]⁴; *WITH ILLUSTRATIONS BY/S. H. SIME* on copyright page. (B) Cancel title leaf mounted on stub; *WITH ILLUSTRATIONS BY/S. H. SIME* on title page. No statement of printing on copyright page. Note: Integral title leaf occurs with bindings A and C; cancel title leaf occurs with binding B; no copies in binding C have been observed with cancel title leaf.

THE EVIL KETTLE.*London & New York: G. P. Putnam's Sons, [1925].*
Wrappers. *First printed separately, November 1925* on copyright page. Reprint. Collected earlier in ALEXANDER & THREE SMALL PLAYS.

FAME AND THE POET.*London & New York: G. P. Putnam's Sons, n.d.*
Wrappers. No statement of printing on copyright page. Reprint. Collected earlier in PLAYS OF NEAR & FAR.

FIFTY-ONE TALES. *London: Elkin Mathews, MCMXV.*
Boards with cloth shelf back. No statement of printing on copyright page. Reissued as THE FOOD OF DEATH: FIFTY-ONE TALES.

FIVE PLAYS.*London: Grant Richards, MDCCCCXIV.*
No statement of printing on copyright page.

THE FLIGHT OF THE QUEEN.*London & New York: G. P. Putnam's Sons, n.d.*
Wrappers. No statement of printing on copyright page. Reprint. Collected earlier in PLAYS OF NEAR & FAR.

THE FOOD OF DEATH: FIFTY-ONE TALES.*Hollywood, Calif.: Newcastle Publishing Company, Inc., 1974.*
Wrappers. *First printing: September, 1974* on copyright page. Reprint of FIFTY-ONE TALES.

*THE FORTRESS UNVANQUISHABLE, SAVE FOR SACNOTH.*Sheffield: The School of Art Press, 1910.*
Blue boards with cloth shelf back. Limited to 30 numbered copies. Reprint. Collected earlier in THE SWORD OF WELLERAN AND OTHER STORIES.

THE FOURTH BOOK OF JORKENS.*London, New York, Melbourne, Sydney, Cape Town: Jarrolds Publishers (London) Limited, [1947].*
Two bindings, no priority established, but probably as listed: (A) Black cloth, spine lettered in gold; (B) Pale blue-green cloth, spine lettered in black. No statement of printing on copyright page.

GODS, MEN AND GHOSTS.*New York: Dover Publications, Inc.*, [*1972*].
  Wrappers. . . . *first published by Dover Publications, Inc., in 1972* . . . on copyright page.
  All material reprinted from earlier books.

THE GODS OF PEGĀNA.*London: Elkin Mathews, 1905.*
  Boards with cloth shelf back. No statement of printing on copyright page.

A GOOD BARGAIN.*London & New York: G. P. Putnam's Sons, n.d.*
  Wrappers. No statement of printing on copyright page. Reprint. Collected earlier in PLAYS
  OF NEAR & FAR.

GUERRILLA.*London :: Toronto: William Heinemann Ltd*, [*1944*].
  First published 1944 on copyright page.

HIS FELLOW MEN.*London New York Melbourne Sydney Cape Town: Jarrolds Publishers
(London) Ltd*, [*1952*].
  First published 1952 on copyright page.

IF: A PLAY IN FOUR ACTS.*London: G. P. Putnam's Sons*, [*1921*].
  Two issues, no priority: (A) Large paper issue (not seen); (B) Cloth. Trade issue. *First
  Published September, 1921* on copyright page.

IF SHAKESPEARE LIVED TODAY. *London & New York: G. P. Putnam's Sons, n.d.* [*1923?*].
  Wrappers. Two printings, no priority established: (A) *Made and Printed in Great Britain
  at the/Botolph Printing Works, Gate Street, Kingsway, W.C. 2* on copyright page.
  (B) *Made in Great Britain/BOTOLPH PRINTING WORKS/GATE ST., KINGSWAY,
  W. C. 2* on copyright page. No statement of printing on copyright page. Reprint. Collected
  earlier in PLAYS OF NEAR & FAR.

JORKENS BORROWS ANOTHER WHISKEY.*London: Michael Joseph*, [*1954*].
  First published . . . 1954 on copyright page.

JORKENS HAS A LARGE WHISKEY.*London: Putnam*, [*1940*].
  First published September 1940 on copyright page.

JORKENS REMEMBERS AFRICA.*New York—Toronto: Longmans Green & Co., 1934.*
  First edition so stated on copyright page. Issued later in Great Britain as MR. JORKENS
  REMEMBERS AFRICA.

THE JOURNEY OF THE SOUL.*London & New York: G. P. Putnam's Sons*, [*1928*].
  Wrappers. . . . *first/printed separately September 1928* on copyright page. Reprint. Collected earlier in SEVEN MODERN COMEDIES.

THE KING OF ELFLAND'S DAUGHTER.*London & New York: G. P. Putnam's Sons*, [*1924*].
  Cloth with paper vellum shelf back, leather label on spine. *First printed May 1924* on
  copyright page. 250 numbered copies signed by Dunsany and illustrator Sidney H. Sime.

THE LAST BOOK OF WONDER.*Boston: John W. Luce & Company*, [*1916*].
  Boards with cloth shelf back. No statement of printing on copyright page. Reprint. Issued
  earlier in Great Britain as TALES OF WONDER.

THE LAST REVOLUTION.*London New York Melbourne Sydney Cape Town: Jarrolds Publishers (London) Ltd*, [*1951*].
  First published—1951 on copyright page.

THE LAUGHTER OF THE GODS. *London: G. P. Putnam's Sons, Ltd.*, [*1922*].
  Wrappers. *First published 1918/Reprinted 1922* on copyright page. Reprint. Collected
  earlier in PLAYS OF GODS AND MEN. Note: This 1922 printing is apparently the first
  separate edition.

THE LITTLE TALES OF SMETHERS. *London New York Melbourne Sydney Cape Town : Jarrolds Publishers (London) Ltd, [1952].*
 Two bindings, priority as listed: (A) Black cloth, spine lettered in gold; (B) Green boards, spine lettered in black. *First published 1952* on copyright page.

LORD ADRIAN: A PLAY IN THREE ACTS. *Waltham Saint Lawrence in Berkshire: Printed and made in Great Britain by the Golden Cockerel Press, [1933].*
 Boards with leather shelf back. No statement of printing on copyright page.
 325 numbered copies printed.

THE MAN WHO ATE THE PHOENIX. *London New York Melbourne Sydney Cape Town: Jarrolds Publishers (London) Ltd., [1949].*
 No statement of printing on copyright page.

MR. FAITHFUL: A COMEDY IN THREE ACTS. *New York Los Angeles: Samuel French/London: Samuel French Ltd, 1935.*
 Wrappers. No statement of printing on copyright page.

MR. JORKENS REMEMBERS AFRICA. *London & Toronto: William Heinemann Ltd., [1934].*
 First published 1934 on copyright page. Issued earlier in the U.S. as JORKENS REMEMBERS AFRICA.

MY TALKS WITH DEAN SPANLEY. *London :: Toronto: William Heinemann Ltd, [1936].*
 No statement of printing on copyright page.

A NIGHT AT AN INN A PLAY IN ONE ACT. *New York: The Sunwise Turn, Inc., 1916.*
 Wrappers. *1st Printing* on copyright page. *Neighborhood Playhouse Plays No. 1.* Later collected in PLAYS OF GODS AND MEN.

THE OLD FOLK OF THE CENTURIES. *London: Elkin Mathews & Marrot, [1930].*
 Boards with cloth shelf back. No statement of printing on copyright page. 900 numbered copies, the first 100 signed by the author, the last 50 for presentation.

THE OLD KING'S TALE. *London & New York: G. P. Putnam's Sons, [1925].*
 Wrappers. *First printed separately, November 1925* on copyright page. Reprint. Collected earlier in ALEXANDER & THREE SMALL PLAYS.

OVER THE HILLS AND FAR AWAY. *New York: Ballantine Books, [1974].*
 Wrappers. *First Printing: April, 1974* on copyright page. *Ballantine 23886* ($1.25). Reprint collection. All material collected from earlier books.

PLAYS FOR EARTH AND AIR. *London :: Toronto: William Heinemann Ltd, [1937].*
 First published 1937 on copyright page.

PLAYS OF GODS AND MEN. *Dublin: The Talbot Press, Limited, 1917.*
 Boards with cloth shelf back. Three issues, priority as listed: (A) Talbot Press imprint on title page; (B) Title page has a cancel with the T. Fisher Unwin imprint pasted over Talbot imprint; (C) Title page imprinted with Unwin imprint. No statement of printing on copyright page.

PLAYS OF NEAR & FAR. *London & New York: G. P. Putnam's Sons, [1922].*
 First printed December, 1922 on copyright page. 500 copies printed.

 ALSO: *New York and London: G. P. Putnam's Sons, 1923.* Boards with cloth shelf back. No statement of printing on copyright page. Adds author's ''Preface to American Edition.''

THE QUEEN'S ENEMIES. *London: G. P. Putnam's Sons, Ltd., [1922].*
 Wrappers. *First published 1918/Reprinted 1922* on copyright page. Reprint. Collected earlier in PLAYS OF GODS AND MEN. Note: This 1922 printing is apparently the first separate edition.

RORY AND BRAN. *London :: Toronto: William Heinemann Ltd*, [*1936*].
   First published 1936 on copyright page.

SELECTIONS FROM THE WRITINGS OF LORD DUNSANY. *Churchtown Dundrum: The Cuala Press, MCMXII*.
   Boards with cloth shelf back. No statement of printing. 250 copies printed.

SEVEN MODERN COMEDIES. *London & New York: G. P. Putnam's Sons*, [*1928*].
   First published September 1928 on copyright page. 250 numbered copies.

THE STORY OF MONA SHEEHY. *London :: Toronto: William Heinemann Ltd*, [*1939*].
   First published 1939 on copyright page.

THE STRANGE JOURNEYS OF COLONEL POLDERS. *London New York Melbourne Sydney Cape Town: Jarrolds Publishers London Limited*, [*1950*].
   First published 1950 on copyright page.

THE SWORD OF WELLERAN AND OTHER STORIES. *London: George Allen & Sons, mcmviii*.
   No statement of printing on copyright page.

THE SWORD OF WELLERAN AND OTHER TALES OF ENCHANTMENT. *New York: The Devin-Adair Company, 1954*.
   Boards. No statement of printing on copyright page. All stories reprinted from earlier books.

TALES OF THREE HEMISPHERES. *Boston: John W. Luce & Company*, [*1919*].
   Boards with cloth shelf back. No statement of printing on copyright page. Note: The British issue consisted of the sheets of the U.S. printing with a cancel title leaf imprinted *London: T. Fisher Unwin, Ltd., 1920* on recto. *Printed in U.S.A.* is rubber-stamped below copyright notice on verso.

TALES OF WAR. *Dublin: The Talbot Press Ltd. London: T. Fisher Unwin Ltd*, [*1918*].
   Boards with cloth shelf back. *First published in 1918* on copyright page.

TALES OF WONDER. *London: Elkin Mathews, MCMXVI*.
   Boards with cloth shelf back. *First Published . . . October, 1916* on copyright page. Issued later in the U.S. as THE LAST BOOK OF WONDER.

THE TENTS OF THE ARABS. *N.p., n.d.* [*London, 1917?*].
   Wrappers. No statement of printing. Cover title. Collected in PLAYS OF GODS AND MEN. Note: British Library assigns a tentative printing date of 1917. Possibly printed prior to collection in PLAYS OF GODS AND MEN.

TIME AND THE GODS. *London: William Heinemann, 1906*.
   Two bindings, priority as listed: (A) Brown boards with green cloth shelf back; (B) Green boards. No statement of printing on copyright page.

   ALSO: *London & New York: G. P. Putnam's Sons, 1922*. No statement of printing on copyright page. 250 numbered copies signed by Dunsany and illustrator Sidney H. Sime.

THE TRAVEL TALES OF MR. JOSEPH JORKENS. *London & New York: G. P. Putnam's Sons*, [*1931*].
   First published April 1931 on copyright page.

UNHAPPY FAR-OFF THINGS. *London: Elkin Mathews, MCMXIX*.
   Boards with cloth shelf back. No statement of printing on copyright page.

UP IN THE HILLS. *London :: Toronto: William Heinemann Ltd*, [*1935*].
   First published 1935 on copyright page.

*WHY THE MILKMAN SHUDDERS WHEN HE PERCEIVES THE DAWN. *Fostoria, Ohio: Privately Printed, 1925.*
  Wrappers. *Put into type and printed by Edwin Uhler Sowers, 2nd, in December 1925 . . .* 100 copies printed. Reprint. Collected earlier in THE LAST BOOK OF WONDER.

Autobiography

Patches of Sunlight. *London :: Toronto: William Heinemann Ltd., [1938].*
  First published 1938 on copyright page.

The Sirens Wake. *London: New York: Melbourne: Sydney: Jarrolds Publishers (London) Limited, [1945].*
  Made and printed in Great Britain . . . 1945 on copyright page.

While the Sirens Slept. *London :: New York :: Melbourne: Jarrolds (Publishers) London Limited, [1944].*
  No statement of printing on copyright page.

Reference

Biography of Lord Dunsany, [by] Mark Amory. *London: Collins, [1972].*
  Boards. *First published 1972* on copyright page.

Dunsany the Dramatist, by Edward Hale Bierstadt. *Boston: Little, Brown, and Company, 1917.*
  Published, February, 1917 on copyright page. Includes Dunsany letters and a bibliography.

  ALSO: *Boston: Little, Brown, and Company, 1919. Published, October, 1919* on copyright page. New and revised edition.

Lord Dunsany: King of Dreams . . ., by Hazel Littlefield. *New York: Exposition Press, [1959].*
  First edition so stated on copyright page.

Eric Rücker Eddison
(1882–1945)

A FISH DINNER IN MEMISON. *New York: E. P. Dutton & Co., Inc., [1941]*.
    First edition so stated on copyright page. 998 numbered copies.

THE MEZENTIAN GATE. [*Plaistow: The Curwen Press, 1958.*]
    No statement of printing on copyright page.

MISTRESS OF MISTRESSES. *London: Faber & Faber Limited, [1935]*.
    First published in January MCMXXXV on copyright page.

STYRBIORN THE STRONG. *London: Jonathan Cape, [1926]*.
    First published in mcmxxvi on copyright page.

THE WORM OUROBOROS. *London: Jonathan Cape, [1922]*.
    First published 1922 on copyright page.

Translated Fiction

Egil's Saga: Done into English Out of the Icelandic. . . . *Cambridge: At the University Press, 1930.*
    No statement of printing on copyright page. Translated, with introduction, notes, and essay, by Eddison.

George Alec Effinger
(b. 1947)

ESCAPE TO TOMORROW. *New York: Award Books*, [*1975*].
Wrappers. *First Award printing 1975* on copyright page. *An Award Science Fiction Novel AN1407* (95¢).

FELICIA. *New York: Berkley Publishing Corporation*, [*1976*].
No statement of printing on copyright page.

IRRATIONAL NUMBERS. *Garden City: Doubleday & Company, Inc.*, *1976*.
Boards. First edition so stated on copyright page.

JOURNEY INTO TERROR. *New York: Award Books*, [*1975*].
Wrappers. *First Award Printing 1975* on copyright page. *An Award Science Fiction Novel AN1436* (95¢).

LORD OF THE APES. *New York: Award Books*, [*1976*].
Wrappers. *First Award printing 1976* on copyright page. *Award Books AN1488* (95¢).

MAN THE FUGITIVE. *New York: Award Books*, [*1974*].
Wrappers. *First Award Printing 1974* on copyright page. *Award Books AN1373* (95¢). *Planet of the Apes* at head of title.

MIXED FEELINGS. *New York, Evanston, San Francisco, London: Harper & Row, Publishers*, [*1974*].
Half boards and cloth. First edition so stated on copyright page.

NIGHTMARE BLUE. [*New York*]: *Published by Berkley Publishing Corporation*, [*1975*].
Wrappers. *October, 1975* on copyright page. *A Berkley Medallion Book N2819* (95¢). With GARDNER DOZOIS.

RELATIVES. *New York, Evanston, San Francisco, London: Harper & Row, Publishers*, [*1973*].
Boards with cloth shelf back. First edition so stated on copyright page.

THOSE GENTLE VOICES. [*New York*]: *Warner Books*, [*1976*].
Wrappers. *First Printing: March, 1976* on copyright page. *Warner Books 86–113* ($1.25).

WHAT ENTROPY MEANS TO ME. *Garden City: Doubleday & Company, Inc.*, *1972*.
First edition so stated on copyright page.

Gordon Eklund

(b. 1945)

ALL TIMES POSSIBLE. *New York: DAW Books, Inc.,* [*1974*].
Wrappers. *First printing, June 1974/1 2 3 4 5 6 7 8 9* on copyright page. *DAW: sf Books No. 108 UQ1117* (95¢).

BEYOND THE RESURRECTION. *Garden City: Doubleday & Company, Inc., 1973.*
First edition so stated on copyright page.

DANCE OF THE APOCALYPSE. *Toronto • New York • London: Laser Books,* [*1976*].
Wrappers. *First published November 1976* on copyright page. *Laser Books 72046* ($1.25).

THE ECLIPSE OF DAWN. *New York: Ace Books,* [*1971*].
Wrappers. No statement of printing on copyright page. *An Ace Science Fiction Special 18630* (75¢).

FALLING TOWARD FOREVER. [*Don Mills, Ontario*]: *Laser Books,* [*1975*].
Wrappers. *First published 1975* on copyright page. *Laser Books 72010* (95¢).

THE GRAYSPACE BEAST. *Garden City: Doubleday & Company, Inc., 1976.*
Boards. First edition so stated on copyright page.

IF THE STARS ARE GODS. *New York: Published by Berkley Publishing Corporation,* [*1977*].
No statement of printing on copyright page. With GREGORY BENFORD.

INHERITORS OF EARTH. *Radnor, Pennsylvania: Chilton Book Company,* [*1974*].
First edition so stated on copyright page. With POUL ANDERSON.

SERVING IN TIME. [*Don Mills, Ontario*]: *Laser Books,* [*1975*].
Wrappers. *First published 1975* on copyright page. *Laser Books 72006* (95¢).

A TRACE OF DREAMS. *New York: Ace Books,* [*1972*].
Wrappers. No statement of printing on copyright page. *Ace Book SF 82070* (95¢).

Harlan Jay Ellison
(b. 1934)

ALL THE SOUNDS OF FEAR. [*St. Albans*]: *Panther*, [*1973*].
Wrappers. *First published in 1973* . . . on copyright page. *Panther 586 03899 X* (30p).
Abridged reprint. Collects eight of the twenty stories from ALONE AGAINST TOMORROW.

ALONE AGAINST TOMORROW. *New York: The Macmillan Company*, [*1971*].
First printing so stated on copyright page.

APPROACHING OBLIVION. *New York: Walker and Company, 1974*.
Boards. First edition so stated on copyright page.

THE BEAST THAT SHOUTED LOVE AT THE HEART OF THE WORLD. [*New York*]: *Avon*, [*1969*].
Wrappers. *First Avon Printing, July, 1969* on copyright page. *Avon V2300* (75¢). Note:
Contains changes made without the author's permission.

ALSO: *New York: Avon*, [*1970*]. Boards. Code *05 L* on page 243. No statement of printing
on copyright page. First hardcover edition. Notes: (1) Issued by the Science Fiction Book
Club. (2) The authorized text.

ALSO: [*London*]: *Millington*, [*1976*]. Boards. *First published in Great Britain in 1976* . . .
on copyright page. Abridged. Drops three stories appearing in the U.S. editions, "Along
the Scenic Route," "The Place With No Name," and "Shattered Like a Glass Goblin."
Note: Photo-offset from plates of the U.S. book club edition.

THE CITY ON THE EDGE OF FOREVER. *Toronto New York London: Bantam Books*, [*1977*].
Wrappers. *November 1977/. . .0 9 8 7 6 5 4 3 2 1* on copyright page. *A Bantam Book
11345–3* ($1.95). *Star Trek* at head of title.

THE DEADLY STREETS. *New York: Ace Books, Inc.*, [*1958*].
Wrappers. No statement of printing on copyright page. *Ace Book D–312* (35¢).

ALSO: *New York: Pyramid Books*, [*1975*]. Wrappers. *First Pyramid Edition: September
1975* on copyright page. *Pryamid V3931* ($1.25). Enlarged edition. Adds new introduction
and five stories, "Rat Hater," "The Man with the Golden Tongue," "The Hippie-
Slayer," "Sob Story" (in collaboration with Henry Slesar), and "Ship-Shape Pay-Off"
(in collaboration with Robert Silverberg).

DEATHBIRD STORIES. *New York Evanston San Francisco London: Harper & Row, Publishers*, [*1975*].
Boards with cloth shelf back. First edition so stated on copyright page.

DOOMSMAN. *New York: Belmont Books*, [*1967*].
Wrappers. *August 1967* on copyright page. *A Belmont Double Book B50–799* (50¢).
Bound with TELEPOWER by Lee Hoffman.

EARTHMAN, GO HOME. *New York: Paperback Library, Inc.*, [*1964*].
Wrappers. *First Printing: June, 1962/Second Printing: December, 1964* on copyright
page. *Paperback Library 52–508* (50¢). Reprint of ELLISON WONDERLAND.

ELLISON WONDERLAND. *New York: Paperback Library*, [*1962*].
Wrappers. *First printing: June, 1962* on copyright page. *Paperback Library Silver Edition
52–149* (50¢). Reissued as EARTHMAN, GO HOME.

ALSO: *[New York]: New American Library*, *[1974]*. Wrappers. *First Printing, August, 1974/1 2 3 4 5 6 7 8 9* on copyright page. *Signet Y6041* ($1.25). New introduction and notes by the author. Drops "The Forces That Crush" and adds "Back to the Drawing Boards."

FROM THE LAND OF FEAR. *New York: Belmont Books*, *[1967]*.
Wrappers. *December 1967* on copyright page. *Belmont Science Fiction B60–069* (60¢).

GENTLEMAN JUNKIE. *Evanston, Illinois: Regency Books*, *[1961]*.
Wrappers. *Published June 1961* on copyright page. *RB 102* (50¢).

ALSO: *New York: Pyramid Books*, *[1975]*. Wrappers. *First Pyramid Edition: August 1975* on copyright page. *Pyramid V3933* ($1.25). Revised edition. Preface replaced with new introduction. Drops "The Time of the Eye" and adds "Turnpike." Some stories revised.

I HAVE NO MOUTH AND I MUST SCREAM. *New York: Pyramid Books*, *[1967]*.
Wrappers. *First printing April, 1967* on copyright page. *Pyramid Science Fiction X–1611* (60¢).

THE JUVIES. *New York: Ace Books, Inc.*, *[1961]*.
Wrappers. No statement of printing on copyright page. *Ace D–513* (35¢).

LOVE AIN'T NOTHING BUT SEX MISSPELLED. *New York: Trident Press*, *[1968]*.
Boards with cloth shelf back. No statement of printing on copyright page.

ALSO: *New York: Pyramid Books*, *[1976]*. Wrappers. *First Pyramid edition: February 1976* on copyright page. *Pyramid M3798* ($1.75). New edition. Drops old introduction and adds a new one; drops nine stories and adds one story and two nonfiction pieces.

THE MAN WITH NINE LIVES. *New York: Ace Books, Inc.*, *[1960]*.
Wrappers. No statement of printing on copyright page. *Ace Double Novel Books D–413* (35¢). Bound with A TOUCH OF INFINITY by Ellison.

NO DOORS, NO WINDOWS. *New York: Pyramid Books*, *[1975]*.
Wrappers. *Pyramid edition published November 1975* on copyright page. *Pyramid A3799* ($1.50).

OVER THE EDGE. *New York: Belmont Books*, *[1970]*.
Wrappers. *May 1970* on copyright page. *Belmont B75–1091* (75¢).

PAINGOD AND OTHER DELUSIONS. *New York: Pyramid Books*, *[1965]*.
Wrappers. *First printing, December 1965* on copyright page. *Pyramid Science Fiction R–1270* (50¢). Note: Second printing (not so marked) retains the first printing notice but bears stock number X–1991 and the price is increased to 60¢.

ALSO: *New York: Pyramid Books*, *[1975]*. Wrappers. *Pyramid edition published March 1975* on copyright page. *Pyramid V3646* ($1.25). Enlarged edition. Adds new introduction and short story "Sleeping Dogs." Some story notes revised.

PARTNERS IN WONDER. *New York: Walker and Company*, *1971*.
Boards. *First published in the United States of America in 1971* on copyright page. Short stories by Ellison, most in collaboration with others.

PHOENIX WITHOUT ASHES. *Greenwich, Connecticut: Fawcett Publications, Inc.*, *[1975]*.
Wrappers. *First printing: February 1975/1 2 3 4 5 6 7 8 9 10* on copyright page. *Fawcett Gold Medal M3188* (95¢). With EDWARD BRYANT.

ROCKABILLY. *Greenwich, Conn.: Fawcett Publications, Inc.*, *[1961]*.
Wrappers. *First printing October 1961* on copyright page. *Gold Medal Book s1161* (35¢). Reprinted as SPIDER KISS.

RUMBLE. *New York: Pyramid Books*, [*1958*].
Wrappers. *Pyramid Books Edition 1958* on copyright page. *Pyramid Books G352* (35¢).
Reissued as WEB OF THE CITY.

SEX GANG. *N.p.: Nightstand Books*, [*1959*].
Wrappers. No statement of printing on copyright page. *NB 1503 aSn* (50¢). *Paul Merchant, pseudonym.*

SPIDER KISS. *New York: Pyramid Books*, [*1975*].
Wrappers. *Pyramid edition published July 1975* on copyright page. *Pyramid V3883* ($1.25). Originally published as ROCKABILLY. Textural revisions and new "Author's Note."

THE TIME OF THE EYE. [*Frogmore, St Albans*]: *Panther*, [*1974*].
Wrappers. *First published in Great Britain in 1974* on copyright page. *Panther 586 03935 X* (35p). Abridged reprint. Collects twelve of the twenty stories from ALONE AGAINST TOMORROW.

A TOUCH OF INFINITY. *New York: Ace Books, Inc.*, [*1960*].
Wrappers. No statement of printing on copyright page. *Ace Double Novel Books D-413* (35¢). Bound with THE MAN WITH NINE LIVES by Ellison.

WEB OF THE CITY. *New York: Pyramid Books*, [*1975*].
Wrappers. *New Pyramid edition: December 1975* on copyright page. *Pyramid A4061* ($1.50). Reissue of RUMBLE with new introduction by Ellison.

Autobiography:

Memos from Purgatory. *Evanston, Ill.: Regency Books*, [*1961*].
Wrappers. *Published September 1961* on copyright page. *Regency Books RB 106* (50¢).

ALSO: [*Reseda, California: Powell Publications, 1969.*] Wrappers. No statement of printing on copyright page. *Powell Fact Book PP154* (95¢). Adds new introduction "Memo 69."

ALSO: *New York: Pyramid Books*, [*1975*]. Wrappers. *Pyramid edition published April 1975* on copyright page. *Pyramid V3706* ($1.25). Adds new introduction "Memo '75."

Edited Fiction

Again, Dangerous Visions. *Garden City: Doubleday & Company, Inc.*, *1972.*
Contrary to this publisher's normal practice, no printing statement appears on copyright page. 6500 copies printed. Two printings, priority as listed: (A) Code *N7* at base of right margin on page 760 (approximately 4500 copies printed); (B) Code *N40* at base of right margin on page 760 (approximately 2000 copies printed). Drops a black "spot" (the title of the story) preceding *Gahan Wilson* in table of contents, page viii, line 10. Edited, with introductions, by Ellison. Note: it is rumored that an earlier state of this book exists with code *N3* at base of right margin on page 760. Reportedly 10 to 20 copies were produced. No such copy has been observed nor has any correspondent reliably confirmed same.

Dangerous Visions. *Garden City: Doubleday & Company, Inc.*, *1967.*
First edition so stated on copyright page. Edited, with introductions and short story "The Prowler in the City at the Edge of the World," by Ellison.

ALSO: Dangerous Visions #1 [through #3]. [*New York*]: *Published by Berkley Publishing Corporation*, [*1969*]. Three volumes as follows: (1) *May, 1969* on copyright page. *A*

Berkley Medallion Book N1686 (95¢). (2)*June, 1969* on copyright page. *A Berkley Medallion Book N1704* (95¢). (3)*July, 1969* on copyright page. *A Berkley Medallion Book N1714* (95¢). New introductions by Ellison in volumes two and three.

Nightshade & Damnations, by Gerald Kersh. *Greenwich, Conn.: Fawcett Publications, Inc., [1968]*.
    Wrappers. No statement of printing on copyright page. *A Fawcett Gold Medal Book R1887* (60¢). Edited, with introduction, by Ellison.

Reference

The Book of Ellison, edited by Andrew Porter. *[New York]: Algol Press, [1978]*.
    2000 copies printed. Two issues, no priority: (A) Cloth. 200 copies. (B) Wrappers. 1800 copies. *First Edition, October 1978* on copyright page. Material by and about Ellison, including a checklist of his non-fiction writings by Leslie Kay Swigart.

Harlan Ellison: A Bibliographical Checklist, compiled by Leslie Kay Swigart. *Dallas: Williams Publishing Co., 1973*.
    Wrappers. No statement of printing on copyright page. 1000 numbered copies. Note: An updated checklist of Ellison's writings compiled by Swigart appears in *The Magazine of Fantasy and Science Fiction*, July 1977.

Harlan Ellison: Unrepentant Harlequin, [by] George Edgar Slusser. *San Bernardino, California: R. Reginald, The Borgo Press, MCMLXXVII*.
    Wrappers. *First Edition———April, 1977* on copyright page. *The Milford Series Popular Writers of Today Volume Six* at head of title.

George Allan England
(1877–1936)

ADVENTURE ISLE. *New York & London: The Century Co.*, [*1926*].
No statement of printing on copyright page.

THE AFTERGLOW. *New York: Avalon Books*, [*1967*].
No statement of printing on copyright page. Abridged reissue. Last half of book three of DARKNESS AND DAWN.

THE AIR TRUST. *St. Louis: Published by Phil Wagner*, [*1915*].
No statement of printing on copyright page.

THE ALIBI. *Boston: Small, Maynard & Company Publishers*, [*1916*].
No statement of printing on copyright page.

BEYOND THE GREAT OBLIVION. *New York: Avalon Books*, [*1965*].
No statement of printing on copyright page. Abridged reissue. First half of book two of DARKNESS AND DAWN.

CURSED. *Boston: Small, Maynard & Company Publishers*, [*1919*].
No statement of printing on copyright page.

DARKNESS AND DAWN. *Boston: Small, Maynard and Company Publishers*, [*1914*].
No statement of printing on copyright page. Reprinted in five volumes as DARKNESS AND DAWN, BEYOND THE GREAT OBLIVION, THE PEOPLE OF THE ABYSS, OUT OF THE ABYSS, and THE AFTERGLOW.

ALSO: *New York: Avalon Books*, [*1965*]. No statement of printing on copyright page. Abridged reissue. Book one of DARKNESS AND DAWN.

THE FLYING LEGION. *Chicago: A. C. McClurg & Co.*, *1920*.
Published July, 1920 on copyright page.

THE GIFT SUPREME. *New York: George H. Doran Company*, [*1916*].
No statement of printing on copyright page.

THE GOLDEN BLIGHT. *New York: The H. K. Fly Company Publishers*, [*1916*].
No statement of printing on copyright page.

THE GREATER CRIME. *London, New York, Toronto and Melbourne: Cassell and Company, Ltd.*, [*1917*].
First published 1917 on copyright page.

KEEP OFF THE GRASS. *Boston: Publishers Small Maynard & Company*, [*1919*].
Boards. No statement of printing on copyright page.

OUT OF THE ABYSS. *New York: Avalon Books*, [*1967*].
No statement of printing on copyright page. Abridged reissue. First half of book three of DARKNESS AND DAWN.

THE PEOPLE OF THE ABYSS. *New York: Avalon Books*, [*1966*].
No statement of printing on copyright page. Abridged reissue. Second half of book two of DARKNESS AND DAWN.

POD, BENDER & CO. *New York: Robert M. McBride & Company, 1916.*
Published October, 1916 on copyright page.

Translated Fiction

Their Son, the Necklace, by Eduardo Zamacois. *New York: Boni and Liveright, 1919.*
No statement of printing on copyright page. Translated with preface, by England.

Philip José Farmer
(b. 1918)

THE ADVENTURE OF THE PEERLESS PEER. *Boulder, Colorado: The Aspen Press, 1974.*
First edition so stated on copyright page. *John H. Watson, M.D., pseudonym.*

THE ALLEY GOD. *New York: Ballantine Books, [1962].*
Wrappers. No statement of printing on copyright page. *An Original Ballantine Book F 588* (50¢).

ALSO: *London: Sidgwick & Jackson, [1970].* Boards. *First Published in Great Britain 1970* on copyright page. First hardcover edition.

BEHIND THE WALLS OF TERRA. *New York: Ace Publishing Corporation, [1970].*
Wrappers. No statement of printing on copyright page. *Ace Book 71135* (75¢).

BLOWN OR SKETCHES AMONG THE RUINS OF MY MIND. *North Hollywood: An Essex House Original, [1969].*
Wrappers. No statement of printing on copyright page. *Essex House 020139* ($1.95).

THE BOOK OF PHILIP JOSÉ FARMER. *New York: DAW Books, Inc., [1973].*
Wrappers. *First printing, July 1973/1 2 3 4 5 6 7 8 9* on copyright page. *DAW: sf Books No. 63 UQ1063* (95¢).

ALSO: *[Morley]: The Elmfield Press, [1976].* Boards. *Published in the United Kingdom in 1976* on copyright page. First hardcover edition.

CACHE FROM OUTER SPACE. *New York: Ace Books, Inc., [1962].*
Wrappers. No statement of printing on copyright page. *Ace Double F–165* (40¢). Bound with THE CELESTIAL BLUEPRINT by Farmer.

THE CELESTIAL BLUEPRINT. *New York: Ace Books, Inc., [1962].*
Wrappers. No statement of printing on copyright page. *Ace Double F–165* (40¢). Bound with CACHE FROM OUTER SPACE.

DARE. *New York: Ballantine Books, [1965].*
Wrappers. *First Ballantine Printing: February 1965* on copyright page. *A Ballantine Science Fiction Original U2193* (50¢).

THE DARK DESIGN. *New York: Published by Berkley Publishing Corporation, [1977].*
No statement of printing on copyright page.

THE DAY OF THE TIMESTOP. *New York: Lancer Books, [1968].*
Wrappers. *A Lancer Book • 1968* on copyright page. *Lancer Books 73–715* (60¢). Reissue of A WOMAN A DAY.

DOC SAVAGE: HIS APOCALYPTIC LIFE. *Garden City: Doubleday & Company, Inc., 1973.*
First edition so stated on copyright page.

ALSO: *Toronto New York London: Bantam Books, [1975].* Wrappers. *Bantam Book/July 1975* on copyright page. *A Bantam Book Q8834* ($1.25). Corrected and enlarged edition.

DOWN IN THE BLACK GANG. *Garden City: Nelson Doubleday, Inc., [1971].*
Two printings, priority as listed: (A) Code *18 M* on page 211; (B) Code *D 44* on page 214. No statement of printing on copyright page. Note: Issued by the Science Fiction Book Club.

THE FABULOUS RIVERBOAT. *New York: G. P. Putnam's Sons*, [1971].
Boards. No statement of printing on copyright page.

A FEAST UNKNOWN. *North Hollywood, Calif.: An Essex House Original*, [1969].
Wrappers. No statement of printing on copyright page. *EH 0121* ($1.95). Note: Subtitle reads *Volume IX of The Memoirs of Lord Grandrith/edited by Philip José Farmer*.

ALSO: [*Kansas City*]: *The Fokker D–LXIX Press A Subsidiary of Acme Zeppelin Company*, [1975]. 1000 copies printed. Two binding states, no priority: (A) Boards. Note: No limitation notice appears in these copies. In a letter to the compiler, undated but circa 6 June, 1977, the publisher states: "Two hundred of these were bound in hard covers and signed by the author and artist [Richard Corben] (with the exception of those which were received by the same)." First hardcover edition. (B) Wrappers. 800 copies. No statement of printing on copyright page.

FIRE AND THE NIGHT. *Evanston, Illinois: Regency Books*, [1962].
Wrappers. *Published April, 1962* on copyright page. *Regency RB 118* (50¢).

FLESH. [*New York*]: *Beacon Books*, [1960].
Wrappers. *First printing —1960* on page [1]. *Beacon Book No. 277* (35¢).

ALSO: *Garden City: Doubleday & Company, Inc.*, *1968*. First edition so stated on copyright page. First hardcover edition. Revised text.

FLIGHT TO OPAR. *New York: DAW Books, Inc.*, [1976].
Wrappers. *First printing, June 1976/1 2 3 4 5 6 7 8 9* on copyright page. *DAW: sf Books No. 197 UW1238* ($1.50).

THE GATE OF TIME. *New York: Belmont Books*, [1966].
Wrappers. *October 1966* on copyright page. *Belmont Science Fiction B50–717* (50¢).

THE GATES OF CREATION. *New York: Ace Books, Inc.*, [1966].
Wrappers. No statement of printing on copyright page. *Ace Book F–412* (40¢).

THE GREEN ODYSSEY. *New York: Ballantine Books*, [1957].
Two bindings, no priority: (A) Cloth; (B) Wrappers. *Ballantine Books 210* (35¢). No statement of printing on copyright page.

HADON OF ANCIENT OPAR. *New York: DAW Books, Inc.*, [1974].
Wrappers. *First printing, April, 1974/1 2 3 4 5 6 7 8 9* on copyright page. *DAW: sf Books No. 100 UY1107* ($1.25).

THE IMAGE OF THE BEAST. *North Hollywood: An Essex House Original*, [1968].
Wrappers. No statement of printing on copyright page. *EH0108* ($1.95).

INSIDE OUTSIDE. *New York: Ballantine Books*, [1964].
Wrappers. No statement of printing on copyright page. *Ballantine Books U2192*. (50¢).

IRONCASTLE. *New York: DAW Books, Inc.*, [1976].
Wrappers. *First printing, March 1976/1 2 3 4 5 6 7 8 9* on copyright page. *DAW: sf Books No. 187 UY1225* ($1.25). Note: Translated and adapted by Farmer from the French of J.-H. Rosney Aîné.

THE LAVALITE WORLD. *New York: Ace Books*, [1977].
Wrappers. *First Ace Printing: December 1977* on copyright page. *Ace 47420–9* ($1.75).

LORD OF THE TREES. *New York: Ace Books*, [1970].
Wrappers. No statement of printing on copyright page. *Ace Double 51375* (75¢). Bound with THE MAD GOBLIN by Farmer.

LORD TYGER. *Garden City: Doubleday & Company, Inc., 1970.*
First edition so stated on copyright page.

LOVE SONG. *North Hollywood: A Brandon House Book, [1970].*
Wrappers. No statement of printing on copyright page. *Brandon House 9BH-6134* ($1.95).

THE LOVERS. *New York: Ballantine Books, [1961].*
Wrappers. No statement of printing on copyright page. *Ballantine Books 507 K* (35¢).

THE MAD GOBLIN. *New York: Ace Books, [1970].*
Wrappers. No statement of printing on copyright page. *Ace Double 51375* (75¢). Bound with LORD OF THE TREES by Farmer.

THE MAKER OF UNIVERSES. *New York: Ace Books Inc., [1965].*
Wrappers. No statement of printing on copyright page. *Ace Book F–367* (40¢).

ALSO: *[New York & London: Garland Publishing, Inc., 1975.]* No statement of printing on copyright page. First hardcover edition. Notes: (1) Photographically reproduced from the 1970 Sphere Books edition. (2) Not issued in dust jacket.

NIGHT OF LIGHT. *[New York]: Published by Berkley Publishing Corporation, [1966].*
Wrappers. *June, 1966* on copyright page. *Berkley Medallion F 1248* (50¢).

ALSO: *[New York & London: Garland Publishing, Inc., 1975.]* No statement of printing on copyright page. First hardcover edition. Notes: (1) Photographically reproduced from the 1966 Berkley edition. (2) Not issued in dust jacket.

THE OTHER LOG OF PHILEAS FOGG. *New York: DAW Books, Inc., [1973].*
Wrappers. *First Printing, March 1973* on copyright page. Also, *First Printing* [through] *Tenth Printing* set in ten lines following the dedication on copyright page. *DAW: sf Books No. 48 UQ 1048* (95¢).

A PRIVATE COSMOS. *New York: Ace Books, Inc., [1968].*
Wrappers. No statement of printing on copyright page. *An Ace Book G–724* (50¢).

THE STONE GOD AWAKENS. *New York: Ace Books, [1970].*
Wrappers. No statement of printing on copyright page. *Ace Book 78650* (75¢).

STRANGE RELATIONS. *New York: Ballantine Books, [1960].*
Wrappers. No statement of printing on copyright page. *Ballantine Books 391 K* (35¢).

ALSO: *London: Victor Gollancz Ltd, 1964.* Boards. No statement of printing on copyright page. First hardcover edition.

TARZAN ALIVE. *Garden City: Doubleday & Company, Inc., 1972.*
First edition so stated on copyright page.

TIME'S LAST GIFT. *New York: Ballantine Books, [1972].*
Wrappers. *First Printing: January, 1972* on copyright page. *Ballantine Books Science Fiction 02468–0–095* (95¢).

ALSO: *New York: Ballantine Books, [1977].* Wrappers. *Revised Edition:/ First Printing: July 1977* on copyright page. *Ballantine 25843* ($1.50). Revised text.

TIMESTOP! *New York: Lancer Books, [1970].*
Wrappers. No statement of printing on copyright page. *Lancer Books 74616–075* (75¢). Reissue of A WOMAN A DAY.

TO YOUR SCATTERED BODIES GO. *New York: G. P. Putnam's Sons*, [*1971*].
No statement of printing on copyright page.

TONGUES OF THE MOON. *New York: Pyramid Books*, [*1964*].
Wrappers. *First printing, August 1964* on copyright page. *Pyramid Books R–1055* (50¢).

TRAITOR TO THE LIVING. *New York: Ballantine Books*, [*1973*].
Wrappers. *First Printing: November, 1973* on copyright page. *Ballantine Books 23613* ($1.25).

VENUS ON THE HALF-SHELL. [*New York*]: *A Dell Book*, [*1975*].
Wrappers. *First printing—February 1975* on copyright page. *Dell 6149* (95¢). *Kilgore Trout, pseudonym.*

THE WIND WHALES OF ISHMAEL. *New York: Ace Books*, [*1971*].
Wrappers. No statement of printing on copyright page. *Ace Book 89237* (75¢).

A WOMAN A DAY. [*New York*]: *Beacon Books*, [*1960*].
Wrappers. *First printing—1960* on page [1]. *Beacon Book No. 291 (Galaxy Novel #43)* (35¢). Reissued as THE DAY OF THE TIMESTOP and later as TIMESTOP!

Edited Fiction

Mother Was a Lovely Beast. *Radnor, Pennsylvania: Chilton Book Company*, [*1974*].
First edition so stated on copyright page. Edited, with foreword, afterword, notes, and pseudoautobiography "Extracts from the Memoirs of 'Lord Greystoke,' " by Farmer.

Reference

The First Editions of Philip Jose Farmer, [by Lawrence Knapp]. [*Menlo Park, California: David G. Turner, 1976.*]
Wrappers. *First edition/June, 1976* on copyright page.

Charles Grandison Finney

(b. 1905)

THE CIRCUS OF DR. LAO. *New York: Published by the Viking Press, 1935.*
Published July 1935 on copyright page.

THE GHOSTS OF MANACLE. *New York: Pyramid Books,* [*1964*].
Wrappers. *First printing, July 1964* on copyright page. *Pyramid Book R–1042* (50¢).

PAST THE END OF THE PAVEMENT. *New York: Henry Holt and Company,* [*1939*].
No statement of printing on copyright page. Reissued as THIS IS PAST THE END OF THE
PAVEMENT: THE STORY OF TOM AND WILLIE FARRIER.

THE UNHOLY CITY. *New York: The Vanguard Press, 1937.*
No statement of printing on copyright page.

ALSO: *New York: Pyramid Books,* [*1968*]. Wrappers. *Pyramid edition published June,
1968* on copyright page. *Pyramid Books X–1818* (60¢). Enlarged edition. Adds ''The
Magician Out of Manchuria.''

Walter Braden Finney
(b. 1911)

ASSAULT ON A QUEEN. *New York: Simon and Schuster, 1959.*
Boards with cloth shelf back. First printing so stated on copyright page. *Jack Finney, pseudonym.*

THE BODY SNATCHERS. *[New York]: A Dell First Edition, [1955].*
Wrappers. No statement of printing on copyright page. *Dell First Edition 42 (25¢). Jack Finney, pseudonym.* Note: The July 1961 Dell reprint bears cover title *The Invasion of the Body Snatchers.*

ALSO: *London: Eyre & Spottiswoode, 1955.* Boards. No statement of printing on copyright page. First hardcover edition.

THE CLOCK OF TIME. *London: Eyre & Spottiswoode, 1958.*
Boards. *First published in Great Britain 1958* on copyright page. *Jack Finney, pseudonym.* Issued earlier in the U.S. as THE THIRD LEVEL.

5 AGAINST THE HOUSE. *Garden City: Doubleday & Company, Inc., 1954.*
First edition so stated on copyright page. *Jack Finney, pseudonym.*

GOOD NEIGHBOR SAM. *New York: Simon and Schuster, 1963.*
Boards with cloth shelf back. First printing so stated on copyright page. *Jack Finney, pseudonym.*

THE HOUSE OF NUMBERS. *[New York]: A Dell First Edition, [1957].*
Wrappers. *First printing —May, 1957* on copyright page. *Dell First Edition A139 (25¢). Jack Finney, pseudonym.*

ALSO: *London: Eyre & Spottiswoode, 1957.* Boards. No statement of printing on copyright page. First hardcover edition.

I LOVE GALESBURG IN THE SPRINGTIME. *New York: Simon and Schuster, 1963.*
First printing so stated on copyright page. *Jack Finney, pseudonym.*

THE INVASION OF THE BODY SNATCHERS. See THE BODY SNATCHERS.

MARION'S WALL. *New York: Simon and Schuster, [1973].*
First printing so stated on copyright page. *Jack Finney, pseudonym.*

THE NIGHT PEOPLE. *Garden City: Doubleday & Company, Inc., 1977.*
Boards with cloth shelf back. First edition so stated on copyright page. *Jack Finney, pseudonym.*

*TELEPHONE ROULETTE: A COMEDY IN ONE ACT. *Chicago: Dramatic Pub. Co., [1956].*
Wrappers. Note: U.S. Copyright Office records with comment:''Author states is a dramatization of the short story 'Take a Number.' ''

THE THIRD LEVEL. *New York Toronto: Rinehart & Company, Inc., [1957].*
Boards. First printing has *R* on copyright page. *Jack Finney, pseudonym.* Issued later in Great Britain as THE CLOCK OF TIME.

TIME AND AGAIN. *New York: Simon and Schuster*, [*1970*].
   First printing so stated on copyright page. *Jack Finney, pseudonym.* Note: Book of the Month Club printing retains first printing statement on copyright page but can be distinguished from the trade printing as follows: (A) Trade printing: No small embossed square in lower right corner of rear cover; dust jacket does not note the title as a book club selection. (B) Book club issue: Small embossed square in lower right corner of rear cover; at head of front dust jacket flap *BOOK-OF-THE-MONTH-CLUB*SELECTION* is printed in red ink.

THE WOODROW WILSON DIME. *New York: Simon and Schuster*, [*1968*].
   First printing so stated on copyright page. *Jack Finney, pseudonym.*

Homer Eon Flint

(189?–1924)

THE BLIND SPOT. *Philadelphia: Prime Press*, [*1951*].
First edition so stated on copyright page. With AUSTIN HALL.

THE DEVOLUTIONIST AND THE EMANCIPATRIX. *New York: Ace Books, Inc.*, [*1965*].
Wrappers. No statement of printing on copyright page. *Ace Science Fiction Classic F–355*
(40¢).

THE LORD OF DEATH AND THE QUEEN OF LIFE. *New York: Ace Books, Inc.*, [*1965*].
Wrappers. No statement of printing on copyright page. *Ace Science Fiction Classic F–345*
(40¢).

Alan Dean Foster
(b. 1946)

BLOODHYPE. *New York: Ballantine Books*, [1973].
Wrappers. *First Printing: March, 1973* on copyright page. *Ballantine Books Science Fiction 03163–6–125* ($1.25).

DARK STAR. *New York: Ballantine Books*, [1974].
Wrappers. *First Printing: October, 1974* on copyright page. *Ballantine Novel 24267* ($1.25).

THE END OF THE MATTER. *New York: Ballantine Books*, [1977].
Wrappers. *First Edition: November 1977* on copyright page. *Ballantine 25861* ($1.75).

ICERIGGER. *New York: Ballantine Books*, [1974].
Wrappers. *First Printing: March, 1974* on copyright page. *Ballantine Books Science Fiction 23836* ($1.25).

ALSO: *[London]: New English Library*, [1976]. Boards. *First published in Great Britain . . . in 1976* on copyright page. First hardcover edition.

LUANA. *New York: Ballantine Books*, [1974].
Wrappers. *First Printing: February, 1974* on copyright page. *Ballantine 23793* ($1.25).

MIDWORLD. *Garden City: Nelson Doubleday, Inc.*, [1975].
Boards. Code *41 R* on page 177. No statement of printing on copyright page. Note: Issued by the Science Fiction Book Club.

ORPHAN STAR. *New York: Ballantine Books*, [1977].
Wrappers. *First Edition: March 1977* on copyright page. *Ballantine 25507* ($1.50).

STAR TREK LOG ONE. *New York: Ballantine Books*, [1974].
Wrappers. *First Printing: June, 1974* on copyright page. *Ballantine 24014* (95¢).

ALSO: *Leyden, Mass.: Aeonian Press*, [1975]. First edition so stated on copyright page. First hardcover edition.

STAR TREK LOG TWO. *New York: Ballantine Books*, [1974].
Wrappers. *First Printing: September, 1974* on copyright page. *Ballantine 24184* (95¢).

ALSO: *Leyden, Mass.: Aeonian Press*, [1975]. First edition so stated on copyright page. First hardcover edition.

STAR TREK LOG THREE. *New York: Ballantine Books*, [1975].
Wrappers. *First Printing: January, 1975* on copyright page. *Ballantine/Science Fiction 24260* ($1.25).

ALSO: *Leyden, Mass.: Aeonian Press*, [1975]. First edition so stated on copyright page. First hardcover edition.

STAR TREK LOG FOUR. *New York: Ballantine Books*, [1975].
Wrappers. *First Printing: March, 1975* on copyright page. *Ballantine/Science Fiction 24435* ($1.25).

ALSO: *Leyden, Mass.: Aeonian Press*, [1975]. First edition so stated on copyright page. First hardcover edition.

STAR TREK LOG FIVE. *New York: Ballantine Books*, [*1975*].
Wrappers. *First Printing: August, 1975* on copyright page. *Ballantine/Science Fiction 24532* ($1.25).

ALSO:*Leyden, Mass.: Aeonian Press*, [*1976*]. First edition so stated on copyright page. First hardcover edition.

STAR TREK LOG SIX.*New York: Ballantine Books*, [*1976*].
Wrappers. *First Edition: March, 1976* on copyright page. *Ballantine Science Fiction 24655* ($1.50).

ALSO:*Leyden, Mass.: Aeonian Press*, [*1976*]. First edition so stated on copyright page. First hardcover edition.

STAR TREK LOG SEVEN.*New York: Ballantine Books*, [*1976*].
Wrappers. *First Edition: June, 1976* on copyright page. *Ballantine Science Fiction 24965* ($1.50).

ALSO: *Mattituck, [New York]: Aeonian Press*, [*1977*]. *First edition, 1976* . . . on copyright page. First hardcover edition. Note: Despite publisher's statement of printing on copyright page, this edition followed Ballantine's and was issued in November 1977.

STAR TREK LOG EIGHT. *New York: Ballantine Books*, [*1976*].
Wrappers. *First Edition: August, 1976* on copyright page. *Ballantine Science Fiction 25141* ($1.50).

STAR TREK LOG NINE. *New York: Ballantine Books*, [*1977*].
Wrappers. *First Edition: February 1977* on copyright page. *Ballantine Science Fiction 25557* ($1.50).

STAR WARS. *New York: Ballantine Books*, [*1976*].
Wrappers. *First Edition: December 1976* on copyright page. *Ballantine Books 26061* ($1.50). *George Lucas, pseudonym.*

ALSO: New York: Ballantine Books, [*1977*]. Boards. Three printings, priority as listed: (A) Code *S27* on page 183; (B) Code *S31* on page 183; (C) Code *S33* on page 183. No statement of printing on copyright page. First hardcover edition. Note: Issued by the Science Fiction Book Club.

THE TAR-AIYM KRANG. *New York: Ballantine Books*, [*1972*].
Wrappers. *First Printing: March, 1972* on copyright page. *Ballantine Books Science Fiction 02547–4–095* (95¢).

WITH FRIENDS LIKE THESE . . .*New York: Ballantine Books*, [*1977*].
Wrappers. *First Edition: December 1977* on copyright page. *Ballantine 25701* ($1.75).

Jerrold David Friedman
(b. 1944)

BATTLE FOR THE PLANET OF THE APES. *New York: Award Books*, [*1973*].
Wrappers. No statement of printing on copyright page. *Aware Books AN1139* (95¢). *David Gerrold, pseudonym*. Note: Novelization of a screenplay by John William Corrington and Joyce Hooper Corrington.

THE FLYING SORCERERS. *New York: Ballantine Books*, [*1971*].
Wrappers. *First Printing: August, 1971* on copyright page. *Ballantine Books Science Fiction 02331–5–095* ($1.95). *David Gerrold, pseudonym*. With LARRY NIVEN.

THE MAN WHO FOLDED HIMSELF. *New York: Random House*, [*1973*].
Boards. First edition so stated on copyright pate. *David Gerrold, pseudonym*.

MOONSTAR ODYSSEY. [*New York*]: *New American Library*, [*1977*].
Wrappers. *First Signet Printing, February, 1977/1 2 3 4 5 6 7 8 9* on copyright page. *Signet 451–W7372* ($1.50). *David Gerrold, pseudonym*.

SPACE SKIMMER. *New York: Ballantine Books*, [*1972*].
Wrappers. *First Printing; June, 1972* on copyright page. *Ballantine Books Science Fiction 02644–6–095* (95¢). *David Gerrold, pseudonym*.

THE TROUBLE WITH TRIBBLES. *New York: Ballantine Books*, [*1973*].
Wrappers. *First Printing: May, 1973* on copyright page. *Ballantine Books 23402–2–150* ($1.50). *David Gerrold, pseudonym*. Note: Includes text of the "revised final draft" of "The Trouble With Tribbles" as well as the premise and outline for the Star Trek episode. Also nonfiction material.

WHEN HARLIE WAS ONE. *Garden City: Nelson Doubleday, Inc.*, [*1972*].
Boards. No statement of printing on copyright page. Code *C22* on page 246. *David Gerrold, pseudonym*. Note: Issued by the Science Fiction Book Club.

WITH A FINGER IN MY I. *New York: Ballantine Books*, [*1972*].
Wrappers. *First Printing: June, 1972* on copyright page. *Ballantine Books Science Fiction 02645–4–095* (95¢). *David Gerrold, pseudonym*.

YESTERDAY'S CHILDREN. [*New York*]: *A Dell Book*, [*1972*].
Wrappers. *First printing—July 1972* on copyright page. *Dell 9780* (95¢). *David Gerrold, pseudonym*.

ALSO: *London: Faber and Faber*, [*1974*]. Boards. *First published in Great Britain in 1974* on copyright page. First hardcover edition.

Edited Fiction

Alternities. [*New York*]: *A Dell Book*, [*1974*].
Wrappers. *First printing—July 1974* on copyright page. *Dell 3195* (95¢). Edited, with introduction, by Friedman. *David Gerrold, pseudonym*. With STEPHEN GOLDIN.

Ascents of Wonder. *New York: Popular Library*, [*1977*].
Wrappers. *December, 1977* on copyright page. *Popular Library Science Fiction 0–445–04128–5* ($1.50). Edited, with introduction, by Friedman. *David Gerrold, pseudonym*. With STEPHEN GOLDIN.

Generation. [*New York*]: *A Dell Book*, [*1972*].
  Wrappers. *First printing, July, 1972* on copyright page. *Dell 2833* (95¢). Edited, with introduction, notes and short story "All Of Them Were Empty," by Friedman. *David Gerrold, pseudonym.* With STEPHEN GOLDIN.

Protostars. *New York • London: Ballantine Books*, [*1971*].
  Wrappers. *First Printing: October, 1971* on copyright page. *Ballantine Books Science Fiction 02393–5–095* (95¢). Edited, with introduction, notes, and short story "Afternoon With a Dead Bus," by Friedman. *David Gerrold, pseudonym.* With STEPHEN GOLDIN.

Science Fiction Emphasis I. *New York: Ballantine Books*, [*1974*].
  Wrappers. *First Printing: May, 1974* on copyright page. *Ballantine 23962* ($1.25). Edited, with introduction, by Friedman. *David Gerrold, pseudonym.* With STEPHEN GOLDIN.

Nonfiction (Dealing with the Fantasy Genre only)

The World of Star Trek. *New York: Ballantine Books*, [*1973*].
  Wrappers. *First Printing: May, 1973* on copyright page. *Ballantine Books 23403–0–150* ($1.50). *David Gerrold, pseudonym.*

Daniel Francis Galouye
(1920–1976)

COUNTERFEIT WORLD. *London: Victor Gollancz Ltd, 1964*.
Boards. No statement of printing on copyright page. Issued later in the U.S. as SIMULACRON-3.

DARK UNIVERSE. *New York: Bantam Books, [1961]*.
Wrappers. *Published September 1961* on copyright page. *Bantam Book J2266* (40¢).

ALSO: *London: Victor Gollancz Ltd, 1962*. Boards. No statement of printing on copyright page. First hardcover edition.

THE INFINITE MAN. *Toronto New York London: Bantam Books, [1973]*.
Wrappers. *Published April 1973* on copyright page. *A Bantam Book N7130* (95¢).

THE LAST LEAP AND OTHER STORIES OF THE SUPER MIND. *London: Transworld Publishers, [1964]*.
Wrappers. *First publication in Great Britain . . . 1964* on copyright page. *Corgi Science Fiction GS7043* (3/6).

LORDS OF THE PSYCHON. *New York: Bantam Books, [1963]*.
Wrappers. *Published April 1963* on copyright page. *A Bantam Book J2555* (40¢).

THE LOST PERCEPTION. *London: Victor Gollancz Ltd, 1966*.
Boards. No statement of printing on copyright page. Issued later in the U.S. as A SCOURGE OF SCREAMERS.

PROJECT BARRIER. *London: Victor Gollancz Ltd, 1968*.
Boards. No statement of printing on copyright page.

A SCOURGE OF SCREAMERS. *Toronto New York London: Bantam Books, [1968]*.
Wrappers. *Published January 1968* on copyright page. *A Bantam Book F3585* (50¢).
Issued earlier in Great Britain as THE LOST PERCEPTION.

SIMULACRON-3. *New York: Bantam Books, [1964]*.
Wrappers. *Published July 1964* on copyright page. *A Bantam Book J2797* (40¢). Issued earlier in Great Britain as COUNTERFEIT WORLD.

Gordon Randall Philip David Garrett

(b. 1927)

ANYTHING YOU CAN DO. . . .*Garden City: Doubleday & Company, Inc., 1963*.
Boards with cloth shelf back. First edition so stated on copyright page. *Darrell T. Langart, pseudonym.*

BRAIN TWISTER.*New York: Pyramid Books, [1962]*.
Wrappers. *First printing, August 1962* on copyright page. *Pyramid Books F–783* (40¢).
With LARRY M. HARRIS. *Mark Phillips, pseudonym.*

THE DAWNING LIGHT. *New York: Gnome Press, Inc., [1959]*.
Boards. First edition so stated on copyright page. With ROBERT SILVERBERG. *Robert Randall, pseudonym.*

THE IMPOSSIBLES.*New York: Pyramid Books, [1963]*.
Wrappers. *First printing: June 1963* on copyright page. *Pyramid Books F–875* (40¢). With
LARRY M. HARRIS.*Mark Phillips, pseudonym.*

PAGAN PASSIONS.*New York: Galaxy Publishing Corp., [1959]*.
Wrappers. No statement of printing on copyright page. Beacon Book No. 263 (35¢). With
LARRY M. HARRIS.

THE SHROUDED PLANET.*New York: Gnome Press, Inc., Publishers, 1957*.
Boards. First edition so stated on copyright page. With ROBERT SILVERBERG. *Robert Randall, pseudonym.*

SUPERMIND.*New York: Pyramid Publications, [1963]*.
Wrappers. *First printing, September 1963* on copyright page. *Pyramid Books F–909* (40¢).
With LARRY M. HARRIS. *Mark Phillips, pseudonym.*

TOO MANY MAGICIANS.*Garden City: Doubleday & Company, Inc., 1967*.
First edition so stated on copyright page.

UNWISE CHILD. *Garden City: Doubleday & Company, Inc., 1962*.
Two issues, no priority: (A) Cloth, top edge not stained, dust jacket bears price *$3.50* in
upper right corner of front flap. Trade issue. (B) Boards, top edge stained yellow, no price
on front dust jacket flap, *BOOK CLUB/EDITION* in lower right corner of front dust
jacket flap. Book club issue. First edition so stated on copyright page. Note: Both trade and
book club copies produced from same press run. Both bear code *D29* at base of page 215;
both issued in September 1962.

Jane Gaskell (Lynch)
(b. 1941)

ALL NEAT IN BLACK STOCKINGS. [*London*]: *Hodder & Stoughton*, [*1966*].
  Boards. No statement of printing on copyright page.

ATLAN. [*London*]: *Hodder and Stoughton*, [*1965*].
  Boards. *First printed 1965* on copyright page.

ATTIC SUMMER. [*London*]: *Hodder and Stoughton*, [*1963*].
  Boards. *First printed 1963* on copyright page.

THE CITY. [*London*]: *Hodder and Stoughton*, [*1966*].
  Boards. *First printed 1966* on copyright page.

THE DRAGON. See THE SERPENT.

THE FABULOUS HEROINE. [*London*]: *Hodder and Stoughton*, [*1965*].
  Boards. *First Printed 1965* on copyright page.

*KING'S DAUGHTER. *London: Hutchinson*, [*1958*].

THE SERPENT. [*London*]: *Hodder and Stoughton*, [*1963*].
  Boards with cloth shelf back. *First printed 1965* on copyright page. Note: Issued in the
  U.S. in 1977 by St. Martin's Press in two volumes as THE SERPENT and THE DRAGON.

THE SHINY NARROW GRIN. [*London*]: *Hodder and Stoughton*, [*1964*].
  Boards with cloth shelf back. *First printed 1964* on copyright page.

SOME SUMMER LANDS. *London Sydney Auckland Toronto: Hodder and Stoughton*, [*1977*].
  Boards. *First printed 1977* on copyright page.

STRANGE EVIL. *London: Hutchinson*, [*1957*].
  Boards. *First published 1957* on copyright page.

SUMMER COMING. *London • Sydney • Auckland • Toronto: Hodder and Stoughton*, [*1972*].
  Boards. *First printed 1972* on copyright page.

A SWEET SWEET SUMMER. [*London*]: *Hodder and Stoughton*, [*1969*].
  Boards. *First printed 1969* on copyright page.

Hugo Gernsback
(1884–1967)

RALPH 124C 41+: A ROMANCE OF THE YEAR 2660. *Boston: The Stratford Company, Publishers, 1925.*
> Two bindings, no priority established: (A) *Stratford* at base of spine measures 1.5 cm; (B) *Stratford* measures 2 cm. No statement of printing on copyright page.

> ALSO: *New York: Frederick Fell, Inc., [1950]. Second edition* . . . on copyright page. New preface by Gernsback. Note: Reprinted with second edition statement on copyright page, on cheap pulp paper and bound in pictorial wrappers for circulation circa 1952 to U.S. military personnel.

ULTIMATE WORLD. *New York: Walker and Company, [1971].*
> Boards. *First published in the United States of America in 1971* . . . on copyright page.

Nonfiction (Dealing with the Fantasy Genre only)

Concrete Science Fiction. Address by Hugo Gernsback Editor Radio-Electronics Before Eastern Science Fiction Association Newark, N. J. March 12, 1961 [*New York?: Hugo Gernsback, 1961.*]
> Six leaves, printed on rectos only, stapled. No statement of printing. Offset from typewritten copy. Cover title.

Evolution of Modern Science Fiction. [*New York: Hugo Gernsback, 1952.*]
> Wrappers. No statement of printing. Offset from typewritten copy. Caption title.

Science Fiction vs Reality. Address by Hugo Gernsback Publisher Radio-Electronics Before the Massachusetts Institute of Technology Science Fiction Society October 21, 1960. [*New York: Hugo Gernsback, 1960.*]
> Self wrappers. No statement of printing. Mimeographed, stapled. Cover title. Note: Prepared for the use of the author and perhaps for distribution at the lecture.

Reference

Hugo Gernsback: Father of Science Fiction, by Sam Moskowitz. *New York: Criterion Linotyping & Printing Co., Inc., 1959.*
> Wrappers. No statement of printing. 300 copies printed.

Mark Symington Geston
(b. 1946)

THE DAY STAR. *New York: DAW Books, Inc.*, [*1972*].
Wrappers. *DAW: sf Books No. 6 UQ1006* (95¢). Note: First printing has no printing statement on copyright page. A later printing has been noted with *First Printing, May, 1972* on copyright page.

LORDS OF THE STARSHIP. *New York: Ace Books, Inc.*, [*1967*].
Wrappers. No statement of printing on copyright page. *An Ace Book G-673* (50¢).

ALSO: *London: Michael Joseph*, [*1971*]. Boards. *First published in Great Britain . . . 1971* on copyright page. First hardcover edition.

OUT OF THE MOUTH OF THE DRAGON. *New York: An Ace Book*, [*1969*].
Wrappers. No statement of printing on copyright page. *Ace Book 64460* (60¢).

ALSO: *London: Michael Joseph*, [*1972*]. Boards. *First published in Great Britain in 1972* on copyright page. First hardcover edition.

THE SIEGE OF WONDER. *Garden City: Doubleday & Company, Inc.*, *1976*.
Boards. First edition so stated on copyright page.

Horace Leonard Gold

(b. 1914)

THE OLD DIE RICH. *New York: Crown Publishers, Inc.*, *[1955]*.
    No statement of printing on copyright page.

Edited Fiction

Bodyguard and Four Other Short Novels From Galaxy. *Garden City: Doubleday & Company, Inc.*, *1960*.
    First edition so stated on copyright page. Edited by Gold.

The Fifth Galaxy Reader. *Garden City: Doubleday & Company, Inc.*, *1961*.
    First edition so stated on copyright page. Edited, with introduction, by Gold.

Five Galaxy Short Novels. *Garden City: Doubleday & Company, Inc.*, *1958*.
    First edition so stated on copyright page. Edited, with introduction, by Gold.

The Fourth Galaxy Reader. *Garden City: Doubleday & Company, Inc.*, *1959*.
    First edition so stated on copyright page. Edited, with introduction, by Gold.

Galaxy Reader of Science Fiction. *New York: Crown Publishers, Inc.*, *[1952]*.
    No statement of printing on copyright page. Edited, with introduction and note, by Gold.

    ALSO: *London: Grayson & Grayson Ltd.*, *[1953]*. Boards. *First published in Great Britain in 1953* . . . on copyright page. Abridged reprint. Collects thirteen of the thirty-three stories.

The Galaxy Science Fiction Omnibus. *[London]: Grayson & Grayson*, *[1955]*.
    First published in 1955 . . . on copyright page. Abridged reprint. Twenty stories selected from *The Second Galaxy Reader of Science Fiction.*

Mind Partner and 8 Other Novelets from Galaxy. *Garden City: Doubleday & Company, Inc.*, *1961*.
    First edition so stated on copyright page. Edited, with introduction, by Gold.

The Second Galaxy Reader of Science Fiction. *New York: Crown Publishers • Inc.*, *[1954]*.
    Two bindings, priority as listed: (A) Green cloth; (B) Brown boards. No statement of printing on copyright page. Edited, with introduction, by Gold. Later abridged as *The Galaxy Science Fiction Omnibus.*

The Sixth Galaxy Reader. *Garden City: Doubleday & Company, Inc.*, *1962*.
    First edition so stated on copyright page. Edited, with introduction and short story "Personnel Problem," by Gold.

The Third Galaxy Reader. *Garden City: Doubleday & Company, Inc.*, *1958*.
    First edition so stated on copyright page. Edited, with introduction, by Gold.

The Weird Ones. *New York: Belmont Books*, *[1962]*.
    Wrappers. *First Printing July 1962* on copyright page. *Belmont L92–541* (50¢). Compiled, with introduction, by Gold.

ALSO: *London: Dennis Dobson, [1965].* Boards. *First published in Great Britain in 1965*
. . . on copyright page. First hardcover edition.

The World That Couldn't Be and 8 Other Novelets from Galaxy. *Garden City: Doubleday &*
Company, Inc., 1959.
  First edition so stated on copyright page. Edited, with introduction, by Gold.

Ronald Joseph Goulart

(b. 1933)

AFTER THINGS FELL APART. *New York: Ace Publishing Corporation,* [*1970*].
Wrappers. *An Ace Science Fiction Special 00950 (75¢).*

ALSO: *Boston: Gregg Press, 1977. First Printing, June 1977* on copyright page. First hardcover edition. Note: Not issued in dust jacket.

BLACK CHARIOTS. [*New York*]: *Warner Paperback Library,* [*1974*].
Wrappers. *First Printing: November, 1974* on copyright page. *Warner Paperback Library 75-720 (95¢). Kenneth Robeson, pseudonym. The Avenger* at head of title.

THE BLOOD COUNTESS. [*New York*]: *Warner Paperback Library,* [*1975*].
Wrappers. *First Printing: February, 1975* on copyright page. *Warner Paperback Library 75-783 (95¢). Kenneth Robeson, pseudonym. The Avenger* at head of title.

BLOOD WEDDING. *New York: Warner Books,* [*1976*].
Wrappers. *First Printing: March, 1976* on copyright page. *Warner Books 86–088* ($1.25). *Vampirella #4* at head of title.

BLOODSTALK. [*New York*]: *Warner Books,* [*1975*].
Wrappers. *First Printing: November, 1975* on copyright page. *Warner Books 76–928* ($1.25). Note: Issued as *Vampirella #1*.

BROKE DOWN ENGINE. *New York: The Macmillan Company. London: Collier-Macmillan Ltd.,* [*1971*].
First printing so stated on copyright page.

THE CARTOON CRIMES. [*New York*]: *Warner Paperback Library,* [*1974*].
Wrappers. *First Printing: December, 1974* on copyright page. *Warner Paperback Library 75–769 (95¢). Kenneth Robeson, pseudonym. The Avenger* at head of title.

CHAINS. [*New York*]: *Warner Paperback Library,* [*1973*].
Wrappers. *First Printing; November, 1973* on copyright page. *Warner Paperback Library 76–465* ($1.25). *Howard Lee, pseudonym. Kung Fu #2* at head of title.

CHALLENGERS OF THE UNKNOWN. [*New York*]: *A Dell Book,* [*1977*].
Wrappers. *First printing—November 1977* on copyright page. *Dell 11337* ($1.50).

THE CHAMELEON CORPS & OTHER SHAPE CHANGERS. *New York: The Macmillan Company. London: Collier-Macmillan Ltd.,* [*1972*].
First printing so stated on copyright page.

CLEOPATRA JONES. [*New York*]: *Warner Paperback Library,* [*1973*].
Wrappers. *First Printing: July, 1973* on copyright page. *Warner Paperback Library 76–388* ($1.25).

CLEOPATRA JONES AND THE CASINO OF GOLD. [*New York*]: *Warner Paperback Library,* [*1975*].
Wrappers. *First Printing: July, 1975* on copyright page. *Warner Paperback Library 76–805* ($1.25).

CLOCKWORK'S PIRATES. *New York: Ace Books*, [*1971*].
Wrappers. No statement of printing on copyright page. *Ace Double 11182* (75¢). Bound with GHOST BREAKER by Goulart.

CRACKPOT. *Garden City: Doubleday & Company, Inc.*, *1977*.
Boards. First edition so stated on copyright page.

DEADWALK. [*New York*]: *Warner Books*, [*1976*].
Wrappers. *First Printing: January, 1976* on copyright page. *Warner Books 76–930* ($1.25). *Vampirella #3* at head of title.

DEATH CELL. *New York: Beagle Books*, [*1971*].
Wrappers. *First printing: July, 1971* on copyright page. *Beagle Boxer Science Fiction Novel 95111* (95¢).

THE DEATH MACHINE. [*New York*]: *Warner Paperback Library*, [*1975*].
Wrappers. *First Printing: January, 1975* on copyright page. *Warner Paperback Library 75–770* (95¢). *Kenneth Robeson, pseudonym. The Avenger* at head of title.

DEATHGAME. [*New York*]: *Warner Books*, [*1976*].
Wrappers. *First Printing: May, 1976* on copyright page. *Warner Books 86–089* ($1.25). *Vampirella #5* at head of title.

DEMON ISLAND. [*New York*]: *Warner Paperback Library*, [*1975*].
Wrappers. *First Printing: May, 1975* on copyright page. *Warner Paperback Library 75–858* (95¢). *Kenneth Robeson, pseudonym. The Avenger* at head of title.

DR. TIME. [*New York*]: *Warner Paperback Library*, [*1974*].
Wrappers. *First Printing: September, 1974* on copyright page. *Warner Paperback Library 75–594* (95¢). *Kenneth Robeson, pseudonym. The Avenger* at head of title.

EASY MONEY. [*New York*]: *Warner Books*, [*1976*].
Wrappers. Code *10 9 8 7 6 5 4 3 2 1* on copyright page. *Warner Books 88–295* ($1.50). *Con Steffanson, pseudonym. Laverne and Shirley #2* at head of title.

THE EMPEROR OF THE LAST DAYS. *New York: Popular Library*, [*1977*].
Wrappers. *April, 1977* on copyright page. *Popular Library 445–03201–150* ($1.50).

THE ENORMOUS HOURGLASS. *New York: Award Books*, [*1976*].
Wrappers. *First Award Printing 1976* on copyright page. *An Award Science Fiction Novel AQ1510* ($1.25).

EYE OF THE VULTURE. [*New York*]: *Published by Jove Books/Harcourt, Brace Jovanovich*, [*1977*].
Wrappers. *Jove/HBJ Books Edition Published October, 1977* on copyright page. *A Jove Book A4293* ($1.50).

THE FIRE-EATER. *New York: Ace Books*, [*1970*].
Wrappers. No statement of printing on copyright page. *Ace Book 28860* (75¢).

FLUX. *New York: DAW Books, Inc.*, [*1974*].
Wrappers. *First printing, June, 1974/1 2 3 4 5 6 7 8 9* on copyright page. *DAW: sf Books No. 107 UQ1116* (95¢).

GADGET MAN. *Garden City: Doubleday & Company, Inc.*, *1971*.
First edition so stated on copyright page.

GHOST BREAKER. *New York: Ace Books*, [*1971*].
Wrappers. No statement of printing on copyright page. *Ace Double 11182* (75¢). Bound with CLOCKWORK'S PIRATES by Goulart.

THE GLASS MAN. [*New York*]: *Warner Paperback Library*, [*1975*].
Wrappers. *First Printing: March, 1975* on copyright page. *Warner Paperback Library 75-802* (95¢). *Kenneth Robeson, pseudonym. The Avenger* at head of title.

THE GOGGLE-EYED PIRATES. [*New York*]: *Avon*, [*1974*].
Wrappers. *First Avon Printing, February, 1974* on copyright page. *Avon 18184* (95¢). *Lee Falk, pseudonym. The Story of the Phantom* at head of title. Note: Goulart used the pen name Frank S. Shawn for the books he wrote for this series. The publisher inadvertently left the pseudonym off this title.

GOLD RUSH. [*New York*]: *Warner Books*, [*1976*].
Wrappers. Code *10 9 8 7 6 5 4 3 2 1* on copyright page. *Warner Books 88-296* ($1.50). *Con Steffanson, pseudonym. Laverne and Shirley #3* at head of title.

THE GOLDEN CIRCLE. [*New York*]: *Avon*, [*1973*].
Wrappers. *First Avon Printing, May, 1973* on copyright page. *Avon 14894* (75¢). *Frank S. Shaw* [sic], *pseudonym. The Story of the Phantom* at head of title. Note: Goulart's pen name misprinted "Shaw" on this title.

HAWKSHAW. *Garden City: Doubleday & Company, Inc., 1972*.
First edition so stated on copyright page.

THE HELLHOUND PROJECT. *Garden City: Doubleday & Company, Inc., 1975*.
Boards. First edition so stated on copyright page.

THE HYDRA MONSTER. [*New York*]: *Avon*, [*1973*].
Wrappers. *First Avon Printing, October, 1973* on copyright page. *Avon 17061* (75¢). *Frank S. Shawn, pseudonym. The Story of the Phantom* at the head of title.

IF DYING WAS ALL. *New York: Ace Books*, [*1971*].
Wrappers. No statement of printing on copyright page. *An Ace Book 36300* (75¢).

THE IRON SKULL. [*New York*]: *Warner Paperback Library*, [*1975*].
Wrappers. *First Printing: April, 1975* on copyright page. *Warner Paperback Library 75-848* (95¢). *Kenneth Robeson, pseudonym. The Avenger* at head of title.

THE ISLAND OF DR. MOREAU. *New York: Ace Books*, [*1977*].
Wrappers. *First Ace Printing: July 1977* on copyright page. *Ace 37421-2* ($1.95). *Joseph Silva, pseudonym.*

ALSO: *Garden City: Nelson Doubleday, Inc.*, [*1977*]. Boards. No statement of printing on copyright page. Code *S 29* on page 229. First hardcover edition. Notes: (1) In addition to the Goulart adaptation of the screenplay, this edition prints the text of the Wells novel. (2) Issued by the Science Fiction Book Club.

THE LION MEN OF MONGO. [*New York*]: *Avon*, [*1974*].
Wrappers. *First Avon Printing, March, 1974* on copyright page. *Avon 18515* (95¢). *Con Steffanson, pseudonym. Flash/Gordon/Alex/Raymond's/Original Story* at head of title.

THE MAN FROM ATLANTIS. [*New York*]: *Warner Paperback Library*, [*1974*].
Wrappers. *First Printing: June, 1974* on copyright page. *Warner Paperback Library 75-609* (95¢). *Kenneth Robeson, pseudonym. The Avenger* at head of title.

THE MYSTERY OF THE SEA HORSE. *[New York]: Avon, [1973]*.
Wrappers. *First Avon Printing, August 1973* on copyright page. *Avon 15867 (75¢). Frank S. Shawn, pseudonym. The Story of the Phantom* at head of title.

NEMO. *[New York]: A Berkley Medallion Book Published by Berkley Publishing Corporation, [1977]*.
Wrappers. *May, 1977* on copyright page. *A Berkley Medallion Book 0-425-03395-3* ($1.25).

THE NIGHTWITCH DEVIL. *[New York]: Warner Paperback Library, [1974]*.
Wrappers. *First Printing: October, 1974* on copyright page. *Warner Paperback Library 75-672 (95¢). Kenneth Robeson, pseudonym. The Avenger* at head of title.

NUTZENBOLTS AND MORE TROUBLES WITH MACHINES. *New York: Macmillan Publishing Co., Inc., [1975]*.
Boards. *First printing 1975* on copyright page.

ODD JOB #101. *New York: Charles Scribner's Sons, [1975]*.
Boards. Code *1 3 5 7 9 11 13 15 17 19 C/C 20 18 16 14 12 10 8 6 4 2* on copyright page.

ON ALIEN WINGS. *[New York]: Warner Books, [1975]*.
Wrappers. *First Printing: December, 1975* on copyright page. *Warner Books 76-929* ($1.25). *Vampirella #2* at head of title.

ONE GRAVE TOO MANY. *New York: Ace Books, [1974]*.
Wrappers. *First Ace Printing: December 1974* on copyright page. *An Ace Book 40591* (95¢).

THE PANCHRONICON PLOT. *New York: DAW Books, Inc., [1977]*.
Wrappers. *First printing, February 1977/1 2 3 4 5 6 7 8 9* on copyright page. *DAW: sf Books No. 231 UY1283* ($1.25).

THE PLAGUE OF SOUND. *[New York]: Avon, [1974]*.
Wrappers. *First Avon Printing, May, 1974* on copyright page. *Avon 19166 (95¢). Con Steffanson, pseudonym. Flash/Gordon/Alex Raymond's/Original Story* at head of title.

PLUNDER. *New York: Beagle Books, [1972]*.
Wrappers. *First Printing: February 1972* on copyright page. *A Beagle Science Fiction Novel 95210* (95¢).

THE PURPLE ZOMBIE. *[New York]: Warner Paperback Library, [1974]*.
Wrappers. *First Printing: August, 1974* on copyright page. *Warner Paperback Library 75-611 (95¢). Kenneth Robeson, pseudonym. The Avenger* at head of title.

QUEST OF THE GYPSY. *New York: Pyramid Books, [1976]*.
Wrappers. *Pyramid Edition published September, 1976* on copyright page. *Pyramid A4034* ($1.50). *Weird Heroes Volume 3* at head of title.

RED MOON. *[New York]: Warner Paperback Library, [1974]*.
Wrappers. *First Printing: July, 1974* on copyright page. *Warner Paperback Library 75-610 (95¢). Kenneth Robeson, pseudonym. The Avenger* at head of title.

THE SAME LIE TWICE. *New York: Ace Books, [1973]*.
Wrappers. *First Ace printing: January, 1973* on copyright page. *An Ace Book 75945* (75¢).

SHAGGY PLANET. *New York: Lancer Books*, [*1973*].
Wrappers. No statement of printing on copyright page. *A Lancer Science Fiction Original 75420–095* (95¢).

SNAKEGOD. [*New York*]: *Warner Books*, [*1976*].
Wrappers. *First Printing: July, 1976* on copyright page. *Warner Paperback Library 86–090* ($1.25). *Vampirella #6* at head of title.

THE SPACE CIRCUS. [*New York*]: *Avon*, [*1974*].
Wrappers. *First Avon Printing, July, 1974* on copyright page. *Avon 19695* (95¢). *Con Steffanson, pseudonym. Flash Gordon* at head of title.

SPACEHAWK, INC. *New York: DAW Books, Inc.*, [*1974*].
Wrappers. *First printing, December 1974/1 2 3 4 5 6 7 8 9* on copyright page. *DAW: sf Books No. 132 UQ1149* (95¢).

[SUPERSTITION.] [*New York*]: *Warner Paperback Library*, [*1973*].
Wrappers. *First Printing: December, 1973* on copyright page. *Warner Paperback Library 76–466* ($1.25). *Howard Lee, pseudonym. Kung Fu #3* on title page. Note: Book title does not appear on title page.

THE SWAMP RATS. [*New York*]: *Avon*, [*1974*].
Wrappers. *First Avon Printing, April, 1974* on copyright page. *Avon 18820* (95¢). *Frank S. Shawn, pseudonym. The Story of the Phantom* at head of title.

THE SWORD SWALLOWER. *Garden City: Doubleday & Company, Inc.*, *1968*.
First edition so stated on copyright page.

A TALENT FOR THE INVISIBLE. *New York: DAW Books, Inc.*, [*1973*].
Wrappers. *First printing, January 1973* on copyright page. *DAW: sf Books No. 37 UQ1037* (95¢).

TEAMWORK. [*New York*]: *Warner Books*, [*1976*].
Wrappers. *First Printing: October, 1976* on copyright page. *Warner Books 88–294* ($1.50). *Con Steffanson, pseudonym. Laverne and Shirley #1* at head of title.

THE TIN ANGEL. *New York: DAW Books, Inc.*, [*1973*].
Wrappers. *First printing, November 1973/1 2 3 4 5 6 7 8 9* on copyright page. *DAW: sf Books No. 80 UQ1083* (95¢).

TOO SWEET TO DIE. *New York: Ace Books*, [*1972*].
Wrappers. No statement of printing on copyright page. *An Ace Book 40590* (75¢).

THE TREMENDOUS ADVENTURES OF BERNIE WINE. [*New York*]: *Warner Paperback Library*, [*1975*].
Wrappers. *First Printing: March, 1975* on copyright page. *Warner Paperback Library 78–416* ($1.50).

THE VEILED LADY. [*New York*]. *Avon*, [*1973*].
Wrappers. *First Avon Printing, March, 1973* on copyright page. *Avon 14498* (75¢). *Frank S. Shawn, pseudonym. The Story of the Phantom* at head of title.

WHAT'S BECOME OF SCREWLOOSE? *New York: Charles Scribner's Sons*, [*1971*].
Boards with cloth shelf back. Code *A–4.71 (C)* on copyright page.

WHEN THE WAKER SLEEPS. *New York: DAW Books, Inc.*, [*1975*].
Wrappers. *First printing, December 1975/1 2 3 4 5 6 7 8 9* on copyright page. *DAW: sf Books No. 175 UY1210* ($1.25).

A WHIFF OF MADNESS. *New York: DAW Books, Inc.*, [*1976*].
  Wrappers. *First printing, August 1976/1 2 3 4 5 6 7 8 9* on copyright page. *DAW: sf Books No. 207 UY1250* ($1.25).

WILDSMITH. *New York: Ace Books*, [*1972*].
  Wrappers. No statement of printing on copyright page. *Ace Book SF 8872* (75¢).

Edited Fiction

The Hardboiled Dicks. *Los Angeles: Sherbourne Press, Inc.*, [*1965*].
  First edition so stated on copyright page. Edited, with introduction and notes, by Goulart.

Nonfiction (Dealing with the Fantasy Genre only)

Cheap Thrills: An Informal History of the Pulp Magazines. *New Rochelle, N. Y.: Arlington House*, [*1972*].
  Boards. No statement of printing on copyright page.

Joseph Lee Green
(b. 1931)

AN AFFAIR WITH GENIUS. *London: Victor Gollancz Ltd, 1969.*
Boards. No statement of printing on copyright page.

CONSCIENCE INTERPLANETARY. *London: Victor Gollancz Ltd, 1972.*
Boards. No statement of printing on copyright page.

GOLD THE MAN. *London: Victor Gollancz Ltd, 1971.*
Boards. No statement of printing on copyright page. Issued later in the U.S. as THE MIND BEHIND THE EYE.

THE HORDE. *Toronto • New York • London: Laser Books,* [1976].
Wrappers. *First published April 1976* on copyright page. *Laser Books 72027* (95¢).

THE LOAFERS OF REFUGE. *London: Victor Gollancz Ltd, 1965.*
Boards. No statement of printing on copyright page.

THE MIND BEHIND THE EYE. *New York: DAW Books, Inc.,* [1972].
Wrappers. *DAW: sf Books No. 2 UQ1002* (95¢). Note: No statement of printing on copyright page of first printing; second printing marked *Second printing, April, 1972* on copyright page. Issued earlier in Great Britain as GOLD THE MAN.

STAR PROBE. [*London*]*: Millington Books,* [1976].
Boards. No statement of printing on copyright page.

George Chetwynd Griffith-Jones
(1857–1906)

THE ANGEL OF THE REVOLUTION. *London: Tower Publishing Company Limited, 1893.*
First edition so stated on title page.

BRITON OR BOER? *London: F.V. White & Co., 1897.*
Two issues, priority as listed: (A) No statement of printing on title page; pages 297–304
comprise publisher's advertisements dated *January 1897*; (B) Title page bears statement
SECOND EDITION; this issue comprises first edition sheets with title leaf and conjugate
leaf xiii/blank reprinted.

BROTHERS OF THE CHAIN. *London: F. V. White & Co., 1899.*
Chocolate brown pebbled cloth stamped in black and gold. Two issues, priority as listed:
(A) Integral title leaf with publisher's imprint as above. Four pages of undated publisher's
advertisements paged 309–12 with page 309 headed *F. V. White & Co.'s/Catalogue of
Publications* inserted at rear. (B) Title leaf is a cancel with publisher's imprint reading
London: F. V. White & Co., 1900. Two variants: (1) Inserted publisher's catalogue as per
issue A. (2) No inserted catalogue (copy thus received at British Library 14 September
1900). Note: The colonial printing (issue?) from the same plates as the domestic printing
(issue?) may precede. Publisher's imprint reads *London: George Bell & Sons and Bombay,
1899.* Red vertically ribbed cloth, spine stamped in blind and gold, front and rear cover in
blind; integral title leaf; [16]-page publisher's catalogue dated *March, 1899* inserted at rear.
No statement of printing on copyright page.

CAPTAIN ISHMAEL. *London: Hutchinson & Co., 1901.*
No statement of printing on copyright page. Pages [345–48] comprise publisher's advertisements dated *Autumn 1901.*

A CONQUEST OF FORTUNE. *London: F. V. White & Co., Limited, 1906.*
No statement of printing on copyright page.

A CRIMINAL CROESUS. *London: John Long, 1904.*
No statement of printing on copyright page.

DENVER'S DOUBLE. *London: F. V. White & Co., 1901.*
No statement of printing on copyright page.

THE DESTINED MAID. *London: F. V. White & Co., 1898.*
No statement of printing on copyright page.

*THE DIAMOND DOG. *London: C. Arthur Pearson, [1913].*
Wrappers? Reprint? Notes: (1) Possibly a paperback reprint of South African crime stories
collected from an earlier book, KNAVES OF DIAMONDS, which contains a story titled "The
Diamond Dog." (2) *English Catalogue of Books* dates September 1913.

GAMBLES WITH DESTINY. *London: F. V. White & Co., 1899.*
No statement of printing on copyright page. Undated 16-page publisher's catalogue at rear.

THE GOLD-FINDER. *London: F. V. White & Co., 1898.*
No statement of printing on copyright page.

THE GREAT PIRATE SYNDICATE. *London: F. V. White & Co., 1899.*
No statement of printing on copyright page. Two variants: (1) No inserted publisher's
catalogue; (2) Undated 10-page publisher's catalogue inserted at rear.

THE GREAT WEATHER SYNDICATE. *London: F. V. White and Co., Limited, 1906.*
No statement of printing on copyright page.

*A HEROINE OF THE SLUMS. *London: The Tower Publishing Co., n.d. [ca. 1894].*
Wrappers. No statement of printing on copyright page. Note: *English Catalogue of Books* dates April 1894.

HIS BEAUTIFUL CLIENT. *London: F. V. White & Co. Ltd., 1906.*
No statement of printing on copyright page.

HIS BETTER HALF. *London: F. V. White & Co., Ltd., 1905.*
No statement of printing on copyright page.

A HONEYMOON IN SPACE. *London: C. Arthur Pearson Ltd., 1901.*
No statement of printing on copyright page. 16 pages of publisher's advertisements (paged 8 + 8) at rear dated *Spring 1901.*

AN ISLAND LOVE-STORY. *London: F. V. White & Co. Ltd., 1905.*
Two bindings, priority as listed: (A) Red cloth lettered in black; (B) Blue cloth lettered in black. Times binding. No statement of printing on copyright page. Note: Copies in both bindings carry 6 pages of undated publisher's advertisements on pages [307–12].

JOHN BROWN, BUCCANEER. *London: F. V. White & Co., Ltd., 1908.*
No statement of printing on copyright page. [8] pages of undated publisher's advertisements at rear.

THE JUSTICE OF REVENGE. *London: F. V. White & Co., 1901.*
No statement of printing on copyright page. 7 pages of undated publisher's advertisements at rear.

KNAVES OF DIAMONDS. *London: C. Arthur Pearson Limited, 1899.*
Two issues (printings?), priority as listed: (A) Domestic issue. Blue cloth stamped in gold and silver; publisher's imprint on title page as above; no publisher's catalogue inserted at rear. No statement of printing on copyright page. (B) Colonial issue. Red vertically ribbed cloth, spine stamped in gold, front and rear cover in blind; signature [a]⁸ has typographical alterations, remainder as per Pearson issue; publisher's imprint reads *London: George Bell & Sons and Bombay, 1899;* 16-page publisher's catalogue dated *November, 1898* inserted at rear. No statement of printing on copyright page.

THE KNIGHTS OF THE WHITE ROSE. *London: F. V. White & Co., 1897.*
No statement of printing on copyright page.

THE LAKE OF GOLD. *London: F. V. White & Co., Limited, 1903.*
No statement of printing on copyright page.

THE LORD OF LABOUR. *London: F. V. White & Co. Ltd., 1911.*
No statement of printing on copyright page.

A MAYFAIR MAGICIAN. *London: F. V. White & Co., Ltd., 1905.*
No statement of printing on copyright page. Note: Reissued in the 1920s or 1930s in paper covers as THE MAN WITH THREE EYES (not seen).

THE MISSIONARY. *London: F. V. White & Co., Ltd., 1902.*
No statement of printing on copyright page.

THE MUMMY AND MISS NITOCRIS. *London: T. Werner Laurie*, [*1906*].
No statement of printing on copyright page. Title page printed in green and black. Note: Reissued in late 1930s in paper covers as THE MUMMY AND THE GIRL (not seen).

OLGA ROMANOFF. *London: Tower Publishing Company Limited, 1894*.
Two issues, priority as listed: (A) Green silk cloth; frontispiece by Edwin S. Hope; errata leaf tipped in between pages viii and 1 which bears a notice directing the reader to the ninth edition of THE ANGEL OF THE REVOLUTION and the following: "In footline to frontispiece, for 'page 388' read 'page 338' ", pages [378–80] comprise publisher's advertisements with page [378] headed *Now ready, Eighth Edition . . . /THE ANGEL OF THE REVOLU-TION*. No statement of printing. (B) Green silk cloth; title page dated 1895 bearing the statement *new edition;* omits the Hope frontispiece; adds 16 plates by Fred T. Jane; same errata leaf tipped in between pages [x] and 1; list of illustrations mispaged "vi"; same advertisements on pages [378–80]. The title leaf, the list of illustrations leaf, and the 16 plates are tipped in. Note: Issue B has not been examined; information from George Locke in *Science Fiction First Editions* (London: Ferret Fantasy, 1978), pp. 31–32. Locke also reports a blue cloth binding on copies of the "new edition" of unknown status.

THE OUTLAWS OF THE AIR. *London: Tower Publishing Company Limited, 1895*.
No statement of printing on copyright page.

THE RAID OF 'LE VENGEUR' AND OTHER STORIES. [*London*]: *Ferret Fantasy Ltd, mcmlxxiv*.
Wrappers. No statement of printing on copyright page. 900 copies printed.

THE ROMANCE OF THE GOLDEN STAR. *London: F. V. White & Co., 1897*.
No statement of printing on copyright page. Undated publisher's catalogue, pages [285]–300.

THE ROSE OF JUDAH. *London: C. Arthur Pearson Limited, 1899*.
No statement of printing on copyright page. Pages [341–44] comprise undated publisher's advertisements.

THE SACRED SKULL. *London: Everett & Co., 1908*.
No statement of printing on copyright page. Title page printed in red and black.

THE STOLEN SUBMARINE. *London: F. V. White & Co., Ltd., 1904*.
No statement of printing on copyright page.

"THOU SHALT NOT —." *London: C. Arthur Pearson, Limited, 1900*.
No statement of printing on copyright page. *Stanton Morich, pseudonym*.

VALDAR THE OFT-BORN. *London: C. Arthur Pearson, Limited, 1895*.
Three bindings, priority as listed: (A) Red cloth, design and lettering in black and gold on front cover, lettering in gold on spine; (B) Red cloth, lettering in black on front cover, lettering in gold on spine; (C) Red cloth, lettering in black on front cover and spine. No statement of printing on copyright page.

THE VIRGIN OF THE SUN. *London: C. Arthur Pearson Limited, 1898*.
Two bindings, no priority established but probably simultaneous: (A) Japan vellum stamped in gold; top edge gilt, other edges untrimmed. Note: Possibly a presentation binding. Copy examined in the collection of George Locke bears a signed inscription by Griffith dated "March 1898." (B) Green cloth stamped in gold and red; top edge plain, all edges trimmed. Trade binding. No statement of printing on copyright page.

THE WHITE WITCH OF MAYFAIR. *London: F. V. White & Co., Ltd., 1902*.
No statement of printing on copyright page.

A WOMAN AGAINST THE WORLD. *London: F. V. White & Co., Limited, 1903.*
  No statement of printing on copyright page.

THE WORLD MASTERS. *London: John Long, 1903.*
  No statement of printing on copyright page.

THE WORLD PERIL OF 1910. *London: F. V. White & Co., Ltd., 1907.*
  No statement of printing on copyright page.

Translated Fiction

*The Hope of the Family, by Alphonse Daudet, translated and adapted from the French. . . .
London: C. Arthur Pearson, 1898.
  Levin Carnac, pseudonym.

Reference

The Raid of 'Le Vengeur' and Other Stories, by George Griffith. [*London*]: *Ferret Fantasy
Ltd, mcmlxxiv.*
  Wrappers. No statement of printing on copyright page. 900 copies printed. Note: Includes
  biography of Griffith by Sam Moskowitz and bibliography of his writings by George
  Locke.

James Edwin Gunn

(b. 1923)

BREAKING POINT. *New York: Walker and Company*, [*1972*].
Boards. *First published in the United States of America in 1972* on copyright page.

THE BURNING. [*New York*]: *A Dell Book*, [*1972*].
Wrappers. *First printing —February 1972* on copyright page. *Dell 0861* (95¢).

THE END OF THE DREAMS. *New York: Charles Scribner's Sons*, [*1975*].
Boards. Code *1 3 5 7 9 11 13 15 17 19 H/C 20 18 16 14 12 10 8 6 4 2* on copyright page.

FUTURE IMPERFECT. *New York: Bantam Books*, [*1964*].
Wrappers. *Published January 1964* on copyright page. *A Bantam Book J2717* (40¢).

THE IMMORTAL. *Toronto New York London: Bantam Books*, [*1970*].
Wrappers. *Published October 1970* on copyright page. *A Bantam Book S5924* (75¢).

THE IMMORTALS. *New York: Bantam Books*, [*1962*].
Wrappers. *Published November 1962* on copyright page. *A Bantam Book J2484* (40¢).

THE JOY MAKERS. *New York: Bantam Books*, [*1961*].
Wrappers. *Published March 1961* on copyright page. *A Bantam Book A2219* (35¢).

ALSO: *London: Victor Gollancz Ltd, 1963*. Boards. No statement of printing on copyright page. First hardcover edition.

KAMPUS. *Toronto New York London: Bantam Books*, [*1977*].
Wrappers. *July 1977* on copyright page. *Bantam Science Fiction 02693–3* ($1.75).

THE LISTENERS. *New York: Charles Scribner's Sons*, [*1972*].
Boards. Code *A–10.72 (C)* on copyright page.

THE MAGICIANS. *New York: Published by Charles Scribner's Sons*, [*1976*].
Boards. Code *1 3 5 7 9 11 13 15 17 19 C/C 20 18 16 14 12 10 8 6 4 2* on copyright page.

SOME DREAMS ARE NIGHTMARES. *New York: Charles Scribner's Sons*, [*1974*].
Boards. Code *1 3 5 7 9 11 13 15 17 19 C/C 20 18 16 14 12 10 8 6 4 2* on copyright page.

STAR BRIDGE. *New York: Gnome Press, Inc. Publishers*, [*1955*].
Boards with cloth shelf back. First edition so stated on copyright page. With JACK WILLIAMSON.

STATION IN SPACE. *New York: Bantam Books*, [*1958*].
Wrappers. *Published September, 1958* on copyright page. *A Bantam Book A1825* (35¢).

THIS FORTRESS WORLD. *New York: Gnome Press*, [*1955*].
Two bindings, priority as listed: (A) Blue-gray boards with light blue cloth shelf back, spine printed in black; (B) Tan boards, spine printed in black. First edition so stated on copyright page.

THE WITCHING HOUR. [*New York*]: *A Dell Book*, [*1970*].
   Wrappers. *First printing—June 1970* on copyright page. *Dell 9605* (60¢).

Edited Fiction

Nebula Award Stories 10. *London: Victor Gollancz Ltd, 1975*.
   Boards. No statement of printing on copyright page. Edited, with introduction and notes, by Gunn.

   ALSO: *New York Evanston San Francisco London: Harper & Row, Publishers*, [*1975*].
   Half boards and cloth. First edition so stated on copyright page. Enlarged edition.

The Road to Science Fiction: From Gilgamesh to Wells. *New York: New American Library*, [*1977*].
   Wrappers. *First Mentor printing, September, 1977/1 2 3 4 5 6 7 8 9* on copyright page. *Mentor ME1578* ($2.25). Edited, with introduction and notes, by Gunn.

Nonfiction (Dealing with the Fantasy Genre only)

Alternate Worlds: The Illustrated History of Science Fiction. *Englewood Cliffs, N.J.: Prentice-Hall, Inc.*, [*1975*].
   No statement of printing on copyright page.

The Discovery of the Future: The Ways Science Fiction Developed. *College Station, Texas: Texas A & M University Library, 1975*.
   Wrappers. No statement of printing. Offset.

Joseph W. Haldeman
(b. 1943)

ALL MY SINS REMEMBERED. *New York: St. Martin's Press*, [*1977*].
  Boards. First edition so stated on copyright page.

ATTAR'S REVENGE. *New York: Pocket Books*, [*1975*].
  Wrappers. *March, 1975* on copyright page. *Pocket Books 77988 (95¢). Robert Graham, pseudonym.*

THE FOREVER WAR. *New York: St. Martin's Press*, [*1974*].
  Boards. First printing so stated on copyright page.

MINDBRIDGE. *New York: St. Martin's Press*, [*1976*].
  Boards. No statement of printing on copyright page.

PLANET OF JUDGMENT. *Toronto New York London: Bantam Books*, [*1977*].
  Wrappers. *Published August 1977* on copyright page. *A Bantam Book 11145-0* ($1.75).

WAR OF NERVES. *New York: Pocket Books*, [*1975*].
  Wrappers. *March, 1975* on copyright page. *Pocket Books 77989 (95¢). Robert Graham, pseudonym.*

WAR YEAR. *New York Chicago San Francisco: Holt, Rinehart and Winston*, [*1972*].
  Boards. First edition so stated on copyright page.

Edited Fiction

Cosmic Laughter. *New York Chicago San Francisco: Holt, Rinehart and Winston*, [*1974*].
  First edition so stated on copyright page. Edited, with introduction and short story ''I of Newton,'' by Haldeman.

Study War No More: A Selection of Alternatives. *New York: St. Martin's Press*, [*1977*].
  Boards. No statement of printing on copyright page. Edited, with introduction, notes, and short story ''To Howard Hughes: A Modest Proposal,'' by Haldeman.

Austin Hall
(1882?–1933)

THE BLIND SPOT. *Philadelphia: Prime Press*, *[1951]*.
First edition so stated on copyright page. With HOMER EON FLINT.

PEOPLE OF THE COMET. *[Los Angeles]: Griffin Publishing House*, *1948*.
No statement of printing on copyright page.

THE SPOT OF LIFE. *New York: Ace Books, Inc.*, *[1965]*.
Wrappers. No statement of printing on copyright page. *Ace Science Fiction Classic F–318*
(40¢).

Edmond Moore Hamilton
(1904–1977)

BATTLE FOR THE STARS. *New York: A Torquil Book Distributed by Dodd, Mead & Company,* *[1961]*.
    Boards. Two issues, priority of release as listed: (A) Price *$2.95* appears in upper right corner of front dust jacket flap. Trade issue. (B) No price, *BOOK CLUB/EDITION* in lower right corner of front dust jacket flap. Book club issue. No statement of printing on copyright page. Note: Trade issue was published in November 1961 while the book club issue was a December 1961 selection. Both issues from same press run; both have printing code *C42* on page 206.

THE BEST OF EDMOND HAMILTON. *Garden City: Nelson Doubleday, Inc.,* *[1977]*.
    Boards. No statement of printing on copyright page. Code *H 10* on page 333. Note: Issued by the Science Fiction Book Club.

BEYOND THE MOON. *[New York]: The New American Library,* *[1950]*.
    Wrappers. *First printing, September, 1950* on copyright page. *Signet Books 812* (25¢). Reissue of THE STAR KINGS.

CALLING CAPTAIN FUTURE. *New York: Popular Library,* *[1969]*.
    Wrappers. No statement of printing on copyright page. *Popular Library 60–2421* (60¢).

CAPTAIN FUTURE AND THE SPACE EMPEROR. *New York: Popular Library,* *[1969]*.
    Wrappers. No statement of printing on copyright page. *Popular Library 60–2457* (60¢).

CAPTAIN FUTURE'S CHALLENGE. *New York: Popular Library,* *[1969]*.
    Wrappers. No statement of printing on copyright page. *Popular Library 60–2430* (60¢).

CITY AT WORLD'S END. *New York: Frederick Fell, Inc.,* *[1951]*.
    Boards. *First Printing February 1951* on copyright page.

THE CLOSED WORLDS. *New York: Ace Books, Inc.,* *[1968]*.
    Wrappers. No statement of printing on copyright page. *Ace Book G–701* (50¢).

THE COMET KINGS. *New York: Popular Library,* *[1969]*.
    Wrappers. No statement of printing on copyright page. *Popular Library 60–2407* (60¢).

CRASHING SUNS. *New York: Ace Books, Inc.,* *[1965]*.
    Wrappers. No statement of printing on copyright page. *Ace Book F–319* (40¢).

DANGER PLANET. *New York: Popular Library,* *[1968]*.
    Wrappers. No statement of printing on copyright page. *Popular Library 60–2335* (60¢). *Brett Sterling, pseudonym.*

DOOMSTAR. *New York: Belmont Books,* *[1966]*.
    Wrappers. *January 1966* on copyright page. *Belmont Science Fiction B50–657* (50¢).

FUGITIVE OF THE STARS. *New York: Ace Books, Inc.,* *[1965]*.
    Wrappers. No statement of printing on copyright page. *Ace Double M–111* (45¢). Bound with LAND BEYOND THE MAP by Kenneth Bulmer.

GALAXY MISSION. *New York: Popular Library*, [*1969*].
Wrappers. No statement of printing on copyright page. *Popular Library 60–2437* (60¢).

THE HAUNTED STARS. *New York: A Torquil Book Distributed by Dodd, Mead & Company*, [*1960*].
Boards. Two issues, priority of release not established but probably simultaneous: (A) Price $2.95 appears in the upper right corner of front dust jacket flap. Trade issue. (B) No price, *BOOK CLUB/EDITION* in lower right corner of front dust jacket flap. Book club issue. No statement of printing on copyright page. Note: Both issues released in March 1960. Both were printed from same press run and have printing code *B3* on page 192. A second book club printing is identified by code *B–18* on page 192.

THE HORROR ON THE ASTEROID. *London: Philip Allan, 1936.*
No statement of printing on copyright page.

THE MAGICIAN OF MARS. *New York: Popular Library*, [*1959*].
Wrappers. No statement of printing on copyright page. *Popular Library 60–2450* (60¢).

THE METAL GIANTS. *Washborn* [sic], *N. Dakota: Swanson Book Co., Publishers*, [*1932?*].
Self wrappers. No statement of printing. Cover title. Mimeographed. *Science Fiction Reprints No. 1* at head of title. Notes: (1) Advertised in *Science Fiction Digest*, October 1932 as available. Pavlat and Evans in *Fanzine Index* (1965), assign a 1933 printing date. (2) Washburn is misspelled in cover title.

THE MONSTERS OF JUNTONHEIM. *Manchester: Distributed by World Distributors Manchester Ltd . . . In collaboration with Sydney Pemberton Publisher*, [*1950*].
Wrappers. No statement of printing on copyright page. *A World Fantasy Classic* (1'6). Issued later in the U.S. as A YANK AT VALHALLA.

MURDER IN THE CLINIC. [*London: Utopian Publications Ltd.*], *n.d.* [*ca. 1946*].
Wrappers. No statement of printing. Cover title. *Printed in Eire* on page 36. Issued as *American Fiction No. 7* (One Shilling Net). Note: In addition to title story, includes "The Island of Unreason" by Hamilton.

OUTLAW WORLD. *New York: Popular Library*, [*1969*].
Wrappers. No statement of printing on copyright page. *Popular Library 60–2376* (60¢).

OUTLAWS OF THE MOON. *New York: Popular Library*, [*1969*].
Wrappers. No statement of printing on copyright page. *Popular Library 60–2399* (60¢).

OUTSIDE THE UNIVERSE. *New York: Ace Books, Inc.*, [*1964*].
Wrappers. No statement of printing on copyright page. *Ace Science Fiction Classic F–271* (40¢).

PLANETS IN PERIL. *New York: Popular Library*, [*1969*].
Wrappers. No statement of printing on copyright page. *Popular Library 60–2416* (60¢).

QUEST BEYOND THE STARS. *New York: Popular Library*, [*1969*].
Wrappers. No statement of printing on copyright page. *Popular Library 60–2389* (60¢).

RETURN TO THE STARS. *New York: Lancer Books*, [*1970*].
Wrappers. No statement of printing on copyright page. *Lancer Books 74612–075* (75¢).

THE STAR KINGS. *New York: Frederick Fell, Inc.*, [*1949*].
First printing, October 1949 on copyright page. Reissued as BEYOND THE MOON.

THE STAR OF LIFE. *New York: A Torquil Book Distributed by Dodd, Mead & Company,* [*1959*].

Boards. Two issues, priority of release as listed: (A) Price *$2.95* appears in upper right corner of front dust jacket flap. Trade issue. (B) No price, *BOOK CLUB/EDITION* in lower right corner of front dust jacket flap. Book club issue. No statement of printing on copyright page. Note: Trade issue published in February 1959, book club issue an April 1959 selection. Both issues from same press run; both have printing code *4* on page 192. A second book club printing is identified by the code *A14* on page 192.

THE SUN SMASHER. *New York: Ace Books, Inc.,* [*1959*].

Wrappers. No statement of printing on copyright page. *Ace Double Novel Books D–351* (35¢). Bound with STARHAVEN by Ivar Jorgenson.

THARKOL, LORD OF THE UNKNOWN. *Manchester: Distributed by World Distributors Manchester Ltd . . . . In collaboration with Sydney Pemberton Publisher,* [*1950*].

Wrappers. No statement of printing on copyright page. *World Fantasy Classics* (1'6).

TIGER GIRL. [*London: Utopian Publications Ltd.*], *n.d.* [*ca. 1945*].

Self wrappers. No statement of printing. Cover title. *Printed in Eire* at base of page 36. Note: In addition to the Hamilton contribution, includes ''Apprentice Magician'' by E. Hoffmann Price.

THE VALLEY OF CREATION. *New York: Lancer Books,* [*1964*].

Wrappers. *A Lancer Book • 1964* on copyright page. *Lancer Science Fiction Library 72–721* (50¢).

THE WEAPON FROM BEYOND. *New York: Ace Books, Inc.,* [*1967*].

Wrappers. No statement of printing on copyright page. *Ace Book G–639* (50¢).

WHAT'S IT LIKE OUT THERE? *New York: Ace Books,* [*1974*].

Wrappers. No statement of printing on copyright page. *An Ace Book 88065* (95¢).

WORLD OF THE STARWOLVES. *New York: Ace Books, Inc.,* [*1968*].

Wrappers. No statement of printing on copyright page. *Ace Book G–766* (50¢).

A YANK AT VALHALLA. *New York: Ace Books,* [*1973*].

Wrappers. *March, 1973* on copyright page. *Ace Double 93900* (95¢). Bound with THE SUN DESTROYERS by Ross Rocklynne. Issued earlier in Great Britain as THE MONSTERS OF JUNTONHEIM.

Edited Fiction

The Best of Leigh Brackett. *Garden City: Nelson Doubleday, Inc.,* [*1977*].

Boards. No statement of printing on copyright page. Code *S24* on page [367]. Edited, with introduction, by Hamilton. Note: Issued by the Science Fiction Book Club.

Charles Leonard Harness

(b. 1915)

FLIGHT INTO YESTERDAY. *New York: Bouregy & Curl, Inc. Publishers, [1953].*
  Boards. First edition so stated on copyright page. Reissued as THE PARADOX MEN.

THE PARADOX MEN. *New York: Ace Books, Inc., [1955].*
  Wrappers. No statement of printing on copyright page. *Ace Double Novel Books D–118*
  (35¢). Bound with DOME AROUND AMERICA by Jack Williamson. Reissue of FLIGHT INTO
  YESTERDAY.

THE RING OF RITORNEL. *London: Victor Gollancz Ltd, 1968.*
  Boards. No statement of printing on copyright page.

THE ROSE. *London: Published by Roberts & Vinter Ltd, [1966].*
  Wrappers. No statement of printing on copyright page. *Compact SF F295* (3/6).

  ALSO: *London: Sidgwick & Jackson, [1968]. This edition published 1968* on copyright
  page. First hardcover edition.

John Wyndham Parkes Lucas Beynon Harris
(1903–1969)

THE BEST OF JOHN WYNDHAM. *London: Sphere Books Limited*, [*1973*].
Wrappers. *First published in Great Britain . . . 1973* on copyright page. *Sphere 0 7221 9369 6 (40p). John Wyndham, pseudonym.* Reissued without introduction and bibliography as THE MAN FROM BEYOND AND OTHER STORIES.

CHOCKY. *New York: Ballantine Books*, [*1968*].
Wrappers. *First Printing: February, 1968* on copyright page. *A Ballantine Science Fiction Original U6119 (75¢). John Wyndham, pseudonym.*

ALSO: *London: Michael Joseph*, [*1968*]. Boards. *First published in Great Britain . . . 1968* on copyright page. First hardcover edition.

THE CHRYSALIDS. *London: Michael Joseph*, [*1955*].
Boards. *First published . . . 1955* on copyright page. *John Wyndham, pseudonym.* Issued earlier in the U.S. with textual differences as RE-BIRTH.

CONSIDER HER WAYS & OTHERS. *London: Michael Joseph*, [*1961*].
Boards. *First published . . .1961* on copyright page. *John Wyndham, pseudonym.*

THE DAY OF THE TRIFFIDS. *Garden City: Doubleday & Company, Inc., 1951.*
First edition so stated on copyright page. *John Wyndham, pseudonym.* Reissued as REVOLT OF THE TRIFFIDS.

ALSO: *London: Michael Joseph*, [*1951*]. *First published . . . 1951* on copyright page. Textual differences.

FOUL PLAY SUSPECTED. *London: George Newnes, Limited*, [*1935*].
No statement of printing on copyright page. *John Beynon, pseudonym.*

THE INFINITE MOMENT. *New York: Ballantine Books*, [*1961*].
Wrappers. No statement of printing on copyright page. *Ballantine Books 546 (35¢). John Wyndham, pseudonym.*

JIZZLE. *London: Dennis Dobson*, [*1954*].
Boards. *First published in Great Britain in MCMLIV* on copyright page. *John Wyndham, pseudonym.* Note: Two states of the dust jacket, priority as listed: (A) Rear panel carries advertisements for two titles, headed *MAN WITH A BACKGROUND OF FLAMES/Richard Johns;* (B) Rear panel lists ten titles, headed *Some imaginative fiction.*

THE JOHN WYNDHAM OMNIBUS. *London: Michael Joseph*, [*1964*].
Boards. *First published . . . 1964* on copyright page. Reprint. Collects THE DAY OF THE TRIFFIDS, THE KRAKEN WAKES, and THE CHRYSALIDS. *John Wyndham, pseudonym.*

THE KRAKEN WAKES. *London: Michael Joseph*, [*1953*].
Boards. *First published . . . 1953* on copyright page. *John Wyndham, pseudonym.* Issued later with textual changes in the U.S. as OUT OF THE DEEPS.

LOVE IN TIME. [*London: Utopian Publications Ltd.*], *n.d.* [*ca. 1945–1946*].
Wrappers. No statement of printing. Cover title. *Printed in Eire* on page 36. *Johnson Harris, pseudonym.*

THE MAN FROM BEYOND AND OTHER STORIES. *London: Michael Joseph*, [*1975*].
Boards. *This edition first published in Great Britain . . . 1975* on copyright page. *John Wyndham, pseudonym*. Reissue of THE BEST OF JOHN WYNDHAM. Drops introduction by Leslie Flood and bibliography.

THE MIDWICH CUCKOOS. *London: Michael Joseph*, [*1957*].
Boards. *First published . . . 1957* on copyright page. *John Wyndham, pseudonym*.

ALSO: *New York: Ballantine Books*, [*1958*]. No statement of printing on copyright page. Textual changes. Reissued following this text as VILLAGE OF THE DAMNED.

OUT OF THE DEEPS. *New York: Ballantine Books*, [*1953*].
Two issues, no priority: (A) Boards; (B) Wrappers. *Ballantine Books 50* (35¢). No statement of printing on copyright page. *John Wyndham, pseudonym*. Issued earlier in Great Britain with textual differences as THE KRAKEN WAKES.

THE OUTWARD URGE. *London: Michael Joseph*, [*1959*].
Boards. *First published . . . 1959* on copyright page. *John Wyndham and Lucas Parkes, pseudonyms*.

ALSO: *London: The Science Fiction Book Club, 1961*. Boards. No statement of printing on copyright page. Adds "The Emptiness of Space: A.D. 2194."

PLANET PLANE. *London: Newnes*, [*1936*].
No statement of printing on copyright page. *John Beynon, pseudonym*. Revised as STOWAWAY TO MARS.

RE-BIRTH. *New York: Ballantine Books*, [*1955*].
Two issues, no priority: (A) Cloth; (B) Wrappers. *Ballantine Books 104* (35¢). No statement of printing on copyright page. *John Wyndham, pseudonym*. Issued later in Great Britain with textual differences as THE CHRYSALIDS.

REVOLT OF THE TRIFFIDS. *New York: Popular Library*, [*1952*].
Wrappers. *March, 1952* on copyright page. *Popular Library 411* (25¢). *John Wyndham, pseudonym*. Reissue of THE DAY OF THE TRIFFIDS.

THE SECRET PEOPLE. *London: George Newnes, Limited*, [*1935*].
Three bindings, no priority established: (A) Green cloth, spine lettered in black; (B) Red cloth, spine lettered in gold; (C) Brown cloth, spine lettered in gold. No statement of printing on copyright page. *John Beynon, pseudonym*. Note: Issued in the U.S. in 1973 by Fawcett Publications under the John Wyndham pseudonym.

THE SEEDS OF TIME. *London: Michael Joseph*, [*1956*].
Boards. *First published . . . 1956* on copyright page. *John Wyndham, pseudonym*.

SLEEPERS OF MARS. *London: Hodder Paperbacks Ltd.*, [*1973*].
Wrappers. *First published in this form . . . 1973* on copyright page. *Coronet Science Fiction 17326 2* (30p).

STOWAWAY TO MARS. *London: Nova Publications Ltd.*, [*1953*].
Wrappers. No statement of printing on copyright page. *Nova Science Fiction Novels No. 1* (1'6). *John Beynon, pseudonym*. Revised text. Originally published as PLANET PLANE.

TALES OF GOOSEFLESH AND LAUGHTER. *New York: Ballantine Books*, [*1956*].
Wrappers. No statement of printing on copyright page. *John Wyndham, pseudonym*.

TROUBLE WITH LICHEN. *London: Michael Joseph*, [*1960*].
Boards. *First published . . . 1960* on copyright page. *John Wyndham, pseudonym*.

ALSO: *New York: Ballantine Books,* [*1960*]. Wrappers. No statement of printing on copyright page. *Ballantine Science Fiction 449 K* (35¢). Textual differences.

ALSO: *New York: Walker and Company,* [*1969*]. Boards. *Published in the United States of America in 1969 . . .* on copyright page. First U.S. hardcover edition. Follows the 1960 Ballantine Books text.

VILLAGE OF THE DAMNED. *New York: Ballantine Books,* [*1960*].
Wrappers. No statement of printing on copyright page. *Ballantine Books 453K* (35¢). *John Wyndham, pseudonym.* Reissue of THE MIDWICH CUCKOOS. Note: Follows the 1958 Ballantine Books text.

WANDERERS OF TIME. *London: Hodder Paperbacks Ltd.,* [*1973*].
Wrappers. *First published in this form . . . 1973* on copyright page. *Coronet Science Fiction 17306 8* (30p).

Associational

The Triffids, adapted by Patrick Nobes from The Day of the Triffids by John Wyndham. *London: Hutchinson,* [*1973*].
Wrappers. *This adaptation first published 1973* on copyright page. *Bulls-Eye Book.*

Harry Maxwell Harrison

(b. 1925)

THE ADVENTURES OF THE STAINLESS STEEL RAT. *Garden City: Nelson Doubleday, Inc.*, [*1977*].
>Boards. No statement of printing on copyright page. Code *H 47* on page 405. Reprint. Collects THE STAINLESS STEEL RAT, THE STAINLESS STEEL RAT'S REVENGE, and THE STAINLESS STEEL RAT SAVES THE WORLD. Note: Issued by the Science Fiction Book Club.

THE BEST OF HARRY HARRISON. *New York: Published by Pocket Books*, [*1976*].
>Wrappers. *Published June, 1976* on copyright page. *Pocket Books Sci-Fi 80525* ($1.95).

>ALSO:*London: Sidgwick & Jackson*, [*1976*]. Boards. *First published in this edition in Great Britain in 1976 . . .* on copyright page. First hardcover edition. Note: Drops the introduction by Barry N. Malzberg and "Not Me, Not Amos Cabot!" and adds "The Wicked Flee" and "We Ate the Whole Thing."

BILL, THE GALACTIC HERO. *Garden City: Doubleday & Company, Inc.*, *1965*.
>First edition so stated on copyright page.

THE CALIFORNIA ICEBERG. *London: Faber and Faber*, [*1975*].
>Boards. *First published in 1975* on copyright page.

CAPTIVE UNIVERSE. *New York: G. P. Putnam's Sons*, [*1969*].
>Boards. No statement of printing on copyright page.

THE DALETH EFFECT. *New York: G. P. Putnam's Sons*, [*1970*].
>No statement of printing on copyright page. Issued later in Great Britain as IN OUR HANDS, THE STARS.

DEATHWORLD. *New York: Bantam Books*, [*1960*].
>Wrappers. *Published September 1960* on copyright page. *A Bantam Book A2160* (35¢). Later collected in THE DEATHWORLD TRILOGY.

DEATHWORLD 2. *Toronto New York London: Bantam Books*, [*1964*].
>Wrappers. *Published September 1964* on copyright page. *A Bantam Fifty F2838* (50¢). Issued later in Great Britain as THE ETHICAL ENGINEER. Later collected in THE DEATHWORLD TRILOGY.

DEATHWORLD 3. [*New York*]: *A Dell Book*, [*1968*].
>Wrappers. *First printing—May 1968* on copyright page. *Dell 1849* (60¢). Later collected in THE DEATHWORLD TRILOGY.

>ALSO:*London: Faber and Faber*, [*1969*]. *First published in England in 1969* on copyright page. First hardcover edition.

THE DEATHWORLD TRILOGY. *Garden City: Nelson Doubleday, Inc.*, [*1974*].
>Boards. No statement of printing on copyright page. Code *40 Q* on page 437. Reprint. Collects DEATHWORLD, DEATHWORLD 2, and DEATHWORLD 3. First hardcover edition of DEATHWORLD; first U.S. hardcover edition of DEATHWORLD 2 and DEATHWORLD 3. Note: Issued by the Science Fiction Book Club.

THE ETHICAL ENGINEER. *London: Victor Gollancz Ltd*, *1964*.
>Boards. No statement of printing on copyright page. Issued earlier in the U.S. as DEATHWORLD 2.

IN OUR HANDS, THE STARS. *London: Faber and Faber, [1970].*
  First published in England in 1970 on copyright page. Issued earlier in the U.S. as THE DALETH EFFECT.

THE JUPITER LEGACY. *Toronto New York London: Bantam Books, [1970].*
  Wrappers. *New Bantam edition published July 1970* on copyright page. *A Bantam Book S5445* (75¢). Reissue of PLAGUE FROM SPACE.

THE LIFESHIP. *New York, Hagerstown, San Francisco, London: Harper & Row, Publishers, [1976].*
  Boards with cloth shelf back. First edition so stated on copyright page. With GORDON R. DICKSON.

MAKE ROOM! MAKE ROOM! *Garden City: Doubleday & Company, Inc., 1966.*
  First edition so stated on copyright page.

THE MAN FROM P.I.G. *[New York]: An Avon Camelot Book, [1968].*
  Wrappers. *First Printing (Camelot Edition), May, 1968* on copyright page. *Avon ZS136* (60¢). Later collected in THE MAN FROM P.I.G. AND R.O.B.O.T.

THE MAN FROM P.I.G. AND R.O.B.O.T. *London: Faber & Faber Ltd, [1974].*
  Boards. *First published in 1974* on copyright page.

MONTEZUMA'S REVENGE. *Garden City: Doubleday & Company, Inc., 1972.*
  First edition in the United States of America on copyright page.

ONE STEP FROM EARTH. *[New York]: The Macmillan Company, [1970].*
  First printing so stated on copyright page.

PLAGUE FROM SPACE. *Garden City: Doubleday & Company, Inc., 1965.*
  First edition so stated on copyright page. Reissued as THE JUPITER LEGACY.

PLANET OF THE DAMNED. *New York: Bantam Books, [1962].*
  Wrappers. *Published January 1962* on copyright page. *A Bantam Book J2316* (40¢). Issued later in Great Britain as SENSE OF OBLIGATION.

PRIME NUMBER. *[New York]: Published by Berkley Publishing Corporation, [1970].*
  Wrappers. *July, 1970* on copyright page. *A Berkley Medallion Book S1857* (75¢).

QUEEN VICTORIA'S REVENGE. *Garden City: Doubleday & Company, Inc., 1974.*
  First edition so stated on copyright page.

SENSE OF OBLIGATION. *London: Dennis Dobson, [1967].*
  Boards. *First published in Great Britain in 1967* on copyright page. Issued earlier in the U.S. as PLANET OF THE DAMNED.

SKYFALL. *London: Faber and Faber, [1976].*
  Boards. *First published in 1976* on copyright page.

SPACESHIP MEDIC. *London: Faber and Faber, [1970].*
  First published in 1970 on copyright page.

THE STAINLESS STEEL RAT. *New York: Pyramid Books, [1961].*
  Wrappers. *First printing: November 1961* on copyright page. *Pyramid Books F672* (40¢).

  ALSO: *New York: Walker and Company, [1970].* Boards. *Published in the United States of America in 1970 . . .* on copyright page. First hardcover edition. Later collected in THE ADVENTURES OF THE STAINLESS STEEL RAT.

THE STAINLESS STEEL RAT SAVES THE WORLD. *New York: G. P. Putnam's Sons*, [*1972*].
No statement of printing on copyright page. Later collected in THE ADVENTURES OF THE STAINLESS STEEL RAT.

THE STAINLESS STEEL RAT'S REVENGE. *New York: Walker and Company*, [*1970*].
Boards. *First published in the United States of America in 1970 . . .* on copyright page. Later collected in THE ADVENTURES OF THE STAINLESS STEEL RAT.

STAR SMASHERS OF THE GALAXY RANGERS. *New York: G. P. Putnam's Sons*, [*1973*].
No statement of printing on copyright page.

STONEHENGE. *London: Peter Davies*, [*1972*].
Boards. *First published 1972* on copyright page. With LEON E. STOVER.

THE TECHNICOLOR® TIME MACHINE. *Garden City: Doubleday & Company, Inc.*, 1967.
First edition so stated on copyright page.

A TRANSATLANTIC TUNNEL, HURRAH! *London: Faber and Faber*, [*1972*].
Boards. *First published in Great Britain in 1972* on copyright page. Issued earlier in the U.S. as TUNNEL THROUGH THE DEEPS.

TUNNEL THROUGH THE DEEPS. *New York: G. P. Putnam's Sons*, [*1972*].
Boards. No statement of printing on copyright page. Issued later in Great Britain as A TRANSATLANTIC TUNNEL, HURRAH!

TWO TALES AND 8 TOMORROWS. *London: Victor Gollancz Ltd*, 1965.
Boards. No statement of printing on copyright page.

*VENDETTA FOR THE SAINT. *Garden City: Doubleday & Company, Inc.*, 1964.
First edition so stated on copyright page. *Leslie Charteris, pseudonym.*

WAR WITH THE ROBOTS. *New York: Pyramid Books*, [*1962*].
Wrappers. *First printing, September 1962* on copyright page. *Pyramid Books F–771* (40¢).

ALSO: *London: Dennis Dobson*, [*1967*]. Boards. *First published in Great Britain in 1967* on copyright page. First hardcover edition.

Edited Fiction

Ahead of Time. *Garden City: Doubleday & Company, Inc.*, 1972.
First edition so stated on copyright page. Edited, with introduction, by Harrison. With THEODORE J. GORDON.

All About Venus. [*New York*]: *A Dell Book*, [*1968*].
Wrappers. *First printing—October 1968* on copyright page. *Dell 0085* (60¢). Edited, with foreword, introductions, and notes, by Harrison. With BRIAN W. ALDISS. A much enlarged edition was issued later the same month in Great Britain as *Farewell, Fantastic Venus!*

Apeman, Spaceman. *Garden City: Doubleday & Company, Inc.*, 1968.
First edition so stated on copyright page. Edited, with introduction, by Harrison. With LEON E. STOVER.

Astounding: John W. Campbell Memorial Anthology. *New York: Random House*, [*1973*].
Boards with cloth shelf back. First edition so stated on copyright page. Edited, with afterword and short story "The Mothballed Spaceship," by Harrison.

The Astounding • Analog Reader. *Garden City: Doubleday & Company, Inc.*, 1972-1973.
First edition so stated on copyright pages. Two volumes. Edited, with introductions and short story "Rescue Operation," by Harrison. With BRIAN W. ALDISS.

Backdrop of Stars. *London: Dennis Dobson*, [*1968*].
  Boards. *First published in Great Britain in 1968* on copyright page. Edited, with introduction, by Harrison. Issued later in the U.S. as *SF: Author's Choice* [*1*].

Best SF: 1967. [*New York*]: *Published by Berkley Publishing Corporation*, [*1968*].
  Wrappers. *March, 1968* on copyright page. *Berkley S1529* (75¢). Edited, with introduction, by Harrison. With BRIAN W. ALDISS. Issued the same month in Great Britain as *The Year's Best Science Fiction No. 1*.

Best SF: 1968. *New York: G. P. Putnam's Sons*, [*1969*].
  No statement of printing on copyright page. Edited, with introduction, by Harrison. With BRIAN W. ALDISS. Issued earlier with textual differences in Great Britain as *The Year's Best Science Fiction No. 2*.

Best SF: 1969. *New York: G. P. Putnam's Sons*, [*1970*].
  Boards. No statement of printing on copyright page. Edited, with introduction, by Harrison. With BRIAN W. ALDISS. Issued earlier in Great Britain as *The Year's Best Science Fiction No. 3*.

Best SF: 1970. *New York: G. P. Putnam's Sons*, [*1970*].
  No statement of printing on copyright page. Edited, with introduction, by Harrison. With BRIAN W. ALDISS. Issued earlier in Great Britain as *The Year's Best Science Fiction No. 4*.

Best SF: 1971. *New York: G. P. Putnam's Sons*, [*1972*].
  No statement of printing on copyright page. Edited, with introduction, by Harrison. With BRIAN W. ALDISS. Published the same month in Great Britain, possibly simultaneously, as *The Year's Best Science Fiction No. 5*.

Best SF: 1972. *New York: G. P. Putnam's Sons*, [*1973*].
  No statement of printing on copyright page. Edited, with introduction, by Harrison. With BRIAN W. ALDISS. Issued later in Great Britain as *The Year's Best Science Fiction No. 6*.

Best SF 73. [*New York*]: *Published by Berkley Publishing Corporation*, [*1974*].
  Wrappers. *June, 1974* on copyright page. *A Berkley Medallion Book 425–02581–095* (95¢). Edited, with introduction, by Harrison. With BRIAN W. ALDISS. Issued later in Great Britain with abridgment as *The Year's Best Science Fiction No. 7*.

  ALSO: New York: G. P. Putnam's Sons, [*1975*]. Boards. No statement of printing on copyright page. First hardcover edition.

Best SF 1974. *Indianapolis/New York: The Bobbs-Merrill Company, Inc.*, [*1975*].
  Boards with cloth shelf back. First printing so stated on copyright page. Edited, with editorial, by Harrison. With BRIAN W. ALDISS. Issued later in Great Britain as *The Year's Best Science Fiction No. 8* without poem "Eyes of a Woman—From a Portrait by Picasso" by Lisa Conesa.

Best SF: 75. The Ninth Annual. *Indianapolis/New York: The Bobbs-Merrill Company, Inc.*, [*1976*].
  Boards with cloth shelf back. First printing so stated on copyright page. Edited, with introduction, by Harrison. With BRIAN W. ALDISS. Issued earlier in Great Britain as *The Year's Best Science Fiction No. 9*.

Blast Off: S. F. for Boys. *London: Faber and Faber Ltd*, [*1969*].
  First published in 1969 on copyright page. Edited, with introduction and short story "Rocket Pilot," by Harrison.

Decade the 1940s. [*London*]: *M*[*acmillan London Limited, 1975*].
  Boards. *First published 1975* . . . on copyright page. Edited by Harrison. With BRIAN W. ALDISS.

Decade the 1950s. *[London]: M[acmillan London Limited, 1976]*.
Boards. *First published 1976* . . . on copyright page. Edited, with introduction, by Harrison. With BRIAN W. ALDISS.

Decade the 1960s. *[London]: M[acmillan, 1977]*.
Boards. *First published 1977* . . . on copyright page. Edited by Harrison. With BRIAN W. ALDISS.

Farewell, Fantastic Venus! *[London]: Macdonald Science Fiction, [1968]*.
Boards. *First published in Great Britain in 1968* on copyright page. Edited, with foreword, introductions, and notes, by Harrison. With BRIAN W. ALDISS. Issued earlier the same month in the U.S. in a much abridged format as *All About Venus*.

Four For the Future. *[London]: Macdonald Science Fiction, [1969]*.
Boards. *First published in Great Britain in 1969* on copyright page. Edited, with introduction and two short stories, "The Gods Themselves Throw Incense" and "The Ghoul Squad," by Harrison.

The Light Fantastic. *New York: Charles Scribner's Sons, [1971]*.
Boards with cloth shelf back. Code *A–3.71 (C)* on copyright page. Edited, with afterword, by Harrison.

Nebula Award Stories Two. *Garden City: Doubleday and Company, Inc., 1967*.
First edition so stated on copyright page. Edited, with introduction and afterword, by Harrison. With BRIAN W. ALDISS.

Nova 1. *New York: Delacorte Press, [1970]*.
Boards with cloth shelf back. First printing so stated on copyright page. Edited, with introduction, by Harrison.

ALSO: *London: Robert Hale & Company, [1976]*. Boards. *This edition 1976* on copyright page. Abridged text.

Nova 2. *New York: Walker and Company, [1972]*.
Boards. *First published in the United States of America in 1972* on copyright page. Edited, with introduction, by Harrison.

Nova 3. *New York: Walker and Company, [1973]*.
Boards. *First published in the United States of America in 1973* on copyright page. Edited, with introduction, by Harrison. Reissued as *The Outdated Man*.

Nova 4. *New York: Walker and Company, [1975]*.
Boards. *First published in the United States of America in 1974* on copyright page. Edited, with notes and afterword, by Harrison. Note: Publication date was 31 January 1975.

The Outdated Man. *[New York]: A Dell Book, [1975]*.
Wrappers. *First Dell printing —April 1975* on copyright page. *Dell 6661* (95¢). Edited, with introduction, by Harrison. Reissue of *Nova 3*.

SF: Authors' Choice. *[New York]: Published by Berkley Publishing Corporation, [1968]*.
Wrappers. *June, 1968* on copyright page. *A Berkley Medallion Book S1567* (75¢). Edited, with introduction, by Harrison. Issued earlier in Great Britain as *Backdrop of Stars*.

SF: Authors' Choice 2. *[New York]: Published by Berkley Publishing Corporation, [1970]*.
Wrappers. *May, 1970* on copyright page. *A Berkley Medallion Book S1837* (75¢). Edited, with introduction, by Harrison.

SF: Authors' Choice 3. *New York: G. P. Putnam's Sons, [1971]*.
No statement of printing on copyright page. Edited, with introduction and short story "By the Falls," by Harrison.

SF: Authors' Choice 4. *New York: G. P. Putnam's Sons, [1974]*.
No statement of printing on copyright page. Edited, with introduction, by Harrison.

Science Fiction Novellas. *New York: Charles Scribner's Sons, [1975]*.
Wrappers. Code *1 3 5 7 9 11 13 15 17 19 M/P 20 18 16 14 12 10 8 6 4 2* on copyright page. Edited, with foreword and notes, by Harrison. With WILLIS E. McNELLY.

A Science Fiction Reader. *New York: Charles Scribner's Sons, [1973]*.
Wrappers. Code *A–11.72 (C)* on copyright page. Issued as *Scribner Student Paperbacks SSP 31*. Edited, with foreword and notes, by Harrison. With CAROL PUGNER.

Worlds of Wonder. *Garden City: Doubleday & Company, Inc., [1969]*.
First edition so stated on copyright page. Edited, with introduction and short story "If," by Harrison.

The Year 2000. *Garden City: Doubleday & Company, Inc., 1970*.
First edition so stated on copyright page. Edited, with introduction and short story "American Dead," by Harrison.

The Year's Best Science Fiction. *[London]: Severn House, [1977]*.
Boards. *The first British hardcover edition published in 1977 . . .* on copyright page. Edited, with foreword, by Harrison. With BRIAN W. ALDISS. Issued earlier as *The Year's Best Science Fiction No. 2*.

The Year's Best Science Fiction No. 1. *London: Sphere Books Limited, [1968]*.
Wrappers. *First published in Great Britain 1968 . . .* on copyright page. *Sphere Science Fiction 43311* (5/0). Edited, with introduction, by Harrison. With BRIAN W. ALDISS. Issued the same month in the U.S. as *Best SF: 1967*.

The Year's Best Science Fiction No. 2. *London: Sphere Books Limited, [1969]*.
Wrappers. *First published in Great Britain in 1969 . . .* on copyright page. *Sphere 43354* (5/–). Edited, with introduction, by Harrison. With BRIAN W. ALDISS. Drops "The Serpent of Kundalini" by Aldiss but does include "Like Young" by Theodore Sturgeon. Issued later in Great Britain as *The Year's Best Science Fiction*. Issued later in the U.S. with the Aldiss story and without the Sturgeon story as *Best SF: 1968*.

The Year's Best Science Fiction No. 3. *London: Sphere Books Limited, [1970]*.
Wrappers. *First published in Great Britain in 1970* on copyright page. *Sphere Science Fiction 43419* (30p). Edited, with introduction, by Harrison. With BRIAN W. ALDISS. Issued later in the U.S. as *Best SF: 1969*.

The Year's Best Science Fiction No. 4. *London: Sphere Books Limited, [1971]*.
Wrappers. *First published in Great Britain in 1971 . . .* on copyright page. *Science Fiction Sphere 43435* (30p). Edited, with introduction, by Harrison. With BRIAN W. ALDISS. Issued later in the U.S. as *Best SF: 1970*.

The Year's Best Science Fiction No. 5. *London: Sphere Books Limited, [1972]*.
Wrappers. *First published in Great Britain in 1972* on copyright page. *Sphere Science Fiction 43443* (35p). Edited, with introduction, by Harrison. With BRIAN W. ALDISS. Published the same month in the U.S., possibly simultaneously, as *Best SF: 1971*.

The Year's Best Science Fiction No. 6. *London: Sphere Books Limited, [1973]*.
Wrappers. *First published in Great Britain in 1973 . . .* on copyright page. *Sphere Science*

Fiction 0 7221 4355 9 (35p.) Edited, with introduction, by Harrison. With BRIAN W. ALDISS. Note: Reprinted in November 1973 with cover title reading *The Year's Best S.F. 1972*. Issued earlier in the U.S. as *Best SF: 1972*.

The Year's Best Science Fiction No. 7. *London: Sphere Books Limited, [1975]*. Wrappers. *First published in Great Britain . . . 1975* on copyright page. *Sphere Science Fiction 0 7221 4361 3* (55p). Edited, with introduction, by Harrison. With BRIAN W. ALDISS. This abridged edition omits the five poems, four stories, and afterword by Aldiss following "La Befana" by Gene Wolfe. Complete text issued earlier in the U.S. as *Best SF 73*.

The Year's Best Science Fiction No. 8. *London: Sphere Books Limited, [1976]*. Wrappers. *First published in Great Britain . . . 1976* on copyright page. *Sphere 0 7221 4398 2* (65p). Edited, with introduction, by Harrison. With BRIAN W. ALDISS. Deletes poem by Lisa Conesa. Issued earlier in the U.S. as *Best SF 1974*.

The Year's Best Science Fiction No. 9. *[London]: Futura Publications Limited, [1976]*. Wrappers. *First published in Great Britain in 1976 . . .* on copyright page. *Orbit Science Fiction 0 8600 7894 9* (65p). Edited, with introduction, by Harrison. With BRIAN W. ALDISS. Issued later in the U.S. as *Best SF: 75. The Ninth Annual*.

ALSO: *London: Weidenfeld and Nicolson, [1976]*. Boards. No statement of printing on copyright page. First British hardcover edition.

Nonfiction (Dealing with the Fantasy Genre only)

Great Balls of Fire. *[London: Pierrot Publishing Limited, 1977.]*
   Two issues, no priority: (A) Boards; (B) Wrappers. *First published in Great Britain in 1977./PIERROT PUBLISHING LIMITED/London* on copyright page. Note: Sheets of the Pierrot and U.S. issues published by Grosset & Dunlap were produced from the same press run, but the British version was released in September 1977 while the U.S. was distributed in December 1977.

Edited Nonfiction (Dealing with the Fantasy Genre only)

Collected Editorials from Analog, by John W. Campbell. *Garden City: Doubleday & Company, Inc., 1966*.
   First edition so stated on copyright page. Edited, with introduction, by Harrison.

Hell's Cartographers. *[London]: Weidenfeld and Nicolson, [1975]*.
   Boards. No statement of printing on copyright page. Edited, with contribution "The Beginning of the Affair," by Harrison. With BRIAN W. ALDISS.

Reference

Harry Harrison: Bibliographia (1951–1965), compiled by Francesco Biamonti, with annotations by Harry Harrison. *[Trieste: Printed by Editoriale Libraria, S. p. A., 1965.]*
   Wrappers. No statement of printing.

Michael John Harrison
(b. 1945)

THE CENTAURI DEVICE. *Garden City: Doubleday & Company, Inc., 1974.*
  Boards. First edition so stated on copyright page.

THE COMMITTED MEN. [*London: Hutchinson, 1971.*]
  Boards. *First published 1971* on copyright page.

  ALSO: *Garden City: Doubleday & Company, Inc., 1971. First edition in the United States of America* on copyright page. Textual differences.

THE MACHINE IN SHAFT TEN AND OTHER STORIES. [*Frogmore*]: *Panther,* [*1975*].
  Wrappers. *First published in 1975 . . .* on copyright page. *Panther 586 04191 5* (50p).

PASTEL CITY. [*London*]: *New English Library,* [*1971*].
  Wrappers. *First NEL paperback edition 1971* on copyright page. *New English Library 450 00764 2* (30p).

  ALSO: *Garden City: Doubleday & Company, Inc., 1972. First edition in the United States of America* on copyright page. First hardcover edition.

Robert Anson Heinlein

(b. 1907)

ASSIGNMENT IN ETERNITY. *Reading, Pennsylvania: Fantasy Press*, [*1953*].
Three bindings, priority as listed: (A) Brick red cloth, spine stamped in gold, including six bands, *HEINLEIN* is set in type 3 mm high; (B) Green boards, spine lettered in black. Remainder binding, Greenberg variant; (C) Red cloth, spine stamped in gold in a manner similar to first binding, but *HEINLEIN* set in type 2 mm high. Remainder binding, Grant variant. Two issues, no priority: (A) 500 copies with numbered leaf signed by Heinlein inserted; (B) Trade issue. First edition so stated on copyright page.

THE BEST OF ROBERT HEINLEIN. *London: Sidgwick & Jackson*, [*1973*].
Boards. *First published in Great Britain in 1973* on copyright page. Reprint collection. Note: Reprinted as a one-volume paperback by Sphere Books Limited in 1975. In 1977 the collection was divided into two paperback volumes and issued by Sphere as THE BEST OF ROBERT HEINLEIN 1939–1942 and THE BEST OF ROBERT HEINLEIN 1947–1959. The latter contains a bibliography revised through 1976.

BETWEEN PLANETS. *New York: Charles Scribner's Sons, 1951*.
First printing has *A* and Scribner seal on copyright page.

BEYOND THIS HORIZON. *Reading, Pennsylvania: Fantasy Press, 1948*.
Two issues, no priority: (A) 500 copies with numbered leaf signed by Heinlein inserted; (B) Trade issue. First edition so stated on copyright page.

CITIZEN OF THE GALAXY. *New York: Charles Scribner's Sons*, [*1957*].
First printing has *A* and code *7.57v* on copyright page.

THE DAY AFTER TOMORROW. [*New York*]: *The New American Library*, [*1951*].
Wrappers. *First printing, September, 1951* on copyright page. *N.A.L. Signet Books 882* (25¢). Reissue of SIXTH COLUMN.

THE DOOR INTO SUMMER. *Garden City: Doubleday & Company, Inc., 1957*.
First edition so stated on copyright page.

DOUBLE STAR. *Garden City: Doubleday & Company, Inc., 1956*.
Boards. First edition so stated on copyright page.

FARMER IN THE SKY. *New York: Charles Scribner's Sons, 1950*.
First printing has *A* and Scribner seal on copyright page.

FARNHAM'S FREEHOLD. *New York: G.P. Putnam's Sons*, [*1964*].
No statement of printing on copyright page.

GLORY ROAD. *New York: G.P. Putnam's Sons*, [*1963*].
No statement of printing on copyright page.

THE GREEN HILLS OF EARTH. *Chicago: Shasta Publishers*, [*1951*].
Boards with cloth shelf back. First edition so stated on copyright page.

HAVE SPACE SUIT—WILL TRAVEL. *New York: Charles Scribner's Sons*, [*1958*].
First printing has code *A.9–58* [*MJ*] on copyright page.

A HEINLEIN TRIAD. *London: Victor Gollancz Ltd, 1966.*
Boards. No statement of printing on copyright page. Reprint. Collects THE PUPPET MASTERS and WALDO AND MAGIC, INC. Issued earlier in the U.S. as THREE BY HEINLEIN.

I WILL FEAR NO EVIL. *New York: G. P. Putnam's Sons, [1970].*
No statement of printing on copyright page.

LOST LEGACY. *London: Brown, Watson Ltd, [1960].*
Wrappers. No statement of printing on copyright page. *Digit Books D386* (2/–). Reprints two stories from ASSIGNMENT IN ETERNITY.

THE MAN WHO SOLD THE MOON. *Chicago: Shasta Publishers, [1950].*
Boards with cloth shelf back. First edition so stated on copyright page.

ALSO: [*New York*]: *Published by The New American Library, [1951].* Wrappers. *First printing, March, 1951* on copyright page. *N.A.L. Signet Books 847* (25¢). Abridged edition.

THE MENACE FROM EARTH. *Hicksville, New York: The Gnome Press, Inc., [1959].*
First edition so stated on copyright page.

METHUSELAH'S CHILDREN. *Hicksville, N.Y.: Gnome Press, [1958].*
Two bindings, probable priority as listed: (A) Black boards, spine printed in red: (B) Gray cloth, spine printed in red. No statement of printing on copyright page. Notes: (1) According to Owings and Chalker in *The Index to the Science-Fantasy Publishers,* there were 1500 copies of the first printing and a second printing in 1959 of 1000 copies. So far no copies of the second printing have been identified. (2) All dust jackets observed print the publisher's address ''80 East 11th St., New York 3'' at base of rear panel. George Locke in *Science Fiction First Editions* (London: Ferret Fantasy, 1978), p.87, reports a variant jacket with ''80 East 11th St.,'' and ''3'' removed.

THE MOON IS A HARSH MISTRESS. *New York: G. P. Putnam's Sons, [1966].*
No statement of printing on copyright page.

ORPHANS OF THE SKY. *London: Victor Gollancz Ltd, 1963.*
Boards. No statement of printing on copyright page.

THE PAST THROUGH TOMORROW. *New York: G. P. Putnam's Sons, [1967].*
No statement of printing on copyright page. Reprint collection. Note: Omnibus collection of the novels and stories comprising the ''Future History'' series reprinted from earlier books.

ALSO: [*London*]: *New English Library, [1977].* Boards. Two volumes. *First published in Great Britain . . . in 1977* on copyright pages. Abridged reprint. Drops METHUSELAH'S CHILDREN.

PODKAYNE OF MARS. *New York: G. P. Putnam's Sons, [1963].*
No statement of printing on copyright page.

THE PUPPET MASTERS. *Garden City: Doubleday & Company, Inc., 1951.*
First edition so stated on copyright page.

RED PLANET. *New York: Charles Scribner's Sons, 1949.*
First printing has *A* and Scribner seal on copyright page.

REVOLT IN 2100. *Chicago: Shasta Publishers, [1953].*
Boards with cloth shelf back. First edition so stated on copyright page.

A ROBERT HEINLEIN OMNIBUS. *London: Sidgwick & Jackson*, [*1966*].
Boards. No statement of printing on copyright page. Reprint. Collects BEYOND THIS HORIZON, THE MAN WHO SOLD THE MOON, and THE GREEN HILLS OF EARTH.

THE ROBERT HEINLEIN OMNIBUS. *London: The Science Fiction Book Club by arrangement with Sidgwick and Jackson, 1958.*
Boards. *This Science Fiction Book Club edition was produced in 1958 for sale to its members only* on copyright page. Reprint. Collects THE MAN WHO SOLD THE MOON and THE GREEN HILLS OF EARTH.

ROCKET SHIP GALILEO. *New York: Charles Scribner's Sons*, [*1947*].
First printing has *A* and Scribner seal on copyright page.

THE ROLLING STONES. *New York: Charles Scribner's Sons*, [*1952*].
First printing has *A* and Scribner seal on copyright page. Reissued in Great Britain as SPACE FAMILY STONE.

6 x H. *New York: Pyramid Books*, [*1961*].
Wrappers. *First printing, August 1961* on copyright page. *Pyramid G642* (35¢). Reprint of THE UNPLEASANT PROFESSION OF JONATHAN HOAG.

SIXTH COLUMN. *New York: Gnome Press*, [*1949*].
First edition so stated on copyright page. Reissued as THE DAY AFTER TOMORROW.

SPACE CADET. *New York: Charles Scribner's Sons, 1948.*
First printing has *A* and Scribner seal on copyright page.

SPACE FAMILY STONE. *London: Victor Gollancz Ltd, 1969.*
Boards. No statement of printing on copyright page. Issued earlier in the U.S. as THE ROLLING STONES.

THE STAR BEAST. *New York: Charles Scribner's Sons*, [*1954*].
First printing has *A* and Scribner seal on copyright page.

STARMAN JONES. *New York: Charles Scribner's Sons*, [*1953*].
First printing has *A* and Scribner seal on copyright page.

STARSHIP TROOPERS. *New York: G. P. Putnam's Sons*, [*1959*].
No statement of printing on copyright page.

STRANGER IN A STRANGE LAND. *New York: G. P. Putnam's Sons*, [*1961*].
No statement of printing on copyright page.

THREE BY HEINLEIN. *Garden City: Doubleday & Company, Inc., 1965.*
No statement of printing on copyright page. Code *G39* at base of page 426. Reprint. Collects THE PUPPET MASTERS and WALDO AND MAGIC, INC. Issued later in Great Britain as A HEINLEIN TRIAD.

TIME ENOUGH FOR LOVE. . . . *New York: G. P. Putnam's Sons*, [*1973*].
No statement of printing on copyright page.

TIME FOR THE STARS. *New York: Charles Scribner's Sons*, [*1956*].
First printing has code *A–8.56* [*v*] on copyright page.

TUNNEL IN THE SKY. *New York: Charles Scribner's Sons*, [*1955*].
First printing has *A* on copyright page.

UNIVERSE. *New York: Published by Dell Publishing Company, Inc.,* [*1951*].
  Wrappers. No statement of printing on copyright page. *Dell Book 36* (10¢). *Adventure on a Gigantic Spaceship* at head of title.

THE UNPLEASANT PROFESSION OF JONATHAN HOAG. *Hicksville, New York: The Gnome Press, Inc.,* [*1959*].
  First edition so stated on copyright page. Reissued as 6 x H.

WALDO AND MAGIC, INC. *Garden City: Doubleday & Company, Inc., 1950.*
  First edition so stated on copyright page. Reissued as WALDO: GENIUS IN ORBIT.

WALDO: GENIUS IN ORBIT. *New York: Avon Publications, Inc.,* [*1958*].
  Wrappers. No statement of printing on copyright page. *Avon T–261* (35¢). Reissue of WALDO AND MAGIC, INC.

THE WORLDS OF ROBERT A. HEINLEIN. *New York: Ace Books, Inc.,* [*1966*].
  Wrappers. No statement of printing on copyright page. *Ace Book F–375* (40¢).

Edited Fiction

Tomorrow, the Stars. *Garden City: Doubleday & Company, Inc., 1952.*
  First edition so stated on copyright page. Edited, with preface, by Heinlein.

Nonfiction (Dealing with the Fantasy Genre only)

The Discovery of the Future . . . Speech Delivered by Guest of Honor at 3d World Science Fiction Convention. . . . [*Los Angeles*]: *A Novacious Publication,* [*1941*].
  Wrappers. *Ltd. first edit./(200)* on front wrapper. Cover title. Spirit duplication, stapled. Limited to 200 copies.

Reference

The Classic Years of Robert A. Heinlein, by George Edgar Slusser. *San Bernardino, California: R. Reginald The Borgo Press, MCMLXXVII.*
  Wrappers. Two states, priority as listed: (A) "The looser structures seem . . . ," page 6, line 1; (B) "Hamilton Felix to do his part).", page 6, line 1. *First Edition———October, 1977* on copyright page. *The Milford Series Popular Writers of Today Volume Eleven* at head of title.

Heinlein in Dimension, by Alexei Panshin. *Chicago: Advent: Publishers, Inc., 1968.*
  First edition so stated on copyright page.

Robert A. Heinlein, edited by Joseph D. Olander and Martin Harry Greenberg. *New York: Taplinger Publishing Company,* [*1978*].
  Two bindings, no priority: (A) Boards with cloth shelf back; (B) Wrappers. First edition so stated on copyright page.

Robert A. Heinlein: A Bibliography, by Mark Owings. *Baltimore: Croatan House,* [*1973*].
  Wrappers. No statement of printing on copyright page. Offset from typewritten copy.

Robert A. Heinlein Stranger in His Own Land, by George Edgar Slusser. *San Bernardino: R. Reginald The Borgo Press, MCMLXXVI.*
  Wrappers. *First Printing—March, 1976/1 2 3 4 5 6 7 8 9 10 11 12 13 14 15* on copyright page. *The Milford Series Popular Writers of Today Volume One* at head of title.

Stranger in a Strange Land & Other Works: Notes . . . , by Baird Searles. *Lincoln, Nebraska: Cliffs Notes Incorporated, [1975].*
  Wrappers. No statement of printing on copyright page.

Zenna Henderson
(b. 1917)

THE ANYTHING BOX. *Garden City: Doubleday & Company, Inc., 1965.*
  First edition so stated on copyright page.

HOLDING WONDER. *Garden City: Doubleday & Company, Inc., 1971.*
  First edition so stated on copyright page.

THE PEOPLE NO DIFFERENT FLESH. *London: Victor Gollancz Ltd, 1966.*
  No statement of printing on copyright page.

PILGRIMAGE. *Garden City: Doubleday & Company, Inc., 1961.*
  First edition so stated on copyright page.

Frank Patrick Herbert

(b. 1920)

THE BEST OF FRANK HERBERT. *London: Sidgwick & Jackson*, [*1975*].
Boards. *First published in Great Britain in 1975* on copyright page. Note: In 1976 this collection was divided into two paperback volumes and issued THE BEST OF FRANK HERBERT 1952–1964 and THE BEST OF FRANK HERBERT 1965–1970.

THE BOOK OF FRANK HERBERT. *New York: DAW Books, Inc.*, [*1973*].
Wrappers. *First printing, January 1973* on copyright page. *DAW: sf Books No. 39 UQ 1039* (95¢).

CHILDREN OF DUNE. *New York: Published by Berkley Publishing Corporation*, [*1976*].
No statement of printing on copyright page.

DESTINATION: VOID. [*New York*]: *Published by Berkley Publishing Corporation*, [*1966*].
Wrappers. *June, 1966* on copyright page. *Berkley Medallion F1249* (50¢).

THE DOSADI EXPERIMENT. *New York: G. P. Putnam's Sons*, [*1977*].
No statement of printing on copyright page.

THE DRAGON IN THE SEA. *Garden City: Doubleday & Company, Inc.*, *1956*.
Boards. First edition so stated on copyright page. Reissued as 21ST CENTURY SUB and later as UNDER PRESSURE.

DUNE. *Philadelphia/New York: Chilton Books a division of Chilton Company*, [*1965*].
Copyright page of the first printing of the first edition reads *Copyright © 1965 by Frank Herbert/First Edition/All Rights Reserved/Published in Philadelphia by Chilton Company and simultaneously/in Toronto, Canada, by Ambassador Books, Ltd./Library of Congress Catalog Card Number 65–22547/Manufactured in the United States of America.* The book has been reprinted at least once with the first edition statement retained on the copyright page but no indication of later printing. The copyright page of this later printing (apparently the fifth) reads *Copyright © 1965 by Frank Herbert/First Edition/All Rights Reserved/Published in Philadelphia by Chilton Book Company and simultaneously/in Ontario, Canada by Thomas Nelson & Sons, Ltd./5 6 7 8 9 0 4 3 2 1 0 9 8 7 6/ISBN 0–8019–5077–5 Library of Congress Catalog Card Number 65–22547/Manufactured in the United States of America.*

DUNE MESSIAH. *New York: G. P. Putnam's Sons*, [*1969*].
Boards. No statement of printing on copyright page.

ALSO: [*New York*]: *Published by Berkley Publishing Corporation*, [*1975*]. Wrappers. *September, 1975* on copyright page. *A Berkley Medallion Book D2952* ($1.50). Minor textual changes.

THE EYES OF HEISENBERG. [*New York*]: *Published by Berkley Publishing Corporation*, [*1966*].
Wrappers. *November, 1966* on copyright page. *Berkley Medallion F1283* (50¢).

ALSO: [*London*]: *New English Library*, [*1975*]. Boards. *First published in hardcover . . . 1975* on copyright page. First hardcover edition.

THE GOD MAKERS. *New York: G. P. Putnam's Sons*, [*1972*].
  Boards. No statement of printing on copyright page.

THE GREEN BRAIN. *New York: Ace Books, Inc.*, [*1966*].
  Wrappers. No statement of printing on copyright page. *Ace Book F–379* (40¢).

THE HEAVEN MAKERS. [*New York*]: *An Avon Book*, [*1968*].
  Wrappers. *First Avon Printing, November, 1968* on copyright page. *An Avon Original S319* (60¢).

  ALSO: *New York: Ballantine Books*, [*1977*]. Wrappers. *First Ballantine Books Edition: March 1977* on copyright page. *Ballantine 25304* ($1.50). Textual revisions.

HELLSTROM'S HIVE. *Garden City: Nelson Doubleday, Inc.*, [*1973*].
  Boards. Three printings, priority as listed: (A) Code *42P* at base of page 277; (B) Code *12Q* at base of page 277; (C) Code *29Q* at base of page 277. No statement of printing on copyright page. Note: Issued by the Science Fiction Book Club.

THE SANTAROGA BARRIER. [*New York*]: *Published by Berkley Publishing Corporation*, [*1968*].
  Wrappers. *October, 1968* on copyright page. *A Berkley Medallion Book S1615* (75¢).

  ALSO: [*London*]: *Rapp + Whiting*, [*1970*]. Boards. *First Published in Great Britain in 1970* on copyright page. First hardcover edition.

SOUL CATCHER. *New York: G. P. Putnam's Sons*, [*1972*].
  No statement of printing on copyright page.

21ST CENTURY SUB. *New York: Avon Publications, Inc.*, [*1956*].
  Wrappers. No statement of printing on copyright page. *Avon T–146* (35¢). Reissue of THE DRAGON IN THE SEA.

UNDER PRESSURE. *New York: Ballantine Books*, [*1974*].
  Wrappers. *First Printing: March, 1974* on copyright page. *Ballantine Books 23835 Science Fiction* ($1.25). Reissue of THE DRAGON IN THE SEA.

WHIPPING STAR. *New York: G. P. Putnam's Sons*, [*1970*].
  Boards. No statement of printing on copyright page.

  ALSO: [*New York*]: *Published by Berkley Publishing Corporation*, [*1977*]. Wrappers. *September, 1977/Sixth Printing* on copyright page. *A Berkley Medallion Book 0–425–03504–2* ($1.50). Revised text.

THE WORLDS OF FRANK HERBERT. [*London*]: *New English Library*, [*1970*].
  Wrappers. *First NEL paperback edition December 1970* on copyright page. *New English Library Science Fiction 2814* (30p).

  ALSO: *New York: Ace Books*, [*1971*]. Wrappers. No statement of printing on copyright page. *Ace Book 90925* (75¢). Adds "By the Book."

Edited Fiction

Tomorrow, and Tomorrow, and Tomorrow. . . . *New York Chicago San Francisco Atlanta Dallas: Holt, Rinehart and Winston, Inc.*, [*1974*].
  Wrappers. First printing has code *4 5 6 7 059 9 8 7 6 5 4 3 2 1* on copyright page. Edited (with three other collaborators) by Herbert, who supplied introduction and short story "The Nothing."

Reference

Herbert's Dune and Other Works: Notes . . . , by L. David Allen. *Lincoln, Nebraska: Cliffs Notes*, [*1975*].

   Wrappers. No statement of printing on copyright page.

Roger Sherman Hoar
(1887–1963)

DANGEROUS LOVE. [*London: Utopian Publications Ltd.*], *n.d.* [*1946*].
Wrappers. No statement of printing. Caption title. *Ralph Milne Farley, pseudonym.* Note: *English Catalogue of Books* dates May 1946.

AN EARTHMAN ON VENUS. *N[ew] Y[ork]: Avon Publishing Co., Inc.,* [*1950*].
Wrappers. No statement of printing on copyright page. *Avon 285 (25¢). Ralph Milne Farley, pseudonym.* Reissue of THE RADIO MAN.

THE HIDDEN UNIVERSE. *Los Angeles: Fantasy Publishing Company, Inc., 1950.*
No statement of printing on copyright page. *Ralph Milne Farley, pseudonym.* Note: Sheets of this book were later combined with those of THE RADIO MAN by Farley and issued in 1953 as [STRANGE WORLDS]. According to Owings and Chalker in *The Index to the Science-Fantasy Publishers,* approximately 500 copies were so bound.

THE IMMORTALS. *Toronto: Popular Publications, Inc.,* [*1947*].
Wrappers. No statement of printing on copyright page. *A Popular Science Novel (1/–). Ralph Milne Farley, pseudonym.*

THE OMNIBUS OF TIME. *Los Angeles: Fantasy Publishing Company, Inc, 1950.*
No statement of printing on copyright page. *Ralph Milne Farley, pseudonym.*

THE RADIO BEASTS. *New York: Ace Books, Inc.,* [*1964*].
Wrappers. No statement of printing on copyright page. *Ace Science Fiction Classic F–304 (40¢). Ralph Milne Farley, pseudonym.*

THE RADIO MAN. *Los Angeles: Fantasy Publishing Co., Inc., 1948.*
First edition so stated on copyright page. *Ralph Milne Farley, pseudonym.* Notes: (1) This book occurs in a number of bindings. The earliest is pebbled blue cloth, spine lettered in gold. The earliest dust jacket is white paper stock, printed in light green and black. (2) Sheets were later combined with those of THE HIDDEN UNIVERSE by Farley and issued in 1953 as [STRANGE WORLDS]. According to Owings and Chalker in *The Index to the Science-Fantasy Publishers,* approximately 500 copies were so bound. Reissued as AN EARTHMAN ON VENUS.

THE RADIO PLANET. *New York: Ace Books, Inc.,* [*1964*].
Wrappers. No statement of printing on copyright page. *Ace Book F-312 (40¢). Ralph Milne Farley, pseudonym.*

[STRANGE WORLDS.] See THE HIDDEN UNIVERSE and THE RADIO MAN.

William Hope Hodgson

(1877–1918)

THE BOATS OF THE 'GLEN CARRIG.'*London: Chapman and Hall, Ltd., 1907.*
No statement of printing on copyright page.

CAPTAIN GAULT: BEING THE EXCEEDINGLY PRIVATE LOG OF A SEA-CAPTAIN.*London: Eveleigh Nash Company Limited, 1917.*
No statement of printing on copyright page.

ALSO:*New York: Robert M. McBride & Co., 1918. Published April, 1918* on copyright page. Deletes the two poems in the Nash edition.

CARGUNKA AND POEMS AND ANECDOTES.*New York: R. Harold Paget/London: A. P. Watt & Son, 1914.*
Wrappers. No statement of printing on copyright page. Note: "D.C.O. Cargunka: The Bells of the 'Laughing Sally' " was collected later in THE LUCK OF THE STRONG.

CARNACKI THE GHOST-FINDER.*London: Eveleigh Nash, 1913.*
No statement of printing on copyright page. Publisher's advertisements on page [288]. 16-page publisher's catalogue inserted at rear.

ALSO:*Sauk City: Mycroft and Moran, 1947.* No statement of printing on copyright page. Enlarged edition. Adds three stories, "The Haunted Jarvee," "The Find," and "The Hog."

CARNACKI, THE GHOST FINDER AND A POEM.*London [1910].*
Wrappers. No statement of printing on copyright page. Note: "Carnacki" is a summary of four of the six episodes, "The House Among the Laurels," "The Gateway of the Monster," "The Horse of the Invisible" (retitled "The Thing Invisible"), and "The Whistling Room" appearing in CARNACKI THE GHOST-FINDER (1913). British Library copy received 19 January 1910.

ALSO:*New York: Paul R. Reynolds, [1910].* Self wrappers? No statement of printing on copyright page. Note: The only located copy of this printing, the Library of Congress copyright deposit copy, has been bound in vertically ribbed red cloth with front cover stamped *CARNACKI THE GHOST FINDER AND A POEM BY WILLIAM HOPE HODGSON*. This appears to be a binding prepared by the library, not the publisher. Received by the Library of Congress 20 January 1910. Listed in *The American Catalogue 1908–1910*, priced at 25¢.

DEEP WATERS.*Sauk City: Arkham House: Publishers, 1967.*
No statement of printing on copyright page. Note: Some first edition material (from periodicals and unpublished manuscripts) with remainder reprinted from MEN OF THE DEEP WATERS.

THE DREAM OF X.*West Kingston, Rhode Island: Donald M. Grant, Publisher, 1977.*
Two issues, no priority: (A) 203 numbered copies signed by artist Stephen E. Fabian. Limited issue, slipcased. (B) Trade issue. *First published in this form, 1977, in an edition of 2500 copies* on page [143]. Note: "The Dream of X" is a rewritten, revised, and condensed version of THE NIGHT LAND. It was prepared by the author, combined with thirteen of his poems, and issued in Great Britain and the U.S. as "POEMS" AND "THE DREAM OF X" in 1912 to protect the U.S. copyright of THE NIGHT LAND. The 1912 printings may not have been commercially distributed.

THE GHOST PIRATES. *London: Stanley Paul & Co., 1909.*
  Two bindings, probable priority as listed: (A) Red cloth lettered in gold on spine and front cover (British Library and Library of Congress copies thus); (B) Green cloth lettered on spine in gold and black, front cover in black. No statement of printing on copyright page. [12] pages of publisher's advertisements at rear.

THE GHOST PIRATES A CHAUNTY AND ANOTHER STORY. *New York: Paul R. Reynolds, 1909.*
  Wrappers. No statement of printing on copyright page. Note: "The Ghost Pirates" is abridged.

THE HOUSE ON THE BORDERLAND. *London: Chapman and Hall, Ltd., 1908.*
  No statement of printing on copyright page. [4] pages of advertisements at rear.

THE HOUSE ON THE BORDERLAND AND OTHER NOVELS. *Sauk City: Arkham House, 1946.*
  No statement of printing on copyright page. Reprint. Collects THE BOATS OF THE 'GLEN CARRIG,' THE HOUSE ON THE BORDERLAND, THE GHOST PIRATES, and THE NIGHT LAND.

THE LUCK OF THE STRONG. *London: Eveleigh Nash Company Limited, 1916.*
  No statement of printing on copyright page. Publisher's advertisements pages [319–20]. Inserted 8-page publisher's catalogue dated *Spring 1916* at rear.

MASTERS OF TERROR. VOLUME ONE. *[Ealing, London]: Corgi Books, [1977].*
  Wrappers. *First publication in Great Britain . . . Corgi edition published 1977* on copyright page. *Corgi 0 552 10662 3* (80p). Reprint collection. All stories from earlier books.

MEN OF THE DEEP WATERS. *London: Eveleigh Nash, 1914.*
  Two bindings, priority as listed: (A) Red cloth lettered in gold on spine and front cover; (B) Pink boards lettered in black on spine. No statement of printing on copyright page.

THE NIGHT LAND. *London: Eveleigh Nash, 1912.*
  Two bindings, priority not established but probably simultaneous: (A) Dark blue cloth lettered in gold. Note: Perhaps a special binding for the author. The only examined copy with this imprint and binding bears a signed inscription by Hodgson dated 22 March 1912 (the book was published in April 1912). (B) Red cloth stamped in gold and blind. No statement of printing on copyright page. Note: Sam Moskowitz records a colonial issue with the title page bearing the imprint *G. Bell & Sons Ltd.* Copies with this imprint were bound in blue cloth and in Wrappers for Bell's Indian and Colonial Library. As there are minor changes in the preliminary matter, it is probable that the first signature is a variant state or that a few leaves have been removed and cancel leaves substituted. The Nash issue carried no advertisements while the Bell issue contains a 16-page publisher's catalogue inserted at the rear. Moskowitz states that this issue was provided for in Hodgson's contract with Nash and that both Nash and Bell issues were "turned out simultaneously." Bell issue not seen. Information from Moskowitz's introduction to William Hope Hodgson's *Out of the Storm* (West Kingston, R.I.: Grant, 1975), pp. 94–95.

  ALSO: *London: Holden & Hardingham, Ltd., [1921].* Boards. *Abridged edition 1921* on copyright page. Abridged text.

  OUT OF THE STORM: UNCOLLECTED FANTASIES . . . . *West Kingston, Rhode Island: Donald M. Grant, Publisher, 1975.*
  First edition so stated on copyright page.

"POEMS" AND "THE DREAM OF X." *London: A. P. Watt & Son, 1912.*
  No statement of printing on copyright page. Notes: (1) The only located copy of this printing, the British Library copy received 2 February 1912, is bound in brown cloth with front cover lettered in white. This appears to be the original binding. (2) "The Dream of

X'' is a rewritten, revised, and condensed version of THE NIGHT LAND. ''The Dream of X'' was reprinted in 1977 by Donald M. Grant.

ALSO:*New York: R. Harold Paget, 1912.* Wrappers or self wrappers? Note: The only located copy of this printing, the Library of Congress copyright deposit copy, has been rebound. No statement of printing on copyright page.

Reference

Out of the Storm: Uncollected Fantasies, by William Hope Hodgson. *West Kingston, Rhode Island: Donald M. Grant, Publisher, 1975.*
   First edition so stated on copyright page. ''William Hope Hodgson,'' a critical biography by Sam Moskowitz, comprises pages 9–117.

William Hope Hodgson: A Centenary Tribute 1877–1977, [compiled by The British Fantasy Society]. [*Dagenham, Essex: The British Fantasy Society, 1977.*]
   Wrappers. *First Printing: November 1977* on rear wrapper. Note: Two stories by Hodgson, ''The Riven Night'' and ''The Phantom Ship,'' and an essay on Hodgson by Peter Tremayne.

Stanley Bennett Hough
(b. 1917)

THE ALSCOTT EXPERIMENT.*London: Hodder and Stoughton*, [*1954*].
Boards. *First printed 1954* on copyright page. *Bennett Stanley, pseudonym.*

BEYOND THE ELEVENTH HOUR.*London: Hodder and Stoughton*, [*1961*].
Boards. *First printed 1961* on copyright page.

THE BRONZE PERSEUS.*London: Secker & Warburg, 1959.*
Boards. *First published 1959 . . .* on copyright page. Reissued as THE TENDER KILLER.

DEAR DAUGHTER DEAD.*London: Victor Gollancz Ltd, 1965.*
Boards. No statement of printing on copyright page.

EXTINCTION BOMBER.*London: The Bodley Head*, [*1956*].
Boards. *First published 1956* on copyright page.

FEAR FORTUNE, FATHER.*London: Victor Gollancz Ltd, 1974.*
Boards. No statement of printing on copyright page.

FIRST ON MARS.*New York: Ace Books*, [*1957*].
Wrappers. No statement of printing on copyright page. *Ace Book D–233* (35¢). *Rex Gordon, pseudonym.* Issued earlier in Great Britain as NO MAN FRIDAY.

FIRST THROUGH TIME.*New York: Ace Books, Inc.*, [*1962*].
Wrappers. No statement of printing on copyright page. *Ace Book F–174* (40¢). *Rex Gordon, pseudonym.* Issued later in Great Britain as THE TIME FACTOR.

FIRST TO THE STARS.*New York: Ace Books, Inc.*, [*1959*].
Wrappers. No statement of printing on copyright page. *Ace Book D–405* (35¢). *Rex Gordon, pseudonym.* Issued later in Great Britain as THE WORLDS OF ECLOS.

FRONTIER INCIDENT.*London: Hodder & Stoughton*, [*1951*].
Boards. *First printed . . 1951* on copyright page.

GOVERNMENT CONTRACT.*London: Hodder and Stoughton*, [*1956*].
Boards. *First Printed . . 1956* on copyright page. *Bennett Stanley, pseudonym.*

MISSION IN GUEMO.*London: Hodder & Stoughton*, [*1953*].
Boards. *First printed 1953* on copyright page.

MOMENT OF DECISION.*London: Hodder and Stoughton*, [*1952*].
First printed . . . 1952 on copyright page.

NO MAN FRIDAY.*Melbourne :: London :: Toronto: William Heinemann Ltd*, [*1956*].
Boards. *First published 1956* on copyright page. *Rex Gordon, pseudonym.* Issued later in the U.S. as FIRST ON MARS.

THE PAW OF GOD.*London: Anthony Gibbs Library 33 Limited*, [*1967*].
Boards. *First Published . . . 1967* on copyright page. *Rex Gordon, pseudonym.* Issued earlier in the U.S. as UTOPIA MINUS X.

THE PRIMITIVES. London: Hodder and Stoughton, [*1954*].
Boards. *First printed 1954* on copyright page.

SEA STRUCK. *New York: Thomas Y. Crowell Company*, [*1953*].
Boards. No statement of printing on copyright page. *Bennett Stanley, pseudonym.* Issued later in Great Britain with textual differences as SEA TO EDEN.

SEA TO EDEN. *London: Hodder and Stoughton*, [*1954*].
Boards. *First Printed -- 1954* on copyright page. *Bennett Stanley, pseudonym.* Issued earlier in the U.S. with textual differences as SEA STRUCK.

THE SEAS SOUTH. *London: Hodder and Stoughton*, [*1953*].
Boards. *First printed -- 1953* on copyright page.

SWEET SISTER SEDUCED. *London: Victor Gollancz Ltd*, *1968*.
Boards. No statement of printing on copyright page.

THE TENDER KILLER. [*Hornchurch, Essex*]: *Ian Henry Publications*, *1975*.
Boards. *This edition, 1975* on copyright page. Reissue of THE BRONZE PERSEUS.

THE TIME FACTOR. *London: Anthony Gibbs and Phillips Ltd.*, [*1964*].
Boards. *First published in Great Britain . . . MCMLXIV* on copyright page. *Rex Gordon, pseudonym.* Issued earlier in the U.S. as FIRST THROUGH TIME.

UTOPIA MINUS X. *New York: Ace Books, Inc.*, [*1966*].
Wrappers. No statement of printing on copyright page. *Ace Book F-416* (40¢). *Rex Gordon, pseudonym.* Issued later in Great Britain as THE PAW OF GOD.

UTOPIA 239. *Melbourne :: London :: Toronto: William Heinemann Ltd*, [*1955*].
First published 1955 on copyright page. *Rex Gordon, pseudonym.*

THE WORLDS OF ECLOS. *London: World Distributors*, [*1961*].
Wrappers. *This Consul edition, complete and unabridged, published in England, 1961 . . .* on copyright page. *Consul Books 1050* (2'6). *Rex Gordon, pseudonym.* Issued earlier in the U.S. as FIRST TO THE STARS.

THE YELLOW FRACTION. *New York: Ace Publishing Corporation*, [*1969*].
Wrappers. No statement of printing on copyright page. *Ace Book 94350* (60¢). *Rex Gordon, pseudonym.*

ALSO: *London: Dennis Dobson*, [*1972*]. Boards. *First published in Great Britain in 1972* on copyright page. First hardcover edition.

John Hayden Howard

THE ESKIMO INVASION. *New York: Ballantine Books*, [*1967*].
   Wrappers. *First Edition: November, 1967* on copyright page. *A Ballantine Science Fiction Original U6112* (75¢).

Robert Ervin Howard
(1906–1936)

ALMURIC.*New York: Ace Books, Inc.*, [*1964*].
Wrappers. No statement of printing on copyright page. *Ace Book F–305* (40¢).

ALSO:*West Kingston, Rhode Island: Donald M. Grant, Publisher, 1975.*
First published in this form—1975 on copyright page. First hardcover edition.

BLACK VULMEA'S VENGEANCE & OTHER TALES OF PIRATES.*West Kingston, Rhode Island:*
Donald M. Grant, Publisher, 1976.
First edition so stated on copyright page.

BLADES FOR FRANCE.*Yorba Linda, California: George T. Hamilton, Publisher, 1975.*
Wrappers. First edition so stated on copyright page. 300 copies printed.

BLOODSTAR.*Leawood/New York: The Morning Star Press*, [*1976*].
First Printing, 1976 on copyright page. 5000 numbered copies of which the first 1500 are
signed by artist Richard Corben. Note: A comic strip adaptation of Robert E. Howard's
"Valley of the Worm" by Corben with additional material by John Jakes.

THE BOOK OF ROBERT E. HOWARD.*New York: Zebra Books*, [*1976*].
Wrappers. *First Printing: February, 1976* on copyright page. *Zebra 163* ($1.95). Some
material appears for the first time in book form.

BRAN MAK MORN. [*New York*]: *A Dell Book*, [*1969*].
Wrappers. *First printing—September 1969* on copyright page. *Dell 0774* (60¢).

THE CHALLENGE FROM BEYOND. N.p.: [*A Weltschmerz Publication/Bill Evans/Franklin Ker-*
khof, Printer/The Pennsylvania Dutch Cheese Press/February 1954].
Self wrappers. No statement of printing. Mimeographed, stapled. Cover title. With C. L.
MOORE, A. MERRITT, H.P. LOVECRAFT, and FRANK BELKNAP LONG. Notes: (1) Published by
William H. Evans for distribution through the Fantasy Amateur Press Association
(FAPA). (2) Not to be confused with a booklet of identical title and format with a different
round-robin story by Stanley G. Weinbaum and others.

THE COMING OF CONAN.*New York: Gnome Press, Inc.*, [*1953*].
Boards. First edition so stated on copyright page.

CONAN.*New York: Lancer Books*, [*1967*].
Wrappers. *A Lancer Book • 1967* on copyright page. *Lancer Books 73–685* (60¢). With
LIN CARTER and L. SPRAGUE DE CAMP.

CONAN OF AQUILONIA. See under Lin Carter or L. Sprague de Camp.

CONAN OF CIMMERIA. *New York: Lancer Books*, [*1969*].
Wrappers. *A Lancer Book • 1969* on copyright page. *Lancer Books 75–072* (95¢). With
LIN CARTER and L. SPRAGUE DE CAMP.

CONAN OF THE ISLES. See under Lin Carter or L. Sprague de Camp.

CONAN THE ADVENTURER. *New York: Lancer Books*, [*1966*].
Wrappers. *A Lancer Book • 1966* on copyright page. *Lancer Books 73–526* (60¢). With
L. SPRAGUE DE CAMP.

CONAN THE AVENGER. See under L. Sprague de Camp.

CONAN THE BARBARIAN. *New York: Gnome Press, Inc., Publishers,* [*1954*].
Boards. First edition so stated on copyright page.

CONAN THE BUCCANEER. See under Lin Carter or L. Sprague de Camp.

CONAN THE CONQUEROR. *New York: Gnome Press, Inc., Publishers,* [*1950*].
First printing so stated on copyright page. Reissued as THE HOUR OF THE DRAGON.

ALSO: *New York: Lancer Books,* [*1967*]. Wrappers. *A Lancer Book • 1967* on copyright page. *Lancer Books 73–572* (60¢). Editorial changes and introduction by L. Sprague de Camp.

CONAN THE FREEBOOTER. *New York: Lancer Books,* [*1968*].
Wrappers. *A Lancer Book • 1968* on copyright page. *Lancer Books 74–963* (75¢). With L. SPRAGUE DE CAMP.

CONAN THE USURPER. *New York: Lancer Books,* [*1967*].
Wrappers. *A Lancer Book • 1967* on copyright page. *Lancer Books 73–599* (60¢). One story appears for the first time. With L. SPRAGUE DE CAMP.

CONAN THE WANDERER. *New York: Lancer Books,* [*1968*].
Wrappers. *A Lancer Book • 1968* on copyright page. *Lancer Books 74–976* (95¢). With LIN CARTER and L. SPRAGUE DE CAMP. Note: Ad on page [223] lists six Conan titles. A later printing with the same stock number has been noted with the statement *A Lancer Book* but no date following on the copyright page and the ad on page [223] listing ten Conan titles.

CONAN THE WARRIOR. *New York: Lancer Books,* [*1967*].
Wrappers. *A Lancer Book • 1967* on copyright page. *Lancer Books 73–549* (60¢).

THE DARK MAN AND OTHERS. *Sauk City: Arkham House: Publishers, 1963.*
No statement of printing on copyright page.

THE DEVIL IN IRON. *West Kingston, Rhode Island: Donald M. Grant, Publisher, 1976.*
First published 1976 on copyright page. Reprint. Collects "Shadows in Zamboula" and "The Devil in Iron."

ETCHINGS IN IVORY. *Pasadena, Texas: Glenn Lord, 1968.*
Wrappers. No statement of printing on copyright page. 268 copies printed. Note: This printing differs from a look-alike reprint in the following ways. Original is printed on laid paper watermarked "Tweedweave" and *ROBERT E. HOWARD* is printed on the front wrapper in 18-point Bodoni Modern in capital letters.

A GENT FROM BEAR CREEK. *London: Herbert Jenkins Limited,* [*1937*].
First printed . . 1937 on copyright page.

THE GREY GOD PASSES. [*Columbia, Pennsylvania: Charles Miller, 1975.*]
Wrappers. First edition so stated on copyright page.

THE GRIM LAND AND OTHERS. [*Lamoni, Iowa: Stygian Isle Press, 1976.*]
Wrappers. No statement of printing on copyright page. 450 numbered copies only. Note: Poetry, save for a prose fragment completed by Tevis Clyde Smith.

THE HAND OF KANE. *New York: Centaur Press,* [*1970*].
Wrappers. *October 1970* on copyright page. *Time-Lost Series* (75¢). Reprint. Collects four stories from RED SHADOWS.

THE HOUR OF THE DRAGON. *New York: Published by Berkley Publishing Corporation,* [*1977*].
　　Wrappers. *August, 1977* on copyright page. *A Berkley Medallion Book 0–425–03608–1* ($1.95). *Conan* at head of title. Note: Revision of CONAN THE CONQUEROR. Follows the text of the five-part serial appearing in *Weird Tales,* December 1935 through April 1936.

　　ALSO:*New York: G. P. Putnam's Sons,* [*1977*]. No statement of printing on copyright page. *Conan* at head of title. First hardcover edition.

THE ILLUSTRATED GODS OF THE NORTH. [*West Warwick, Rhode Island*]: *Necronomicon Press,* [*1977*].
　　Wrappers. No statement of printing on copyright page. 750 numbered copies printed.

THE INCREDIBLE ADVENTURES OF DENNIS DORGAN. [*West Linn, Oregon*]: *FAX Collector's Editions,* [*1974*].
　　No statement of printing on copyright page.

THE IRON MAN. [*New York*]: *Zebra Books,* [*1976*].
　　Wrappers. *First Printing: March, 1976* on copyright page. *Zebra 171* ($1.50).

　　ALSO: THE IRON MAN & OTHER TALES OF THE RING. *West Kingston, Rhode Island: Donald M. Grant, Publisher, 1976.* First edition so stated on copyright page. First hardcover edition.

ISLE OF PIRATE'S DOOM. *Yorba Linda, California: George T. Hamilton, Publisher, 1975.*
　　Wrappers. First edition so stated on copyright page. 302 copies printed.

KING CONAN. *New York: Gnome Press, Inc. Publishers,* [*1953*].
　　First printing so stated on copyright page.

KING KULL. *New York: Lancer Books,* [*1967*].
　　Wrappers. *A Lancer Book • 1967* on copyright page. *Lancer Books 73–650* (60¢). With LIN CARTER.

THE KING'S SERVICE. *Yorba Linda, California: George T. Hamilton, 1976.*
　　Wrappers. First edition so stated on copyright page. 310 copies printed.

THE LOST VALLEY OF ISKANDER. [*West Linn, Oregon*]: *FAX Collector's Editions, 1974.*
　　No statement of printing on copyright page.

MARCHERS OF VALHALLA. *West Kingston, R.I.: Donald M. Grant, Publisher, 1972.*
　　First edition so stated on copyright page.

　　ALSO:*London: Sphere Books Limited,* [*1977*]. Wrappers. *First published in Great Britain . . . 1977* on copyright page. *Sphere 0 7221 4728 7* (65p). Enlarged edition. Adds six stories.

　　ALSO:*West Kingston, Rhode Island: Donald M. Grant, Publisher, 1977.* Abridged reprint. "The Grey God Passes" appears for the first time in hardcover.

THE MOON OF SKULLS. *New York: Centaur Press,* [*1969*].
　　Wrappers. *November 1969* on copyright page. *Time-Lost Series* (60¢). Reprint. Three stories collected from RED SHADOWS.

THE PEOPLE OF THE BLACK CIRCLE. *West Kingston, Rhode Island: Donald M. Grant, Publisher, 1974.*
　　Boards with cloth shelf back. *First published 1974* on copyright page.

THE PEOPLE OF THE BLACK CIRCLE. [*New York*]: *Published by Berkley Publishing Corporation*, [*1977*].
   Wrappers. *September, 1977* on copyright page. *A Berkley Medallion Book 0–425–03609–X* ($1.95). *Conan* at head of title. Reprint collection. Prints four stories using original *Weird Tales* texts.

PIGEONS FROM HELL. [*New York*]: *Kensington Publishing Corp.*, [*1976*].
   Wrappers. *First Printing: June, 1976* on copyright page. *Zebra Books 189* ($1.95). Reprint. Includes thirteen of the fifteen stories collected in THE DARK MAN AND OTHERS.

THE PRIDE OF BEAR CREEK. *West Kingston, Rhode Island: Donald M. Grant, Publisher, 1966*.
   First edition so stated on copyright page.

RED BLADES OF BLACK CATHAY. *West Kingston, Rhode Island: Donald M. Grant, Publisher, 1971*.
   First edition so stated on copyright page. With TEVIS CLYDE SMITH.

RED NAILS. *West Kingston, Rhode Island: Donald M. Grant, Publisher, 1975*.
   Boards with cloth shelf back. Reprint. Originally collected in THE SWORD OF CONAN.

RED NAILS. [*New York*]: *Published by Berkley Publishing Corporation*, [*1977*].
   Wrappers. *October, 1977* on copyright page. *A Berkley Medallion Book 0–425–03610–3* ($1.95). *Conan* at head of title. Reprint collection. Prints three stories using original *Weird Tales* texts and ''The Hyborian Age.''

RED SHADOWS. *West Kingston, Rhode Island: Donald M. Grant, Publisher, 1968*.
   First edition so stated on copyright page. This short story collection was reprinted in three volumes: THE MOON OF SKULLS, THE HAND OF KANE, and SOLOMON KANE.

THE RETURN OF CONAN. See under L. Sprague de Camp.

THE RETURN OF SKULL-FACE. [*West Linn, Oregon*]: *FAX Collector's Editions*, [*1977*].
   Two issues, no priority: (A) Boards with cloth shelf back. 215 copies signed by Lupoff and illustrator Stephen E. Leialoha, comprising 150 numbered copies for sale and 65 unnumbered copies for presentation. (B) Boards. 1450 trade copies. No statement of printing on copyright page. With RICHARD A. LUPOFF.

THE ROBERT E. HOWARD OMNIBUS. [*London*]: *Futura Publications Limited*, [*1977*].
   Wrappers. *First published in Great Britain . . . 1977* on copyright page. *Orbit 0 8600 7955 4* (90p).

ROGUES IN THE HOUSE. *West Kingston, Rhode Island: Donald M. Grant, Publisher, 1976*.
   Boards with cloth shelf back. *Deluxe edition—First Published 1976* on copyright page. Reprint. Collects ''Rogues in the House'' and ''The Frost-Giant's Daughter.''

THE SECOND BOOK OF ROBERT HOWARD. [*New York*]: *Kensington Publishing Corp.*, [*1976*].
   Wrappers. *First Printing: May, 1976* on copyright page. *Zebra 183* ($1.95).

THE SHADOW OF THE BEAST. *Yorba Linda, California: George T. Hamilton, Publisher, 1977*.
   Wrappers. First edition so stated on copyright page. 280 copies printed.

SHADOW OF THE HUN. *Yorba Linda, California: George T. Hamilton, Publisher, 1975*.
   Wrappers. First edition so stated on copyright page. 318 copies printed.

SKULL-FACE AND OTHERS. *Sauk City: Arkham House, 1946*.
   No statement of printing on copyright page.

SOLOMON KANE. *New York: Centaur Press*, [*1971*].
Wrappers. *February 1971* on copyright page. *Time-Lost Series* (75¢). Reprint. Seven stories previously collected in RED SHADOWS.

SON OF THE WHITE WOLF. [*West Linn, Oregon*]: *Published by FAX*, 1977.
No statement of printing on copyright page.

THE SOWERS OF THE THUNDER. *West Kingston, Rhode Island: Donald M. Grant, Publisher,* 1973.
First edition so stated on copyright page.

THE SWORD OF CONAN. *New York: Gnome Press, Inc. Publishers*, [*1952*].
First edition so stated on copyright page.

THE SWORD WOMAN. [*New York*]: *Kensington Publishing Corp.*, [*1977*].
Wrappers. *First Printing: May, 1977* on copyright page. *Zebra 261* ($1.50).

SWORDS OF SHAHRAZAR. [*London*]: *Futura Publications Limited*, [*1976*].
Wrappers. *First published in Great Britain in 1976* on copyright page. *Orbit Science Fiction 0 8600 7881 7* (50p).

ALSO: [*West Linn, Oregon*]: *FAX Collector's Editions*, [*1976*]. No statement of printing on copyright page. Note: Story titled ''Swords of Shahrazar'' in the Orbit edition is here titled ''The Treasure of Shaibar Khan.'' First hardcover edition.

TALES OF CONAN. *New York: Gnome Press Inc. Publishers*, [*1955*].
Five bindings, earliest as listed, sequence for the remainder not established: (A) Red boards lettered in black; (B) Green (boards?) lettered in black (not seen); (C) Black boards lettered in red; (D) Gray boards lettered in red; (E) Gray cloth lettered in red. First edition so stated on copyright page. Howard story drafts revised and altered by L. SPRAGUE DE CAMP.

THREE-BLADED DOOM. [*New York*]: *Kensington Publishing Corp.*, [*1977*].
Wrappers. *First Printing: July, 1977* on copyright page. *Zebra 277* ($1.50).

TIGERS OF THE SEA. *West Kingston, Rhode Island: Donald M. Grant, Publisher, 1974*.
First edition so stated on copyright page.

THE TOWER OF THE ELEPHANT. *West Kingston, Rhode Island: Donald M. Grant, Publisher,* 1975.
Boards with cloth shelf back. Reprint. Collects ''The Tower of the Elephant'' and ''The God in the Bowl'' (the latter collected earlier in THE COMING OF CONAN in a slightly different version edited by L. Sprague de Camp).

TWO AGAINST TYRE. [*Memphis, Tenn.: Dennis McHaney, 1976.*]
Wrappers. Two issues, no priority: (A) 600 numbered copies on 70-pound Strathmore Artlaid paper; (B) 900 unnumbered trade copies. No statement of printing on copyright page.

VALLEY OF THE LOST. [*Columbia, Pennsylvania: Charles Miller, 1975.*]
Wrappers. No statement of printing on copyright page. 777 numbered copies only.

THE VULTURES. SHOWDOWN AT HELL'S CANYON. *Lakemont, Georgia: Fictioneer Books Ltd.,* [*1973*].
Fabrikoid. First edition so stated on copyright page.

ALSO: THE VULTURES OF WHAPETON. [*New York*]: *Kensington Publishing Corp.*, [*1975*]. Wrappers. *First Printing: November, 1975* on copyright page. *Zebra 144* ($1.50). Enlarged edition. Adds two stories.

A WITCH SHALL BE BORN. *West Kingston, Rhode Island: Donald M. Grant, Publisher, 1975.*
Boards with cloth shelf back. Reprint. Collected earlier in CONAN THE BARBARIAN.

WOLFSHEAD. *New York: Lancer Books, [1968].*
Wrappers. *A Lancer Book • 1968* on copyright page. *Lancer Books 73–721* (60¢). First
book publication for "The House of Arabu"; other stories collected earlier in SKULL-FACE
AND OTHERS.

WORMS OF THE EARTH. *West Kingston, Rhode Island: Donald M. Grant, Publisher, 1974.*
First edition so stated on copyright page. Reprint. All stories previously collected in BRAN
MAK MORN.

Nonfiction (Dealing with the Fantasy Genre only)

The Hyborian Age, by Robert E. Howard, and A Probable Outline of Conan's Career by P.
Schuyler Miller and John D. Clark. *Los Angeles: LANY Coöperative Publications, 1938.*
Wrappers. No statement of printing. Mimeographed, stapled.

Letters

Runes of Ahrh • Eih • Eche. *[Lamoni, Iowa: Jonathan Bacon, 1976.]*
Wrappers. *1st Edition* on inside front wrapper. Cover title. 1000 numbered copies signed
by editor Jonathan Bacon. Prints twenty-six letters by Howard.

Reference

The Annotated Guide to Robert E. Howard's Sword & Sorcery, [by] Robert Weinberg. *[West
Linn, Oregon]: Starmont House, [1976].*
Wrappers. No statement of printing on copyright page.

Bicentennial Tribute to Robert E. Howard, [edited by George T. Hamilton]. *Yorba Linda,
California: George T. Hamilton, Publisher, 1976.*
Wrappers. *First edition-1976* on copyright page. 194 copies printed. Note: Although a
publication date of 1976 is indicated, it appears that this booklet was issued in 1977.

The Blade of Conan, edited by L. Sprague de Camp. *New York: Ace Books, [1979].*
Wrappers. *First Ace printing: May 1979* on copyright page. *Ace 11670–1* ($1.95).

Conan's World and Robert E. Howard, by Darrell Schweitzer. *San Bernardino, California:
R. Reginald/The Borgo Press, MCMLXXVIII.*
Wrappers. *First Edition—November, 1978* on copyright page. *The Milford Series Popular
Writers of Today Volume Seventeen* at head of title.

The Fiction of Robert E. Howard: A Pocket Checklist, by Dennis McHaney & Glenn Lord.
N.p.: [Published by D. McHaney & T. Foster, 1975].
Wrappers. No statement of printing.

A Gazeteer of the Hyborian World of Conan Including Also the World of Kull . . . , compiled by Lee N. Falconer. *West Linn, Oregon: Starmont House, [1977].*
Wrappers. No statement of printing on copyright page.

The Howard Collector: By and About Robert E. Howard, edited by Glenn Lord. *New York: Ace Books, [1979]*.
   Wrappers. *First Ace printing: April 1979* on copyright page. *Ace 34458–5* ($1.95). Note: Miscellany printing short stories, poems, and letters by Howard, as well as letters. memoirs, poems, and commentary by others on Howard's life and work.

The Last Celt: A Bio-bibliography of Robert Ervin Howard, edited and compiled by Glenn Lord. *West Kingston, Rhode Island: Donald M. Grant, Publisher, 1976*.
   First edition so stated on copyright page. Contains material by and about Howard.

The Miscast Barbarian: A Biography of Robert E. Howard (1906–1936), by L. Sprague de Camp. *Saddle River, N.J.: Published by Gerry de la Ree, 1975*.
   Two bindings, no priority: (A) 130 numbered copies in cloth; (B) 900 numbered copies in wrappers. No statement of printing. A second printing of 512 copies can be identified by absence of a limitation statement on the outside rear cover.

The Ultimate Guide to Howardia 1925–1975, edited by Wayne Warfield. *[Aberdeen, Maryland]: Hall Publications, 1976*.
   Wrappers. No statement of printing on copyright page. Caption title.

Fred Hoyle
(b. 1915)

A FOR ANDROMEDA. *[London]: Souvenir Press*, [1962].
  Boards. *First published 1962* on copyright page. With JOHN ELLIOT.

ANDROMEDA BREAKTHROUGH. *[London]: Souvenir Press*, [1964].
  Boards. *First published 1964* on copyright page. With JOHN ELLIOT.

THE BLACK CLOUD. *London Melbourne Toronto: Heinemann*, [1957].
  Boards. *First published 1957* on copyright page.

ELEMENT 79. *[New York]: The New American Library*, [1967].
  First printing so stated on copyright page.

FIFTH PLANET. *London Melbourne Toronto: Heinemann*, [1963].
  Boards. *First published 1963* on copyright page. With GEOFFREY HOYLE.

THE INCANDESCENT ONES. *New York, Hagerstown San Francisco London: Harper & Row, Publishers*, [1977].
  Boards with cloth shelf back. First edition so stated on copyright page. With GEOFFREY HOYLE.

THE INFERNO. *London: Heinemann*, [1973].
  Boards. *First published 1973* on copyright page. With GEOFFREY HOYLE.

INTO DEEPEST SPACE. *New York Evanston San Francisco London: Harper & Row, Publishers*, [1974].
  Boards with cloth shelf back. First edition so stated on copyright page. With GEOFFREY HOYLE.

THE MOLECULE MEN AND THE MONSTER OF LOCH NESS. *London: Heinemann*, [1971].
  Boards. *First published 1971* on copyright page. With GEOFFREY HOYLE.

OCTOBER THE FIRST IS TOO LATE. *London: Heinemann*, [1966].
  Boards. *First published 1966* on copyright page.

OSSIAN'S RIDE. *London Melbourne Toronto: Heinemann*, [1959].
  Boards. *First published 1959* on copyright page.

ROCKETS IN URSA MAJOR. *London: Heinemann*, [1969].
  Boards. *First published 1969* on copyright page. With GEOFFREY HOYLE.

SEVEN STEPS TO THE SUN. *London: Heinemann*, [1970].
  Boards. *First published 1970* on copyright page. With GEOFFREY HOYLE.

La Fayette Ronald Hubbard

(b. 1911)

BUCKSKIN BRIGADES. *New York: The Macaulay Company, [1937]*.
No statement of printing on copyright page.

DEATH'S DEPUTY. *Los Angeles: Fantasy Publishing Co., Inc., 1948*.
Two bindings, priority as listed: (A) Cloth; (B) Boards with Gnome Press imprint at base of spine. No statement of printing on copyright page. First edition sheets were later combined with those of THE KINGSLAYER and issued in 1953 as [FROM DEATH TO THE STARS]. According to Owings and Chalker in *The Index to the Science-Fantasy Publishers*, approximately 500 copies were so bound.

FEAR & THE ULTIMATE ADVENTURE. *[New York]: Berkley Publishing Corporation, [1970]*.
Wrappers. *March 1970* on copyright page. *A Berkley Medallion Book S1811* (75¢). First book appearance for "The Ultimate Adventure."

FINAL BLACKOUT. *Providence, R.I.: Hadley Publishing Co., [1948]*.
No statement of printing on copyright page.

[FROM DEATH TO THE STARS.] See DEATH'S DEPUTY and THE KINGSLAYER.

THE KINGSLAYER. *Los Angeles: Fantasy Publishing Co., Inc., 1949*.
Two printings noted, probably priority as listed: (A) Printed on laid paper; 18.8 cm tall; white wove endpapers; (B) Printed on wove paper; 19 cm tall; blue wove endpapers. No statement of printing on copyright page. Reissued as SEVEN STEPS TO THE ARBITER. Note: First printing sheets were later combined with those of DEATH'S DEPUTY and issued in 1953 as [FROM DEATH TO THE STARS]. According to Owings and Chalker in *The Index to the Science-Fantasy Publishers*, approximately 500 copies were so bound.

OLE DOC METHUSELAH. *Austin, Texas: Theta Press, [1970]*.
Boards. First edition so stated on copyright page.

RETURN TO TOMORROW. *New York: Ace Books, Inc., [1954]*.
Wrappers. No statement of printing on copyright page. *Ace Books S–66* (25¢).

ALSO: *[New York & London: Garland Publishing, Inc., 1975.]* No statement of printing on copyright page. First hardcover edition. Notes: (1) Photo-offset from 1954 Ace Books edition. (2) Not issued in dust jacket.

[SCIENCE-FANTASY QUINTETTE]. See TRITON AND BATTLE OF WIZARDS.

SEVEN STEPS TO THE ARBITER. *Chatsworth, California: Major Books, [1975]*.
Wrappers. No statement of printing on copyright page. *Major Books 3018* ($1.25). Reissue of THE KINGSLAYER.

SLAVES OF SLEEP. *Chicago: Shasta Publishers, 1948*.
First edition so stated on copyright page.

TRITON AND BATTLE OF WIZARDS. *Los Angeles: Fantasy Publishing Co., Inc., 1949*.
Two bindings, priority as listed: (A) Cloth; (B) Boards with Gnome Press imprint at base of spine. No statement of printing on copyright page. Note: Sheets of this book were later combined with those of THE RADIUM POOL by Ed Earl Repp and issued in 1953 as [SCIENCE-FANTASY QUINTETTE]. According to Owings and Chalker in *The Index to the Science-Fantasy Publishers*, approximately 500 copies were so bound.

TWO NOVELS. See TYPEWRITER IN THE SKY/FEAR.

TYPEWRITER IN THE SKY/FEAR. *New York: Gnome Press, Inc.*, [*1951*].
  First edition so stated on copyright page. *Two Novels* at head of title.

THE ULTIMATE ADVENTURE. See FEAR & THE ULTIMATE ADVENTURE.

Piers Anthony Dillingham Jacob
(b. 1934)

AMAZON SLAUGHTER. [*New York*]: *Published by Berkley Publishing Corporation*, [*1976*].
Wrappers. *April, 1976* on copyright page. *A Berkley Medallion Book Z3090* ($1.25). *Piers Anthony, pseudonym*. With ROBERTO FUENTES.

THE BAMBOO BLOODBATH. [*New York*]: *Published by Berkley Publishing Corporation*, [*1974*].
Wrappers. *December, 1974* on copyright page. *A Berkley Medallion Book N2716* (95¢). *Piers Anthony, pseudonym*. With ROBERTO FUENTES.

BUT WHAT OF EARTH? *Toronto • New York • London: Laser Books*, [*1976*].
Wrappers. *A Laser Book/first published October 1976* on copyright page. *Laser Books 72044* ($1.25). *Piers Anthony, pseudonym*. With ROBERT COULSON.

CHTHON. *New York: Ballantine Books*, [*1967*].
Wrappers. *First U.S. edition: July, 1967* on copyright page. *A Ballantine Science Fiction Original U6107* (75¢). *Piers Anthony, pseudonym*.

ALSO: [*London*]: *Macdonald*, [*1970*]. Boards. *First published in Great Britain in 1970* on copyright page. First hardcover edition.

CLUSTER. [*New York*]: *Avon*, [*1977*].
Wrappers. *First Avon Printing, October, 1977* on copyright page. *Avon 34686* ($1.75). *Piers Anthony, pseudonym*.

THE E.S.P. WORM. *New York: Paperback Library*, [*1970*].
Wrappers. *First Printing: June, 1970* on copyright page. *Paperback Library 63–357* (60¢). *Piers Anthony, pseudonym*. With ROBERT MARGROFF.

HASAN. *San Bernardino, California: R. Reginald The Borgo Press, MCMLXXVII*.
Wrappers. *First Edition—October, 1977* on copyright page. *Borgo Press B–215* ($3.95). *Piers Anthony, pseudonym*.

KIAI! [*New York*]: *Published by Berkley Publishing Corporation*, [*1974*].
Wrappers. *February, 1974* on copyright page. *Berkley Medallion 425–02511–095* (95¢). *Piers Anthony, pseudonym*. With ROBERT FUENTES.

MACROSCOPE. [*New York*]: *Avon*, [*1969*].
Wrappers. *First Avon Printing, October, 1969* on copyright page. *Avon W166* ($1.25). *Piers Anthony, pseudonym*.

ALSO: *London: Sphere Books Limited*, [*1972*]. Wrappers. *First published in Great Britain in 1972 . . .* on copyright page. *Sphere Science Fiction 11762* (50p). Abridged text.

MISTRESS OF DEATH. [*New York*]: *Published by Berkley Publishing Corporation*, [*1974*].
Wrappers. *July, 1974* on copyright page. *A Berkley Medallion Book 425–02623–095* (95¢). *Piers Anthony, pseudonym*. With ROBERTO FUENTES.

NEQ THE SWORD. [*London*]: *Corgi Books*, [*1975*].
Wrappers. *First publication in Great Britain 1975* on copyright page. *Corgi Science Fiction 0 552 09824 8* (40p). *Piers Anthony, pseudonym*.

NINJA'S REVENGE. [*New York*]: *Published by Berkley Publishing Corporation*, [*1975*].
Wrappers. *May, 1975* on copyright page. *Berkley Medallion Book N2821* (95¢). *Piers Anthony, pseudonym*. With ROBERTO FUENTES.

OMNIVORE. *New York: Ballantine Books*, [*1968*].
Wrappers. *First Printing: December, 1968* on copyright page. *A Ballantine Science Fiction Original 72014* (75¢). *Piers Anthony, pseudonym*.

ALSO: *London: Faber and Faber*, [*1969*]. *First published in England in 1969* on copyright page. First hardcover edition. Note: British edition was published in May 1969 and precedes the U.S. Science Fiction Book Club edition which was the July 1969 selection.

ORN. *Garden City: Nelson Doubleday, Inc.*, [*1971*].
Boards. Two printings, priority as listed: (A) Code *B37* on page 246; (B) Code *C 1* on page 246. No statement of printing on copyright page. *Piers Anthony, pseudonym*. Note: Issued by the Science Fiction Book Club.

OX. *Garden City: Nelson Doubleday, Inc.*, [*1976*].
Boards. No statement of printing on copyright page. Code *G 3* on page 215. *Piers Anthony, pseudonym*. Note: Issued by the Science Fiction Book Club.

PHTHOR. [*New York*]: *Published by Berkley Publishing Corporation*, [*1975*].
Wrappers. *December, 1975* on copyright page. *A Berkley Medallion Book Z3011* ($1.25). *Piers Anthony, pseudonym*.

PROSTHO PLUS. *London: Victor Gollancz Limited, 1971*.
Boards. No statement of printing on copyright page. *Piers Anthony, pseudonym*.

RACE AGAINST TIME. *New York: Hawthorn Books, Inc.*, [*1973*].
Code *1 2 3 4 5 6 7 8 9 10* on copyright page. *Piers Anthony, pseudonym*.

THE RING. *New York: Ace Books, Inc.*, [*1968*].
Wrappers. No statement of printing on copyright page. *Ace Book A–19* (75¢). *Piers Anthony, pseudonym*. With ROBERT E. MARGROFF.

ALSO: [*London*]: *Macdonald Science Fiction*, [*1969*]. Boards. *First published in Great Britain in 1969* on copyright page. First hardcover edition.

RINGS OF ICE. [*New York*]: *Avon*, [*1974*].
Wrappers. *First Avon Printing, June, 1974* on copyright page. *Avon Science Fiction 19448* (95¢). *Piers Anthony, pseudonym*.

ALSO: [*London*]: *Millington*, [*1975*]. Boards. *First published 1975 . . .* on copyright page. First hardcover edition.

SOS THE ROPE. *New York: Pyramid Books*, [*1968*].
Wrappers. *First printing October, 1968* on copyright page. *Pyramid Science Fiction X–1890* (60¢). *Piers Anthony, pseudonym*.

ALSO: *London: Faber and Faber*, [*1970*]. *First published in England in 1970* on copyright page. First hardcover edition.

A SPELL FOR CHAMELEON. *New York: Ballantine Books*, [*1977*].
Wrappers. *First Edition: September 1977* on copyright page. *Ballantine 25855* ($1.95). *Piers Anthony, pseudonym*.

STEPPE. [*London*]: *Millington*, [*1976*].
Boards. No statement of printing on copyright page. *Piers Anthony, pseudonym*.

TRIPLE DETENTE. *New York: DAW Books, Inc., [1974]*.
Wrappers. *First printing, September 1974/1 2 3 4 5 6 7 8 9* on copyright page. *DAW: sf Books No. 118 UQ1130 (95¢). Piers Anthony, pseudonym.*

VAR THE STICK. *London: Faber and Faber, [1972]*.
First published in 1972 on copyright page. *Piers Anthony, pseudonym.*

ALSO: *Toronto New York London: Bantam Books, [1973]*. Wrappers. *Published December 1973* on copyright page. *A Bantam Book N6948 (95¢)*. Textual changes; "expurgated," according to Jacob.

Montague Rhodes James
(1862–1936)

BEST GHOST STORIES OF M. R. JAMES. *Cleveland and New York: The World Publishing Company*, [*1944*].
Boards. *Tower Books Edition/First Printing March 1944* on copyright page. Reprint collection.

THE COLLECTED GHOST STORIES. *London: Edward Arnold & Co.*, [*1931*].
Collected edition first published, 1931 on copyright page. Reprint except for "Preface," "There Was a Man Dwelt by a Churchyard," "Rats," "After Dark in the Playing Fields," and "Stories I Have Tried to Write."

THE FIVE JARS. *London: Edward Arnold & Co.*, *1922*.
No statement of printing on copyright page.

GHOST-STORIES OF AN ANTIQUARY. *London: Edward Arnold, 1904.*
No statement of printing on copyright page. 16-page publisher's catalogue dated *November, 1904* inserted at rear.

MORE GHOST STORIES OF AN ANTIQUARY. *London: Edward Arnold, 1911.*
No statement of printing on copyright page. Publisher's advertisements on pages [275–76]. Inserted 24-page publisher's catalogue dated *Autumn 1911* at rear. Reissued in 1959 by Penguin Books as MORE GHOST STORIES.

SELECTED GHOST STORIES. *New York: Editions for the Armed Services, Inc.*, [*1945*].
Wrappers. No statement of printing on copyright page. *Armed Services Edition O–28.* Reprint collection. All stories from earlier books.

A THIN GHOST AND OTHERS. *London: Edward Arnold, 1919.*
No statement of printing on copyright page.

WAILING WELL. *Stanford Dingley: The Mill House Press, MCMXXVIII.*
157 copies. Two issues, no priority: (A) Seven copies signed by the author with title page printed in blue and black; (B) 150 numbered unsigned copies with title page printed in black. No statement of printing on copyright page.

A WARNING TO THE CURIOUS AND OTHER GHOST STORIES. *London: Edward Arnold & Co.*, *1925.*
No statement of printing on copyright page.

Translated Fiction

Forty Stories, [by] Hans Andersen. *London: Faber & Faber Limited*, [*1930*].
First published in MCMXXX on copyright page. Translated by James.

The Little Mermaid, [by] Hans Christian Andersen. *New York: Holiday House, 1935.*
No statement of printing on copyright page. Translated by James. Reprint. Collected earlier in *Forty Stories.*

The Nightingale, [by] Hans Christian Andersen. *London: Kaye & Ward Ltd/New York: Van Nostrand Reinhold Company, [1972]*.

   Boards. *Published in the United States of America 1972 . . . First published in Great Britain . . . 1972* on copyright page. Translated by James. Reprint. Collected earlier in *Forty Stories*.

The Princess and the Swineherd, [by] Hans Christian Andersen. *New York: Van Nostrand Reinhold Company, [1972]*.

   Boards. First printing has code *16 15 14 13 12 11 10 9 8 7 6 5 4 3 2 1* on front paste-down. Translated by James. Reprint. Collected earlier in *Forty Stories*.

Thumbelina, [by] Hans Christian Andersen. *London: Kaye & Ward Ltd/New York: Van Nostrand Reinhold Company, [1972]*.

   Boards. *Published in the United States of America 1972 . . . First published in Great Britain . . . 1973 . . . Printed in England by Bookprint International Ltd. 1972* on copyright page. Translated by James. Reprint. Collected earlier in *Forty Stories*.

Edited Fiction

Madam Crowl's Ghost and Other Tales of Mystery, by Joseph Sheridan Le Fanu. *London: G. Bell and Sons, Ltd., 1923*.

   No statement of printing on copyright page. Edited, with prologue and epilogue, by James.

Letters

Letters to a Friend. *London: Edward Arnold (Publishers) Ltd., [1956]*.

   First published, 1956 on copyright page.

Reference

A Memoir of Montague Rhodes James, by S. G. Lubbock. *Cambridge: At the University Press, 1939*.

   No statement of printing on copyright page. Includes a comprehensive bibliography of James's writings by A. F. Scholfield.

Malcolm Jameson
(1891–1945)

ATOMIC BOMB. [*Hollywood*]: *A Bond-Charteris Publication*, [*1945*].
  Wrappers. No statement of printing on copyright page. *A Bonded Special* (25¢).

BULLARD OF THE SPACE PATROL. *Cleveland and New York: The World Publishing Company*, [*1951*].
  First edition so stated on copyright page.

TARNISHED UTOPIA. *New York: Galaxy Publishing Corp.*, [*1956*].
  Wrappers. No statement of printing on copyright page. *Galaxy Novel No. 27* (35¢).

Frederick Thomas Jane
(1865–1916)

BLAKE OF THE "RATTLESNAKE" OR THE MAN WHO SAVED ENGLAND A STORY OF TORPEDO WARFARE IN 189-. *London: Tower Publishing Company Limited, 1895.*
No statement of printing on copyright page.

EVER MOHUN. *London: John Macqueen, 1901.*
Two bindings, priority as listed: (A) Red cloth stamped in blind and gold on spine and front cover; (B) Blue cloth, author's name and title stamped in gold on spine and front cover. No statement of printing on copyright page.

THE INCUBATED GIRL. *London: Tower Publishing Company Limited, 1896.*
No statement of printing on copyright page. Four pages of undated publisher's advertisements at rear; *NEW AND FORTHCOMING WORKS . . . THE PEOPLE OF THE PERIOD . . .* at head of page [349]. *BLAKE OF THE "RATTLESNAKE"* is advertised as "Now ready" on page [351].

THE LORDSHIP THE PASSEN, AND WE. *London: A. D. Innes & Co., 1897.*
No statement of printing on copyright page. Publisher's advertisements at rear dated *October 1897.*

THE PORT GUARD SHIP: A ROMANCE OF THE PRESENT DAY NAVY. *London: Hurst and Blackett Limited, 1900.*
No statement of printing on copyright page.

A ROYAL BLUEJACKET. *London: Sampson Low, Marston & Co., Ltd., 1908.*
No statement of printing on copyright page.

TO VENUS IN FIVE SECONDS. BEING AN ACCOUNT OF THE STRANGE DISAPPEARANCE OF THOMAS PLUMMER, PILL-MAKER. *London: A. D. Innes & Co., 1897.*
Two bindings, no priority: (A) Yellow cloth lettered in black; (B) Gray wrappers. No statement of printing on copyright page.

THE VIOLET FLAME. *London: Ward, Lock & Co., Limited, 1899.*
No statement of printing on copyright page. Publisher's advertisements pages [247–48].

William Fitzgerald Jenkins
(1896–1975)

THE ALIENS. *[New York]: Published by the Berkley Publishing Corporation, [1960].*
Wrappers. *March, 1960* on copyright page. *Berkley Medallion G410* (35¢). *Murray Leinster, pseudonym.*

THE BEST OF MURRAY LEINSTER. *[London]: Corgi Books, [1976].*
Wrappers. *First publication in Great Britain . . . Corgi edition published 1976* on copyright page. *Corgi 0 552 10333 0* (60p). *Murray Leinster, pseudonym.*

THE BLACK GALAXY. *New York: Galaxy Publishing Corp., [1954].*
Wrappers. No statement of printing on copyright page. *Galaxy Science Fiction Novel 20* (35¢). *Murray Leinster, pseudonym.*

BLACK SHEEP. *New York: Julian Messer, Inc., [1936].*
No statement of printing on copyright page.

THE BRAIN-STEALERS. *New York: Ace Books, Inc., [1954].*
Wrappers. No statement of printing on copyright page. *Ace Double Novel Books D–79* (35¢). *Murray Leinster, pseudonym.* Bound with ATTA by Francis Rufus Bellamy.

CATTLE RUSTLERS. *London and Melbourne: Ward, Lock & Co., Limited, [1952].*
First published . . . 1952 on copyright page. *Murray Leinster, pseudonym.*

THE CHALLENGE FROM BEYOND. *N.p.: [A Weltschmerz Publication/Bill Evans Franklin Kerkhof, Printer/The Pennsylvania Dutch Cheese Press/February 1954].*
Self wrappers. No statement of printing. Mimeographed, stapled. Cover title. *Murray Leinster, pseudonym.* With STANLEY G. WEINBAUM, DONALD WANDREI, EDWARD E. SMITH, and HARL VINCENT. Notes: (1) Published by William H. Evans for distribution through the Fantasy Amateur Press Association (FAPA). (2) Not to be confused with a booklet of identical title and format with a different round-robin story by C. L. Moore and others.

CHECKPOINT LAMBDA. *[New York]: Published by the Berkley Publishing Corporation, [1966].*
Wrappers. *July, 1966* on copyright page. *Berkley Medallion F1263* (50¢). *Murray Leinster, pseudonym.* Later collected in A MURRAY LEINSTER OMNIBUS.

CITY ON THE MOON. *New York: Avalon Books, [1957].*
No statement of printing on copyright page. *Murray Leinster, pseudonym.*

COLONIAL SURVEY. *New York: Gnome Press, [1957].*
Boards. First edition so stated on copyright page. *Murray Leinster, pseudonym.* Reissued as PLANET EXPLORER.

CREATURES OF THE ABYSS. *[New York]: Published by the Berkley Publishing Corporation, [1961].*
Wrappers. *August, 1961* on copyright page. *Berkley Medallion G549* (35¢). *Murray Leinster, pseudonym.* Issued later in Great Britain as THE LISTENERS.

DALLAS. *New York: Fawcett Publications, Inc., 1950.*
Wrappers. No statement of printing on copyright page. *Gold Medal Book 126* (25¢).

DESTROY THE U.S.A. *Toronto London New York: A News Stand Library Pocket Edition*, [*1950*].
Wrappers. *First Printing/September 1950* on page [2]. *News Stand Library 141* (25¢). Reissue of THE MURDER OF THE U.S.A.

DOCTOR TO THE STARS. *New York: Pyramid Books*, [*1964*].
Wrappers. *Published March 1964* on copyright page. *Pyramid Books F –987* (40¢). *Murray Leinster, pseudonym.*

THE DUPLICATORS. *New York: Ace Books, Inc.*, [*1964*].
Wrappers. No statement of printing on copyright page. *Ace Double F –275* (40¢). *Murray Leinster, pseudonym.* Bound with NO TRUCE WITH TERRA by Philip E. High.

FIGHT FOR LIFE. *New York: Crestwood Publishing Co., Inc., n.d.* [*ca. 1949–1950*].
Wrappers. No statement of printing on copyright page. *Prize Science-Fiction Novels No. 10* (25¢). *Murray Leinster, pseudonym.*

FIGHTING HORSE VALLEY. *New York: Alfred H. King*, [*1934*].
No statement of printing on copyright page.

THE FORGOTTEN PLANET. *New York: Gnome Press, Inc.*, [*1954*].
Four bindings, first two probably as listed, last two later: (A) Cream cloth lettered in yellow-green (copy thus deposited in the Library of Congress); (B) Cream boards with yellow-green marbled pattern lettered in green; (C) Tan boards lettered in green; (D) Gray cloth lettered in red. First edition so stated on copyright page. *Murray Leinster, pseudonym.* Note: The dust jacket incorporates a map design. A variant dust jacket depicting a man confronted by a giant scarab beetle was prepared to promote the only title in the short-lived Gnome Press ''Gnome Juniors'' experiment, an attempt to reach the public library juvenile market. Publisher Martin Greenberg states that this design was commercially unattractive and all copies of this title were issued with the map jacket. However, examples of the beetle variant survive and infrequently appear on copies of the book.

FOUR FROM PLANET 5. *Greenwich, Conn.: Fawcett Publications, Inc.*, [*1959*].
Wrappers. *First Printing, November 1959* on copyright page. *Gold Medal Book s937* (35¢). *Murray Leinster, pseudonym.*

ALSO: *London - New York - Sydney: White Lion Publishers Limited*, [*1974*]. Boards. *White Lion edition, 1974* on copyright page. First hardcover edition.

THE GAMBLIN' KID. *New York: Alfred H. King*, [*1933*].
No statement of printing on copyright page.

GATEWAY TO ELSEWHERE. *New York: Ace Books, Inc.*, [*1954*].
Wrappers. No statement of printing on copyright page. *Ace Double Novel Books D–53* (35¢). *Murray Leinster, pseudonym.* Bound with THE WEAPON SHOPS OF ISHER by A.E. van Vogt.

GET OFF MY WORLD! *New York: Belmont Books*, [*1966*].
Wrappers. *April 1966* on copyright page. *Belmont Science Fiction B50–676* (50¢). *Murray Leinster, pseudonym.*

THE GREKS BRING GIFTS. [*New York*]: *A Macfadden-Bartell Book*, [*1964*].
Wrappers. *A Macfadden book . . . 1964* on copyright page. *Macfadden Books 50–224* (50¢). *Murray Leinster, pseudonym.*

GUNS FOR ACHIN. *London: Wright & Brown*, [*1936*].
No statement of printing on copyright page. *Murray Leinster, pseudonym.*

THE HOT SPOT. *New York: Pyramid Books*, [*1969*].
 Wrappers. *First printing April, 1969* on copyright page. *Pyramid Science Fiction X–1921* (60¢). *Land of the Giants #2* at head of title. *Murray Leinster, pseudonym.*

INVADERS OF SPACE. [*New York*]: *Published by Berkley Publishing Corporation*, [*1964*].
 Wrappers. *December, 1964* on copyright page. *Berkley Medallion F1022* (50¢). *Murray Leinster, pseudonym.* Later collected in A MURRAY LEINSTER OMNIBUS.

KID DEPUTY. [*New York*]: *Alfred H. King Publisher*, [*1935*].
 No statement of printing on copyright page.

LAND OF THE GIANTS. *New York: Pyramid Books*, [*1968*].
 Wrappers. *First printing, September 1968* on copyright page. *Pyramid Science Fiction X–1846* (60¢). *Murray Leinster, pseudonym.*

LAND OF THE GIANTS #2. See THE HOT SPOT.

LAND OF THE GIANTS #3. See UNKNOWN DANGER.

THE LAST SPACE SHIP. *New York: Frederick Fell, Inc.*, [*1949*].
 Boards with cloth shelf back. *First printing November 1949* on copyright page. *Murray Leinster, pseudonym.*

THE LISTENERS. *London: Sidgwick & Jackson*, [*1969*].
 Boards. *First published in Great Britain 1969* on copyright page. *Murray Leinster, pseudonym.* Issued earlier in the U.S. as CREATURES OF THE ABYSS.

THE MAN WHO FEARED. *New York: Gateway Books, 1942.*
 First Printing, September 1942 on copyright page.

 ALSO: *New York: Published by Journal of Living Publishing Corp., n.d.* Wrappers. No statement of printing on copyright page. *A Hangman's House Mystery 4* (25¢). Abridged text. Issued circa 1945–1946.

MEN INTO SPACE. [*New York*]: *Published by the Berkley Publishing Corporation*, [*1960*].
 Wrappers. *October, 1960* on copyright page. *Berkley Medallion G461* (35¢). *Murray Leinster, pseudonym.*

MEXICAN TRAIL. *New York: Alfred H. King, Inc.*, [*1933*].
 No statement of printing on copyright page.

MINERS IN THE SKY. [*New York*]: *An Avon Book*, [*1967*].
 Wrappers. *First Avon Printing, April, 1967* on copyright page. *Avon G1310* (50¢). *Murray Leinster, pseudonym.*

THE MONSTER FROM EARTH'S END. *Greenwich, Conn.: Fawcett Publications, Inc.*, [*1959*].
 Wrappers. *First Printing, January 1959* on copyright page. *Gold Medal S 832* (35¢). *Murray Leinster, pseudonym.*

 ALSO: *London and New York: White Lion Publishers*, [*1973*]. Boards. *This White Lion edition, 1973* on copyright page. First hardcover edition.

MONSTERS AND SUCH. *New York: Avon Book Division*, [*1959*].
 Wrappers. No statement of printing on copyright page. *Avon T–345* (35¢). *Murray Leinster, pseudonym.*

MURDER IN THE FAMILY. *London: Publishers John Hamilton, Ltd*, [*1935*].
 No statement of printing on copyright page. 32-page publisher's catalogue inserted at rear. *Murray Leinster, pseudonym.*

MURDER MADNESS. *New York: Brewer and Warren Inc., MCMXXXI.*
No statement of printing on copyright page. *Murray Leinster, pseudonym.*

THE MURDER OF THE U.S.A. *New York: Crown Publishers, [1946].*
No statement of printing on copyright page. Reissued as DESTROY THE U.S.A.

MURDER WILL OUT. *London: John Hamilton Ltd. Publishers, [1932].*
No statement of printing on copyright page. *Murray Leinster, pseudonym.*

A MURRAY LEINSTER OMNIBUS. *London: Sidgwick & Jackson, [1968].*
Boards. No statement of printing on copyright page. Reprint. Collects OPERATION TER-
ROR, INVADERS OF SPACE, and CHECKPOINT LAMBDA. *Murray Leinster, pseudonym.* Note:
First hardcover edition for all titles.

THE MUTANT WEAPON. *New York: Ace Books, Inc., [1959].*
Wrappers. No statement of printing on copyright page. *Ace Double Novel Books D-403*
(35¢). *Murray Leinster, pseudonym.* Bound with THE PIRATES OF ZAN by Leinster.

NO CLUES. *London: Wright and Brown, [1935].*
No statement of printing on copyright page. Publisher's advertisements pages [252–256].
Murray Leinster, pseudonym.

OPERATION: OUTER SPACE. *Reading, Pennsylvania: Fantasy Press, [1954].*
Four bindings noted, priority as listed: (A) Dark blue cloth, spine stamped in gold; (B) Red
boards printed in black; (C) Blue boards printed in black; (D) Wrappers. Two issues, no
priority: (A) 300 copies with numbered leaf signed by the author inserted; (B) Trade issue.
First edition so stated on copyright page. *Murray Leinster, pseudonym.*

OPERATION TERROR. *[New York]: Published by Berkley Publishing Corp., [1962].*
Wrappers. No statement of printing on copyright page. *Berkley Medallion F694* (50¢).
Murray Leinster, pseudonym. Later collected in A MURRAY LEINSTER OMNIBUS.

THE OTHER SIDE OF HERE. *New York: Ace Books, Inc., [1955].*
Wrappers. No statement of printing on copyright page. *Ace Double Novel Books D-94*
(35¢). *Murray Leinster, pseudonym.* Bound with ONE AGAINST ETERNITY by A. E. van
Vogt.

THE OTHER SIDE OF NOWHERE. *[New York]: Published by Berkley Publishing Corporation,*
[1964].
Wrappers. *May, 1964* on coypright page. *Berkley Medallion F918* (50¢). *Murray Lein-*
ster, pseudonym.

OUT OF THIS WORLD. *New York: Avalon Books, [1958].*
No statement of printing on copyright page. *Murray Leinster, pseudonym.*

*OUTLAW DEPUTY. 1954.
Wrappers. *Harlequin 281.* Reprint? *Murray Leinster, pseudonym.*

OUTLAW SHERIFF. *New York: Alfred H. King, [1934].*
No statement of printing on copyright page. Issued later in Great Britain as RUSTLIN'
SHERIFF.

THE PIRATES OF ZAN. *New York: Ace Books, Inc., [1959].*
Wrappers. No statement of printing on copyright page. *Ace Double Novel Books D-403*
(35¢). *Murray Leinster, pseudonym.* Bound with THE MUTANT WEAPON by Leinster.

PLANET EXPLORER. *New York: Avon Publications, Inc., [1957].*
Wrappers. No statement of printing on copyright page. *Avon T-202* (35¢). *Murray Lein-*
ster, pseudonym. Reissue of COLONIAL SURVEY.

RUSTLIN' SHERIFF. *Mayfair, London: Eldon Press Limited*, [*1934*].
First Published . . . 1934 on copyright page. Publisher's advertisements pages [279–88].
Issued earlier the same year in the U.S. as OUTLAW SHERIFF.

S.O.S. FROM THREE WORLDS. *New York: Ace Books, Inc.*, [*1966*].
Wrappers. No statement of printing on copyright page. *Ace Book G–647* (50¢). *Murray Leinster, pseudonym.*

SCALPS. *New York: Brewer & Warren Inc.*, *1930*.
No statement of printing on copyright page. *Murray Leinster, pseudonym.* Issued later in Great Britain as WINGS OF CHANCE.

SIDEWISE IN TIME. *Chicago: Shasta Publishers, 1950*.
First edition so stated on copyright page. *Murray Leinster, pseudonym.*

SON OF THE FLYING "Y". *New York: Fawcett Publications, Inc.*, [*1951*].
Wrappers. No statement of printing on copyright page. *Gold Medal Books 161* (25¢).

SPACE CAPTAIN. *New York: Ace Books, Inc.*, [*1966*].
Wrappers. No statement of printing on copyright page. *Ace Double M–135* (45¢). *Murray Leinster, pseudonym.* Bound with THE MAD METROPOLIS by Philip E. High.

SPACE GYPSIES. [*New York*]: *An Avon Book*, [*1967*].
Wrappers. *First Avon Printing, June, 1967* on copyright page. *Avon G1318* (50¢). *Murray Leinster, pseudonym.*

SPACE PLATFORM. *Chicago: Shasta Publishers*, [*1953*].
First edition so stated on copyright page. *Murray Leinster, pseudonym.*

SPACE TUG. *Chicago: Shasta Publishers*, [*1953*].
First edition so stated on copyright page. *Murray Leinster, pseudonym.*

SWORD OF KINGS. *London: John Long, Limited*, [*1933*].
No statement of printing on copyright page. 40-page publisher's catalogue dated *Autumn, 1932* inserted at rear. *Murray Leinster, pseudonym.*

TALENTS, INCORPORATED. *New York: Avon Book Division*, [*1962*].
Wrappers. No statement of printing on copyright page. *Avon G–1120* (50¢). *Murray Leinster, pseudonym.*

THIS WORLD IS TABOO. *New York: Ace Books, Inc.*, [*1961*].
Wrappers. No statement of printing on copyright page. *Ace Book D–525* (35¢). *Murray Leinster, pseudonym.*

TIME TUNNEL. *New York: Pyramid Books*, [*1964*].
Wrappers. *First printing, July 1964* on copyright page. *Pyramid Books R–1043* (50¢). *Murray Leinster, pseudonym.*

THE TIME TUNNEL. *New York: Pyramid Books*, [*1967*].
Wrappers. *First printing January, 1967* on copyright page. *Pyramid R–1522* (50¢). *Murray Leinster, pseudonym.* Note: Differs from the preceding novel.

ALSO: *London: Sidgwick & Jackson*, [*1971*]. Boards. *First published in Great Britain in 1971* on copyright page. First hardcover edition.

TIMESLIP! *New York: Pyramid Books*, [*1967*].
Wrappers. *First printing, July, 1967* on copyright page. *Pyramid R–1680* (50¢). *Murray Leinster, pseudonym.* Note: *Time Tunnel Adventure #2* at head of title on front cover.

TWISTS IN TIME. *New York: Avon Book Division*, [*1960*].
  Wrappers. No statement of printing on copyright page. *Avon T–389* (35¢). *Murray Leinster, pseudonym.*

UNKNOWN DANGER. *New York: Pyramid Books*, [*1969*].
  Wrappers. *First printing, November 1969* on copyright page. *Pyramid Science Fiction X–2105* (60¢). *Land of the Giants #3* at head of title. *Murray Leinster, pseudonym.*

THE WAILING ASTEROID. *New York: Avon Book Division*, [*1960*].
  Wrappers. No statement of printing on copyright page. *Avon T–483* (35¢). *Murray Leinster, pseudonym.*

WANTED DEAD OR ALIVE! *London: Wright & Brown Limited*, [*1950*].
  First Published 1950 on copyright page. *Murray Leinster, pseudonym.*

WAR WITH THE GIZMOS. *Greenwich, Conn.: Fawcett Publications, Inc.*, [*1958*].
  Wrappers. *First Printing, March 1958* on copyright page. *Gold Medal Book s751* (35¢). *Murray Leinster, pseudonym.*

WINGS OF CHANCE. *London: John Hamilton Ltd. Publishers*, [*1935*].
  No statement of printing on copyright page. *Murray Leinster, pseudonym.* Issued earlier in the U.S. as SCALPS.

Edited Fiction

Great Stories of Science Fiction. *New York: Random House*, [*1951*].
  First printing so stated on copyright page. Edited, with preface and two stories, ''Symbiosis'' and ''The Strange Case of John Kingman,'' by Jenkins. *Murray Leinster, pseudonym.*

Dennis Feltham Jones
(c. 1915)

COLOSSUS. *London: Rupert Hart-Davis, 1966.*
  Boards. *First published 1966* on copyright page.

COLOSSUS AND THE CRAB. *[New York]: Published by Berkley Publishing Corporation,*
[1977].
  Wrappers. *August, 1977* on copyright page. *A Berkley Medallion Book 0-425-03467-4*
  ($1.50).

DENVER IS MISSING. *New York: Walker and Company, [1971].*
  Boards. *First published in the United States of America in 1971* . . . on copyright page.
  Issued later in Great Britain as DON'T PICK THE FLOWERS.

DON'T PICK THE FLOWERS. *[London]: Panther, [1971].*
  Wrappers. *First published in 1971* . . . on copyright page. *Panther Science Fiction 586*
  035575 (35p). Issued earlier in the U.S. as DENVER IS MISSING.

THE FALL OF COLOSSUS. *New York: G. P. Putnam's Sons, [1974].*
  Boards. No statement of printing on copyright page.

THE FLOATING ZOMBIE. *[New York]: Published by Berkley Publishing Corporation, [1975].*
  Wrappers. *November, 1975* on copyright page. *A Berkley Medallion Book Z2980* ($1.25).

IMPLOSION. *London: Rupert Hart-Davis, 1967.* — BGRKLLET, SFBC
  Boards. *First published 1967* on copyright page.

Raymond F. Jones
(b. 1915)

THE ALIEN. *New York: World Editions, Inc.*, [*1951*].
   Wrappers. No statement of printing on copyright page. *Galaxy Science Fiction Novel No. 6* (35¢).

THE CYBERNETIC BRAINS. *New York: Avalon Books*, [*1962*].
   No statement of printing on copyright page.

THE DEVIATES. *New York: Published by Galaxy Publishing Corp.*, [*1959*].
   Wrappers. No statement of printing on copyright page. *Beacon Book 242* (35¢). Reissue of THE SECRET PEOPLE.

THE KING OF EOLIM. [*Don Mills*]: *Laser Books*, [*1975*].
   Wrappers. *First published 1975* on copyright page. Laser Books 72012 (95¢).

MAN OF TWO WORLDS. *New York: Pyramid Books*, [*1963*].
   Wrappers. *Pyramid edition published November 1963* on copyright page. *Pyramid Books F–941* (40¢). Reissue of RENAISSANCE.

MOONBASE ONE. *London, New York, Toronto: Criterion Books*, [*1972*].
   Two issues, probable priority as listed: (A) Cloth, price *$4.95* on front dust jacket flap. U.S. issue. (B) Boards, price £*1.25* on front dust jacket flap. British issue. *First published in Great Britain in 1972* on copyright page. The U.S. issue was published 15 March 1972; according to *Whitaker's Cumulative Book List*, the British issue was published in April 1972.

THE NON-STATISTICAL MAN. *New York: Belmont Books*, [*1964*].
   Wrappers. *May 1964* on copyright page. *Belmont Future Series L92–588* (50¢).

PLANET OF LIGHT. *Philadelphia Toronto: The John C. Winston Company*, [*1953*].
   First edition so stated on copyright page.

RENAISSANCE. *New York: Gnome Press*, [*1951*].
   First edition so stated on copyright page. Reissued as MAN OF TWO WORLDS.

RENEGADES OF TIME. [*Don Mills*]: *Laser Books*, [*1975*].
   Wrappers. *First published 1975* on copyright page. *Laser Books 72001* (95¢).

THE RIVER AND THE DREAM. *Toronto • New York • London: Laser Books*, [*1977*].
   Wrappers. *First published January 1977* on copyright page. *Laser Books 72054* ($1.25).

THE SECRET PEOPLE. *New York: Avalon Books*, [*1956*].
   No statement of printing on copyright page. Reissued as THE DEVIATES.

SON OF THE STARS. *Philadelphia • Toronto: The John C. Winston Company*, [*1952*].
   First edition so stated on copyright page.

SYN. *New York: Belmont Books*, [*1969*].
   Wrappers. *June 1969* on copyright page. *Belmont B60–1018* (60¢).

THIS ISLAND EARTH. *Chicago: Shasta Publishers*, [*1952*].
  Boards with cloth shelf back. First edition so stated on copyright page.

THE TOYMAKER. *Los Angeles: Fantasy Publishing Company, Inc., 1951*.
  Two bindings, priority as listed: (A) Cloth; (B) Boards with Gnome Press imprint on spine.
  First edition so stated on copyright page.

VOYAGE TO THE BOTTOM OF THE SEA. *Racine: Whitman Publishing Company*, [*1965*].
  Boards. No statement of printing on copyright page.

THE YEAR WHEN STARDUST FELL. *Philadelphia Toronto: The John C. Winston Company*,
[*1958*].
  First edition so stated on copyright page.

David Henry Keller

(1880–1966)

THE DEVIL AND THE DOCTOR. *New York: Simon and Schuster, 1940.*
No statement of printing on copyright page.

THE ETERNAL CONFLICT. *Philadelphia: Prime Press, 1949.*
Three quarter cloth and boards. No statement of printing on copyright page. 400 copies only, numbered and signed. Note: Issued without dust jacket, slipcased.

FIGMENT OF A DREAM. *[Baltimore]: An Anthem "Limited Edition" Produced by Jack L. Chalker, [1962].*
Wrappers. *Published on or about December 1, 1962* on copyright page. Mimeographed. Limited to "approximately" 175 numbered copies.

THE FINAL WAR. *Portland, Oregon: Perri Press, 1949.*
Wrappers. No statement of printing. Mimeographed on paper marked *Wekoosu MIMEO BOND,* stapled. Note: Although Keller states in the foreword, "The author wishes to thank the artists for their courtesy in allowing him to use their pictures to illustrate his story. It is to be hoped that they will be pleased with the combination," the illustrations inspiring this short story were issued earlier as a portfolio and are not generally found with, nor are they part of, this booklet.

THE FOLSOM FLINT. *Sauk City: Arkham House, 1969.*
No statement of printing on copyright page.

THE HOMUNCULUS. *Philadelphia: Prime Press, 1949.*
Two issues, no priority: (A) 112 copies, numbered and signed, slipcased; (B) Trade issue. No statement of printing on copyright page.

THE LADY DECIDES. *Philadelphia: Prime Press, 1950.*
Three-quarter cloth and boards. No statement of printing on copyright page. 400 copies only, numbered and signed. Note: Issued without dust jacket, slipcased.

LIFE EVERLASTING. *Newark, New Jersey: The Avalon Company, 1947.*
No statement of printing on copyright page. 1000 numbered copies. Notes: (1) Early copies (not more than 200, according to Sam Moskowitz) were signed on the frontispiece or limitation leaf by Keller. (2) A booklet containing a bibliography of Keller's writings was issued with this volume.

MEN OF AVALON. *[Everett, Penna.: Fantasy Publications, ca. 1935.]*
Wrappers. Two bindings, no priority established: (A) Length of rule on front wrapper is 2.2 cm and incorporates two dots; (B) Length of rule on front wrapper is 2.5 cm and incorporates three dots. No statement of printing. Bound with THE WHITE SYBIL by Clark Ashton Smith.

THE SIGN OF THE BURNING HART. *N.p.: Published by The National Fantasy Fan Federation, [1948].*
First American edition on copyright page. 250 copies printed. Note: Offset from the first edition printed in Saint-Lo, France, in 1938 in an edition of 100 numbered copies bound in wrappers.

THE SOLITARY HUNTERS AND THE ABYSS. *Philadelphia: New Era Publishers, 1948.*
First edition so stated on copyright page.

TALES FROM UNDERWOOD. *New York: Published for Arkham House by Pellegrini & Cudahy,* [*1952*].
   No statement of printing on copyright page.

THE TELEVISION DETECTIVE. [*Los Angeles*]: *LASFL, Mar*[*ch 19*]*38.*
   Self wrappers. No statement of printing. Mimeographed on paper watermarked
   PEN-TYPE MIMEOGRAPH, stapled. Caption title. Note: Issued as volume one, number
   one of *Mikros*, a fanzine issued by the Los Angeles Science Fiction League.

THE THING IN THE CELLAR. *Millheim, Penna.: The Bizarre Series, n.d.* [*1940*].
   Wrappers. No statement of printing.

THE THOUGHT PROJECTOR. *New York: Stellar Publishing Corporation,* [*1930*].
   Wrappers. No statement of printing. Cover title. Issued as *Science Fiction Series No. 2*.

THE WATERS OF LETHE. *Great Barrington, Mass.: Hayward S. Kirby, Publisher,* [*cop. 1937*].
   Wrappers. No statement of printing.

WOLF HOLLOW BUBBLES. *Jamaica, New York: The ARRA Printers, n.d.* [*1934?*].
   Self wrappers. No statement of printing. Cover title. Issued as *Scientific Detective Series Number One*. Notes: (1) Advertised in *Science Fiction Digest*, May 1933. (2) Dated 1934
   by Pavlat and Evans in *Fanzine Index* (1965).

Reference

David H. Keller, M.D. Lieut. Col., U.S.A., Ret. Bibliography. *N.p., n.d.*
   Self wrappers. No statement of printing. Caption title. Note: Issued with LIFE EVERLAST-
   ING by Keller.

Daniel Keyes
(b. 1927)

THE CONTAMINATED MAN. *[Frogmore]: Mayflower*, *[1977]*.
   Wrappers. *Published in 1977* on copyright page. *Mayflower 583 12434 8* (65p). Reissue of THE TOUCH.

FLOWERS FOR ALGERNON. *New York: Harcourt, Brace & World, Inc.*, *[1966]*.
   First edition so stated on copyright page.

THE TOUCH. *New York: Harcourt, Brace & World, Inc.*, *[1968]*.
   First edition so stated on copyright page. Issued later in Great Britain as THE CONTAMI-
   NATED MAN.

Associational

Flowers for Algernon: A Full-length Play by David Rogers, Based Upon the Novel by Daniel
Keyes. *Chicago: The Dramatic Publishing Company*, *[1969]*.
   Wrappers. No statement of printing on copyright page. Note: Adapted by Rogers from the
   novel, FLOWERS FOR ALGERNON, by Keyes.

Stephen King
(b. 1946)

CARRIE. *Garden City: Doubleday & Company, Inc., 1974.*
First edition so stated on copyright page. Note: The two deposit copies at the Library of Congress are advance readers' copies bound in printed white wrappers with *SPECIAL EDITION NOT FOR SALE/TO BE PUBLISHED APRIL 1974 BY DOUBLEDAY & COMPANY, INC.* on rear cover.

'SALEM'S LOT. *Garden City: Doubleday & Company, Inc., 1975.*
Boards with cloth shelf back. First edition so stated on copyright page.

THE SHINING. *Garden City: Doubleday & Company, Inc., 1977.*
Boards with cloth shelf back. First edition so stated on copyright page.

Philip J. Klass
(b. 1920)

THE HUMAN ANGLE.*New York: Ballantine Books*, [*1956*].
Two issues, no priority: (A) Cloth; (B) Wrappers. *Ballantine Books 159* (35¢). No statement of printing on copyright page. *William Tenn, pseudonym.*

A LAMP FOR MEDUSA.*New York: Belmont Books*, [*1968*].
Wrappers. *June 1968* on copyright page. *Belmont B60–077* (60¢). *William Tenn, pseudonym.* Bound with THE PLAYERS OF HELL by Dave Van Arnam.

OF ALL POSSIBLE WORLDS.*New York: Ballantine Books*, [*1955*].
Two issues, no priority: (A) Cloth; (B) Wrappers. *Ballantine Books 99* (35¢). No statement of printing on copyright page. *William Tenn, pseudonym.*

ALSO:*London: Michael Joseph*, [*1956*]. Boards. *First published . . . 1956* on copyright page. Adds three stories not in the U.S. collection, "Generation of Noah," "Project Hush," and "Party of the Two Parts" and excludes two, "Me, Myself, and I" and "Everybody Loves Irving Bomber."

OF MEN AND MONSTERS.*New York: Ballantine Books*, [*1968*].
Wrappers. *First Printing: June, 1968* on copyright page. *Ballantine Science Fiction U6131* (75¢). *William Tenn, pseudonym.*

ALSO:*New York: Walker and Company*, [*1969*]. Boards. *Published in the United States of America in 1969* on copyright page. First hardcover edition.

THE SEVEN SEXES.*New York: Ballantine Books*, [*1968*].
Wrappers. *First Printing: June, 1968* on copyright page. *Ballantine Science Fiction U6134* (75¢). *William Tenn, pseudonym.*

THE SQUARE ROOT OF MAN.*New York: Ballantine Books*, [*1968*].
Wrappers. *First Printing: June, 1968* on copyright page. *Ballantine Science Fiction U6132* (75¢). *William Tenn, pseudonym.*

TIME IN ADVANCE.*New York: Bantam Books*, [*1958*].
Wrappers. *Published June 1958* on copyright page. *A Bantam Book A1786* (35¢). *William Tenn, pseudonym.*

ALSO:*London: Victor Gollancz Ltd, 1963*. Boards. No statement of printing on copyright page. First hardcover edition.

THE WOODEN STAR.*New York: Ballantine Books*, [*1968*].
Wrappers. *First Printing: June, 1968* on copyright page. *Ballantine Science Fiction U6133* (75¢). *William Tenn, pseudonym.*

Edited Fiction

Children of Wonder. *New York: Simon and Schuster, 1953.*
Boards with cloth shelf back. First printing so stated on copyright page. Edited, with introduction and short story "Errand Boy," by Klass. *William Tenn, pseudonym.* Reissued as *Outsiders: Children of Wonder.*

Once Against the Law. *New York: The Macmillan Company*, [*1968*].
  First printing so stated on copyright page. Edited by Klass with DONALD E. WESTLAKE.
  William Tenn, pseudonym.

Outsiders: Children of Wonder. *Garden City: Permabooks*, [*1954*].
  Wrappers. *1st printing . . . May, 1954* on copyright page. *Perma P291* (35¢). Edited, with
  introduction and short story "Errand Boy," by Klass. *William Tenn, pseudonym.* Reissue
  of *Children of Wonder.*

Otis Adelbert Kline
(1891–1946)

THE BRIDE OF OSIRIS. See STORIES. . . .

CALL OF THE SAVAGE. *New York: Edward J. Clode Inc.*, [*1937*].
No statement of printing on copyright page. Reissued as JAN OF THE JUNGLE.

JAN IN INDIA. *Lakemont, Georgia: Fictioneer Books Ltd.*, *1974* .
Wrappers. *First Edition/1974* on page [191].

JAN OF THE JUNGLE. *New York: Ace Books*, [*1966*].
Wrappers. No statement of printing on copyright page. *Ace Science Fiction Classic F-400*
(40¢). Reissue of CALL OF THE SAVAGE.

THE MAN WHO LIMPED AND OTHER STORIES. *Hollywood, California: Saint Enterprises Inc.*
Publishers, [*1946*].
Wrappers. *First book publication* on copyright page. *Chartered Collection 22* (25¢).

MAZA OF THE MOON. *Chicago: A. C. McClurg & Co.*, *1930*.
No statement of printing on copyright page. McClurg seal on copyright page.

THE OUTLAWS OF MARS. *New York: Avalon Books*, [*1961*].
No statement of printing on copyright page.

THE PLANET OF PERIL. [*Chicago*]: *A. C. McClurg & Co.*, *1929*.
First edition so stated on copyright page.

THE PORT OF PERIL. *Providence, Rhode Island: The Grandon Company*, *1949*.
No statement of printing on copyright page.

THE PRINCE OF PERIL. *Chicago: A. C. McClurg & Co.*, *1930*.
First edition so stated on copyright page.

STORIES BY OTIS ADELBERT KLINE. [*Oak Lawn, Ill.: Published by Robert Weinberg*, *1975*.]
Wrappers. No statement of printing on copyright page. *Lost Fantasies, Number 1*. Note:
Cover title reads *The Bride of Osiris*.

THE SWORDSMAN OF MARS. *New York: Avalon Books*, [*1960*].
No statement of printing on copyright page.

TAM, SON OF THE TIGER. *New York: Avalon Books*, [*1962*].
No statement of printing on copyright page.

Thomas Nigel Kneale
(b. 1922)

QUATERMASS AND THE PIT. *[Harmondsworth]: Penguin Books, [1960]*.
  Wrappers. *First published 1960* on copyright page. *Penguin Books 1449* (2'6).

THE QUATERMASS EXPERIMENT. *[Harmondsworth]: Penguin Books, [1959]*.
  Wrappers. *First published 1959* on copyright page. *Penguin Books 1421* (2'6).

QUATERMASS II. *[Harmondsworth]: Penguin Books, [1960]*.
  Wrappers. *First published 1960* on copyright page. *Penguin Books 1448* (2'6).

TOMATO CAIN. *London: Collins, 1949*.
  No statement of printing on copyright page.

THE YEAR OF THE SEX OLYMPICS AND OTHER TV PLAYS. *[London]: Ferret Fantasy Ltd, mcmlxxvi*.
  Two issues, no priority: (A) Cloth. *Of this First Edition . . . one/hundred numbered copies have been bound in buckram and signed/by the author . . .* on copyright page. Limited issue. (B) Boards. No statement of printing on copyright page. Trade issue.

Damon Francis Knight

(b. 1922)

A FOR ANYTHING. *London: The New English Library Ltd*, [*1961*].
Wrappers. *First published in England by Four Square Books in 1961* on copyright page, *Four Square 382* (2'6). First printing of complete text of THE PEOPLE MAKER.

ALSO: *New York: Walker and Company*, [*1970*]. Boards. *Published in 1970* on copyright page. First hardcover edition. Note: Offset from plates of the 1965 Berkley Publishing Corporation edition.

ANALOGUE MEN. [*New York*]: *Berkley Publishing Corporation*, [*1962*].
Wrappers. No statement of printing on copyright page. *Berkley Medallion F647* (50¢). Reissue of HELL'S PAVEMENT.

THE BEST OF DAMON KNIGHT. *Garden City: Nelson Doubleday, Inc.*, [*1976*].
Boards. Two printings, priority as listed: (A) Code *G 17* at base of page 306; (B) Code *H 11* at base of page 306. No statement of printing on copyright page. Note: Issued by the Science Fiction Book Club.

BEYOND THE BARRIER. *Garden City: Doubleday & Company, Inc.*, *1964*.
First edition so stated on copyright page.

THE EARTH QUARTER. See WORLD WITHOUT CHILDREN AND THE EARTH QUARTER.

FAR OUT. *New York: Simon and Schuster*, *1961*.
Boards. First printing so stated on copyright page.

HELL'S PAVEMENT. *New York: Lion Books, Inc.*, [*1955*].
Wrappers. *Lion Library Edition published February, 1955* on copyright page. *Lion Library LL 13* (35¢). Reissued as ANALOGUE MEN.

IN DEEP. [*New York*]: *Berkley Publishing Corporation*, [*1963*].
Wrappers. *May, 1963* on copyright page. *Berkley Medallion F760* (50¢).

ALSO: *London: Victor Gollancz Ltd*, *1964*. Boards. No statement of printing on copyright page. First hardcover edition. Drops one story, "The Handler."

MASTERS OF EVOLUTION. *New York: Ace Books, Inc.*, [*1959*].
Wrappers. No statement of printing on copyright page. *Ace Double Novel Books D–375* (35¢). Bound with FIRE IN THE HEAVENS by George O. Smith.

MIND SWITCH. [*New York*]: *Berkley Publishing Corporation*, [*1965*].
Wrappers. *November, 1965* on copyright page. *Berkley Medallion F1160* (50¢). Reissued as THE OTHER FOOT.

NATURAL STATE AND OTHER STORIES. *London and Sydney: Pan Books*, [*1975*].
Wrappers. *This edition published 1975 . . .* on copyright page. *Pan Science Fiction 0 330 24442 6* (60p). Reprint. Issued earlier in the U.S. as THREE NOVELS.

OFF CENTER. *New York: Ace Books, Inc.*, [*1965*].
Wrappers. No statement of printing on copyright page. *Ace Double M–113* (45¢). Bound with THE RITHIAN TERROR by Knight.

ALSO: OFF CENTRE. *London: Victor Gollancz Ltd, 1969.* Boards. No statement of printing on copyright page. Three additional stories, "Dulcie and Decorum," "Masks," and "To Be Continued." First hardcover edition.

THE OTHER FOOT. *London: Ronald Whiting & Wheaton, [1966].*
Boards. *First published in Great Britain 1966* on copyright page. Issued earlier in the U.S. as MIND SWITCH.

THE PEOPLE MAKER. *Rockville Center, N.Y.: Zenith Books, Inc., [1959].*
Wrappers. *Zenith Books edition published February, 1959* on copyright page. *Zenith Books ZB–14* (35¢). Enlarged as A FOR ANYTHING.

THE RITHIAN TERROR. *New York: Ace Books, Inc., [1965].*
Wrappers. No statement of printing on copyright page. *Ace Double M–113* (45¢). Bound with OFF CENTER by Knight.

THE SUN SABOTEURS. *New York: Ace Books, Inc., [1961].*
Wrappers. No statement of printing on copyright page. *Ace Double Novels F–108* (40¢). Bound with THE LIGHT OF LILITH by G. McDonald Wallis. Reissued as THE EARTH QUARTER. See WORLD WITHOUT CHILDREN AND THE EARTH QUARTER and TWO NOVELS.

THREE NOVELS. *Garden City: Doubleday & Company, Inc., 1967.*
First edition so stated on copyright page. Issued later in Great Britain as NATURAL STATE AND OTHER STORIES.

TURNING ON. *Garden City: Doubleday & Company, Inc., 1966.*
First edition so stated on copyright page.

ALSO: *London: Victor Gollancz Ltd, 1967.* Boards. No statement of printing on copyright page. Adds "The Handler."

TWO NOVELS. *London: Victor Gollancz Ltd, 1974.*
Boards. No statement of printing on copyright page. Collects "The Earth Quarter" (originally published as THE SUN SABOTEURS) and "Double Meaning."

WORLD WITHOUT CHILDREN AND THE EARTH QUARTER. *New York: Lancer Books, [1970].*
Wrappers. No statement of printing on copyright page. *Lancer Books, 74-601* (75¢). THE EARTH QUARTER was published earlier as THE SUN SABOTEURS.

Translated Fiction

Ashes, Ashes, [by] René Barjavel. *Garden City: Doubleday & Company, Inc., 1967.*
First Edition in the United States of America on copyright page. Translated by Knight.

Thirteen French Science-Fiction Stories. See Edited Fiction.

Edited Fiction

Best Stories from Orbit: Volumes 1–10. *[New York]: Published by Berkley Publishing Company, [1975].*
No statement of printing on copyright page. Edited, with introduction and notes, by Knight.

Beyond Tomorrow. *New York: Harper & Row, Publishers, [1965].*
Boards. First edition so stated on copyright page. Edited, with introduction, by Knight.

A Century of Great Short Science Fiction Novels. *New York: Delacorte Press,* [*1964*].
   No statement of printing on copyright page. Edited, with introduction and notes, by
   Knight.

A Century of Science Fiction. *New York: Simon and Schuster, 1962.*
   Boards. First printing so stated on copyright page. Edited, with introduction, by Knight.

Cities of Wonder. *Garden City: Doubleday & Company, Inc., 1966.*
   First edition so stated on copyright page. Edited, with introduction, by Knight.

The Dark Side. *Garden City: Doubleday & Company, Inc., 1965.*
   First edition so stated on copyright page. Edited, with introduction, by Knight.

Dimension X. *New York: Simon and Schuster,* [*1970*].
   Boards. First printing so stated on copyright page. Compiled, with introductory notes, by
   Knight.

First Contact. *New York: Pinnacle Books,* [*1971*].
   Wrappers. *First printing, November, 1971* on copyright page. *Pinnacle Books P062N*
   (95¢). Edited, with introduction, by Knight.

First Flight. *New York: Lancer Books,* [*1963*].
   Wrappers. *A Lancer Book • 1963* on copyright page. *Lancer Books 72–672* (50¢). Edited,
   with introduction, by Knight. Reissued as *Now Begins Tomorrow.*

The Golden Road. *New York: Simon and Schuster,* [*1973*].
   Boards. First printing so stated on copyright page. Edited, with introduction, by Knight.

Happy Endings. *Indianapolis New York: The Bobbs-Merrill Company, Inc.,* [*1974*].
   Boards. First printing so stated on copyright page. Edited, with introduction, by Knight.

The Metal Smile. *New York: Belmont Books,* [*1968*].
   Wrappers. *October 1968* on copyright page. *Belmont Science Fiction B60–082* (60¢).
   Edited by Knight.

Nebula Award Stories 1965. *Garden City: Doubleday & Company, Inc., 1966.*
   First edition so stated on copyright page. Edited, with introduction, by Knight.

Now Begins Tomorrow. *New York: Lancer Books,* [*1969*].
   Wrappers. No statement of printing on copyright page. *Lancer Books 74–585* (75¢).
   Edited, with introduction, by Knight. Reissue of *First Flight.*

One Hundred Years of Science Fiction. *New York: Simon and Schuster,* [*1968*].
   Boards. First printing so stated on copyright page. Edited, with introduction, by Knight.

Orbit 1. *New York: G. P. Putnam's Sons,* [*1966*].
   No statement of printing on copyright page. Edited, with introduction and notes, by
   Knight.

Orbit 2. *New York: G. P. Putnam's Sons,* [*1967*].
   No statement of printing on copyright page. Edited, with introductory notes, by Knight.

Orbit 3. *New York: G. P. Putnam's Sons,* [*1968*].
   No statement of printing on copyright page. Edited, with introductory notes, by Knight.

Orbit 4. *New York: G. P. Putnam's Sons,* [*1968*].
   Boards. No statement of printing on copyright page. Edited, with introductory notes, by
   Knight.

Orbit 5. *New York: G. P. Putnam's Sons*, [*1969*].
No statement of printing on copyright page. Edited by Knight.

Orbit 6. *New York: G. P. Putnam's Sons*, [*1970*].
No statement of printing on copyright page. Edited by Knight.

Orbit 7. *New York: G. P. Putnam's Sons*, [*1970*].
Boards. No statement of printing on copyright page. Edited by Knight.

Orbit 8. *New York: G. P. Putnam's Sons*, [*1970*].
No statement of printing on copyright page. Edited by Knight.

Orbit 9. *New York: G. P. Putnam's Sons*, [*1971*].
No statement of printing on copyright page. Edited by Knight.

Orbit 10. *New York: G. P. Putnam's Sons*, [*1972*].
No statement of printing on copyright page. Edited by Knight.

Orbit 11. *New York: G. P. Putnam's Sons*, [*1972*].
No statement of printing on copyright page. Edited by Knight.

Orbit 12. *New York: G. P. Putnam's Sons*, [*1973*].
No statement of printing on copyright page. Edited by Knight.

Orbit 13. *New York: Berkley Publishing Corporation*, [*1974*].
Boards. No statement of printing on copyright page. Edited by Knight.

Orbit 14. *New York, Evanston, San Francisco, London: Harper & Row, Publishers*, [*1974*].
Boards with cloth shelf back. First edition so stated on copyright page. Edited, with notes, by Knight.

Orbit 15. *New York, Evanston, San Francisco, London: Harper & Row, Publishers*, [*1974*].
Boards with cloth shelf back. First edition so stated on copyright page. Edited by Knight.

Orbit 16. *New York, Evanston, San Francisco, London: Harper & Row, Publishers*, [*1975*].
Boards with cloth shelf back. First edition so stated on copyright page. Edited, with foreword and biographies, by Knight.

Orbit 17. *New York, Evanston, San Francisco, London: Harper & Row, Publishers*, [*1975*].
Boards with cloth shelf back. First edition so stated on copyright page. Edited, with notes, by Knight.

Orbit 18. *New York, Hagerstown, San Francisco, London: Harper & Row, Publishers*, [*1976*].
Boards with cloth shelf back. First edition so stated on copyright page. Edited, with afterword, by Knight.

Orbit 19. *New York, Hagerstown, San Francisco, London: Harper & Row, Publishers*, [*1977*].
Boards with cloth shelf back. First edition so stated on copyright page. Edited by Knight.

Perchance to Dream. *Garden City: Doubleday & Company, Inc., 1972.*
First edition so stated on copyright page. Edited, with introduction, by Knight.

A Pocketful of Stars. *Garden City: Doubleday & Company, Inc., 1971.*
First edition so stated on copyright page. Edited, with introduction and short story ''Masks,'' by Knight.

A Science Fiction Argosy. *New York: Simon and Schuster,* [*1972*].
First printing so stated on copyright page. Edited, with introduction, by Knight.

Science Fiction Inventions. *New York: Lancer Books,* [*1967*].
Wrappers. *A Lancer Book • 1967* on copyright page. *Lancer Books 73–691* (60¢). Edited, with introduction and notes, by Knight.

Science Fiction of the Thirties. *Indianapolis/New York: The Bobbs-Merrill Company, Inc.,* [*1975*].
Boards with cloth shelf back. First printing so stated on copyright page. Edited, with foreword and commentary, by Knight.

The Shape of Things. *New York: Popular Library,* [*1965*].
Wrappers. No statement of printing on copyright page. *Popular Library SP352* (50¢). Edited, with introduction and notes, by Knight.

A Shocking Thing. *New York: Published by Pocket Books,* [*1974*].
Wrappers. *November, 1974* on copyright page. *Pocket Books 77775* (95¢). Edited by Knight.

Thirteen French Science-Fiction Stories. *Toronto New York London: Bantam Books,* [*1965*].
Wrappers. *Published August 1965* on copyright page. *A Bantam Fifty F2817* (50¢). Edited, with translations and introduction, by Knight.

Tomorrow and Tomorrow. *New York: Simon and Schuster,* [*1973*].
Code *1 2 3 4 5 6 7 8 9 10* on copyright page. Edited, with foreword, by Knight.

Tomorrow × 4. *Greenwich, Conn.: Fawcett Publications, Inc.,* [*1964*].
Wrappers. No statement of printing on copyright page. *Gold Medal d1428* (50¢). Edited by Knight.

Toward Infinity. *New York: Simon & Schuster,* [*1968*].
Boards. First printing so stated on copyright page. Edited, with introduction and notes, by Knight.

Westerns of the 40's: Classics From the Great Pulps. *Indianapolis/New York: The Bobbs-Merrill Company, Inc.,* [*1977*].
Boards with cloth shelf back. First printing so stated on copyright page. Edited by Knight.

Worlds to Come. *New York, Evanston, and London: Harper & Row, Publishers,* [*1967*].
Boards. First edition so stated on copyright page. Edited, with introduction, by Knight.

Nonfiction (Dealing with the Fantasy Genre only)

The Futurians: The Story of the Science Fiction "Family" of the 30's that Produced Today's Top SF Writers and Editors. *New York: John Day,* [*1977*].
Boards with cloth shelf back. Code *1 3 5 7 9 10 8 6 4 2* on copyright page.

In Search of Wonder. *Chicago: Advent: Publishers, 1956.*
First edition so stated on copyright page.

ALSO:*Chicago: Advent: Publishers, 1967.* Second edition, revised and enlarged.

Edited nonfiction (Dealing with the Fantasy Genre only)

Turning Points Essays on the Art of Science Fiction. *New York Hagerstown San Francisco London: Harper & Row, Publishers, [1977]*.

    Boards with cloth shelf back. First edition so stated on copyright page. Edited, with introduction and contributions "What Is Science Fiction?" and "Writing and Selling Science Fiction," by Knight.

Cyril M. Kornbluth
(1923–1958)

THE BEST OF C. M. KORNBLUTH. *Garden City: Nelson Doubleday, Inc.*, [*1976*].
Boards. No statement of printing on copyright page. Code *G35* on page [311]. Note: Issued by the Science Fiction Book Club.

BEST SF STORIES. . . .*London: Faber and Faber*, [*1968*].
First published in mcmlxviii on copyright page. Note: All stories reprinted from earlier books; one appears for the first time in a collection solely by Kornbluth.

CHRISTMAS EVE. *London: Michael Joseph*, [*1956*].
Boards. *First published . . . 1956* on copyright page. Issued earlier in the U.S. as NOT THIS AUGUST.

CRITICAL MASS. *Toronto New York London: Bantam Books*, [*1977*].
Wrappers. *October 1977* on copyright page. *Bantam Science Fiction 10948–0* ($1.75). With FREDERIK POHL.

THE EXPLORERS. *New York: Ballantine Books*, [*1954*].
Wrappers. No statement of printing on copyright page. *Ballantine Books 86* (35¢).

GLADIATOR-AT-LAW. *New York: Ballantine Books*, [*1955*].
Two issues, no priority: (A) Cloth; (B) Wrappers. *Ballantine Books 107* (35¢). No statement of printing on copyright page. With FREDERIK POHL.

GUNNER CADE. *New York: Simon and Schuster*, 1952.
Boards. First printing so stated on copyright page. *Cyril Judd, pseudonym.* With JUDITH MERRIL.

HALF. *New York: Lion Books, Inc.*, [*1953*].
Wrappers. *Lion edition published/March, 1953* on copyright page. *Lion 135* (25¢). *Jordan Park, pseudonym.*

THE MAN OF COLD RAGES. *New York: Pyramid Books*, [*1958*].
Wrappers. *Pyramid Books edition 1958* on copyright page. *Pyramid G368* (35¢). *Jordan Park, pseudonym.*

THE MARCHING MORONS. *New York: Ballantine Books*, [*1959*].
Wrappers. No statement of printing on copyright page. *Ballantine Books 303 K* (35¢).

A MILE BEYOND THE MOON. *Garden City: Doubleday, Inc.*, 1958.
First edition so stated on copyright page.

ALSO: [*New York*]: *A Macfadden Book*, [*1962*]. Wrappers. *A Macfadden Book . . . 1962* on copyright page. *MB40–100* (40¢). Abridged reprint. Drops four stories.

THE MINDWORM. *London: Michael Joseph*, [*1955*].
Boards. *First published . . . 1955* on copyright page. Note: Includes four short stories collected for the first time in book form.

. . .THE NAKED STORM. *New York: A Lion Book*, [*1952*].
Wrappers. *Lion Edition published November, 1952* on copyright page. *Lion 109* (25¢). *Simon Eisner, pseudonym.*

NOT THIS AUGUST.*Garden City: Doubleday & Company, Inc., 1955.*
Boards. First edition so stated on copyright page. Issued later in Great Britain as
CHRISTMAS EVE.

OUTPOST MARS.*New York: Abelard Press,* [*1952*].
No statement of printing on copyright page. *Cyril Judd, pseudonym.* With JUDITH MERRIL.
Revised as SIN IN SPACE.

PRESIDENTIAL YEAR.*New York: Ballantine Books,* [*1956*].
Two bindings, no priority: (A) Cloth: (1) Green cloth, spine lettered in blue; (2) Red cloth,
spine lettered in blue. Both cloth bindings received at Library of Congress 7 June 1956. (B)
Wrappers. *Ballantine Books 144* (35¢). No statement of printing on copyright page. With
FREDERIK POHL.

SEARCH THE SKY.*New York: Ballantine Books,* [*1954*].
Two issues, no priority: (A) Boards; (B) Wrappers. *Ballantine Books 61* (35¢). No statement of printing on copyright page. With FREDERIK POHL.

SIN IN SPACE.*New York: Galaxy Publishing Corporation,* [*1961*].
Wrappers No statement of printing on copyright page. *Beacon Book No. 312* (35¢). *Cyril
Judd, pseudonym.* With JUDITH MERRIL. Revised text of OUTPOST MARS.

SORORITY HOUSE.*New York City: Lion Library Editions,* [*1956*].
Wrappers. *Published May, 1956* on copyright page. *Lion Library LL 97* (35¢). With
FREDERIK POHL. *Jordan Park, pseudonym.*

THE SPACE MERCHANTS.*New York: Ballantine Books,* [*1953*].
Two issues, no priority: (A) Boards; (B) Wrappers. *Ballantine Books 21* (35¢). No statement of printing on copyright page. With FREDERIK POHL.

THE SYNDIC.*Garden City: Doubleday & Company, Inc., 1953.*
First edition so stated on copyright page.

TAKEOFF.*Garden City: Doubleday & Company, Inc., 1952.*
Boards. First edition so stated on copyright page.

THIRTEEN O'CLOCK.*[New York]: A Dell Book,* [*1970*].
Wrappers. *First printing —December 1970* on copyright page. *Dell 8731* (75¢).

ALSO:*London: Robert Hale & Company, 1972.* Boards. *First published in Great Britain
1972* on copyright page. First hardcover edition.

A TOWN IS DROWNING.*New York: Ballantine Books,* [*1955*].
Two bindings, no priority: (A) Cloth: (1) Red cloth, spine lettered in blue; (2) Dark blue
cloth, spine lettered in light blue. Both cloth bindings received at Library of Congress 2
February 1956. (B) Wrappers. *Ballantine Books 123* (35¢). No statement of printing on
copyright page. With FREDERIK POHL.

VALERIE.*New York: A Lion Book,* [*1953*].
Wrappers. *November, 1953* on copyright page. *A Lion Book 176* (25¢). *Jordan Park,
pseudonym.*

WOLFBANE.*New York: Ballantine Books,* [*1959*].
Wrappers. *First Ballantine Edition* on copyright page. *Ballantine Books 335 K* (35¢). With
FREDERIK POHL.

ALSO:*London: Victor Gollancz Ltd, 1960.* Boards. No statement of printing on copyright
page. First hardcover edition.

THE WONDER EFFECT. *New York: Ballantine Books*, [*1962*].
  Wrappers. No statement of printing on copyright page. *An Original Ballantine Book F 638* (50¢). With FREDERIK POHL.

  ALSO:*London: Victor Gollancz Ltd*, *1967*. Boards. No statement of printing on copyright page. First hardcover edition.

Henry Kuttner
(1915–1958)

AHEAD OF TIME. *New York: Ballantine Books,* [*1953*].
　　Two bindings, no priority: (A) Boards; (B) Wrappers. *Ballantine Books 30* (35¢). No statement of printing on copyright page.

THE BEST OF HENRY KUTTNER. *Garden City: Nelson Doubleday, Inc.,* [*1975*].
　　Boards. Two printings, priority as listed: (A) Code *01 R* on page 335; (B) Code *H 15* on page 337. No statement of printing on copyright page. Note: Issued by the Science Fiction Book Club.

THE BEST OF KUTTNER VOLUME 1. [*London*]: *A Mayflower-Dell Paperback,* [*1965*].
　　Wrappers. *First Publication in this form . . . November 1965* on copyright page. *Mayflower-Dell Science Fiction 0547* (5/–).

THE BEST OF KUTTNER VOLUME 2. [*London*]: *A Mayflower-Dell Paperback,* [*1966*].
　　Wrappers. *May 1966* on copyright page. *Mayflower Dell 0547* (5/–).

BEYOND EARTH'S GATES. *New York: Ace Books, Inc.,* [*1954*].
　　Wrappers. No statement of printing on copyright page. *Ace Double Novel Books D–69* (35¢). *Lewis Padgett, pseudonym.* With C. L. MOORE. Bound with DAYBREAK—2250 A.D. by Andre Norton.

THE BRASS RING. *New York: Duell, Sloan and Pearce,* [*1946*].
　　First printing so stated on copyright page. *Lewis Padgett, pseudonym.* With C. L. MOORE. Reissued as MURDER IN BRASS.

BYPASS TO OTHERNESS. *New York: Ballantine Books,* [*1961*].
　　Wrappers. No statement of printing on copyright page. *Ballantine Books 497 K* (35¢).

CHESSBOARD PLANET. *New York: Galaxy Publishing Corp.,* [*1956*].
　　Wrappers. No statement of printing on copyright page. *Galaxy Novel 26* (35¢). *Lewis Padgett, pseudonym.* With C. L. MOORE. Reissue of THE FAIRY CHESSMEN (see TOMORROW AND TOMORROW AND THE FAIRY CHESSMEN).

THE CREATURE FROM BEYOND INFINITY. *New York: Popular Library,* [*1968*].
　　Wrappers. No statement of printing on copyright page. *Popular Library 60–2355* (60¢).

THE DARK WORLD. *New York: Ace Books, Inc.,* [*1965*].
　　Wrappers. No statement of printing on copyright page. *Ace Book F–327* (40¢).

THE DAY HE DIED. *New York: Duell, Sloan and Pearce,* [*1947*].
　　First printing so stated on copyright page. *Lewis Padgett, pseudonym.* With C. L. MOORE.

DESTINATION INFINITY. *New York: Avon Publications, Inc.,* [*1958*].
　　Wrappers. No statement of printing on copyright page. *Avon T–275* (35¢). With the anonymous collaboration of C. L. MOORE. Reissue of FURY.

DR. CYCLOPS. *New York: Popular Library,* [*1967*].
　　Wrappers. No statement of printing on copyright page. *Popular Library 445–02485–060* (60¢). Notes: (1) The text is that of the novelette originally appearing in *Thrilling Wonder Stories,* June 1940. According to C. L. Moore, Kuttner has noted on his file card for this

work, "magazine version from movie script." Moore states that Kuttner "did the rephrasing of the script but not the original story." A novel with the same title was published under the house pseudonym Will Garth by Phoenix Press Publishers of New York in 1940. The 1940 novel version is often credited to Kuttner but it appears that he did not write it. The Library of Congress attributes LAWLESS GUNS, a western novel published under the Will Garth pseudonym by Dodge Publishing Company of New York in 1937, to Kuttner as well. C. L. Moore comments, "As for LAWLESS GUNS, I have no record of it. I've consulted friends who worked at a literary agency with Hank before he and I met, and they have no recollection of this title, nor of any particular interest he ever had in westerns. It may not be impossible that it was his, but very improbable." (2) In addition to the Kuttner novelette, this volume includes "Too Late for Eternity" by Bryce Walton and "The Harpers of Titan" by Edmond Hamilton.

EARTH'S LAST CITADEL. *New York: Ace Books, Inc.*, [*1964*].
Wrappers. No statement of printing on copyright page. *Ace Book F–306* (40¢). With C. L. MOORE.

THE FAR REALITY. *London: World Distributors*, [*1963*].
Wrappers. *This Consul edition, complete and unabridged, published in England, 1963* . . . on copyright page. *Consul Books Selected Science Fiction 1266* (2'6). *Lewis Padgett, pseudonym.* With C. L. MOORE. Reissue of THE FAIRY CHESSMEN (see TOMORROW AND TOMORROW AND THE FAIRY CHESSMEN).

FURY. *New York: Grosset & Dunlap Publishers*, [*1950*].
Boards. No statement of printing on copyright page. With the anonymous collaboration of C. L. MOORE. Reissued as DESTINATION INFINITY.

ALSO: *New York: Lancer Books*, [*1972*]. Wrappers. No statement of printing on copyright page. *Lancer Books 75413–095* (95¢). New introduction by Moore.

A GNOME THERE WAS. *New York: Simon and Schuster*, *1950*.
Boards. No statement of printing on copyright page. *Lewis Padgett, pseudonym.* With C. L. MOORE.

LINE TO TOMORROW. *New York: Bantam Books*, [*1954*].
Wrappers. *A Bantam Book Published August, 1954* on copyright page. *Bantam Books 1251* (25¢). *Lewis Padgett, pseudonym.* With C. L. MOORE.

MAN DROWNING. *New York: Harper & Brothers Publishers*, [*1952*].
Boards. First edition so stated on copyright page.

THE MASK OF CIRCE. *New York: Ace Books*, [*1971*].
Wrappers. No statement of printing on copyright page. *Ace Book SF 52075* (60¢). With the anonymous collaboration of C. L. MOORE.

MURDER IN BRASS. *New York: Bantam Books*, [*1947*].
Wrappers. *Bantam Edition Published/August, 1947* on copyright page. *Bantam Books 107* (25¢). *Lewis Padgett, pseudonym.* With C. L. MOORE. Reissue of THE BRASS RING.

MURDER OF A MISTRESS. *New York: Permabooks*, [*1957*].
Wrappers. *Permabook edition published July, 1957/1st printing . . . May, 1957* on copyright page. *Permabooks M–4082* (35¢).

MURDER OF A WIFE. *New York: Permabooks*, [*1958*].
Wrappers. *Permabook edition published March, 1958/1st printing January, 1958* on copyright page. *Permabooks M 4096* (35¢).

THE MURDER OF ANN AVERY.*Garden City: Permabooks*, *[1956]*.
  Wrappers. *1st printing . . . September, 1956* on copyright page. *Permabooks 3058* (25¢).

THE MURDER OF ELEANOR POPE.*New York: Permabooks*, *[1956]*.
  Wrappers. *Permabook edition published July, 1956/1st printing . . . May, 1956* on copyright page. *Permabooks M–3046* (25¢).

MUTANT.*New York: Gnome Press, Inc., Publishers*, *[1953]*.
  Boards. First edition so stated on copyright page. *Lewis Padgett, pseudonym*. With C. L. MOORE.

NO BOUNDARIES.*New York: Ballantine Books*, *[1955]*.
  Two bindings, no priority: (A) Cloth; (B) Wrappers. *Ballantine Books 122* (35¢). No statement of printing on copyright page. With C. L. MOORE.

RETURN TO OTHERNESS.*New York: Ballantine Books*, *[1962]*.
  Wrappers. No statement of printing on copyright page. *An Original Ballantine Book F619* (50¢).

ROBOTS HAVE NO TAILS.*New York: Gnome Press Inc.*, *[1952]*.
  Boards. First edition so stated on copyright page. *Lewis Padgett, pseudonym*.

THE TIME AXIS.*New York: Ace Books, Inc.*, *[1965]*.
  Wrappers. No statement of printing on copyright page. *Ace Science Fiction Classic F–356* (40¢). With the anonymous collaboration of C. L. MOORE.

TOMORROW AND TOMORROW AND THE FAIRY CHESSMEN.*New York: Gnome Press, Inc. Publishers*, *[1951]*.
  Boards. First edition so stated on copyright page. *Lewis Padgett, pseudonym*. With C. L. MOORE. Note: THE FAIRY CHESSMEN was reissued as CHESSBOARD PLANET and later as THE FAR REALITY.

TOMORROW AND TOMORROW.*London: World Distributors*, *[1963]*.
  Wrappers. *This Consul edition complete and unabridged, published in England, 1963 . . .* on copyright page. *Consul Books Selected Science Fiction 1265* (2'6). *Lewis Padgett, pseudonym*. With C. L. MOORE. Reprint. Collected earlier in TOMORROW AND TOMORROW AND THE FAIRY CHESSMEN.

VALLEY OF THE FLAME.*New York: Ace Books, Inc.*, *[1964]*.
  Wrappers. No statement of printing on copyright page. *Ace Book F–297* (40¢). With the anonymous collaboration of C. L. MOORE.

WELL OF THE WORLDS.*New York: Galaxy Publishing Corp.*, *[1953]*.
  Wrappers. No statement of printing on copyright page. *Galaxy Science Fiction Novel No. 17* (35¢). *Lewis Padgett, pseudonym*. With C. L. MOORE.

Associational

A Play in One Act: Mimsy Were the Borogoves, by Charles G. Taylor, Adapted From the Story by Lewis Padgett . . . *Chicago: The Dramatic Publishing Company*, *[1965]*.
  Wrappers. Two printings noted, probable priority as listed: (A) Second line on copyright page reads: *Permission for an amateur performance of this play/*; (B) Second line on copyright page reads: *The royalty fee, payable in advance, for each amateur/*. No state-

ment of printing on copyright page. Note: Adapted by Taylor from the short story "Mimsy Were the Borogoves," by Kuttner.

Reference

*Henry Kuttner: A Memorial Symposium, edited by Karen Anderson. *Berkeley: Sevagram Enterprises, Aug 1958.*
  Self wrappers? Mimeographed. Includes bibliography compiled by Donald H. Tuck.

Raphael Aloysius Lafferty

(b. 1914)

APOCALYPSES. *Los Angeles: Pinnacle Books*, [1977].
Wrappers. *First printing, October 1977* on copyright page. *Futorian Science Fiction/Pinnacle Books 40–148* ($1.95).

ARRIVE AT EASTERWINE. *New York: Charles Scribner's Sons*, [1971].
Boards with cloth shelf back. Code *A–6.71 (C)* on copyright page.

THE DEVIL IS DEAD. [*New York*]: *Avon*, [1971].
Wrappers. *First Avon Printing, May, 1971* on copyright page. *Avon Science Fiction Original V2406* (75¢).

ALSO: *Boston: Gregg Press, 1977. First Printing, June 1977* on copyright page. First hardcover edition. Note: Not issued in dust jacket.

DOES ANYONE ELSE HAVE SOMETHING FURTHER TO ADD? *New York: Charles Scribner's Sons*, [1974].
Code *1 3 5 7 9 11 13 15 17 19 c/c 20 18 16 14 12 10 8 6 4 2* on copyright page.

THE FLAME IS GREEN. *New York: Walker and Company*, [1971].
Boards. *First published in the United States of America in 1971* on copyright page.

FOURTH MANSIONS. *New York: An Ace Book*, [1969].
Wrappers. No statement of printing on copyright page. *An Ace Science Fiction Special 24590* (75¢).

ALSO: *London: Dennis Dobson*, [1972]. Boards. *First published in Great Britain in 1972* on copyright page. First hardcover edition.

FUNNYFINGERS & CABRITO. *Portland: Pendragon Press*, [1976].
800 copies printed. Three issues, no priority: (A) 50 copies hardbound in boards lettered a–ax signed by the author; (B) 100 copies bound in wrappers numbered 1–100 signed by the author; (C) 650 copies bound in wrappers numbered 101–750, unsigned. *First printing/1976 September* on copyright page.

HORNS ON THEIR HEADS. *Portland: Pendragon Press*, [1976].
800 copies printed. Three issues, no priority: (A) 50 copies hardbound in boards lettered a–ax signed by the author; (B) 100 copies bound in wrappers numbered 1–100 signed by the author; (C) 650 copies bound in wrappers numbered 101–750, unsigned. *First printing/1976 September* on copyright page.

NINE HUNDRED GRANDMOTHERS. *New York: Ace Publishing Corporation*, [1970].
Wrappers. No statement of printing on copyright page. *An Ace Science Fiction Special 58050* (95¢).

ALSO: *London: Dennis Dobson*, [1975]. Boards. *First published in Great Britain in 1975* on copyright page. First hardcover edition.

NOT TO MENTION CAMELS. *Indianapolis/New York: The Bobbs-Merrill Company, Inc.*, [1976].
Boards. First printing so stated on copyright page.

OKLA HANNALI. *Garden City: Doubleday & Company, Inc., 1972.*
First edition so stated on copyright page.

PAST MASTER. *New York: Ace Books, Inc.* [*1968*].
Wrappers. No statement of printing on copyright page. *Ace Science Fiction Special H–54* (60¢).

ALSO: *London: Rapp & Whiting,* [*1968*]. Boards. *First published in Great Britain 1968* on copyright page. First hardcover edition.

THE REEFS OF EARTH. [*New York*]: *Published by Berkley Publishing Corporation,* [*1968*].
Wrappers. *March, 1968* on copyright page. *Berkley Medallion X1528* (60¢).

ALSO: *London: Dennis Dobson,* [*1970*]. Boards. *First published in Great Britain in 1970* on copyright page. First hardcover edition.

SPACE CHANTEY. *New York: Ace Books, Inc.,* [*1968*].
Wrappers. No statement of printing on copyright page. *Ace Double H–56* (60¢). Bound with PITY ABOUT EARTH by Ernest Hill.

ALSO: *London: Dennis Dobson,* [*1976*]. Boards. *First published in Great Britain in 1976* . . . on copyright page. First hardcover edition.

STRANGE DOINGS. *New York: Charles Scribner's Sons,* [*1971*].
Boards with cloth shelf back. Code *A–12.71* [*c*] on copyright page.

John Frederick Lange, Jr.

(b. 1931)

ASSASSIN OF GOR. *New York: Ballantine Books*, [*1970*].
Wrappers. *First Printing: December, 1970* on copyright page. *Ballantine Books Fantasy Adventure 02094–4–095* (95¢). *John Norman, pseudonym.*

CAPTIVE OF GOR. *New York: Ballantine Books*, [*1972*].
Wrappers. *First Printing: December, 1972* on copyright page. *Ballantine Books Fantasy Adventure 02994–1–095* (95¢). *John Norman, pseudonym.*

GOR OMNIBUS. *London: Sidgwick & Jackson*, [*1972*].
Boards. No statement of printing on copyright page. Reprint. Collects OUTLAW OF GOR, TARNSMAN OF GOR, and PRIEST KINGS OF GOR. *John Norman, pseudonym.*

HUNTERS OF GOR. *New York: DAW Books, Inc.*, [*1974*].
Wrappers. *First printing: March 1974/1 2 3 4 5 6 7 8 9* on copyright page. *DAW: sf Books No. 96 UW1102* ($1.50). *John Norman, pseudonym.*

MARAUDERS OF GOR. *New York: DAW Books, Inc.*, [*1975*].
Wrappers. *First printing, March 1975/1 2 3 4 5 6 7 8 9* on copyright page. *DAW: sf Books No. 141 UW1160* ($1.50). *John Norman, pseudonym.*

NOMADS OF GOR. *New York: Ballantine Books*, [*1969*].
Wrappers. *First Printing: November, 1969* on copyright page. *Ballantine Books Fantasy Adventure 01765–075* (75¢). *John Norman, pseudonym.*

OUTLAW OF GOR. *New York: Ballantine Books*, [*1967*].
Wrappers. *First Edition: December, 1967* on copyright page. *A Ballantine Fantasy Adventure Original U6072* (75¢). *John Norman, pseudonym.* Later collected in GOR OMNIBUS.

ALSO: *London: Sidgwick & Jackson*, [*1970*]. Boards. *First published in Great Britain 1970* on copyright page. First hardcover edition.

PRIEST-KINGS OF GOR. *New York: Ballantine Books*, [*1968*].
Wrappers. *First Edition: December, 1968* on copyright page. *A Ballantine Fantasy Adventure Original 72015* (75¢). *John Norman, pseudonym.* Later collected in GOR OMNIBUS.

ALSO: *London: Sidgwick & Jackson*, [*1971*]. Boards. *First published in Great Britain 1971* on copyright page. First hardcover edition.

RAIDERS OF GOR. *New York: Ballantine Books*, [*1971*].
Wrappers. *First Printing: December, 1971* on copyright page. *Ballantine Books Fantasy Adventure 02447–8–095* (95¢). *John Norman, pseudonym.*

SLAVE GIRL OF GOR. *New York: DAW Books, Inc.*, [*1977*].
Wrappers. *First printing, March 1977/1 2 3 4 5 6 7 8 9* on copyright page. *DAW: sf Books No. 232 UJ1285* ($1.95). *John Norman, pseudonym.*

TARNSMAN OF GOR. *New York: Ballantine Books*, [*1966*].
Wrappers. *First Edition: December, 1966* on copyright page. *A Ballantine Fantasy Adventure Original U6071* (75¢). *John Norman, pseudonym.* Later collected in GOR OMNIBUS.

ALSO: *London: Sidgwick & Jackson*, [*1969*]. Boards. *First published in Great Britain 1969* on copyright page. First hardcover edition.

TIME SLAVE. *New York: DAW Books, Inc.*, [*1975*].
  Wrappers. *First printing, November 1975/1 2 3 4 5 6 7 8 9* on copyright page. *DAW: sf Books No. 169 UW1204* ($1.50). *John Norman, pseudonym.*

TRIBESMEN OF GOR. *New York: DAW Books, Inc.*, [*1976*].
  Wrappers. *First printing, March 1976/1 2 3 4 5 6 7 8 9* on copyright page. *DAW: sf Books No. 185 UW1223* ($1.50). *John Norman, pseudonym.*

Sterling E. Lanier
(b. 1927)

HIERO'S JOURNEY.*Radnor: Chilton Book Company*, [*1973*].
   Boards with cloth shelf back. First edition so stated on copyright page.

THE PECULIAR EXPLOITS OF BRIGADIER FFELLOWES.*New York: Walker and Company*,
[*1971*].
   Boards. *First published in the United States of America in 1971* on copyright page.

THE WAR FOR THE LOT.*Chicago New York: Follett Publishing Company*, [*1969*].
   Two bindings, no priority: (A) Pictorial cloth reproducing dust jacket design. ''Titan
   edition.'' Library binding. (B) Boards. ''Trade edition.'' Trade binding. *First Printing/I*
   on copyright page.

John Keith Laumer

(b. 1925)

THE AFRIT AFFAIR. *[New York]: Published by Berkley Publishing Corporation, [1968]*.
Wrappers. *April, 1968* on copyright page. *A Berkley Medallion Book X1547 (60¢). The Avengers #5* at head of title.

ASSIGNMENT IN NOWHERE. *[New York]: Published by Berkley Publishing Corporation, [1968]*.
Wrappers. *August, 1968* on copyright page. *A Berkley Medallion Book X1596 (60¢)*.

ALSO: *London: Dennis Dobson, [1972]*. Boards. *First published in Great Britain in 1972* on copyright page. First hardcover edition.

THE BEST OF KEITH LAUMER. *New York: Published by Pocket Books, [1976]*.
Wrappers. *March, 1976* on copyright page. *Pocket Books 80310* ($1.75).

THE BIG SHOW. *New York: Ace Books, [1972]*.
Wrappers. *First Ace printing: October, 1972* on copyright page. *An Ace Book 06177* (75¢).

ALSO: *London: Robert Hale & Company, [1976]*. Boards. *This edition 1976* on copyright page. First hardcover edition.

BOLO. *New York: Published by Berkley Publishing Corporation, [1976]*.
No statement of printing on copyright page.

CATASTROPHE PLANET. *[New York]: Published by Berkley Publishing Corporation, [1966]*.
Wrappers. *August 1966* on copyright page. *Berkley Medallion F1273 (50¢)*.

ALSO: *London: Dennis Dobson, [1970]*. Boards. *First published in Great Britain in 1970* on copyright page. First hardcover edition.

THE DAY BEFORE FOREVER AND THUNDERHEAD. *Garden City: Doubleday & Company, Inc. 1968*.
First edition so stated on copyright page.

DEADFALL. *Garden City: Doubleday & Company, Inc., 1971*.
First edition so stated on copyright page. Reissued as FAT CHANCE.

DINOSAUR BEACH. *[New York]: Charles Scribner's Sons, [1971]*.
Boards with cloth shelf back. Code *A–9.71 [C]* on copyright page.

THE DROWNED QUEEN. *[New York]: Published by Berkley Publishing Corporation, [1968]*.
Wrappers. *June, 1968* on copyright page. *A Berkley Medallion Book X1565 (60¢). The Avengers #6* at head of title.

EARTHBLOOD. *Garden City: Doubleday & Company, Inc., 1966*.
First edition so stated on copyright page. With ROSEL GEORGE BROWN.

EMBASSY. *New York: Pyramid Books, [1965]*.
Wrappers. *First printing, March 1965* on copyright page. *Pyramid Books X–1145 (60¢)*.

ENEMIES FROM BEYOND.*New York: Pyramid Books*, [*1967*].
Wrappers. *First printing October, 1967* on copyright page. *Pyramid Books X–1689* (60¢).
Note: *The Invaders Number 2* at head of title on front cover.

ENVOY TO NEW WORLDS.*New York: Ace Books, Inc.*, [*1963*].
Wrappers. No statement of printing on copyright page. *Ace Double F–223* (40¢). Bound
with FLIGHT FROM YESTERDAY by Robert Moore Williams.

ALSO:*London: Dennis Dobson*, [*1972*]. Boards. *First published in Great Britain in 1972*
on copyright page. First hardcover edition.

FAT CHANCE.*New York: Published by Pocket Books*, [*1975*].
Wrappers. *March, 1975* on copyright page. *Pocket Books 78899* ($1.25). Reissue of
DEADFALL.

GALACTIC DIPLOMAT.*Garden City: Doubleday & Company, 1965*.
First edition so stated on copyright page.

GALACTIC ODYSSEY. [*New York*]: *Published by Berkley Publishing Corporation*, [*1967*].
Wrappers. *September, 1967* on copyright page. *Berkley Medallion X1447* (60¢).

ALSO:*London: Dennis Dobson*, [*1968*]. Boards. *First published in Great Britain in 1968*
on copyright page. First hardcover edition.

THE GLORY GAME.*Garden City: Doubleday & Company, Inc., 1973*.
First edition so stated on copyright page.

THE GOLD BOMB. [*New York*]: *Published by Berkley Publishing Corporation*, [*1968*].
Wrappers. *September, 1968* on copyright page. *A Berkley Medallion Book X1592* (60¢).
The Avengers #7 at head of title.

THE GREAT TIME MACHINE HOAX.*New York: Simon and Schuster, 1964*.
First printing so stated on copyright page.

GREYLORN. [*New York*]: *Published by Berkley Publishing Corporation*, [*1968*].
Wrappers. *February, 1968* on copyright page. *Berkley Medallion X1514* (60¢). Issued
later in Great Britain as THE OTHER SKY.

THE HOUSE IN NOVEMBER.*New York: G. P. Putnam's Sons*, [*1970*].
Boards. No statement of printing on copyright page.

THE INFINITE CAGE.*New York: G. P. Putnam's Sons*, [*1972*].
Boards. No statement of printing on copyright page.

THE INVADERS.*New York: Pyramid Books*, [*1967*].
Wrappers. *First printing August, 1967* on copyright page. *Pyramid R–1664* (50¢). Issued
later in Great Britain as THE METEOR MEN.

IT'S A MAD, MAD, MAD GALAXY. [*New York*]: *Published by Berkley Publishing Corporation*,
[*1968*].
Wrappers. *December, 1968* on copyright page. *A Berkley Medallion Book X1641* (60¢).

ALSO:*London: Dennis Dobson*, [*1969*]. Boards. *First published in Great Britain 1969* on
copyright page. First hardcover edition.

THE LONG TWILIGHT.*New York: G. P. Putnam's Sons*, [*1969*].
Boards. No statement of printing on copyright page.

THE METEOR MEN. *[London]: Corgi Books, [1968]*.
Wrappers. *Corgi Edition published 1968* on copyright page. *Souvenir Press/Corgi Science Fiction GS7836* (3s. 6d.). *Anthony LeBaron, pseudonym*. Issued earlier in the U.S. as THE INVADERS.

THE MONITORS. *[New York]: Published by Berkley Publishing Corporation, [1966]*.
Wrappers. *December, 1966* on copyright page. *Berkley Medallion X1340* (60¢).

ALSO:*London: Dennis Dobson, [1968]*. Boards. *First published in Great Britain 1968* on copyright page. First hardcover edition.

NIGHT OF DELUSIONS. *New York: G. P. Putnam's Sons, [1972]*.
Boards. No statement of printing on copyright page.

NINE BY LAUMER. *Garden City: Doubleday & Company, Inc., 1967*.
First edition so stated on copyright page.

ONCE THERE WAS A GIANT. *Garden City: Doubleday & Company, Inc., 1971*.
First edition so stated on copyright page.

THE OTHER SIDE OF TIME. *[New York]: Published by Berkley Publishing Corporation, [1965]*.
Wrappers. *August, 1965* on copyright page. *Berkley Medallion F1129* (50¢).

ALSO:*London: Dennis Dobson, [1968]*. Boards. *First published in Great Britain in 1968* on copyright page. First hardcover edition.

THE OTHER SKY. *London: Dennis Dobson, [1968]*.
Boards. *First published in Great Britain 1968* on copyright page. Issued earlier in the U.S. as GREYLORN.

A PLAGUE OF DEMONS. *[New York]: Published by Berkley Publishing Corporation, [1965]*.
Wrappers. *May, 1965* on copyright page. *Berkley Medallion F1086* (50¢).

ALSO:*[London]: Millington, [1975]*. Boards. *First published 1975 . . .* on copyright page. First hardcover edition.

PLANET RUN. *Garden City: Doubleday & Company, Inc., 1967*.
First edition so stated on copyright page. With GORDON R. DICKSON.

RETIEF: AMBASSADOR TO SPACE. *Garden City: Doubleday & Company, Inc., 1969*.
First edition so stated on copyright page.

RETIEF AND THE WARLORDS. *Garden City: Doubleday & Company, Inc., 1968*.
First edition so stated on copyright page.

RETIEF EMISSARY TO THE STARS. *[New York]: A Dell Book, [1975]*.
Wrappers. *First printing—December 1975* on copyright page. *Dell 7425* (95¢).

RETIEF OF THE CDT. *Garden City: Doubleday & Company, Inc., 1971*.
First edition so stated on copyright page.

RETIEF'S RANSOM. *New York: G. P. Putnam's Sons, [1971]*.
Boards. No statement of printing on copyright page.

RETIEF'S WAR. *Garden City: Doubleday & Company, Inc., 1966*.
First edition so stated on copyright page.

THE SHAPE CHANGER. *New York: G. P. Putnam's Sons, [1972]*.
Boards. No statement of printing on copyright page.

THE STAR TREASURE. *New York: G. P. Putnam's Sons*, [*1971*].
No statement of printing on copyright page.

THE TIME BENDER. [*New York*]: *Published by Berkley Publishing Corporation*, [*1966*].
Wrappers. *February, 1966* on copyright page. *Berkley Medallion F1185* (50¢).

ALSO: *London: Dennis Dobson*, [*1971*]. Boards. *First published in Great Britain in 1975* on copyright page. First hardcover edition.

TIME TRAP. *New York: G. P. Putnam's Sons*, [*1970*].
Boards. No statement of printing on copyright page.

TIMETRACKS. *New York: Ballantine Books*, [*1972*].
Wrappers. *First Printing: April, 1972* on copyright page. *Ballantine Books Science Fiction 02575–X–095* (95¢).

A TRACE OF MEMORY. [*New York*]: *Published by Berkley Publishing Corporation*, [*1963*].
Wrappers. *June, 1963* on copyright page. *Berkley Medallion F780* (50¢).

THE UNDEFEATED. [*New York*]: *A Dell Book*, [*1974*].
Wrappers. *First printing—June 1974* on copyright page. *Dell 9285* (95¢).

THE WORLD SHUFFLER. *New York: G. P. Putnam's Sons*, [*1970*].
Boards. No statement of printing on copyright page.

WORLDS OF THE IMPERIUM. *New York: Ace Books, Inc.*, [*1962*].
Wrappers. No statement of printing on copyright page. *Ace Double Novel F–127* (40¢).
Bound with SEVEN FROM THE STARS by Marion Zimmer Bradley.

ALSO: *London: Dennis Dobson*, [*1967*]. Boards. *First published in Great Britain 1967* on copyright page. First hardcover edition.

Edited Fiction

Five Fates. *Garden City: Doubleday & Company, Inc.*, [*1970*].
First edition so stated on copyright page. Anonymously edited, with story "Of Death What Dreams," by Laumer.

Ursula Kroeber Le Guin

(b. 1929)

CITY OF ILLUSIONS. *New York: Ace Books, Inc., [1967]*.
  Wrappers. No statement of printing on copyright page. *Ace Book G–626* (50¢).

  ALSO: *London: Victor Gollancz, 1971*. Boards. No statement of printing on copyright page.
  First hardcover edition.

THE DISPOSSESSED. *New York Evanston San Francisco London: Harper & Row, Publishers,*
[1974].
  Boards with cloth shelf back. First edition so stated on copyright page.

EARTHSEA. *London: Victor Gollancz Ltd, 1977*.
  Boards. No statement of printing on copyright page. Reprint. Collects A WIZARD OF
  EARTHSEA, THE TOMBS OF ATUAN, and THE FARTHEST SHORE.

THE FARTHEST SHORE. *New York: Atheneum, 1972*.
  Two bindings, priority as listed: (A) Black cloth stamped on spine and front cover in silver
  with a purple tint. Dust jacket reads at head of front flap *Reinforced Binding $6.25*. Note:
  The only trade binding of this title. *Cumulative Book Index* terms it a "library" binding.
  (B) Pictorial cloth reproducing dust jacket design. *A Guild Book* printed on spine. Junior
  Literary Guild binding. Not seen; reported by Jeff Levin. First edition so stated on
  copyright page.

  ALSO: *London: Victor Gollancz Ltd, 1973*. Boards. No statement of printing on copyright
  page. Drops three long speeches by Ged at the suggestion of her British editor. See Le
  Guin's *Dreams Must Explain Themselves*, page 13.

THE LATHE OF HEAVEN. *New York: Charles Scribner's Sons, [1971]*.
  Boards with cloth shelf back. Code *A–10.71 (C)* on copyright page.

THE LEFT HAND OF DARKNESS. *New York: An Ace Book, [1969]*.
  Wrappers. No statement of printing on copyright page. *An Ace Science Fiction Special*
  47800 (95¢). Note: First printing does not mention Hugo and Nebula awards won by Le
  Guin. Second printing bearing same stock number and price carries notices of Hugo and
  Nebula awards.

  ALSO: *New York: Walker and Company, [1969]*. Boards. *Published in the United States of*
  America in 1969 . . . on copyright page. First hardcover edition.

  ALSO: *New York: Ace Books, [1976]*. Wrappers. Twelve line printing history on copyright
  page with line twelve reading: *Twelfth Ace printing: July, 1976. Ace 47805* ($1.95). New
  introduction by Le Guin.

ORSINIAN TALES. *New York, Hagerstown, San Francisco, London: Harper & Row, Pub-*
lishers, [1976].
  Boards with cloth shelf back. First edition so stated on copyright page.

PLANET OF EXILE. *New York: Ace Books, Inc., [1966]*.
  Wrappers. No statement of printing on copyright page. *Ace Double G–597* (50¢). Bound
  with MANKIND UNDER THE LEASH by Thomas M. Disch.

  ALSO: *[New York & London: Garland Publishing, Inc., 1975.]* No statement of printing on
  copyright page. First hardcover edition. Notes: (1) Photo-reproduction of the 1972 Tandem
  edition. (2) Not issued in dust jacket.

ROCANNON'S WORLD.*New York: Ace Books, Inc., [1966].*
Wrappers. No statement of printing on copyright page. *Ace Double G–574* (50¢). Bound with THE KAR-CHEE REIGN by Avram Davidson.

ALSO: [*New York & London: Garland Publishing, Inc., 1975.*] No statement of printing on copyright page. First hardcover edition. Notes: (1) Photo-reproduction of the 1966 Ace Books edition. (2) Not issued in dust jacket.

ALSO:*New York, Hagerstown, San Francisco, London: Harper & Row, Publishers, [1977].* Boards with cloth shelf back. First printing has code *77 78 79 80 81 10 9 8 7 6 5 4 3 2 1* on copyright page. Note: Photo-offset of the second Ace Books printing with new introduction and a few textual corrections by Le Guin.

THE TOMBS OF ATUAN.*New York: Atheneum, 1971.*
First edition so stated on copyright page. Two states of copyright notice: (1) Notice on copyright page reads *Copyright © 1971 by Ursula K. Le Guin.* (2) Original notice altered by a cancel affixed to copyright page to read *Copyright © 1970, 1971 by Ursula K. Le Guin.* Two dust jacket states: (1) Newbery Honor Book seal not pasted on front panel. (2) Silver circular seal pasted on front panel identifying this title as a *Newbery Honor Book.* Note: Copies with and without the cancel copyright notice have been observed in jacket with the Newbery seal.

VERY FAR AWAY FROM ANYWHERE ELSE.*New York: Atheneum, 1976.*
First edition so stated on copyright page. Note: Published in Great Britain as A VERY LONG WAY FROM ANYWHERE ELSE. This title is taken directly from a line in the novel and is preferred by the author.

THE WATER IS WIDE.*Portland: Pendragon Press, [1976].*
1000 copies printed. Three issues, no priority: (A) 50 copies hardbound in boards lettered a–ax signed by the author, illustrators Leo and Diane Dillon, and calligrapher Robert J. Palladino; (B) 200 copies bound in wrappers numbered 1–200 signed by the author; (C) 750 copies bound in wrappers numbered 201–950, unsigned. *First printing/1976 September* on copyright page.

THE WIND'S TWELVE QUARTERS.*New York, Evanston San Francisco, London: Harper & Row, Publishers, [1975].*
Boards with cloth shelf back. First edition so stated on copyright page.

A WIZARD OF EARTHSEA.*Berkeley: Parnassus Press, [1968].*
No statement of printing on copyright page. Three printings, priority as listed: (A) First printing. 6,800 copies. All examined copies have a faint vertical line or smudge from the top to the base of the title page, generally running through the *r* or *d* of *wizard* to the *p* or *s* of *press.* Two bindings, no priority: (1) Library binding. The illustration on front cover and lettering on spine and rear cover are stamped (embossed); rear cover embossed with rectangular box enclosing a note on the binding headed *PARNASSUS* [publisher's logo] *LIBRARY EDITION;* inner hinges reinforced with a visible strip of white linen tape pasted under the endpapers. (2) Trade binding: Illustration on the front cover and lettering on spine are embossed; rear cover is blank; inner hinges not reinforced. The same dust jacket was used for both bindings with *$3.95 1 1up* in upper right corner of front flap and *Library Edition $3.90* in lower right corner. Generally the trade price is clipped from the jackets on the library binding and the library price is clipped from those on the trade binding. (B) Later printings. Two printings totalling 16,200 copies. Vertical line is not present on title page; front cover illustration and spine lettering are printed without embossment; rear cover is blank; no inner linen hinge; dust jacket does not bear a printed price (in most cases these copies have various prices handwritten by the publisher).

THE WORD FOR WORLD IS FOREST. *New York: Published by Berkley Publishing Corporation,* [*1976*].

    No statement of printing on copyright page. Note: First separate edition in English. Originally appeared in *Again, Dangerous Visions,* edited by Harlan Ellison.

    ALSO:*London: Victor Gollancz Ltd, 1977.* Boards. No statement of printing on copyright page. Adds "Author's Introduction."

Edited Fiction

Nebula Award Stories 11. *London: Victor Gollancz Limited, 1976.*

    Boards. No statement of printing on copyright page. Edited, with introduction, by Le Guin.

Nonfiction (Dealing with the Fantasy Genre only)

Dreams Must Explain Themselves. [*New York*]: *Algol Press,* [*1975*].

    Wrappers. Two printings, priority as listed: (A) Statement on copyright page reads *This volume is printed in a limited edition of 1,000 copies. This is/copy number . . .* (B) Limitation notice removed. Note: Le Guin's short story "The Rule of Names" appears for the first time in book form.

From Elfland to Poughkeepsie. *Portland, Oregon: Pendragon Press, 1973.*

    776 copies printed. Three issues, no priority: (A) 26 copies hardbound in boards lettered a–z signed by the author, Vonda N. McIntyre, and the photographer; (B) 100 copies bound in wrappers numbered 1–100 signed by the author; (C) 600 copies bound in wrappers numbered 101–750, unsigned. *First printing/1973 June* on copyright page.

Reference

The Farthest Shores of Ursula K. Le Guin, [by] George Edgar Slusser. *San Bernardino: R. Reginald The Borgo Press, MCMLXXVI.*

    Wrappers. *First Printing——September, 1976/1 2 3 4 5 6 7 8 9 10* on copyright page. *The Milford Series Popular Writers of Today Volume Three* at head of title.

Ursula K. LeGuin: Voyager to Inner Lands and to Outer Space, edited by Joe De Bolt. . . . *Port Washington, N.Y. // London: Kennikat Press, 1979.*

    Boards. No statement of printing on copyright page. Note: Not issued with dust jacket.

Fritz Reuter Leiber, Jr.

(b. 1910)

THE BEST OF FRITZ LEIBER.*London: Sphere Books Limited*, [*1974*].
Wrappers. *First published in Great Britain . . . 1974* on copyright page. *Sphere 0 7221 5474 7* (60p).

ALSO:*London: Sidgwick & Jackson*, [*1974*]. Boards. *First published in Great Britain in 1974* on copyright page. Note: Sphere and Sidgwick & Jackson editions printed from same plates and published in May and November respectively.

ALSO:*Garden City: Nelson Doubleday, Inc.*, [*1974*]. Boards. Three printings, priority as listed: (A) Code *E 22* on page 299; (B) Code *32 Q* on page 297; (C) Code *44R* on page 297. No statement of printing on copyright page. First hardcover edition. Notes: (1) Published as the June 1974 selection of the Science Fiction Book Club. (2) Story contents of British and U.S. editions are the same. British editions drop the introduction by Poul Anderson and substitute the afterword by Leiber. British editions have a bibliography by Gerald Bishop not appearing in the U.S. version.

THE BIG TIME.*New York: Ace Books, Inc.*, [*1961*].
Wrappers. No statement of printing on copyright page. *Ace Double Novel Books D-491* (35¢). Bound with THE MIND SPIDER AND OTHER STORIES by Leiber.

ALSO:*Boston: Gregg Press, 1976. First Printing, June 1976* on copyright page. First hardcover edition. Notes: (1) Photo-reproduction of the 1961 Ace edition. (2) Not issued in dust jacket.

THE BOOK OF FRITZ LEIBER.*New York: DAW Books, Inc.*, [*1974*].
Wrappers. *First printing, January 1974/1 2 3 4 5 6 7 8 9* on copyright page. *DAW: sf Books No. 87 UQ1091* (95¢).

CONJURE WIFE.*New York: Twayne Publishers, Inc.*, [*1953*].
No statement of printing on copyright page. Reissued by Berkley in 1962 with cover title BURN WITCH BURN. Note: The first separate edition. Originally collected in book form in 1952 as part of *Witches Three* edited by Fletcher Pratt.

DESTINY TIMES THREE.*New York: Galaxy Publishing Corp.*, [*1957*].
Wrappers. No statement of printing on copyright page. *Galaxy Novel No. 28* (35¢).

GATHER, DARKNESS!*New York: Pellegrini & Cudahy*, [*1950*].
No statement of printing on copyright page.

THE GREEN MILLENNIUM.*New York: Abelard Press*, [*1953*].
Boards. No statement of printing on copyright page. Note: The first British edition was issued in 1959 and comprised the U.S. sheets with title leaf a cancel and the publisher's imprint reading *Abelard-Schuman London and New York*. The dust jacket is that of the U.S. edition, with British price and address overprinted.

THE MIND SPIDER AND OTHER STORIES.*New York: Ace Books, Inc.*, [*1961*].
Wrappers. No statement of printing on copyright page. *Ace Double Novel Books D-491* (35¢). Bound with THE BIG TIME by Leiber.

ALSO: *New York: Ace Books*, [*1976*]. Wrappers. No statement of printing on copyright page. *Ace 53330* ($1.50). New foreword by Leiber. Drops "Try and Change the Past" and adds "Midnight in the Mirror World."

NIGHT MONSTERS.*New York: An Ace Book*, [*1969*].
  Wrappers. No statement of printing on copyright page. *Ace Double 30300* (60¢). Bound with THE GREEN MILLENNIUM by Leiber.

NIGHT MONSTERS.*London: Victor Gollancz Ltd, 1974*.
  Boards. No statement of printing on copyright page. Note: Differs from the U.S. collection of the same title. Contains three of the four stories there collected; drops "The Casket-Demon" and adds "The Creature From Cleveland Depths," "The Oldest Soldier," "The Girl With the Hungry Eyes," and "A Bit of the Dark World."

THE NIGHT OF THE WOLF.*New York: Ballantine Books*, [*1966*].
  Wrappers. *First printing: July, 1966* on copyright page. *A Ballantine Science Fiction Original U2254* (50¢).

NIGHT'S BLACK AGENTS.*Sauk City: Arkham House, 1947*.
  No statement of printing on copyright page. Reissued in slightly abridged format as TALES FROM NIGHT'S BLACK AGENTS.

OUR LADY OF DARKNESS.*New York: Published by Berkley Publishing Corporation*, [*1977*].
  No statement of printing on copyright page.

A PAIL OF AIR.*New York: Ballantine Books*, [*1964*].
  Wrappers. *First printing July 1964* on copyright page. *Ballantine Books U2216* (50¢).

RIME ISLE.[*Chapel Hill, N.C.*]: *Whispers Press, 1977*.
  2500 copies printed. Three issues, no priority: (A) 26 lettered copies signed by the author, artist Tim Kirk, and designer Stuart David Schiff; (B) 250 numbered copies signed by author, artist, and designer; (C) Trade issue. *This first separate edition of the entire novel published . . .* on copyright page.

THE SECOND BOOK OF FRITZ LEIBER.*New York: DAW Books, Inc.*, [*1975*].
  Wrappers. *First Printing, September 1975/1 2 3 4 5 6 7 8 9* on copyright page. *DAW: sf Books No. 164 UY1195* ($1.25).

THE SECRET SONGS.*London: Rupert Hart-Davis, 1968*.
  Boards. *First published 1968* on copyright page.

SHADOWS WITH EYES.*New York: Ballantine Books*, [*1962*].
  Wrappers. No statement of printing on copyright page. *Ballantine Books 577* (35¢).

SHIPS TO THE STARS.*New York: Ace Books, Inc.*, [*1964*].
  Wrappers. No statement of printing on copyright page. *Ace Double F–285* (40¢). Bound with THE MILLION YEAR HUNT by Kenneth Bulmer.

THE SILVER EGGHEADS.*New York: Ballantine Books*, [*1962*].
  Wrappers. No statement of printing on copyright page. *Ballantine Books F 561* (50¢).

THE SINFUL ONES.*New York: Universal*, [*1953*].
  Wrappers. No statement of printing on copyright page. *Universal Giant Edition No. 5* (50¢). Bound with BULLS, BLOOD AND PASSION by David Williams. Revised and condensed text published later as "You're All Alone."

A SPECTER IS HAUNTING TEXAS.*New York: Walker and Company*, [*1969*].
  Boards. *First published as a book in the United States of America in 1969 . . .* on copyright page.

SWORDS AGAINST DEATH. *New York: An Ace Book*, [*1970*].
Wrappers. No statement of printing on copyright page. *Ace Book 79150* (75¢). Note: Seven of the ten stories collected earlier as TWO SOUGHT ADVENTURE.

ALSO:*Boston: Gregg Press*, [*1977*]. *First Printing, December 1977* on copyright page. First hardcover edition.

SWORDS AGAINST WIZARDRY. *New York: Ace Books, Inc.*, [*1968*].
Wrappers. No statement of printing on copyright page. *An Ace Book H–73* (60¢).

ALSO:*Boston: Gregg Press*, [*1977*]. *First Printing, December 1977* on copyright page. First hardcover edition.

SWORDS AND DEVILTRY. *New York: An Ace Book*, [*1970*].
Wrappers. No statement of printing on copyright page. *Ace Book 79170* (75¢).

ALSO:*Boston: Gregg Press*, [*1977*]. *First Printing, December 1977* on copyright page. First hardcover edition. Adds introduction by Leiber.

SWORDS AND ICE MAGIC. *New York: Ace Books*, [*1977*].
Wrappers. *First Ace printing: July 1977* on copyright page. *Ace 79166–2* ($1.50).

ALSO:*Boston: Gregg Press*, [*1977*]. *First Printing, December 1977* on copyright page. First hardcover edition.

SWORDS IN THE MIST. *New York: Ace Books, Inc.*, [*1968*].
Wrappers. No statement of printing on copyright page. *Ace Book H–90* (60¢).

ALSO:*Boston: Gregg Press*, [*1977*]. *First Printing, December 1977* on copyright page. First hardcover edition.

THE SWORDS OF LANKHMAR. *New York: Ace Books, Inc.*, [*1968*].
Wrappers. No statement of printing on copyright page. *Ace Book H–38* (60¢).

ALSO:*London: Rupert Hart-Davis*, *1969*. Boards. *First published in Great Britain 1969* on copyright page. First hardcover edition.

TALES FROM NIGHT'S BLACK AGENTS. *New York: Ballantine Books*, [*1961*].
Wrappers. *June 1961* on copyright page. *Ballantine Books 508K* (35¢). Reprint. Includes nine of the ten stories originally collected in NIGHT'S BLACK AGENTS.

TARZAN AND THE VALLEY OF GOLD. *New York: Ballantine Books*, [*1966*].
Wrappers. *First edition: April, 1966* on copyright page. *Ballantine Book U6125* (75¢).

TWO SOUGHT ADVENTURE. *New York: Gnome Press, Inc.*, [*1957*].
Two bindings, priority as listed: (A) Black boards stamped in red; (B) Gray cloth stamped in red. First edition so stated on copyright page.

THE WANDERER. *New York: Ballantine Books*, [*1964*].
Wrappers. No statement of printing on copyright page. *An Original Ballantine Book U6010* (75¢).

ALSO:*London: Dennis Dobson*, [*1967*]. Boards. *First published in Great Britain in 1967* on copyright page. First hardcover edition.

THE WORLDS OF FRITZ LEIBER. *New York: Ace Books*, [*1976*].
Wrappers. *First ACE printing: November, 1976* on copyright page. *Ace 91640* ($1.95).

YOU'RE ALL ALONE. *New York: Ace Books*, [*1972*].
Wrappers. No statement of printing on copyright page. *Ace Book SF 95146* (95¢). Note: Title story is revised and condensed version of THE SINFUL ONES.

Clive Staples Lewis
(1898–1963)

THE DARK TOWER AND OTHER STORIES. *London: Collins, 1977.*
Boards. *First published 1977* on copyright page.

THE GREAT DIVORCE. *London: Geoffrey Bles: The Centenary Press, [1945].*
First Published November 1945 on copyright page.

THE HORSE AND HIS BOY. *London: Geoffrey Bles, [1954].*
Boards. *First published 1954* on copyright page.

THE LAST BATTLE: A STORY FOR CHILDREN. *London: The Bodley Head, 1956.*
First Published 1956 on copyright page.

THE LION, THE WITCH AND THE WARDROBE. *London: Geoffrey Bles, [1950].*
First published 1950 on copyright page.

THE MAGICIAN'S NEPHEW. *London: The Bodley Head, 1955.*
Boards. *First Published 1955* on copyright page.

OF OTHER WORLDS. *London: Geoffrey Bles, [1966].*
Boards. No statement of printing on copyright page. Edited by Walter Hooper. Note:
Includes three short stories and the draft of an unfinished novel.

OUT OF THE SILENT PLANET. *London: John Lane The Bodley Head, [1938].*
Two bindings, priority as listed: (A) Brick red cloth, spine lettered in gold; (B) Scarlet
cloth, spine lettered in black. *First published in 1938* on copyright page.

PERELANDRA. *London: John Lane The Bodley Head, [1943].*
First published 1943 on copyright page. Reissued as VOYAGE TO VENUS.

THE PILGRIM'S REGRESS. *London: J. M. Dent and Sons Ltd, [1933].*
First published 1933 on copyright page.

PRINCE CASPIAN: THE RETURN TO NARNIA. *London: Geoffrey Bles, [1951].*
Boards. *First published 1951* on page [196].

THE SCREWTAPE LETTERS. *London: Geoffrey Bles, [1942].*
First published 1942 on copyright page.

   ALSO: THE SCREWTAPE LETTERS AND SCREWTAPE PROPOSES A TOAST. *London: Geoffrey
   Bles, 1961.* Boards. *This new edition 1961* on copyright page. Enlarged edition.

THE SILVER CHAIR. *London: Geoffrey Bles, [1953].*
Boards. *First published 1953* on copyright page.

THAT HIDEOUS STRENGTH. *London: John Lane The Bodley Head, [1945].*
First published 1945 on copyright page.

   ALSO: *London: Pan Books Ltd. [1955].* Wrappers. *This edition, abridged by the author,
   published 1955 . . .* on copyright page. *Pan 321.* Abridged text; adds new author's "preface." The abridged text was reissued as THE TORTURED PLANET. Note: Price does not
   appear on the book.

TILL WE HAVE FACES. *London: Geoffrey Bles, 1956.*
  Boards. *First published 1956* on copyright page.

THE TORTURED PLANET *New York: Avon Publications, Inc., [1958].*
  Wrappers. No statement of printing on copyright page. *Avon T–211* (35¢). Reissue of
  THAT HIDEOUS STRENGTH with text abridged by Lewis and a new preface.

THE VOYAGE OF THE DAWN TREADER. *London: Geoffrey Bles, [1952].*
  Boards. *First published 1952* on page [224].

VOYAGE TO VENUS. *London: Pan Books Ltd, [1953].*
  Wrappers. *This edition published 1953 . . .* on copyright page. *Pan 253* (2'-). Reissue of
  PERELANDRA.

Associational

*Dear Wormwood: A Play in Three Acts, by James Forsyth based upon C.S. Lewis's Book
The Screwtape Letters. *Elgin, Illinois: Dramatic Publishing Company, 1961.*
  Wrappers.

C. S. Lewis' The Lion, the Witch and the Wardrobe, Dramatized by Don Quinn. *Chicago:
The Dramatic Publishing Company, [1968].*
  Wrappers. No statement of printing on copyright page. Earliest printing bound in pale blue
  wrappers lettered in black; later in yellow wrappers lettered in black. Note: Adapted by
  Quinn from the novel, THE LION, THE WITCH AND THE WARDROBE, by Lewis.

Autobiography and Letters

Letters of C. S. Lewis. *London: Geoffrey Bles Ltd, [1966].*
  Boards. No statement of printing on copyright page.

Letters to an American Lady. *Grand Rapids, Michigan: William B. Eerdmans Publishing
Company, [1967].*
  No statement of printing on copyright page. Edited, with preface and notes, by Clyde S.
  Kilby.

Surprised by Joy: The Shape of My Early Life. *London: Geoffrey Bles, 1955.*
  First published in 1955 on copyright page.

Reference

For a more exhaustive listing of pre-1974 material about Lewis refer to *C. S. Lewis: An
Annotated Checklist of Writings About Him and His Works,* compiled by Christopher and
Ostling listed below.

Bright Shadow of Reality, by Corbin Scott Carnell. *Grand Rapids: William B. Eerdmans
Publishing Company, [1974].*
  Wrappers. No statement of printing on copyright page.

C. S. Lewis a Biography, [by] Roger Lancelyn Green & Walter Hooper. *New York and
London: Harcourt Brace Jovanovich, [1974].*
  First American edition on copyright page.

C. S. Lewis: An Annotated Checklist of Writings About Him and His Works, compiled by Joe R. Christopher and Joan K. Ostling. [*Kent, Ohio*]: *The Kent State Press*, [*1973*].
    First edition so stated on copyright page.

C. S. Lewis: Apostle to the Skeptics, by Chad Walsh. *New York: The Macmillan Company, 1949.*
    First printing so stated on copyright page.

C. S. Lewis: Images of His World, [by] Douglas Gilbert [and] Clyde S. Kilby. *Grand Rapids, Michigan: William B. Eerdmans Publishing Company,* [*1973*].
    Boards. No statement of printing on copyright page.

C. S. Lewis: The Shape of His Faith and Thought, [by] Paul L. Holmer. *New York • Hagerstown • San Francisco • London: Harper & Row • Publishers,* [*1976*].
    Boards with cloth shelf back. First edition so stated on copyright page.

The Christian World of C. S. Lewis, by Clyde S. Kilby. *Grand Rapids, Michigan: Wm B. Eerdmans Publishing Company,* [*1964*].
    No statement of printing on copyright page.

The Image of Man in C. S. Lewis, [by] William Luther White. *Nashville and New York: Abingdon Press,* [*1969*].
    No statement of printing on copyright page.

Light on Lewis, edited by Jocelyn Gibb. *London: Geoffrey Bles, 1965.*
    Boards. No statement of printing on copyright page. Includes bibliography of Lewis's writings by Walter Hooper.

The Literary Legacy of C. S. Lewis, [by] Chad Walsh. *New York and London: Harcourt Brace Jovanovich,* [*1979*].
    Two bindings, no priority: (A) Boards with cloth shelf back; (B) Wrappers. First edition so stated on copyright page.

The Longing for a Form: Essays on the Fiction of C. S. Lewis, edited by Peter J. Schakel. [*Kent, Ohio*]: *The Kent State University Press,* [*1977*].
    No statement of printing on copyright page.

Lord of the Elves and Eldils: Fantasy and Philosophy in C. S. Lewis and J. R. R. Tolkien, by Richard Purtill. *Grand Rapids, Michigan: Zondervan Publishing House,* [*1974*].
    Wrappers. No statement of printing on copyright page. *Zondervan Books 12267p* ($1.50).

Shadows of Imagination: The Fantasies of C. S. Lewis, J. R. R. Tolkien and Charles Williams, edited by Mark R. Hillegas. *Carbondale and Edwardsville: Southern Illinois University Press. London and Amsterdam: Feffer & Simons, Inc.,* [*1969*].
    No statement of printing on copyright page.

    ALSO:*Carbondale and Edwardsville: Southern Illinois University Press/London and Amsterdam: Feffer & Simons, Inc.,* [*1979*]. No statement of printing on copyright page. Enlarged edition.

Robert Arthur Ley
(1921–1968)

INTERMIND. *[New York]: A Banner Book, [1967].*
   Wrappers. *First Banner Printing, October, 1967* on copyright page. *A Banner Original B50–117* (50¢). *Ray Luther, pseudonym.*

   ALSO: *London: Dennis Dobson, [1969].* Boards. *First published in Great Britain in 1969* on copyright page. *Arthur Sellings, pseudonym.* First hardcover edition.

JUNK DAY. *London: Dennis Dobson, [1970].*
   Boards. *First published in Great Britain in 1970* on copyright page. *Arthur Sellings, pseudonym.*

THE LONG EUREKA. *London: Dennis Dobson, [1968].*
   Boards. *First published in 1968* on copyright page. *Arthur Sellings, pseudonym.*

THE POWER OF X. *London: Dennis Dobson, [1968].*
   Boards. *First published in 1968* on copyright page. *Arthur Sellings, pseudonym.*

THE QUY EFFECT. *London: Dennis Dobson, [1966].*
   Boards. *First published in Great Britain in 1966* on copyright page. *Arthur Sellings, pseudonym.*

THE SILENT SPEAKERS. *London: Dennis Dobson, [1963].*
   Boards. *First published in Great Britain in 1963* on copyright page. *Arthur Sellings, pseudonym.* Issued earlier in the U.S. as TELEPATH.

TELEPATH. *New York: Ballantine Books, [1962].*
   Wrappers. No statement of printing on copyright page. *A Ballantine Book F 609* (50¢). *Arthur Sellings, pseudonym.* Issued later in Great Britain as THE SILENT SPEAKERS.

TIME TRANSFER AND OTHER STORIES. *London: Michael Joseph, [1956].*
   Boards. *First published . . . 1956* on copyright page. *Arthur Sellings, pseudonym.*

THE UNCENSORED MAN. *London: Dennis Dobson, [1964].*
   Boards. *First published in Great Britain in 1964* on copyright page. *Arthur Sellings, pseudonym.*

David Lindsay
(1876–1945)

ADVENTURES OF MONSIEUR DE MAILLY.*London & New York: Andrew Melrose Ltd., 1926.*
No statement of printing on copyright page. Issued later in the U.S. as A BLADE FOR SALE.

A BLADE FOR SALE THE ADVENTURES OF MONSIEUR DE MAILLY.*New York: Robert M. McBride & Company, MCMXXVII.*
First Published March, 1927 on copyright page. Issued earlier in Great Britain as ADVENTURES OF MONSIEUR DE MAILLY.

DEVIL'S TOR.*London: G. P. Putnam's Sons, [1932].*
Two bindings, priority as listed: (A) Black cloth, spine lettered in gold; (B) Blue cloth, spine lettered in black. *First Published April 1932* on copyright page.

THE HAUNTED WOMAN.*London: Methuen & Co., Ltd., [1922].*
First Published in 1922 on copyright page.

SPHINX.*London: John Long, Limited, [1923].*
No statement of printing on copyright page.

THE VIOLENT APPLE & THE WITCH.*[Chicago]: Chicago Review Press, [1976].*
Two bindings, no priority: (A) Boards; (B) Wrappers. No statement of printing on copyright page. Edited by J. B. Pick.

A VOYAGE TO ARCTURUS.*London: Methuen & Co., Ltd., [1920].*
Two bindings, priority as listed: (A) Red cloth, spine stamped in gold, front panel in blind. 8-page publisher's catalogue inserted at rear. (B) A later binding reported by George Locke. Not seen; no details available. *First Published in 1920* on copyright page.

Reference

The Strange Genius of David Lindsay: An Appreciation by J. B. Pick, Colin Wilson & E. H. Visiak. *London: John Baker, [1970].*
Boards. *First published in 1970 . . .* on copyright page.

Paul Myron Anthony Linebarger
(1913–1966)

ATOMSK. *New York: Duell, Sloan and Pearce, [1949].*
First printing so stated on copyright page. *Carmichael Smith, pseudonym.*

THE BEST OF CORDWAINER SMITH. *Garden City: Nelson Doubleday, Inc., [1975].*
Boards. No statement of printing on copyright page. Code *24 R* on page 337. *Cordwainer Smith, pseudonym.* Notes: (1) Edited, with introduction and notes, by J.J. Pierce. (2) Issued by the Science Fiction Book Club.

CAROLA. *New York: Duell, Sloan and Pearce, [1948].*
First edition so stated on copyright page. *Felix C. Forrest, pseudonym.*

NORSTRILIA. *New York: Ballantine Books, [1975].*
Wrappers. *First Printing: February, 1975* on copyright page. *Ballantine Books SF 24366* ($1.50). *Cordwainer Smith, pseudonym.* Note: Complete texts of THE PLANET BUYER and THE UNDERPEOPLE.

THE PLANET BUYER. *New York: Pyramid Books, [1964].*
Wrappers. *October 1964* on copyright page. *Pyramid Books R–1084* (50¢). *Cordwainer Smith, pseudonym.* Note: Complete text later collected in NORSTRILIA.

QUEST OF THE THREE WORLDS. *New York: Ace Books, Inc., [1966].*
Wrappers. No statement of printing on copyright page. *Ace Book F–402* (40¢). *Cordwainer Smith, pseudonym.*

RIA. *New York: Duell, Sloan and Pearce, [1947].*
First edition so stated on copyright page. *Felix C. Forrest, pseudonym.*

SPACE LORDS. *New York: Pyramid Books, [1965].*
Wrappers. *First printing, May 1965* on copyright page. *Pyramid Science Fiction R–1183* (50¢). *Cordwainer Smith, pseudonym.*

ALSO: *London: Sidgwick & Jackson, [1969]. Boards. First published in Great Britain 1969 on copyright page. First hardcover edition.*

STARDREAMER. *New York: Beagle Books, [1971].*
Wrappers. *First printing: August, 1971* on copyright page. *A Beagle Boxer Science Fiction Story Collection 95127* (95¢). *Cordwainer Smith, pseudonym.*

UNDER OLD EARTH AND OTHER EXPLORATIONS. *[London]: Panther Science Fiction, [1970].*
Wrappers. *First published by Panther Books 1970* on copyright page. *Panther Science Fiction 586 033025* (25p). *Cordwainer Smith, pseudonym.*

THE UNDERPEOPLE. *New York: Pyramid Books, [1968].*
Wrappers. *First printing, November, 1968* on copyright page. *Pyramid Science Fiction X–1910* (60¢). *Cordwainer Smith, pseudonym.* Note: Complete text later collected in NORSTRILIA.

YOU WILL NEVER BE THE SAME. *Evanston: Regency Books, [1963].*
Wrappers. No statement of printing on copyright page. *Regency RB 309* (50¢). *Cordwainer Smith, pseudonym.*

ALSO:[*New York & London: Garland Publishing, Inc., 1975.*] No statement of printing on copyright page. First hardcover edition. Notes: (1) Photo-reproduction of the 1970 Berkley Publishing Corporation edition. (2) Not issued in dust jacket.

Reference

Exploring Cordwainer Smith, [compiled by Andrew Porter]. *New York: Algol Press, [1975]*. Wrappers. No statement of printing on copyright page.

Frank Belknap Long
(b. 1903)

. . . AND OTHERS SHALL BE BORN. *New York: Belmont Books, [1968]*.
Wrappers. *January 1968* on copyright page. *Belmont Double B50–809* (50¢). Bound with
THE THIEF OF THOTH by Lin Carter.

THE ANDROIDS. *[New York]: A Tower Book, [1969]*.
Wrappers. No statement of printing on copyright page. *Tower T–060–3* (60¢). Reissue of
LEST EARTH BE CONQUERED.

THE BLACK DRUID AND OTHER STORIES. *[Frogmore]: Panther, [1975]*.
Wrappers. Published in 1975 . . . on copyright page. *Panther 586 04182 6* (50p). Reprint.
Eleven stories selected from THE HOUNDS OF TINDALOS.

THE CHALLENGE FROM BEYOND. *N.p.: [A Weltschmerz Publication/Bill Evans/Franklin Ker-*
khof, Printer/The Pennsylvania Dutch Cheese Press/February 1954].
Self wrappers. No statement of printing. Mimeographed, stapled. Cover title. With C.L.
MOORE, A. MERRITT, H.P. LOVECRAFT, and ROBERT E. HOWARD. Notes: (1) Published by
William H. Evans for distribution through Fantasy Amateur Press Association
(FAPA). (2) Not to be confused with a booklet of identical title and format with a different
round-robin story by Stanley G. Weinbaum and others.

CRUCIBLE OF EVIL. *[New York]: Avon, [1974]*.
Wrappers. *First Avon Printing, July, 1974* on copyright page. *Avon Gothic Original 19646*
(95¢). *Lyda Belknap Long, pseudonym*.

THE DARK BEASTS. *New York: Belmont Books, [1964]*.
Wrappers. *First printing January 1964* on copyright page. *Belmont L92–579* (50¢). Reprint. Nine stories selected from THE HOUNDS OF TINDALOS.

THE EARLY LONG. *Garden City: Doubleday & Company, Inc., 1975*.
Boards. First edition so stated on copyright page.

FIRE OF THE WITCHES. *New York: Popular Library, [1971]*.
Wrappers. No statement of printing on copyright page. *Popular Library 445–00310–095*
(95¢). *Lyda Belknap Long, pseudonym*.

THE HORROR EXPERT. *New York: Belmont Books, [1961]*.
Wrappers. *First Printing December 1961* on copyright page. *Belmont 246* (35¢).

THE HORROR FROM THE HILLS. *Sauk City: Arkham House: Publishers, 1963*.
No statement of printing on copyright page. Note: Copyright notice was inadvertently left
off verso of title page. Copies of this book have been observed with and without a copyright
notice printed on a small cancel label affixed to the title page verso.

THE HORROR FROM THE HILLS. *London: Brown, Watson Ltd., [1965]*.
Wrappers. *This edition published 1965 . . .* on copyright page. *Digit R907* (2/6). Note: A
reissue of ODD SCIENCE FICTION, not a reprint of the Arkham House edition of THE HORROR
FROM THE HILLS.

THE HOUNDS OF TINDALOS. *Sauk City: Arkham House, 1946*.
No statement of printing on copyright page.

ALSO: *New York: Belmont Books, [1963]*. Wrappers. *First Printing August 1963* on copyright page. *Belmont L92–569* (50¢). Abridged reprint. Prints nine of the twenty-one stories.

HOUSE OF THE DEADLY NIGHTSHADE. *New York: Beagle Books, [1972]*.
Wrappers. *First printing: March 1972* on copyright page. *A Beagle Gothic 94223* (75¢). *Lyda Belknap Long, pseudonym.*

IT WAS THE DAY OF THE ROBOT. *New York: Belmont Books, [1963]*.
Wrappers. *First printing March 1963* on copyright page. *Belmont 90–277* (40¢).

ALSO: *London: Dennis Dobson, [1964]*. Boards. *First Published in Great Britain in 1964* on copyright page. First hardcover edition.

JOHN CARSTAIRS SPACE DETECTIVE. *New York: Frederick Fell, Inc., [1949]*.
First printing September 1949 on copyright page.

JOURNEY INTO DARKNESS. *New York: Belmont Books, [1967]*.
Wrappers. *April 1967* on copyright page. *Belmont Science Fiction B50–757* (50¢).

LEGACY OF EVIL. *New York: Beagle Books, [1973]*.
Wrappers. *First printing: June 1973* on copyright page. *A Beagle Gothic 94376* (75¢). *Lyda Belknap Long, pseudonym.*

LEST EARTH BE CONQUERED. *New York: Belmont Books, [1966]*.
Wrappers. *December 1966* on copyright page. *Belmont Science Fiction B50–726* (50¢). Reissued as THE ANDROIDS.

MARS IS MY DESTINATION. *New York: Pyramid Books, [1962]*.
Wrappers. *First printing, June 1962* on copyright page. *Pyramid Books F–742* (40¢).

THE MARTIAN VISITORS. *New York: Avalon Books, [1964]*.
No statement of printing on copyright page.

THE MATING CENTER. *N.p., [cop. 1961]*.
Wrappers. No statement of printing on copyright page. *A Chariot Book CB 162* (50¢).

MISSION TO A STAR. *New York: Avalon Books, [1964]*.
No statement of printing on copyright page.

MONSTER FROM OUT OF TIME. *New York: Popular Library, [1970]*.
Wrappers. No statement of printing on copyright page. *Popular Library 445–02474–060* (60¢).

ALSO: *London: Robert Hale, [1971]*. Boards *First Published in Great Britain 1971* on copyright page. First hardcover edition.

THE NIGHT OF THE WOLF. *New York: Popular Library, [1972]*.
Wrappers. No statement of printing on copyright page. *Popular Library 445–01562–075* (75¢).

ODD SCIENCE FICTION. *New York: Belmont Books, [1964]*.
Wrappers. *August 1964* on copyright page. *Belmont Future Series L92–600* (50¢). Note: In addition to reprinting THE HORROR FROM THE HILLS, this collection includes two short stories, "The Flame of Life" and "Giant in the Forest." Reprinted in Great Britain as THE HORROR FROM THE HILLS.

THE RIM OF THE UNKNOWN. *Sauk City: Arkham House, 1972*.
No statement of printing on copyright page.

THE SHAPE OF FEAR. *New York: Beagle Books*, [*1971*].
Wrappers. *First printing: July, 1971* on copyright page. *A Beagle Gothic 94106* (75¢).
Lyda Belknap Long, pseudonym. Note: The pseudonym appears incorrectly on front cover
and spine as *Lydia Belknap Long*.

SO DARK A HERITAGE. [*New York: Lancer Books, Inc., 1966.*]
Wrappers. *A Lancer Book • 1966* on copyright page. *Lancer Books 72–106* (50¢).

SPACE STATION 1. *New York: Ace Books*, [*1957*].
Wrappers. No statement of printing on copyright page. *Ace Double Novel Books D–242*
(35¢). Bound with EMPIRE OF THE ATOM by A. E. van Vogt.

SURVIVAL WORLD. *New York: Lancer Books*, [*1971*].
Wrappers. No statement of printing on copyright page. *Lancer Books 74750–075* (75¢).

THIS STRANGE TOMORROW. *New York: Belmont Books*, [*1966*].
Wrappers. *February 1966* on copyright page. *Belmont Science Fiction B50–663* (50¢).

THE THREE FACES OF TIME. [*New York*]: *A Tower Book*, [*1969*].
Wrappers. No statement of printing on copyright page. *Tower 43–251* (60¢).

THREE STEPS SPACEWARD. *New York: Avalon Books*, [*1963*].
No statement of printing on copyright page.

TO THE DARK TOWER. *New York: Lancer Books*, [*1969*].
Wrappers. *A Lancer Book • 1969* on copyright page. *Lancer Books 73–840* (60¢). *Lyda
Belknap Long, pseudonym*.

THE WITCH TREE. *New York: Lancer Books*, [*1971*].
Wrappers. No statement of printing on copyright page. *Lancer Books 74772–075* (75¢).
Lyda Belknap Long, pseudonym.

WOMAN FROM ANOTHER PLANET. *N.p.*, [*cop. 1960*].
Wrappers. No statement of printing on copyright page. *A Chariot Book CB 123* (50¢).

Nonfiction (Dealing with the Fantasy Genre only)

Howard Phillips Lovecraft: Dreamer on the Nightside. *Sauk City: Arkham House, 1975*.
No statement of printing on copyright page.

Howard Phillips Lovecraft
(1890–1937)

This checklist includes all books, pamphlets, and ephemeral material by Lovecraft including those completed by other hands. Reprint collections with title changes or rearrangement of contents are recorded. The checklist is arranged in two sections. The first lists all items comprised wholly or in part of his fictional work, including writings by others revised or rewritten by Lovecraft. The second lists all other prose, poetry, and edited books.

Fiction

AT THE MOUNTAINS OF MADNESS AND OTHER NOVELS. *Sauk City: Arkham House: Publishers, 1964.*
No statement of printing on copyright page. Four printings, priority as listed: (A) First printing. *Three thousand copies of this book have been printed . . .* on page [434]. No headbands. Issued in a dust jacket printed in green and black ink. (B) Second printing so indicated on page [433]. Headbands. Issued in dust jacket printed in red and black ink. (C) Third printing so indicated on page [433]. Headbands. Issued in dust jacket printed in red and black ink. (D) Fourth printing so indicated on page [433]. Headbands. Issued in dust jacket printed in red and black ink. Edited, with introduction, by August Derleth. All fiction reprinted from earlier books.

ALSO: AT THE MOUNTAINS OF MADNESS AND OTHER TALES OF TERROR. *[London]: A Panther Book, [1968].* Wrappers. *Panther edition published 1968* on copyright page. *Panther 025960 (5/–).* Abridged reprint. Collects six of the eight stories in the Arkham House collection.

ALSO: *New York: Beagle Books, [1971].* Wrappers. *First printing: January 1971* on copyright page. *A Beagle Horror Collection 95041 (95¢).* Abridged reprint. Prints four of the eight stories in the Arkham House collection.

THE BATTLE THAT ENDED THE CENTURY (MS. FOUND IN A TIME MACHINE). *[De Land, Florida: Robert H. Barlow, 1934.]*
Mimeographed on two sheets of 8½ x 14 paper. Printed on rectos only. Caption title. Note: L. Sprague de Camp, in *Lovecraft: A Biography* (Garden City: Doubleday, 1975), p. 394, states, "While Lovecraft was at De Land, he and Barlow composed a little literary spoof called 'The Battle That Ended the Century.' . . . Barlow printed the composition as a brochure [sic] and mailed it out to other fans and members of the Lovecraft circle."

BEST SUPERNATURAL STORIES OF H. P. LOVECRAFT. *Cleveland and New York: The World Publishing Company, [1945].*
TOWER BOOKS EDITION/First Printing April 1945 on copyright page. Edited, with introduction, by August Derleth. All fiction reprinted from earlier books. Note: So far no copy stating "first printing" without the "Tower Books Edition" on the copyright page has been located. *Cumulative Book Index* lists only the initial Tower Books printing in 1945 with a list price of 49¢. The deposit copy of this printing was received at the Library of Congress 28 April 1945. All three Tower printings were printed on high pulp content wartime paper stock. Reprinted in 1950 on better quality text paper and listed at $1.49. This reprint has no statement of printing on copyright page, but code *WP 9–50* is present.

BEYOND THE WALL OF SLEEP. *Sauk City: Arkham House, 1943.*
No statement of printing on copyright page. Collected, with introduction, by August Derleth and Donald Wandrei.

THE CASE OF CHARLES DEXTER WARD. *London: Victor Gollancz Ltd, 1951.*
No statement of printing on copyright page. Collected earlier in BEYOND THE WALL OF
SLEEP. Notes: (1) The text of the Gollancz edition is basically the version printed in the
anthology *Night's Yawning Peal* edited by August Derleth, with Lovecraft's antiquated
spelling modernized and a number of serious misprints. (2) *Whitaker's Cumulative Book
List* assigns a publication date of February 1952.

THE CATS OF ULTHAR. *[Cassia, Florida: The Dragon-Fly Press], Christmas 1935.*
Wrappers. 42 copies printed. Two issues, no priority: (A) Two copies on Red Lion Text.
Verso of title page blank. No statement of printing or limitation. Note: Printed by Robert
H. Barlow. The Barlow inscription in Lovecraft's copy (now in the John Hay Library,
Brown University) reads, "Dear HP—/Here is the booklet/I so long ago promised!/There
were forty copies/on ordinary paper, and only/two on Red Lion Text. This/is one of the
latter./RHB." (B) 40 copies on ordinary paper. Verso of title page reads, *Forty copies of
this booklet have/been printed at the Dragon-/Fly Press, Cassia, Florida./Copyright 1926,
Popular Fiction Pub. Co.*

THE CHALLENGE FROM BEYOND. *N.p.: [A Weltschmerz Publication/Bill Evans/Franklin Kerkhof, Printer/The Pennsylvania Dutch Cheese Press/February 1954].*
Self wrappers. No statement of printing. Mimeographed, stapled. Cover title. With C. L.
MOORE, A. MERRITT, ROBERT E. HOWARD, and FRANK BELKNAP LONG. Notes: (1) Published
by William H. Evans for distribution through the Fantasy Amateur Press Association
(FAPA). (2) Not to be confused with a booklet of identical title and format with a different
round-robin story by Stanley G. Weinbaum and others.

COLLAPSING COSMOSES. *[West Warwick, R.I.: Necronomicon Press, 1977.]*
Wrappers. *This edition, the first . . . is limited to a numbered prin-/ting of 500 copies* on
page [8]. Offset from typewritten copy. Issued as *F & SF Fragments 1.*

THE COLOUR OUT OF SPACE. *New York: Lancer Books, [1964].*
Wrappers. *A Lancer Book • 1964* on copyright page. *Lancer Books 73–425* (60¢). Reprint
collection.

CRY HORROR! *New York: Avon Publications, Inc., [1958].*
Wrappers. No statement of printing on copyright page. *Avon T–284* (35¢). Reprint of the
1947 Avon edition of THE LURKING FEAR AND OTHER STORIES.

THE CURSE OF YIG. *Sauk City: Arkham House, 1953.*
No statement of printing on copyright page. Short stories written by Lovecraft from plot
outlines by Zealia B. Bishop. All fiction printed here originally collected in BEYOND THE
WALL OF SLEEP and MARGINALIA.

DAGON AND OTHER MACABRE TALES. *Sauk City: Arkham House: Publishers, 1965.*
No statement of printing on copyright page. Four printings, priority as listed: (A) First
printing. *Thirty-five hundred copies of this book have been printed . . .* on page [414].
(B) Second printing. *Three thousand copies of this book have been printed . . .* on page
[414]. (C) Third printing so indicated on page [414]. (D) Fourth printing so indicated on
page [414]. Edited, with introduction, by August Derleth. All fiction reprinted from
earlier books.

ALSO: *[London]: A Panther Book, [1969].* Wrappers. *These stories were first published in
Great Britain as part of a/collection, Dagon and other macabre tales, by Victor
Gollancz/Limited 1967* on copyright page. *Panther 586 02866 8* (30p). Abridged reprint.
Collects fifteen of the thirty-eight pieces.

THE DARK BROTHERHOOD. *Sauk City: Arkham House: Publishers, 1966.*
No statement of printing on copyright page. Edited, with an introduction, by August
Derleth. Note: Includes collaborations with DERLETH and C. M. EDDY, JR.

THE DOOM THAT CAME TO SARNATH. *New York: Ballantine Books*, [*1971*].
Wrappers. *First Printing: February, 1971* on copyright page. *Ballantine Books 02146-0-095* (95¢). Edited, with introduction and notes, by Lin Carter. All fiction reprinted from earlier books.

THE DREAM QUEST OF UNKNOWN KADATH. *Buffalo: Shroud, Publishers, 1955*.
1500 numbered copies printed. Binding sequence presumed as listed: (A) Sheets stapled into printed orange wrappers reinforced with black cloth tape or brown paper tape on spine. Earliest distributed copies have dust jacket of white paper stock printed in red and black ink with publisher's address *819 Michigan Avenue/Buffalo 3, New York* on rear panel. Later examples of this dust jacket are rubber-stamped *NOTE NEW ADDRESS/332 So. Abbott Rd. R. D. 1/Hamburg, New York*. (B) Sheets stapled into printed orange wrappers reinforced with black cloth tape or brown paper tape. Later dust jacket of yellow paper stock printed in black ink with rear panel advertising THE MOON MAKER by Train and Wood and carrying the publisher's *332 SOUTH ABBOTT ROAD HAMBURG, NEW YORK* address. Not distributed prior to 1958. (C) Sheets stapled into printed orange wrappers, under an additional stiff yellow wrapper mimeographed in black ink. Not distributed before 1958, as THE MOON MAKER is listed on rear of yellow wrapper. (D) Black cloth, spine stamped in gold. Two variants: (1) Limitation notice glued in stating that 50 copies were so bound. (2) Lacking the glued-in limitation notice. Both variants occur in first and second state dust jackets. Note: More than 50 copies were bound in cloth. Owings and Chalker in *The Index to the Science-Fantasy Publishers* state that copies numbered 451–500 were hardbound. Hardbound copies numbered 51, 285, 623, 643, and 644 have been reported or observed. Shroud probably bound cloth copies and distributed both cloth and wrappered states out of numerical sequence and thus copy numbers do not reflect sequence of issue. (E) Boards. Not seen. Listed in Spring 1970 catalogue from Carl's Bookstore, Tacoma, Washington, item 29. (F) De la Ree binding. In 1972 fantasy collector/dealer Gerry de la Ree specially bound 12 copies in black cloth stamped in gold. These copies have a label affixed to the colophon page reading #[number inserted] *of 12 specially bound copies of THE DREAM QUEST OF UNKNOWN KADATH. First edition/First printing, November 1955* on copyright page. Collected earlier in BEYOND THE WALL OF SLEEP. Note: Text of the Shroud edition is offset from the serial printing in *The Arkham Sampler*, Winter–Autumn 1948.

THE DREAM-QUEST OF UNKNOWN KADATH. *New York: Ballantine Books*, [*1970*].
Wrappers. *First Printing: May, 1970* on copyright page. *Ballantine Books 01923-7-095* (95¢). Edited, with introduction, by Lin Carter. All fiction reprinted from earlier books.

DREAMS AND FANCIES. *Sauk City: Arkham House: Publishers, 1962*.
No statement of printing on copyright page. All fiction reprinted from earlier books.

THE DUNWICH HORROR. *New York: Published by Bartholomew House, Inc.*, [*1945*].
Wrappers. No statement of printing on copyright page. *Bart House Mystery 12* (25¢). Reprint collection.

THE DUNWICH HORROR AND OTHER WEIRD TALES. *New York: Editions for the Armed Services, Inc.*, [*1945*].
Wrappers. No statement of printing on copyright page. *Armed Services Edition 730*. Selected, with introduction, by August Derleth. All fiction reprinted from earlier books. Differs from the Bart House collection.

THE DUNWICH HORROR AND OTHERS. *Sauk City: Arkham House: Publishers, 1963*.
No statement of printing on copyright page. Four printings, priority as listed: (A) First printing. No headbands. Dust jacket price is $5.00. (B) Second printing. Headbands, count 14 black alternating with 14 white stripes. Dust jacket price is $6.50. (C) Third printing. Headbands, count 10 black alternating with 10 white stripes. Dust jacket price is $6.50. (D) Fourth printing so indicated on page [432]. Page 19, line 1, "Elio" corrected to read

"Eliot." Edited, with new introduction, by August Derleth. All fiction reprinted from earlier books. Note: Pages 10–309 are offset from the World Publishing Company text of BEST SUPERNATURAL STORIES OF H. P. LOVECRAFT.

ALSO: *New York: Lancer Books, [1963]*. Wrappers. *A Lancer Book • 1963* on copyright page. *Lancer Books 72–702* (50¢). Abridged reprint. Prints seven stories from the Arkham House collection.

EX OBLIVIONE. *[Glendale: Roy A. Squires], 1969.*
Wrappers. *One hundred twenty-five copies . . . have been printed during November of 1969* on page [12]. Two issues, no priority: (A) 99 numbered copies; (B) 26 copies lettered A–Z. Reprinted from BEYOND THE WALL OF SLEEP.

THE HAUNTER OF THE DARK. *London: Victor Gollancz Ltd, 1951.*
No statement of printing on copyright page. Edited, with introduction, by August Derleth. All fiction reprinted from earlier books. Note: Proof copies have title pages dated 1950.

HERBERT WEST REANIMATOR. *[West Warwick, R. I.]: Necronomicon Press, 1977.*
Wrappers. *One thousand copies of this edition - the first - . . . have been printed. This is copy number . . .* on copyright leaf. Offset reproduction printed on rectos only, stapled. Note: This six-part series is reproduced in facsimile from its original serialized appearance in six issues of *Home Brew*, February–July, 1922.

THE HORROR IN THE BURYING GROUND AND OTHER TALES. *[Frogmore]: Panther, [1975].*
Wrappers. *First published in Great Britain in 1975 . . .* on copyright page. *Panther Fiction/Fantasy & Horror 586 04231 8* (60p). Abridged reprint. All stories reprinted from the Arkham House edition of THE HORROR IN THE MUSEUM AND OTHER REVISIONS.

THE HORROR IN THE MUSEUM AND OTHER REVISIONS. *Sauk City: Arkham House: Publishers, 1970.*
No statement of printing on copyright page. Two printings, priority as listed: (A) First printing. *Four thousand copies of this book have been printed . . .* on page [384]. (B) Second printing. *A second printing of four thousand copies of this book has been made in April 1976 . . .* on page [390]. Edited, with introduction, by August Derleth. Two revisions, "Till All the Seas" by Robert H. Barlow and "Two Black Bottles" by Wilfred B. Talman, appear for the first time in book form with the remainder reprinted from earlier collections. Abridged reprint collection issued later as NINE STORIES FROM THE HORROR IN THE MUSEUM AND OTHER REVISIONS.

ALSO: THE HORROR IN THE MUSEUM AND OTHER TALES. *[Frogmore]: Panther, [1975].*
Wrappers. *First published in Great Britain in 1975 . . .* on copyright page. *Panther Fiction/Fantasy & Horror 586 04230 X* (50p). Abridged reprint. Collects nine of the twenty stories.

THE LURKER AT THE THRESHOLD. *Sauk City: Arkham House, 1945.*
No statement of printing on copyright page. With AUGUST DERLETH.

THE LURKING FEAR AND OTHER STORIES. *New York: Avon Book Company, [1947].*
Wrappers. No statement of printing on copyright page. *Avon 136* (25¢). Reprint collection. Reissued as CRY HORROR!

THE LURKING FEAR AND OTHER STORIES. *[London]: A Panther Book, [1964].*
Wrappers. *This collection first published in Great Britain . . . November 1964* on copyright page. *Panther 1759* (3'6). Reprint collection. Contents differ from 1947 Avon collection.

THE LURKING FEAR AND OTHER STORIES.*New York: Beagle Books*, [*1971*].
> Wrappers. *First printing: January 1971* on copyright page. *A Beagle Horror Collection 95042* (95¢). Reprint collection. Contents differ from 1947 Avon and 1964 Panther collections.

MARGINALIA.*Sauk City: Arkham House, 1944.*
> No statement of printing on copyright page. Edited by August Derleth and Donald Wandrei.

MEMORY.*[Glendale: Roy A. Squires], 1969.*
> Wrappers. *One hundred twenty-five copies . . . have been printed during October of 1969* on page [12]. Two issues, no priority: (A) 99 numbered copies; (B) 26 copies lettered A–Z. Reprinted from BEYOND THE WALL OF SLEEP.

NINE STORIES FROM THE HORROR IN THE MUSEUM AND OTHER REVISIONS.*New York: Beagle Books*, [*1971*].
> Wrappers. *First printing: October 1971* on copyright page. *A Beagle Boxer Horror Anthology 95159* (95¢). Abridged reprint. Collects ten (not nine) of the twenty stories in the Arkham House edition of THE HORROR IN THE MUSEUM AND OTHER REVISIONS.

NYARLATHOTEP.*[Glendale: Roy A. Squires], 1970.*
> Wrappers. *This booklet . . . has been printed as an edition of 125 copies during December of 1969* on page [16]. Two issues, no priority: (A) 99 numbered copies; (B) 26 copies lettered A–Z. Reprinted from BEYOND THE WALL OF SLEEP.

THE OUTSIDER AND OTHERS.*Sauk City: Arkham House, 1939.*
> No statement of printing on copyright page. Edited, with introduction, by August Derleth and Donald Wandrei. Note: Various auction and bookseller catalogues have recorded a "second state" dust jacket. Arkham House produced one printing of the jacket. In 1974 Gerry de la Ree of Saddle River, N.J., produced a facsimile reprint, and this later reprint has been incorrectly termed "second state." Commenting on the original dust jacket, August Derleth remarked, "I'm sorry, but no kind of 'Outsider' d/j is still around. I suppose these were destroyed. When A[rkham] H[ouse] was begun, I didn't know enough about publishing to have extra d/j [s] made . . ." (letter to Gerry de la Ree from Derleth written in 1970, quoted in Gerry de la Ree, ed., *Fantasy Collector's Annual—1974* [Saddle River, N.J.: Gerry de la Ree, 1974], p. 5).

THE SHADOW OUT OF TIME AND OTHER TALES OF HORROR.*London: Victor Gollancz Ltd, 1968.*
> Boards. No statement of printing on copyright page. Ten of these sixteen stories were written by AUGUST DERLETH from story fragments and plot outlines by Lovecraft. All stories reprinted from earlier collections. Note: All observed copies have the half title mounted on a stub.

THE SHADOW OVER INNSMOUTH.*Everett, Pennsylvania: Visionary Publishing Co., 1936.*
> *Published, April, 1936* on copyright page. Note: Publisher states that approximately 400 copies were printed, of which about 200 were bound with the remainder later destroyed. See William L. Crawford, "Lovecraft's First Book," *The Shuttered Room* (Sauk City: Arkham House: Publishers, 1959), pp. 287–90. Earliest copies contain numerous corrections in ink in Lovecraft's holograph. An errata leaf and dust jacket were added later. In some cases these were supplied to those receiving early copies without them. Two dust jacket variants: (1) White paper stock printed in yellow; (2) White paper stock, lettering in silver, illustration in green.

THE SHADOW OVER INNSMOUTH AND OTHER STORIES OF HORROR.*New York Toronto London Auckland Sydney: Scholastic Book Services*, [*1971*].
> Wrappers. *1st printing . . . December 1971* on copyright page. *Scholastic TK1934* (75¢). Reprint collection. All stories reprinted from earlier books.

THE SHUNNED HOUSE. *Athol, Mass.: Published by W. Paul Cook The Recluse Press, 1928.* No statement of printing on copyright page. 300 copies printed. Paper stock watermarked "Canterbury Laid." Priority of circulation as follows: (A) Copyright notice on verso of title page reading *COPYRIGHT 1928/by W. PAUL COOK* uncanceled. Note: Occurs in sets of unbound sheets and in a few copies cased in Arkham House bindings. (B) Copies distributed by Robert H. Barlow: (1) Cancel copyright notice reading *Copyright 1935/R. H. Barlow* set in italics, pasted over the original Cook copyright. Note: Copies with printed 1935 Barlow copyright have been observed (a) as unbound sheets; (b) hand-trimmed and stapled into wrappers; (c) bound in heavy green buckram; (2) Copyright notice in holograph reading . . . *1936 . . . R. H. Barlow.* A single copy recorded bound in decorated boards with cloth spine stamped in silver; (3) Copyright notice in holograph, dated 1938 (reported, but not seen). Note: It is estimated that Barlow received approximately 225 sets of sheets (some of which he reported had been soiled and were unusable) in 1934. It is rumored that no more than seven copies were cased or given paper covers, and the remainder of the copies he distributed were sets of unbound sheets. Additionally, one copy was bound in full brown leather and presented to Lovecraft in 1935. (C) Copies distributed by Arkham House: (1) Circa 1952? Commenced marketing approximately 50 sets of unbound sheets; (2) 1961. 100 sets of sheets bound in black cloth. Most copies distributed by Arkham House contain a cancel copyright notice listing copyrights for 1936, 1937, 1939, and 1947. This cancel occurs in two states: (a) book and magazine titles set in bold face; (b) book and magazine titles set in italics. Notes: (1) Arkham House obtained approximately 150 sets of sheets, (2) One set of unbound sheets has been observed with both Barlow and Arkham House cancels.

THE FORGERY: An unknown number of copies were produced circa 1965–1966 using the photo-offset process, printed on laid paper watermarked "Chantry." Probably of British origin. The first recorded copy was located in London in June 1966. A reproduction of the Arkham cancel was affixed to the copyright page but the original Cook copyright does not appear under it. All recorded copies are bound in red cloth with quarter crushed red morocco spine lettered in gold, bottom to top, *THE SHUNNED HOUSE—LOVECRAFT—1928.*

THE SHUTTERED ROOM AND OTHER PIECES. *Sauk City: Arkham House: Publishers, 1959.* No statement of printing on copyright page. Edited with completions, by August Derleth.

THE SHUTTERED ROOM AND OTHER TALES OF HORROR. *London: A Panther Book, [1970].* Wrappers. *Panther Books edition published 1970* on copyright page. *Panther 586 033998* (30p). With AUGUST DERLETH. Abridged reprint. Collects the ten Lovecraft/Derleth collaborations from THE SHADOW OUT OF TIME AND OTHER TALES OF HORROR.

THE SHUTTERED ROOM AND OTHER TALES OF TERROR. *New York: Beagle Books, [1971].* Wrappers. *First printing: April 1971* on copyright page. *A Beagle Horror Anthology 95068* (95¢). With AUGUST DERLETH. Reprint collection. Contents differ from 1959 Arkham House and 1970 Panther Books collections.

SOMETHING ABOUT CATS. *Sauk City: Arkham House, 1949.* No statement of printing on copyright page. Edited, with preface, by August Derleth.

THE SURVIVOR AND OTHERS. *Sauk City: Arkham House: Publishers, 1957.* No statement of printing on copyright page. With AUGUST DERLETH.

3 TALES OF HORROR. *[Sauk City]: Arkham House, [1967].* No statement of printing on copyright page. Stories reprinted from earlier books.

THE TOMB AND OTHER TALES. *[London]: A Panther Book, [1969].* Wrappers. *These stories were first published in Great Britain as part/of a collection, Dagon and other macabre tales, by Victor/Gollancz Limited 1967. Panther edition of the Tomb pub-/lished 1969* on copyright page. *Panther 586 02903 6* (25p). Reprint collection. All stories reprinted from earlier books.

THE WATCHERS OUT OF TIME AND OTHERS. *Sauk City: Arkham House: Publishers, 1974.*
   No statement of printing on copyright page. With AUGUST DERLETH. Reprint collection
   with the exception of "The Watchers Out of Time."

THE WEIRD SHADOW OVER INNSMOUTH AND OTHER STORIES OF THE SUPERNATURAL. *New
York: Published by Bartholomew House, Inc., [1944].*
   Wrappers. No statement of printing on copyright page. *Bart House Novel 4* (25¢). Reprint
   collection.

WHAT THE MOON BRINGS. *[Glendale: Roy A. Squires], 1970.*
   Wrappers. *One hundred twenty-five copies . . . have been printed during January and
   February of 1970* on page [16]. Two issues, no priority: (A) 99 numbered copies; (B) 26
   copies lettered A–Z. Reprinted from BEYOND THE WALL OF SLEEP.

Nonfiction; Essays, Poetry, Autobiographies, Letters, and Miscellanea

The Amateur Journalist. *[North Tonawanda, N. Y.]: SSR [Publications], 1955.*
   Wrappers. *First Printing: January, 1955* on copyright page. Mimeographed, stapled. 75
   numbered copies. Edited by George Wetzel. *The Lovecraft Collectors Library, Volume
   Five.*

Antarktos. *Warren, Ohio: Fantome Press, [1977].*
   Wrappers. *This poetry folio was set and printed by C. M. James/during Jan. 1977 . . .
   /This is copy* [holograph number inserted] *of an edition of 150 copies* on page [8]. Reprint.
   Collected earlier in *Fungi From Yuggoth.*

Autobiography: Some Notes on a Nonentity. *Sauk City: Printed for Arkham House: Publishers . . . by Villiers Publications, Ltd., London, N. W. 5., England, 1963.*
   Wrappers. No statement of printing on copyright page. 500 copies printed. Collected
   earlier in BEYOND THE WALL OF SLEEP. Extensive annotations by August Derleth printed
   for the first time.

Beyond the Wall of Sleep. *Sauk City: Arkham House, 1943.*
   No statement of printing on copyright page. Collected, with introduction, by August
   Derleth and Donald Wandrei. Includes nonfictional writings by Lovecraft.

The Californian 1934–1938. *[West Warwick, R. I.]: Necronomicon Press, 1977.*
   Wrappers. *One thousand copies of this edition, the first . . . have been printed* on copyright
   leaf. Offset reproduction printed on rectos only, stapled. Numbered and signed by compiler Marc A. Michaud.

Charleston. *N.p., n.d. [but 1936].*
   22 leaves mimeographed on rectos only and three photostat reproductions of maps and
   sketches by Lovecraft. Stapled into brown paper folder, buff label pasted to front wrapper
   with typewritten text reading *CHARLESTON/ by H. P. Lovecraft.* Caption title. Some
   copies have two laid-in pages of errata in Lovecraft's holograph reproduced by photolithog-
   raphy. Note: Published version was preceded by a preliminary printing of very limited
   circulation. It comprised 22 leaves mimeographed on rectos only, was not accompanied by
   the photostat reproductions, and was not bound. The first leaf is headed *January 12,
   1936./Dear Ech-Si-Kheh:.* A copy of this preliminary version was sent by publisher H. C.
   Koenig to Lovecraft, whose extensive revisions were incorporated in the published version.

Collected Poems. *Sauk City: Arkham House: Publishers, 1963.*
   No statement of printing on copyright page.

*The Conservative Complete 1915–1923. [*West Warwick, R.I.*]: *Necronomicon Press*, *1976*.
   Wrappers. Offset reproduction printed on rectos only, stapled. 50 numbered copies.

*The Crime of Crimes. [*Llandudno, Wales, England: Printed and Published by A. Harris*], *n.d.* [*probably 1915*].
   Single sheet folded into four pages. Not seen. Description based on examination of a photocopy. Note: The poem on the sinking of the Lusitania was first published in *Interesting Items*, July 1915.

Dagon and Other Macabre Tales. *Sauk City: Arkham House: Publishers, 1965*.
   No statement of printing on copyright page. Four printings; see Section I for details.
   Reprints "Supernatural Horror in Literature."

The Dark Brotherhood and Other Pieces. *Sauk City: Arkham House: Publishers, 1966*.
   No statement of printing on copyright page. Edited, with introduction, by August Derleth.
   Includes nonfictional writings by Lovecraft.

The Doom That Came to Sarnath. *New York: Ballantine Books*, [*1971*].
   Wrappers. *First Printing: February, 1971* on copyright page. *Ballantine Books 02146–0–095* (95¢). Edited, with introduction and notes, by Lin Carter. Prints "Nathicana," a poem collected earlier in *Selected Poetry* [*Second Series*].

Dreams and Fancies. *Sauk City: Arkham House: Publishers, 1962*.
   No statement of printing on copyright page. Includes Lovecraft letters published for the first time.

Ec'h-Pi-El Speaks: An Autobiographical Sketch. . . . *Saddle River, N.J.: Published by Gerry de la Ree, 1972*.
   Three bindings, no priority: (A) One copy bound in black cloth, front cover stamped in gold; (B) 25 copies bound in maroon cloth, front cover stamped in gold; (C) 474 copies in pictorial wrappers. *Five hundred copies . . . have been printed on 70-pound parchment. This is copy No.* [ink holograph number] on rear wrapper.

Exponent of Amateur Journalism. See United Amateur Press Association: Exponent of Amateur Journalism.

First Writings Pawtuxet Valley Gleaner 1906. [*West Warwick, R.I.*]: *Necronomicon Press*, *1976*.
   Wrappers. No statement of printing on copyright leaf. Offset reproduction printed on rectos only, stapled. 500 numbered copies.

Fungi From Yuggoth. [*Salem, Oregon*]: *Bill Evans, June 1943*.
   Self wrappers. No statement of printing. Cover title. Mimeographed, stapled. Approximately 65 copies printed. Note: Collects the first thirty-three of thirty-six poems in this sonnet sequence.

   ALSO: [*West Warwick, R.I.*]: *Necronomicon Press*, [*1977*]. Wrappers. *Four hundred and seventy-five copies of/this edition, the first . . . have been printed* on copyright page. Enlarged edition. Adds three sonnets.

Fungi From Yuggoth and Other Poems. *New York: Ballantine Books*, [*1971*].
   Wrappers. *First Printing: February, 1971* on copyright page. *Ballantine Books 02147–9–095* (95¢). Omits "To the American Flag," otherwise a reprint of *Collected Poems*.

Further Criticism of Poetry. [*Louisville: Press of Geo. G. Fetter Co., 1932.*]
   Self wrappers. No statement of printing.

H P L. [*Belleville, N.J.: Printed by Corwin Stickney, 1937.*]
   Wrappers. No statement of printing. Cover title. Note: A memorial booklet containing eight Lovecraft poems. 25 copies were printed and distributed to subscribers of the *Amateur Correspondent*.

Hail, Klarkash-Ton! Being Nine Missives Inscribed Upon Postcards, by H. P. Lovecraft to Clark Ashton Smith. [*Glendale: Roy A. Squires, 1971.*]
   Wrappers. No statement of printing. 89 copies printed. Two issues, no priority: (A) 80 numbered copies; (B) Nine lettered copies containing an original holograph postcard from Lovecraft to Smith.

A History of The Necronomicon. *Oakman, Alabama: Wilson H. Shepherd The Rebel Press, n.d.* [*but 1938*].
   Single sheet folded into four pages. No statement of printing. Fewer than 100 copies printed.

Looking Backward. *Haverhill, Mass.: C. W. Smith, n.d.* [*but probably 1920*].
   Wrappers. No statement of printing. Sewn. Cover title. Note: Printed from the same setting of type used for the essay's initial appearance in *The Tryout*, February–June, 1920.

Lovecraft at Last. *Arlington: Carrollton-Clark,* [*1975*].
   3000 copies printed. Three issues, no priority: (A) "Presentation" issue. Red cloth, black leather label on spine, lettered in gold; top edge not stained. 25 copies numbered P-I-P-XXV signed by Conover and designer Robert L. Dothard on page [273]. *This presentation copy of/Lovecraft at Last . . . on page* [273]. Enclosed in a paper slipcase. (B) "Collectors" issue. Red cloth, spine lettering in gold on black background; top edge stained red. 1000 copies numbered 1—1000. *This collectors edition of /Lovecraft at Last . . .* on page [273]. Enclosed in a paper slipcase. (C) Trade issue. Red cloth, spine lettering in gold on black background; top edge not stained. No statement of limitation on page [273]. Not issued with slipcase. No statement of printing on copyright page. With WILLIS CONOVER. Prints the Lovecraft/Conover correspondence with narrative continuity by Conover. Note: Subscribers to this volume received a premium booklet containing a facsimile of Lovecraft's 1936 revision of "Supernatural Horror in Literature."

The Lovecrafter. See A Sonnet.

Marginalia. *Sauk City: Arkham House, 1944.*
   No statement of printing on copyright page. Edited by August Derleth and Donald Wandrei. Includes nonficational writings by Lovecraft.

*The Materialist Today. *N.p., n.d.* [*North Montpelier, Vermont? May 1926.*]
   Self wrappers? Apparently an off-print of Lovecraft's essay, "The Materialist Today," which appeared in *Driftwind*, October 1926. No copy of this pamphlet has been located. Entries in earlier Lovecraft bibliographies appear to be based on a description provided by Walter J. Coates, "Check List of Publications of Driftwind Press," *Driftwind*, 6, No. 3 (November 1931), page 17 where it is entered as "THE MATERIALIST TODAY. Howard P. Lovecraft. n.p., n.d. [May 1926]. *Not for sale*. 12mo, pa, 8pp. Only 15 copies printed."

Medusa: A Portrait. [*New York: Printed for Tom Collins by Ronald Gordon at The Oliphant Press, 1975.*]
   Wrappers. No statement of printing. 526 copies printed. Two issues, no priority: (A) 500 numbered copies; (B) 26 copies lettered A–Z.

Memoirs of an Inconsequential Scribbler. [*West Warwick, R.I.*]: *Necronomicon Press,* [*1977*].
   Wrappers. *This first printing . . . is limited to 500 copies . . .* on page [8]. Offset from

typewritten copy. Cover title. Issued as *F & SF Self-Portraits 3*. Collects "The Brief Autobiography of an Inconsequential Scribbler" and "Autobiography of Howard Phillips Lovecraft."

The Notes & Commonplace Book Employed by the Late H. P. Lovecraft. . . . *Lakeport, California: The Futile Press, MDCCCCXXXVIII.*
    Boards. *75 copies . . . have been printed by THE FUTILE PRESS in May and June, 1938 . . .* on copyright page. 75 numbered copies prepared but not all were bound. Perhaps half the edition comprises gathered and padded sheets lacking the board casing.

The Occult Lovecraft by H. P. Lovecraft [and Others]. *Saddle River, N.J.: Published by Gerry de la Ree, 1975.*
    1118 copies printed. Two issues, no priority: (A) 128 numbered copies in cloth; (B) 990 numbered copies in wrappers. First edition so stated on rear wrapper. Includes two essays by Lovecraft extracted from his letters.

The Outsider and Others. *Sauk City: Arkham House, 1939.*
    No statement of printing on copyright page. Edited, with introduction, by August Derleth and Donald Wandrei. Includes Lovecraft's "The Supernatural Horror in Literature."

Selected Essays [First Series]. *North Tonawanda, New York: SSR Publications, 1952.*
    Wrappers. *First printing: December 1952* on page ii. Mimeographed, stapled. 75 numbered copies. Edited by George Wetzel. *The Lovecraft Collectors Library, Volume One.*

Selected Essays [Second Series]. *North Tonawanda, New York: SSR Publications, 1953.*
    Wrappers. *First printing: February 1952* [sic, i.e., February 1953] on copyright page. Mimeographed, stapled. 75 numbered copies. Edited by George Wetzel. *The Lovecraft Collectors Library, Volume Two.*

Selected Letters 1911–1924. *Sauk City: Arkham House: Publishers, 1965.*
    No statement of printing on copyright page. Two printings, priority as listed: (A) First printing. *Twenty-five hundred copies of this book have been printed . . .* on page [363]. (B) Second printing so indicated on page [363]. Edited, with preface, by August Derleth and Donald Wandrei.

Selected Letters 1925–1929. *Sauk City: Arkham House: Publishers, 1968.*
    No statement of printing on copyright page. Two printings, priority as listed: (A) First printing. *Twenty-five hundred copies of this book have been printed . . .* on page [360]. (B) Second printing so indicated on page [360]. Edited, with preface, by August Derleth and Donald Wandrei.

Selected Letters 1929–1931. *Sauk City: Arkham House: Publishers, 1971.*
    No statement of printing on copyright page. Edited, with preface, by August Derleth and Donald Wandrei.

Selected Letters 1932–1934. *Sauk City: Arkham House Publishers, Inc., 1976.*
    No statement of printing on copyright page. Edited by August Derleth and James Turner with preface by the latter.

Selected Letters 1934–1937. *Sauk City: Arkham House Publishers, Inc., 1976.*
    No statement of printing on copyright page. Edited by August Derleth and James Turner with preface by the latter.

Selected Poetry [First Series]. *North Tonawanda, New York: SSR Publications, 1953.*
    Wrappers. *First Printing: October, 1953* on copyright page. Mimeographed, stapled. 75 numbered copies. Edited by George Wetzel. *The Lovecraft Collectors Library, Volume Three.*

Selected Poetry [Second Series]. [*North Tonawanda, New York*]: *SSR* [*Publications, 1955*]. Wrappers. Verso of title leaf blank. *This first printing is limited to seventy-five numbered copies . . .* on half title leaf. Mimeographed, stapled. Edited by George Wetzel. *The Lovecraft Collectors Library, Volume Four*.

The Shuttered Room and Other Pieces. *Sauk City: Arkham House: Publishers, 1959*. No statement of printing on copyright page. Edited by August Derleth. Includes nonfictional writings by Lovecraft.

Some Current Motives and Practices. [*De Land, Florida: Robert H. Barlow, 1936?*] Four pages, mimeographed on two sheets of 8 ½ × 14 paper. Caption title. Dated and signed in type *June 4, 1936 H. P. Lovecraft* at conclusion of text on page [4]. Notes: (1) Probably printed by Barlow for Lovecraft. Unknown number of copies printed. (2) Lovecraft's holograph manuscript of the open letter is dated "June 4, 1936."

Something About Cats and Other Pieces. *Sauk City: Arkham House, 1949*. No statement of printing on copyright page. Edited, with preface, by August Derleth. Includes nonfictional writings by Lovecraft.

A Sonnet. *N.p.: Printed with the Deep Gratitude and Best Wishes of Wilson Shepherd and Donald A. Wollheim, August 20, 1936*. Broadside. Two issues, no priority: (A) Printed on rag stock. Note: Copy in the John Hay Library, Brown University has a manuscript note reading, "About 15 copies printed on cheap stock, in addition to this one for the author." (B) Printed on wood pulp stock. Issued as *The Lovecrafter, Fourty* [sic] *-Sixth Anniversary Issue, Vol. 47, No. 1*. Note: The only issue of *The Lovecrafter*, prepared for Lovecraft's forty-sixth birthday.

Supernatural Horror in Literature. *New York: Ben Abramson Publisher, 1945*. No statement of printing on copyright page. Two printings, priority not established but probably as listed: (A) Black cloth; "elft" for "left," line one, page 66; printed on wove paper watermarked "Suede/D [within a diamond]/Finish." (B) Red cloth; "left," line one, page 66; unwatermarked wove text paper; endpapers on wove paper watermarked "Eagle—A quality Text." Notes: (1) Copies of the latter printing have been noted with publisher's "review copy" stamp on the front free endpaper. (2) A presumed copy of printing B has been described as "Printed by offset on paper watermarked 'Eagle—A Quality Text.'" Not seen. Information from undated catalogue no 8. *H. P. Lovecraft and the Lovecraft Circle: Books & Autographs*, issued by Roy A. Squires, Glendale, California, item 40.

Supernatural Horror in Literature as Revised in 1936. [*Arlington: Carrollton: Clark, 1974.*] Wrappers. No statement of printing. Cover title. 2000 numbered copies. Facsimile reproduction of the original typescript.

To Quebec and the Stars. *West Kingston, Rhode Island: Donald M. Grant, Publisher, 1976*. First edition so stated on copyright page. Edited, with introduction and notes, by L. Sprague de Camp.

United Amateur Press Association: Exponent of Amateur Journalism. *N.p.: United Amateur Press Association, n.d.* [*ca. 1916*]. Self wrappers. No statement of printing. Caption title. Signed in type *H. P. LOVECRAFT,/Vice President* at base of text on page [12].

A Winter Wish. [*Chapel Hill, N.C.*]: *Whispers Press, 1977*. 2385 copies printed. Three issues, no priority: (A) 26 copies lettered A–Z signed by editor Tom Collins, artist Stephen E. Fabian, and designer Stuart David Schiff; (B) 200 numbered copies signed by editor, artist, and designer; (C) Trade issue. First edition so stated on copyright page.

Writings in the Tryout . . . . [*West Warwick, R.I.*]: *Necronomicon Press, 1977.*
Wrappers. *One thousand copies of this edition, the first . . . have been printed* on copyright leaf. Offset reproduction printed on rectos only, stapled. Compiled by Marc A. Michaud.

Writings in the United Amateur 1915–1925. [*West Warwick, R.I.*]: *Necronomicon Press, 1976.*
Wrappers. No statement of printing. Offset reproduction printed on rectos only, stapled. 500 numbered copies printed. Compiled by Marc A. Michaud.

Edited Books

The Poetical Works of Jonathan E. Hoag. *New York 1923.*
No statement of printing on copyright page. Anonymously edited by Lovecraft, who contributed preface and six poems.

Thoughts and Pictures, by Eugene B. Kuntz, D.D. *Haverhill, Mass.: Co-operatively Published by H. P. Loveracft* [sic] *and C. W. Smith, Jan. 1932.*
Wrappers. No statement of printing. Cover title. Contains foreword by Lovecraft, probably the anonymous editor of this booklet.

White Fire, by John Ravenor Bullen. *Athol, Massachusetts: The Recluse Press, 1927.*
304 copies printed. Two bindings, no priority: (A) Green leather stamped in gold. 24 copies. (B) Gray cloth, printed paper labels on front cover and spine. 280 copies. Note; No limitation notice appears in the book. Limitation cited by Will Ranson in *Private Presses and Their Books* (New York: R. R. Bowker, 1929), p. 394. No statement of printing on copyright page. Edited anonymously, with preface, by Lovecraft.

Reference

Beyond the Wall of Sleep, by H. P. Lovecraft. *Sauk City: Arkham House, 1943.*
No statement of printing on copyright page. Edited, with introduction, by August Derleth and Donald Wandrei. Contains "The Cthulhu Mythology: A Glossary" by Francis T. Laney and reprints "An Appreciation of H. P. Lovecraft" by W. Paul Cook.

Bibliographies, [compiled by George Wetzel and Robert E. Briney]. [*North Tonawanda, New York*]: *SSR* [*Publications*], *1955.*
Wrappers. *This first printing is limited to seventy-five numbered copies . . .* on half title leaf. Mimeographed, stapled. Edited by George Wetzel. *The Lovecraft Collectors Library, Volume Seven.*

Bibliotheca: H. P. Lovecraft, [compiled by David A. Sutton]. [*Kings Norton, Birmingham: Produced by David A. Sutton, 1971.*]
Front wrapper only. . . . *printed in a limited run of one hundred numbered copies* on page [2]. Mimeographed, stapled. Caption title.

A Catalog of Lovecraftiana: the Grill/Binkin Collection Catalogued and Annotated by Mark Owings and Irving Binkin. *Baltimore: The Mirage Press, Ltd., 1975.*
No statement of printing on copyright page. 2000 copies printed. Two issues, no priority: (A) 500 copies in black cloth, spine stamped in gold; (B) 1500 copies in wrappers. Note: 668 entries, including letters and manuscripts which are briefly abstracted.

Commentaries . . . , edited by G[eorge] Wetzel. [*North Tonawanda, New York*]: *SSR* [*Publications*], *1955.*
Wrappers. *First Printing: August, 1955* on copyright page. Mimeographed, stapled. 75 numbered copies. Edited by George Wetzel. *The Lovecraft Collectors Library, Volume Six.*

The Curse of Yig, [by] Zealia B. Bishop. *Sauk City: Arkham House, 1953.*
No statement of printing on copyright page. Includes ''H. P. Lovecraft: A Pupil's View''
by Bishop.

The Dark Brotherhood and Other Pieces, by H. P. Lovecraft & Divers Hands. *Sauk City:
Arkham House: Publishers, 1966.*
No statement of printing on copyright page. Memoirs, essays and other material, including
an extensive and useful bibliography by Jack L. Chalker.

The Dream Quest of H. P. Lovecraft, [by] Darrell Schweitzer. *San Bernardino, California:
R. Reginald The Borgo Press, MCMLXXVIII.*
Wrappers. *First Edition— May, 1978* on copyright page. *The Milford Series Popular
Writers of Today Volume Twelve* at head of title.

Essays Lovecraftian, edited by Darrell Schweitzer. *Baltimore: T–K Graphics, 1976.*
Wrappers. No statement of printing on copyright page.

The Gentleman From Angell Street, by Muriel E. Eddy. [*Providence, Rhode Island: The
Author, 1961.*]
Wrappers. No statement of printing. Mimeographed. Cover title. 100 copies only, pri-
vately printed and distributed.

HPL, [compiled by Meade and Penny Frierson]. [*Birmingham, Alabama: Meade & Penny
Frierson, 1972.*]
1000 copies printed. Two issues, no priority: (A) 965 copies in pictorial wrappers; (B) 35
copies bound in black cloth, front cover stamped in gold, with numbered limitation leaf
inserted. No statement of printing. Note: A second printing produced in 1973 is identical
with the first, except *Second Printing $4.00* is rubber-stamped on front cover and at base of
page 3 (not seen; information from Stuart Schiff).

H. P. L. ''The Man and the Image.'' See Howard Phillips Lovecraft: The Man and the
Image.

H. P. L.: A Memoir, by August Derleth. *New York: Ben Abramson, Publisher, 1945.*
No statement of printing on copyright page.

H. P. Lovecraft: A Bibliography, compiled by Joseph Payne Brennan. *Washington: Biblio
Press,* [*1952*].
Self wrappers. *Revised edition* on copyright page. A revised version of *A Select Biblio-
graphy of H. P. Lovecraft.*

H P Lovecraft: A Portrait, by W Paul Cook. *Baltimore: Mirage, 1968.*
Wrappers. No statement of printing on copyright page. 500 numbered copies. Reprint of *In
Memoriam Howard Phillips Lovecraft . . .* with new preface ''Notes on W. Paul Cook''
by Jack L. Chalker.

H. P. Lovecraft: A Symposium. [*Los Angeles*]: *Sponsored by the Los Angeles Science
Fantasy Society. Printed by The Riverside Quarterly,* [*1964*].
Wrappers. No statement of printing. Offset. Errata leaf laid in. Note: The first printing has
17 pages of text. A reprint with textual corrections has 14 pages.

H. P. Lovecraft: An Evaluation, by Joseph Payne Brennan. [*New Haven, Connecticut:
Macabre House, 1955.*]
Wrappers. No statement of printing. Multilithographed. Cover title. 75 numbered copies
only.

The H. P. Lovecraft Companion, [by] Philip A. Shreffler. *Westport, Connecticut • London,
England: Greenwood Press,* [*1977*].
First published in 1977 on copyright page.

Howard Phillips Lovecraft: Dreamer on the Nightside, by Frank Belknap Long. *Sauk City: Arkham House, 1975.*
　　No statement of printing on copyright page.

Howard Phillips Lovecraft 1890–1937: A Tentative Bibliography, [compiled by Francis T. Laney and William H. Evans]. *[Los Angeles]: An "Acolyte" Publication Francis T. Laney William H. Evans FAPA, Winter —1943.*
　　Wrappers. No statement of printing. Mimeographed, stapled. Cover title.

Howard Phillips Lovecraft: Memoirs Critiques & Bibliographies, edited by George Wetzel. *[North Tonawanda, New York]: SSR [Publications], 1955.*
　　Wrappers. *This volume has been published in an edition of 200 copies in August 1955* on inside rear wrapper. Mimeographed, stapled.

Howard Phillips Lovecraft: The Man and the Image, by Muriel E. Eddy. *[Providence, Rhode Island: Muriel E. Eddy, 1969.]*
　　Wrappers. No statement of printing. Mimeographed, stapled. Caption title. Cover title reads: *H. P. L. "The Man and the Image."*

The Howard Phillips Lovecraft We Knew, by Muriel E. Eddy. *N.p., n.d.*
　　Wrappers. No statement of printing. Mimeographed, stapled. Caption title. Privately printed and distributed circa 1968.

In Memoriam Howard Phillips Lovecraft: Recollections Appreciations Estimates, by W. Paul Cook. *[North Montpelier, Vt.: The Author, 1942.]*
　　Wrappers. No statement of printing. 94 copies printed. Collected in BEYOND THE WALL OF SLEEP and later reprinted as *H P Lovecraft: A Portrait.*

Lovecraft a Biography, by L. Sprague de Camp. *Garden City: Doubleday & Company, Inc., 1975.*
　　Boards. First edition so stated on copyright page. Note: Third printing (not so identified) has textual corrections. The following are representative: Page 4, line 18, "half a dozen" changed to "ten or more;" page 12, line 23, "1835" changed to "1853."

Lovecraft: A Look Behind the "Cthulhu Mythos," by Lin Carter. *New York: Ballantine Books, [1972].*
　　Wrappers. *First printing: February, 1972* on copyright page. *Ballantine Books 02427–3–095* (95¢).

Lovecraft and Benefit Street, by Dorothy C. Walter. *[North Montpelier, Vermont: The Driftwind Press, 1943.]*
　　Wrappers. No statement of printing. 150 copies printed. Reprinted from *The Ghost*, Spring 1943.

Lovecraft in the Cinema, by Darrell Schweitzer. *[Baltimore: T K Graphics, 1975.]*
　　Wrappers. No statement of printing.

Lovecraft: The Fiction. An Index to Dagon and Other Macabre Tales, The Dunwich Horror and Others, At the Mountains of Madness and Other Novels, [compiled by Donald E. Cochran]. *[Jackson, Mississippi: Donald E. Cochran, 1974.]*
　　Self wrappers. No statement of printing. Mimeographed, stapled. Cover title.

Lovecraft: The Revisions. An Index to The Horror in the Museum and Other Revisions, [compiled by Donald E. Cochran]. *[Jackson, Mississippi: Donald E. Cochran, 1975.]*
　　Self wrappers. No statement of printing. Mimeographed, stapled. Cover title.

The Major Works of H. P. Lovecraft, [by] John Taylor Gatto. *[New York]: Monarch Press, [1977].*
　　Wrappers. Code *1 2 3 4 5 6 7 8 9 10* on copyright page.

Marginalia, by H. P. Lovecraft. *Sauk City: Arkham House, 1944.*
No statement of printing on copyright page. Edited, with foreword, by August Derleth and Donald Wandrei. Includes a number of memoirs and appreciations of Lovecraft.

Mirage on Lovecraft: A Literary View, edited by Jack L. Chalker. *Baltimore: Jack L. Chalker & Mark Owings: Publishers, 1965.*
Wrappers. No statement of printing on copyright page. Mimeographed, stapled. "Approximately" 200 numbered copies.

The Necronomicon: A Study, by Mark Owings. *[Baltimore]: Mirage, 1967.*
Wrappers. No statement of printing on copyright page. 600 numbered copies.

The New H. P. Lovecraft Bibliography, compiled and edited by Jack L. Chalker and Divers Hands. *Baltimore: The Anthem Press, 1962.*
Wrappers. No statement of printing on copyright page. Mimeographed, stapled.
. . . *mimeographed in an/edition of 100 copies . . .* on page [4]. Note: According to Mark Owings and Jack L. Chalker in *The Index to the Science-Fantasy Publishers,* 110 copies were printed.

The Normal Lovecraft, [compiled by Gerry de la Ree]. *Saddle River, N.J.: Published by Gerry de la Ree, 1973.*
This first edition limited to 600 copies on copyright page. Two bindings, no priority:
(A) 535 numbered copies in pictorial wrappers; (B) 65 numbered copies bound in black cloth, spine and front cover stamped in gold.

The Occult Lovecraft, by H. P. Lovecraft. With Additional Material and Interpretations by Anthony Raven [and Others]. *Saddle River, N.J.: Published by Gerry de la Ree, 1975.*
1118 copies printed. Two issues, no priority: (A) 990 numbered copies in wrappers;
(B) 128 numbered copies in cloth. First edition so stated on rear wrapper.

A Reader's Guide to the Cthulhu Mythos, by Robert Weinberg. *Hillside, New Jersey: Robert Weinberg, 1969.*
Self wrappers. *Published July 1969* on page 9. Mimeographed, printed on rectos only, stapled.

ALSO: *Albuquerque, New Mexico: The Silver Scarab Press, [1973].* 1200 copies printed. Two bindings, no priority: (A) 200 copies in cloth; (B) 1000 copies in pictorial wrappers. Second edition, revised and enlarged. With EDWARD P. BERGLUND.

The Revised H. P. Lovecraft Bibliography, by Mark Owings with Jack L. Chalker. *Baltimore: The Mirage Press, Ltd., 1973.*
Wrappers. No statement of printing on copyright page. Approximately 1500 copies printed.

Rhode Island on Lovecraft, edited by Donald M. Grant and Thomas P. Handley. *Providence: Grant-Handley, 1945.*
Wrappers. *Set up and printed by Will Sykora* at base of copyright page. No statement of printing on copyright page. Note: Second printing is so indicated on copyright page.

The Roots of Horror in the Fiction of H. P. Lovecraft, by Barton Levi St. Armand. *Elizabethtown, New York: Dragon Press, 1977.*
First edition so stated on copyright page. Note: Not issued with dust jacket.

A Select Bibliography of H. P. Lovecraft, compiled by Joseph Payne Brennan. *N.p.: [Joseph Payne Brennan, 1952].*
Self wrappers. No statement of printing. Privately printed in a small edition and circulated by the compiler.

The Shuttered Room and Other Pieces, by H. P. Lovecraft & Divers Hands. *Sauk City: Arkham House: Publishers, 1959.*
    No statement of printing on copyright page. Compiled, with foreword, by August Derleth.
    Includes memoirs, tributes, and essays.

Some Notes on H. P. Lovecraft . . . , by August Derleth. *[Sauk City]: Arkham House: Publishers, 1959.*
    Wrappers. No statement of printing.

Robert Augustine Ward Lowndes
(b. 1916)

BELIEVERS' WORLD. *New York: Avalon Books*, [*1961*].
  No statement of printing on copyright page.

THE DUPLICATED MAN. *New York: Avalon Books*, [*1959*].
  No statement of printing on copyright page. With JAMES BLISH.

MYSTERY OF THE THIRD MINE. *Philadelphia Toronto: The John C. Winston Company*, [*1953*].
  First edition so stated on copyright page.

THE PUZZLE PLANET. *New York: Ace Books, Inc.*, [*1961*].
  Wrappers. No statement of printing on copyright page. *Ace D–485* (35¢). Bound with THE
  ANGRY ESPERS by Lloyd Biggle, Jr.

Nonfiction (Dealing with the Fantasy Genre only)

Three Faces of Science Fiction. *Boston: The NESFA Press, 1973*.
  First edition so stated on copyright page. 500 numbered copies signed by the author.

Richard Allen Lupoff

(b. 1935)

THE CRACK IN THE SKY. [*New York*]: *A Dell Book*, [*1976*].
Wrappers. *First printing —February 1976* on copyright page. *Dell 5419* ($1.25).

INTO THE AETHER. [*New York*]: *A Dell Book*, [*1974*].
Wrappers. *First printing —January 1974* on copyright page. *Dell 3830* (95¢).

LISA KANE. *Indianapolis/New York: The Bobbs-Merrill Company, Inc.*, [*1976*].
First printing so stated on copyright page.

ONE MILLION CENTURIES. *New York: Lancer Books*, [*1967*].
Wrappers. No statement of printing on copyright page. *Lancer Books 74–892* (75¢).

THE RETURN OF SKULL-FACE. [*West Linn, Oregon*]: *Fax Collector's Editions*, [*1977*].
Two issues, no priority: (A) Boards with cloth shelf back. 215 copies signed by Lupoff and illustrator Stephen E. Leialoha, comprising 150 numbered copies for sale and 65 unnumbered copies for presentation. (B) Boards. 1450 trade copies. No statement of printing on copyright page. With ROBERT E. HOWARD.

SACRED LOCOMOTIVE FLIES. *New York: Beagle Books*, [*1971*].
Wrappers. *First printing: September 1971* on copyright page. *Beagle Boxer Science Fiction 95143* (95¢).

SANDWORLD. [*New York*]: *Published by Berkley Publishing Corporation*, [*1976*].
Wrappers. *May, 1976* on copyright page. *A Berkley Medallion Book Z3116* ($1.25).

SWORD OF THE DEMON. *New York, Hagerstown, San Francisco, London: Harper & Row, Publishers*, [*1977*].
Boards with cloth shelf back. First edition so stated on copyright page.

THE TRIUNE MAN. *New York: Published by Berkley Publishing Corporation*, [*1976*].
No statement of printing on copyright page.

Nonfiction (Dealing with the Fantasy Genre only)

Barsoom: Edgar Rice Burroughs and the Martian Vision. *Baltimore: The Mirage Press, Ltd.*, *1976*.
  First printing: October 1, 1976 on page [162].

Edgar Rice Burroughs: Master of Adventure. *New York: Canaveral Press, 1965*.
  Two issues, priority not determined but probably simultaneous: (A) Boards with cloth shelf back. No statement of printing. Trade issue. (B) Pebbled cloth. 150 numbered copies and a few out-of-series copies signed by the author. The following statement is printed on the front pastedown: *First Edition/Limited to 150 numbered copies/on Number Seventy, plate finish opaque paper./Signed by the Author./This copy is No* [holograph number or "out of series" notation]/[signature]. Limited issue.

  ALSO: *New York: Ace Books, Inc.*, [*1968*]. Wrappers. No statement of printing on copyright page. *Ace Book N–6* (95¢). Revised and enlarged edition.

ALSO: *New York: Ace Books, Inc., [1968]*. Wrappers. No statement of printing on copyright page. *Ace 18771* ($1.25). Adds author's "Introduction to the Centennial Edition."

Edited Nonfiction (Dealing with the Fantasy Genre only)

The Reader's Guide to Barsoom and Amtor, by David G. Van Arnam and Others. [*New York: Richard Lupoff, 1963.*]

Issued as loose sheets, offset. 500 copies printed. Two states, no priority: (A) *The/first printing is limited to 200 copies,/numbered and signed* on verso of title leaf; (B) Printing statement removed from verso of title leaf. Edited, with preface, afterword, and essay, by Lupoff.

Anne Inez McCaffrey
(b. 1926)

DECISION AT DOONA. *New York: Ballantine Books*, [1969].
Wrappers. *First Printing: April, 1969* on copyright page. *Ballantine Science Fiction 01576* (75¢).

ALSO: [*London*]: *Rapp + Whiting*, [1970]. Boards. *First published in Great Britain in 1970* on copyright page. First hardcover edition.

DRAGONFLIGHT. *New York: Ballantine Books*, [1968].
Wrappers. *First Printing: July, 1968* on copyright page. *Ballantine Science Fiction U6124* (75¢).

ALSO: *New York: Walker and Company*, [1969]. Boards. *Published in the United States of America in 1969* on copyright page.

DRAGONQUEST. *New York and London: Ballantine Books*, [1971].
Wrappers. *First Printing: May, 1971* on copyright page. *Ballantine Books Fantasy Adventure 02245–9–095* (95¢).

ALSO: [*London*]: *Rapp + Whiting/André Deutsch*, [1973]. Boards. *First published 1973* on copyright page. First hardcover edition.

DRAGONSINGER. *New York: Atheneum*, 1977.
First edition so stated on copyright page.

DRAGONSONG. *New York: Atheneum*, 1976.
First edition so stated on copyright page.

ALSO: *London: Sidgwick & Jackson*, [1976]. Boards. *First published in Great Britain in 1976* on copyright page. Note: Printed from plates of the Atheneum edition, but drops author's autobiographical sketch appearing on page [203].

GET OFF THE UNICORN. *New York: Ballantine Books*, [1977].
Wrappers. *First Edition: June 1977* on copyright page. *Ballantine 25666* ($1.75).

THE KILTERNAN LEGACY. [*New York*]: *A Dell Book*, [1975].
Wrappers. *First printing—December, 1975* on copyright page. *Dell 7195* ($1.25).

ALSO: [*London*]: *Millington*, [1976]. Boards. *First published in Great Britain in 1976* . . . on copyright page. First hardcover edition.

THE MARK OF MERLIN. [*New York*]: *A Dell Book*, [1971].
Wrappers. *First printing—May, 1971* on copyright page. *Dell 5466* (75¢).

ALSO: [*London*]: *Millington*, [1977]. Boards. *First published in Great Britain in 1977* on copyright page. First hardcover edition.

RESTOREE. *New York: Ballantine Books*, [1967].
Wrappers. *First printing: September, 1967* on copyright page. *A Ballantine Science Fiction Original U6108* (75¢).

ALSO: *London: Rapp & Whiting*, [1968]. Boards. No statement of printing on copyright page. First hardcover edition.

RING OF FEAR. *[New York]: A Dell Book, [1971]*.
Wrappers. *First printing—November 1971* on copyright page. *Dell 7445* (75¢).

THE SHIP WHO SANG. *New York: Walker and Company, [1969]*.
Boards. *Published in the United States of America in 1969 . . .* on copyright page.

A TIME WHEN. *[Cambridge, Massachusetts]: Nesfa Press, [1975]*.
820 copies signed by the author and illustrator Bonnie Dalzell. Two issues, no priority:
(A) 20 lettered copies bound in three-quarter leather and marbled boards. ''Finebound''
issue. (B) 800 numbered copies bound in cloth. No statement of printing on copyright
page.

TO RIDE PEGASUS. *New York: Ballantine Books, [1973]*.
Wrappers. *First Printing: August, 1973* on copyright page. *Ballantine Books 23417–0–125*
($1.25).

ALSO: *London: J M Dent & Sons Ltd, [1974]*. Boards. *First published in Great Britain
1974* on copyright page. First hardcover edition.

Edited Fiction

Alchemy and Academe. *Garden City: Doubleday & Company, Inc., 1970.*
First edition so stated on copyright page. Edited, with foreword, by McCaffrey.

Reference

*Anne McCaffrey: A Dragondex & Bibliography, by Glasser and Whyte. *Cambridge, 1975?*
Wrappers.

James Murdoch Macgregor
(b. 1925)

BORN LEADER. *Garden City: Doubleday & Company, Inc., 1954.*
Boards. First edition so stated on copyright page. *J. T. McIntosh, pseudonym.* Reissued as
WORLDS APART.

A COAT OF BLACKMAIL. *[London]: Frederick Muller, [1970].*
Boards. *First published in Great Britain 1970* on copyright page. *J. T. McIntosh, pseudonym.*

THE COSMIC SPIES. *London: Robert Hale & Company, [1972].*
Boards. *First published in Great Britain 1972* on copyright page. *J. T. McIntosh, pseudonym.*

A CRY TO HEAVEN. *London Melbourne Toronto: Heinemann, [1961].*
Boards. *First published in Great Britain 1961* on copyright page.

THE FITTEST. *Garden City: Doubleday & Company, Inc., 1955.*
Boards. First edition so stated on copyright page. *J. T. McIntosh, pseudonym.* Reissued as
THE RULE OF THE PAGBEASTS.

FLIGHT FROM REBIRTH. *[New York]: Avon, [1971].*
Wrappers. *First Avon Printing, July, 1971* on copyright page. *Avon Science Fiction Original V2411* (75¢). *J. T. McIntosh, pseudonym.*

ALSO: *London: Robert Hale & Company, [1973].* Boards. *First published in Great Britain 1973* on copyright page. First hardcover edition.

GALACTIC TAKEOVER BID. *London: Robert Hale & Company, [1973].*
Boards. *First published in Great Britain 1973* on copyright page. *J. T. McIntosh, pseudonym.*

INCIDENT OVER THE PACIFIC. *Garden City: Doubleday & Company, Inc., 1960.*
First edition so stated on copyright page.

THE IRON RAIN. *London Melbourne Toronto: Heinemann, [1962].*
First published 1962 on copyright page.

THE MILLION CITIES. *New York: Pyramid Books, [1963].*
Wrappers. *Published August 1963* on copyright page. *Pyramid Books F–898* (40¢). *J. T. McIntosh, pseudonym.*

NORMAN CONQUEST 2066. *[London]: Corgi Books, [1977].*
Wrappers. *First publication in Great Britain . . . Corgi edition published 1977* on copyright page. *A Corgi Book 0 552 10484 1* (70p). *J. T. McIntosh, pseudonym.*

THE NORMAN WAY. *London: Brown, Watson Ltd., [1964].*
Wrappers. *First published . . . 1964* on copyright page. *Digit Book R882* (2'6). *J. T. McIntosh, pseudonym.*

ONE IN THREE HUNDRED. *Garden City: Doubleday & Company, Inc., 1954.*
Boards. First edition so stated on copyright page. *J. T. McIntosh, pseudonym.*

OUT OF CHAOS.*London: Brown, Watson Ltd.*, [*1965*].
  Wrappers. *First published in Digit Books 1965* on copyright page. *Digit Books Science Fiction R888* (2'6). *J. T. McIntosh, pseudonym.*

THE RULE OF THE PAGBEASTS.*Greenwich, Conn.: Fawcett Publications, Inc.*, [*1956*].
  Wrappers. *November 1956* on copyright page. *Crest Book 150* (25¢). *J. T. McIntosh, pseudonym.* Reissue of THE FITTEST.

RULER OF THE WORLD.*Toronto • New York • London: Laser Books*, [*1976*].
  Wrappers. *First published March 1976* on copyright page. *Laser Books 72024* (95¢). *J. T. McIntosh, pseudonym.*

SIX GATES FROM LIMBO.*London: Michael Joseph*, [*1968*].
  Boards. *First published in Great Britain . . . 1968* on copyright page.*J. T. McIntosh, pseudonym.*

SNOW WHITE AND THE GIANTS.[*New York*]: *An Avon Book*, [*1968*].
  Wrappers. *First Avon Printing, May, 1968* on copyright page. *Avon Original S347* (60¢). *J. T. McIntosh, pseudonym.* Reissue of TIME FOR A CHANGE.

THE SPACE SORCERERS.*London: Robert Hale & Company*, [*1972*].
  Boards. *First published in Great Britain 1972* on copyright page.*J. T. McIntosh, pseudonym.*

THE SUICIDERS. [*New York*]*: Avon*, [*1973*].
  Wrappers. *First Avon Printing, November, 1973* on copyright page. *Avon Science Fiction 17889* (75¢). *J. T. McIntosh, pseudonym.*

TAKE A PAIR OF PRIVATE EYES. [*London*]*: Frederick Muller*, [*1968*].
  Boards. *First published in Great Britain 1968 . . .* on copyright page.*J. T. McIntosh, pseudonym.*

THIS IS THE WAY THE WORLD BEGINS. [*London*]*: Corgi Books*, [*1977*].
  Wrappers. *First publication in Great Britain . . . Corgi edition published 1977* on copyright page. *Corgi 0 552 10432 9* (70p). *J. T. McIntosh, pseudonym.*

TIME FOR A CHANGE.*London: Michael Joseph*, [*1967*].
  Boards. *First published in Great Britain . . . 1967* on copyright page.*J. T. McIntosh, pseudonym.* Reissued as SNOW WHITE AND THE GIANTS.

TRANSMIGRATION. [*New York*]*: Avon*, [*1970*].
  Wrappers. *First Avon Printing, December, 1970* on copyright page. *Avon Science Fiction Original V2375* (75¢). *J. T. McIntosh, pseudonym.*

200 YEARS TO CHRISTMAS.*New York: Ace Books, Inc.*, [*1961*].
  Wrappers. No statement of printing on copyright page. *Ace Double Novel F–113* (40¢). *J. T. McIntosh, pseudonym.* Bound with REBELS OF THE RED PLANET by Charles L. Fontenay.

WHEN THE SHIP SANK.*Garden City: Doubleday & Company, Inc.*, 1959.
  First edition so stated on copyright page.

WORLD OUT OF MIND.*Garden City: Doubleday & Company, Inc.*, 1953.
  Boards. First edition so stated on copyright page.*J. T. M'Intosh, pseudonym.*

WORLDS APART.*New York: Avon Publications, Inc.*, [*1958*].
  Wrappers. No statement of printing on copyright page. *Avon T–249* (35¢). *J. T. McIntosh, pseudonym.* Reissue of BORN LEADER.

David McIlwain
(b. 1921)

ALPH.*Garden City: Nelson Doubleday, Inc.*, [*1972*].
Boards. Four printings, priority as listed: (A) Code *28N* on page 213; (B) Code *D 24* on page 217; (C) Code *D43* on page 217; (D) Code *F2* on page 217. No statement of printing on copyright page. *Charles Eric Maine, pseudonym.* Revised and expanded version of WORLD WITHOUT MEN. Note: Issued by the Science Fiction Book Club.

B.E.A.S.T. [*London*]: *Hodder and Stoughton*, [*1966*].
Boards. *First printed 1966* on copyright page. *Charles Eric Maine, pseudonym.*

CALCULATED RISK.*London: Hodder and Stoughton*, [*1960*].
Boards. No statement of printing on copyright page. *Charles Eric Maine, pseudonym.*

COUNT-DOWN.*London: Hodder and Stoughton*, [*1959*].
Boards. No statement of printing on copyright page. *Charles Eric Maine, pseudonym.* Issued later in the U.S. as FIRE PAST THE FUTURE.

CRISIS 2000.*London: Hodder and Stoughton*, [*1956*].
Boards. *First printed 1956* on copyright page. *Charles Eric Maine, pseudonym.*

THE DARKEST OF NIGHTS. *London: Hodder & Stoughton*, [*1962*].
Boards. *First printed 1962* on copyright page. *Charles Eric Maine, pseudonym.* Issued later in the U.S. as SURVIVAL MARGIN.

DARLING DAUGHTER.*London: Robert Hale Limited*, [*1961*].
Boards. *First published in Great Britain 1961* on copyright page. *Richard Rayner, pseudonym.*

DIG DEEP FOR JULIE.*London: Robert Hale Limited*, [*1963*].
Boards. *First published in Great Britain 1963* on copyright page. *Richard Rayner, pseudonym.*

ESCAPEMENT.*London: Hodder and Stoughton*, [*1956*].
Boards. *First printed 1956* on copyright page. *Charles Eric Maine, pseudonym.* Issued later in the U.S. as THE MAN WHO COULDN'T SLEEP.

FIRE PAST THE FUTURE.*New York: Ballantine Books*, [*1960*].
Wrappers. No statement of printing on copyright page. *Ballantine Books 360K (35¢). Charles Eric Maine, pseudonym.* Issued earlier in Great Britain as COUNT-DOWN.

HE OWNED THE WORLD.*New York: Avalon Books*, [*1960*].
No statement of printing on copyright page. *Charles Eric Maine, pseudonym.* Issued later in Great Britain as THE MAN WHO OWNED THE WORLD.

HIGH VACUUM.*London: Hodder and Stoughton*, [*1957*].
Boards. *First Printed 1957* on copyright page. *Charles Eric Maine, pseudonym.*

THE ISOTOPE MAN.*London: Hodder and Stoughton*, [*1957*].
Boards. *First printed 1957* on copyright page. *Charles Eric Maine, pseudonym.*

THE MAN WHO COULDN'T SLEEP.*Philadelphia New York: J.B. Lippincott Company, 1958*.
Boards. No statement of printing on copyright page. *Charles Eric Maine, pseudonym.* Issued earlier in Great Britain as ESCAPEMENT.

THE MAN WHO OWNED THE WORLD. *London: Hodder and Stoughton*, [*1961*].
Boards. *First printed in Great Britain in 1961 . . . on copyright page. Charles Eric Maine, pseudonym.* Issued earlier in the U.S. as HE OWNED THE WORLD.

THE MIND OF MR. SOAMES. *London: Hodder and Stoughton*, [*1961*].
Boards. *First printed 1961* on copyright page. *Charles Eric Maine, pseudonym.*

NEVER LET UP. [*London*]*: Hodder and Stoughton*, [*1964*].
Boards. *First printed 1964* on copyright page. *Charles Eric Maine, pseudonym.*

THE RANDOM FACTOR. *London Sydney Auckland Toronto: Hodder and Stoughton*, [*1971*].
Boards. *First printed 1971* on copyright page. *Charles Eric Maine, pseudonym.*

SPACEWAYS. *London: Hodder and Stoughton*, [*1953*].
Boards. *First printed 1953* on copyright page. *Charles Eric Maine, pseudonym.* Issued later in the U.S. with textual differences as SPACEWAYS SATELLITE.

STAND IN FOR DANGER. *London: Robert Hale Limited*, [*1963*].
Boards. *First published in Great Britain 1963* on copyright page. *Richard Rayner, pseudonym.*

SUBTERFUGE. *London: Hodder and Stoughton*, [*1959*].
Boards. No statement of printing on copyright page. *Charles Eric Maine, pseudonym.*

SURVIVAL MARGIN. *Greenwich, Conn.: Fawcett Publications, Inc.*, [*1968*].
Wrappers. No statement of printing on copyright page. *Fawcett Gold Medal Book R1918* (60¢). *Charles Eric Maine, pseudonym.* Issued earlier in Great Britain as THE DARKEST OF NIGHTS.

THIRST! *London: Sphere Books Limited*, [*1977*].
Wrappers. *Published in Great Britain . . . 1977* on copyright page. *Sphere 0 7221 5720 7* (65p). *Charles Eric Maine, pseudonym.* Revised text of THE TIDE WENT OUT.

THE TIDE WENT OUT. *London: Hodder and Stoughton*, [*1958*].
Boards. No statement of printing on copyright page. *Charles Eric Maine, pseudonym.* Revised as THIRST!

TIMELINER. *London: Hodder and Stoughton*, [*1955*].
Boards. *First printed 1955* on copyright page. *Charles Eric Maine, pseudonym.*

THE TROUBLE WITH RUTH. *London: Robert Hale Limited*, [*1960*].
Boards. *First published in Great Britain, 1960* on copyright page. *Richard Rayner, pseudonym.*

WORLD WITHOUT MEN. *New York: Ace Books, Inc.*, [*1958*].
Wrappers. No statement of printing on copyright page. *Ace Double-Sized Books D–274* (35¢). *Charles Eric Maine, pseudonym.* Revised and expanded as ALPH.

Vonda N. McIntyre
(b. 1948)

THE EXILE WAITING. *Garden City: Nelson Doubleday, Inc., [1975]*.
Boards. Two printings, priority of printing but not distribution as listed: (A) Code *30 R* on page 211; (B) Code *32 R* on page 211. No statement of printing on copyright page. Notes: (1) Issued by the Science Fiction Book Club; (2) Two printings before simultaneous distribution to members.

ALSO: *London: Victor Gollancz Ltd, 1976*. Boards. No statement of printing on copyright page. Textual differences.

Edited Fiction

Aurora: Beyond Equality. *Greenwich, Connecticut: Fawcett Publications, Inc., [1976]*. Wrappers. *First printing: May 1976/1 2 3 4 5 6 7 8 9 10* on copyright page. *Fawcett Gold Medal P3515* ($1.25). Edited by McIntyre with SUSAN JANICE ANDERSON.

Katherine Anne MacLean
(b. 1925)

COSMIC CHECKMATE. *New York: Ace Books, Inc.,* [*1962*].
  Wrappers. No statement of printing on copyright page. *Ace Double F–149* (40¢). With
  CHARLES V. DEVET. Bound with KING OF THE FOURTH PLANET by Robert Moore Williams.

THE DIPLOIDS. *New York: Avon Book Division,* [*1962*].
  Wrappers. No statement of printing on copyright page. *An Avon Book G–1143* (50¢).

THE MAN IN THE BIRD CAGE. *New York: Ace Books,* [*1971*].
  Wrappers. No statement of printing on copyright page. *Ace Book 51800* (75¢).

MISSING MAN. *New York: Published by Berkley Publishing Corporation,* [*1975*].
  No statement of printing on copyright page.

TROUBLE WITH TREATIES. [*Tacoma, Washington*]: *The Lanthorne Press, 1975*.
  Wrappers. No statement of printing on copyright page. 200 numbered copies only. With
  TOM CONDIT. First separate printing. Collected earlier in *Star Science Fiction Stories No. 5*
  edited by Frederik Pohl.

Barry N. Malzberg
(b. 1939)

ACTS OF MERCY. *New York: G. P. Putnam's Sons*, [1977].
No statement of printing on copyright page. With BILL PRONZINI. Note: Prepublication title was RIDE THE TIGER.

THE ART OF THE FUGUE. [*New York*]: *The Traveller's Companion Series*, [1970].
Wrappers. No statement of printing on copyright page. *The Traveller's Companion Series TC–483*. ($1.95). *Gerrold Watkins, pseudonym*.

BAY PROWLER. [*New York*]: *Published by Berkley Publishing Corporation*, [1973].
Wrappers. *October, 1973* on copyright page. *A Berkley Medallion Book 425–02430–095* (95¢). *Mike Barry, pseudonym*. #2 *The Lone Wolf* at head of title.

A BED OF MONEY. [*New York*]: *The Traveller's Companion Series*, [1970].
Wrappers. No statement of printing on copyright page. *The Traveller's Companion Series TC–474*. ($1.95). *Gerrold Watkins, pseudonym*.

THE BEST OF BARRY N. MALZBERG. *New York: Published by Pocket Books*, [1976].
Wrappers. *Published January, 1976* on copyright page. *Pocket Books 80256* ($1.95).

BEYOND APOLLO. *New York: Random House*, [1972].
Boards with cloth shelf back. First edition so stated on copyright page.

BORN TO GIVE. [*New York*]: *A Midwood Book*, [1969].
Wrappers. No statement of printing on copyright page. *Midwood 37–232* ($1.25). *Mel Johnson, pseudonym*. Bound with SWAP CLUB by Greg Hamilton and WILD IN BED by Dirk Malloy.

BOSTON AVENGER. [*New York*]: *Published by Berkley Publishing Corporation*, [1973].
Wrappers. *October, 1973* on copyright page. *A Berkley Medallion Book 425–02431–095* (95¢). *Mike Barry, pseudonym*. #3 *The Lone Wolf* at head of title.

THE BOX. *New York: Oracle Books*, [1969].
Wrappers. *An Oracle Book • 1969* on copyright page. *Oracle Books 88–603* ($1.25). *Mel Johnson, pseudonym*.

CAMPUS DOLL. [*New York*]: *A Midwood Book*, [1969].
Wrappers. No statement of printing on copyright page. *Midwood 35–241* (95¢). *Mel Johnson, pseudonym*. Bound with HIGH SCHOOL STUD by Robert Hadley.

THE CASE FOR ELIZABETH MOORE. See HORIZONTAL WOMAN.

CHAINED. [*New York*]: *A Midwood Book*, [1968].
Wrappers. No statement of printing on copyright page. *Midwood 37–157* ($1.25). *Mel Johnson, pseudonym*. Bound with LOVE CAPTIVE by Dallas Mayo.

CHICAGO SLAUGHTER. [*New York*]: *Published by Berkley Publishing Corporation*, [1974].
Wrappers. *May, 1974* on copyright page. *A Berkley Medallion Book 425–02555–095* (95¢). *Mike Barry, pseudonym*. #6 *The Lone Wolf* at head of title.

THE CIRCLE. [*New York*]: *The Traveller's Companion Series*, [*1969*].
  Wrappers. No statement of printing on copyright page. *The Traveller's Companion Series TC–444* ($1.75). *Francine di Natale, pseudonym.*

CONFESSIONS OF WESTCHESTER COUNTY. [*New York*]: *The Olympia Press, Inc.*, [*1971*].
  Wrappers. No statement of printing on copyright page. *The Olympia Press OPS–29* ($1.95).

CONVERSATIONS. *Indianapolis/New York: The Bobbs-Merrill Company, Inc.*, [*1975*].
  Boards. First printing so stated on copyright page.

THE DAY OF THE BURNING. *New York: Ace Books*, [*1974*].
  Wrappers. No statement of printing on copyright page. *Ace 13902* (95¢).

DESERT STALKER. [*New York*]: *Published by Berkley Publishing Corporation*, [*1974*].
  Wrappers. *January, 1974* on copyright page. *A Berkley Medallion Book 425–02204–095* (95¢). *Mike Barry, pseudonym.* #4 The Lone Wolf at head of title.

THE DESTRUCTION OF THE TEMPLE. *New York: Published by Pocket Books*, [*1974*].
  Wrappers. *Published February, 1974* on copyright page. *Pocket Books 77696* (95¢).

DETROIT MASSACRE. [*New York*]: *Published by Berkley Publishing Corporation*, [*1975*].
  Wrappers. *April, 1975* on copyright page. *A Berkley Medallion Book N2793* (95¢). *Mike Barry, pseudonym.* #11 The Lone Wolf at head of title.

DIARY OF A PARISIAN CHAMBERMAID. [*New York*]: *The Collectors Classic Series*, [*1969*].
  Wrappers. No statement of printing on copyright page. *A Midwood Book 37–206* ($1.25). *Claudine Dumas, pseudonym.*

DO IT TO ME. [*New York*]: *A Midwood Book*, [*1969*].
  Wrappers. No statement of printing on copyright page. *Midwood 35–227* (95¢). *Mel Johnson, pseudonym.* Bound with HOT BLONDE by Jim Conroy.

DOWN HERE IN THE DREAM QUARTER. *Garden City: Doubleday & Company, Inc.*, 1976.
  Boards. First edition so stated on copyright page.

DWELLERS OF THE DEEP. *New York: Ace Books*, [*1970*].
  Wrappers. No statement of printing on copyright page. *Ace Double 27400* (75¢). *K. M. O'Donnell, pseudonym.* Bound with THE GATES OF TIME by Neal Barrett, Jr.

THE EMPTY PEOPLE. *New York: Lancer Books*, [*1969*].
  Wrappers. *A Lancer Book • 1969* on copyright page. *Lancer Books 74–546* (75¢). *K. M. O'Donnell, pseudonym.*

THE FALLING ASTRONAUTS. *New York: Ace Books*, [*1971*].
  Wrappers. No statement of printing on copyright page. *Ace Book 22690* (75¢).

FINAL WAR AND OTHER FANTASIES. *New York: An Ace Book*, [*1969*].
  Wrappers. No statement of printing on copyright page. *Ace Double 23775* (75¢). *K. M. O'Donnell, pseudonym.* Bound with TREASURE OF TAU CETI by John Rackham.

GALAXIES. *New York: Pyramid Books*, [*1975*].
  Wrappers. *Published August 1975* on copyright page. *Pyramid V3734* ($1.25).

THE GAMESMAN. *New York: Published by Pocket Books*, [*1975*].
  Wrappers. *Published December, 1975* on copyright page. *Pocket Books 80174* ($1.25).

GATHER IN THE HALL OF THE PLANETS. *New York: Ace Books*, [*1971*].
Wrappers. No statement of printing on copyright page. *Ace Double 27415* (75¢). *K. M. O'Donnell, pseudonym*. Bound with IN THE POCKET AND OTHER S-F STORIES by O'Donnell.

GIVING IT AWAY. [*New York*]: *The Traveller's Companion Series*, [*1970*].
Wrappers. No statement of printing on copyright page. *The Traveller's Companion Series TC 479*. ($1.95). *Gerrold Watkins, pseudonym*.

GUERNICA NIGHT. *Indianapolis/New York: The Bobbs-Merrill Company, Inc.*, [*1974*].
Boards. First printing so stated on copyright page.

HARLEM SHOWDOWN. [*New York*]: *Published by Berkley Publishing Corporation*, [*1975*].
Wrappers. *February, 1975* on copyright page. *A Berkley Medallion Book N2761* (95¢). *Mike Barry, pseudonym*. *#10 in the savage quest of The Lone Wolf* at head of title.

HAVANA HIT. [*New York*]: *Published by Berkley Publishing Corporation*, [*1974*].
Wrappers. *March, 1974* on copyright page. *A Berkley Medallion Book 425–02527–095* (95¢). *Mike Barry, pseudonym*. *The Lone Wolf* at head of title.

HEROVIT'S WORLD. *New York: Random House*, [*1973*].
First edition so stated on copyright page.

HORIZONTAL WOMAN. *New York: Leisure Books*, [*1972*].
Wrappers. *A Leisure Book — 1972* on copyright page. *Leisure Books LB124 ZK* ($1.25). Reissued as THE SOCIAL WORKER. Note: This novel was scheduled in 1972 by Belmont Books as THE CASE FOR ELIZABETH MOORE but the first printing appeared under the Leisure Books imprint as HORIZONTAL WOMAN.

I, LESBIAN. [*New York*]: *A Midwood Book*, [*1968*].
Wrappers. No statement of printing on copyright page. *Midwood 34–943* (75¢). *M. L. Johnson, pseudonym*.

IN MY PARENTS' BEDROOM. *New York: The Olympia Press, Inc.*, [*1971*].
Wrappers. No statement of printing on copyright page. *Olympia Press OPS–17* ($1.25).

IN THE ENCLOSURE. [*New York*]: *Avon*, [*1973*].
Wrappers. *First Avon Printing, May, 1973* on copyright page. *Avon Science Fiction 15073* (95¢).

ALSO: *London: Robert Hale & Company*, [*1976*]. Boards. *First published in Great Britain 1976* on copyright page. First hardcover edition.

IN THE POCKET AND OTHER S-F STORIES. *New York: Ace Books*, [*1971*].
Wrappers. No statement of printing on copyright page. *Ace Double 27415* (75¢). *K. M. O'Donnell, pseudonym*. Bound with GATHER IN THE HALL OF THE PLANETS by O'Donnell.

INSTANT SEX. [*New York*]: *A Midwood Book*, [*1968*].
Wrappers. No statement of printing on copyright page. *Midwood 34–994* (75¢). *Mel Johnson, pseudonym*.

JUST ASK. [*New York*]: *A Midwood Book*, [*1968*].
Wrappers. No statement of printing on copyright page. *Midwood 35–983* (95¢). *Mel Johnson, pseudonym*. Bound with PLAYGIRL by Lou Craig.

THE KILLING RUN. [*New York*]: *Published by Berkley Publishing Corporation*, [*1975*].
Wrappers. *August, 1975* on copyright page. *A Berkley Medallion Book N2920* (95¢). *Mike Barry, pseudonym*. *#13 The Lone Wolf* at head of title.

KISS AND RUN. [*New York*]: *A Midwood Book*, [*1968*].
Wrappers. No statement of printing on copyright page. *Midwood 37–179* ($1.25). *Mel Johnson, pseudonym*. Bound with SEX ON THE SAND by Sheldon Lord and ODD GIRL by March Hastings.

LADY OF A THOUSAND SORROWS. [*Chicago*]: *Playboy Press Paperbacks*, [*1977*].
Wrappers. First edition so stated on copyright page. *Playboy Press 16362* ($1.95). *Lee W. Mason, pseudonym*.

THE LAST TRANSACTION. *Los Angeles: Pinnacle Books*, [*1977*].
Wrappers. *First printing, November 1977* on copyright page. *Futorian Science Fiction/Pinnacle Books 40–174* ($1.75).

LOS ANGELES HOLOCAUST. [*New York*]: *Published by Berkley Publishing Corporation*, [*1974*].
Wrappers. *September, 1974* on copyright page. *A Berkley Medallion Book N2665* (95¢). *Mike Barry, pseudonym*. #8 *The Lone Wolf* at head of title.

LOVE DOLL. *New York: Soft Cover Library, Inc.*, [*1967*].
Wrappers. No statement of printing on copyright page. *Soft Cover Library B1076N K* (95¢). *Mel Johnson, pseudonym*. Bound with THE SEX PROS by Orrie Hitt.

THE MANY WORLDS OF BARRY MALZBERG. *New York: Popular Library*, [*1975*].
Wrappers. No statement of printing on copyright page. *Popular Library 445–00298–125* ($1.25).

THE MASOCHIST. *New York: Belmont/Tower Books*, [*1972*].
Wrappers. *August 1972* on copyright page. *Belmont Tower 50261* ($1.25).

THE MEN INSIDE. *New York: Lancer Books*, [*1973*].
Wrappers. No statement of printing on copyright page. *Lancer 75486–095* (95¢). Note: Malzberg's name appears on cover but not on title page.

MIAMI MARAUDER. [*New York*]: *Published by Berkley Publishing Corporation*, [*1974*].
Wrappers. *December, 1974* on copyright page. *A Berkley Medallion Book N2715* (95¢). *Mike Barry, pseudonym*. The *Lone Wolf* at head of title.

NIGHT RAIDER. [*New York*]: *Published by Berkley Publishing Corporation*, [*1973*].
Wrappers. *October, 1973* on copyright page. *A Berkley Medallion Book 425–02429–095* (95¢). *Mike Barry, pseudonym*. #1 *The Lone Wolf* at head of title.

NYMPHO NURSE. [*New York*]: *A Midwood Book*, [*1969*].
Wrappers. No statement of printing on copyright page. *Midwood 37–199* ($1.25). *Mel Johnson, pseudonym*. Bound with YOUNG AND EAGER by Jim Conroy and QUICKIE by Gene Evans.

ON A PLANET ALIEN. *New York: Published by Pocket Books*, [*1974*].
Wrappers. *Published October, 1974* on copyright page. *Pocket Books 77766* (95¢).

ORACLE OF THE THOUSAND HANDS. *New York: The Olympia Press, Inc.*, [*1968*].
This edition of/ ORACLE OF THE/THOUSAND HANDS/published by arrangement with/The Traveller's Companion, Inc./and the Olympia Press, Inc./has been especially designed and bound/for the members of/THE OLYMPIA/BOOK SOCIETY/a division of/The Olympia Press, Inc./P.O. Box 440, Madison Square Station/New York, New York 10010/ © Barry N. Malzberg 1968 on copyright page.

OUT FROM GANYMEDE. [*New York*]: *Warner Paperback Library*, [*1974*].
Wrappers. *First Printing: December, 1974* on copyright page. *Warner Paperback Library 76–538* ($1.25).

OVERLAY. *New York: A Lancer Book*, [*1972*].
Wrappers. No statement of printing on copyright page. *Lancer Books 75345–095* (95¢).

PERUVIAN NIGHTMARE. [*New York*]: *Published by Berkley Publishing Corporation*, [*1974*].
Wrappers. *July, 1974* on copyright page. *A Berkley Medallion Book 425–02624–095* (95¢). *Mike Barry, pseudonym. #7 The Lone Wolf* at head of title.

PHASE IV. *New York: Published by Pocket Books*, [*1973*].
Wrappers. *Published November, 1973* on copyright page. *Pocket Books 77710* (95¢).

PHILADELPHIA BLOWUP. [*New York*]: *Published by Berkley Publishing Corporation*, [*1975*].
Wrappers. *October, 197*[sic] on copyright page. *A Berkley Medallion Book N2960* (95¢).
Mike Barry, pseudonym. The Lone Wolf at head of title.

PHOENIX INFERNO. [*New York*]: *Published by Berkley Publishing Corporation*, [*1975*].
Wrappers. *June, 1975* on copyright page. *A Berkley Medallion Book N2858* (95¢). *Mike Barry, pseudonym. #12 The Lone Wolf* at head of title.

REVELATIONS. *New York: Warner Paperback Library*, [*1972*].
Wrappers. *First Printing: October, 1972* on copyright page. *Warner Paperback Library 64–947* (75¢).

ALSO: [*New York*]: *Published by Avon Books*, [*1977*]. Wrappers. *First Equinox Printing, March, 1977* on copyright page. *Equinox 31716* ($2.25). Adds "Afterword: April 1976" by Malzberg.

THE RUNNING OF BEASTS. *New York: G. P. Putnam's Sons*, [*1976*].
No statement of printing on copyright page. With BILL PRONZINI.

THE SADIST. [*New York*]: *A Midwood Book*, [*1969*].
Wrappers. No statement of printing on copyright page. *Midwood 35–200* (95¢). *Mel Johnson, pseudonym.* Bound with FLESH by Max Collier.

A SATYR'S ROMANCE. [*New York*]: *The Traveller's Companion Series*, [*1970*].
Wrappers. No statement of printing on copyright page. *The Traveller's Companion Series TC 476.* ($1.95). *Gerrold Watkins, pseudonym.*

SCOP. *New York: Pyramid Book*, [*1976*].
Wrappers. *Published April 1976* on copyright page. *Pyramid V3895* ($1.25).

SCREEN. *New York: The Olympia Press, Inc.*, [*1968*].
This edition of/SCREEN/published by arrangement with/The Traveller's Companion, Inc./and the Olympia Press, Inc./has been especially designed and bound/for the members of/THE OLYMPIA/BOOK SOCIETY/a division of/The Olympia Press, Inc./P.O. Box 440, Madison Square Station/New York, New York 10010/© Barry N. Malzberg 1968 on copyright page.

THE SOCIAL WORKER. *New York: Leisure Books*, [*1977*].
Wrappers. No statement of printing on copyright page. *Leisure Book LB 511 DK* ($1.50). Reissue of HORIZONTAL WOMAN.

THE SODOM AND GOMORRAH BUSINESS. *New York: Published by Pocket Books* [*1974*].
Wrappers. *Published December, 1974* on copyright page. *Pocket Books 77789* (95¢).

SOUTHERN COMFORT. *[New York]: The Traveller's Companion Series*, *[1969]*.
Wrappers. No statement of printing on copyright page. *The Traveller's Companion Series TC-460* ($1.75). *Gerrold Watkins, pseudonym.*

THE SPREAD. *New York: Belmont Books*, *[1971]*.
Wrappers. *October 1971* on copyright page. *Belmont B75-2167* (75¢).

TACTICS OF CONQUEST. *New York: Pyramid Books*, *[1974]*.
Wrappers. *First edition published February 1974* on copyright page. *Pyramid N3330* (95¢).

UNDERLAY. *[New York]: Avon*, *[1974]*.
Wrappers. *First Avon Printing, January, 1974* on copyright page. *Avon 17939* ($1.50).
Note: Prepublication title was THE SEASON OF CHANGES.

UNIVERSE DAY. *[New York]: Avon*, *[1971]*.
Wrappers. *First Avon Printing, April, 1971* on copyright page. *Avon Science Fiction Original V2394* (75¢). *K. M. O'Donnell, pseudonym.*

THE WAY OF THE TIGER, THE SIGN OF THE DRAGON. *[New York]: Warner Paperback Library*, *[1973]*.
Wrappers. *First printing: October, 1973* on copyright page. *Warner Paperback Library 76-464* ($1.25). *Howard Lee, pseudonym. Kung Fu #1* at head of title. Note: Subsequent titles in this series were not written by Malzberg.

A WAY WITH ALL MAIDENS. *New York: Oracle Books*, *[1969]*.
Wrappers. *An Oracle Book • 1969* on copyright page. *Oracle Books 88-605* ($1.25). *Mel Johnson, pseudonym.*

Edited Fiction

Arena: Sports SF. *Garden City: Doubleday & Company, Inc.*, *1976*.
Boards. First edition so stated on copyright page. Edited, with afterword, notes, and short story "Closed Sicilian," by Malzberg. With EDWARD L. FERMAN.

Final Stage. *New York: Charterhouse*, *[1974]*.
Boards. Edited, with introduction, by Malzberg with EDWARD L. FERMAN. Includes short story "The Wonderful, All-Purpose Transmogrifier" by Malzberg. Note: This edition was heavily rewritten and cut by the publisher without the consent of the authors or editors.

ALSO: *[Harmondsworth, Middlesex]: Penguin Books*, *[1975]*. Wrappers. *Published by Penguin Books, 1975* on copyright page. *Penguin 4039* (75p). Note: Prints the original versions of the authors' stories.

Graven Images. *Nashville New York: Thomas Nelson Inc., Publishers*, *[1977]*.
Boards with cloth shelf back. First edition so stated on copyright page. Edited, with introduction and short story "Choral," by Malzberg. With EDWARD L. FERMAN.

George R. R. Martin
(b. 1948)

DYING OF THE LIGHT. [*New York*]: *Simon and Schuster*, [*1977*].
  Boards. Code *1 2 3 4 5 6 7 8 9 10* on copyright page.

A SONG FOR LYA AND OTHER STORIES. [*New York*]: *Avon*, [*1976*].
  Wrappers. *First Avon Printing, February, 1976* on copyright page. *Avon Science Fiction 27581* ($1.25).

SONGS OF STARS AND SHADOWS. *New York: Published by Pocket Books*, [*1977*].
  Wrappers. *July, 1977* on copyright page. *Pocket 81277* ($1.75).

Edited Fiction

New Voices in Science Fiction: Stories by Campbell Award Nominees. *New York: Macmillan Publishing Co., Inc., London: Collier Macmillan Publishers*, [*1977*].
  Boards. *First printing 1977* on copyright page. Edited, with notes and short story ''The Stone City,'' by Martin.

Douglas Rankine Mason
(b. 1918)

ANDROID PLANET. *[London]: Futura Publications Limited, [1976]*.
Wrappers. *First published in Great Britain in 1976* on copyright page. *Orbit 0 8600 7903 1* (50p). *Space 1999* at head of title. *John Rankine, pseudonym*.

ALSO: *London: Arthur Barker Limited, [1976]*. Boards. No statement of printing on copyright page. First hardcover edition. Note: Possibly published simultaneously with the Futura edition.

ASTRAL QUEST. *London: Dennis Dobson, [1975]*.
Boards. *This edition first published in Great Britain in 1975* on copyright page. *John Rankine, pseudonym. Space: 1999 6* at head of title.

ALSO: *[London]: Futura Publications Limited, [1975]*. Wrappers. *First published in Great Britain in 1975* on copyright page. *Orbit Science Fiction 0 8600 78787* (50p). *Space 1999* at head of title. Note: *Whitaker's Cumulative Book List* records both editions as published December 1975. Possible simultaneous publication, but the Dobson appears to have preceded the Orbit edition, which was received by the British Library 26 August 1976.

BINARY Z. *London: Dennis Dobson, [1969]*.
Boards. *First published in Great Britain in 1969* on copyright page. *John Rankine, pseudonym*.

THE BLOCKADE OF SINITRON. FOUR ADVENTURES OF DAG FLETCHER. *[London]: Nelson, [1966]*.
Boards. *First published 1966* on copyright page. *John Rankine, pseudonym*.

THE BROMIUS PHENOMENON. *New York: Ace Books, [1973]*.
Wrappers. *First Ace printing: August, 1973* on copyright page. *An Ace Book 08145* (95¢). *John Rankine, pseudonym*.

ALSO: *London: Dennis Dobson, [1976]*. Boards. *First published in Great Britain in 1976* . . . on copyright page. First hardcover edition.

DILATION EFFECT. *New York: Ballantine Books, [1971]*.
Wrappers. *First Printing: March, 1971* on copyright page. *Ballantine Books 02180-0-095* (95¢).

EIGHT AGAINST UTOPIA. *New York: Paperback Library, Inc., [1967]*.
Wrappers. *First Printing: December, 1967* on copyright page. *A Paperback Library Science Fiction Novel 52-599* (50¢). Reissue of FROM CARTHAGE THEN I CAME.

THE END BRINGERS. *New York: Ballantine Books, [1973]*.
Wrappers. *First Printing: June, 1973* on copyright page. *Ballantine Books 03366-3-125* ($1.25).

ALSO: *London: Robert Hale & Company, [1975]*. Boards. *First published in Great Britain 1975* on copyright page. First hardcover edition.

EUPHOR UNFREE. *London: Robert Hale, [1977]*.
Boards. *First published in Great Britain 1977* on copyright page.

THE FINGALNAN CONSPIRACY.*London: Sidgwick & Jackson, [1973]*.
Boards. *First published in Great Britain in 1973* on copyright page. *John Rankine, pseudonym*.

FROM CARTHAGE THEN I CAME.*Garden City: Doubleday & Company, 1966*.
First edition so stated on copyright page. Reissued as EIGHT AGAINST UTOPIA.

HORIZON ALPHA.*New York: Ballantine Books, [1971]*.
Wrappers. *First Printing: March, 1971* on copyright page. *Ballantine Books 02179-7-095* (95¢).

INTERSTELLAR TWO-FIVE.*London: Dennis Dobson, [1966]*.
Boards. *First published in Great Britain in 1966* on copyright page. *John Rankine, pseudonym*.

THE JANUS SYNDROME.*London: Robert Hale, [1969]*.
Boards. *First published in Great Britain 1969* on copyright page.

LANDFALL IS A STATE OF MIND.*London: Robert Hale, [1968]*.
Boards. *First published in Great Britain 1968* on copyright page.

LUNAR ATTACK.*[London]: Futura Publications Limited, [1975]*.
Wrappers. *First published in Great Britain in 1975* on copyright page. *Orbit 0 8600 7875 2* (45p). *Space 1999* at head of title. *John Rankine, pseudonym*.

ALSO: *London: Dennis Dobson, [1975]*. Boards. *This edition first published in Great Britain in 1975* on copyright page. *Space 1999 5* at head of title. First hardcover edition.

MATRIX.*New York: Ballantine Books, [1970]*.
Wrappers. *First Printing: January, 1970* on copyright page. *Ballantine Books Science Fiction 01816-075* (75¢).

ALSO:*London: Robert Hale & Company, [1971]*. Boards. *First published in Great Britain 1971* on copyright page. First hardcover edition.

MOON ODYSSEY.*[London]: Futura Publications Limited, [1975]*.
Wrappers. *First published in Great Britain in 1975* on copyright page. *Orbit 0 8600 7844 2* (35p). *John Rankine, pseudonym*.

ALSO:*London: Dennis Dobson, [1975]*. Boards. *This edition first published in Great Britain in 1975* on copyright page. *Space: 1999 2* at head of title. First hardcover edition.

MOONS OF TRIOPUS.*London: Dennis Dobson, [1969]*.
Boards. *First published in Great Britain in 1968* on copyright page. *John Rankine, pseudonym*. Note: Published January 1969.

NEVER THE SAME DOOR.*London: Dennis Dobson, [1967]*.
Boards. *First published in Great Britain 1967* on copyright page. *John Rankine, pseudonym*.

THE OMEGA WORM.*London: Robert Hale & Company, [1976]*.
Boards. *First published in Great Britain 1976* on copyright page.

ONE IS ONE.*London: Dennis Dobson, [1968]*.
Boards. *First published in Great Britain in 1968* on copyright page. *John Rankine, pseudonym*.

OPERATION UMANAG. *New York: Ace Books*, [*1973*].
Wrappers. *First Ace printing: February, 1973* on copyright page. *Ace 63590* (75¢). *John Rankine, pseudonym.*

ALSO:*London: Sidgwick & Jackson*, [*1974*]. Boards. *First published in Great Britain in 1974* on copyright page. First hardcover edition.

THE PHAETON CONDITION. *New York: G. P. Putnam's Sons*, [*1973*].
No statement of printing on copyright page.

PHOENIX OF MEGARON. *New York: Published by Pocket Books*, [*1976*].
Wrappers. *Published November, 1976* on copyright page. *Pocket Books 80764* ($1.50). *John Rankine, pseudonym.* Note: Copyright page of the Pocket Books edition states: "Futura Publications edition published 1976." Futura did not produce an edition of this book. In a letter to the compiler the publisher notes: "This book was scheduled to be published by Futura but unfortunately due to a change in publishing policy it was decided that we could not go ahead." No British edition has been located, nor is one listed in the 1976 or 1977 *Cumulative Book List.*

PITMAN'S PROGRESS. [*Morley, Yorkshire*]: *The Elmfield Press*, [*1976*].
Boards. *Published 1976* . . . on copyright page.

THE PLANTOS AFFAIR. *London: Dennis Dobson*, [*1971*].
Boards. *First published in Great Britain in 1971* on copyright page. *John Rankine, pseudonym.*

THE RESURRECTION OF ROGER DIMENT. *New York: Ballantine Books*, [*1972*].
Wrappers. *First Printing: April, 1972* on copyright page. *Ballantine Books Science Fiction 02573–3–095* (95¢).

THE RING OF GARAMAS. *London: Dennis Dobson*, [*1971*].
Boards. *First published in 1971* on copyright page. *John Rankine, pseudonym.*

RING OF VIOLENCE. *London: Robert Hale*, [*1968*].
Boards. *First published in Great Britain 1968* on copyright page.

SATELLITE 54-ZERO. *New York: Ballantine Books*, [*1971*] .
Wrappers. *First Printing: January, 1971* on copyright page. *Ballantine Books Science Fiction 02108–8–095* (95¢).

THE THORBURN ENTERPRISE. *London: Dennis Dobson*, [*1977*].
Boards. *First published in Great Britain 1977* on copyright page. *John Rankine, pseudonym.*

THE TOWER OF RIZWAN. *London: Robert Hale*, [*1968*].
Boards. *First published in Great Britain 1968* on copyright page.

THE WEISMAN EXPERIMENT. *London: Dennis Dobson*, [*1969*].
Boards. *First published in Great Britain in 1969* on copyright page. *John Rankine, pseudonym.*

David I. Masson
(b. 1915)

THE CALTRAPS OF TIME. *London: Faber and Faber*, [*1968*].
   First published in mcmlxviii on copyright page.

Richard Burton Matheson
(b. 1926)

THE BEARDLESS WARRIORS. *Boston Toronto: Little, Brown and Company*, [*1960*].
First edition so stated on copyright page.

BID TIME RETURN. *New York: The Viking Press*, [*1975*].
Boards with cloth shelf back. *First published in 1975* on copyright page.

BORN OF MAN AND WOMAN. *Philadelphia: The Chamberlain Press, Inc.*, *1954*.
First edition so stated on copyright page. Thirteen of the seventeen stories were later reprinted in THIRD FROM THE SUN.

ALSO: *London: Max Reinhardt*, [*1956*]. Boards. *First published in Great Britain 1956* on copyright page. Drops the Robert Bloch introduction and four stories, ''Full Circle,'' ''Disappearing Act,'' ''The Wedding,'' and ''The Traveller.''

FURY ON SUNDAY. *New York: Lion Books, Inc.*, [*1953*].
Wrappers. *Lion edition published December, 1953* on copyright page. *A'Lion Book 180* (25¢).

HELL HOUSE. *New York: The Viking Press*, [*1971*].
Boards with cloth shelf back. *First published in 1971* on copyright page.

I AM LEGEND. *New York: Fawcett Publications, Inc.*, [*1954*].
Wrappers. *First Printing, July 1954* on copyright page. *Gold Medal Book 417* (25¢).

ALSO: *New York: Walker and Company*, [*1970*]. Boards. *Published in the United States of America in 1970 . . .* on copyright page. First hardcover edition.

RIDE THE NIGHTMARE. *New York: Ballantine Books*, [*1959*].
Wrappers. No statement of printing on copyright page. *A Ballantine Suspense Novel 301 K* (35¢).

SHOCK! [*New York: Dell Publishing Co., Inc., 1961.*]
Wrappers. *First printing—June, 1961* on copyright page. *Dell B195* (35¢).

SHOCK II. [*New York*]: *A Dell Book*, [*1964*].
Wrappers. *First Dell printing—October, 1964* on copyright page. *Dell 7829* (50¢).

SHOCK III. [*New York*]: *A Dell Book*, [*1966*].
Wrappers. *First Dell Printing—March, 1966* on copyright page. *Dell 7830* (50¢).

SHOCK WAVES. [*New York*]: *A Dell Book*, [*1970*].
Wrappers. *First printing—October 1970* on copyright page. *Dell 7831* (75¢).

THE SHORES OF SPACE. *New York: Bantam Books*, [*1957*].
Wrappers. *Published February 1957* on copyright page. *Bantam Books A1571* (35¢).

THE SHRINKING MAN. *New York: Fawcett Publications, Inc.*, [*1956*].
Wrappers. *First Printing, May 1956* on copyright page. *Gold Medal Giant s577* (35¢).

ALSO: *London: David Bruce & Watson*, [*1973*]. Boards. *This edition published in 1973* on copyright page. First hardcover edition.

SOMEONE IS BLEEDING. *New York: Lion Books, Inc., [1953].*
  Wrappers. *Lion edition published/April, 1953* on copyright page. *A Lion Book 137* (25¢).

A STIR OF ECHOES. *Philadelphia and New York: J. B. Lippincott Company, [1958].*
  Boards. First edition so stated on copyright page.

THIRD FROM THE SUN. *New York: Bantam Books, [1955].*
  Wrappers. *Bantam edition published February 1955/1st Printing . . . January 1955* on
  copyright page. *Bantam Books 1294* (25¢). Thirteen stories reprinted from BORN OF MAN
  AND WOMAN.

Associational

The Beat Generation, by Albert Zugsmith. Based on a Screenplay by Richard Matheson and
Lewis Meltzer. *New York: Bantam Books, [1959].*
  Wrappers. *Published April 1959* on copyright page. *A Bantam Book 1965* (25¢). Note:
  Novel by Zugsmith adapted from the screenplay by Matheson and Lewis.

De Sade, by Henry Clement. Based on the Screenplay by Richard Matheson. *[New York]:
Published by The New American Library, [1969].*
  Wrappers. *First printing, September, 1969* on copyright page. *A Signet Novel T 3952*
  (75¢). Note: Novel by Clement adapted from the screenplay by Matheson.

Tales of Terror, by Edgar Allan Poe. Based on the American-International Picture, adapted
by Eunice Sudak from the screenplay by Richard Matheson. *New York: Lancer Books,
[1962].*
  Wrappers. *A Lancer original • Never before published* on copyright page. *Lancer Original
  71–325* (35¢).

Judith Merril

(b. 1923)

THE BEST OF JUDITH MERRIL. [*New York*]: *Warner Books*, [*1976*].
Wrappers. *First Printing: January, 1976* on copyright page. *Warner Books 86–058* ($1.25).

DAUGHTERS OF EARTH. *London: Victor Gollancz Ltd, 1968.*
Boards. No statement of printing on copyright page.

GUNNER CADE. *New York: Simon and Schuster, 1952.*
Boards. First printing so stated on copyright page. *Cyril Judd, pseudonym.* With C. M. KORNBLUTH.

OUT OF BOUNDS. *New York: Pyramid Books*, [*1960*].
Wrappers. *First printing: April 1960* on copyright page. *Pyramid G499* (35¢).

OUTPOST MARS. *New York: Abelard Press*, [*1952*].
No statement of printing on copyright page. *Cyril Judd, pseudonym.* With C. M. KORNBLUTH. Reissued with textual changes as SIN IN SPACE.

SHADOW ON THE HEARTH. *Garden City: Doubleday & Company, Inc., 1950.*
Boards. First edition so stated on copyright page.

ALSO: *London: Published by Roberts & Vinter Ltd*, [*1966*]. Wrappers. No statement of printing on copyright page. *Compact SF F325* (3/6). Textual revisions.

SIN IN SPACE. *New York: Galaxy Publishing Corporation*, [*1961*].
Wrappers. No statement of printing on copyright page. *Beacon Book No. 312* (35¢). *Cyril Judd, pseudonym.* With C. M. KORNBLUTH. Revised edition of OUTPOST MARS.

SURVIVAL SHIP AND OTHER STORIES. *Toronto: Kakabeka Publishing Company*, [*1974*].
Wrappers. No statement of printing on copyright page. *Kak Min. Books 919588* ($1.95). Note: Copyright page lists ISBN numbers for two issues, "paper" and "cloth," but no hardcover issue was published.

THE TOMORROW PEOPLE. *New York: Pyramid Books*, [*1960*].
Wrappers. *First printing: May 1960* on copyright page. *Pyramid G502* (35¢).

Edited Fiction

The Best of Sci-Fi. [*London*]: *A Mayflower Paperback*, [*1963*].
Wrappers. *First publication in Great Britain . . . 1963* on copyright page. *Mayflower Dell 0543–8* (5/–). Edited, with introduction and afterword, by Merril. Issued earlier in the U.S. as *The 6th Annual of the Year's Best S-F.*

The Best of Sci Fi—Two. [*London*]: *A Mayflower-Dell Paperback*, [*1964*].
Wrappers. *First publication in Great Britain . . . 1964* on copyright page. *Mayflower Dell 9773* (5/–). Edited, with afterword, by Merril. Issued earlier in the U.S. as *The 7th Annual of the Year's Best S-F.*

The Best of Sci-Fi No. 4. [*London*]: *A Mayflower-Dell Paperback*, [*1965*].
   Wrappers. *First publication in Great Britain . . . August 1965* on copyright page.
   Mayflower Dell 0544 (5/–). Edited, with afterword, by Merril. Issued earlier in the U.S. as
   The 8th Annual of the Year's Best SF.

The Best of Sci-Fi 5. [*London*]: *A Mayflower-Dell Paperback*, [*1966*].
   Wrappers. *First publication in Great Britain/Published . . . October 1966* on copyright
   page. *Mayflower-Dell 0531* (5/–). Edited, with introduction and notes, by Merril. Issued
   earlier in the U.S. as *The 5th Annual of the Year's Best S-F*.

The Best of Sci-Fi No. 9. See 9th Annual of the Year's Best SF.

The Best of Sci-Fi No. 10. See 10th Annual Edition of the Year's Best SF.

The Best of Sci-Fi 12. [*London*]: *A Mayflower Paperback*, [*1970*].
   Wrappers. *First published in Great Britain . . . 1970* on copyright page. *Mayflower
   Science Fiction 583 11784 8* (35p). Edited, with introduction and notes, by Merril. Issued
   earlier in the U.S. as *SF 12*.

Beyond Human Ken. *New York: Random House*, [*1952*].
   Boards with cloth shelf back. First printing so stated on copyright page. Edited, with
   preface, by Merril. Abridged collection reprinted as *Selections From Beyond Human Ken*.

   ALSO:*London: Grayson & Grayson, Ltd.*, [*1953*]. Boards. *First published in Great Britain
   in 1953* on copyright page. Abridged reprint. Collects fifteen of the twenty-one stories.

Beyond the Barriers of Space and Time. *New York: Random House*, [*1954*].
   First printing so stated on copyright page. Edited, with preface, by Merril.

The 8th Annual of the Year's Best SF. *New York: Simon and Schuster, 1963*.
   Boards. First printing so stated on copyright page. Edited, with afterword, by Merril.
   Issued later in Great Britain as *The Best of Sci-Fi No. 4*.

11th Annual Edition the Year's Best S-F. *New York: Delacorte Press*, [*1966*].
   First printing so stated on copyright page. Edited, with introduction, afterword, and notes,
   by Merril.

England Swings SF. *Garden City: Doubleday & Company, Inc., 1968*.
   First edition so stated on copyright page. Edited, with introduction, by Merril. Abridged
   collection issued later in Great Britain as *The Space-Time Journal*.

The 5th Annual of the Year's Best S-F. *New York: Simon and Schuster, 1960*.
   Boards with cloth shelf back. First printing so stated on copyright page. Edited, with
   introduction and afterword, by Merril. Issued later in Great Britain as *The Best of Sci-Fi
   No. 5*.

Galaxy of Ghouls. *New York: A Lion Library Edition*, [*1955*].
   Wrappers. *Lion Library Edition published May, 1955* on copyright page. *Lion Library
   LL25* (35¢). Edited, with notes, by Merril. Reissued as *Off the Beaten Orbit*.

Human? *New York: A Lion Book*, [*1954*].
   Wrappers. *Lion edition published April, 1954* on copyright page. *A Lion Book 205* (25¢).
   Edited, with introductions and notes, by Merril.

The 9th Annual of the Year's Best SF. *New York: Simon and Schuster, 1964*.
   Boards. First printing so stated on copyright page. Edited, with preface and afterword, by
   Merril. Issued later in Great Britain as *9th Annual S-F* (cover title reads *The Best of
   Sci-Fi/9th Annual S-F*).

Off the Beaten Orbit. *New York: Pyramid Books, [1959]*.
   Wrappers. *Pyramid Books Edition 1959* on copyright page. *Pyramid G397* (35¢). Edited, with notes, by Merril. Reissue of *Galaxy of Ghouls*.

Selections From Beyond Human Ken. *New York: Pennant Books, [1954]*.
   Wrappers. *Pennant Edition Published June, 1954/1st Printing . . . May, 1954* on copyright page. *Pennant Books P56* (25¢). Edited, with notes, by Merril. Reprints twelve stories from *Beyond Human Ken*.

The 7th Annual of the Year's Best S-F. *New York: Simon and Schuster, 1962*.
   Boards with cloth shelf back. First printing so stated on copyright page. Edited, with afterword, by Merril. Issued later in Great Britain as *The Best of Sci Fi—Two*.

SF the Best of the Best. *New York: Delacorte Press, [1967]*.
   First printing so stated on copyright page. Edited, with introduction, by Merril.

S-F the Year's Greatest Science-Fiction and Fantasy. *[New York: Dell Publishing Company, Inc., 1956.]*
   Wrappers. No statement of printing on copyright page. *Dell First Edition B103* (35¢). Edited, with preface and afterword, by Merril.

   ALSO: *New York: Gnome Press, Inc. Publishers, [1956]*. Two bindings, probable priority as listed: (A) Cloth; (B) Boards. First edition so stated on copyright page. Note: Dell and Gnome Press editions published simultaneously.

SF the Year's Greatest Science-Fiction and Fantasy: Second Annual Volume. *[New York: Dell Publishing Company, Inc., 1957.]*
   Wrappers. *First printing—June, 1957* on copyright page. *Dell First Edition B110* (35¢). Edited, with afterword, by Merril.

   ALSO: SF: '57. *New York: The Gnome Press Inc., [1957]*. First edition so stated on copyright page. Note: Dell and Gnome Press editions published simultaneously.

SF the Year's Greatest Science-Fiction and Fantasy: Third Annual Volume. *[New York: Dell Publishing Company, Inc., 1958.]*
   Wrappers. *First printing—July, 1958* on copyright page. *Dell First Edition B119* (35¢). Edited, with introduction, afterword and article, by Merril.

   ALSO: SF: '58. *Hicksville, New York: The Gnome Press, [1958]*. Two bindings, probable priority as listed: (A) Boards; (B) Cloth. First printing so stated on copyright page. Note: Dell and Gnome Press editions published simultaneously.

SF the Year's Greatest Science-Fiction and Fantasy: Fourth Annual Volume. *[New York: Dell Publishing Company, Inc., 1959.]*
   Wrappers. *First printing—June, 1959* on copyright page. *Dell First Edition B129* (35¢). Edited, with introduction, afterword, and article, by Merril.

   ALSO: SF: '59. *Hicksville, New York: The Gnome Press Inc., [1959]*. Three bindings, probable priority as listed: (A) Red boards; (B) Green boards; (C) Red cloth. First printing so stated on copyright page. Note: Dell and Gnome Press editions published simultaneously.

SF 12. *[New York]: Delacorte Press, [1968]*.
   Boards with cloth shelf back. First printing so stated on copyright page. Edited, with introduction and notes, by Merril. Issued later in Great Britain as *The Best of Sci-Fi 12*.

Shot in the Dark. *New York: Bantam Books, [1950]*.
   Wrappers. *Published January 1950* on copyright page. *A Bantam Book 751* (25¢). Edited by Merril.

The 6th Annual of the Year's Best S-F. *New York: Simon and Schuster, 1961*.
Boards. First printing so stated on copyright page. Edited, with introduction and afterword,
by Merril. Issued later in Great Britain as *The Best of Sci-Fi*.

The Space-Time Journal. *[London]: Panther, [1972]*.
Wrappers. *First published in 1972* on copyright page. *Panther Science Fiction 586 03837
X* (30p). Edited by Merril. Reprints twenty-one stories from *England Swings SF*.

10th Annual Edition the Year's Best SF. *New York: Delacorte Press, [1965]*.
First printing so stated on copyright page. Edited, with afterword, by Merril. Issued later in
Great Britain as *10th Annual S-F*. Note: "The Best of Sci-Fi No. 10" does not appear on
the title page or cover, although it is so listed by *Whitaker's Cumulative Book List*.

Abraham Merritt

(1884–1943)

THE BLACK WHEEL. *New York: New Collectors' Group, 1947.*
Two bindings, priority as listed: (A) Title set in three lines on front cover *THE/BLACK/ WHEEL*. Issued in plain white paper dust jacket. (B) Title set in one line. Issued in printed yellow dust jacket. Note: This state comprises sheets bound by fantasy collector/dealer Julius Unger. First edition so stated on copyright page. Limited to 1000 numbered copies. This fantasy by Merritt was completed by HANNES BOK. Notes: (1) Observed with and without cancel copyright notice affixed to copyright page. (2) Although stated limitation was 1000 copies, more were printed. Unnumbered copies have been observed.

BURN WITCH BURN! *New York: Liveright • Inc • Publishers, [1933].*
No statement of printing on copyright page.

THE CHALLENGE FROM BEYOND. *N.p.: [A Weltschmerz Publication/Bill Evans/Franklin Kerkhof, Printer/The Pennsylvania Dutch Cheese Press/February 1954].*
Self wrappers. No statement of printing. Mimeographed, stapled. Cover title. With ROBERT E. HOWARD, FRANK BELKNAP LONG, H. P. LOVECRAFT, and C. L. MOORE. Notes: (1) Published by William H. Evans for distribution through the Fantasy Amateur Press Association (FAPA). (2) Not to be confused with a booklet of identical title and format with a different round-robin story by Stanley G. Weinbaum and others.

CREEP, SHADOW! *Garden City: Doubleday, Doran & Company, Inc., 1934.*
First edition so stated on copyright page.

THE DRONE MAN. *N.p., n.d. [but 1948].*
Wrappers. No statement of printing on copyright page. Mimeographed, stapled. Collected later in THE FOX WOMAN & OTHER STORIES.

DWELLERS IN THE MIRAGE. *New York: Liveright • Inc • Publishers, [1932].*
No statement of printing on copyright page.

ALSO: *New York: Avon Book Company, [1944].* Wrappers. No statement of printing on copyright page. *Murder Mystery Monthly 24* (25¢). Note: Restores the original "unhappy" ending published in *Argosy,* 23 January–27 February 1932.

DWELLERS IN THE MIRAGE AND THE FACE IN THE ABYSS. *New York: Liveright Publishing Corporation, [1953].*
No statement of printing on copyright page. Reprint. Collects DWELLERS IN THE MIRAGE and THE FACE IN THE ABYSS.

THE FACE IN THE ABYSS. *New York: Horace Liveright, Inc., [1931].*
No statement of printing on copyright page.

THE FOX WOMAN/THE BLUE PAGODA. *New York: New Collectors Group, 1946.*
Two bindings, priority as listed: (A) Tight weave mesh (nearly smooth) black cloth. Issued in plain paper dust jacket. (B) Glossy pebbled black cloth. Issued without dust jacket. Two states, simultaneous issue: (A) Illustration on page [19] depicting nude woman; (B) Illustration on page [19] depicting nude man. First edition so stated on copyright page. Contains "The Fox Woman," a short fantasy by Merritt completed by HANNES BOK, and Bok's short story "The Blue Pagoda." Notes: (1) Although stated limitation was 1000 copies, more

were printed. Unnumbered copies have been observed; in some cases booksellers numbered them. (2) It is possible that part of the edition was never bound. A number of sets of gathered and padded sheets lacking cloth casing have been observed.

THE FOX WOMAN & OTHER STORIES. *New York: Avon Publishing Company, Inc.*, [*1949*].
Wrappers. No statement of printing on copyright page. *Avon 214* (25¢). Note: 300 copies were hardbound by Lloyd A. Eshbach. "I bound 300 copies, most of them in black pebble cloth, though I believe there were also a few in a light blue cloth, the bindery running out of the black stuff. . . .I sold them at $3.00 per copy . . ." (letter from Eshbach to the compiler).

THE METAL MONSTER. *New York: Avon Book Company*, [*1946*].
Wrappers. No statement of printing on copyright page. *Murder Mystery Monthly 41* (25¢).

ALSO: *Westport, Connecticut: Hyperion Press, Inc.*, [*1974*]. Hyperion reprint edition 1974 on copyright page. First hardcover edition. Note: Not issued in dust jacket.

THE MOON POOL. *New York and London: G. P. Putnam's Sons, 1919*.
Two printings, priority as listed: (A) No advertisement on page [434]; sheets bulk 3.2 cm; *Putnam* is set in upper- and lowercase letters at base of spine. (B) Advertisement on page [434]; sheets bulk 2.6 cm; *PUTNAM* is set in capital letters at base of spine. Note: Later Liveright printings delete a portion of the conclusion and retitle the final chapter.

THE PEOPLE OF THE PIT. *N.p., n.d.* [*but 1948*].
Wrappers. No statement of printing on copyright page. Mimeographed, stapled. Collected later in THE FOX WOMAN & OTHER STORIES.

RHYTHM OF THE SPHERES. *N.p., n.d.* [*but 1948*].
Wrappers. No statement of printing. Mimeographed, stapled. Caption title. Collected later as "The Last Poet and the Robots" in THE FOX WOMAN & OTHER STORIES.

7 FOOTPRINTS TO SATAN. *New York: Boni and Liveright, 1928*.
No statement of printing on copyright page. Boni and Liveright monogram on copyright page.

SEVEN FOOTPRINTS TO SATAN AND BURN WITCH BURN! *New York: Liveright Publishing Corporation*, [*1952*].
No statement of printing on copyright page. Reprint. Collects 7 FOOTPRINTS TO SATAN and BURN WITCH BURN!

THE SHIP OF ISHTAR. *New York and London: G. P. Putnam's Sons, 1926*.
Numerous bindings, no priority established: (A) Red-brown mesh weave cloth with orange lettering, top edge not stained (dedication copy so bound); (B) Red-brown mesh weave cloth with tan lettering, top edge stained red; (C) Red-brown mesh weave cloth with yellow lettering, top edge not stained; (D) Red mesh weave cloth with yellow lettering, top edge not stained; (E) Copies reported in light and dark brown cloth with orange lettering, red-brown cloth with cream lettering, green cloth with yellow lettering, green cloth with lime lettering, red cloth with black lettering, and blue cloth with black lettering, with cloth types ranging from smooth to mesh weave. No statement of printing on copyright page. Seal of the Knickerbocker Press on copyright page. Note: Although Wentz notes "several printings" and G. Gordon Dewey in *Fantasy Advertiser*, December 1948 notes five "printings," there was but a single printing. According to Sam Moskowitz in *Explorers of the Infinite* (Cleveland: World, 1963), page 203, ". . . Putnam had been unable to sell a pitifully small edition of a thousand copies of *The Ship of Ishtar* in book form and the sheets for the last three hundred copies were finally purchased by Munsey, and were bound and distributed to readers of *Argosy—All-Story Magazine*."

ALSO: *Los Angeles* • *Toronto: Borden Publishing Company,* [*1949*]. The "Memorial Edition." No statement of printing on copyright page. Text differs; follows version published in *Argosy—All-Story Magazine* in 1924.

THREE LINES OF OLD FRENCH. *Milheim, Pennsylvania: The Bizarre Series, n.d.* [*but 1937*]. Wrappers. No statement of printing on copyright page. Issued as *Bizarre Number 1.* Note: Reviewed in *The Science Fiction News Letter,* 4 December 1937.

THRU THE DRAGON GLASS. *Jamaica, New York: The ARRA Printers, n.d.* [*but 1932*]. Wrappers. No statement of printing. Cover title. Note: Advertised in the September and October 1932 issues of the *Science Fiction Digest,* the latter announcement implying that it was available.

WOMAN OF THE WOOD. *N.p., n.d.* [*but 1948*]. Wrappers. No statement of printing. Mimeographed, stapled. Caption title. Collected later in THE FOX WOMAN & OTHER STORIES.

Reference

A. Merritt: A Bibliography of Fantastic Writings, [compiled by] Walter James Wentz. *Roseville, California: Published by George A. Bibby, 1965.* Wrappers. *First edition September, 1965* on title page. Also 25 numbered complimentary copies with a special title page.

Walter Michael Miller, Jr.
(b. 1923)

A CANTICLE FOR LEIBOWITZ. *Philadelphia & New York: J. B. Lippincott Company, 1960.*
Boards with cloth shelf back. First edition so stated on copyright page.

CONDITIONALLY HUMAN. *New York: Ballantine Books, [1962].*
Wrappers. No statement of printing on copyright page. *Ballantine Books F 626* (50¢).

ALSO: *London: Victor Gollancz Ltd, 1963.* Boards. No statement of printing on copyright page. First hardcover edition.

THE VIEW FROM THE STARS. *New York: Ballantine Books, [1965].*
Wrappers. *First Ballantine Printing: January 1965* on copyright page. *A Ballantine Science Fiction Original U2212* (50¢).

ALSO: *London: Victor Gollancz Ltd, 1965.* Boards. No statement of printing on copyright page. First hardcover edition.

Reference

*A Canticle for Leibowitz: Notes and Questions Prepared by Kenneth J. Weber. *Toronto: Macmillan, [1968].*
Wrappers?

Michael John Moorcock
(b. 1939)

THE ADVENTURES OF UNA PERSSON AND CATHERINE CORNELIUS IN THE TWENTIETH CENTURY. *London: Quartet Books, [1976].*
Boards. *First published . . . 1976* on copyright page. Note: A remainder issue was released circa Spring (?) 1979 comprising first printing sheets perfect bound, with dust jacket folded over unprinted stiff white wrappers.

AN ALIEN HEAT. *London: MacGibbon & Kee, [1972].*
Boards. *First published in Great Britain 1972* on copyright page.

THE BANE OF THE BLACK SWORD. *New York: DAW Books, Inc., [1977].*
Wrappers. *First DAW printing, August 1977/1 2 3 4 5 6 7 8 9* on copyright page. *DAW: sf Books No. 254 UY 1316* ($1.25). Publisher's note: "Part of this book originally appeared in a volume entitled *The Stealer of Souls* published in the U.S. by Lancer Books in 1967. This revised version contains a section never previously published in chronological sequence but which appeared out of context in a collection *The Singing Citadel* published in the U.S. by Berkley Medallion Books in 1970. This is the first time this revised edition has been published in any country."

THE BARBARIANS OF MARS. *London: Published by Roberts & Vinter Ltd, [1965].*
Wrappers. No statement of printing on copyright page. *Compact SF F291* (3/6). *Edward P Bradbury, pseudonym.* Reissued as THE MASTERS OF THE PIT.

BEHOLD THE MAN. *London: Allison & Busby, [1969].*
Boards. No statement of printing on copyright page.

THE BLACK CORRIDOR. *[London]: A Mayflower Paperback, [1969].*
Wrappers. *Mayflower Original 1969* on copyright page. *Mayflower 583 11640 x* (25p).

ALSO: *New York: An Ace Book, [1969].* Wrappers. No statement of printing on copyright page. *An Ace Science Fiction Special 06530* (75¢). Minor textual differences; slightly cut.

ALSO: *New York: Ace Books, Inc., [1970].* Boards. No statement of printing on copyright page. Code *16 L* at base of page 181. First hardcover edition. Note: Issued by the Science Fiction Book Club with, according to Moorcock, "a slightly, but crucially edited text."

BLADES OF MARS. *London: Compact Books, [1965].*
Wrappers. No statement of printing on copyright page. *Compact SF F279* (3/6). *Edward P Bradbury, pseudonym.* Reissued as THE LORD OF THE SPIDERS.

THE BLOOD RED GAME. *London: Sphere Books Limited, [1970].*
Wrappers. *First Sphere Books Edition 1970* on copyright page. *Sphere Science Fiction 62154* (5/–). Reissue of THE SUNDERED WORLDS.

BREAKFAST IN THE RUINS. *[London]: New English Library, [1972].*
Boards. *First N E L hardback edition 1972* on copyright page.

THE BULL AND THE SPEAR. *[London]: Allison & Busby, [1973].*
Boards. No statement of printing on copyright page.

CARIBBEAN CRISIS. *London: Sexton Blake Library Fleetway Publications Ltd., [1962].*
Wrappers. *First Printing, June 1962* on copyright page. *Sexton Blake Library No. 501* (1'). *Desmond Reid, pseudonym.* Note: Desmond Reid is a house pseudonym and this is the only time it was used by Moorcock. Written in collaboration with Jim Cawthorn.

THE CHAMPION OF GARATHORM. [*London*]: *Mayflower*, [*1973*].
Wrappers. *First published in 1973* . . . on copyright page. *Mayflower 583 12199 3* (30p).

THE CHINESE AGENT. [*New York*]: *The Macmillan Company*, [*1970*].
Boards. First printing so stated on copyright page. Note: Extensively rewritten version of SOMEWHERE IN THE NIGHT.

THE CITY OF THE BEAST. *New York: Lancer Books*, [*1970*].
Wrappers. No statement of printing on copyright page. *Lancer Books 74668–075* (75¢). Published earlier in Great Britain and in the U.S. (Lancer, 1966) as WARRIORS OF MARS under the pseudonym Edward P Bradbury. Note: The 1970 Lancer edition is the first to acknowledge Moorcock's authorship and the first to carry the title THE CITY OF THE BEAST.

THE CONDITION OF MUZAK. *London: Allison & Busby*, [*1977*].
Two issues, no priority: (A) Boards; (B) Wrappers. *ISBN: 0 85031 214 0* (£1.95). No statement of printing on copyright page. Later collected with some textual changes in THE CORNELIUS CHRONICLES.

THE CORNELIUS CHRONICLES. [*New York*]: *Avon*, [*1977*].
Wrappers. *First Avon Printing, August, 1977* on copyright page. *Avon 31468* ($2.95). Reprint. Collects THE FINAL PROGRAMME, A CURE FOR CANCER, THE ENGLISH ASSASSIN, and THE CONDITION OF MUZAK. The four novels have minor textual revisions by Moorcock for this edition.

COUNT BRASS. [*London*]: *Mayflower*, [*1973*].
Wrappers. *First published in 1973* . . . on copyright page. *Mayflower Science Fantasy 583 121198 5* (30p).

A CURE FOR CANCER. *London: Allison & Busby*, [*1971*].
Two bindings, priority as listed: (A) Brown boards, spine lettered in gold; buff endpapers; triple sewn; dust jacket on white stock printed in brown and orange, price at base of front flap £1.50/30s. (B) Black boards, spine lettered in gold; white endpapers; quadruple sewn; dust jacket on white stock printed in black and green, price at base of front flap £3.50. Not issued prior to 1976. No statement of printing on copyright page. Later collected with some textual changes in THE CORNELIUS CHRONICLES.

THE DEEP FIX. *London: Published by Roberts & Vinter Ltd*, [*1966*].
Wrappers. No statement of printing on copyright page. *Compact SF F305* (3/6). *James Colvin, pseudonym.*

THE DISTANT SUNS. [*Nant Gwilw, Llanfynydd, Carmarthen, Dyfed: Unicorn, 1975.*]
Wrappers. No statement of printing on copyright page. Caption title. *Unicorn SF* (75p). With PHILIP JAMES (pseudonym of James Cawthorn).

THE DREAMING CITY. *New York: Lancer Books*, [*1972*].
Wrappers. No statement of printing on copyright page. *Lancer Books 75376–095* (95¢). An edited version of ELRIC OF MELNIBONÉ with changes not authorized by Moorcock.

ELRIC OF MELNIBONÉ. *London: Hutchinson*, [*1972*].
Boards. *First published 1972* on copyright page. Issued later in the U.S. with unauthorized changes as THE DREAMING CITY.

ELRIC THE RETURN TO MELNIBONÉ. [*Brighton: Unicorn Bookshop, 1973.*]
Wrappers. No statement of printing. Cover title. Pictorial format with graphics by Philippe Druillet.

THE END OF ALL SONGS. *New York, Hagerstown San Francisco London: Harper & Row, Publishers*, [*1976*].
  Boards with cloth shelf back. First edition so stated on copyright page. Note: Author's name misspelled *Moorock* on spine.

THE ENGLISH ASSASSIN. *London: Allison & Busby*, [*1972*].
  Boards. *First published in Great Britain in 1972* on copyright page. Later collected with some textual changes in THE CORNELIUS CHRONICLES.

THE ETERNAL CHAMPION. [*New York*]: *A Dell Book*, [*1970*].
  Wrappers. *First printing—April 1970* on copyright page. *Dell 2383* (60¢).

THE FINAL PROGRAMME. [*New York*]: *An Avon Book*, [*1968*].
  Wrappers. *First Avon Printing, March, 1968* on copyright page. *Avon Original S351* (60¢). Contains many unauthorized textual changes.

  ALSO: [*London*]: *Allison & Busby*, [*1969*]. Boards. *First published in Great Britain 1969* on copyright page. First hardcover edition. Text follows the original manuscript. Later collected with some textual changes in THE CORNELIUS CHRONICLES.

THE FIRECLOWN. *London: Published by Roberts & Vinter Ltd*, [*1965*].
  Wrappers. No statement of printing on copyright page. *Compact SF F281* (3/6). Reissued as THE WINDS OF LIMBO.

THE HOLLOW LANDS. *New York, Evanston, San Francisco, London: Harper & Row, Publishers*, [*1974*].
  Boards with cloth shelf back. First edition so stated on copyright page.

THE ICE SCHOONER. *London: Sphere Books Limited*, [*1969*].
  Wrappers. *First published in Great Britain in 1969 . . .* on copyright page. *Sphere Science Fiction 62162* (5/0).

  ALSO: *New York, Hagerstown, San Francisco, London: Harper & Row, Publishers*, [*1977*]. Boards. Code *77 78 79 80 10 9 8 7 6 5 4 3 2 1* on copyright page. First hardcover edition. Includes textual revisions by the author.

THE JADE MAN'S EYES. *Brighton-Seattle: Unicorn Bookshop*, [*1973*].
  Wrappers. No statement of printing on copyright page.

THE JEWEL IN THE SKULL. *New York: Lancer Books*, [*1967*].
  Wrappers. *A Lancer Book • 1967* on copyright page. *Lancer Books 73–688* (60¢).

  ALSO: *London and New York: White Lion Publishers*, [*1973*]. Boards. *This White Lion edition, 1973* on copyright page. First hardcover edition.

  ALSO: *New York: DAW Books, Inc.*, [*1977*]. Wrappers. *First DAW printing, January 1977/1 2 3 4 5 6 7 8 9* on copyright page. *DAW: sf Books No. 225 UY1276* ($1.25). Revised text.

THE KING OF THE SWORDS. [*New York*]: *Published by Berkley Publishing Corporation*, [*1971*].
  Wrappers. *October, 1971* on copyright page. *A Berkley Medallion Book S2070* (75¢).

THE KNIGHT OF THE SWORDS. [*London*]: *Mayflower*, [*1971*].
  Wrappers. *First published in 1971* on copyright page. *Mayflower 583 11860 7* (25p).

  ALSO: *London: Allison & Busby*, [*1977*]. Boards. *Published in Great Britain 1977 . . .* on copyright page. First hardcover edition.

THE LAND LEVIATHAN. *London: Quartet Books,* [*1974*].
Two issues, no priority: (A) Boards; (B) Wrappers. [*Midway 7043 3013 X (£1.25).*] *First published . . . 1974* on copyright page.

LEGENDS FROM THE END OF TIME. *New York, Evanston, San Francisco, London: Harper & Row, Publishers,* [*1976*].
Boards with cloth shelf back. First edition so stated on copyright page.

THE LIVES AND TIMES OF JERRY CORNELIUS. *London: Allison and Busby,* [*1976*].
Boards. No statement of printing on copyright page.

THE LORD OF THE SPIDERS. *New York: Lancer Books,* [*1970*].
Wrappers. No statement of printing on copyright page. Two printings, probable priority as listed: (A) First title listed in publisher's advertisement on page [160] is *THE FANTASTIC FOUR;* edges stained purple; (B) First title listed in advertisement on page [160] is *CONAN THE WANDERER;* edges stained yellow. *Lancer Books 74736–075* (75¢). Issued earlier in Great Britain and the U.S. (Lancer, 1966) as BLADES OF MARS under the pseudonym Edward P Bradbury. Note: 1970 Lancer edition is the first to acknowledge Moorcock's authorship and the first to carry the title THE LORD OF THE SPIDERS.

THE LSD DOSSIER. *London: Published by Roberts & Vinter Ltd,* [*1966*].
Wrappers. No statement of printing on copyright page. *Compact F 303* (3/6). Note: This novel, written by and credited to Roger Harris, was anonymously rewritten by Moorcock.

THE MAD GOD'S AMULET. [*London*]: *A Mayflower Paperback,* [*1969*].
Wrappers. *First published in Great Britain . . . 1969* on copyright page. *Mayflower 113850* (3/6). Issued earlier in the U.S. as SORCERER'S AMULET.

ALSO: *London and New York: White Lion Publishers,* [*1973*]. Boards. *This White Lion edition, 1973* on copyright page. First hardcover edition.

ALSO: *New York: DAW Books, Inc.* [*1977*]. Wrappers. *First DAW printing, April 1977/1 2 3 4 5 6 7 8 9* on copyright page. *DAW: sf Books No. 238 UY1289* ($1.25). Revised text.

THE MASTERS OF THE PIT. *New York: Lancer Books,* [*1970*].
Wrappers. No statement of printing on copyright page. *Lancer Books 75199–095* (95¢). Issued earlier in Great Britain and the U.S. (Lancer, 1966) as THE BARBARIANS OF MARS under the pseudonym Edward P Bradbury. Note: 1970 Lancer edition is the first to acknowledge Moorcock's authorship and the first to carry the title THE MASTERS OF THE PIT.

MOORCOCK'S BOOK OF MARTYRS. *London: Quartet Books,* [*1976*].
Wrappers. *First published . . . 1976* on copyright page. *A Quartet Book 0 704 31265 4* (65p).

THE OAK AND THE RAM. [*London*]: *Allison & Busby,* [*1973*].
Boards. No statement of printing on copyright page.

PHOENIX IN OBSIDIAN. [*London*]: *A Mayflower Paperback,* [*1970*].
Wrappers. *First published . . . 1970* on copyright page. *Mayflower 583 11800 3* (5/–). Issued later in the U.S. as THE SILVER WARRIORS.

PRINTER'S DEVIL. *London: Published by Roberts & Vinter Ltd.,* [*1966*].
Wrappers. No statement of printing on copyright page. *Compact F322* (3/6). *Bill Barclay, pseudonym.*

THE QUEEN OF THE SWORDS. *[New York]: Published by Berkley Publishing Corporation,* *[1971]*.
   Wrappers. *August, 1971* on copyright page. *A Berkley Medallion Book S1999* (75¢).

THE QUEST FOR TANELORN. *[Frogmore]: Mayflower, [1975]*.
   Wrappers. *First published in 1975 . . .* on copyright page. *Mayflower 583 12200 0* (35p).

THE RITUALS OF INFINITY. *[London]: Arrow Books, [1971]*.
   Wrappers. *First published in book form by Arrow Books Ltd 1971* on copyright page. *SF 488* (25p). Note: Follows text of the original serial version in *New Worlds*, November 1965–January 1966, with minor revisions. Issued earlier in the U.S. with textual differences as THE WRECKS OF TIME.

THE RUNESTAFF. *[London]: A Mayflower Paperback, [1969]*.
   Wrappers. *A Mayflower Original 1969* on copyright page. *Mayflower 114997* (5/–). Issued earlier in the U.S. as THE SECRET OF THE RUNESTAFF.

   ALSO: *London and New York: White Lion Publishers, [1974]*. Boards. *First British Hard Cover Edition . . . 1974* on copyright page. First hardcover edition.

   ALSO: *New York: DAW Books, Inc., [1977]*. Wrappers. *First DAW printing, September 1977/1 2 3 4 5 6 7 8 9* on copyright page. *DAW: sf Books No. 257 UY1324* ($1.25). Revised text.

THE SAILOR ON THE SEAS OF FATE. *London: Quartet Books, [1976]*.
   Boards. *First published . . . 1976* on copyright page. Note: Originally announced as VOYAGE ON A DARK SHIP.

THE SECRET OF THE RUNESTAFF. *New York: Lancer Books, [1969]*.
   Wrappers. *A Lancer Book • 1969* on copyright page. *Lancer Books 73–824* (60¢). Issued later in Great Britain as THE RUNESTAFF.

THE SHORES OF DEATH. *London: Sphere Books Limited, [1970]*.
   Wrappers. *First Sphere Books edition, 1970* on copyright page. *Sphere Science Fiction 62146* (25p.) Reissue of THE TWILIGHT MAN.

THE SILVER WARRIORS. *[New York]: A Dell Book, [1973]*.
   Wrappers. *First printing—September, 1973* on copyright page. *Dell 7994* (95¢). Issued earlier in Great Britain as PHOENIX IN OBSIDIAN.

THE SINGING CITADEL. *[London]: A Mayflower Paperback, [1970]*.
   Wrappers. *Published . . . 1970* on copyright page. *Mayflower Science Fiction 583 116701* (25p).

THE SLEEPING SORCERESS. *[London]: New English Library, [1971]*.
   Boards. *First published 1971* on copyright page. Reissued in the U.S. as THE VANISHING TOWER.

   ALSO: *New York: Lancer Books, [1972]*. Wrappers. No statement of printing on copyright page. *Lancer Books 75375–095* (95¢). Unauthorized text, reedited without the author's consent.

SOJAN. *[Manchester]: Savoy, [1977]*.
   Wrappers. No statement of printing on copyright page.

SOMEWHERE IN THE NIGHT. *London: Published by Roberts & Vinter Ltd, [1966]*.
   Wrappers. No statement of printing on copyright page. *Compact F 309* (3/6). *Bill Barclay, pseudonym*. Later rewritten as THE CHINESE AGENT.

SORCERER'S AMULET. *New York: Lancer Books, [1968]*.
 Wrappers. *A Lancer Book • 1968* on copyright page. *Lancer Books 73–707* (60¢). Issued later in Great Britain as THE MAD GOD'S AMULET.

THE STEALER OF SOULS. *London: Neville Spearman Ltd, 1963*.
 Two bindings, priority as listed: (A) Orange boards, spine lettered in black; (B) Green boards, spine lettered in black. No statement of printing on copyright page.

STORMBRINGER. *London: Herbert Jenkins, [1965]*.
 Boards. *First published . . . 1965* on copyright page.

 ALSO: *New York: DAW Books, Inc., [1977]*. Wrappers. *First DAW printing, November 1977/1 2 3 4 5 6 7 8 9* on copyright page. *DAW: sf Books No. 264 UW 1335* ($1.50). First printing of the complete text.

THE SUNDERED WORLDS. *London: Published by Roberts & Vinter Ltd., [1965]*.
 Wrappers. No statement of printing on copyright page. *Compact SF F266* (3/6). Reissued as THE BLOOD RED GAME.

THE SWORD AND THE STALLION. *[New York]: Published by Berkley Publishing Corporation, [1974]*.
 Wrappers. *April, 1974* on copyright page. *A Berkley Medallion Book 425–02548–075* (75¢).

 ALSO: *[London]: Allison & Busby, [1974]*. Boards. No statement of printing on copyright page. First hardcover edition.

SWORD OF THE DAWN. *New York: Lancer Books, [1968]*.
 Wrappers. *A Lancer Book • 1968* on copyright page. *Lancer Books 73–761* (60¢).

 ALSO: *London and New York: White Lion Publishers, [1973]*. Boards. *First British Hard-Cover Edition . . . 1973* on copyright page. First hardcover edition.

 ALSO: *New York: DAW Books, Inc., [1977]*. Wrappers. *First DAW printing, July 1977/1 2 3 4 5 6 7 8 9* on copyright page. *DAW: sf Books No. 249 UYl310* ($1.25). Revised text.

THE SWORDS TRILOGY. *[New York]: Published by Berkley Publishing Corporation, [1977]*.
 Wrappers. *August, 1977* on copyright page. *A Berkley Medallion Book 0–425–03468–2* ($1.95). Reprint. Collects THE KNIGHT OF THE SWORDS, THE QUEEN OF THE SWORDS, and THE KING OF THE SWORDS.

THE TIME DWELLER. *London: Rupert Hart-Davis, 1969*.
 Boards. *First published 1969* on copyright page.

THE TRANSFORMATION OF MISS MAVIS MING. *London: W. H. Allen, 1977*.
 Boards. No statement of printing on copyright page.

THE TWILIGHT MAN. *London: Published by Roberts & Vinter Ltd., [1966]*.
 Wrappers. No statement of printing on copyright page. *Compact SF F313* (3/6). Reissued as THE SHORES OF DEATH.

THE VANISHING TOWER. *New York: DAW Books, Inc., [1977]*.
 Wrappers. *First DAW printing, June 1977/1 2 3 4 5 6 7 8 9* on copyright page. *DAW: sf Books No. 245 UYl304* ($1.25). Text of the 1970 New English Library edition published as THE SLEEPING SORCERESS.

THE WARLORD OF THE AIR. *New York: Ace Books, [1971]*.
 Wrappers. No statement of printing on copyright page. *Ace Book Science Fiction 87060* (75¢). Text follows the author's manuscript.

ALSO:[*London*]: *New English Library*, [*1971*]. Boards. *First published 1971* on copyright page. First hardcover edition. Text edited by the publisher.

WARRIORS OF MARS. *London: Published by Roberts & Vinter Ltd*, [*1965*].
Wrappers. No statement of printing on copyright page. *Compact SF F275* (3/6). *Edward P Bradbury, pseudonym*. Reissued as THE CITY OF THE BEAST.

THE WEIRD OF THE WHITE WOLF. *New York: DAW Books, Inc.*, [*1977*].
Wrappers. *First DAW printing, March 1977/1 2 3 4 5 6 7 8 9* on copyright page. *DAW: sf Books No. 233 UY1286* ($1.25). Publisher's note: "Part of this book originally appeared in a volume entitled *The Stealer of Souls*, published in the U.S.A. by Lancer Books in 1967. This revised version contains two sections never previously published in chronological sequence but which appeared out of context in a collection entitled *The Singing Citadel* published in the U.S.A. by Berkley Medallion Books in 1970. This is the first time this revised edition has been published in any country."

THE WINDS OF LIMBO. *New York: Paperback Library*, [*1969*].
Wrappers. *Second Printing: July, 1969* on copyright page. *Paperback Library 63–149* (60¢). Reissue of THE FIRE CLOWN. Note: First printing with this unauthorized title change.

THE WRECKS OF TIME. *New York: Ace Books, Inc.*, [*1967*].
Wrappers. No statement of printing on copyright page. *Ace Double H–36* (60¢). Bound with TRAMONTANE by Emil Petaja. Note: A copy-edited version of the original *New Worlds* text. Issued later with original text as THE RITUALS OF INFINITY.

Associational

Queens of Deliria, [by] Michael Butterworth. [*London*]: *A Star Book*, [*1977*].
Wrappers. *Published in 1977 . . .* on copyright page. *Star 39602* (80p). This novel by Butterworth is developed from an idea by Moorcock. A sequel to *The Time of the Hawklords*.

The Time of the Hawklords, [by] Michael Moorcock and Michael Butterworth.
[*Henley-on-Thames*]: *Aidan Ellis*, [*1976*].
Boards. No statement of printing on copyright page. Although Moorcock is credited with joint authorship of this novel, it was written entirely by Butterworth. Moorcock notes in a letter to the compiler, "Only broad idea was mine."

Edited Fiction

Before Armageddon. *London: W. H. Allen*, *1975*.
Boards. No statement of printing on copyright page. Edited, with introduction, by Moorcock.

The Best of New Worlds. *London: Published by Roberts & Vinter Ltd*, [*1965*].
Wrappers. No statement of printing on copyright page. *Compact SF H287* (5/–). Edited, with introduction and short story "The Time Dweller," by Moorcock.

Best S.F. Stories from New Worlds. [*London*]: *A Panther Book*, [*1967*].
Wrappers. *First published . . . 1967* on copyright page. *Panther Books 2243* (3/6). Edited, with introduction, by Moorcock.

Best S.F. Stories from New Worlds 2. [*London*]: *A Panther Book*, [*1968*].
Wrappers. *First published . . . 1968* on copyright page. *Panther Books 23690* (3/6). Edited, with introduction, by Moorcock.

Best S.F. Stories from New Worlds 3. [*London*]: *Panther Science Fiction*, [*1968*].
Wrappers. *First published . . . 1968* on copyright page. *Panther Books 24956* (3/6).
Edited, with introduction, by Moorcock.

Best SF Stories from New Worlds 4. [*London*]: *Panther Science Fiction*, [*1969*].
Wrappers. *First published by Panther Books 1969* on copyright page. *Panther Science Fiction 027947* (25p). Edited, with introduction, by Moorcock.

Best S.F. Stories from New Worlds 5. [*London*]: *Panther Science Fiction*, [*1969*].
Wrappers. *First published . . . 1969* on copyright page. *Panther 586 02964 8* (5/–). Edited, with introduction, by Moorcock.

Best S.F. Stories from New Worlds 6. [*London*]: *Panther Science Fiction*, [*1970*].
Wrappers. *First published . . . 1970* on copyright page. *Panther 586 03283 5* (25p). Edited, with introduction and short story "The Delhi Division," by Moorcock.

Best S.F. Stories from New Worlds 7. [*London*]: *Panther Science Fiction*, [*1971*].
Wrappers. *First published . . . 1971* on copyright page. *Panther 586 03449 8* (25p). Edited, with introduction and short story "The Tank Trapeze," by Moorcock.

Best S.F. Stories from New Worlds 8. [*Frogmore*]: *Panther*, [*1974*].
Wrappers. *First published in 1974* on copyright page. *Panther Science Fiction 586 03803 5* (35p). Edited by Moorcock.

England Invaded. *London: W. H. Allen, 1977.*
Boards. No statement of printing on copyright page. Edited, with introduction, by Moorcock.

The Inner Landscape. *London: Allison & Busby,* [*1969*].
Boards. *First published in Great Britain 1969* on copyright page. Edited anonymously by Moorcock.

The Nature of the Catastrophe. *London: Hutchinson,* [*1971*].
Boards. *First published 1971* on copyright page. Edited by Moorcock with LANGDON JONES. Includes five short stories by Moorcock.

New Worlds Quarterly. *London: Sphere Books Limited,* [*1971*].
Wrappers. *First published . . . 1971 . . .* on copyright page. *Sphere SF 62081* (5/–). Edited, with introduction, by Moorcock. Note: Cover title reads *NEW/WORLDS 1/THE SCIENCE FICTION/QUARTERLY.*

New Worlds Quarterly 2. *London: Sphere Books Limited,* [*1971*].
Wrappers. *First published . . . 1971 . . .* on copyright page. *Sphere SF 62103* (6/–). Edited, with introduction, by Moorcock. Note: Cover title reads *NEW/WORLDS 2/THE SCIENCE FICTION/QUARTERLY.*

New Worlds Quarterly 3. *London: Sphere Books Limited,* [*1972*].
Wrappers. *First published . . . 1972 . . .* on copyright page. *Sphere 62111* (30p). Edited, with introduction, by Moorcock.

New Worlds Quarterly 4. *London: Sphere Books Limited,* [*1972*].
Wrappers. *First published . . . 1972 . . .* on copyright page. *Sphere 62200* (35p). Edited by Moorcock.

New Worlds Quarterly 5. *London: Sphere Books Limited,* [*1973*].
Wrappers. *First published in Great Britain in 1973 . . .* on copyright page. *Sphere 62006* (40p). Edited, with introduction, by Moorcock. Note: Cover title reads *NEW/WORLDS 5.*

New Worlds 6: The Science Fiction Quarterly. *London: Sphere Books Limited,* [*1973*].
   Wrappers. *First published in Great Britain . . . 1973* on copyright page. Sphere *0 7221
   6201 4* (40p). Edited, with introduction, by Moorcock. With CHARLES PLATT. Note: Published in the U.S. in 1974 by Avon as *New Worlds #5.*

The Traps of Time. *London: Rapp & Whiting,* [*1968*].
   Boards. *First published in Great Britain 1968* on copyright page. Edited, with introduction, by Moorcock.

Reference

The Chronicles of Moorcock, compiled by A. J. Callow. [*Worcester: Published by A. J.
Callow, 1978.*]
   Wrappers. *First edition published in Great Britain in 1978* on copyright page. Offset from
   typewritten copy. Cover title reads: *The Chronicles of Moorcock a Bibliography.*

Michael Moorcock: A Bibliography, [by] Andrew Harper & George McAulay. [*Baltimore:
T–K Graphics, 1976.*]
   Wrappers. No statement of printing.

Catherine Lucile Moore
(Catherine Kuttner Reggie)
(b. 1911)

THE BEST OF C. L. MOORE. *Garden City: Nelson Doubleday, Inc., [1975]*.
Boards. No statement of printing on copyright page. Code *42 R* on page 307. Note: Issued by the Science Fiction Book Club.

BEYOND EARTH'S GATES. *New York: Ace Books, Inc., [1954]*.
Wrappers. No statement of printing on copyright page. *Ace Double Novel Books D–69* (35¢). *Lewis Padgett, pseudonym*. With HENRY KUTTNER. Bound with DAYBREAK—2250 A.D. by Andre Norton.

BLACK GOD'S SHADOW. *West Kingston, Rhode Island: Donald M. Grant, Publisher, 1977*.
Two issues, no priority: (A) 149 numbered plus three special unnumbered copies signed by the author. In publisher's paper slipcase. (B) Trade issue of approximately 2250 copies. First edition so stated on copyright page. Reissue of JIREL OF JOIRY. First hardcover edition of this collection.

THE BRASS RING. *New York: Duell, Sloan and Pearce, [1946]*.
First printing so stated on copyright page. *Lewis Padgett, pseudonym*. With HENRY KUTT-NER. Reissued as MURDER IN BRASS.

THE CHALLENGE FROM BEYOND. *N.p.: [A Weltschmerz Publication/Bill Evans/Franklin Kerkhof, Printer/The Pennsylvania Dutch Cheese Press/February 1954]*.
Self wrappers. No statement of printing. Mimeographed, stapled. Cover title. With ROBERT E. HOWARD, FRANK BELKNAP LONG, H. P. LOVECRAFT, and A. MERRITT. Notes: (1) Published by William H. Evans for distribution through the Fantasy Amateur Press Association (FAPA). (2) Not to be confused with a booklet of identical title and format with a different round-robin story by Stanley G. Weinbaum and others.

CHESSBOARD PLANET. *New York: Galaxy Publishing Corp., [1956]*.
Wrappers. No statement of printing on copyright page. *Galaxy Novel 26* (35¢). *Lewis Padgett, pseudonym*. With HENRY KUTTNER. Reissue of THE FAIRY CHESSMEN (see TOMORROW AND TOMORROW AND THE FAIRY CHESSMEN).

THE DAY HE DIED. *New York: Duell, Sloan and Pearce, [1947]*.
First printing so stated on copyright page. *Lewis Padgett, pseudonym*. With HENRY KUTT-NER.

DESTINATION INFINITY. *New York: Avon Publications, Inc., [1958]*.
Wrappers. No statement of printing on copyright page. *Avon T–275* (35¢). Anonymous collaboration with HENRY KUTTNER. Reissue of FURY.

DOOMSDAY MORNING. *Garden City: Doubleday & Company, Inc., 1957*.
Boards. First edition so stated on copyright page.

EARTH'S LAST CITADEL. *New York: Ace Books, Inc., [1964]*.
Wrappers. No statement of printing on copyright page. *Ace Book F–306* (40¢). With HENRY KUTTNER.

THE FAR REALITY. *London: World Distributors*, [*1963*].
Wrappers. *This Consul edition, complete and unabridged, published in England, 1963 . . .* on copyright page. *Consul Books Selected Science Fiction 1266* (2'6). *Lewis Padgett, pseudonym.* With HENRY KUTTNER. Reissue of THE FAIRY CHESSMEN (see TOMORROW AND TOMORROW AND THE FAIRY CHESSMEN).

FURY. *New York: Grosset & Dunlap Publishers*, [*1950*].
Boards. No statement of printing on copyright page. Anonymous collaboration with HENRY KUTTNER. Reissued as DESTINATION INFINITY.

ALSO: *New York: Lancer Books*, [*1972*]. Wrappers. No statement of printing on copyright page. *Lancer Books 75413–095* (95¢). New introduction by Moore.

A GNOME THERE WAS. *New York: Simon and Schuster, 1950*.
Boards. No statement of printing on copyright page. *Lewis Padgett, pseudonym.* With HENRY KUTTNER.

JIREL OF JOIRY. *New York: Paperback Library*, [*1969*].
Wrappers. *First Printing: August, 1969* on copyright page. *Paperback Library Science Fantasy 63–166* (60¢). Reprint collection. All stories previously collected in SHAMBLEAU and NO BOUNDARIES. Reissued as BLACK GOD'S SHADOW.

JUDGMENT NIGHT. *New York: Gnome Press Publishers*, [*1952*].
Two bindings, priority as listed: (A) Cloth; (B) Boards. First edition so stated on copyright page.

LINE TO TOMORROW. *New York: Bantam Books*, [*1954*].
Wrappers. *A Bantam Book Published August, 1954* on copyright page. *Bantam Books 1251* (25¢). *Lewis Padgett, pseudonym.* With HENRY KUTTNER.

THE MASK OF CIRCE. *New York: Ace Books*, [*1971*].
Wrappers. No statement of printing on copyright page. *Ace Book SF 52075* (60¢). Anonymous collaboration with HENRY KUTTNER.

MURDER IN BRASS. *New York: Bantam Books*, [*1947*].
Wrappers. *Bantam Edition Published/August, 1947* on copyright page. *Bantam Books 107* (25¢). *Lewis Padgett, pseudonym.* With HENRY KUTTNER. Reissue of THE BRASS RING.

MUTANT. *New York: Gnome Press, Inc., Publishers*, [*1953*].
Boards. First edition so stated on copyright page. *Lewis Padgett, pseudonym.* With HENRY KUTTNER.

NO BOUNDARIES. *New York: Ballantine Books*, [*1955*].
Two bindings, no priority: (A) Cloth; (B) Wrappers. *Ballantine Books 122* (35¢). No statement of printing on copyright page. With HENRY KUTTNER.

NORTHWEST OF EARTH. *New York: Gnome Press, Inc. Publishers*, [*1954*].
Boards. First edition so stated on copyright page.

SHAMBLEAU AND OTHERS. *New York: Gnome Press, Inc. Publishers*, [*1953*].
Boards. First edition so stated on copyright page.

ALSO: SHAMBLEAU. *New York: Galaxy Publishing Corp.*, [*1958*]. Wrappers. *Reprinted by Galaxy Publishing Corporation . . .* on copyright page. *Galaxy Science Fiction Novel No. 31* (35¢). Abridged reprint. Contains three of the seven stories.

ALSO: SHAMBLEAU. *London: World Distributors*, [*1961*]. Wrappers. *This Consul edition published in England, 1961 . . .* on copyright page. *Consul Books SF 1009* (2'6). Abridged reprint. Contains six of the seven stories.

THE TIME AXIS.*New York: Ace Books, Inc.*, [*1965*].
 Wrappers. No statement of printing on copyright page. *Ace Science Fiction Classic F–356* (40¢). Anonymous collaboration with HENRY KUTTNER.

TOMORROW AND TOMORROW.*London: World Distributors*, [*1963*].
 Wrappers. *This Consul edition complete and unabridged, published in England, 1963 . . .* on copyright page. *Consul Books Selected Science Fiction 1265* (2'6). *Lewis Padgett, pseudonym*. With HENRY KUTTNER. Reprint. Collected earlier in TOMORROW AND TOMOR-ROW AND THE FAIRY CHESSMEN.

TOMORROW AND TOMORROW AND THE FAIRY CHESSMEN.*New York: Gnome Press, Inc. Publishers*, [*1951*].
 Boards. First edition so stated on copyright page. *Lewis Padgett, pseudonym*. With HENRY KUTTNER. THE FAIRY CHESSMEN was reissued as CHESSBOARD PLANET and later as THE FAR REALITY.

VALLEY OF THE FLAME.*New York: Ace Books, Inc.*, [*1964*].
 Wrappers. No statement of printing on copyright page. *Ace Book F–297* (40¢). Anonymous collaboration with HENRY KUTTNER.

WELL OF THE WORLDS.*New York: Galaxy Publishing Corp.*, [*1953*].
 Wrappers. No statement of printing on copyright page. *Galaxy Science Fiction Novel No. 17* (35¢). *Lewis Padgett, pseudonym*. With HENRY KUTTNER.

Sam Moskowitz

(b. 1920)

Nonfiction (Dealing with the Fantasy Genre only)

A Canticle for P. Schuyler Miller. [*Newark: Sam Moskowitz, 1975.*]
   Front wrapper only. *Published in a limited printing of not over 300 copies . . .* on page [1].
   Mimeographed. Cover title.

Charles Fort: A Radical Corpuscle. *Newark, N.J.: Sam Moskowitz, 1976.*
   Wrappers. No statement of printing. Mimeographed, stapled. Caption title. Approximately
   300 copies printed.

Explorers of the Infinite. *Cleveland and New York: The World Publishing Company, [1963].*
   First edition so stated on copyright page.

How Science Fiction Got Its Name. [*New York: Compliments of Hugo Gernsback*], n.d.
[*Circa 1957.*]
   Self wrappers. No statement of printing. Caption title. Cover title reads: *The Origin of the
   Term Science Fiction.* Note: Offprint from *The Magazine of Fantasy and Science Fiction,*
   February 1957.

Hugo Gernsback: Father of Science Fiction. *New York: Criterion Linotyping & Printing Co.,
Inc., 1959.*
   Wrappers. No statement of printing. 300 copies printed.

The Immortal Storm. *N.p.: Sam Moskowitz, November 1951.*
   Wrappers. No statement of printing. Mimeographed. 150 copies printed.

   ALSO:*Atlanta: The Atlanta Science Fiction Organization Press, 1954.* No statement of
   printing. 1000 copies printed. First hardcover edition.

Seekers of Tomorrow. *Cleveland and New York: The World Publishing Company, [1966].*
   First edition so stated on copyright page.

Strange Horizons: The Spectrum of Science Fiction. *New York: Charles Scribner's Sons,
[1976].*
   Boards. Code *1 3 5 7 9 11 13 15 17 19 H/C 20 18 16 14 12 10 8 6 4 2* on copyright page.

Edited Fiction

Alien Earth and Other Stories. [*New York*]: *A Macfadden-Bartell Book, [1969].*
   Wrappers. No statement of printing on copyright page. *MB 75–219 (75¢).* Edited by
   Moskowitz with ROGER ELWOOD.

Alien Worlds. *New York: Paperback Library, Inc., [1964].*
   Wrappers. *First Printing: September, 1964* on copyright page. *Paperback Library 52–320*
   (50¢). Compiled anonymously by Moskowitz. With ROGER ELWOOD.

The Award Science Fiction Reader. *New York: Award Books, [1966].*
   Wrappers. *First Printing 1966* on copyright page. *Award Books A 181X* (60¢). Compiled
   anonymously by Moskowitz, who also supplied the introduction bearing his byline. With
   ALDEN H. NORTON.

The Coming of the Robots. *New York: Collier Books, [1963].*
   Wrappers. First edition so stated on copyright page. *Collier AS 548* (95¢). Edited, with
   introduction, by Moskowitz.

Contact. *New York: Paperback Library, Inc., [1963].*
  Wrappers. *First Printing: May, 1963* on copyright page. *Paperback Library 52-211* (50¢).
  Edited, with introduction, by NOEL KEYES. Note: Moskowitz served as an anonymous
  collaborator and selected some of the contents of this book.

The Crystal Man, Landmark Science Fiction, by Edward Page Mitchell. *Garden City:*
Doubleday & Company, Inc., 1973.
  First edition so stated on copyright page. Edited, with introduction, by Moskowitz.

Doorway Into Time. *[New York]: A Macfadden-Bartell Book, [1966].*
  Wrappers. No statement of printing on copyright page. *Macfadden Books 50–311* (50¢).
  Edited, with introduction, by Moskowitz. Reprint. Collects six stories from *Modern Mas-*
  terpieces of Science Fiction.

Editor's Choice in Science Fiction. *New York: The McBride Company, [1954].*
  Boards. No statement of printing on copyright page. Compiled, with introduction, by
  Moskowitz.

Exploring Other Worlds. *New York: Collier Books, [1963].*
  Wrappers. First edition so stated on copyright page. *Collier AS 551* (95¢). Edited, with
  introduction and short story "Man of the Stars," by Moskowitz.

Futures to Infinity. *New York: Pyramid Books, [1970].*
  Wrappers. *First printing, September 1970* on copyright page. *Pyramid Science Fiction*
  T2312 (75¢). Edited, with notes and short story "The Way Back," by Moskowitz.

Ghostly by Gaslight. *New York: Pyramid Books, [1971].*
  Wrappers. *First printing, February 1971* on copyright page. *Pyramid T2416* (75¢). Edited,
  with introduction and notes, by Moskowitz with ALDEN H. NORTON.

Great Railroad Stories of the World. *New York: The McBride Company, [1954].*
  No statement of printing on copyright page. Edited, with notes, by Moskowitz. Note:
  Includes fiction and nonfiction selections.

Great Spy Novels and Stories. *New York: Pyramid Books, [1965].*
  Wrappers. *First printing, August 1965* on copyright page. *Pyramid Books R–1219* (50¢).
  Edited by Moskowitz with ROGER ELWOOD.

Great Untold Stories of Fantasy and Horror. *New York: Pyramid Books, [1969].*
  Wrappers. *First printing, October, 1969* on copyright page. *Pyramid Books T–2093* (75¢).
  Edited, with notes, by Moskowitz with ALDEN H. NORTON.

Hauntings and Horrors. *[New York]: Published by Berkley Publishing Corporation, [1969].*
  Wrappers. *March, 1969* on copyright page. *A Berkley Medallion Book X1674* (60¢).
  Compiled anonymously by Moskowitz. With ALDEN H. NORTON. Moskowitz is credited
  with the introduction and notes on the title page.

Horrors in Hiding. *[New York]: Published by Berkley Publishing Corporation, [1973].*
  Wrappers. *February, 1973* on copyright page. *A Berkley Medallion Book S2303* (75¢).
  Edited, with introduction, by Moskowitz with ALDEN H. NORTON.

Horror Times Ten. *[New York]: Published by Berkley Publishing Corporation, [1967].*
  Wrappers. *June, 1967* on copyright page. *Berkley X1414* (60¢). Compiled anonymously by
  Moskowitz. With ALDEN H. NORTON. Moskowitz is credited for notes on the title page.

Horrors Unknown. *New York: Walker and Company, [1971].*
  Boards. *First published in the United States of America in 1971 . . .* on copyright page.
  Edited, with introduction and notes, by Moskowitz.

Horrors Unseen. [*New York*]: *Published by Berkley Publishing Corporation*, [*1974*].
Wrappers. *June, 1974* on copyright page. *A Berkley Medallion Book 425–02583–075*
(75¢). Edited, with introduction and notes, by Moskowitz.

The Human Zero and Other Science-Fiction Masterpieces. [*New York*]: *A Tower Book*,
[*1967*].
Wrappers. No statement of printing on copyright page. *Tower 43–906* (60¢).

Invasion of the Robots. *New York: Paperback Library, Inc.*, [*1965*].
Wrappers. *First Printing: April, 1965* on copyright page. *Paperback Library 52–519*
(50¢). Compiled anonymously by Moskowitz. With ROGER ELWOOD.

Life Everlasting, by David H. Keller. *Newark, New Jersey: The Avalon Company, 1947*.
No statement of printing on copyright page. 1000 numbered copies. Edited, with introduction, by Moskowitz. With WILL SYKORA.

The Man Who Called Himself Poe. *Garden City: Doubleday & Company, Inc., 1969*.
First edition so stated on copyright page. Edited, with introduction and notes, by Moskowitz.

A Martian Odyssey, [by] Stanley Weinbaum. *New York: Lancer Books*, [*1962*].
Wrappers. No statement of printing on copyright page. *The Lancer Science Fiction Library 74–808* (75¢). Edited, with introduction, by Moskowitz.

A Martian Odyssey and Other Science Fiction Tales: The Collected Short Stories of Stanley
G. Weinbaum. *Westport, Connecticut: Hyperion Press, Inc.*, [*1974*].
Hyperion edition 1974 on copyright page. Collected, with introduction, by Moskowitz.
Note: Issued without dust jacket.

Masterpieces of Science Fiction. *Cleveland and New York: The World Publishing Company*,
[*1966*].
First edition so stated on copyright page. Edited, with introduction and notes, by Moskowitz.

Masters of Horror. [*New York*]: *Published by Berkley Publishing Corporation*, [*1968*].
Wrappers. *April, 1968* on copyright page. *Berkley X1497* (60¢). Compiled anonymously
by Moskowitz. With ALDEN H. NORTON. Moskowitz is credited with the introduction and
notes on the title page.

Microcosmic God and Other Stories from Modern Masterpieces of Science Fiction. [*New
York*]: *A Macfadden-Bartell Book*, [*1968*].
Wrappers. No statement of printing on copyright page. *Macfadden Books 60–335* (60¢).
Edited by Moskowitz. Reprint. Collects seven stories from *Modern Masterpieces of Science Fiction*.

Modern Masterpieces of Science Fiction. *Cleveland and New York: The World Publishing
Company*, [*1965*].
First edition so stated on copyright page. Edited, with introduction, by Moskowitz.

The Moon Era. *New York: Curtis Books*, [*1969*].
Wrappers. No statement of printing on copyright page. *Curtis Books 123–07014–075*
(75¢). Edited, with introduction, by Moskowitz. Issued earlier as *Three Stories*.

Other Worlds, Other Times. [*New York*]: *A Macfadden-Bartell Book*, [*1969*].
Wrappers. No statement of printing on copyright page. *Macfadden Books 75–238* (75¢).
Edited by Moskowitz with ROGER ELWOOD.

Out of the Storm: Uncollected Fantasies, by William Hope Hodgson. *West Kingston, Rhode Island: Donald M. Grant, Publisher, 1975.*
  First edition so stated on copyright page. Edited, with introduction, by Moskowitz.

The Pulps: Fifty Years of American Pop Culture, compiled and edited by Tony Goodstone. *New York: Chelsea House, [1970].*
  First edition so stated on copyright page. Moskowitz and his wife, Christine E. Haycock, collaborated with Goodstone in the compilation of this book.

Science Fiction by Gaslight: A History and Anthology of Science Fiction in Popular Magazines, 1891–1911. *Cleveland and New York: The World Publishing Company, [1968].*
  First printing so stated on copyright page. Edited, with preface, introduction, and notes, by Moskowitz.

A Sense of Wonder. *London: Sidgwick & Jackson, [1967].*
  Boards. *First published in Great Britain 1967* on copyright page. Edited, with introduction, by Moskowitz. The introduction is abridged. Issued earlier in the U.S. as *Three Stories.*

The Space Magicians. *New York: Pyramid Books, [1971].*
  Wrappers. *First printing, January 1971* on copyright page. *Pyramid Science Fiction T2393* (75¢). Edited, with notes, by Moskowitz with ALDEN H. NORTON.

Strange Signposts. *New York Chicago San Francisco: Holt, Rinehart and Winston, [1966].*
  Boards. First edition so stated on copyright page. Edited by Moskowitz with ROGER ELWOOD.

Three in One. *New York: Pyramid Books, [1963].*
  Wrappers. *First printing, August 1963* on copyright page. *Pyramid Books F–899* (40¢). Edited anonymously by Moskowitz. With LEO MARGULIES. Note: Although the introduction to this volume is credited to Margulies, in a letter to the compiler dated 2 December 1977 Moskowitz states that he wrote it.

Three Stories. *Garden City: Doubleday & Company, Inc., 1967.*
  First edition so stated on copyright page. Edited, with introduction, by Moskowitz. Issued later in Great Britain as *A Sense of Wonder* and in the U.S. as *The Moon Era.*

Three Times Infinity. *Greenwich, Conn.: Fawcett Publications, [1958].*
  Wrappers. *First Gold Medal Printing, January 1958* on copyright page. *Gold Medal Giant s726* (35¢). Compiled anonymously by Moskowitz. With LEO MARGULIES.

The Time Curve. *[New York]: A Tower Book, [1968].*
  Wrappers. No statement of printing on copyright page. *Tower 43–986* (60¢). Edited, with short story "Death of a Dinosaur," by Moskowitz. With ROGER ELWOOD.

Ultimate World, [by] Hugo Gernsback. *New York: Walker and Company, [1971].*
  Boards. *First published in the United States of America in 1971 . . .* on copyright page. Edited, with introduction, by Moskowitz.

Under the Moons of Mars: A History and Anthology of "The Scientific Romance" in the Munsey Magazines, 1912–1920. *New York Chicago San Francisco: Holt, Rinehart and Winston, [1970].*
  First edition so stated on copyright page. Edited, with preface, essay, and notes, by Moskowitz.

The Vortex Blasters and Other Stories from Modern Masterpieces of Science Fiction. [*New York*]: *A Macfadden-Bartell Book*, [*1968*].
>   Wrappers. No statement of printing on copyright page. *Macfadden Books 60–325* (60¢). Edited by Moskowitz. Reprint. Collects seven stories from *Modern Masterpieces of Science Fiction*.

Weird Tales. *New York: Pyramid Books*, [*1964*].
>   Wrappers. *Published May 1964* on copyright page. *Pyramid Books R–1029* (50¢). Compiled anonymously by Moskowitz. With LEO MARGULIES.

When Women Rule. *New York: Walker and Company*, [*1972*].
>   Boards. *First published in the United States of America in 1972* . . . on copyright page. Edited, with introduction, by Moskowitz.

Worlds of the Weird. *New York: Pyramid Books*, [*1965*].
>   Wrappers. *First printing, January 1965* on copyright page. *Pyramid Books R–1125* (50¢). Edited, with introduction and notes, by Moskowitz. With LEO MARGULIES.

Edited Nonfiction (Dealing with the Fantasy Genre only)

After Ten Years: A Tribute to Stanley G. Weinbaum 1902–1935. *Westwood, N.J.: Published by Gerry de la Ree, November, 1945*.
>   Wrappers. No statement of printing. Mimeographed, stapled. 100 copies printed. Compiled by Moskowitz and GERRY DE LA REE with an essay by the former.

John Middleton Murry
(b. 1926)

BREAKTHROUGH.*London: Dennis Dobson*, [*1967*].
Boards. *First published in Great Britain in 1967* on copyright page. *Richard Cowper, pseudonym.*

CLONE.*London: Victor Gollancz Ltd*, *1972*.
Boards. No statement of printing on copyright page. *Richard Cowper, pseudonym.*

THE CUSTODIANS AND OTHER STORIES.*London: Victor Gollancz Ltd*, *1976*.
Boards. No statement of printing on copyright page. *Richard Cowper, pseudonym.*

DOMINO.*London: Dennis Dobson*, [*1971*].
Boards. *First published in Great Britain in 1971* on copyright page. *Richard Cowper, pseudonym.*

THE GOLDEN VALLEY.*London: Hutchinson*, [*1958*].
Boards. *First published 1958* on copyright page. *Colin Murry, pseudonym.*

KULDESAK.*London: Victor Gollancz Ltd*, *1972*.
Boards. No statement of printing on copyright page. *Richard Cowper, pseudonym.*

A PATH TO THE SEA.*London: Hutchinson*, [*1961*].
Boards. *First published 1961* on copyright page. *Colin Murry, pseudonym.*

PHOENIX.*London: Dennis Dobson*, [*1968*].
Boards. *First published in Great Britain in 1968* on copyright page. *Richard Cowper, pseudonym.*

PRIVATE VIEW.*London: Dennis Dobson*, [*1972*].
Boards. *First published in 1972* on copyright page. *Colin Murry, pseudonym.*

RECOLLECTIONS OF A GHOST.*London: Hutchinson*, [*1960*].
Boards. *First published 1960* on copyright page. *Colin Murry, pseudonym.*

TIME OUT OF MIND.*London: Victor Gollancz Ltd*, *1973*.
Boards. No statement of printing on copyright page. *Richard Cowper, pseudonym.*

THE TWILIGHT OF BRIAREUS.*London: Victor Gollancz Ltd*, *1974*.
Boards. No statement of printing on copyright page. *Richard Cowper, pseudonym.*

WORLDS APART.*London: Victor Gollancz Ltd*, *1974*.
Boards. No statement of printing on copyright page. *Richard Cowper, pseudonym.*

Autobiography

One Hand Clapping. *London: Victor Gollancz Ltd*, *1975*.
Boards. No statement of printing on copyright page. *Colin Middleton Murry, pseudonym.*

Shadows on the Grass. *London: Victor Gollancz Ltd*, *1977*.
Boards. No statement of printing on copyright page. *Colin Middleton Murry, pseudonym.*

Laurence Van Cott Niven
(b. 1938)

ALL THE MYRIAD WAYS.*New York: Ballantine Books*, [*1971*].
  Wrappers. *First Printing: June, 1971* on copyright page. *Ballantine Books 02280–7–095* (95¢).

THE FLIGHT OF THE HORSE.*New York: Ballantine Books*, [*1973*].
  Wrappers. *First Printing: September, 1973* on copyright page. *Ballantine Books 23487* ($1.25).

THE FLYING SORCERERS.*New York: Ballantine Books*, [*1971*].
  Wrappers. *First Printing: August, 1971* on copyright page. *Ballantine Books Science Fiction 02331–5–095* (95¢). With DAVID GERROLD.

A GIFT FROM EARTH.*New York: Ballantine Books*, [*1968*].
  Wrappers. *First Printing: September, 1968* on copyright page. *Ballantine Science Fiction Original 72113* (75¢).

  ALSO: [*London*]: *Macdonald Science Fiction*, [*1969*]. Boards. *First published in Great Britain in 1969* on copyright page. First hardcover edition.

A HOLE IN SPACE.*New York: Ballantine Books*, [*1974*].
  Wrappers. *First Printing: June, 1974* on copyright page. *Ballantine 24011* ($1.25).

INCONSTANT MOON.*London: Victor Gollancz Ltd, 1973*.
  Boards. No statement of printing on copyright page.

INFERNO.*New York: Published by Pocket Books*, [*1976*].
  Wrappers. *May, 1976* on copyright page. *Pocket Books S/F 80490* ($1.75). With JERRY POURNELLE.

  ALSO:*London: Allan Wingate, 1977*. Boards. *First British edition, 1977* on copyright page. First hardcover edition.

THE LONG ARM OF GIL HAMILTON.*New York: Ballantine Books*, [*1976*].
  Wrappers. *First Printing: February, 1976* on copyright page. *Ballantine Books 24868* ($1.50).

LUCIFER'S HAMMER. [*Chicago*]: *A Playboy Press Book*, [*1977*].
  Boards with cloth shelf back. First edition so stated on copyright page. With JERRY POURNELLE.

THE MOTE IN GOD'S EYE. *New York: Simon and Schuster*, [*1974*].
  Boards with cloth shelf back. Code *1 2 3 4 5 6 7 8 9 10* on copyright page. With JERRY POURNELLE.

NEUTRON STAR. *New York: Ballantine Books*, [*1968*].
  Wrappers. *First Printing: April, 1968* on copyright page. *A Ballantine Original Science Fiction U6120* (75¢).

  ALSO: [*London*]: *Macdonald Science Fiction*, [*1969*]. Boards. *First published in Great Britain in 1969* on copyright page. First hardcover edition.

PROTECTOR. *New York: Ballantine Books*, [*1973*].
Wrappers. *First Printing: September, 1973* on copyright page. *Ballantine Books 23486* ($1.25).

ALSO: [*Tisbury, Wiltshire*]: *Compton Russell*, [*1976*]. Boards. *This hardcover edition first published in Great Britain in 1976* . . . on copyright page. First hardcover edition.

RINGWORLD. *New York: Ballantine Books*, [*1970*].
Wrappers. *First Printing: October, 1970* on copyright page. *Ballantine Books Science Fiction 02046–4–095* (95¢).

ALSO: *London: Victor Gollancz Ltd, 1972*. Boards. No statement of printing on copyright page. First hardcover edition.

ALSO: *New York: Holt, Rinehart and Winston*, [*1977*]. Boards with cloth shelf back. *First published in hardcover in 1977* . . . *10 9 8 7 6 5 4 3 2 1* on copyright page. Adds ''Author's Note.''

THE SHAPE OF SPACE. *New York: Ballantine Books*, [*1969*].
Wrappers. *First Printing: September, 1969* on copyright page. *Ballantine Books Science Fiction 01712 075* (75¢).

TALES OF KNOWN SPACE. *New York: Ballantine Books*, [*1975*].
Wrappers. *First Printing: August, 1975* on copyright page. *Ballantine Books SF 24563* ($1.50).

WORLD OF PTAVVS. *New York: Ballantine Books*, [*1966*].
Wrappers. *First Edition: August, 1966* on copyright page. *A Ballantine Science Fiction Original U2328* (50¢).

ALSO: *London: Macdonald Science Fiction*, [*1968*]. Boards. *First published in Great Britain in 1968* on copyright page. First hardcover edition.

A WORLD OUT OF TIME. *New York: Holt, Rinehart and Winston*, [*1976*].
Boards with cloth shelf back. First edition so stated on copyright page.

Andre Norton

(b. 1912)

ANDROID AT ARMS. *New York: Harcourt Brace Jovanovich, Inc.*, [*1971*].
First edition so stated on copyright page.

AT SWORDS' POINTS. *New York: Harcourt, Brace and Company*, [*1954*].
Boards. First edition so stated on copyright page.

THE BEAST MASTER. *New York: Harcourt, Brace and Company*, [*1959*].
First edition so stated on copyright page.

ALSO: *New York: Ace Books, Inc.*, [*1961*]. Wrappers. No statement of printing on
copyright page. *Ace Double Novel Books D–509* (35¢). Abridged text.

BERTIE AND MAY. *New York and Cleveland: The World Publishing Company*, [*1969*].
No statement of printing on copyright page. Code *1 2 3 4 5 73 72 71 70 69* on page [176].
With BERTHA STEMM NORTON.

THE BOOK OF ANDRE NORTON. *New York: DAW Books, Inc.*, [*1975*].
Wrappers. *First printing, October 1975/1 2 3 4 5 6 7 8 9* on copyright page. *DAW: sf Books
No. 165 UY1198* ($1.25). Reissue of THE MANY WORLDS OF ANDRE NORTON.

BREED TO COME. *New York: The Viking Press*, [*1972*].
Boards. First edition so stated on copyright page.

CATSEYE. *New York: Harcourt, Brace & World, Inc.*, [*1961*].
First edition so stated on copyright page.

THE CROSSROADS OF TIME. *New York: Ace Books*, [*1956*].
Wrappers. No statement of printing on copyright page. *Ace Double Novel Books D–164*
(35¢). Bound with MANKIND ON THE RUN by Gordon R. Dickson.

CROSSTIME AGENT. *London: Victor Gollancz Ltd*, *1975*.
Boards. No statement of printing on copyright page. Issued earlier in the U.S. as QUEST
CROSSTIME.

THE CRYSTAL GRYPHON. *New York: Atheneum*, *1972*.
First edition so stated on copyright page.

DARK PIPER. *New York: Harcourt, Brace & World, Inc.*, [*1968*].
First edition so stated on copyright page.

THE DAY OF THE NESS. *New York: Walker and Company*, [*1975*].
Boards. Code *10 9 8 7 6 5 4 3 2 1* on copyright page. With MICHAEL GILBERT.

DAYBREAK—2250 A.D. *New York: Ace Books, Inc.*, [*1954*].
Wrappers. No statement of printing on copyright page. *Ace Double Novel Books D–69*
(35¢). Bound with BEYOND EARTH'S GATES by Lewis Padgett and C. L. Moore. Reissue of
STAR MAN'S SON 2250 A.D.

THE DEFIANT AGENTS. *Cleveland and New York: The World Publishing Company*, [*1962*].
First edition so stated on copyright page.

DRAGON MAGIC. *New York: Thomas Y. Crowell Company*, [*1972*].
  Code *1 2 3 4 5 6 7 8 9 10* on copyright page.

DREAD COMPANION. *New York: Harcourt Brace Jovanovich, Inc.*, [*1970*].
  Two bindings, probable priority as listed: (A) Slate gray endpapers; (B) White endpapers.
  Remaindered copies thus. First edition so stated on copyright page.

EXILES OF THE STARS. *New York: The Viking Press*, [*1971*].
  Two bindings, no priority: (A) Undecorated cloth. Trade binding. (B) Pictorial cloth
  reproducing dust jacket design. Library binding. First edition so stated on copyright page.

EYE OF THE MONSTER. *New York: Ace Books, Inc.*, [*1962*].
  Wrappers. No statement of printing on copyright page. *Ace Double F–147* (40¢). Bound
  with SEA SIEGE by Norton.

FOLLOW THE DRUM: BEING THE VENTURES AND MISADVENTURES OF ONE JOHANNA LOVELL,
SOMETIME LADY OF CATKEPT MANOR IN KENT COUNTY OF LORD BALTIMORE'S PROPRIETARY
OF MARYLAND, IN THE GRACIOUS REIGN OF KING CHARLES THE SECOND. *New York: Wm.
Penn Publishing Corp.*, [*1942*].
  No statement of printing on copyright page.

FORERUNNER FORAY. *New York: The Viking Press*, [*1973*].
  Boards. First edition so stated on copyright page.

FUR MAGIC. *Cleveland and New York: The World Publishing Company*, [*1968*].
  No statement of printing on copyright page.

GALACTIC DERELICT. *Cleveland and New York: The World Publishing Company*, [*1959*].
  First edition so stated on copyright page.

GARAN THE ETERNAL. *Alhambra, California: Fantasy Publishing Co., Inc.*, [*1972*].
  Boards. First edition so stated on copyright page.

GRAY MAGIC. *New York • London • Richmond Hill, Ontario: Scholastic Book Services,*
[*1967*].
  Wrappers. *1st printing . . . April 1967* on copyright page. SBS TX 919 (50¢). Reissue
  of STEEL MAGIC.

HERE ABIDE MONSTERS. *New York: Atheneum, 1973.*
  First edition so stated on copyright page.

HIGH SORCERY. *New York: An Ace Book*, [*1970*].
  Wrappers. No statement of printing on copyright page. *Ace Book 33700* (60¢).

HUON OF THE HORN, BEING A TALE OF THAT DUKE OF BORDEAUX WHO CAME TO SORROW
AT THE HAND OF CHARLEMAGNE AND YET WON THE FAVOR OF OBERON, THE ELF KING, TO
HIS LASTING FAME AND GREAT GLORY. *New York: Harcourt, Brace and Company*, [*1951*].
  Boards with cloth shelf back. First edition so stated on copyright page.

ICE CROWN. *New York: The Viking Press*, [*1970*].
  Two bindings, no priority: (A) Undecorated cloth. Trade binding. (B) Pictorial cloth
  reproducing the dust jacket design. Library binding. First edition so stated on copyright
  page. Note: First printing bears code *1 2 3 4 5 74 73 72 71 70* on copyright page. Second
  printing retains first edition statement, but code on copyright page reads *2 3 4 5 74 73 72*.

IRON CAGE. *New York: The Viking Press*, [*1974*].
  First edition so stated on copyright page.

ISLAND OF THE LOST. *London: Staples Press Limited*, [*1953*].
Boards. *First published in Great Britain 1953* on copyright page. Issued earlier in the
U.S. as SWORD IN SHEATH.

THE JARGOON PARD. *New York: Atheneum*, *1974*.
First edition so stated on copyright page.

JUDGMENT ON JANUS. *New York: Harcourt, Brace & World, Inc.*, [*1963*].
First edition so stated on copyright page. Note: Second printing retains first edition
statement but adds code *B.2.66*.

KEY OUT OF TIME. *Cleveland and New York: The World Publishing Company*, [*1963*].
First edition so stated on copyright page.

KNAVE OF DREAMS. *New York: The Viking Press*, [*1975*].
Boards with cloth shelf back. First edition so stated on copyright page.

THE LAST PLANET. *New York: Ace Books*, [*1955*].
Wrappers. No statement of printing on copyright page. *Ace Book D–96* (35¢). Bound with
A MAN OBSESSED by Alan E. Nourse. Reissue of STAR RANGERS.

LAVENDER-GREEN MAGIC. *New York: Thomas Y. Crowell Company*, [*1974*].
Code *1 2 3 4 5 6 7 8 9 10* on copyright page.

LORD OF THUNDER. *New York: Harcourt, Brace & World, Inc.*, [*1962*].
First edition so stated on copyright page.

THE MANY WORLDS OF ANDRE NORTON. *Radnor, Pennsylvania: Chilton Book Company*,
[*1974*].
First edition so stated on copyright page.

MERLIN'S MIRROR. *New York: DAW Books, Inc.*, [*1975*].
Wrappers. *First printing, June 1975/1 2 3 4 5 6 7 8 9* on copyright page. *DAW: sf Books
No. 152 UY1175* ($1.25).

ALSO: *London: Sidgwick & Jackson*, [*1976*]. Boards. *First published in Great Britain in
1976* on copyright page. First hardcover edition.

MOON OF THREE RINGS. *New York: The Viking Press*, [*1966*].
First published in 1966 on copyright page.

MURDERS FOR SALE. *London: Hammond, Hammond & Company*, [*1954*].
Boards. No statement of printing on copyright page. *Allen Weston, pseudonym* for Norton
and GRACE ALLEN HOGARTH.

NIGHT OF MASKS. *New York: Harcourt, Brace & World, Inc.*, [*1964*].
First edition so stated on copyright page.

NO NIGHT WITHOUT STARS. *New York: Atheneum*, *1975*.
First edition so stated on copyright page.

OCTAGON MAGIC. *Cleveland and New York: The World Publishing Company*, [*1967*].
No statement of printing on copyright page.

THE OPAL-EYED FAN. *New York: E. P. Dutton*, [*1977*].
Boards with cloth shelf back. First edition so stated on copyright page.

OPERATION TIME SEARCH. *New York: Harcourt, Brace & World, Inc., [1967]*.
  First edition so stated on copyright page.

ORDEAL IN OTHERWHERE. *Cleveland and New York: The World Publishing Company,*
[1964].
  First edition so stated on copyright page.

OUTSIDE. *New York: Walker and Company, [1974, i.e. 1975]*.
  Boards. Code *10 9 8 7 6 5 4 3 2 1* on copyright page. Note: Originally scheduled for release
  in December 1974, the book was published 28 February 1975.

PERILOUS DREAMS. *New York: DAW Books, Inc., [1976]*.
  Wrappers. *First printing, June 1976/1 2 3 4 5 6 7 8 9* on copyright page. *DAW: sf Books*
  No. 196 UY1237 ($1.25).

PLAGUE SHIP A DANE THORSON-SOLAR QUEEN ADVENTURE. *New York: Gnome Press Inc.*
Publishers, [1956].
  Three bindings, probable priority as listed: (A) Tan boards lettered in black (copy thus
  deposited 29 October 1956 at the Library of Congress); (B) Tan cloth lettered in black;
  (C) Red boards lettered in black. First edition so stated on copyright page. *Andrew North,*
  pseudonym.

POSTMARKED THE STARS. *New York: Harcourt, Brace & World, Inc., [1969]*.
  First edition so stated on copyright page.

THE PRINCE COMMANDS, BEING THE SUNDRY ADVENTURES OF MICHAEL KARL, SOMETIME
CROWN PRINCE & PRETENDER TO THE THRONE OF MORVANIA. *New York London: D.*
Appleton-Century Company, 1934.
  First printing so stated on copyright page. *(1)* at base of page [269].

QUEST CROSSTIME. *New York: The Viking Press, [1965]*.
  Bindings, no priority: (A) Red cloth, spine lettered in black. Trade binding. (B) Pictorial
  boards reproducing dust jacket design. *Viking Library Binding* on rear cover. *First pub-*
  lished in 1965 on copyright page. Issued later in Great Britain as CROSSTIME AGENT.

RALESTONE LUCK. *New York London: D. Appleton-Century Company Incorporated, 1938.*
  No statement of printing on copyright page. Code *(1)* at base of text on page 296.

REBEL SPURS. *Cleveland and New York: The World Publishing Company, [1962]*.
  First edition so stated on copyright page.

RED HART MAGIC. *[New York]: Thomas Y. Crowell Company, [1976]*.
  Code *1 2 3 4 5 6 7 8 9 10* on copyright page.

RIDE PROUD, REBEL! *Cleveland and New York: The World Publishing Company, [1961]*.
  First edition so stated on copyright page.

ROGUE REYNARD BEING A TALE OF THE FORTUNES AND MISFORTUNES AND DIVERS MISDEEDS
OF THAT GREAT VILLAIN, BARON REYNARD, THE FOX, AND HOW HE WAS SERVED WITH KING
LION'S JUSTICE. BASED UPON THE BEAST SAGA. *Boston: Houghton Mifflin Company, 1947.*
  No statement of printing on copyright page.

SARGASSO OF SPACE. *New York: Gnome Press, [1955]*.
  Bindings, probable priority as listed: (A) Gray cloth lettered in black (copy thus deposited 2
  December 1955 at the Library of Congress); (B) Tan boards lettered in black. First edition
  so stated on copyright page. *Andrew North, pseudonym. A Dane Thorson-Solar Queen*
  Adventure at head of title.

SCARFACE BEING THE STORY OF ONE JUSTIN BLADE, LATE OF THE PIRATE ISLE OF TORTUGA, AND HOW FATE DID JUSTLY DEAL WITH HIM, TO HIS GREAT PROFIT.*New York: Harcourt, Brace and Company*, [*1948*].
   No statement of printing on copyright page. Code *I* on copyright page.

SEA SIEGE. *New York: Harcourt, Brace and Company*, [*1957*].
   First edition so stated on copyright page.

SECRET OF THE LOST RACE.*New York: Ace Books, Inc.*, [*1959*].
   Wrappers. No statement of printing on copyright page. *Ace Double Novel Books D–381* (35¢). Bound with ONE AGAINST HERCULUM by Jerry Sohl. Issued later in Great Britain as WOLFSHEAD.

SHADOW HAWK.*New York: Harcourt, Brace and Company*, [*1960*].
   First edition so stated on copyright page.

THE SIOUX SPACEMAN.*New York: Ace Books, Inc.*, [*1960*].
   Wrappers. No statement of printing on copyright page. *Ace Double Novel Books D–437* (35¢). Bound with AND THEN THE TOWN TOOK OFF by Richard Wilson.

   ALSO:*London: Robert Hale & Company*, [*1976*]. Boards. *First published in Great Britain 1976* on copyright page. First hardcover edition.

SORCERESS OF THE WITCH WORLD.*New York: Ace Books, Inc.*, [*1968*].
   Wrappers. No statement of printing on copyright page. *An Ace Book H–84* (60¢).

   ALSO:*Boston: Gregg Press, 1977. First Printing, March 1977* on copyright page. First hardcover edition.

SPELL OF THE WITCH WORLD.*New York: DAW Books, Inc.*, [*1972*].
   Wrappers. No statement of printing on copyright page. *DAW: sf Books No. 1 UQ1001–095* (95¢). Note: Second printing so marked on copyright page.

   ALSO:*Boston: Gregg Press, 1977. First Printing, March 1977* on copyright page. First hardcover edition.

STAND TO HORSE.*New York: Harcourt, Brace and Company*, [*1956*].
   First edition so stated on copyright page.

STAR BORN.*Cleveland and New York: The World Publishing Company*, [*1957*].
   First edition so stated on copyright page.

STAR GATE.*New York: Harcourt, Brace and Company*, [*1958*].
   First edition so stated on copyright page.

   ALSO:*New York: Ace Books, Inc.*, [*1963*]. Wrappers. No statement of printing on copyright page. *Ace Book F–231* (40¢). Adds "Prologue" by Norton.

STAR GUARD.*New York: Harcourt, Brace and Company*, [*1955*].
   First edition so stated on copyright page.

STAR HUNTER. *New York: Ace Books, Inc.*, [*1961*].
   Wrappers. No statement of printing on copyright page. *Ace Double Novel Books D–509* (35¢). Bound with THE BEAST MASTER by Norton.

STAR HUNTER & VOODOO PLANET.*New York: Ace Books, Inc.*, [*1968*].
   Wrappers. No statement of printing on copyright page. *An Ace Book G–723* (50¢). Reprint. Collects STAR HUNTER and VOODOO PLANET.

STAR KA'AT.*New York: Walker and Company*, [*1976*].
Boards. Code *10 9 8 7 6 5 4 3 2 1* on copyright page. With DOROTHY MADLEE.

STAR MAN'S SON 2250 A.D.*New York: Harcourt, Brace and Company*, [*1952*].
Two bindings, no priority established: (A) Boards with cloth shelf back; (B) Boards. First edition so stated on copyright page. Reissued as DAY-BREAK—2250 A.D.

STAR RANGERS.*New York: Harcourt, Brace and Company*, [*1953*].
First edition so stated on copyright page. Reissued as THE LAST PLANET.

THE STARS ARE OURS!*Cleveland and New York: The World Publishing Company*, [*1954*].
First edition so stated on copyright page.

STEEL MAGIC.*Cleveland and New York: The World Publishing Company*, [*1965*].
First edition so stated on copyright page. Reissued as GRAY MAGIC.

STORM OVER WARLOCK.*Cleveland and New York: The World Publishing Company*, [*1960*].
First edition so stated on copyright page.

SWORD IN SHEATH.*New York: Harcourt, Brace and Company*, [*1949*].
First edition so stated on copyright page. Issued later in Great Britain as ISLAND OF THE LOST.

THE SWORD IS DRAWN. [*Boston*]: *Houghton Mifflin Company, 1944* .
No statement of printing on copyright page.

THREE AGAINST THE WITCH WORLD.*New York: Ace Books, Inc.*, [*1965*].
Wrappers. No statement of printing on copyright page. *Ace Book F–332* (40¢).

ALSO:*Boston: Gregg Press, 1977. First Printing, March 1977* on copyright page. First hardcover edition.

THE TIME TRADERS.*Cleveland and New York: The World Publishing Company*, [*1958*].
First edition so stated on copyright page.

TREY OF SWORDS.*New York: Grosset & Dunlap*, [*1977*].
First printing 1977 on copyright page.

UNCHARTED STARS.*New York: The Viking Press*, [*1969*].
First published in 1969 . . . on copyright page.

VELVET SHADOWS.*Greenwich, Connecticut: Fawcett Publications, Inc.*, [*1977*].
Wrappers. Code *10 9 8 7 6 5 4 3 2 1* on copyright page. *Fawcett Crest 2–3135–6* ($1.50).

VICTORY ON JANUS.*New York: Harcourt, Brace & World, Inc.*, [*1966*].
First edition so stated on copyright page.

VOODOO PLANET.*New York: Ace Books, Inc.*, [*1959*].
Wrappers. No statement of printing on copyright page. *Ace Double Novel Books D–345* (35¢). *Andrew North, pseudonym*. Bound with PLAGUE SHIP by North.

WARLOCK OF THE WITCH WORLD.*New York: Ace Books Inc.*, [*1967*].
Wrappers. No statement of printing on copyright page. *Ace Book G–630* (50¢).

ALSO: *Boston: Gregg Press, 1977. First Printing, March 1977* on copyright page. First hardcover edition.

WEB OF THE WITCH WORLD. *New York: Ace Books Inc.*, *[1964]*.
Wrappers. No statement of printing on copyright page. *Ace Book F–263*.

ALSO: *Boston: Gregg Press, 1977. First Printing, March 1977* on copyright page. First hardcover edition.

THE WHITE JADE FOX. *New York: E. P. Dutton & Co., Inc.*, *[1975]*.
Boards with cloth shelf back. First edition so stated on copyright page.

WITCH WORLD. *New York: Ace Books, Inc.*, *[1963]*.
Wrappers. No statement of printing on copyright page. *Ace Book F–197* (40¢).

ALSO: *Boston: Gregg Press, 1977. First Printing, March 1977* on copyright page. First hardcover edition.

WOLFSHEAD. *London: Robert Hale*, *[1977]*.
Boards. *This edition 1977* on copyright page. Issued earlier in the U.S. as SECRET OF THE LOST RACE.

WRAITHS OF TIME. *New York: Atheneum, 1976.*
First edition so stated on copyright page.

THE X FACTOR. *New York: Harcourt, Brace & World, Inc.*, *[1965]*.
First edition so stated on copyright page.

YANKEE PRIVATEER. *Cleveland & New York: The World Publishing Company*, *[1955]*.
First edition so stated on copyright page.

YEAR OF THE UNICORN. *New York: Ace Books Inc.*, *[1965]*.
Wrappers. No statement of printing on copyright page. *Ace Book F–357* (40¢).

ALSO: *Boston: Gregg Press, 1977. First Printing, March 1977* on copyright page. First hardcover edition.

THE ZERO STONE. *New York: The Viking Press*, *[1968]*.
First published in 1968 . . . on copyright page.

Edited Fiction

Baleful Beasts and Eerie Creatures. *Chicago/New York/San Francisco: Rand McNally & Company*, *[1976]*.
Two bindings, no priority: (A) Boards. Trade binding with sticker showing *$5.95* price on front cover and ISBN *528–82171–7* printed on rear cover uncanceled. (B) Boards. Library binding with no price sticker and ISBN printed on rear cover canceled with a label reading *528–80211–9–5.97. First printing, 1976* on copyright page. Edited, with introduction, by Norton.

Bullard of the Space Patrol, by Malcolm Jameson. *Cleveland and New York: The World Publishing Company*, *[1951]*.
First edition so stated on copyright page. Edited by Norton.

Gates of Tomorrow. *New York: Atheneum, 1973.*
First edition so stated on copyright page. Edited, with introduction, by Norton. With ERNESTINE DONALDY.

Small Shadows Creep. *New York: E. P. Dutton & Co., Inc.*, *[1974]*.
Boards with cloth shelf back. First edition so stated on copyright page. Compiled, with introduction, by Norton.

Space Pioneers. *New York and Cleveland: The World Publishing Company,* [*1954*].
  First edition so stated on copyright page. Edited, with introduction and notes, by Norton.

Space Police. *Cleveland and New York: The World Publishing Company,* [*1956*].
  First edition so stated on copyright page. Edited, with foreword, by Norton.

Space Service. *Cleveland and New York: The World Publishing Company,* [*1953*].
  First printing so stated on copyright page. Edited, with introduction and notes, by Norton.

Reference

The First Editions of Andre Norton, [compiled by David G. Turner]. [*Menlo Park, California: Published by David G. Turner — Bookman, 1974.*]
  Wrappers. First edition so stated on copyright page. Offset from typewritten copy. Issued as *Science Fiction Bibliographies–1*.

Alan Edward Nourse
(b. 1928)

BEYOND INFINITY.*London: Transworld Publishers*, [*1964*].
Wrappers. No statement of printing on copyright page. *Corgi Science Fiction GS1526* (3/6). Reissue of TIGER BY THE TAIL.

THE BLADERUNNER.*New York: David McKay Company, Inc.*, [*1974*].
Boards. No statement of printing on copyright page.

THE COUNTERFEIT MAN.*New York: David McKay Company, Inc.*, [*1963*].
No statement of printing on copyright page.

THE INVADERS ARE COMING!*New York: Ace Books, Inc.*, [*1959*].
Wrappers. No statement of printing on copyright page. *Ace Book D–366* (35¢). With J. A. MEYER.

JUNIOR INTERN.*New York: Harper & Brothers*, [*1955*].
First edition so stated on copyright page.

A MAN OBSESSED.*New York: Ace Books, Inc.*, [*1955*].
Wrappers. No statement of printing on copyright page. *Ace Double Novel Books D–96* (35¢). Bound with THE LAST PLANET by Andre Norton. Expanded version issued later as THE MERCY MEN.

THE MERCY MEN.*New York: David McKay Company, Inc.*, [*1968*].
No statement of printing on copyright page. Enlarged version of A MAN OBSESSED.

PSI HIGH AND OTHERS.*New York: David McKay Company, Inc.*, [*1967*].
No statement of printing on copyright page.

RAIDERS FROM THE RINGS.*New York: David McKay Company, Inc.*, [*1962*].
First edition so stated on copyright page.

ROCKET TO LIMBO.*New York: David McKay Company, Inc.*, [*1957*].
No statement of printing on copyright page.

Rx FOR TOMORROW.*New York: David McKay Company, Inc.*, [*1971*].
No statement of printing on copyright page.

SCAVENGERS IN SPACE.*New York: David McKay Company, Inc.*, [*1959*].
No statement of printing on copyright page.

STAR SURGEON.*New York: David McKay Company, Inc.*, [*1960*].
No statement of printing on copyright page.

TIGER BY THE TAIL.*New York: David McKay Company, Inc.*, [*1961*].
No statement of printing on copyright page. Reissued as BEYOND INFINITY.

TROUBLE ON TITAN.*Philadelphia Toronto: The John C. Winston Company*, [*1954*].
First edition so stated on copyright page.

THE UNIVERSE BETWEEN.*New York: David McKay Company, Inc.*, [*1965*].
No statement of printing on copyright page.

Symmes Chadwick Oliver

(b. 1928)

ANOTHER KIND. *New York: Ballantine Books*, [*1955*].
Three bindings, no priority of issue: (A) Tan cloth lettered in red; (B) Red cloth lettered in dark red; (C) Wrappers. *Ballantine Books 113* (35¢). No statement of printing on copyright page.

THE EDGE OF FOREVER. *Los Angeles: Sherbourne Press, Inc.*, [*1971*].
Boards. First printing so stated on copyright page. Note: Includes biography and checklist of the author's writings by William F. Nolan.

GIANTS IN THE DUST. *New York: Pyramid Books*, [*1976*].
Wrappers. *March 1976* on copyright page. *Pyramid V3670* ($1.25).

MISTS OF DAWN. *Philadelphia Toronto: The John C. Winston Company*, [*1952*].
First edition so stated on copyright page.

SHADOWS IN THE SUN. *New York: Ballantine Books*, [*1954*].
Three bindings, no priority of issue: (A) Tan cloth lettered in black; (B) Blue cloth lettered in black; (C) Wrappers. *Ballantine Books 91* (35¢). No statement of printing on copyright page.

THE SHORES OF ANOTHER SEA. [*New York*]: *New American Library*, [*1971*].
Wrappers. *First printing, February, 1971* on copyright page. *Signet Science Fiction T4526* (75¢).

ALSO: *London: Victor Gollancz Limited, 1971*. Boards. No statement of printing on copyright page. First hardcover edition.

UNEARTHLY NEIGHBORS. *New York: Ballantine Books*, [*1960*].
Wrappers. No statement of printing on copyright page. *Ballantine Books 365K* (35¢).

THE WINDS OF TIME. *Garden City: Doubleday & Company, Inc., 1957*.
First edition so stated on copyright page.

THE WOLF IS MY BROTHER. [*New York*]: *Published by The New American Library*, [*1967*].
Wrappers. *First Printing, January, 1967* on copyright page. *Signet D3081* (50¢).

ALSO: *London: Herbert Jenkins*, [*1968*]. Boards. *First published in Great Britain . . . 1968* on copyright page. First hardcover edition.

Edgar Pangborn
(1909–1976)

A-100: A MYSTERY STORY. *New York: E. P. Dutton & Co., Inc.*, [*1930*].
First edition so stated on copyright page. *Bruce Harrison, pseudonym*.

THE COMPANY OF GLORY. *New York: Pyramid Books*, [*1975*].
Wrappers. *January 1975* on copyright page. *Pyramid Science Fiction V3568* ($1.25).

DAVY. *New York: St. Martin's Press*, [*1964*].
Boards with cloth shelf back. No statement of printing on copyright page.

GOOD NEIGHBORS AND OTHER STRANGERS. *New York: The Macmillan Company*, [*1972*].
First printing so stated on copyright page.

THE JUDGMENT OF EVE. *New York: Simon and Schuster*, [*1966*].
Boards with cloth shelf back. First printing so stated on copyright page.

A MIRROR FOR OBSERVERS. *Garden City: Doubleday & Company, Inc.*, *1954*.
Boards. First edition so stated on copyright page.

THE TRIAL OF CALLISTA BLAKE. *New York: St Martin's Press*, [*1961*].
Boards with cloth shelf back. No statement of printing on copyright page.

WEST OF THE SUN. *Garden City: Doubleday & Company, Inc.*, *1953*.
Boards. First edition so stated on copyright page.

WILDERNESS OF SPRING. *New York Toronto: Rinehart & Company, Inc.*, [*1958*].
Boards with cloth shelf back. No statement of printing on copyright page. Rinehart monogram on copyright page.

Alexei Panshin
(b. 1940)

FAREWELL TO YESTERDAY'S TOMORROW. *New York: G. P. Putnam's Sons*, [*1975*].
Boards. No statement of printing on copyright page.

ALSO: [*New York*]: *Published by Berkley Publishing Corporation*, [*1976*].
Wrappers. *September, 1976* on copyright page. *A Berkley Medallion Book 23211* ($1.25).
Enlarged edition. Adds "Lady Sunshine and the Magoon of Beatus."

MASQUE WORLD. *New York: An Ace Book*, [*1969*].
Wrappers. No statement of printing on copyright page. *Ace Book 02320* (60¢).

RITE OF PASSAGE. *New York: Ace Books, Inc.*, [*1968*].
Wrappers. No statement of printing on copyright page. *An Ace Science Fiction Special A–16* (75¢).

ALSO: *London: Sidgwick & Jackson*, [*1969*]. Boards. *First published in Great Britain 1969* on copyright page. First hardcover edition.

ALSO: *Boston: Gregg Press, 1976. First Printing, June 1976* on copyright page. New introduction by the author. Note: Not issued in dust jacket.

STAR WELL. *New York: Ace Books, Inc.*, [*1968*].
Wrappers. No statement of printing on copyright page. *Ace Book G–756* (50¢).

THE THURB REVOLUTION. *New York: Ace Books, Inc.*, [*1968*].
Wrappers. No statement of printing on copyright page. *Ace Book G–762* (50¢).

Nonfiction (Dealing with the Fantasy Genre only)

Heinlein in Dimension: A Critical Analysis. *Chicago: Advent: Publishers, Inc., 1968*.
First edition so stated on copyright page.

SF in Dimension: A Book of Explorations. *Chicago: Advent: Publishers, Inc., 1976*.
First edition so stated on copyright page. With CORY PANSHIN.

Mervyn Laurence Peake
(1911–1968)

BOY IN DARKNESS. *[Exeter]: Wheaton, [1976].*
  Wrappers. *This edition 1976* on copyright page. First separate printing. Collected earlier in the anthology *Sometime, Never*.

CAPTAIN SLAUGHTERBOARD DROPS ANCHOR. *[London: Country Life, 1939.]*
  Boards with cloth shelf back. No statement of printing. Note: Publisher's imprint appears at base of front cover. No copyright page.

GORMENGHAST. *London: Eyre & Spottiswoode, MCML.*
  First published in 1950 on copyright page.

LETTERS FROM A LOST UNCLE. *London: Published by Eyre and Spottiswoode (Publishers) Ltd., 1948.*
  First edition so stated on page [2].

MR. PYE. *Melbourne :: London :: Toronto: William Heinemann Ltd, [1953].*
  First published 1953 on copyright page.

TITUS ALONE. *London: Eyre & Spottiswoode, 1959.*
  First published 1959 on copyright page.

  ALSO: *London: Eyre & Spottiswoode, [1970]. This edition, reset and illustrated, first published 1970* . . . on copyright page. Revised and enlarged text. Note: Restores deletions in the 1959 edition. Follows Peake's manuscript with illegible text interpreted by Langdon Jones.

TITUS GROAN. *[London]: Eyre & Spottiswoode, MCMXLVI.*
  This book first published MCMXLVI on copyright page.

Reference

A Guide to the Gormenghast Trilogy, [by] Arthur Metzger. *[Baltimore: T–K Graphics, 1976.]*
  Wrappers. No statement of printing on copyright page.

Mervyn Peake, [by] John Watney. *London: Michael Joseph, [1976].*
  Boards. *First published in Great Britain* . . . *1976* on copyright page. Includes bibliography.

Mervyn Peake: A Biographical and Critical Exploration, [by] John Batchelor. *[London]: Duckworth, [1974].*
  First published in 1974 on copyright page. Includes bibliography.

Mervyn Peake: Writings & Drawings, [by] Maeve Gilmore & Shelagh Johnson. *London: Academy Editions/New York: St Martin's Press, [1974].*
  Boards. *First published in Great Britain in 1974* . . . *First published in the U.S.A. in 1974* . . . on copyright page. Includes previously unpublished literary material by Peake and bibliography.

A World Away: A Memoir of Mervyn Peake, by Maeve Gilmore. *London: Victor Gollancz Ltd, 1970.*

Boards. No statement of printing on copyright page.

Horace Beam Piper
(1904–1964)

THE COSMIC COMPUTER. *New York: Ace Books, Inc.*, [*1964*].
Wrappers. No statement of printing on copyright page. *Ace Book F–274* (40¢). Reissue of JUNKYARD PLANET.

CRISIS IN 2140. *New York: Ace Books*, [*1957*].
Wrappers. No statement of printing on copyright page. *Ace Double Novel Books D–227* (35¢). With JOHN J. McGUIRE. Bound with GUNNER CADE by Cyril Judd.

FOUR-DAY PLANET. *New York: G. P. Putnam's Sons*, [*1961*].
No statement of printing on copyright page.

THE FUZZY PAPERS. *Garden City: Nelson Doubleday, Inc.*, [*1977*].
Boards. No statement of printing on copyright page. Code *H 03* on page 308. Collects LITTLE FUZZY and THE OTHER HUMAN RACE (a.k.a. FUZZY SAPIENS). First hardcover edition for both titles. Note: Issued by the Science Fiction Book Club.

FUZZY SAPIENS. *New York: Ace Books*, [*1976*].
Wrappers. *First Ace Printing: June 1976* on copyright page. *Ace SF 26190* ($1.50). Reissue of THE OTHER HUMAN RACE. Later collected in THE FUZZY PAPERS.

JUNKYARD PLANET. *New York: G. P. Putnam's Sons*, [*1963*].
No statement of printing on copyright page. Reissued as THE COSMIC COMPUTER.

LITTLE FUZZY. *New York: Avon Book Division*, [*1962*].
Wrappers. No statement of printing on copyright page. *Avon F–118* (40¢). Later collected in THE FUZZY PAPERS.

LORD KALVAN OF OTHERWHEN. *New York: Ace Books, Inc.*, [*1965*].
Wrappers. No statement of printing on copyright page. *Ace Book F–342* (40¢).

ALSO: [*New York & London: Garland Publishing, Inc.*, *1975*.] No statement of printing on copyright page. First hardcover edition. Notes: (1) Photo-offset from Ace Books edition of 1965. (2) Not issued in dust jacket.

MURDER IN THE GUN ROOM. *New York: Alfred A. Knopf, 1953*.
Boards. First edition so stated on copyright page.

THE OTHER HUMAN RACE. [*New York*] : *An Avon Book*, [*1964*].
Wrappers. No statement of printing on copyright page. *Avon G1220* (50¢). Reissued as FUZZY SAPIENS. Later collected in THE FUZZY PAPERS.

A PLANET FOR TEXANS. *New York: Ace Books, Inc.*, [*1958*].
Wrappers. No statement of printing on copyright page. *Ace Double Novel Books D–299* (35¢). With JOHN J. McGUIRE. Bound with STAR BORN by Andre Norton.

SPACE VIKING. *New York: Ace Books, Inc.*, [*1963*].
Wrappers. No statement of printing on copyright page. *Ace Book F–225* (40¢).

ALSO: [*New York & London: Garland Publishing, Inc.*, *1975*.] No statement of printing on copyright page. First hardcover edition. Notes: (1) Photo-offset from Ace Books edition of 1963. (2) Not issued in dust jacket.

Frederik Pohl

(b. 1919)

THE ABOMINABLE EARTHMAN. *New York: Ballantine Books*, [*1963*].
Wrappers. No statement of printing on copyright page. *An Original Ballantine Book F685*
(50¢).

THE AGE OF THE PUSSYFOOT. *New York: Trident Press*, [*1969*].
Boards with cloth shelf back. No statement of printing on copyright page.

ALTERNATING CURRENTS. *New York: Ballantine Books*, [*1956*].
Two bindings, no priority: (A) Cloth; (B) Wrappers. *Ballantine Books 130* (35¢). No
statement of printing on copyright page.

ALSO: [*Harmondsworth*]: *Penguin Books*, [*1966*]. Wrappers. *Published in Penguin Books
1966* on copyright page. *Penguin Science Fiction 2452* (3'6). Replaces "Happy Birthday,
Dear Jesus" with "The Children of Night."

THE BEST OF FREDERIK POHL. *Garden City: Nelson Doubleday, Inc.*, [*1975*].
Boards. No statement of printing on copyright page. Two printings, priority as listed:
(A) Code *Q 6* on page 306; (B) Code *Q 24* on page 306. Note: Issued by the Science Fiction
Book Club.

THE CASE AGAINST TOMORROW. *New York: Ballantine Books*, [*1957*].
Wrappers. No statement of printing on copyright page. *Ballantine Books 206* (35¢).

CRITICAL MASS. *Toronto New York London: Bantam Books*, [*1977*].
Wrappers. *October 1977* on copyright page. *Bantam Science Fiction 19048–0* ($1.75).
With CYRIL M. KORNBLUTH.

DAY MILLION. *New York: Ballantine Books*, [*1970*].
Wrappers. *First Printing: June, 1970* on copyright page. *Ballantine Books Science Fiction
01939–3–095* (95¢).

ALSO: *London: Victor Gollancz Ltd, 1971*. Boards. No statement of printing on copyright
page. First hardcover edition.

DIGITS AND DASTARDS. *New York: Ballantine Books*, [*1966*].
Wrappers. *First Edition: June, 1966* on copyright page. *A Ballantine Science Fiction
Original U2178* (50¢).

ALSO: *London: Dennis Dobson*, [*1968*]. Boards. *First published in Great Britain 1968* on
copyright page. First hardcover edition. Note: Author's name misspelled *Frederick* on title
page.

DRUNKARD'S WALK. *New York: Ballantine Books*, [*1960*].
Wrappers. No statement of printing on copyright page. *Ballantine Books 439K* (35¢).

ALSO: *Hicksville, New York: The Gnome Press, Inc.*, [*1961*]. Boards. No statement of
printing on copyright page. First hardcover edition. Note: Ballantine and Gnome editions
printed from the same plates.

THE EARLY POHL. *Garden City: Doubleday & Company, Inc.*, *1976*.
Boards. First edition so stated on copyright page.

EDGE OF THE CITY. *New York: Ballantine Books*, [*1957*].
Wrappers. No statement of printing on copyright page. *Ballantine Books 199* (35¢). Note: Novelization of the screenplay by Robert Alan Aurthur.

FARTHEST STAR. *New York: Ballantine Books*, [*1975*].
Wrappers. *First Printing: February, 1975* on copyright page. *Ballantine Books SF 24330* ($1.50). With JACK WILLIAMSON.

THE FREDERIK POHL OMNIBUS. *London: Victor Gollancz Ltd, 1966*.
Boards. No statement of printing on copyright page.

GATEWAY. *New York: St. Martin's Press*, [*1977*].
Boards. No statement of printing on copyright page.

GLADIATOR-AT-LAW. *New York: Ballantine Books*, [*1955*].
Two bindings, no priority: (A) Cloth; (B) Wrappers. *Ballantine Books 107* (35¢). No statement of printing on copyright page. With C. M. KORNBLUTH.

THE GOD OF CHANNEL 1. *New York: Ballantine Books*, [*1956*].
Two bindings, no priority: (A) Blue cloth, spine lettered in dark blue; (B) Wrappers. *Ballantine Books 137* (35¢). No statement of printing on copyright page. *Donald Stacy, pseudonym*. Note: Pohl collaborated anonymously on this novel.

THE GOLD AT THE STARBOW'S END. *New York: Ballantine Books*, [*1972*].
Wrappers. *First Printing: August, 1972* on copyright page. *Ballantine Books Science Fiction 02775–2–125* ($1.25).

ALSO: *London: Victor Gollancz Ltd, 1973*. Boards. No statement of printing on copyright page. First hardcover edition.

IN THE PROBLEM PIT. *Toronto New York London: Bantam Books*, [*1976*].
Wrappers. *June 1976* on copyright page. *Bantam Science Fiction T8857* ($1.50).

MAN PLUS. *New York: Random House*, [*1976*].
Boards. First edition so stated on copyright page.

THE MAN WHO ATE THE WORLD. *New York: Ballantine Books*, [*1960*].
Wrappers. No statement of printing on copyright page. *Ballantine Books 397 K* (35¢).

A PLAGUE OF PYTHONS. *New York: Ballantine Books*, [*1965*].
Wrappers. *First Printing: September 1965* on copyright page. *A Ballantine Science Fiction Original U2174* (50¢).

ALSO: *London: Victor Gollancz Ltd, 1966*. Boards. No statement of printing on copyright page. First hardcover edition.

PREFERRED RISK. *New York: Simon and Schuster, 1955*.
Boards with cloth shelf back. First printing so stated on copyright page. With LESTER DEL REY. *Edson McCann, pseudonym*.

PRESIDENTIAL YEAR. *New York: Ballantine Books*, [*1956*].
Two bindings, no priority: (A) Cloth: (1) Green cloth, spine lettered in blue; (2) Red cloth, spine lettered in blue. Both cloth bindings received at the Library of Congress 7 June 1956. (B) Wrappers. *Ballantine Books 144* (35¢). No statement of printing on copyright page. With C. M. KORNBLUTH.

THE REEFS OF SPACE. *New York: Ballantine Books*, [*1964*].
Wrappers. *First Ballantine Printing September 1964* on copyright page. *Ballantine Books U2172* (50¢). With JACK WILLIAMSON. Collected later in THE STARCHILD TRILOGY.

ALSO: *London: Dennis Dobson,* [*1965*]. Boards. *First published in Great Britain in 1965* on copyright page. First hardcover edition.

ROGUE STAR. *New York: Ballantine Books,* [*1969*].
Wrappers. *First Printing: December, 1969* on copyright page. *Ballantine Books Science Fiction 01797–075* (75¢). With JACK WILLIAMSON. Collected later in THE STARCHILD TRILOGY.

ALSO: *London: Dennis Dobson,* [*1972*]. Boards. *First published in Great Britain in 1972* on copyright page. First hardcover edition. Note: Author's name misspelled *Frederick* on title page.

SEARCH THE SKY. *New York: Ballantine Books,* [*1954*].
Two bindings, no priority: (A) Boards; (B) Wrappers. *Ballantine Books 61* (35¢). No statement of printing on copyright page. With C. M. KORNBLUTH.

SLAVE SHIP. *New York: Ballantine Books,* [*1957*].
Two bindings, no priority: (A) Cloth; (B) Wrappers. *Ballantine Books 192* (35¢). No statement of printing on copyright page.

SORORITY HOUSE. *New York: Lion Library Editions,* [*1956*].
Wrappers. *Published May, 1956* on copyright page. *Lion Library LL 97* (35¢). With C. M. KORNBLUTH. *Jordan Park, pseudonym.*

THE SPACE MERCHANTS. *New York: Ballantine Books,* [*1953*].
Two bindings, no priority: (A) Boards; (B) Wrappers. *Ballantine Books 21* (35¢). No statement of printing on copyright page. With C. M. KORNBLUTH.

STARCHILD. *New York: Ballantine Books,* [*1965*].
Wrappers. *First printing: November, 1965* on copyright page. *A Ballantine Science Fiction Original U2176* (50¢). With JACK WILLIAMSON. Collected later in THE STARCHILD TRILOGY.

ALSO: *London: Dennis Dobson,* [*1966*]. Boards. *First published in Great Britain in 1966* on copyright page. First hardcover edition.

THE STARCHILD TRILOGY. *Garden City: Nelson Doubleday, Inc.,* [*1977*].
Boards. No statement of printing on copyright page. Code *H 36* on page 435. Reprint. Collects THE REEFS OF SPACE, STARCHILD, and ROGUESTAR. With JACK WILLIAMSON. Note: Issued by the Science Fiction Book Club.

TOMORROW TIMES SEVEN. *New York: Ballantine Books,* [*1959*].
Wrappers. No statement of printing on copyright page. *Ballantine Books 325 K* (35¢).

A TOWN IS DROWNING. *New York: Ballantine Books,* [*1955*].
Two bindings, no priority: (A) Cloth: (1) Red cloth, spine lettered in blue; (2) Dark blue cloth, spine lettered in light blue. Both cloth bindings received at the Library of Congress 2 February 1956. (B) Wrappers. *Ballantine Books 123* (35¢). No statement of printing on copyright page. With C. M. KORNBLUTH.

TURN LEFT AT THURSDAY. *New York: Ballantine Books,* [*1961*].
Wrappers. No statement of printing on copyright page. *Ballantine Books 476 K* (35¢).

TURN THE TIGERS LOOSE. *New York: Ballantine Books,* [*1956*].
Two bindings, no priority: (A) Blue cloth, spine lettered in yellow; (B) Wrappers. *Ballantine Books 173* (35¢). No statement of printing on copyright page. Note: Written by and credited to Walter Lasly with the anonymous collaboration of Pohl.

UNDERSEA CITY. *Hicksville, N.Y.: The Gnome Press, Inc., Publishers, [1958]*.
Two bindings, priority as listed: (A) Black boards lettered in red; (B) Gray cloth lettered in red. First edition so stated on copyright page. With JACK WILLIAMSON.

UNDERSEA FLEET. *New York: Gnome Press Inc., Publishers, [1956]*.
Two bindings, probable sequence as listed: (A) Green cloth lettered in brown; (B) Gray boards lettered in red. First edition so stated on copyright page. With JACK WILLIAMSON.

UNDERSEA QUEST. *New York: Gnome Press Inc. Publishers, [1954]*.
First edition so stated on copyright page. With JACK WILLIAMSON.

WOLFBANE. *New York: Ballantine Books, [1959]*.
Wrappers. *First Ballantine Edition* on copyright page. *Ballantine Books 335 K* (35¢). With C. M. KORNBLUTH.

ALSO: *London: Victor Gollancz Ltd, 1960*. Boards. No statement of printing on copyright page. First hardcover edition.

THE WONDER EFFECT. *New York: Ballantine Books, [1962]*.
Wrappers. No statement of printing on copyright page. *An Original Ballantine Book F 638* (50¢). With C. M. KORNBLUTH.

ALSO: *London: Victor Gollancz Ltd, 1967*. Boards. No statement of printing on copyright page. First hardcover edition.

Edited Fiction

Assignment in Tomorrow. *Garden City: Hanover House, [1954]*.
First edition so stated on copyright page. Edited, with introduction, by Pohl.

The Best of C. M. Kornbluth. *Garden City: Nelson Doubleday, Inc., [1976]*.
Boards. No statement of printing on copyright page. Code *G35* on page [311]. Edited, with introduction, by Pohl. Note: Issued by the Science Fiction Book Club.

Best Science Fiction for 1972. *New York: Ace Books, [1972]*.
Wrappers. *First Ace Printing: September, 1972* on copyright page. *Ace Book 91359* ($1.25). Edited, with introduction and short story "Gold At the Starbow's End," by Pohl.

Beyond the End of Time. *Garden City: Permabooks, [1952]*.
Wrappers. No statement of printing on copyright page. *Permabooks P145* (35¢). Edited, with introduction, by Pohl.

Door to Anywhere. *New York: Curtis Books, [1970]*.
Wrappers. No statement of printing on copyright page. *Curtis Books 123–07070–075* (75¢). Edited by Pohl. Reissue of *The Tenth Galaxy Reader*.

The Eighth Galaxy Reader. *Garden City: Doubleday & Company, Inc., 1965*.
First edition so stated on copyright page. Edited, with introduction and short story "Critical Mass" (in collaboration with C. M. Kornbluth), by Pohl. Reissued as *Final Encounter*.

The Eleventh Galaxy Reader. *Garden City: Doubleday & Company, 1969*.
First edition so stated on copyright page. Edited, with introduction, by Pohl.

The Expert Dreamers. *Garden City: Doubleday & Company, Inc., 1962*.
First edition so stated on copyright page. Edited, with introduction and notes, by Pohl.

Final Encounter. *New York: Curtis Books*, [*1970*].
   Wrappers. No statement of printing on copyright page. *Curtis Books 123–07071–075*
   (75¢). Edited, with introduction and short story "Critical Mass" (in collaboration with
   C. M. Kornbluth), by Pohl. Reissue of *The Eighth Galaxy Reader*.

The If Reader of Science Fiction. *Garden City: Doubleday & Company, Inc., 1966*.
   First edition so stated on copyright page. Edited, with introduction and short story "Father
   of the Stars," by Pohl.

Jupiter. *New York: Ballantine Books*, [*1973*].
   Wrappers. *First Printing: December 1973* on copyright page. *Ballantine Books 23662*
   ($1.25). Edited, with preface, by Pohl with CAROL POHL.

Nightmare Age. *New York: Ballantine Books*, [*1970*].
   Wrappers. *First Printing: October 1970* on copyright page. *Ballantine Books Science*
   Fiction 02044–8–095 (95¢). Edited, with introduction and two short stories, "The Census
   Takers" and "The Midas Plague," by Pohl.

The Ninth Galaxy Reader. *Garden City: Doubleday & Company, Inc., 1966.*
   First edition so stated on copyright page. Edited, with introduction and short story "The
   Children of Night," by Pohl.

Science Fiction Discoveries. *Toronto New York London: Bantam Books*, [*1976*].
   Wrappers. *August 1976* on copyright page. *Bantam Books Science Fiction 08635–9*
   ($1.50). Edited, with introduction and notes, by Pohl with CAROL POHL.

The Science Fiction Roll of Honor. *New York: Random House*, [*1975*].
   Boards with cloth shelf back. First edition so stated on copyright page. Edited, with
   introduction and notes, by Pohl.

Science Fiction: The Great Years. *New York: Ace Books*, [*1973*].
   Wrappers. *First Ace printing: January, 1973* on copyright page. *Ace Science Fiction 75430*
   ($1.25). Edited, with introductions, by Pohl with CAROL POHL.

   ALSO: *London: Victor Gollancz Ltd, 1974*. Boards. No statement of printing on copyright
   page. First hardcover edition.

Science Fiction: The Great Years. Volume II. *New York: Ace Books*, [*1976*].
   Wrappers. No statement of printing on copyright page. *Ace 75431* ($1.50). Edited, with
   introduction and notes, by Pohl with CAROL POHL.

The Second If Reader of Science Fiction. *Garden City: Doubleday & Company, Inc., 1968.*
   First edition so stated on copyright page. Edited, with introduction and short story "Under
   Two Moons," by Pohl.

The Seventh Galaxy Reader. *Garden City: Doubleday & Company, Inc., 1964.*
   First edition so stated on copyright page. Edited, with introduction and short story "Three
   Portraits and a Prayer," by Pohl.

Shadow of Tomorrow. *Garden City: Permabooks*, [*1953*].
   Wrappers. *1st printing . . . July, 1953* on copyright page. *Permabooks P236* (35¢). Edited,
   with introduction, by Pohl.

Star Fourteen. *London: Ronald Whiting & Wheaton*, [*1966*].
   Boards. *First published in Great Britain 1966* on copyright page. Edited, with introduction, by Pohl. Issued earlier in the U.S. as *Star of Stars*.

Star of Stars. *Garden City: Doubleday & Company, Inc., 1960.*
First edition so stated on copyright page. Edited, with introduction, by Pohl. Issued later in Great Britain as *Star Fourteen.*

Star Science Fiction Stories. *New York: Ballantine Books,* [*1953*].
Two bindings, no priority: (A) Boards; (B) Wrappers. *Ballantine Books 16* (35¢). No statement of printing on copyright page. Edited, with notes, by Pohl.

Star Science Fiction Stories No. 2. *New York: Ballantine Books,* [*1954*].
Two bindings, no priority (A) Boards; (B) Wrappers. *Ballantine Books 55* (35¢). No statement of printing on copyright page. Edited, with notes, by Pohl.

Star Science Fiction Stories No. 3. *New York: Ballantine Books,* [*1955*].
Two bindings, no priority: (A) Cloth; (B) Wrappers. *Ballantine Books 96* (35¢). No statement of printing on copyright page. Edited, with notes, by Pohl.

Star Science Fiction Stories No. 4. *New York: Ballantine Books,* [*1958*].
Wrappers. No statement of printing on copyright page. *Ballantine Books 272K* (35¢). Edited, with introduction and notes, by Pohl.

Star Science Fiction Stories No. 5. *New York: Ballantine Books,* [*1959*].
Wrappers. No statement of printing on copyright page. *Ballantine Books 308 K* (35¢). Edited, with notes, by Pohl.

Star Science Fiction No. 6. *New York: Ballantine Books,* [*1959*].
Wrappers. No statement of printing on copyright page. *Ballantine Books 353 K* (35¢). Edited, with notes, by Pohl. Note: This volume drops ''Stories'' from the title.

Star Short Novels. *New York: Ballantine Books,* [*1954*].
Two bindings, no priority: (A) Cloth; (B) Wrappers. *Ballantine Books 89* (35¢). No statement of printing on copyright page. Edited, with introduction, by Pohl.

The Tenth Galaxy Reader. *Garden City: Doubleday & Company, Inc., 1967.*
First edition so stated on copyright page. Edited, with short story ''The Tunnel Under the World,'' by Pohl. Reissued as *Door to Anywhere.*

Time Waits for Winthrop and Four Other Short Novels from Galaxy. *Garden City: Doubleday & Company, Inc., 1962.*
First edition so stated on copyright page. Edited, with introduction, by Pohl.

Jerry Pournelle

(b. 1933)

BIRTH OF FIRE. *Toronto • New York • London: Laser Books,* [*1976*].
   Wrappers. *First published March 1976* on copyright page. *Laser Books 72023* (95¢).

ESCAPE FROM THE PLANET OF THE APES. *New York: Award Books,* [*1974*].
   Wrappers. No statement of printing on copyright page. *Award Books AN1240* (95¢). Note: Based on the screenplay by Paul Dehn.

HIGH JUSTICE. *New York: Published by Pocket Books,* [*1977*].
   Wrappers. *May, 1977* on copyright page. *Pocket SF 81104* ($1.75).

INFERNO. *New York: Published by Pocket Books,* [*1976*].
   Wrappers. *May, 1976* on copyright page. *Pocket Books S/F 80490* ($1.75). With LARRY NIVEN.

   ALSO: *London: Allan Wingate, 1977.* Boards. *First British edition, 1977* on copyright page. First hardcover edition.

LUCIFER'S HAMMER. [*Chicago*]: A Playboy Press Book, [*1977*].
   Boards with cloth shelf back. First edition so stated on copyright page. With LARRY NIVEN.

THE MERCENARY. *New York: Published by Pocket Books,* [*1977*].
   Wrappers. *February, 1977* on copyright page. *Pocket S/F 80903* ($1.75).

THE MOTE IN GOD'S EYE. *New York: Simon and Schuster,* [*1974*].
   Boards with cloth shelf back. Code *1 2 3 4 5 6 7 8 9 10* on copyright page. With LARRY NIVEN.

RED DRAGON. [*New York*]: *Published by Berkley Publishing Corporation,* [*1971*].
   Wrappers. *May, 1971* on copyright page. *A Berkley Medallion Book S1996* (75¢). *Wade Curtis, pseudonym.*

RED HEROIN. [*New York*]: *Published by Berkley Publishing Corporation,* [*1969*].
   Wrappers. *August, 1969* on copyright page. *A Berkley Medallion Book X1723* (60¢). *Wade Curtis, pseudonym.*

A SPACESHIP FOR THE KING. *New York: DAW Books, Inc.,* [*1973*].
   Wrappers. *First printing, February 1973* on copyright page. *DAW: sf Books No. 42 UQ1042* (95¢).

WEST OF HONOR. *Toronto • New York • London: Laser Books,* [*1976*].
   Wrappers. *First published December 1976* on copyright page. *Laser Books 50* ($1.25).

Edited Fiction

2020 Vision. [*New York*]: *Avon,* [*1974*].
   Wrappers. *First Avon Printing, February, 1974* on copyright page. *Avon Science Fiction 18390* (95¢). Edited, with preface, introduction, and notes, by Pournelle.

Fletcher Pratt
(1897–1956)

ALIEN PLANET. *New York: Avalon Books*, [*1962*].
No statement of printing on copyright page.

THE BLUE STAR. *New York: Ballantine Books*, [*1969*].
Wrappers. *First Ballantine Printing: May, 1969* on copyright page. *Ballantine Books 01602* (95¢). First separate printing. Collected earlier in the anthology *Witches Three*, anonymously edited by Pratt.

THE CARNELIAN CUBE. *New York: Gnome Press, 1948*.
First edition so stated on copyright page. With L. SPRAGUE DE CAMP.

THE CASTLE OF IRON. *New York: Gnome Press*, [*1950*].
Boards. First edition so stated on copyright page. With L. SPRAGUE DE CAMP.

THE COMPLEAT ENCHANTER. *Garden City: Nelson Doubleday, Inc.*, [*1975*].
Boards. No statement of printing on copyright page. Code *44 R* on page 337. Reprint. Collects THE INCOMPLETE ENCHANTER and THE CASTLE OF IRON. With L. SPRAGUE DE CAMP. Note: Issued by the Science Fiction Book Club.

DOUBLE IN SPACE. *Garden City: Doubleday & Company, Inc., 1951*.
Boards. First edition so stated on copyright page.

ALSO: *London/New York: T. V. Boardman & Company, Limited*, [*1954*].
Boards. *First published in Great Britain 1954* on copyright page. Note: Text differs from U.S. edition. Contains "Project Excelsior" but drops "The Wanderer's Return" and substitutes "The Conditioned Captain," issued a year earlier in book form in the U.S. as THE UNDYING FIRE.

DOUBLE JEOPARDY. *Garden City: Doubleday & Company, Inc., 1952*.
Boards. First edition so stated on copyright page.

THE INCOMPLETE ENCHANTER. *New York: Henry Holt and Company*, [*1941*].
No statement of printing on copyright page. With L. SPRAGUE DE CAMP.

INVADERS FROM RIGEL. *New York: Avalon Books*, [*1960*].
No statement of printing on copyright page.

LAND OF UNREASON. *New York: Henry Holt and Company*, [*1942*].
No statement of printing on copyright page. With L. SPRAGUE DE CAMP.

TALES FROM GAVAGAN'S BAR. *N*[*ew*] Y[*ork*]: *Twayne Publishers*, [*1953*].
No statement of printing on copyright page. With L. SPRAGUE DE CAMP.

THE UNDYING FIRE. *New York: Ballantine Books*, [*1953*].
Two bindings, no priority: (A) Boards; (B) Wrappers. *Ballantine Books 25* (35¢). No statement of printing on copyright page.

WALL OF SERPENTS. *New York: Avalon Books*, [*1960*].
No statement of printing on copyright page. With L. SPRAGUE DE CAMP.

THE WELL OF THE UNICORN. *New York: William Sloane Associates, Inc., Publishers, [1948]*. First printing so stated on copyright page. *George U. Fletcher, pseudonym.*

Edited Fiction

Petrified Planet. *New York: Twayne Publishers, 1952.*
No statement of printing on copyright page. Anonymously edited, with short story "The Long View," by Pratt.

Witches Three. *New York: Twayne Publishers, Inc., [1952].*
Two bindings, priority as listed: (A) Lettered in gold; (B) Lettered in yellow. Two issues, priority as listed: (A) Sheets bulk 3.3 cm; (B) Sheets bulk? (not recorded but less than 3.3 cm). No statement of printing on copyright page. Anonymously edited, with novella "The Blue Star," by Pratt.

World of Wonder. *New York: Twayne Publishers, [1951].*
No statement of printing on copyright page. Edited, with introduction, by Pratt.

Christopher Priest

(b. 1943)

DARKENING ISLAND. *New York • Evanston • San Francisco • London: Harper & Row, Publishers, [1972].*
  Boards with cloth shelf back. *First U.S. edition* on copyright page. Issued earlier in Great Britain as FUGUE FOR A DARKENING ISLAND.

A DREAM OF WESSEX. *London: Faber & Faber, [1977].*
  Boards. *First published in 1977* on copyright page. Issued later in the U.S. as THE PERFECT LOVER.

FUGUE FOR A DARKENING ISLAND. *London: Faber and Faber, [1972].*
  First published in 1972 on copyright page. Issued later in the U.S. as DARKENING ISLAND.

INDOCTRINAIRE. *London: Faber and Faber, [1970].*
  First published in 1970 on copyright page.

INVERTED WORLD. *London: Faber and Faber, [1974].*
  Boards. *First published in 1974 . . .* on copyright page.

THE PERFECT LOVER. *New York: Charles Scribner's Sons, [1977].*
  Boards. Code *1 3 5 7 9 11 13 15 17 19 H/C 20 18 16 14 12 10 8 6 4 2* on copyright page. Issued earlier in Great Britain as A DREAM OF WESSEX.

REAL-TIME WORLD. *[London]: New English Library, [1974].*
  Boards. *This collection first published in Great Britain . . . 1974* on copyright page.

THE SPACE MACHINE. *London: Faber and Faber, [1976].*
  Boards. *First published in 1976* on copyright page.

Seabury Grandin Quinn
(1889–1969)

THE ADVENTURES OF JULES DE GRANDIN. *New York: Popular Library*, [*1976*].
Wrappers. *August, 1976* on copyright page. *Popular Library Science Fiction 445–00394–125* ($1.25).

ALIEN FLESH. *Philadelphia: Oswald Train, 1977*.
First edition so stated on copyright page.

THE CASEBOOK OF JULES DE GRANDIN. *New York: Popular Library*, [*1976*].
Wrappers. *September, 1976* on copyright page. *Popular Library Science Fiction 445–00404–125* ($1.25).

THE DEVIL'S BRIDE. *New York: Popular Library*, [*1976*].
Wrappers. *November 1976* on copyright page. *Popular Library 445–00424–125* ($1.25).

THE HELLFIRE FILES OF JULES DE GRANDIN. *New York: Popular Library*, [*1976*].
Wrappers. *December, 1976* on copyright page. *Popular Library 445–00428–125* ($1.25).

THE HORROR CHAMBERS OF JULES DE GRANDIN. *New York: Popular Library*, [*1977*].
Wrappers. No statement of printing on copyright page. *Popular Library Science Fiction 445–03183–150* ($1.50).

IS THE DEVIL A GENTLEMAN? *Baltimore: Mirage, 1970*.
No statement of printing on copyright page. Approximately 1000 numbered copies.

THE PHANTOM-FIGHTER. *Sauk City: Mycroft & Moran: Publishers, . 66*.
No statement of printing on copyright page.

ROADS. *N.p.: Conrad H. Ruppert, Christmas, 1938*.
Wrappers. *Reprinted in this Special Edition from the January, 1938, issue of Weird Tales . . .* on copyright page.

ALSO: *Sauk City: Arkham House, 1948*. No statement of printing on copyright page. First hardcover edition.

THE SKELETON CLOSET OF JULES DE GRANDIN. *New York: Popular Library*, [*1976*].
Wrappers. *October, 1976* on copyright page. *Popular Library Science Fiction 445–08527–125* ($1.25).

Interview

Seabury Quinn Famous Creator of Jules de Grandin Interviewed by Julius Schwartz and Mortimer Weisinger. [*West Warwick, R.I.: Necronomicon Press, 1977.*]
Wrappers. *This edition, the first . . . is limited to a numbered/printing of 500 copies* on page [8]. Caption title. Offset from typewritten copy. Cover title reads: *Seabury Quinn/Creator of Jules de Grandin*. Issued as *F & SF Self-Portraits 2*.

Marta Randall
(b. 1948)

A CITY IN THE NORTH. *[New York]: Warner Books*, *[1976]*.
   Wrappers. *First Printing: May, 1976* on copyright page. *Warner Books 88–117* ($1.50).

ISLANDS. *New York: Pyramid Books*, *[1976]*.
   Wrappers. *Pyramid edition published September 1976* on copyright page. *Pyramid V3664* ($1.25).

Dallas McCord Reynolds

(b. 1917)

ABILITY QUOTIENT.*New York: Ace Books*, [*1975*].
Wrappers. No statement of printing on copyright page. *Ace 00265* ($1.25). *Mack Reynolds, pseudonym.*

AFTER SOME TOMORROW.*New York: Belmont Books*, [*1967*].
Wrappers. *November 1967* on copyright page. *A Belmont Science Fiction B50–795* (50¢). *Mack Reynolds, pseudonym.*

AFTER UTOPIA.*New York: Ace Books*, [*1977*].
Wrappers. *First Ace printing: November 1977* on copyright page. *Ace 00958* ($1.50). *Mack Reynolds, pseudonym.*

AMAZON PLANET.*New York: Ace Books*, [*1975*].
Wrappers. No statement of printing on copyright page. *Ace 01950* ($1.25). *Mack Reynolds, pseudonym.*

THE BEST OF MACK REYNOLDS.*New York: Published by Pocket Books*, [*1976*].
Wrappers. *April, 1976* on copyright page. *Pocket Books 80403* ($1.95). *Mack Reynolds, pseudonym.*

BLACKMAN'S BURDEN.*New York: Ace Books*, [*1972*].
Wrappers. *First Ace printing: August, 1972* on copyright page. *Ace Double 06612* (95¢). *Mack Reynolds, pseudonym.* Bound with BORDER, BREED NOR BIRTH by Reynolds.

BORDER, BREED NOR BIRTH. *New York: Ace Books*, [*1972*].
Wrappers. *First Ace printing: August, 1972* on copyright page. *Ace Double 06612* (95¢). *Mack Reynolds, pseudonym.* Bound with BLACKMAN'S BURDEN by Reynolds.

THE CASE OF THE LITTLE GREEN MEN.[*New York*]: *Phoenix Press*, [*1951*].
No statement of printing on copyright page. *Mack Reynolds, pseudonym.*

CODE DUELLO. *New York: Ace Books, Inc.*, [*1968*].
Wrappers. No statement of printing on copyright page. *Ace Double H–103* (60¢). *Mack Reynolds, pseudonym.* Bound with THE AGE OF RUIN by John M. Faucette.

COMMUNE 2000 A.D.*Toronto New York London: Bantam Books*, [*1974*].
Wrappers. *Published January 1974* on copyright page. *Bantam Science Fiction N8402* (95¢). *Mack Reynolds, pseudonym.*

COMPUTER WAR.*New York: Ace Books, Inc.*, [*1967*].
Wrappers. No statement of printing on copyright page. *Ace Double H–34* (60¢). *Mack Reynolds, pseudonym.* Bound with DEATH IS A DREAM by E. C. Tubb.

COMPUTER WORLD.*New York: Curtis Books*, [*1970*].
Wrappers. No statement of printing on copyright page. *Curtis Books 123–07098–075* (75¢). *Mack Reynolds, pseudonym.*

THE COSMIC EYE.*New York: Belmont Books*, [*1969*].
Wrappers. *September 1969* on copyright page. *Belmont B60–1040* (60¢). *Mack Reynolds, pseudonym.*

DAWNMAN PLANET. *New York: Ace Books, Inc.*, [*1966*].
    Wrappers. No statement of printing on copyright page. *Ace Double G–580* (50¢). *Mack Reynolds, pseudonym*. Bound with INHERIT THE EARTH by Claude Nunes.

DAY AFTER TOMORROW. *New York: Ace Books*, [*1976*].
    Wrappers. No statement of printing on copyright page. *Ace SF 13960* ($1.25). *Mack Reynolds, pseudonym*.

DEPRESSION OR BUST. *New York: Ace Books*, [*1974*].
    Wrappers. No statement of printing on copyright page. *Ace 14250* (95¢). *Mack Reynolds, pseudonym*. Note: Bound with a reissue of DAWNMAN PLANET by Reynolds. Cover title reads *Depression or Bust/and/Dawnman Planet*.

EARTH UNAWARE. *New York: Belmont Books*, [*1966*].
    Wrappers. *Second printing May 1968* on copyright page. *Belmont Science Fiction B50–826* (50¢). *Mack Reynolds, pseudonym*. Note: A reissue of OF GODLIKE POWER and the first printing under the alternate title.

THE EARTH WAR. *New York: Pyramid Books*, [*1963*].
    Wrappers. *First printing, July 1963* on copyright page. *Pyramid Books F–886* (40¢). *Mack Reynolds, pseudonym*.

*EPISODE ON THE RIVIERA. *Derby, Connecticut: Monarch Books, Inc.*, [*1961*].
    Wrappers. *Monarch Books 205*. *Mack Reynolds, pseudonym*.

EQUALITY: IN THE YEAR 2000. *New York: Ace Books*, [*1977*].
    Wrappers. *First Ace Printing: May 1977* on copyright page. *Ace 21430–4* ($1.50). *Mack Reynolds, pseudonym*.

THE FIVE WAY SECRET AGENT. *New York: Ace Books*, [*1975*].
    Wrappers. No statement of printing on copyright page. *Ace 24035* ($1.25). *Mack Reynolds, pseudonym*. Bound with MERCENARY FROM TOMORROW by Reynolds.

GALACTIC MEDAL OF HONOR. *New York: Ace Books*, [*1976*].
    Wrappers. *First Ace printing: August, 1976* on copyright page. *Ace SF 27240* ($1.50). *Mack Reynolds, pseudonym*.

*THE HOME OF THE INQUISITOR. *New York: Beagle Books*, [*1972*].
    Wrappers. *A Beagle Gothic 94312*. *Maxine Reynolds, pseudonym*.

*THE HOUSE IN THE KASBAH. *New York: Beagle Books*, [*1972*].
    Wrappers. *A Beagle Gothic 94283*. *Maxine Reynolds, pseudonym*.

THE JET SET. *Derby, Connecticut: Monarch Books, Inc.*, [*1964*].
    Wrappers. *Published in January, 1964* on copyright page. *Monarch Books 405* (40¢). *Mack Reynolds, pseudonym*. *A Contemporary Novel* at head of title.

*THE KEPT WOMAN. *Derby, Connecticut: Monarch Books, Inc.*, [*1963*].
    Wrappers. *Monarch Books 360*. *Mack Reynolds, pseudonym*.

A KISS BEFORE LOVING. *Derby, Connecticut: Monarch Books, Inc.*, [*1961*].
    Wrappers. *Published in October, 1961* on copyright page. *Monarch Books 214* (35¢). *Mack Reynolds, pseudonym*. *A Contemporary Novel* at head of title.

LOOKING BACKWARD, FROM THE YEAR 2000. *New York: Ace Books*, [*1973*].
    Wrappers. *First Ace printing: March, 1973* on copyright page. *Ace Science Fiction 48970* (95¢). *Mack Reynolds, pseudonym*.

ALSO: [*Morley*]: *The Elmfield Press*, [*1976*]. Boards. *Published in the United Kingdom in 1976 . . . on copyright page*. First hardcover edition.

MERCENARY FROM TOMORROW. *New York: Ace Books, Inc.*, [*1968*].
   Wrappers. No statement of printing on copyright page. *Ace Double H–65 (60¢). Mack Reynolds, pseudonym*. Bound with THE KEY TO VENUDINE by Kenneth Bulmer.

MISSION TO HORATIUS. *Racine, Wis.: Whitman Publishing Division Western Publishing Company, Inc.*, [*1968*].
   Boards. No statement of printing on copyright page. *Mack Reynolds, pseudonym. Star Trek* at head of title.

OF GODLIKE POWER. *New York: Belmont Books*, [*1966*].
   Wrappers. *May 1966* on copyright page. *Belmont Science Fiction B50–680 (50¢). Mack Reynolds, pseudonym*. Reissued as EARTH UNAWARE.

ONCE DEPARTED. *New York: Curtis Books*, [*1970*].
   Wrappers. No statement of printing on copyright page. *Curtis Books 502–06122–060 (60¢). Mack Reynolds, pseudonym*.

PERCHANCE TO DREAM. *New York: Ace Books*, [*1977*].
   Wrappers. *First Ace Printing: December 1977* on copyright page. *Ace 65948 ($1.50). Mack Reynolds, pseudonym*.

PLANETARY AGENT X. *New York: Ace Books, Inc.*, [*1965*].
   Wrappers. No statement of printing on copyright page. *Ace Double M–131 (45¢). Mack Reynolds, pseudonym*. Bound with BEHOLD THE STARS by Kenneth Bulmer. Note: Later reissued bound with THE RIVAL RIGELIANS by Reynolds.

POLICE PATROL: 2000 A.D. *New York: Ace Books*, [*1977*].
   Wrappers. No statement of printing on copyright page. *Ace 67460 ($1.50). Mack Reynolds, pseudonym*.

THE RIVAL RIGELIANS. *New York: Ace Books, Inc.*, [*1967*].
   Wrappers. No statement of printing on copyright page. *Ace Double G–632 (50¢). Mack Reynolds, pseudonym*. Bound with NEBULA ALERT by A. Bertram Chandler. Note: Later reissued bound with PLANETARY AGENT X by Reynolds.

ROLLTOWN. *New York: Ace Books*, [*1976*].
   Wrappers. *First Ace printing: June 1976* on copyright page. *Ace 73450 ($1.50). Mack Reynolds, pseudonym*.

*SATELLITE CITY. *New York: Ace Books*, [*1975*].
   Wrappers. *Ace 75045 ($1.25). Mack Reynolds, pseudonym*.

SECTION G: UNITED PLANETS. *New York: Ace Books*, [*1976*].
   Wrappers. No statement of printing on copyright page. *Ace 75860 ($1.25). Mack Reynolds, pseudonym*.

THE SPACE BARBARIANS. *New York: Ace Publishing Corporation*, [*1969*].
   Wrappers. No statement of printing on copyright page. *Ace 77710 (75¢). Mack Reynolds, pseudonym*. Bound with THE EYES OF BOLSK by Robert Lory.

SPACE PIONEER. [*London*]: *A Four Square Book*, [*1966*].
   Wrappers. *First published in Great Britain . . . in December 1966* on copyright page. *Four Square Science-Fiction 1671 (3/6). Mack Reynolds, pseudonym*.

SPACE VISITOR. *New York: Ace Books*, [*1977*].
  Wrappers. *First Ace printing: August 1977* on copyright page. *Ace 77782–1* ($1.50). *Mack Reynolds, pseudonym*.

STAR TREK: MISSION TO HORATIUS. See MISSION TO HORATIUS.

*THIS TIME WE LOVE. *Derby, Connecticut: Monarch Books, Inc.*, [*1962*].
  Wrappers. *Monarch Books 259. Mack Reynolds, pseudonym*.

TIME GLADIATOR. [*London*]: *A Four Square Book*, [*1966*].
  Wrappers. *First published in Great Britain in March 1966* on copyright page. *Four Square Science-Fiction 1459* (3/6). *Mack Reynolds, pseudonym*.

TOMORROW MIGHT BE DIFFERENT. *New York: Ace Books*, [*1975*].
  Wrappers. No statement of printing on copyright page. *Ace 81670* ($1.25). *Mack Reynolds, pseudonym*.

THE TOWERS OF UTOPIA. *Toronto New York London: Bantam Books*, [*1975*].
  Wrappers. *July 1975* on copyright page. *Bantam Science Fiction T6884* ($1.50). *Mack Reynolds, pseudonym*.

Edited Fiction

Science-Fiction Carnival. *Chicago: Shasta Publishers*, [*1953*].
  Boards with cloth shelf back. First edition so stated on copyright page. Edited, with preface, notes, and short story "The Martians and the Coys," by Reynolds. *Mack Reynolds, pseudonym*. With FREDRIC BROWN.

  ALSO: *New York: Bantam Books*, [*1957*]. Wrappers. *Bantam edition published June 1957* on copyright page. *Bantam Books A1615* (35¢). Abridged reprint. Collects eleven of the thirteen stories.

Keith John Kingston Roberts
(b. 1935)

ANITA. *New York: Ace Books*, [*1970*].
Wrappers. No statement of printing on copyright page. *Ace Book 02295* (75¢).

ALSO: [*London*]: *Millington*, [*1976*]. Boards. *First published in Great Britain in 1976* . . . on copyright page. First hardcover edition.

THE BOAT OF FATE. *London: Hutchinson*, [*1971*].
Boards. *First published 1971* on copyright page.

THE CHALK GIANTS. *London: Hutchinson*, [*1974*].
Boards. *First published 1974* on copyright page.

ALSO: *New York: G. P. Putnam's Sons*, [*1975*]. *First American edition 1975* on copyright page. Textual revisions. — CUT BY D.G. HARTWELL — NOT DESIRABLE

THE FURIES. [*New York*]: *Published by Berkley Publishing Corporation*, [*1966*].
Wrappers. *January, 1966* on copyright page. *Berkley Medallion F1177* (50¢).

ALSO: [*London*]: *Rupert Hart-Davis*, [*1966*]. Boards. *First published 1966* on copyright page. First hardcover edition.

THE GRAIN KINGS. *London: Hutchinson*, [*1976*].
Boards. *First published 1976* on copyright page.

THE INNER WHEEL. *London: Rupert Hart-Davis*, 1970.
Boards. *First published in Great Britain 1970* on copyright page.

MACHINES AND MEN. *London: Hutchinson*, [*1973*].
Boards. *First published 1973* on copyright page.

PAVANE. *London: Rupert Hart-Davis*, 1968.
Boards. *First published 1968* on copyright page.

ALSO: *Garden City: Doubleday & Company, Inc.*, *1968*. First edition so stated on copyright page. Enlarged edition. Adds "The White Boat."

THE PASSING OF THE DRAGONS. [*New York*]. *Published by Berkley Publishing Corporation*, [*1977*].
Wrappers. *April, 1977* on copyright page. *A Berkley Medallion Book 0-425-03477-1* ($1.25).

Frank Malcolm Robinson
(b. 1926)

THE GLASS INFERNO. *Garden City: Doubleday & Company, Inc., 1974.*
First edition so stated on copyright page. With THOMAS N. SCORTIA.

THE POWER. *Philadelphia New York: J. B. Lippincott Company, [1956].*
Boards. First edition so stated on copyright page.

THE PROMETHEUS CRISIS. *Garden City: Doubleday & Company, Inc., 1975.*
Boards with cloth shelf back. First edition so stated on copyright page. With THOMAS N. SCORTIA.

Paul Robinson
(b. 1948)

CALLAHAN'S CROSSTIME SALOON. *New York: Ace Books*, [*1977*].
  Wrappers. *First Ace printing: June 1977* on copyright page. *Ace 09034–6* ($1.50). *Spider Robinson, pseudonym.*

TELEMPATH. *New York: Published by Berkley Publishing Corporation*, [*1976*].
  No statement of printing on copyright page. *Spider Robinson, pseudonym.*

Joanna Russ
(b. 1937)

AND CHAOS DIED. *New York: Ace Publishing Corporation, [1970].*
Wrappers. No statement of printing on copyright page. *An Ace Science Fiction Special 02268 (75¢).*

ALYX. *Boston: Gregg Press, 1976.*
First Printing, June 1976 on copyright page. Note: Not issued in dust jacket.

THE FEMALE MAN. *Toronto New York London: Bantam Books, [1975].*
Wrappers. *February 1975* on copyright page. *A Bantam Book Q8765 ($1.25).*

ALSO: *Boston: Gregg Press, 1977. First Printing, June 1977* on copyright page. First hardcover edition. Note: Not issued in dust jacket.

PICNIC ON PARADISE. *New York: Ace Books, Inc., [1968].*
Wrappers. No statement of printing on copyright page. *An Ace Science Fiction Special H–72 (60¢).*

ALSO: *[London]: Macdonald, [1969].* Boards. *First published in Great Britain in 1969* on copyright page. First hardcover edition.

WE WHO ARE ABOUT TO . . . . *[New York]: A Dell Book, [1977].*
Wrappers. *First printing—July 1977* on copyright page. *Dell SF 19428 ($1.50).*

Eric Frank Russell
(1905–1978)

DARK TIDES.*London: Dennis Dobson*, [*1962*].
Boards.*First published in Great Britain in 1962* on copyright page.

DEEP SPACE.*Reading, Pennsylvania: Fantasy Press, Inc.*, [*1954*].
Two bindings, priority as listed: (A) Dark blue cloth, spine stamped in gold; (B) Greenberg variant binding reported by Owings and Chalker in *The Index to the Science-Fantasy Publishers* (not seen). Two issues, no priority: (A) 300 copies with numbered leaf signed by the author inserted; (B) Trade issue. First edition so stated on copyright page.

ALSO:*New York: Bantam Books*, [*1955*]. Wrappers. *October, 1955* on copyright page. *Bantam Books 1362* (25¢). Drops ''First Person Singular.''

DREADFUL SANCTUARY.*Reading, Pennsylvania: Fantasy Press, 1951*.
Two bindings, priority as listed: (A) Dark blue cloth, spine stamped in gold; (B) Greenberg variant binding reported by Owings and Chalker in *The Index to the Science-Fantasy Publishers* (not seen). Two issues, no priority: (A) 350 copies with numbered leaf signed by the author inserted; (B) Trade issue. First edition so stated on copyright page.

ALSO: *New York: Lancer Books*, [*1963*]. Wrappers. *A Lancer Book • 1963* on copyright page. *The Lancer Science Fiction Library 74–819* (75¢). Revised text.

ALSO:[*London*]: *A Four Square Book*, [*1967*]. Wrappers. *First Four Square Edition, with minor revisions to the text, January 1967* on copyright page. *Four Square Science Fiction 1719* (5/–). Revised text. Differs from Fantasy Press and Lancer editions.

ALSO:*London: Dennis Dobson*, [*1972*]. Boards.*Published in Great Britain in 1972* on copyright page. First hardcover printing with revised text following that of the 1967 Four Square edition.

FAR STARS.*London: Dennis Dobson*, [*1961*].
Boards.*First published in Great Britain in volume form in 1961* on copyright page. Two states of the dust jacket, priority as listed: (A) Price *13'6* at base of front flap; rear panel advertises *Great World Mysteries* by Russell; rear flap advertises Russell's *Three To Conquer*. (B) Price *15s* at base of front flap; list of 23 Dobson titles on rear panel; rear flap advertises *New Writings In S-F*, edited by John Carnell.

THE GREAT EXPLOSION.*London: Dennis Dobson*, [*1962*].
Boards. *First published in Great Britain in 1962* on copyright page.

LIKE NOTHING ON EARTH.*London: Dennis Dobson*, [*1975*].
Boards. *First published in Great Britain in 1975* on copyright page.

MEN, MARTIANS AND MACHINES.*London: Dennis Dobson*, [*1955*].
Boards. *First published in Great Britain in MCMLV* on copyright page. Note: Issued in the U.S. by Roy Publishers in 1956 utilizing sheets of the British printing with new title page mounted on a stub.

THE MINDWARPERS.*New York: Lancer Books*, [*1965*].
Wrappers. *A Lancer Book • 1965* on copyright page. *Lancer Science-Fiction Library 72–942* (50¢). Issued earlier in Great Britain as WITH A STRANGE DEVICE.

NEXT OF KIN.*London: Dennis Dobson*, [*1959*].
  Boards. *First published in Great Britain in 1959* . . . on copyright page. An enlarged version of THE SPACE WILLIES.

SENTINELS FROM SPACE.*New York: Bouregy & Curl, Inc. Publishers*, [*1953*].
  Boards. First edition so stated on copyright page.

SINISTER BARRIER.*Kingswood Surrey: The World's Work (1913) Ltd*, [*1943*].
  First published 1943 on copyright page.

  ALSO:*Reading, Pennsylvania: Fantasy Press, 1948*. Two bindings, priority as listed: (A) Dark blue cloth, spine stamped in gold; (B) Greenberg variant binding reported by Owings and Chalker in *The Index to the Science-Fantasy Publishers* (not seen). Two issues, no priority: (A) 500 copies with numbered leaf signed by the author inserted; (B) Trade issue. First edition so stated on copyright page. New foreword by Russell. Text of the Fantasy Press edition differs substantially from that of The World's Work edition, the former following the original version printed in *Unknown*, March 1939.

SIX WORLDS YONDER.*New York: Ace Books, Inc.*, [*1958*].
  Wrappers. No statement of printing on copyright page. *Ace Double Novel Books D–315* (35¢). Bound with THE SPACE WILLIES by Russell.

SOMEWHERE A VOICE.*London: Dennis Dobson*, [*1965*].
  Boards. *First published in Great Britain in 1965* on copyright page.

THE SPACE WILLIES.*New York: Ace Books, Inc.*, [*1958*].
  Wrappers. No statement of printing on copyright page. *Ace Double Novel Books D–315* (35¢). Bound with SIX WORLDS YONDER by Russell. Later enlarged as NEXT OF KIN.

THREE TO CONQUER.*New York: Avalon Books*, [*1956*].
  No statement of printing on copyright page.

WASP.*New York: Avalon Books*, [*1957*].
  No statement of printing on copyright page.

  ALSO:*London: Dennis Dobson*, [*1958*]. Boards. *First published in Great Britain in 1958* on copyright page. Enlarged text.

WITH A STRANGE DEVICE.*London: Dennis Dobson*, [*1964*].
  Boards. *First published in Great Britain in 1964* on copyright page. Issued later in the U.S. as THE MINDWARPERS.

Fred Thomas Saberhagen

(b. 1930)

BERSERKER. *New York: Ballantine Books*, [1967].
Wrappers. *First Edition: January, 1967* on copyright page. *A Ballantine Science Fiction U5063* (60¢).

BERSERKER'S PLANET. *New York: DAW Books, Inc.*, [1975].
Wrappers. *First printing, April 1975/1 2 3 4 5 6 7 8 9* on copyright page. *DAW: sf Books No. 147 UY1167* ($1.25).

THE BLACK MOUNTAINS. *New York: Ace Books*, [1971].
Wrappers. No statement of printing on copyright page. *Ace Book 06615* (60¢).

THE BOOK OF SABERHAGEN. *New York: DAW Books, Inc.*, [1975].
Wrappers. *First printing, January 1975/1 2 3 4 5 6 7 8 9* on copyright page. *DAW: sf Books No. 136 UY1153* ($1.25).

THE BROKEN LANDS. *New York: Ace Books, Inc.*, [1968].
Wrappers. No statement of printing on copyright page. *Ace Book G–740* (50¢).

BROTHER ASSASSIN. *New York: Ballantine Books*, [1969].
Wrappers. *First Printing: January, 1969* on copyright page. *A Ballantine Science Fiction Original 72018* (75¢). Issued later in Great Britain as BROTHER BERSERKER.

BROTHER BERSERKER. *[London]: Macdonald Science Fiction*, [1969].
Boards. *First published in Great Britain in 1969 . . .* on copyright page. Issued earlier in the U.S. as BROTHER ASSASSIN.

CHANGELING EARTH. *New York: DAW Books, Inc.*, [1973].
Wrappers. *First printing, February, 1973* on copyright page. Also, *First Printing* [through] *Tenth Printing* set in ten lines below the art credit on copyright page. *DAW: sf Books No. 41 UQ1041* (95¢).

THE DRACULA TAPE. *[New York]: Warner Paperback Library*, [1975].
Wrappers. *First Printing: June, 1975* on copyright page. *Warner Paperback Library 78–869* ($1.50).

THE GOLDEN PEOPLE. *New York: Ace Books, Inc.*, [1964].
Wrappers. No statement of printing on copyright page. *Ace Double M–103* (45¢). Bound with EXILE FROM XANADU by Lan Wright.

SPECIMENS. *New York: Popular Library*, [1976].
Wrappers. *January, 1976* on copyright page. *Popular Library 445–00335–125* ($1.25).

THE WATER OF THOUGHT. *New York: Ace Books, Inc.*, [1965].
Wrappers. No statement of printing on copyright page. *Ace Double M–127* (45¢). Bound with WE, THE VENUSIANS by John Rackham.

Margaret St. Clair
(b. 1911)

AGENT OF THE UNKNOWN. *New York: Ace Books*, [*1956*].
  Wrappers. No statement of printing on copyright page. *Ace Double Novel Books D–150* (35¢). Bound with THE WORLD JONES MADE by Philip K. Dick.

CHANGE THE SKY AND OTHER STORIES. *New York: Ace Books*, [*1974*].
  Wrappers. No statement of printing on copyright page. *Ace 10258* (95¢).

THE DANCERS OF NOYO. *New York: Ace Books*, [*1973*].
  Wrappers. *First Ace printing: July 1973* on copyright page. *An Ace Book 13600* (95¢).

THE DOLPHINS OF ALTAIR. [*New York*]: *A Dell Book*, [*1967*].
  Wrappers. *First Dell Printing—May, 1967* on copyright page. *Dell 2079* (50¢).

THE GAMES OF NEITH. *New York: Ace Books, Inc.*, [*1960*].
  Wrappers. No statement of printing on copyright page. *Ace Double Novel Books D–453* (35¢). Bound with THE EARTH GODS ARE COMING by Kenneth Bulmer.

THE GREEN QUEEN. *New York: Ace Books*, [*1956*].
  Wrappers. No statement of printing on copyright page. *Ace Double Novel Books D–176* (35¢). Bound with 3 THOUSAND YEARS by Thomas Calvert McClary.

MESSAGE FROM THE EOCENE. *New York: Ace Books, Inc.*, [*1964*].
  Wrappers. No statement of printing on copyright page *Ace Double M–105* (45¢). Bound with THREE WORLDS OF FUTURITY by St. Clair.

THE SHADOW PEOPLE. [*New York*]: *A Dell Book*, [*1969*].
  Wrappers. *First printing—August 1969* on copyright page. *Dell 7820* (60¢).

SIGN OF THE LABRYS. *New York: Bantam Books*, [*1963*].
  Wrappers. *August 1963* on copyright page. *Bantam Book J2617* (40¢).

THREE WORLDS OF FUTURITY. *New York: Ace Books, Inc.*, [*1964*].
  Wrappers. No statement of printing on copyright page. *Ace Double M–105* (45¢). Bound with MESSAGE FROM THE EOCENE by St. Clair.

James Henry Schmitz

(b. 1911)

AGENT OF VEGA. *Hicksville, New York: The Gnome Press, Inc.,* [*1960*].
Two bindings, priority as listed: (A) Light blue boards, spine lettered in gold; (B) Gray cloth, spine lettered in red. First edition so stated on copyright page.

THE DEMON BREED. *New York: Ace Books, Inc.,* [*1968*].
Wrappers. No statement of printing on copyright page. *An Ace Science Fiction Special H–105* (60¢).

ALSO: *New York: Ace Books, Inc.,* [*1969*]. Boards. No statement of printing on copyright page. Code *24 K* on page 187. First hardcover edition. Note: Issued by the Science Fiction Book Club.

THE ETERNAL FRONTIERS. *New York: G. P. Putnam's Sons,* [*1973*].
Boards. No statement of printing on copyright page.

THE LION GAME. *New York: DAW Books, Inc.,* [*1973*].
Wrappers. *First printing, January 1973* on copyright page. *DAW: sf Books No. 38 UQ1038* (95¢).

ALSO: *London: Sidgwick & Jackson,* [*1976*]. Boards. *First published in Great Britain in 1976* on copyright page. First hardcover edition.

A NICE DAY FOR SCREAMING AND OTHER TALES OF THE HUB. *Philadelphia and New York: Chilton Books,* [*1965*].
First edition so stated on copyright page.

A PRIDE OF MONSTERS. [*New York*]: *The Macmillan Company,* [*1970*].
First printing so stated on copyright page.

A TALE OF TWO CLOCKS. *New York: A Torquil Book Distributed by Dodd, Mead & Company,* [*1962*].
Boards. Two issues, priority of release as listed: (A) Dust jacket has price *$3.50* rubber-stamped in upper right corner of front flap, lower right corner clipped; Trade issue. (B) No price, *BOOK CLUB/EDITION* printed in lower right corner of front dust jacket flap. Book club issue. No statement of printing on copyright page. Note: Trade issue published 15 March 1962, book club issue was an April 1959 selection. Both issues from the same press run; both have printing code *D 6* on page 206. A second book club printing is identified by the code *D 8* on page 206.

THE TELZEY TOY. *New York: DAW Books, Inc.,* [*1973*].
Wrappers. *First printing, December 1973/1 2 3 4 5 6 7 8 9* on copyright page. *DAW: sf Books No. 82 UQ1086* (95¢).

ALSO: *London: Sidgwick & Jackson,* [*1976*]. Boards. *First published in Great Britain in 1976* on copyright page. First hardcover edition.

THE UNIVERSE AGAINST HER. *New York: Ace Books, Inc.,* [*1964*].
Wrappers. No statement of printing on copyright page. *Ace Book F–314* (40¢).

THE WITCHES OF KARRES. *Philadelphia and New York: Chilton Books,* [*1966*].
First edition so stated on copyright page.

Reference

James H. Schmitz: A Bibliography, [compiled by Mark Owings]. *Baltimore: Croatan House*, [*1973*].
   Wrappers. No statement of printing on copyright page. Offset from typewritten copy.

Thomas Nicholas Scortia
(b. 1926)

ARTERY OF FIRE. *Garden City: Doubleday & Company, Inc., 1972.*
First edition so stated on copyright page.

CAUTION! INFLAMMABLE! *Garden City: Doubleday & Company, Inc., 1975.*
Boards. First edition so stated on copyright page.

EARTHWRECK! *Greenwich, Conn.: Fawcett Publications, Inc., [1974].*
Wrappers. *May 1974* on copyright page. *Fawcett Gold Medal M2963* (95¢).

THE GLASS INFERNO. *Garden City: Doubleday & Company, Inc., 1974.*
First edition so stated on copyright page. With FRANK M. ROBINSON.

THE PROMETHEUS CRISIS. *Garden City: Doubleday & Company, Inc., 1975.*
Boards with cloth shelf back. First edition so stated on copyright page. With FRANK M.
ROBINSON.

WHAT MAD ORACLE? *Evanston: Regency Books, [1961].*
Wrappers. *Published December, 1961* on copyright page. *Regency Books RB 111* (50¢).

Edited Fiction

Human-Machines. *New York: Vintage Books, [1975].*
Wrappers. First edition so stated on copyright page. *Vintage V-607* ($2.95). Edited, with
introduction and notes, by Scortia with GEORGE ZEBROWSKI. Contains "Sea Change" by
Scortia.

ALSO: *London: Robert Hale, [1977].* Boards. *First published in Great Britain 1977* on
copyright page. First hardcover edition. Deletes "About the Editors," "About the Con-
tributors," and "Recommended Reading."

Strange Bedfellows. *New York: Random House, [1972].*
Boards with cloth shelf back. First edition so stated on copyright page. Edited, with
introduction, notes, and short story "The Icebox Blonde," by Scortia.

Two Views of Wonder. *New York: Ballantine Books, [1973].*
Wrappers. *First Printing: December 1973* on copyright page. *Ballantine Books 23713*
($1.25). Edited, with introduction, by Scortia with CHELSEA QUINN YARBRO. Contains
"Thou Good and Faithful" by Scortia.

Garrett Putnam Serviss

(1851–1929)

A COLUMBUS OF SPACE. *New York and London: D. Appleton and Company, 1911.*
Published September, 1911 on copyright page. *(1)* at base of text on page [298].

EDISON'S CONQUEST OF MARS. *Los Angeles: Carcosa House, 1947.*
First edition so stated on copyright page. 1500 numbered copies printed. Reissued in an
edited version as INVASION OF MARS.

INVASION OF MARS. [*Reseda, California: Powell Publications, Inc., 1969.*]
Wrappers. *First Printing August, 1969* on copyright page. *Powell Sci-Fi Classic PP 173*
(95¢). Reissue of EDISON'S CONQUEST OF MARS. Note: Text was heavily edited by Forrest
J. Ackerman. Scholars are advised to consult the Carcosa House edition.

THE MOON METAL. *New York and London: Harper & Brothers Publishers, 1900.*
No statement of printing on copyright page.

THE SECOND DELUGE. *New York: McBride, Nast & Company, 1912.*
Published, March, 1912 on copyright page. Note: Issued in Great Britain by Grant
Richards in 1912 utilizing sheets of the McBride, Nast edition. Two bindings, priority as
listed: (A) Blue cloth lettered in gold on spine and front cover; fore edge untrimmed;
(B) Green boards; all edges trimmed. Not seen; recorded by George Locke in *Science
Fiction First Editions* (London: Ferret, 1978), p. 47.

Bob (Robert) Shaw

(b. 1931)

COSMIC KALEIDOSCOPE. *London: Victor Gollancz Ltd, 1976.*
Boards. No statement of printing on copyright page.

ALSO:*Garden City: Doubleday & Company, Inc., 1977.* Boards. First edition so stated on copyright page. Drops "The Brink" and adds "Element of Chance" and "Deflation 2001."

GROUND ZERO MAN. *[New York]: Avon, [1971].*
Wrappers. *First Avon Printing, September, 1971* on copyright page. *Avon Science Fiction Original V2414* (75¢).

MEDUSA'S CHILDREN. *London: Victor Gollancz Ltd, 1977.*
Boards. No statement of printing on copyright page.

NIGHT WALK. *[New York]: A Banner Book, [1967].*
Wrappers. *First Banner Printing, September, 1967* on copyright page. *Banner B60–110* (60¢).

ALSO:*London: Victor Gollancz Ltd, 1976.* Boards. No statement of printing on copyright page. First hardcover edition.

ONE MILLION TOMORROWS. *New York: Ace Books, [1970].*
Wrappers. No statement of printing on copyright page. *An Ace Science Fiction Special 62938* (75¢).

ALSO:*London: Victor Gollancz Limited, 1971.* Boards. No statement of printing on copyright page. First hardcover edition.

ORBITSVILLE. *London: Victor Gollancz Ltd, 1975.*
Boards. No statement of printing on copyright page.

OTHER DAYS, OTHER EYES. *London: Victor Gollancz, 1972.*
Boards. No statement of printing on copyright page.

THE PALACE OF ETERNITY. *New York: An Ace Book, [1969].*
Wrappers. No statement of printing on copyright page. *An Ace Science Fiction Special 65050* (75¢).

ALSO:*London: Victor Gollancz Ltd, 1970.* Boards. No statement of printing on copyright page. First hardcover edition.

SHADOW OF HEAVEN. *[New York]: An Avon Book, [1969].*
Wrappers. *First Avon Printing, June, 1969* on copyright page. *Avon S398* (60¢).

ALSO: *[London]: New English Library, [1970].* Wrappers. *First NEL abridged edition August 1970* on copyright page. *New English Library Science Fiction 2716* (5/–). Abridged text.

TOMORROW LIES IN AMBUSH. *London: Victor Gollancz Ltd, 1973.*
Boards. No statement of printing on copyright page.

ALSO:*New York: Ace Books, [1973].* Wrappers. *First Ace Printing: February, 1973* on copyright page. *Ace Science Fiction 81656* (95¢). Adds two stories, "Stormseeker" and "Element of Chance." Note: Both editions published in February 1973.

THE TWO-TIMERS. *New York: Ace Books, Inc.,* [*1968*].
Wrappers. No statement of printing on copyright page. *An Ace Science Fiction Special H–79* (60¢).

ALSO: *London: Victor Gollancz Ltd, 1969.* Boards. No statement of printing on copyright page. First hardcover edition.

WHO GOES HERE? *London: Victor Gollancz Ltd, 1977.*
Boards. No statement of printing on copyright page.

A WREATH OF STARS. *London: Victor Gollancz Ltd, 1976.*
Boards. No statement of printing on copyright page.

Robert E. Sheckley
(b. 1928)

CALIBRE .50. *New York: Bantam Books*, [*1961*].
Wrappers. *Published March 1961* on copyright page. *A Bantam Mystery A2216* (35¢).

CAN YOU FEEL ANYTHING WHEN I DO THIS? *Garden City: Doubleday & Company, Inc., 1971.*
First edition so stated on copyright page. Reissued as THE SAME TO YOU DOUBLED AND OTHER STORIES.

CITIZEN IN SPACE. *New York: Ballantine Books*, [*1955*].
Two bindings, no priority: (A) Cloth; (B) Wrappers. *Ballantine Books 126* (35¢). No statement of printing on copyright page.

DEAD RUN. *New York: Bantam Books*, [*1961*].
Wrappers. *Published May 1961* on copyright page. *A Bantam Mystery A2240* (35¢).

DIMENSION OF MIRACLES. [*New York*]: *A Dell Book*, [*1968*].
Wrappers. *First Printing—June 1968* on copyright page. *Dell 1940* (50¢).

ALSO: *London: Victor Gollancz, 1969.* Boards. No statement of printing on copyright page. First hardcover edition.

THE GAME OF X. *New York: Delacorte Press*, [*1965*].
No statement of printing on copyright page.

IMMORTALITY DELIVERED. *New York: Avalon Books*, [*1958*].
No statement of printing on copyright page. Note: Text abridged against the author's wishes. Full text published as IMMORTALITY, INC.

IMMORTALITY, INC. *New York: Bantam Books*, [*1959*].
Wrappers. *Bantam edition published October 1959* on copyright page. *A Bantam Book A1991* (35¢). Full text. Issued earlier with abridged text as IMMORTALITY DELIVERED.

ALSO: *London: Victor Gollancz Ltd, 1963.* Boards. No statement of printing on copyright page. First hardcover edition of full text.

JOURNEY BEYOND TOMORROW. [*New York*]: *The New American Library*, [*1962*].
Wrappers. *First Printing, December, 1962* on copyright page. *Signet Books D2223* (50¢).

ALSO: *London: Victor Gollancz Ltd, 1964.* Boards. No statement of printing on copyright page. First hardcover edition.

LIVE GOLD. *New York: Bantam Books*, [*1962*].
Wrappers. *Published July 1962* on copyright page. *A Bantam Mystery J2401* (40¢).

THE MAN IN THE WATER. *Evanston, Illinois: Regency Books*, [*1961*].
Wrappers. *Published December, 1961* on copyright page. *Regency Books RB 112* (50¢).

MINDSWAP. *New York: Delacorte Press*, [*1966*].
First printing so stated on copyright page.

NOTIONS: UNLIMITED. *New York: Bantam Books*, [*1960*].
Wrappers. *Published June 1960* on copyright page. *A Bantam Book A2003* (35¢).

OPTIONS. *New York: Pyramid Books*, [*1975*].
Wrappers. *June 1975* on copyright page. *Pyramid Original V3688* ($1.25).

THE PEOPLE TRAP. [*New York*]: *A Dell Book*, [*1968*].
Wrappers. *First printing—December 1968* on copyright page. *Dell 6881* (60¢).

ALSO: *London: Victor Gollancz Ltd*, *1969*. Boards. No statement of printing on copyright page. First hardcover edition.

PILGRIMAGE TO EARTH. *New York: Bantam Books*, [*1957*].
Wrappers. *Published October 1957* on copyright page. *Bantam Books A1672* (35¢).

THE ROBERT SHECKLEY OMNIBUS. *London: Victor Gollancz Ltd*, *1973*.
Boards. No statement of printing on copyright page.

THE SAME TO YOU DOUBLED AND OTHER STORIES. *London and Sydney: Pan Books Ltd*, [*1974*].
Wrappers. *This edition published 1974* . . . on copyright page. *Pan Science Fiction 0 330 23988 0* (35¢). Reissue of CAN YOU FEEL ANYTHING WHEN I DO THIS?

SHARDS OF SPACE. *New York: Bantam Books*, [*1962*].
Wrappers. *Published July 1962* on copyright page. *Bantam Book J2443* (40¢).

THE STATUS CIVILIZATION. [*New York*]: *Published by The New American Library*, [*1960*].
Wrappers. *First Printing, September, 1960* on copyright page. *Signet Books S1840* (35¢).

ALSO: *London: Victor Gollancz Ltd*, *1976*. Boards. No statement of printing on copyright page. First hardcover edition.

STORE OF INFINITY. *New York: Bantam Books*, [*1960*].
Wrappers. *Published November 1960* on copyright page. *A Bantam Book A2170* (35¢).

THE 10TH VICTIM. *New York: Ballantine Books*, [*1966*].
Wrappers. *First Edition: December, 1965* on copyright page. *An Original Ballantine Book U5050* (60¢). Note: Publisher's review slip gives publication date as 3 January 1966.

TIME LIMIT. *Toronto New York London: Bantam Books*, [*1967*].
Wrappers. *Published April 1967* on copyright page. *A Bantam Mystery F3381* (50¢).

UNTOUCHED BY HUMAN HANDS. *New York: Ballantine Books*, [*1954*].
Two bindings, no priority: (A) Boards; (B) Wrappers. *Ballantine Books 73* (35¢). No statement of printing on copyright page.

ALSO: *London: Michael Joseph*, [*1955*]. Boards. *First published* . . . *1955* on copyright page. Drops two stories appearing in the U.S. collection, "The King's Wishes" and "The Demons," and adds two, "Watchbird" and "Hands Off."

WHITE DEATH. *New York: Bantam Books*, [*1963*].
Wrappers. *Published November 1963* on copyright page. *A Bantam Mystery J2685* (40¢).

Alice Sheldon
(b. 1916)

TEN THOUSAND LIGHT-YEARS FROM HOME. *New York: Ace Books*, [*1973*].
Wrappers. *First Ace printing: July 1973* on copyright page. *An Ace Book 80180* (95¢).
James Tiptree, Jr., pseudonym.

ALSO:*London: Eyre Methuen*, [*1975*]. Boards. *First published in Great Britain 1975* on
copyright page. First hardcover edition.

WARM WORLDS AND OTHERWISE. *New York: Ballantine Books*, [*1975*].
Wrappers. *First Printing: February, 1975* on copyright page. *Ballantine Books SF 24380*
($1.50). *James Tiptree, Jr., pseudonym.*

Reference

The Fiction of James Tiptree, Jr., [by] Gardner Dozois. [*New York*]: *Algol Press*, [*1977*].
Wrappers. *This edition is printed in a limited edition of 1,000 copies* on copyright page.
Note: The essay was originally published as an introduction to the 1976 Gregg Press edition
of TEN THOUSAND LIGHT-YEARS FROM HOME. Adds a checklist of Sheldon's published
fiction by Jeff Smith.

Robert Silverberg

(b. 1935)

Compiler's note: This checklist of Silverberg's fiction is not complete. All science fiction and fantasy titles, including those published under pseudonyms, are listed. Missing are pseudonymous novels in the mystery and western genres (including one revised for W. R. Burnett) as well as romantic fiction published between 1959 and 1966 in pocket book format under various pen names including Don Elliott.

ACROSS A BILLION YEARS. *New York: The Dial Press, Inc., [1969]*.
   First printing so stated on copyright page.

ALIENS FROM SPACE. *New York: Avalon Books, [1958]*.
   No statement of printing on copyright page. *David Osborne, pseudonym*.

THE ANVIL OF TIME. *London: Sidgwick & Jackson, [1969]*.
   Boards. *First published in Great Britain 1969* on copyright page. Issued earlier in the U.S. as HAWKSBILL STATION.

THE BEST OF ROBERT SILVERBERG. *New York: Pocket Books, [1976]*.
   Wrappers. *February, 1976* on copyright page. *Pocket Books 80282 ($1.95)*.

   ALSO: *London: Sidgwick & Jackson, [1977]*. Boards. *First published in Great Britain in 1977 . . .* on copyright page. First hardcover edition.

THE BOOK OF SKULLS. *New York: Charles Scribner's Sons, [1971]*.
   Boards with cloth shelf back. Code *A–12.71 [C]* on copyright page.

BORN WITH THE DEAD. *New York: Random House, [1974]*.
   Boards. First edition so stated on copyright page.

THE CALIBRATED ALLIGATOR. *New York Chicago San Francisco: Holt, Rinehart and Winston, [1969]*.
   Two bindings, no priority: (A) Green boards printed in black. Trade binding. (B) Pictorial cloth reproducing dust jacket design. Library binding. First edition so stated on copyright page.

CAPRICORN GAMES. *New York: Random House, [1976]*.
   Boards. First edition so stated on copyright page.

COLLISION COURSE. *New York: Avalon Books, [1961]*.
   No statement of printing on copyright page.

CONQUERORS FROM THE DARKNESS. *New York • Chicago • San Francisco: Holt, Rinehart and Winston, [1965]*.
   Two bindings, no priority: (A) Boards. Trade binding. (B) Pictorial cloth reproducing dust jacket design. Library binding. First edition so stated on copyright page.

THE CUBE ROOT OF UNCERTAINTY. *[New York]: The Macmillan Company, [1970]*.
   First printing so stated on copyright page.

THE DAWNING LIGHT. *New York: Gnome Press, Inc., [1959]*.
   Boards. First edition so stated on copyright page. With RANDALL GARRETT. *Robert Randall, pseudonym*.

DIMENSION THIRTEEN. *New York: Ballantine Books*, [*1969*].
  Wrappers. *First Printing: May, 1969* on copyright page. *Ballantine Science Fiction 01601*
  (75¢).

DOWNWARD TO THE EARTH. *Garden City: Nelson Doubleday, Inc.*, [*1970*].
  Boards. No statement of printing on copyright page. Four printings, priority as listed:
  (A) Code *28L* at base of page 179; (B) Code *39L* at base of page 179; (C) Code *50M* at base
  of page 179; (D) Code *24N* at base of page 179. Note: Issued by the Science Fiction Book
  Club.

DYING INSIDE. *New York: Charles Scribner's Sons*, [*1972*].
  Boards. Code *A–10.72 (V)* on copyright page.

EARTH'S OTHER SHADOW. [*New York*]: *New American Library*, [*1973*].
  Wrappers. *First Printing, June, 1973* on copyright page. *Signet 451–Q5538* (95¢).

  ALSO: [*London*]: *Millington*, [*1977*]. Boards. *First published in Great Britain in 1977 . . .*
  on copyright page. First hardcover edition.

THE FEAST OF ST. DIONYSUS. *New York: Charles Scribner's Sons*, [*1975*].
  Boards. Code *1 3 5 7 9 11 13 15 17 19 V/C 20 18 16 14 12 10 8 6 4 2* on copyright page.

THE GATE OF WORLDS. *New York Chicago San Francisco: Holt, Rinehart and Winston*,
  [*1967*].
  Two bindings, no priority: (A) Black boards stamped in red. Trade binding. (B) Pictorial
  cloth reproducing dust jacket design. Library binding. First edition so stated on copyright
  page.

GODLING, GO HOME! *New York: Belmont Books*, [*1964*].
  Wrappers. *June 1964* on copyright page. *Belmont Future Series L92–591* (50¢).

HAWKSBILL STATION. *Garden City: Doubleday & Company, Inc.*, *1968*.
  First edition so stated on copyright page. Issued later in Great Britain as THE ANVIL OF
  TIME.

INVADERS FROM EARTH. *New York: Ace Books, Inc.*, [*1958*].
  Wrappers. No statement of printing on copyright page. *Ace Double Novel Books D–286*
  (35¢). Bound with ACROSS TIME by David Grinnell. Note: Abridged as "We, the Marauders." See A PAIR FROM SPACE.

  ALSO: *London: Sidgwick & Jackson*, [*1977*]. Boards. *This edition published in Great*
  Britain in 1977 . . . on copyright page. First separate hardcover edition. Collected earlier
  in hardcover in A ROBERT SILVERBERG OMNIBUS.

INVISIBLE BARRIERS. *New York: Avalon Books*, [*1958*].
  No statement of printing on copyright page. Two states noted, probable sequence as listed:
  (A) First four leaves printed in incorrect sequence as follows: half title/blank, page
  7/copyright page, dedication/blank, title page/page 8; (B) Paged correctly. *David Osborne*,
  pseudonym.

LEST WE FORGET THEE, EARTH. *New York: Ace Books, Inc.*, [*1958*].
  Wrappers. No statement of printing on copyright page. *Ace Double Novel Books D–291*
  (35¢). *Calvin M. Knox, pseudonym*. Bound with PEOPLE MINUS X by Raymond Z. Gallun.

LOST RACE OF MARS. *Philadelphia, Toronto: The John C. Winston Company*, [*1960*].
  First edition so stated on copyright page.

THE MAN IN THE MAZE. *[New York]: An Avon Book, [1969]*.
Wrappers. *First Avon Printing, February, 1969* on copyright page. *An Avon Original V2262 (75¢)*.

ALSO:*London: Sidgwick & Jackson, [1969]*. Boards. *First published in Great Britain 1969* on copyright page. First hardcover edition.

THE MASK OF AKHNATEN. *New York: The Macmillan Company, [1965]*.
Two bindings, no priority: (A) Yellow boards stamped in black. Trade binding. (B) Yellow (?) cloth. Library binding (listed in *Cumulative Book Index;* not seen). First printing so stated on copyright page.

THE MASKS OF TIME. *New York: Ballantine Books, [1968]*.
Wrappers. *First Edition: May, 1968* on copyright page. *Ballantine Science Fiction Original U6121 (75¢)*. Issued later in Great Britain as VORNAN-19.

MASTER OF LIFE AND DEATH. *New York: Ace Books, [1957]*.
Wrappers. No statement of printing on copyright page. *Ace Double Novel Books D–237 (35¢)*. Bound with THE SECRET VISITORS by James White.

ALSO:*London: Sidgwick & Jackson, [1977]*. Boards. *This edition published in Great Britain in 1977 . . .* on copyright page. First separate hardcover edition. Collected earlier in hardcover in A ROBERT SILVERBERG OMNIBUS.

MOONFERNS AND STARSONGS. *New York: Ballantine Books, [1971]*.
Wrappers. *First Printing: June, 1971* on copyright page. *Ballantine Books Science Fiction 02278–5–095 (95¢)*.

NEEDLE IN A TIMESTACK. *New York: Ballantine Books, [1966]*.
Wrappers. *First Edition: November, 1966* on copyright page. *A Ballantine Science Fiction Original U2330 (50¢)*.

NEXT STOP THE STARS. *New York: Ace Books, Inc., [1962]*.
Wrappers. No statement of printing on copyright page. *Ace Double F–145 (40¢)*. Bound with THE SEED OF EARTH by Silverberg.

NIGHTWINGS. *[New York]: Avon, [1969]*.
Wrappers. *First Avon Printing, September, 1969* on copyright page. *An Avon Original V2303 (75¢)*.

ALSO:*New York: Walker and Company, [1970]*. Boards. *First published in book form in the United States of America in 1970 . . .* on copyright page. First hardcover edition.

ONE OF OUR ASTEROIDS IS MISSING. *New York: Ace Books, Inc., [1964]*.
Wrappers. No statement of printing on copyright page. *Ace Double F–253 (40¢)*. *Calvin M. Knox, pseudonym*. Bound with the THE TWISTED MEN by A. E. van Vogt.

A PAIR FROM SPACE. *New York: Belmont Books, [1965]*.
Wrappers. *January 1965* on copyright page. *Belmont 92–612 (50¢)*. Note: A later printing drops *January 1965* from copyright page and carries book number *B50–813*. Contains "We, the Marauders," an abridged version of INVADERS FROM EARTH.

PARSECS AND PARABLES. *Garden City: Doubleday & Company, Inc., 1970*.
First edition so stated on copyright page.

THE PLANET KILLERS. *New York: Ace Books, Inc., [1959]*.
Wrappers. No statement of printing on copyright page. *Ace Double Novel Books D–407 (35¢)*. Bound with WE CLAIM THESE STARS! by Poul Anderson.

PLANET OF DEATH.*New York, Chicago, San Francisco: Holt, Rinehart and Winston*, [*1967*].
Two bindings, no priority: (A) Black boards stamped in white. Trade binding. (B) Pictorial
cloth reproducing dust jacket design. Library binding. First edition so stated on copyright
page.

THE PLOT AGAINST EARTH.*New York: Ace Books, Inc.*, [*1959*].
Wrappers. No statement of printing on copyright page. *Ace Double Novel Books D–358*
(35¢). *Calvin M. Knox, pseudonym.* Bound with RECRUIT FOR ANDROMEDA by Milton
Lesser.

THE REALITY TRIP.*New York: Ballantine Books*, [*1972*].
Wrappers. *First Printing: March, 1972* on copyright page. *Ballantine Books Science
Fiction 02548–2–095* (95¢).

RECALLED TO LIFE.*New York: Lancer Books*, [*1962*].
Wrappers. *A Lancer Science Fiction Classic • 1962* on copyright page. *The Lancer Science
Fiction Library 74–810* (75¢). Note: *Lancer Focus Books 72–156* (50¢) is a reprint.

ALSO:*Garden City: Doubleday & Company, Inc., 1972*. No statement of printing on
copyright page. Code *N24* at base of page 184. Revised text.

REGAN'S PLANET.*New York: Pyramid Books*, [*1964*].
Wrappers. *March 1964* on copyright page. *Pyramid Books F–986* (40¢).

REVOLT ON ALPHA C.*New York: Thomas Y. Crowell Company*, [*1955*].
First printing so stated on copyright page.

A ROBERT SILVERBERG OMNIBUS.*London: Sidgwick & Jackson*, [*1970*].
Boards. No statement of printing on copyright page. Reprint. Collects MASTER OF LIFE
AND DEATH, INVADERS FROM EARTH, and THE TIME-HOPPERS. Note: First hardcover publi-
cation for MASTER OF LIFE AND DEATH and INVADERS FROM EARTH.

THE SECOND TRIP.*Garden City: Nelson Doubleday, Inc.*, [*1972*].
Boards. No statement of printing on copyright page. Code *39N* at base of page 181. Note:
Issued by the Science Fiction Book Club.

THE SEED OF EARTH.*New York: Ace Books, Inc.*, [*1962*].
Wrappers. No statement of printing on copyright page. *Ace Double F–145* (40¢). Bound
with NEXT STOP THE STARS by Silverberg.

SHADRACH IN THE FURNACE.*Indianapolis/New York: The Bobbs-Merrill Company, Inc.*,
[*1976*].
Boards with cloth shelf back. First printing so stated on copyright page.

THE SHORES OF TOMORROW.*Nashville New York: Thomas Nelson Inc., Publishers*, [*1976*].
First edition so stated on copyright page.

THE SHROUDED PLANET.*New York: Gnome Press, Inc., Publishers, 1957.*
Boards. First edition so stated on copyright page. With RANDALL GARRETT.*Robert Randall, pseudonym.*

THE SILENT INVADERS.*New York: Ace Books, Inc.*, [*1963*].
Wrappers. No statement of printing on copyright page. *Ace Double F–195* (40¢). Bound
with BATTLE ON VENUS by William F. Temple.

ALSO:*London: Dennis Dobson*, [*1975*]. Boards. *First published in Great Britain in 1975*
on copyright page. First hardcover edition.

SON OF MAN.*New York: Ballantine Books, [1971]*.
   Wrappers. *First printing: June, 1971* on copyright page. *Ballantine Books 02277–7–125* ($1.25).

STARHAVEN.*New York: Avalon Books, [1958]*.
   No statement of printing on copyright page. *Ivar Jorgenson, pseudonym.*

STARMAN'S QUEST.*Hicksville, N.Y.: Gnome Press, [1959]*.
   Two bindings, priority as listed: (A) Dark blue-gray boards, spine lettered in yellow; (B) Gray cloth, spine lettered in red. First edition so stated on copyright page.

STEPSONS OF TERRA.*New York: Ace Books, Inc., [1958]*.
   Wrappers. No statement of printing on copyright page. *Ace Double Novel Books D–311* (35¢). Bound with A MAN CALLED DESTINY by Lan Wright.

THE STOCHASTIC MAN.*New York/Evanston/San Francisco/London: Harper & Row, Publishers, [1975]*.
   Boards with cloth shelf back. First edition so stated on copyright page.

SUNDANCE AND OTHER SCIENCE FICTION STORIES.*Nashville/New York: Thomas Nelson Inc., [1974]*.
   Boards. First edition so stated on copyright page.

SUNRISE ON MERCURY.*Nashville New York: Thomas Nelson Inc., Publishers, [1975]*.
   Boards. First edition so stated on copyright page.

THE 13TH IMMORTAL.*New York: Ace Books, [1957]*.
   Wrappers. No statement of printing on copyright page. *Ace Double Novel Books D–223* (35¢). Bound with THIS FORTRESS WORLD by James E. Gunn.

THORNS.*New York: Ballantine Books, [1967]*.
   Wrappers. *First Edition: August, 1967* on copyright page. *A Ballantine Science Fiction Original U6097* (75¢).

   ALSO:*New York: Walker and Company, [1969]*. Boards. *Published in the United States of America in 1969* on copyright page. First hardcover edition.

THOSE WHO WATCH.*[New York]: Published by The New American Library, [1967]*.
   Wrappers. *First printing, April, 1967* on copyright page. *Signet Books P3160* (60¢).

THREE SURVIVED.*New York Chicago San Francisco: Holt, Rinehart and Winston, [1969]*.
   Two bindings, no priority: (A) Green boards lettered in black. Trade binding. (B) Green cloth lettered in black. Library binding. First edition so stated on copyright page.

THE TIME-HOPPERS.*Garden City: Doubleday & Company, Inc., 1967*.
   First edition so stated on copyright page.

A TIME OF CHANGES.*Garden City: Nelson Doubleday, Inc., [1971]*.
   Boards. No statement of printing on copyright page. Five printings, priority as listed: (A) Code *22 M* at base of page 179; (B) Code *B22* at base of page 182. Note: *22 M* is apparently simultaneous with *B22* as both are 1971 codes; (C) Code *27N* at base of page 179; (D) Code *D 37* at base of page 181; (E) Code *E40* at base of page 182. Note: Issued by the Science Fiction Book Club.

TIME OF THE GREAT FREEZE.*New York/Chicago/San Francisco: Holt, Rinehart and Winston, [1964]*.
   Two bindings, no priority: (A) Boards. Trade binding. (B) Pictorial cloth reproducing dust jacket design. Library binding. First edition so stated on copyright page.

TO LIVE AGAIN. *Garden City: Doubleday & Company, Inc., 1969.*
First edition so stated on copyright page.

TO OPEN THE SKY. *New York: Ballantine Books, [1967].*
Wrappers. *First Edition: May, 1967* on copyright page. *Ballantine Science Fiction U6093* (75¢).

ALSO: *Boston: Gregg Press, 1977. First Printing, June 1977* on copyright page. First hardcover edition. Note: Not issued in dust jacket.

TO WORLDS BEYOND. *Philadelphia New York: Chilton Books, [1965].*
First edition so stated on copyright page.

TOWER OF GLASS. *New York: Charles Scribner's Sons, [1970].*
Code *A–10.70 (C)* on copyright page.

UNFAMILIAR TERRITORY. *New York: Charles Scribner's Sons, [1973].*
Code *1 3 5 7 9 11 13 15 17 19 C/C 20 18 16 14 12 10 8 6 4 2* on copyright page. Note: The 1975 *Cumulative Book Index* indicates that the 1975 Victor Gollancz edition adds two stories not in the Scribner edition. This is not correct. The Gollancz edition is photo-offset from the Scribner plates and the texts are identical.

UP THE LINE. *New York: Ballantine Books, [1969].*
Wrappers. *First Printing: August, 1969* on copyright page. *Ballantine Books 01680* (75¢).

VALLEY BEYOND TIME. *[New York]: A Dell Book, [1973].*
Wrappers. *First Dell printing—January 1973* on copyright page. *Dell 9249* (95¢).

VORNAN-19. *London: Sidgwick & Jackson, [1970].*
Boards. *First published in Great Britain in 1970* on copyright page. Issued earlier in the U.S. as THE MASKS OF TIME.

WE, THE MARAUDERS. See A PAIR FROM SPACE.

THE WORLD INSIDE. *Garden City: Doubleday & Company, Inc., 1971.*
First edition so stated on copyright page.

WORLD'S FAIR, 1992. *Chicago New York: Follett Publishing Company, [1970].*
Boards. First printing so stated on copyright page.

Edited Fiction

The Aliens. *Nashville New York: Thomas Nelson Inc., Publishers, [1976].*
Boards. First edition so stated on copyright page. Edited, with introduction and short story "Sundance," by Silverberg.

Alpha One. *New York: Ballantine Books, [1970].*
Wrappers. *First Printing: September, 1970* on copyright page. *Ballantine Books Science Fiction 02014–6–095* (95¢). Edited, with introduction, by Silverberg.

Alpha Two. *New York: Ballantine Books, [1971].*
Wrappers. *First Printing: November, 1971* on copyright page. *Ballantine Books Science Fiction 02419–2–095* (95¢). Edited, with introduction and notes, by Silverberg.

Alpha Three. *New York: Ballantine Books, [1972].*
Wrappers. *First Printing: October, 1972* on copyright page. *Ballantine Books Science Fiction 02883–X–125* ($1.25). Edited, with introduction, by Silverberg.

Alpha 4. *New York: Ballantine Books*, [*1973*].
Wrappers. *First Printing: October, 1973* on copyright page. *Ballantine Books 23564* ($1.25). Edited, with introduction, by Silverberg.

Alpha 5. *New York: Ballantine Books*, [*1974*].
Wrappers. *First Printing: August, 1974* on copyright page. *Ballantine Science Fiction 24140* ($1.25). Edited, with introduction and notes, by Silverberg.

Alpha 6. [*New York*]: *Published by Berkley Publishing Corporation*, [*1976*].
Wrappers. *April, 1976* on copyright page. *A Berkley Medallion Book D3048* ($1.50). Edited, with introduction, by Silverberg.

Alpha 7. [*New York*]: *Published by Berkley Publishing Corporation*, [*1977*].
Wrappers. *July, 1977* on copyright page. *A Berkley Medallion Book 0–425–03530–1* ($1.50). Edited, with introduction and notes, by Silverberg.

Alpha 8. [*New York*]: *Published by Berkley Publishing Corporation*, [*1977*].
Wrappers. *November, 1977* on copyright page. *A Berkley Medallion Book 0–425–03561–1* ($1.50). Edited, with introduction, by Silverberg.

Beyond Control. *Nashville Camden New York: Thomas Nelson Inc.*, [*1972*].
Two bindings, no priority established: (A) Dark blue cloth, spine lettered in silver; price in upper right corner of dust jacket flap is *$5.95;* (B) Pictorial boards reproducing the dust jacket design; *A Guild Book* printed on spine; no price on dust jacket flap; *This is a Junior Literary Guild selection* . . . at base of front dust jacket flap. First edition so stated on copyright page. Edited, with introduction and short story "The Iron Chancellor," by Silverberg. Note: Second printing retains the first edition statement but is also marked *Second printing, February 1973* on copyright page.

Chains of the Sea. *Nashville: Thomas Nelson Inc.*, [*1973*].
Boards. First edition so stated on copyright page. Edited, with introduction, by Silverberg.

The Crystal Ship. *Nashville New York: Thomas Nelson Inc., Publishers*, [*1976*].
Boards. First edition so stated on copyright page. Edited, with introduction, by Silverberg.

Dark Stars. *New York: Ballantine Books*, [*1969*].
Wrappers. *First Printing: December, 1969* on copyright page. *Ballantine Books Science Fiction 01796 095* (95¢). Edited, with introduction, notes, and short story "Road to Nightfall," by Silverberg.

The Day the Sun Stood Still. *Nashville New York: Thomas Nelson, Inc.*, [*1972*].
First edition so stated on copyright page. Edited anonymously, with short story "Thomas the Proclaimer," by Silverberg.

Deep Space. *Nashville Camden New York: Thomas Nelson Inc.*, [*1973*].
First edition so stated on copyright page. Edited, with introduction and short story "The Sixth Palace," by Silverberg.

Earth is the Strangest Planet. *Nashville New York: Thomas Nelson Inc., Publishers*, [*1977*].
Boards. First edition so stated on copyright page. Edited, with introduction and short story "When We Went to See the End of the World," by Silverberg.

Earthmen and Strangers. *New York: Duell, Sloan and Pearce*, [*1966*].
First edition so stated on copyright page. Edited, with introduction and short story "Alaree," by Silverberg.

The Ends of Time. *New York: Hawthorn Books, Inc. Publishers, [1970]*.
Code *1 2 3 4 5 6 7 8 9 10* on copyright page. Edited, with introduction and short story "At the End of Days," by Silverberg.

Epoch. *New York: Published by Berkley Publishing Corporation, [1975]*.
No statement of printing on copyright page. Edited, with introduction, by Silverberg with ROGER ELWOOD. Note: Advance copies contained story by Harlan Ellison "Demon With a Glass Hand" deleted from the published edition.

Explorers of Space. *Nashville New York: Thomas Nelson Inc., Publishers, [1975]*.
Boards. First edition so stated on copyright page. Edited, with introduction and short story "Collecting Team," by Silverberg.

Four Futures. *New York: Hawthorn Books, Inc., [1971]*.
Code *1 2 3 4 5 6 7 8 9 10* on copyright page. Anonymously edited, with short story "Going," by Silverberg.

Galactic Dreamers. *New York: Random House, [1977]*.
Boards with cloth shelf back. First edition so stated on copyright page. Edited, with introduction and short story "Breckenridge and the Continuum," by Silverberg.

Great Short Novels of Science Fiction. *New York: Ballantine Books, [1970]*.
Wrappers. *First Printing: July, 1970* on copyright page. *Ballantine Books Science Fiction 01960* (95¢). Edited, with introduction and notes, by Silverberg.

Infinite Jests. *Radnor, Pennsylvania: Chilton Book Company, [1974]*.
First edition so stated on copyright page. Edited, with introduction and short story "(Now+n), (Now−n)," by Silverberg.

The Infinite Web. *New York: The Dial Press, [1977]*.
First printing so stated on copyright page. Edited, with introduction, notes, and short story "The Wind and the Rain," by Silverberg.

Invaders From Space. *New York: Hawthorn Books, Inc., [1972]*.
Code *1 2 3 4 5 6 7 8 9 10* on copyright page. Edited, with introduction and short story "Nightwings," by Silverberg.

Men and Machines. *New York: Meredith Press, [1968]*.
Boards with cloth shelf back. First edition so stated on copyright page. Edited, with introduction and short story "The Macauley Circuit," by Silverberg. Note: Reported in a Junior Literary Guild binding of washable cloth reproducing dust jacket design (not seen).

Mind to Mind. *New York Camden: Thomas Nelson Inc., [1971]*.
First edition so stated on copyright page. Edited, with introduction, notes, and short story "Something Wild is Loose," by Silverberg.

The Mirror of Infinity. *New York, Evanston, and London: Harper & Row, Publishers, [1970]*.
Boards with cloth shelf back. First edition so stated on copyright page. Edited, with introduction, by Silverberg.

Mutants. *Nashville, Tennessee/New York, New York: Thomas Nelson Inc., Publishers, [1974]*.
Boards. First edition so stated on copyright page. Edited, with introduction and short story "The Man Who Never Forgot," by Silverberg.

The New Atlantis. *New York: Hawthorn Books, Inc., [1975]*.
Boards with cloth shelf back. Code *1 2 3 4 5 6 7 8 9 10* on copyright page. Edited, with introduction, by Silverberg.

New Dimensions I. *Garden City: Doubleday & Company, Inc., 1971*.
First edition so stated on copyright page. Edited, with introduction, by Silverberg.

New Dimensions II. *Garden City: Doubleday & Company, Inc., 1972*.
First edition so stated on copyright page. Edited, with introduction, by Silverberg.

New Dimensions 3. *Garden City: Nelson Doubleday, Inc., [1973]*.
Boards. No statement of printing on copyright page. Code *D36* at base of page 211. Edited, with introduction, by Silverberg. Note: Issued by the Science Fiction Book Club.

New Dimensions IV. *[New York]: New American Library, [1974]*.
Wrappers. *First printing, October, 1974/1 2 3 4 5 6 7 8 9* on copyright page. *Signet 451–Y6113–125* ($1.25). Edited, with notes, by Silverberg.

New Dimensions Science Fiction Number 5. *New York Evanston San Francisco London: Harper & Row, Publishers, [1975]*.
Boards with cloth shelf back. First edition so stated on copyright page. Edited, with notes, by Silverberg.

New Dimensions Science Fiction Number 6. *New York Hagerstown San Francisco London: Harper & Row, Publishers, [1976]*.
Boards with cloth shelf back. First edition so stated on copyright page. Edited, with introduction and notes, by Silverberg.

New Dimensions Science Fiction Number 7. *New York, Hagerstown, San Francisco, London: Harper & Row, Publishers, [1977]*.
Boards with cloth shelf back. First edition so stated on copyright page. Two states, priority as listed: (A) Introductory note for John Shirley is duplicated for Gordon Eklund on page [2]; (B) Leaf [A⁵] is a cancel and the note for Eklund is present. Edited, with introductory notes, by Silverberg.

No Mind of Man. *New York: Hawthorn Books, Inc. Publishers, [1973]*.
Boards with cloth shelf back. Code *1 2 3 4 5 6 7 8 9 10* on copyright page. Edited, with foreword and short story "This is the Road," by Silverberg.

Other Dimensions. *New York: Hawthorn Books, Inc. Publishers, [1973]*.
Code *1 2 3 4 5 6 7 8 9 10* on copyright page. Edited, with introduction, by Silverberg.

The Science Fiction Bestiary. *New York Camden: Thomas Nelson Inc., [1971]*.
Boards. First edition so stated on copyright page. Edited, with introduction and short story "Collecting Team," by Silverberg. Note: Second printing retains the first edition statement but is marked *Second printing, March 1973* on copyright page.

Science Fiction Hall of Fame. Volume One. *Garden City: Doubleday & Company, Inc., 1970*.
First edition so stated on copyright page. Edited, with introduction, by Silverberg. Note: Volume two (parts A and B) were edited by Ben Bova.

Strange Gifts. *Nashville New York: Thomas Nelson Inc., Publishers, [1975]*.
Boards. First edition so stated on copyright page. Edited, with introduction, notes, and short story "To Be Continued," by Silverberg.

Threads of Time. *Nashville Camden New York: Thomas Nelson Inc., [1974]*.
   Boards. First edition so stated on copyright page. Edited, with introduction, by Silverberg.

Three For Tomorrow. *New York: Meredith Press, [1969]*.
   Boards with cloth shelf back. First edition so stated on copyright page. Anonymously
   edited, with short story "How It Was When the Past Went Away," by Silverberg. Note:
   British edition, *London: Victor Gollancz Limited, 1970*, credits editorship of this volume to
   Arthur C. Clarke.

Three Trips in Time and Space. *New York: Hawthorn Books, Inc. Publishers, [1973]*.
   Code *1 2 3 4 5 6 7 8 9 10* on copyright page. Edited, with foreword, by Silverberg.

To the Stars. *New York: Hawthorn Books, Inc., [1971]*.
   Code *1 2 3 4 5 6 7 8 9 10* on copyright page. Edited, with introduction, notes, and short
   story "Ozymandias," by Silverberg.

Tomorrow's Worlds. *New York: Meredith Press, [1969]*.
   Boards with cloth shelf back. First edition so stated on copyright page. Edited, with
   introduction and short story "Sunrise on Mercury," by Silverberg. Note: Second printing
   was issued under the Hawthorn Books imprint and has the code *2 3 4 5 6 7 8 9 10* on
   copyright page.

Triax. *Los Angeles: Pinnacle Books, [1977]*.
   Wrappers. *First printing, December 1977* on copyright page. *Futorian Science
   Fiction/Pinnacle Books 40–121–3* ($1.95). Edited, with introduction and notes, by Silver-
   berg.

Trips in Time. *Nashville New York: Thomas Nelson Inc., Publishers, [1977]*.
   Boards. First edition so stated on copyright page. Edited, with introduction and short story
   "MUgwump 4," by Silverberg.

Voyagers in Time. *New York: Meredith Press, [1967]*.
   First edition so stated on copyright page. Edited, with introduction and short story "Abso-
   lutely Inflexible," by Silverberg.

Windows into Tomorrow. *New York: Hawthorn Books, Inc. Publishers, [1974]*.
   Code *1 2 3 4 5 6 7 8 9 10* on copyright page. Edited, with introduction and short story "The
   Pain Peddlers," by Silverberg.

Worlds of Maybe. *New York Camden: Thomas Nelson Inc., [1970]*.
   First edition so stated on copyright page. Edited, with introduction and short story "Trans-
   lation Error," by Silverberg.

Nonfiction (Dealing with the Fantasy Genre only)

Drug Themes in Science Fiction. *Rockville, Maryland: National Institute on Drug Abuse,
1974*.
   Wrappers. *Printed 1975* on verso of title page. Issued as *Research Issues Series 9. DHEW
   Publication No. (ADM) 75–190*.

Clifford Donald Simak

(b. 1904)

ALIENS FOR NEIGHBOURS. *London: Faber and Faber*, [*1961*].
Boards. *First published in mcmlxi* on copyright page. Abridged reprint. Collects nine of the twelve stories originally appearing in THE WORLDS OF CLIFFORD SIMAK.

ALL FLESH IS GRASS. *Garden City: Doubleday & Company, Inc., 1965.*
First edition so stated on copyright page.

ALL THE TRAPS OF EARTH. *Garden City: Doubleday & Company, Inc., 1962.*
First edition so stated on copyright page. Five of these nine stories were reprinted under the title THE NIGHT OF THE PUUDLY.

ALSO: [*New York*]: *A Macfadden Book*, [*1963*]. Wrappers. *A Macfadden Book . . . 1963* on copyright page. *Macfadden Books 50–165* (50¢). Abridged reprint. Collects six of the nine stories.

ALSO: [*London*]: *A Four Square Book*, [*1964*]. Wrappers. *First Four Square edition 1964* on copyright page. *Four Square 993* (2'6). Abridged reprint. Collects four of the nine stories.

THE BEST OF CLIFFORD D. SIMAK. *London: Sidgwick & Jackson*, [*1975*].
Boards. *First published in Great Britain in 1975* on copyright page.

BEST SCIENCE FICTION STORIES OF CLIFFORD SIMAK. *London: Faber and Faber*, [*1967*].
First published in mcmlxvii on copyright page.

CEMETERY WORLD. *New York: G. P. Putnam's Sons*, [*1973*].
Boards. No statement of printing on copyright page.

A CHOICE OF GODS. *New York: G. P. Putnam's Sons*, [*1972*].
Boards. No statement of printing on copyright page.

CITY. [*New York*]: *Gnome Press*, [*1952*].
Boards. First edition so stated on copyright page.

COSMIC ENGINEERS. *New York: Gnome Press, Publishers*, [*1950*].
Two bindings, probable priority as listed: (A) Blue cloth lettered in yellow; (B) Tan boards lettered in black. First edition so stated on copyright page.

THE CREATOR. [*Los Angeles*]: *A Crawford Publication*, [*1946*].
Wrappers. No statement of printing on copyright page.

DESTINY DOLL. *New York: G. P. Putnam's Sons*, [*1971*].
No statement of printing on copyright page.

EMPIRE. *New York: World Editions, Inc.*, [*1951*].
Wrappers. No statement of printing on copyright page. *Galaxy Science Fiction Novel No. 7* (35¢). Note: Original version of EMPIRE was written by John W. Campbell Jr. as a teenager. Unable to find a publisher for it, he turned it over to Simak and asked that he rewrite it for *Astounding*. According to Simak, "EMPIRE was essentially a rewrite of John's plot. I may have taken a few of the ideas and action, but I didn't use any of his words. And I

certainly tried to humanize his characters'' (quote via Muriel Becker). Simak's version was rejected by Campbell and ultimately appeared as a Galaxy Novel.

ENCHANTED PILGRIMAGE. *New York: Published by Berkley Publishing Corporation,* [*1975*].
No statement of printing on copyright page.

FIRST HE DIED. [*New York*]: *A Dell Book,* [*1953*].
Wrappers. No statement of printing on copyright page. *Dell Book 680* (25¢). Reissue of TIME AND AGAIN.

THE GOBLIN RESERVATION. *New York: G. P. Putnam's Sons,* [*1968*].
No statement of printing on copyright page.

A HERITAGE OF STARS. *New York: Published by Berkley Publishing Corporation,* [*1977*].
No statement of printing on copyright page. Note: Bound uncorrected galley proofs were issued with the title PLACE OF GOING TO THE STARS.

THE NIGHT OF THE PUUDLY. [*London*]: *A Four Square Book,* [*1964*].
Wrappers. *First Four Square Edition 1964* on copyright page. *Four Square Science Fiction 1040* (3'6). Abridged reprint. Collects five stories from ALL THE TRAPS OF EARTH with lead story ''Good Night, Mr. James'' retitled ''The Night of the Puudly.''

ALSO: *London, New York, Sydney and Toronto: White Lion Publishers Limited,* [*1975*].
Boards. *White Lion Edition 1975* on copyright page. First hardcover edition of this collection.

OTHER WORLDS OF CLIFFORD SIMAK. *New York: Avon Book Division,* [*1962*].
Wrappers. No statement of printing on copyright page. *An Avon Book G–1124* (50¢).
Reprints six stories from THE WORLDS OF CLIFFORD SIMAK.

OUR CHILDREN'S CHILDREN. *New York: G. P. Putnam's Sons,* [*1974*].
No statement of printing on copyright page.

OUT OF THEIR MINDS. *New York: G. P. Putnam's Sons,* [*1970*].
No statement of printing on copyright page.

RING AROUND THE SUN. *New York: Simon and Schuster, 1953.*
Boards. First printing so stated on copyright page.

SHAKESPEARE'S PLANET. *New York: Published by Berkley Publishing Corporation,* [*1976*].
No statement of printing on copyright page.

SKIRMISH. *New York: Published by G. P. Putnam's Sons,* [*1977*].
Boards with cloth shelf back. No statement of printing on copyright page.

SO BRIGHT THE VISION. *New York: Ace Books, Inc.,* [*1968*].
Wrappers. No statement of printing on copyright page. *Ace Double H–95* (60¢). Bound with THE MAN WHO SAW TOMORROW by Jeff Sutton.

STRANGERS IN THE UNIVERSE. *New York: Simon and Schuster, 1956.*
Boards. First printing so stated on copyright page.

ALSO: *New York: Berkley Publishing Corp.,* [*1957*]. Wrappers. No statement of printing on copyright page. *Berkley Books G–71* (35¢). Abridged reprint containing seven of the eleven stories in the Simon and Schuster edition.

ALSO: *London: Faber and Faber,* [*1958*]. Boards. *First published in mcmlviii* on copyright page. Abridged reprint containing seven of the eleven stories (selection differs from the Berkley edition).

THEY WALKED LIKE MEN.*Garden City: Doubleday & Company, Inc., 1962.*
First edition so stated on copyright page.

TIME AND AGAIN.*New York: Simon and Schuster, 1951.*
Boards with cloth shelf back. No statement of printing on copyright page. Reissued as
FIRST HE DIED.

TIME IS THE SIMPLEST THING.*Garden City: Doubleday & Company, Inc., 1961.*
First edition so stated on copyright page.

THE TROUBLE WITH TYCHO.*New York: Ace Books, Inc., [1961].*
Wrappers. No statement of printing on copyright page. *Ace Double Novel Books D–517*
(35¢). Bound with BRING BACK YESTERDAY by A. Bertram Chandler.

WAY STATION.*Garden City: Doubleday & Company, Inc., 1963.*
First edition so stated on copyright page.

THE WEREWOLF PRINCIPLE.*New York: G. P. Putnam's Sons, [1967].*
No statement of printing on copyright page.

WHY CALL THEM BACK FROM HEAVEN?*Garden City: Doubleday & Company, Inc., 1967.*
First edition so stated on copyright page.

THE WORLDS OF CLIFFORD SIMAK.*New York: Simon and Schuster, 1960.*
Boards. First printing so stated on copyright page.

ALSO:*New York: Avon Book Division, [1961].* Wrappers. No statement of printing on
copyright page. *Avon G–1096* (50¢). Abridged reprint. Collects six of the twelve stories.

WORLDS WITHOUT END.*New York: Belmont Books, [1964].*
Wrappers. *A Belmont Book—April 1964* on copyright page. *Belmont L92–584* (50¢).
Note: Second printing bears no statement of printing on copyright page and book number is
changed to *B50–791*.

ALSO:*London: Herbert Jenkins, [1965].* Boards. *First published in Great Britain . . .
1965* on copyright page. First hardcover edition.

Associational

A One-Act Play: Clifford D. Simak's The Ritual Reading, adapted by Douglas L. Lieberman
From And the Truth Shall Make You Free. *Elgin, Illinois: Performance Publishing, [1972].*
Wrappers. No statement of printing on copyright page. Note: Adapted by Lieberman from
"And the Truth Shall Make You Free" by Simak.

Edited Fiction

Nebula Award Stories Six. *Garden City: Doubleday & Company, Inc., 1971.*
First edition so stated on copyright page. Edited, with introduction, by Simak.

Reference

The Electric Bibliograph, Part I: Clifford D. Simak, compiled by Mark Owings. *Baltimore: Produced by Alice and Jay Haldeman, 1971.*
   Wrappers. No statement of printing. Mimeographed, stapled. Caption title.

John T. Sladek

(b. 1937)

BLACK ALICE. *Garden City: Doubleday & Company, Inc., 1968.*
First edition so stated on copyright page. With THOMAS M. DISCH. *Thom Demijohn, pseudonym.*

BLACK AURA. *London: Jonathan Cape, [1974].*
Boards. *First published 1974* on copyright page.

THE CASTLE AND THE KEY. *New York: Paperback Library, Inc., [1967].*
Wrappers. *First Printing: June, 1967* on copyright page. *A Paperback Library Gothic 52–454* (50¢). *Cassandra Knye, pseudonym.*

THE HOUSE THAT FEAR BUILT. *New York: Paperback Library, Inc., [1966].*
Wrappers. *First Printing: March, 1966* on copyright page. *A Paperback Library Gothic 52–923* (50¢). With THOMAS M. DISCH. *Cassandra Knye, pseudonym.*

INVISIBLE GREEN. *London: Victor Gollancz Ltd, 1977.*
Boards. No statement of printing on copyright page.

MECHASM. *New York: Ace Publishing Corporation, [1969].*
Wrappers. No statement of printing on copyright page. *An Ace Science Fiction Special 71435* (75¢). Issued earlier in Great Britain as THE REPRODUCTIVE SYSTEM.

THE MÜLLER-FOKKER EFFECT. *London: Hutchinson, [1970].*
Boards. *First published 1970* on copyright page.

THE REPRODUCTIVE SYSTEM. *London: Victor Gollancz Ltd, 1968.*
Boards. No statement of printing on copyright page. Issued later in the U.S. as MECHASM.

THE STEAM-DRIVEN BOY. *[Frogmore]: Panther, [1973].*
Wrappers. *First published in Great Britain in 1973* on copyright page. *Panther Science Fiction 586 03801 9* (35¢).

William Milligan Sloane III
(1906–1974)

ART FOR ART'S SAKE. *Boston: Walter H. Baker Company Publishers*, [*1934*].
  Wrappers. No statement of printing on copyright page.

BACK HOME: A GHOST PLAY IN ONE ACT. *New York: Longmans, Green and Co., 1931*.
  Wrappers. First edition so stated on copyright page.

BALLOTS FOR BILL A LIGHT-HEARTED COMEDY OF POLITICS. *New York: Playhouse Plays/Fitzgerald Publishing Corporation*, [*1933*].
  Wrappers. No statement of printing on copyright page. With WILLIAM ELLIS JONES.

CRYSTAL CLEAR: A ROMANCE IN ONE ACT. *New York: Longmans, Green and Co., 1932*.
  Wrappers. First edition so stated on copyright page.

DIGGING UP THE DIRT: A COMEDY IN THREE ACTS. *New York: Longmans, Green and Co., 1931*.
  Wrappers. First edition so stated on copyright page. Note: Adaptation by Sloane of a play by Bert J. Norton.

THE EDGE OF RUNNING WATER. *New York Toronto: Farrar & Rinehart Incorporated*, [*1939*].
  First printing has F&R monogram on copyright page. Reissued as THE UNQUIET CORPSE. Collected later in THE RIM OF MORNING.

GOLD STARS FOR GLORY. *Boston: Walter H. Baker Company Publishers*, [*1935*].
  Wrappers. No statement of printing on copyright page.

THE INVISIBLE CLUE. *New York: Playhouse Plays/Fitzgerald Publishing Corporation*, [*1934*].
  Wrappers. No statement of printing on copyright page. *William Milligan, pseudonym.*

THE RIM OF MORNING. *New York: Dodd, Mead & Company*, [*1964*].
  Boards. *This edition published 1964* on copyright page. Reprint. Collects THE EDGE OF RUNNING WATER and TO WALK THE NIGHT.

RUNNER IN THE SNOW A PLAY OF THE SUPERNATURAL IN ONE ACT. *Boston: Walter H. Baker Company Publishers*, [*1931*].
  Wrappers. No statement of printing on copyright page. Note: Adapted by Sloane from short story "I Saw a Woman Turn Into a Wolf" by W. B. Seabrook.

THE SILENCE OF GOD: A PLAY FOR CHRISTMAS IN ONE ACT. *Boston: Walter H. Baker Company Publishers*, [*1933*].
  Wrappers. No statement of printing on copyright page.

TO WALK THE NIGHT. *New York Toronto: Farrar & Rinehart Incorporated*, [*1937*].
  First printing has *F&R* monogram on copyright page. Later collected in THE RIM OF MORNING.

  ALSO: *New York: Dodd, Mead & Company, 1954*. No statement of printing on copyright page. Revised text.

THE UNQUIET CORPSE. *New York: A Dell Mystery*, [*1956*].
  Wrappers. No statement of printing on copyright page. *Dell 928 (25¢)*. Reissue of THE EDGE OF RUNNING WATER.

Edited Fiction

Space Space Space. *New York: Franklin Watts, Inc.,* [*1953*].
    First printing so stated on copyright page. Edited, with introduction and notes, by Sloane.

Stories for Tomorrow. *New York: Funk & Wagnalls Company, 1954.*
    First printing has *1* on copyright page. Edited, with introduction, notes, and short story "Let Nothing You Dismay," by Sloane.

Clark Ashton Smith
(1893–1961)

THE ABOMINATIONS OF YONDO. *Sauk City: Arkham House, 1960.*
No statement of printing on copyright page.

THE DOUBLE SHADOW. *[Auburn, California: Auburn Journal Print, 1933.]*
Wrappers. No statement of printing. Cover title.

EBONY AND CRYSTAL: POEMS IN VERSE AND PROSE. *[Auburn, California: Clark Ashton Smith, 1923.]*
No statement of printing. 500 (525?) numbered copies signed by the author. Note: Printed limitation statement notes 500 copies. A copy in the collection of Gerry de la Ree has the following colophon statement: *500* [canceled and raised in holograph to 525] *copies of Ebony and Crystal have been printed. This is No.* [number in holograph]/Clark Ashton Smith [in holograph].

FROM THE CRYPTS OF MEMORY. *[Glendale, California]: Roy A Squires, 1973.*
Wrappers. No statement of printing. 198 numbered copies. Reprint. Collected earlier in EBONY AND CRYSTAL.

GENIUS LOCI. *Sauk City: Arkham House, 1948.*
No statement of printing on copyright page.

HYPERBOREA. *New York: Ballantine Books, [1971].*
Wrappers. *First Printing: April, 1971* on copyright page. *Ballantine Books 02206–8–095* (95¢). Reprint collection.

THE IMMORTALS OF MERCURY. *New York: Stellar Publishing Corporation, [1932].*
Wrappers. No statement of printing. Cover title. Issued as *Science Fiction Series No. 16.*

LOST WORLDS. *Sauk City: Arkham House, 1944.*
No statement of printing on copyright page.

THE MORTUARY. *[Glendale, California: Roy A Squires, 1971.]*
Wrappers. *This first printing of/THE MORTUARY/consists of 180 copies of which/this is copy/*[holograph number] on page [10].

OTHER DIMENSIONS. *Sauk City: Arkham House: Publishers, 1970.*
No statement of printing on copyright page.

OUT OF SPACE AND TIME. *[Sauk City]: Arkham House, 1942.*
No statement of printing on copyright page.

POEMS IN PROSE. *Sauk City: Arkham House, 1964.*
No statement of printing on copyright page.

POSEIDONIS. *New York: Ballantine Books, [1973].*
Wrappers. *First Printing: July, 1973* on copyright page. *Ballantine Books 03353–1–125* ($1.25). Reprint collection. Note: "The Double Shadow" follows the text printed in THE DOUBLE SHADOW.

PRINCE ALCOUZ AND THE MAGICIAN. [*Glendale, California*]: *Roy A Squires, 1977.*
  Wrappers. *This first publication of/Clark Ashton Smith's very early tale/PRINCE ALC-OUZ AND THE MAGICIAN/consists of 190 copies printed/on handmade Amatruda paper/from Post Roman types./This is Copy/*[holograph number] on page [8].

SADASTOR. [*Glendale, California: Roy A Squires*], *1972.*
  Wrappers. No statement of printing. 108 numbered copies. Reprint. Collected earlier in OUT OF SPACE AND TIME.

TALES OF SCIENCE AND SORCERY. *Sauk City: Arkham House: Publishers, 1964.*
  No statement of printing on copyright page.

THE WHITE SYBIL. [*Everett, Penna.: Fantasy Publications*], *n.d.* [*ca. 1935*].
  Wrappers. Two bindings, no priority established: (A) Length of rule on front wrapper is 2.2 cm and incorporates two dots; (B) Length of rule on front wrapper is 2.5 cm and incorporates three dots. No statement of printing. Bound with MEN OF AVALON by David H. Keller.

XICCARPH. *New York: Ballantine Books,* [*1972*].
  Wrappers. *First Printing: February, 1972* on copyright page. *Ballantine Books 02501–6–125* ($1.25). Reprint collection. Note: "The Maze of Maal Dweb" follows the text printed in THE DOUBLE SHADOW.

ZOTHIQUE. *New York: Ballantine Books,* [*1970*].
  Wrappers. *First Printing: June, 1970* on copyright page. *Ballantine Books 01938–5–095* (95¢). Note: "The Last Hieroglyph" and "The Death of Ilalotha" are edited from the original manuscript, "The Voyage of King Euvoran" follows the text printed in THE DOUBLE SHADOW, and the remainder follow the texts of the Arkham House collections.

Nonfiction (Dealing with the Fantasy Genre only)

Grotesques and Fantastiques. . . . A Selection of Previously Unpublished Drawings and Poems. *Saddle River, N.J.: Published by Gerry de la Ree, 1973.*
  Two bindings, no priority: (A) Cloth. 50 numbered copies. (B) Wrappers. 600 numbered copies. First edition so stated on copyright page. Note: Includes extracts from Smith letters.

Klarkash-ton and Monstro Lieriv: Previously Unpublished Poems and Art by Clark Ashton Smith (1893-1961) and Virgil Finlay (1914-1971), Including Smith's Correspondence. . . . *Saddle River, N.J.: Published by Gerry de la Ree, 1974.*
  Two bindings, no priority: (A) Cloth. 50 numbered copies. (B) Wrappers. 500 numbered copies. First edition so stated on copyright page. Note: Includes text of three letters from Smith to Finlay.

Planets and Dimensions: Collected Essays. *Baltimore: The Mirage Press, 1973.*
  Two bindings, no priority: (A) Cloth. 500 numbered copies. (B) Wrappers. Approximately 750 unnumbered copies. No statement of printing on copyright page.

Reference

*Clark Ashton Smith, Emperor of Shadows, by Benjamin De Casseres. *N.p., n.d.* [*Lakeport, California: The Futile Press, 1937.*]
  "Two leaves, printed (letterpress from hand set types) on one side of each, measuring 15.9 X 21 cm."—Roy A. Squires, letter to the compiler dated 13 March 1979. 70 copies printed

circa November 1937 according to Donald Sidney-Fryer, *Emperor of Dreams: A Clark Ashton Smith Bibliography* (West Kingston, R.I.: Grant, 1978), p. 233.

Emperor of Dreams: A Clark Ashton Smith Bibliography, compiled by Donald Sidney–Fryer & Divers Hands. *West Kingston, Rhode Island: Donald M. Grant, Publisher, 1978.*
   First edition so stated on copyright page. Includes biographical and critical material.

The Fantastic Art of Clark Ashton Smith, by Dennis Rickard. *Baltimore: The Mirage Press, Ltd., 1973.*
   Wrappers. No statement of printing on copyright page. Approximately 1500 copies printed.

In Memoriam Clark Ashton Smith, edited by Jack L. Chalker. *Baltimore: "anthem" jack l chalker & associates, 1963.*
   Two issues, no priority: (A) Cloth. 10 copies. Typewritten limitation leaf pasted to front flyleaf reads: *Ten copies were casebound in a special edition: 2 copies to the editor/2 copies for the publisher's file/2 copies for persons associated with Clark Ashton Smith/4 copies for sale to collectors. Of that edition, this is copy* # [number inserted]. Not seen; information from Roy A. Squires in *Beyond the Bibliographies* (Glendale, California, [1973]), catalog 7, lots 74 and 75. (B) Wrappers, stapled. No statement of printing. Mimeographed. Note: Colophon notes "approximately" 450 copies printed. Squires (see above) states total edition was 387 copies.

The Last of the Great Romantic Poets, by Donald Sidney-Fryer. *Albuquerque, New Mexico: The Silver Scarab Press, 1973.*
   Wrappers. No statement of printing.

A Listing of the Poems in Manuscript by Clark Ashton Smith in the Berg Collection of the New York City Public Library, [compiled by Alan Lewis]. *[Los Angeles: Alan Lewis], n.d.*
   Single sheet, printed on both sides. Mimeographed. No statement of printing. Note: Donald Sidney-Fryer, *Emperor of Dreams*, dates 1964.

The Tales of Clark Ashton Smith: A Bibliography, [compiled by Thomas G. L. Cockcroft]. *Melling, Lower Hutt, New Zealand: Published by Thomas G. L. Cockcroft, [1951].*
   Wrappers. *Published November, 1951* on copyright page. 500 copies printed. Leaf of addenda laid in.

Edward Elmer Smith
(1890–1965)

THE BEST OF E. E. 'DOC' SMITH. [*London*]: *Futura Publications Limited*, [*1975*].
Wrappers. *First published in 1975* . . . on copyright page. *Orbit Science Fiction 0 8600 7873 6* (75p).

ALSO: *London: Weidenfeld & Nicolson*, [*1976*]. Boards. *First published in hard cover by Weidenfeld and Nicolson* . . . on copyright page. First hardcover edition. Note: Orbit edition was published in November 1975. The Weidenfeld & Nicolson edition was scheduled for October 1975 release but was not published until January 1976.

THE CHALLENGE FROM BEYOND. *N.p.*: [*A Weltschmerz Publication/Bill Evans/Franklin Kerkhof, Printer/The Pennsylvania Dutch Cheese Press/February 1954*].
Self wrappers. No statement of printing. Mimeographed, stapled. Cover title. With STANLEY G. WEINBAUM, DONALD WANDREI, HARL VINCENT, and MURRAY LEINSTER. Notes: (1) Published by William H. Evans for distribution through the Fantasy Amateur Press Association (FAPA). (2) Not to be confused with a booklet of identical title and format with a different round-robin story by C. L. Moore and others.

CHILDREN OF THE LENS. *Reading, Pennsylvania: Fantasy Press, Inc.*, [*1954*].
Four bindings, priority as listed: (A) Blue cloth, spine lettered in gold; (B) Blue cloth, spine lettered in black; (C) Blue boards, spine lettered in black; (D) Gray boards, spine lettered in black. Two issues, no priority: (A) 500 copies with numbered leaf signed by the author inserted; (B) Trade issue. First edition so stated on copyright page.

FIRST LENSMAN. *Reading, Pennsylvania: Fantasy Press, 1950.*
Two issues, no priority: (A) 500 copies with numbered leaf signed by the author inserted; (B) Trade issue. First edition so stated on copyright page.

GALACTIC PATROL. *Reading, Pennsylvania: Fantasy Press, 1950.*
Four bindings, priority as listed: (A) Blue cloth, spine lettered in gold; (B) Red cloth, spine lettered in black; (C) Red boards, spine lettered in black; (D) Gray boards, spine lettered in black. Two issues, no priority: (A) 500 copies with numbered leaf signed by the author inserted; (B) Trade issue. First edition so stated on copyright page.

THE GALAXY PRIMES. *New York: Ace Books, Inc.*, [*1965*].
Wrappers. No statement of printing on copyright page. *Ace Book F–328* (40¢).

GRAY LENSMAN. *Reading, Pennsylvania: Fantasy Press, 1951.*
Two issues, no priority: (A) 500 copies with numbered leaf signed by the author inserted; (B) Trade issue. First edition so stated on copyright page. Notes: (1) Owings and Chalker in *The Index to the Science-Fantasy Publishers* report a Greenberg variant binding for this title. No copy thus bound has been observed. (2) In 1962 Gnome Press produced an offset reprint bearing the title page imprint *The Gnome Press Inc./P.O. Box 161/Hicksville, New York*. This reprint retains the first edition statement on the copyright page.

[THE HISTORY OF CIVILIZATION.] *Reading: Fantasy Press, Inc.*, *1953–1955.*
Cloth with leather shelf back. Six volumes. 75 sets, each volume having a numbered leaf signed by the author inserted. Issued without dust jackets, enclosed in a card-stock box. Reprint. Includes TRIPLANETARY, FIRST LENSMAN, GALACTIC PATROL, GRAY LENSMAN, SECOND STAGE LENSMEN, and CHILDREN OF THE LENS.

IMPERIAL STARS. *New York: Pyramid Books, [1976].*
Wrappers. *February 1976* on copyright page. *Pyramid V3839* ($1.25). With STEPHEN GOLDIN. An enlargement by Goldin of Smith's short novel "The Imperial Stars," which originally appeared in *Worlds of If,* May 1964. Subsequent volumes in The Family d'Alembert series were written by Goldin.

MASTERS OF SPACE. *[London]: Futura Publications Limited, [1976].*
Wrappers. *First published in Great Britain in 1976 . . .* on copyright page. *Orbit 0 8600 7901 5* (50p).

MASTERS OF THE VORTEX. *New York: Pyramid Books, [1968].*
Wrappers. *August, 1968* on copyright page. *Pyramid Science Fiction X–1851* (60¢). Reissue of THE VORTEX BLASTER.

SECOND STAGE LENSMEN. *Reading, Pennsylvania: Fantasy Press, [1953].*
Four bindings, priority as listed: (A) Blue cloth, spine lettered in gold; (B) Blue cloth, spine lettered in black; (C) Blue-gray cloth, spine lettered in black; (D) Red boards, spine lettered in black. Two issues, no priority: (A) 500 copies with numbered leaf signed by the author inserted; (B) Trade issue. First edition so stated on copyright page.

SKYLARK DUQUESNE. *New York: Pyramid Books, [1966].*
Wrappers. *November, 1966* on copyright page. *Pyramid Books X–1539* (60¢).

ALSO: *[New York & London: Garland Publishing, Inc., 1975.]* First hardcover edition. Notes: (1) Offset from the January 1974 eighth printing of the Pyramid Books edition. (2) Not issued in dust jacket.

THE SKYLARK OF SPACE. *[Providence, Rhode Island: The Buffalo Book Co., 1946.]*
No statement of printing on copyright page. With MRS. LEE HAWKINS GARBY.

SKYLARK OF VALERON. *Reading, Pennsylvania: Fantasy Press, 1949.*
Two issues, no priority: (A) 500 copies with numbered leaf signed by the author inserted; (B) Trade issue. First edition so stated on copyright page. Note: An undetermined number of copies of the limited issue have an inserted limitation leaf which lacks the statements *Number* and *of which 500 are numbered and autographed.* All examined copies of this variant have the author's signature or presentation inscription.

SKYLARK THREE. *Reading, Pennsylvania: Fantasy Press, 1948.*
Two issues, no priority: (A) 500 copies with numbered leaf signed by the author inserted; (B) Trade issue. First edition so stated on copyright page.

SPACEHOUNDS OF IPC. *Reading, Pennsylvania: Fantasy Press, 1947.*
Two issues, no priority: (A) 300 copies with numbered leaf signed by the author inserted; (B) Trade issue. Dust jacket occurs in two states, priority as listed: (A) Rear panel lists four titles, the first being *The Legion of Space* by Jack Williamson; (B) Rear panel lists 11 titles, the first being *The Forbidden Garden* by John Taine. Note: This later dust jacket also appears on copies of the second edition published by Fantasy Press in 1949. First edition so stated on copyright page.

SUBSPACE EXPLORERS. *New York: Canaveral Press, Inc., 1965.*
No statement of printing on copyright page.

TRIPLANETARY. *Reading, Pennsylvania: Fantasy Press, 1948.*
Two issues, no priority: (A) 500 copies with numbered leaf signed by the author inserted; (B) Trade issue. First edition so stated on copyright page. Note: *Triplanetary* is printed in red on front panel of dust jacket issued with the first edition. Second edition published by Fantasy Press in 1950 has *Triplanetary* printed in yellow on front panel of dust jacket.

THE VORTEX BLASTER. *Hicksville, New York: Gnome Press, Inc., [1960]*.
  Two issues, priority as listed: (A) With Gnome Press imprint as above. Three bindings,
  priority as listed: (1) Blue boards, spine lettered in yellow; (2) Gray cloth, spine lettered in
  red; (3) Gray wrappers, lettered in black. (B) Imprint reads *Reading, Pa./Fantasy Press*.
  Of the Fantasy Press variant, publisher Lloyd Eshbach remarked in a letter to the compiler
  dated 19 May 1975, "When I printed the overrun of the Gnome Press edition with FP
  imprint, I shot for 100 [copies]. There were a few extras." In a later undated letter (1977)
  he states, "Press run immediately after Gnome Press edition, 300 copies on better book
  paper." First edition so stated on copyright pages of both issues. Reissued as MASTERS OF
  THE VORTEX.

Nonfiction (Dealing with the Fantasy Genre only)

What Does This Convention Mean? A Speech Delivered at The Chicago 1940 World's
Science Fiction Convention . . . *[Bryantville, Mass.]: Published especially for the Denver
1941 World's Science Fiction Convention—by Art Widner jr, [1941]*.
  Self wrappers. No statement of printing. Mimeographed, stapled.

Interview

Galactic Roamer. Dr. E. E. Smith Talks About the Famous "Skylark" Tales and the
"Lensmen" Series in an Interview with Thomas Sheridan. *[West Warwick, R.I.: Nec-
ronomicon Press, 1977.]*
  Wrappers. *This edition, the first, . . . is limited/to a numbered printing of 500 copies* on
  page [8]. Caption title. Offset from typewritten copy. Cover title reads *E. E. "Doc"
  Smith/Father of Star Wars*. Issued as *F & SF Self-Portraits 1*.

Reference

The Universes of E. E. Smith, by Ron Ellik and Bill Evans. *Chicago: Advent: Publishers,
1966*.
  First edition so stated on copyright page.

George Oliver Smith
(b. 1911)

THE BRAIN MACHINE. *New York: Lancer Books,* [*1968*].
Wrappers. *A Lancer Book • 1968* on copyright page. *Lancer Books 74–936* (75¢). Reissue of THE FOURTH "R."

ALSO: [*New York & London: Garland Publishing, Inc., 1975.*] First hardcover edition. Notes: (1) Offset from the 1968 Lancer Books edition. (2) Not issued in dust jacket.

THE COMPLETE VENUS EQUILATERAL. *New York: Ballantine Books,* [*1976*].
Wrappers. *First Edition: November 1976* on copyright page. *Ballantine Books 25551* ($1.95). Reprint. This printing of the enlarged edition is preceded by the two-volume 1975 Orbit edition issued as VENUS EQUILATERAL.

FIRE IN THE HEAVENS. *New York: Avalon Books,* [*1958*].
No statement of printing on copyright page.

THE FOURTH "R." *New York: Ballantine Books,* [*1959*].
Wrappers. No statement of printing on copyright page. *Ballantine Books 316 K* (35¢). Reissued as THE BRAIN MACHINE.

HELLFLOWER. *New York: Abelard Press,* [*1953*].
No statement of printing on copyright page.

HIGHWAYS IN HIDING. *New York: Gnome Press, Inc. Publishers,* [*1956*].
First edition so stated on copyright page. Abridged as THE SPACE PLAGUE.

LOST IN SPACE. *New York: Avalon Books,* [*1959*].
No statement of printing on copyright page.

NOMAD. *Philadelphia: Prime Press,* [*1950*].
No statement of printing on copyright page.

OPERATION INTERSTELLAR. *Chicago: Century Publications,* [*1950*].
Wrappers. No statement of printing on copyright page. *Merit Books B–10* (25¢).

THE PATH OF UNREASON. *Hicksville, New York: Gnome Press, Inc.,* [*1958*].
Boards. First edition so stated on copyright page.

PATTERN FOR CONQUEST. *New York: Gnome Press Publishers,* [*1949*].
First edition so stated on copyright page. Note: Reprinted circa 1952 in paper wrappers for distribution to U.S. military personnel. Although a later printing, the first edition statement is retained on the copyright page.

THE SPACE PLAGUE. *New York: Avon Publications, Inc.,* [*1957*].
Wrappers. No statement of printing on copyright page. *Avon T–180* (35¢). Abridged version of HIGHWAYS IN HIDING. Note: Title page notes that this edition is "revised."

TROUBLED STAR. *New York: Avalon Books,* [*1957*].
No statement of printing on copyright page.

VENUS EQUILATERAL. *Philadelphia: The Prime Press, 1947.*
No statement of printing on copyright page.

ALSO: *[London]: Futura Publications Limited,* [*1975*]. Wrappers. Two volumes. *First published in Great Britain in 1975* on copyright pages. *Orbit 0 8600 7860 4* (75p) and *0 8600 7861 2* (75p). Enlarged edition. Adds "Lost Art," "The External Triangle," and "Identity." This version issued later in the U.S. as THE COMPLETE VENUS EQUILATERAL.

Gerald Allan Sohl
(b. 1913)

THE ALTERED EGO. *New York Toronto: Rinehart & Company, Inc., [1954]*.
  Boards. First printing has Rinehart monogram on copyright page.

THE ANOMALY. *New York: Curtis Books, [1971]*.
  Wrappers. No statement of printing on copyright page. *Curtis Books 502–07151–075* (75¢).

BLOW-DRY. *Greenwich, Connecticut: Fawcett Publications, Inc., [1976]*.
  Wrappers. *First printing: May 1976/1 2 3 4 5 6 7 8 9 10* on copyright page. *Fawcett Gold Medal Q3513* ($1.50). *Nathan Butler, pseudonym.*

COSTIGAN'S NEEDLE. *New York Toronto: Rinehart & Company, Inc., [1953]*.
  Boards. No statement of printing on copyright page.

DR. JOSH. *Greenwich, Conn.: Fawcett Publications, Inc., [1973]*.
  Wrappers. No statement of printing on copyright page. *Fawcett Gold Medal 1–3522–5* ($1.75). *Nathan Butler, pseudonym.*

THE HAPLOIDS. *New York • Toronto: Rinehart & Co., Inc., [1952]*.
  Boards. First printing has Rinehart monogram on copyright page.

I, ALEPPO. *Toronto • New York • London: Laser Books, [1976]*.
  Wrappers. *First published July, 1976* on copyright page. *Laser Books 72035* (95¢).

THE LEMON EATERS. *New York: Simon and Schuster, [1967]*.
  First printing so stated on copyright page.

MAMELLE. *Greenwich, Conn.: Fawcett Publications, Inc., [1974]*.
  Wrappers. No statement of printing on copyright page. *Fawcett Gold Medal 1–3782–1* ($1.50). *Nathan Butler, pseudonym.*

MAMELLE, THE GODDESS. *Greenwich, Connecticut: Fawcett Publications, Inc., [1977]*.
  Wrappers. Code *10 9 8 7 6 5 4 3 2 1* on copyright page. *Fawcett Gold Medal 1–3773–2* ($1.50). *Nathan Butler, pseudonym.*

THE MARS MONOPOLY. *New York: Ace Books, [1956]*.
  Wrappers. No statement of printing on copyright page. *Ace Double Novel Books D–162* (35¢). Bound with THE MAN WHO LIVED FOREVER by R. De Witt Miller and Anna Hunger.

NIGHT SLAVES. *Greenwich, Conn. Fawcett Publications, Inc., [1965]*.
  Wrappers. No statement of printing on copyright page. *A Fawcett Gold Medal Book d1561* (50¢).

THE ODIOUS ONES. *New York Toronto: Rinehart & Company, Inc., [1959]*.
  Boards. First printing has Rinehart monogram on copyright page.

ONE AGAINST HERCULUM. *New York: Ace Books, Inc., [1959]*.
  Wrappers. No statement of printing on copyright page. *Ace Double Novel Books D–381* (35¢). Bound with SECRET OF THE LOST RACE by Andre Norton.

POINT ULTIMATE. *New York •Toronto: Rinehart & Company, Inc.*, [*1955*].
Boards. First printing has Rinehart monogram on copyright page.

PRELUDE TO PERIL. *New York Toronto: Rinehart & Company, Inc.*, [*1957*].
Boards. First printing has Rinehart monogram on copyright page.

THE RESURRECTION OF FRANK BORCHARD. *New York: Simon and Schuster*, [*1973*].
First printing so stated on copyright page.

THE SPUN SUGAR HOLE. *New York: Simon and Schuster*, [*1971*].
First printing so stated on copyright page.

*SUPERMANCHU, MASTER OF KUNG FU. *New York: Ballantine Books*, [*1974*].
Wrappers. *Sean Mei Sullivan, pseudonym.*

THE TIME DISSOLVER. *New York: Avon Publications, Inc.*, [*1957*].
Wrappers. No statement of printing on copyright page. *Avon T–186* (35¢).

THE TRANSCENDENT MAN. *New York, Toronto: Rinehart and Company, Inc.*, [*1953*].
Boards. First printing has Rinehart monogram on copyright page.

Norman Richard Spinrad

(b. 1940)

AGENT OF CHAOS. *New York: Belmont Books,* [*1967*].
Wrappers. *January 1967* on copyright page. *Belmont Science Fiction B50–739* (50¢).

BUG JACK BARRON. [*New York*]*: An Avon Book,* [*1969*].
Wrappers. *First Avon Printing, April, 1969* on copyright page. *Avon N206* (95¢).

ALSO: *New York: Walker and Company,* [*1969*]. Boards. *Published in the United States of America in 1969* on copyright page. Simultaneous publication with Avon edition.

THE IRON DREAM. [*New York*]*: Avon,* [*1972*].
Wrappers. *First Avon Printing, September, 1972* on copyright page. *Avon Science Fiction N448* (95¢).

ALSO: *Boston: Gregg Press, 1977. First Printing, June 1977* on copyright page. First hardcover edition. Note: Not issued in dust jacket.

THE LAST HURRAH OF THE GOLDEN HORDE. *Garden City: Nelson Doubleday, Inc.,* [*1970*].
Boards. No statement of printing on copyright page. *Code 27 L* on page 211. Note: Issued by the Science Fiction Book Club.

THE MEN IN THE JUNGLE. *Garden City: Doubleday & Company, Inc.,* *1967.*
First edition so stated on copyright page.

NO DIRECTION HOME. *New York: Published by Pocket Books,* [*1975*].
Wrappers. *May, 1975* on copyright page. *Pocket Books 78887* ($1.25).

ALSO: [*London*]*: Millington Books,* [*1976*]. Boards. *First British edition published in 1976 . . .* on copyright page. First hardcover edition.

PASSING THROUGH THE FLAME. *New York: G. P. Putnam's Sons,* [*1975*].
No statement of printing on copyright page.

THE SOLARIANS. *New York: Paperback Library, Inc.,* [*1966*].
Wrappers. *First Printing: July, 1966* on copyright page. *Paperback Library 52–985* (50¢).

Edited Fiction

Modern Science Fiction. *Garden City: Anchor Books, 1974.*
Wrappers. First edition so stated on copyright page. *Anchor A–978* ($3.50). Edited, with foreword, introduction, afterword, and short story "No Direction Home," by Spinrad.

ALSO: *Boston: Gregg Press, 1976. First Printing, June 1976* on copyright page. First hardcover edition. Note: Not issued in dust jacket.

The New Tomorrows. *New York: Belmont Books,* [*1971*].
Wrappers. *October 1971* on copyright page. *Belmont B95–2172* (95¢). Edited, with introduction and short story "The Last Hurrah of the Golden Horde," by Spinrad.

Nonfiction (Dealing with the Fantasy Genre only)

Experiment Perilous: Three Essays on Science Fiction, [edited by Andrew Porter]. [*New York*]: *Algol Press*, [*1976*].

> Wrappers. No statement of printing on copyright page. Contains "The Bug Jack Barron Papers" by Spinrad.

Brian M. Stableford

(b. 1948)

THE BLIND WORM. *New York: An Ace Book*, [*1970*].
Wrappers. No statement of printing on copyright page. *Ace Double 06707* (75¢). Bound with SEED OF THE DREAMERS by Emil Petaja.

ALSO: *London: Sidgwick & Jackson*, [*1970*]. Boards. No statement of printing on copyrigh page. First hardcover edition.

CRADLE OF THE SUN. *New York: An Ace Book*, [*1969*].
Wrappers. No statement of printing on copyright page. *Ace Double 12140* (75¢). Bound with THE WIZARDS OF SENCHURIA by Kenneth Bulmer.

ALSO: *London: Sidgwick & Jackson*, [*1969*]. Boards. No statement of printing on copyright page. First hardcover edition.

CRITICAL THRESHOLD. *New York: DAW Books, Inc.*, [*1977*].
Wrappers. *First printing, February 1977/1 2 3 4 5 6 7 8 9* on copyright page. *DAW: sf Books No. 230 UY1282* ($1.25).

DAY OF WRATH. *New York: Ace Books*, [*1971*].
Wrappers. No statement of printing on copyright page. *Ace Book 13972* (75¢).

THE DAYS OF GLORY. *New York: Ace Books*, [*1971*].
Wrappers. No statement of printing on copyright page. *Ace Book 14000* (60¢).

THE FACE OF HEAVEN. *London: Quartet Books*, [*1976*].
Wrappers. *First published . . . 1976 . . .* on copyright page. *Quartet 0 704 31194 1* (60p). Issued later as book one (of three) of THE REALMS OF TARTARUS.

THE FENRIS DEVICE. *New York: DAW Books, Inc.*, [*1974*].
Wrappers. *First printing, December 1974/1 2 3 4 5 6 7 8 9* on copyright page. *DAW: sf Books No. 130 UQ1147* (95¢).

THE FLORIANS. *New York: DAW Books, Inc.*, [*1976*].
Wrappers. *First printing, September 1976/1 2 3 4 5 6 7 8 9* on copyright page. *DAW: sf Books No. 211 UY1255* ($1.25).

THE HALCYON DRIFT. *New York: DAW Books, Inc.*, [*1972*].
Wrappers. *First printing, November, 1972* on copyright page. *DAW: sf Books No. 32 UQ1032* (95¢).

ALSO: *London: J M Dent & Sons Ltd*, [*1974*]. Boards. *First published in Great Britain 1974* on copyright page. First hardcover edition.

IN THE KINGDOM OF THE BEASTS. *New York: Ace Books*, [*1971*].
Wrappers. No statement of printing on copyright page. *Ace Book 37106* (75¢).

MAN IN A CAGE. *New York: The John Day Company*, [*1975*].
Code *10 9 8 7 6 5 4 3 2 1* on copyright page.

THE MIND-RIDERS. *New York: DAW Books, Inc.*, [*1976*].
Wrappers. *First printing, May 1976/1 2 3 4 5 6 7 8 9* on copyright page. *DAW: sf Books No. 194 UY1234* ($1.25).

THE PARADISE GAME. *New York: DAW Books, Inc.*, [*1974*].
Wrappers. *First printing, June 1974/1 2 3 4 5 6 7 8 9* on copyright page. *DAW: sf Books No. 111 UQ1121* (95¢).

ALSO:*London: J M Dent & Sons Ltd*, [*1976*]. Boards. *First published in Great Britain 1976* on copyright page. First hardcover edition.

PROMISED LAND. *New York: DAW Books, Inc.*, [*1974*].
Wrappers. *First printing, February 1974/1 2 3 4 5 6 7 8 9* on copyright page. *DAW: sf Books No. 92 UQ1097* (95¢).

ALSO:*London: J M Dent & Sons Ltd*, [*1975*]. Boards. *First published in Great Britain 1975* on copyright page. First hardcover edition. Adds two-page introduction by Stableford.

THE REALMS OF TARTARUS. *New York: DAW Books, Inc.*, [*1977*].
Wrappers. *First printing, July 1977/1 2 3 4 5 6 7 8 9* on copyright page. *DAW: sf Books No. 248 UJ1309* ($1.95). Book one (of three) was issued earlier as THE FACE OF HEAVEN.

RHAPSODY IN BLACK. *New York: DAW Books, Inc.*, [*1973*].
Wrappers. *First printing, June 1973/1 2 3 4 5 6 7 8 9* on copyright page. *DAW: sf Books No. 59 UQ1059* (95¢).

ALSO:*London: J M Dent & Sons Ltd*, [*1975*]. Boards. *First published in Great Britain 1975* on copyright page. First hardcover edition. Textual changes. Approximately 5000 words cut from DAW text and 3000 words of new copy added.

SWAN SONG. *New York: DAW Books, Inc.*, [*1975*].
Wrappers. *First printing, May 1975/1 2 3 4 5 6 7 8 9* on copyright page. *DAW: sf Books No. 149 UY1171* ($1.25).

TO CHALLENGE CHAOS. *New York: DAW Books, Inc.*, [*1972*].
Wrappers. No statement of printing on copyright page. *DAW: sf Books No. 7 UQ1007* (95¢).

WILDEBLOOD'S EMPIRE. *New York: DAW Books, Inc.*, [*1977*].
Wrappers. *First printing, October 1977/1 2 3 4 5 6 7 8 9* on copyright page. *DAW: sf Books No. 263 UW1331* ($1.50).

William Olaf Stapledon

(1886–1950)

DARKNESS AND THE LIGHT. *London: Methuen & Co. Ltd.*, *[1942]*.
  First published in 1942 on copyright page.

DEATH INTO LIFE. *London: Methuen & Co. Ltd.*, *[1946]*.
  First published in 1946 on copyright page. Later collected in WORLDS OF WONDER.

THE FLAMES. *London: Secker and Warburg, 1947.*
  Boards with cloth shelf back. *First published 1947* on copyright page. Collected later in
  WORLDS OF WONDER and TO THE END OF TIME.

LAST AND FIRST MEN. *London: Methuen & Co. Ltd.*, *[1930]*.
  First published in 1930 on copyright page. Inserted eight-page publisher's catalogue at rear
  dated *630* at base of page 8. Presumed later copies lacking publisher's catalogue have been
  reported. Note: Dust jacket for first printing does not carry excerpts from reviews in
  Morning Post, Observer, or *Daily Herald* on front panel. Collected later in TO THE END OF
  TIME.

  ALSO: *New York: Jonathan Cape and Harrison Smith,* *[1931]*. Three bindings, priority as
  listed: (A) Purple cloth, spine lettered in gold; (B) Tan cloth, spine lettered in black;
  (C) Peter Smith imprint on spine (not seen). *First published in America, 1931* on copyright
  page. Adds Stapledon's "Foreword to the American Edition."

LAST MEN IN LONDON. *London: Methuen & Co. Ltd.*, *[1932]*.
  First published in 1932 on copyright page. Inserted eight-page publisher's catalogue at rear
  dated *932* at base of page 8. Note: Dust jacket occurs in two states, priority as listed: (A)
  Yellow-orange paper stock printed in black; *7'6* on spine panel. (B) Sea green paper stock
  printed in purple with trident design on front panel; *3'6* on spine panel. This later jacket also
  occurs on copies of the "Second and Cheaper Edition" with *3'6* and later *4'6* on spine
  panel.

A MAN DIVIDED. *London: Methuen & Co. Ltd.*, *[1950]*.
  First published in 1950 on copyright page.

"NEBULA MAKER." *[Hayes, Middlesex]: Bran's Head Books Ltd, [1976]*.
  Boards. *First published 1976* . . . on copyright page.

ODD JOHN. *London: Methuen & Co. Ltd.*, *[1935]*.
  Four bindings, priority as listed: (A) Blue cloth, spine lettered in dark blue; eight-page
  publisher's catalogue inserted at rear. Date *535* at base of page [8], page 1 does not list *Odd
  John.* (B) Blue cloth, spine lettered in dark blue; eight-page publisher's catalogue inserted
  at rear. Date *835* at base of page [8], page 1 advertises *Odd John.* (C) Wrappers. No
  inserted publisher's catalogue; price *2/–* on spine panel. Remainder binding. (D) Wrappers.
  No inserted publisher's catalogue; price *2/6* on spine panel. Remainder binding. *First
  published in 1935* on copyright page. Collected later in TO THE END OF TIME.

OLD MAN IN NEW WORLD. *London: George Allen & Unwin Ltd, [1944]*.
  Boards. *First published in 1944* on copyright page. Collected later in WORLDS OF WONDER.

SIRIUS. *London: Secker & Warburg, 1944.*
  First published January, 1944 on copyright page. Collected later in TO THE END OF TIME.

STAR MAKER. *London: Methuen & Co. Ltd.,* [*1937*].
Two bindings, priority as listed: (A) Blue cloth, spine lettered in purple; (B) Cream wrappers. Price 2/– on spine panel. Remainder binding. *First published in 1937* on copyright page. Note: George Locke in *Science Fiction First Editions* (London: Ferret, 1978), pp. 88–89 reports that the 1938 "Second and Cheaper Edition" is a later state of the first edition with [1]^2 and [1]^7 (conjugate leaves comprising the title leaf and the first leaf of text) reprinted. Red cloth, spine lettered in black. *First published . . . June 24th 1937/Second and Cheaper Edition. 1938.* Not seen. Collected later in TO THE END OF TIME.

TO THE END OF TIME. *New York: Funk & Wagnalls Company,* [*1953*].
First printing has *1* at base of copyright page. Reprint. Collects LAST AND FIRST MEN (abridged), STAR MAKER, ODD JOHN, SIRIUS, and THE FLAMES.

WORLDS OF WONDER. *Los Angeles: Fantasy Publishing Co., Inc., 1949.*
No statement of printing on copyright page. Reprint. Collects THE FLAMES, DEATH INTO LIFE, and OLD MAN IN NEW WORLD. Note: Sheets of this book were later combined with those of MURDER MADNESS by Murray Leinster and issued in 1953 as [QUADRATIC]. According to Owings and Chalker in *The Index to the Science-Fantasy Publishers,* approximately 500 copies were so bound.

Harry Clement Stubbs

(b. 1922)

CLOSE TO CRITICAL. *New York: Ballantine Books*, [*1964*].
Wrappers. *First Printing, July, 1964* on copyright page. *Ballantine Book U2215* (50¢).
Hal Clement, pseudonym.

ALSO: *London: Victor Gollancz Ltd, 1966*. Boards. No statement of printing on copyright
page. First hardcover edition.

CYCLE OF FIRE. *New York: Ballantine Books*, [*1957*].
Two issues, no priority: (A) Cloth; (B) Wrappers. *Ballantine Books 200* (35¢). No statement of printing on copyright page. *Hal Clement, pseudonym.*

FROM OUTER SPACE. *New York: Avon Publications, Inc.*, [*1957*].
Wrappers. No statement of printing on copyright page. *Avon T–175* (35¢). *Hal Clement,
pseudonym.* Reissue of NEEDLE.

ICEWORLD. [*New York*]: *Gnome Press, Inc.*, [*1953*].
Boards. First edition so stated on copyright page. *Hal Clement, pseudonym.*

LEFT OF AFRICA. *New Orleans: The Aurian Society Press*, [*1976*].
First edition so stated on copyright page. *Hal Clement, pseudonym.*

MISSION OF GRAVITY. *Garden City: Doubleday & Company, Inc.*, 1954.
Boards. First edition so stated on copyright page. *Hal Clement, pseudonym.*

NATIVES OF SPACE. *New York: Ballantine Books*, [*1965*].
Wrappers. *First Ballantine Printing: April 1965* on copyright page. *A Ballantine Science
Fiction Original U2235* (50¢). *Hal Clement, pseudonym.*

NEEDLE. *Garden City: Doubleday & Company, Inc.*, 1950.
First edition so stated on copyright page. *Hal Clement, pseudonym.* Reissued as FROM
OUTER SPACE.

OCEAN ON TOP. *New York: DAW Books, Inc.*, [*1973*].
Wrappers. *First printing, June 1973/1 2 3 4 5 6 7 8 9* on copyright page. *DAW: sf Books
No. 57 UQ1057* (95¢). *Hal Clement, pseudonym.*

THE RANGER BOYS IN SPACE. *Boston: L. C. Page & Company Publishers*, [*1956*].
First impression/July 1956 on copyright page. *Hal Clement, pseudonym.*

SMALL CHANGES. *Garden City: Doubleday & Company, Inc.*, 1969.
First edition so stated on copyright page. *Hal Clement, pseudonym.* Reissued as SPACE
LASH.

SPACE LASH. [*New York*]: *A Dell Book*, [*1969*].
Wrappers. *First Dell printing—December 1969* on copyright page. *Dell 8039* (60¢). *Hal
Clement, pseudonym.* Reissue of SMALL CHANGES.

STAR LIGHT. *New York: Ballantine Books*, [*1971*].
Wrappers. *First Printing: September, 1971* on copyright page. *Ballantine Books Science
Fiction 02361–7–095* (95¢). *Hal Clement, pseudonym.*

Edited Fiction

First Flights to the Moon. *Garden City: Doubleday & Company, Inc., 1970.*
  First edition so stated on copyright page. Edited, with foreword, notes, and essay, by
  Stubbs. *Hal Clement, pseudonym.*

Theodore Hamilton Sturgeon
(b. 1918)

ALIENS 4. *New York: Avon Publications, Inc.*, [*1959*].
  Wrappers. No statement of printing on copyright page. *An Avon Book T–304* (35¢).

. . . AND MY FEAR IS GREAT/BABY IS THREE. [*New York*]: *Published by Galaxy Publishing Corp.*, [*1965*].
  Wrappers. No statement of printing on copyright page. *Magabook No. 3. Two Complete Novels* at head of title.

BEYOND. *New York: Avon Book Division*, [*1960*].
  Wrappers. No statement of printing on copyright page. *Avon T–439* (35¢).

CASE AND THE DREAMER. *Garden City: Nelson Doubleday, Inc.*, [*1974*].
  Boards. No statement of printing on copyright page. Code *E 10* on page 151. Note: Issued by the Science Fiction Book Club.

CAVIAR. *New York: Ballantine Books*, [*1955*].
  Two issues, no priority: (A) Cloth; (B) Wrappers. *Ballantine Books 119* (35¢). No statement of printing on copyright page.

THE COSMIC RAPE. [*New York*]: *Dell*, [*1958*].
  Wrappers. *First printing—August, 1958* on copyright page. *Dell First Edition B 120* (35¢).

  ALSO: THE COSMIC RAPE AND "TO MARRY MEDUSA." *Boston: Gregg Press 1977. First Printing June 1977* on copyright page. First hardcover edition. Adds "To Marry Medusa." Note: Not issued in dust jacket.

THE DREAMING JEWELS. *New York: Greenberg Publisher*, [*1950*].
  No statement of printing on copyright page. Reissued as THE SYNTHETIC MAN.

E PLURIBUS UNICORN. *New York: Abelard Press*, [*1953*].
  Boards. No statement of printing on copyright page.

I, LIBERTINE. *New York: Ballantine Books*, [*1956*].
  Two issues, no priority: (A) Cloth; (B) Wrappers. *Ballantine Books 165* (35¢). No statement of printing on copyright page. *Frederick R. Ewing, pseudonym.* Note: According to the United States Copyright Office, Ewing is a joint pseudonym for Sturgeon and JEAN SHEPHERD.

"IT." *Philadelphia: The Prime Press*, [*1948*].
  Self wrappers, stapled. Cover title reads *This is "It"/Only One of the Thirteen Great Stories in/THEODORE STURGEON'S New Book/from The Prime Press——/WITHOUT SORCERY/Presented (Without IT's Illustrations) to THE TORCON.* Note: 29 leaves on proof paper, rectos only. Issued in advance of WITHOUT SORCERY as a promotion. Fewer than 200 copies printed.

THE JOYOUS INVASIONS. *London: Victor Gollancz Ltd, 1965.*
  Boards. No statement of printing on copyright page.

THE KING AND FOUR QUEENS. [*New York*]: *A Dell First Edition*, [*1956*].
  Wrappers. *First printing—December, 1956* on copyright page. *Dell First Edition A128* (25¢).

MORE THAN HUMAN. *New York: Farrar, Straus and Young*, [*1953*].
Two issues, no priority: (A) Publisher's imprint as above. Boards with cloth shelf back.
First printing so stated on copyright page. (B) Publisher's imprint reads: *Farrar, Straus and Young with Ballantine Books*. Wrappers. *First printing, 1953* on copyright page.
Ballantine Books 46 (35¢). Note: Format varies slightly but both issues are printed from the same plates.

NOT WITHOUT SORCERY. *New York: Ballantine Books*, [*1961*].
Wrappers. No statement of printing on copyright page. *Ballantine Books 506K* (35¢). Reprints eight stories from WITHOUT SORCERY.

THE PLAYER ON THE OTHER SIDE. *New York: Random House*, [*1963*].
First printing so stated on copyright page. *Ellery Queen, pseudonym*.

THE RARE BREED. *Greenwich, Conn.: Fawcett Publications, Inc.*, [*1966*].
Wrappers. No statement of printing on copyright page. *Fawcett Gold Medal Book d1626* (50¢).

SOME OF YOUR BLOOD. *New York: Ballantine Books*, [*1961*].
Wrappers. No statement of printing on copyright page. *Ballantine Books 458K* (35¢).

STARSHINE. *New York: Pyramid Books*, [*1966*].
Wrappers. *December, 1966* on copyright page. *Pyramid Science Fiction X–1543* (60¢).

ALSO: *London: Victor Gollancz Ltd, 1968*. Boards. No statement of printing on copyright page. First hardcover edition.

STURGEON IN ORBIT. *New York: Pyramid Books*, [*1964*].
Wrappers. *February, 1964* on copyright page. *Pyramid Books F–974* (40¢).

ALSO: *London: Victor Gollancz Limited, 1970*. Boards. No statement of printing on copyright page. Drops introduction. First hardcover edition.

STURGEON IS ALIVE AND WELL. *New York: G. P. Putman's Sons*, [*1971*].
No statement of printing on copyright page.

STURGEON'S WEST. *Garden City: Doubleday & Company, Inc.*, [*1973*].
First edition so stated on copyright page. Three of the stories written in collaboration with DON WARD.

THE SYNTHETIC MAN. *New York: Pyramid Books*, [*1957*].
Wrappers. *Pyramid Books Edition 1957* on copyright page. *Pyramid Books G247* (35¢).
Reissue of THE DREAMING JEWELS.

THUNDER AND ROSES. *London: Michael Joseph*, [*1957*].
Boards. No statement of printing on copyright page. All stories collected earlier in A WAY HOME.

TO HERE AND THE EASEL. *London: Victor Gollancz Ltd, 1973*.
Boards. No statement of printing on copyright page. All stories collected from earlier books.

A TOUCH OF STRANGE. *Garden City: Doubleday & Company, Inc., 1958*.
First edition so stated on copyright page.

ALSO: [*New York*]: *Berkley Publishing Corp.*, [*1959*]. Wrappers. *October, 1959* on copyright page. *Berkley Medallion G280* (35¢). Abridged edition. Drops two stories.

TWO COMPLETE NOVELS. See . . . AND MY FEAR IS GREAT/BABY IS THREE.

VENUS PLUS X. *New York: Pyramid Books*, [*1960*].
   Wrappers. *First printing, September 1960* on copyright page. *Pyramid G544* (35¢).

   ALSO: *London: Victor Gollancz Ltd, 1969*. Boards. No statement of printing on copyright page. First hardcover edition.

VOYAGE TO THE BOTTOM OF THE SEA. *New York: Pyramid Books*, [*1961*].
   Wrappers. *First printing, June 1961* on copyright page. *Pyramid G622* (35¢).

A WAY HOME. *New York: Funk & Wagnalls Company, 1955*.
   First printing has *1* on copyright page. Eight of the eleven stories later collected as THUNDER AND ROSES.

   ALSO: *New York: Pyramid Books*, [*1956*]. Wrappers. No statement of printing on copyright page. *Pyramid Giant G184* (35¢). Abridged edition. Drops two stories.

WITHOUT SORCERY. [*Philadelphia*]: *Prime Press, 1948*.
   Two issues, no priority: (A) Red buckram, spine stamped in gilt; all edges uncut; printed on laid paper; issued in red paper slipcase without dust jacket. Limitation notices in holograph on front pastedown. Wording of the statement varies and in some copies no copy number appears. Copies have been noted giving limitation as 80 and 88 copies respectively:
   (a) "The Publisher certifies that/this is one of an edition/of eighty copies only. This/is # six/The Prime Press." (b) "One of 88 copies on special/paper specially bound. Prime Press." Notes: (1) Variant (a) is a presentation copy inscribed on the front free endpaper by Sturgeon. Signature of illustrator L. Robert Tschirky is not present. (2) Variant (b) is signed by Sturgeon and Tschirky on the front end paper. There were a few extra copies with both signatures on the front endpaper but no statement of limitation. Limited issue.
   (B) Black cloth, spine stamped in gold. Trade issue. No statement of printing on copyright page. Eight of these stories reprinted in NOT WITHOUT SORCERY.

THE WORLDS OF THEODORE STURGEON. *New York: Ace Books*, [*1972*].
   Wrappers. No statement of printing on copyright page. *Ace Book 91060* (95¢).

Thomas Burnett Swann
(1928–1976)

CRY SILVER BELLS. *New York: DAW Books, Inc.,* [*1977*].
Wrappers. *First printing, December 1977/1 2 3 4 5 6 7 8 9* on copyright page. *DAW: sf Books No. 270 UW1345* ($1.50).

DAY OF THE MINOTAUR. *New York: Ace Books, Inc.,* [*1966*].
Wrappers. No statement of printing on copyright page. *Ace Book F–407* (40¢).

THE DOLPHIN AND THE DEEP. *New York: Ace Books, Inc.,* [*1968*].
Wrappers. No statement of printing on copyright page. *Ace Book G–694* (50¢).

THE FOREST OF FOREVER. *New York: Ace Books,* [*1971*].
Wrappers. No statement of printing on copyright page. *Ace Book 24650* (60¢).

THE GOAT WITHOUT HORNS. *New York: Ballantine Books,* [*1971*].
Wrappers. *First Printing: October, 1971* on copyright page. *Ballantine Books Fantasy Adventure 02395–1–095* (95¢).

THE GODS ABIDE. *New York: DAW Books, Inc.,* [*1976*].
Wrappers. *First printing, December 1976/1 2 3 4 5 6 7 8 9* on copyright page. *DAW: sf Books No. 222 UY1272* ($1.25).

GREEN PHOENIX. *New York: DAW Books, Inc.,* [*1972*].
Wrappers. *First printing 1972* on copyright page. *DAW: sf Books No. 27 UQ1027* (95¢).

HOW ARE THE MIGHTY FALLEN. *New York: DAW Books, Inc.,* [*1974*].
Wrappers. *First printing: March 1974/1 2 3 4 5 6 7 8 9* on copyright page. *DAW: sf Books No. 94 UQ1100* (95¢).

LADY OF THE BEES. *New York: Ace Books,* [*1976*].
Wrappers. *First Ace printing: May 1976* on copyright page. *Ace 46850* ($1.25).

THE MINIKINS OF YAM. *New York: DAW Books, Inc.,* [*1976*].
Wrappers. *First printing, February 1976/1 2 3 4 5 6 7 8 9* on copyright page. *DAW: sf Books No. 182 UY1219* ($1.25).

MOONDUST. *New York: Ace Books, Inc.,* [*1968*].
Wrappers. No statement of printing on copyright page. *Ace Book G–758* (50¢).

THE NOT-WORLD. *New York: DAW Books, Inc.,* [*1975*].
Wrappers. *First printing, February 1975/1 2 3 4 5 6 7 8 9* on copyright page. *DAW: sf Books No. 140 UY1158* ($1.25).

QUEENS WALK IN THE DUSK. *Forest Park, Georgia: Heritage Press, Inc.,* 1977.
No statement of printing on copyright page. 2000 numbered copies printed. Note: Issued in an unprinted acetate jacket.

TOURNAMENT OF THORNS. *New York: Ace Books,* [*1976*].
Wrappers. *First Ace printing: July 1976* on copyright page. *Ace 81900* ($1.50).

THE WEIRWOODS. *New York: Ace Books, Inc., [1967].*
   Wrappers. No statement of printing on copyright page. *Ace Book G–640* (50¢).

WHERE IS THE BIRD OF FIRE? *New York: An Ace Book. [1970].*
   Wrappers. No statement of printing on copyright page. *Ace Book 88270* (60¢).

WILL-O-THE-WISP. *[London]: Corgi Books, [1976].*
   Wrappers. *Corgi edition published 1976* on copyright page. *Corgi Science Fantasy 0 552 10358 6* (60p).

WOLFWINTER. *New York: Ballantine Books, [1972].*
   Wrappers. *First Printing: November, 1972* on copyright page. *Ballantine Books Science Fiction 02905–4–125* ($1.25).

John Ronald Reuel Tolkien
(1892–1973)

FARMER GILES OF HAM. *London: George Allen & Unwin Ltd, MCMXLIX.*
Boards. *First published in 1949* on copyright page.

THE FATHER CHRISTMAS LETTERS. *London: George Allen & Unwin Ltd, [1976].*
Boards. *First published in 1976* on page [48]. Note: Issued without dust jacket.

THE FELLOWSHIP OF THE RING. *London: George Allen & Unwin Ltd, 1954.*
First published in 1954 on copyright page.

ALSO: *New York: Ballantine Books, [1965].* Wrappers. *First Printing: October, 1965* on
copyright page. *Ballantine Books U7040* (95¢). [Second edition.] Revised text. Adds new
author's "foreword."

ALSO: *London: George Allen & Unwin Ltd, [1966].* 16-line printing history on copyright
page with line 16 reading: *Second Edition 1966.* First hardcover printing of the second
edition. Minor variations in foreword, otherwise follows the 1965 Ballantine text. Collected later as part of one of THE LORD OF THE RINGS.

THE HOBBIT OR THERE AND BACK AGAIN. *London: George Allen & Unwin Ltd, [1937].*
First Published in 1937 on copyright page. Note: All examined copies of first printing dust
jacket misprint "Dodgeson" for "Dodgson" on rear flap.

* ALSO: *London: George Allen and Unwin Ltd, [1951].* Second edition [fifth impression].
Revised text.

ALSO: *London: Unwin Books, [1966].* Wrappers. 16-line printing history on copyright page
with line 16 reading: *Third edition (sixteenth impression) 1966.* Additional textual revisions.

ALSO: [*London*]: *Longmans, [1966].* Boards. *First published 1937/Second edition (fifth
impression) 1951/Third edition (sixteenth impression) published in the Heritage of Literature Series in 1966 by arrangement with Messrs. George Allen & Unwin Ltd.* on copyright
page. First hardcover printing of the third edition. Note: *Whitaker's Cumulative Book List*
cites June 1966 as month of publication for both Allen and Unwin and Longmans editions.
Possibly published simultaneously but the Longmans edition may precede. The British
Library received the Longmans edition on 6 June 1966 and the Allen and Unwin edition on
11 July 1966.

THE LORD OF THE RINGS. *London: George Allen and Unwin Ltd, [1968].*
Wrappers. *First published in one volume 1968* on copyright page. Reprint. Collects THE
FELLOWSHIP OF THE RING, THE TWO TOWERS, and THE RETURN OF THE KING. Lacks index
and appendices, save for "A Part of the Tale of Aragorn and Arwen." Note: A Canadian
variant was probably produced during the same print run. This issue bears the imprint
Thomas Nelson and Sons (Canada) Ltd on the title page, includes the following statement
on the copyright page: *George Allen & Unwin Ltd have authorized this edition/for sale in
Canada by Thomas Nelson & Sons (Canada) Ltd,* page [1080] is blank, and the publisher's
spine imprint reads *NELSON.*

ALSO: *London: George Allen and Unwin Ltd, [1969]. This India paper edition first published 1969* on copyright page. First hardcover one-volume edition. Follows second edition
text and includes the six appendices and index.

THE RETURN OF THE KING. *London: George Allen & Unwin Ltd, 1955.*
First published in 1955 on copyright page.

ALSO: *New York: Ace Books, Inc., [1965].* Wrappers. No statement of printing on copyright page. *Ace Science Fiction Classic A–6 (75¢).* Abridged. Does not contain appendices. Text follows the 1955 Allen & Unwin edition.

ALSO: *New York: Ballantine Books, [1965].* Wrappers. *First printing: December, 1965* on copyright page. *Ballantine Books U7042 (95¢).* [Second edition.]. Revised text; adds index.

ALSO: *London: George Allen & Unwin Ltd, [1966].* 12-line printing history on copyright page with line 12 reading: *Second Edition 1966.* First hardcover printing of the second edition. Follows the 1965 Ballantine text. Collected later as part three of THE LORD OF THE RINGS.

THE SILMARILLION. International publication date was 19 September 1977. Three editions, simultaneous publication but priority of printing probably as indicated:

(1) Allen & Unwin export edition. *London: George Allen & Unwin, [1977].*
First published in 1977 on copyright page. Printer's imprint at base of copyright page reads *Printed in Great Britain/in 11 on 12 point Imprint type/by William Clowes & Sons, Limited/London, Beccles and Colchester.* Dust jacket has no printed price. Background color of dust jacket design is midnight blue. Note: Allen & Unwin dummy copies occur in two states, priority as listed: (A) Publisher's imprint on title page reads *London/George Allen & Unwin Ltd/Ruskin House Museum Street;* Only the publisher's prefix *0 04* of the ISBN number is present on copyright page; 23 chapters listed on contents page. (B) Publisher's imprint on title page reads *London/George Allen & Unwin/Boston Sydney; ISBN 0 04 823139 8* on copyright page; 24 chapters listed on contents page. Both bear the William Clowes & Sons imprint on copyright page. Export edition is per dummy "B."

(2) Allen & Unwin domestic edition. *London: George Allen & Unwin, [1977].*
First published in 1977 on copyright page. Printer's imprint at base of copyright page reads *Printed in Great Britain by offset lithography by/Billing & Sons Ltd, Guildford, London and Worcester.* Dust jacket has *PRICE NET £4.95/IN U.K. ONLY* in lower right corner of front flap. Background color of dust jacket design is purple.

(3) Houghton Mifflin edition. *Boston: Houghton Mifflin Company, 1977.*
First printing/First American Edition on copyright page. Two printings, probable priority as listed: (A) Green cloth, cover stamped in copper and silver; printed on white wove paper; no loss of text at the end of lines 27–32 on page 229. Note: Publisher's advance copy thus. (B) Green cloth, cover stamped in gold and silver; loss of text at the end of lines 27–32 on page 229. Two variants: (a) Printed on white wove paper; (b) Printed on cream wove paper. Notes: (1) First printing run was set at 150,000 copies but prepublication orders raised the first printing order to 325,000 copies. Five additional printings totaling 375,000 copies followed immediately. The first four of these reprintings totaling 200,000 copies were produced by the printer and binder of the first printing, the fifth reprinting of 175,000 copies prepared simultaneously at another press. A comparison of copies within the 325,000 copy "first printing" indicates at least two printings. (2) Misprint *Father Giles of Ham,* page [3], line 7, present in all copies marked *First printing/First American Edition.* It is not an issue point.

SMITH OF WOOTTON MAJOR. *London: George Allen & Unwin Ltd, [1967].*
First published in 1967 on copyright page. Note: Issued without dust jacket.

THE TOLKIEN READER. *New York: Ballantine Books, [1966].*
Wrappers. *First Edition: September, 1966* on copyright page. *A Ballantine Book U7038 (95¢).*

TREE AND LEAF. *London: George Allen & Unwin Ltd*, [*1964*].
    Boards. *First published . . . 1964* on copyright page. Includes essay "On Fairy Stories,"
short story "Leaf by Niggle," and an introductory note.

TREE AND LEAF/SMITH OF WOOTTON MAJOR/THE HOMECOMING OF BEORHTNOTH
BEORHTHELM'S SON. [*London*]: *Unwin Books*, [*1975*].
    Wrappers. *Unwin Books Edition 1975* on copyright page. Note: "The Homecoming of
Beorhtnoth Beorhthelm's Son," a verse play, is first collected here in a book solely by
Tolkien; fiction is reprinted from earlier books.

THE TWO TOWERS. *London: George Allen & Unwin Ltd, 1954.*
    First published in 1954 on copyright page.

    ALSO: *New York: Ballantine Books*, [*1965*]. Wrappers. *First Printing: November, 1965* on
copyright page. *Ballantine Books U7041* (95¢). [Second edition.] Revised text.

    ALSO: *London: George Allen & Unwin Ltd*, [*1966*]. 13-line printing history on copyright
page with line 13 reading: *Second Edition 1966*. First hardcover printing of second edition.
Follows the 1965 Ballantine text. Collected later as part two of THE LORD OF THE RINGS.

Associational

The Hobbit, Dramatized by Patricia Gray. This Dramatization of The Hobbit is Authorized
by Professor J. R. R. Tolkien. *Chicago: The Dramatic Publishing Company*, [*1968*].
    Wrappers. No statement of printing on copyright page. Note: Adapted by Gray from the
novel, THE HOBBIT, by Tolkien.

A Musical Play: The Hobbit, Music by Allan Jay Friedman, Lyrics by David Rogers, Book
by Ruth Perry. The Adaptation of "The Hobbit" is Authorized by Professor J. R. R.
Tolkien. *Chicago: The Dramatic Publishing Company*, [*1972*].
    Wrappers. No statement of printing on copyright page. Cover title reads: *The Hobbit a
Musical*. Note: Adapted by Friedman, Rogers, and Perry from the novel, THE HOBBIT, by
Tolkien.

Reference

Note: This is a partial listing with emphasis on material published since 1970. For earlier
material see *Tolkien Criticism: An Annotated Checklist* compiled by Richard C. West listed
below.

The Biography of J. R. R. Tolkien: Architect of Middle-Earth, by Daniel Grotta.
Philadelphia: Running Press, [*1978*].
    Two bindings, no priority: (A) Cloth with front and rear panels of the paperback issue
affixed to front and rear covers. "Library Binding." (B) Wrappers. Trade binding. *9 8 7 6
5 4 3 2 1 . . . Second Edition* on copyright page. Redesigned, reset, and enlarged edition of
J. R. R. Tolkien: Architect of Middle Earth. Adds "Epilogue: *The Silmarillion*" and an
index. Note: The author's name is printed *Daniel Grotta-Kurska* in the first edition.

Catalogue of an Exhibition of Drawings by J. R. R. Tolkien at the Ashmolean Museum
Oxford 14th December–27th February 1976–1977 and at The National Book League 7 Al-
bemarle Street London W1 2nd March–7th April 1977. [*Oxford and London: Published
jointly by The Ashmolean Museum and The National Book League, in conjunction with
George Allen & Unwin (Publishers) Ltd, 1976.*]
    Wrappers. *First published 1976* on copyright page.

The Complete Guide to Middle-Earth From The Hobbit to The Silmarillion, [by] Robert Foster. *New York: Ballantine Books*, [*1978*].
> *Revised and enlarged edition: March 1978 (hardbound)* on copyright page. Enlarged version of *A Guide to Middle-Earth*.

Funeral Customs in Tolkien's Trilogy, by Karen Rockow. [*Baltimore*]: *TK Graphics*, [*1973*].
> Wrappers. No statement of printing on copyright page.

Good News from Tolkien's Middle Earth Two Essays on the "Applicability" of The Lord of the Rings, by Gracia Fay Ellwood. *Grand Rapids, Michigan: William B. Eerdmans Publishing Company*, [*1970*].
> Wrappers. No statement of printing on copyright page. Stock number *1285* ($3.25).

A Guide to Middle-Earth, by Robert Foster. *Baltimore: Mirage, 1971*.
> Two issues, no priority: (A) 750 numbered copies in cloth; (B) 1250 copies in wrappers. No statement of printing on copyright page. Later revised as *The Complete Guide to Middle-Earth From The Hobbit to The Silmarillion*.

J. R. R. Tolkien: A Biography, by Humphrey Carpenter. *London: George Allen & Unwin Ltd*, [*1977*].
> *First published in 1977* on copyright page.

J. R. R. Tolkien Architect of Middle Earth: A Biography, by Daniel Grotta-Kurska . . . . *Philadelphia: Running Press*, [*1976*].
> Two bindings, probably issued simultaneously: (A) Buckram with front and rear panels of the paperback issue affixed to front and rear covers. Library issue. (B) Wrappers. Trade issue. No statement of printing on copyright page. Revised as *The Biography of J. R. R. Tolkien: Architect of Middle-Earth*.

J. R. R. Tolkien, Scholar and Storyteller: Essays in Memoriam, edited by Mary Salu and Robert T. Farrell. *Ithaca and London: Cornell University Press*, [*1979*].
> *First published 1979 . . .* on copyright page.

The Languages of Middle Earth, by Ruth Noel. *Baltimore: Mirage, 1974*.
> Wrappers. No statement of printing on copyright page. Note: First issue comprises 500 copies bound in wrappers with *Special World Science Fiction Convention edition* at base of copyright page.

Lightning From a Clear Sky: Tolkien, the Trilogy and The Silmarillion, [by] Richard Mathews. *San Bernardino, California: R. Reginald The Borgo Press, MCMLXXVIII*.
> *Wrappers. First Edition——July, 1978* on copyright page. *The Milford Series Popular Writers of Today Volume Fifteen* at head of title.

Lord of the Elves and Eldils: Fantasy and Philosophy in C. S. Lewis and J. R. R. Tolkien, by Richard Purtill. *Grand Rapids, Michigan: Zondervan Publishing House*, [*1974*].
> Wrappers. No statement of printing on copyright page. *Zondervan Books 12267p* ($1.50).

Master of Middle-Earth: The Fiction of J. R. R. Tolkien, by Paul H. Kocher. *Boston: Houghton Mifflin Company, 1972*.
> *First printing V* on copyright page.

Middle Earth: A World in Conflict, by Stephen O. Miller. [*Baltimore: T–K Graphics, 1975.*]
> Wrappers. No statement of printing on copyright page.

Mithrandir, [by] Stephen O. Miller. [*Baltimore: T–K Graphics, 1974.*]
> Wrappers. No statement of printing.

Modern Heroism Essays on D. H. Lawrence, William Empson, & J. R. R. Tolkien, [by] Roger Sale. *Berkeley, Los Angeles, London: University of California Press, 1973.*
   No statement of printing on copyright page.

Myth, Symbol & Religion in The Lord of the Rings, by Sandra Miesel. [*Baltimore*]: *TK Graphics,* [*1973*].
   Wrappers. No statement of printing.

The Mythology of Middle-Earth, [by] Ruth S. Noel. *Boston: Houghton Mifflin Company, 1977.*
   First printing has code *V 10 9 8 7 6 5 4 3 2 1* on copyright page.

The Silmarillion J. R. R. Tolkien: A Brief Account of the Book and its Making, by Christopher Tolkien. [*Boston*]: *Houghton Mifflin Company,* [*1977*].
   Wrappers. No statement of printing. Cover title.

Tolkien & The Silmarillion, [by] Clyde S. Kilby. *Wheaton, Illinois: Harold Shaw Publishers,* [*1976*].
   Boards. No statement of printing on copyright page.

The Tolkien Companion, [by] J. E. A. Tyler. [*London*]: *M*[*acmillan London Limited, 1976*].
   Boards. *First published in 1976 . . .* on copyright page.

Tolkien Criticism: An Annotated Checklist, Compiled by Richard C. West. [*Kent, Ohio*]: *The Kent State University Press,* [*1970*].
   First edition so stated on copyright page.

Tolkien: Cult or Culture? by J. S. Ryan. *Armidale, N.S.W., Australia: University of New England, 1969.*
   Wrappers. *First published 1969 . . .* on copyright page. Offset from typewritten copy.

Tolkien's World, [by] Randel Helms. *Boston: Houghton Mifflin Company, 1974.*
   First Printing v on copyright page.

Tree By Tolkien, [by] Colin Wilson. [*London: Covent Garden Press Ltd, 1973.*]
   Two issues, no priority: (A) 100 numbered copies signed by the author; (B) 500 unnumbered copies. No statement of printing on copyright page.

The Trees, the Jewels and the Rings A Discursive Enquiry Into Things Little Known on Middle-Earth, by Charles E. Noad. [*Harrow, Middx*]: *Published by the Tolkien Society, 1977.*
   Wrappers. No statement of printing on copyright page. Leaf of errata tipped in on inside rear cover.

Visions of Paradise in LotR, [by] Bruce Palmer. [*Baltimore*]: *T–K Graphics, 1976.*
   Wrappers. No statement of printing. Cover title reads: *Of Orc-Rags, Phials, & a Far Shore: Visions of Paradise in The Lord of the Rings.*

Edwin Charles Tubb

(b. 1919)

ALIEN DUST.*London New York: T. V. Boardman & Company Limited*, [*1955*].
  Boards. *First published 1955* on copyright page.

ALIEN LIFE.*London: Paladin Press Ltd*, [*1954*].
  Wrappers. No statement of printing on copyright page. Price *1/6* printed on front wrapper.

ALIEN SEED.*New York: Published by Pocket Books*, [*1976*].
  Wrappers. *June, 1976* on copyright page. *Pocket Books S/F 80520* ($1.50).

  ALSO:*London: Arthur Barker Limited*, [*1976*]. Boards. No statement of printing on copyright
  page. *Space 1999* at head of title. First hardcover edition.

ALIEN UNIVERSE.*London: Scion Ltd.*, [*1952*].
  Wrappers. *First published 1952* . . . on copyright page. *A Scion Scientific Novel* (1/6).
  Volsted Gridban, pseudonym.

"ARGENTIS."*London: Printed in England & Published by Curtis Warren Ltd.*, [*1952*].
  Wrappers. *Curtis Books* (1/6). *Brian Shaw, pseudonym.*

ASSIGNMENT NEW YORK. [*London*]: *John Spencer*, [*1955*].
  Wrappers. No statement of printing on copyright page. *Mystery Series No. 1* (2/–). *Mike
  Lantry, pseudonym.*

ATILUS THE GLADIATOR. [*London*]: *Futura Publications Limited*, [*1975*].
  Wrappers. *First published in Great Britain in 1975* . . . on copyright page. *Futura Fiction
  0 8600 7229 4* (50p). *Edward Thomson, pseudonym.*

ATILUS THE SLAVE. [*London*]: *Futura Publications Limited*, [*1975*].
  Wrappers. *First published in Great Britain in 1975* . . . on copyright page. *Futura Fiction
  0 8600 7194 4* (45p). *Edward Thomson, pseudonym.*

ATOM WAR ON MARS.*London: Hamilton & Co. (Stafford) Limited*, [*1952*].
  Wrappers. No statement of printing on copyright page. *Panther Books* (1'6).

BEYOND THE GALACTIC LENS.*New York: DAW Books, Inc.*, [*1975*].
  Wrappers. *First printing, December 1975/1 2 3 4 5 6 7 8 9* on copyright page. *DAW: sf
  Books No. 176 UY1211* ($1.25). *Gregory Kern, pseudonym.*

BREAKAWAY. [*London*]: *Futura Publications Limited*, [*1975*].
  Wrappers. *First published in Great Britain in 1975* on copyright page. *Orbit 0 8600 7843 4*
  (35p). *Space 1999* at head of title.

  ALSO:*London: Dennis Dobson*, [*1975*]. Boards. *This edition first published in Great
  Britain in 1975* on copyright page. *Space: 1999* at head of title. First hardcover edition.

CENTURY OF THE MANIKIN.*New York: DAW Books, Inc.*, [*1972*].
  Wrappers. No statement of printing on copyright page. *DAW: sf Books No. 18 UQ1018*
  (95¢).

  ALSO: [*London*]: *Millington*, [*1975*]. Boards. *First British edition published in 1975* . . .
  on copyright page. First hardcover edition.

CITY OF NO RETURN.*London: Scion Limited*, [*1954*].
Wrappers. *First published in Great Britain, 1954* on page [2].

C.O.D. MARS.*New York: Ace Books, Inc.*, [*1968*].
Wrappers. No statement of printing on copyright page. *Ace Double H–40* (60¢). Bound with ALIEN SEA by John Rackham.

COLLISION COURSE. [*London*]: *Futura Publications Limited*, [*1975*].
Wrappers. *First published in Great Britain in 1975* on copyright page. *Orbit 0 8600 78647* (45p). *Space 1999* at head of title.

ALSO:*London: Dennis Dobson*, [*1975*]. Boards. *This edition first published in Great Britain in 1975* on copyright page. *Space 1999 4* at head of title. First hardcover edition.

*COLT VENGEANCE.*London: Spencer*, [*1957*].
Wrappers.*James R. Fenner, pseudonym*.

*COMANCHE CAPTURE.*London: Spencer*, [*1955*].
Wrappers. *E.F. Jackson, pseudonym*.

DE BRACY'S DRUG.*London: Scion*, [*1953*].
Wrappers. *First published in Great Britain 1953* on copyright page. *Volsted Gridban, pseudonym*.

DEATH IS A DREAM.*London: Rupert Hart-Davis, 1967*.
Boards. *First published 1967* on copyright page.

DERAI.*New York: Ace Books, Inc.*, [*1968*].
Wrappers. No statement of printing on copyright page. *Ace Double H–77* (60¢). Bound with THE SINGING STONES by Juanita Coulson.

*DRUMS OF THE PRAIRIE.*London: Spencer*, [*1956*].
Wrappers.*P. Lawrence, pseudonym*.

DYNASTY OF DOOM.*London: Milestone Publications Ltd.*, [*1953*].
Wrappers. *First published in Great Britain 1953* on copyright page. *Milestone 1062* (1/6d). *Charles Grey, pseudonym*.

EARTH ENSLAVED.*New York: DAW Books, Inc.*, [*1974*].
Wrappers. *First printing, June, 1974/1 2 3 4 5 6 7 8 9* on copyright page. *DAW: sf Books UQ1118* (95¢). *Gregory Kern, pseudonym*.

EARTHFALL. [*London*]: *Futura Publications Limited*, [*1977*].
Wrappers. *First published in Great Britain in 1977 . . .* on copyright page. *Orbit Science Fiction 0 8600 7940 6* (80p). *Space 1999* at head of title.

THE EATER OF WORLDS.*New York: DAW Books, Inc.*, [*1974*].
Wrappers. *First printing, May 1974/1 2 3 4 5 6 7 8 9* on copyright page. *DAW: sf Books UQ1113* (95¢). *Gregory Kern, pseudonym*.

ELOISE.*New York: DAW Books, Inc.*, [*1975*].
Wrappers. *First printing: March 1975/1 2 3 4 5 6 7 8 9* on copyright page. *DAW: sf Books No. 143 UY1162* ($1.25).

ENEMY WITHIN THE SKULL.*New York: DAW Books, Inc.*, [*1974*].
Wrappers. *First printing, January 1974/1 2 3 4 5 6 7 8 9* on copyright page. *DAW: sf Book UT1093* (75¢). *Gregory Kern, pseudonym*.

ENTERPRISE 2115. *London: Merit Books*, [*1954*].
Two issues, no priority: (A) Boards; (B) Wrappers. *A Merit Book* (2/–). No statement of printing on copyright page. *Charles Grey, pseudonym*. Issued later in the U.S. as THE MECHANICAL MONARCH.

ESCAPE INTO SPACE. *London: Sidgwick & Jackson*, [*1969*].
Boards. *First published in Great Britain 1969* on copyright page.

THE EXTRA MAN. *London: Milestone*, [*1954*].
Wrappers. *First published in Great Britain, 1954* on copyright page. *Charles Grey, pseudonym*.

EYE OF THE ZODIAC. *New York: DAW Books, Inc.*, [*1975*].
Wrappers. *First Printing, September 1975/1 2 3 4 5 6 7 8 9* on copyright page. *DAW: sf Books No. 163 UY1194* ($1.25).

*THE FIGHTING FURY. *London: Spencer*, [*1955*].
Wrappers. *Paul Schofield, pseudonym*.

FUGITIVE OF TIME. *London: Milestone Publications Ltd.*, [*1953*].
Wrappers. *First published in Great Britain 1953* on copyright page. *Milestone Science* (1'6). *Volsted Gridban, pseudonym*.

GALAXY OF THE LOST. *New York: DAW Books, Inc.*, [*1973*].
Wrappers. *First printing, September 1973/1 2 3 4 5 6 7 8 9* on copyright page. *DAW: sf Books UT 1073* (75¢). *Gregory Kern, pseudonym*.

GATH. *London: Rupert Hart-Davis, 1968*.
Boards. *First published 1968* on copyright page. Issued earlier in the U.S. as THE WINDS OF GATH.

THE GENETIC BUCCANEER. *New York: DAW Books, Inc.*, [*1974*].
Wrappers. *First printing, October 1974/1 2 3 4 5 6 7 8 9* on copyright page. *DAW: sf Books UQ1138* (95¢). *Gregory Kern, pseudonym*.

THE GHOLAN GATE. *New York: DAW Books, Inc.*, [*1974*].
Wrappers. *First printing, April 1974/1 2 3 4 5 6 7 8 9* on copyright page. *DAW: sf Books UQ1108* (95¢). *Gregory Kern, pseudonym*.

THE GHOSTS OF EPIDORIS. *New York: DAW Books, Inc.*, [*1975*].
Wrappers. *First printing, February 1975/1 2 3 4 5 6 7 8 9* on copyright page. *DAW: sf Books UQ1159* (95¢). *Gregory Kern, pseudonym*.

THE HAND OF HAVOC. *London: Merit Books*, [*1954*].
Wrappers. *First published in Great Britain 1954* on copyright page. *A Merit Science Novel* (1/6). *Charles Grey, pseudonym*.

HAVEN OF DARKNESS. *New York: DAW Books, Inc.*, [*1977*].
Wrappers. *First printing, May 1977/1 2 3 4 5 6 7 8 9* on copyright page. *DAW: sf Books No. 242 UW1299* ($1.50).

THE HELL PLANET. *London: Scion Distributors Ltd.*, [*1954*].
Wrappers. *First published in Great Britain, 1954* . . . on page [2].

I FIGHT FOR MARS. *London: Milestone*, [*1953*].
Wrappers. *First published in Great Britain, 1953* on copyright page. *Milestone Books* (1'6). *Charles Grey, pseudonym*.

JACK OF SWORDS. *New York: DAW Books, Inc.*, *[1976]*.
Wrappers. *First printing, June 1976/1 2 3 4 5 6 7 8 9* on copyright page. *DAW: sf Books No. 198 UY1239* ($1.25).

THE JESTER AT SCAR. *New York: Ace Publishing Corporation*, *[1970]*.
Wrappers. No statement of printing on copyright page. *Ace Double 81610* (75¢). Bound with TO VENUS! TO VENUS! by David Grinnell.

JEWEL OF JARHEN. *New York: DAW Books, Inc.*, *[1974]*.
Wrappers. *First printing, February 1974/1 2 3 4 5 6 7 8 9* on copyright page. *DAW: sf Books UQ1098* (95¢). *Gregory Kern, pseudonym*.

JONDELLE. *New York: DAW Books, Inc.*, *[1973]*.
Wrappers. *First printing, October 1973/1 2 3 4 5 6 7 8 9* on copyright page. *DAW: sf Books No. 74 UQ1075* (95¢).

JOURNEY TO MARS. *London: Scion Limited*, *[1954]*.
Wrappers. *First Published in Great Britain 1954* on page [2].

KALIN. *New York: An Ace Book*, *[1969]*.
Wrappers. No statement of printing on copyright page. *Ace Double 42800* (75¢). Bound with THE BANE OF KANTHOS by Alex Dain.

LALLIA. *New York: Ace Books*, *[1971]*.
Wrappers. No statement of printing on copyright page. *Ace Double 71082* (75¢). Bound with RECOIL by Claude and Rhoda Nunes.

THE LIVING WORLD. *[London: C. Arthur Pearson Ltd., 1954.]*
Wrappers. No statement of printing. Caption title. *Tit-Bits Science Fiction Library* (9d). *Carl Maddox, pseudonym*.

MAYENNE. *New York: DAW Books, Inc.*, *[1973]*.
Wrappers. *First printing, May 1973/1 2 3 4 5 6 7 8 9* on copyright page. *DAW: sf Books No. 54 UQ1054* (95¢).

THE MECHANICAL MONARCH. *New York: Ace Books, Inc.*, *[1958]*.
Wrappers. No statement of printing on copyright page. *Ace Double Novel Books D–266* (35¢). Bound with TWICE UPON A TIME by Charles L. Fontenay. Issued earlier in Great Britain as ENTERPRISE 2115 under the pseudonym Charles Grey.

*MEN OF THE LONG RIFLE. *London: Spencer*, *[1955]*.
Wrappers. *J. F. Clarkson, pseudonym*.

*MEN OF THE WEST. *London: Spencer*, *[1956]*.
Wrappers. *Chet Lawson, pseudonym*.

MENACE FROM THE PAST. *[London: C. Arthur Pearson, Ltd., 1954.]*
Wrappers. No statement of printing. Caption title. *Tit-Bits Science Fiction Library* (9d). *Carl Maddox, pseudonym*.

THE METAL EATER. *London: Panther Books*, *[1954]*.
Two issues, no priority: (A) Cloth; (B) Wrappers. *Panther Books 109* (1'6). No statement of printing on copyright page. *Roy Sheldon, pseudonym*.

MIMICS OF DEPHENE. *New York: DAW Books, Inc.*, *[1975]*.
Wrappers. *First printing, April 1975/1 2 3 4 5 6 7 8 9* on copyright page. *DAW: sf Books UY1168* ($1.25). *Gregory Kern, pseudonym*.

MONSTER OF METELAZE.*New York: DAW Books, Inc.*, [*1973*].
Wrappers. *First printing, November 1973/1 2 3 4 5 6 7 8 9* on copyright page. *DAW: sf Books UT1084* (75¢). *Gregory Kern, pseudonym*.

MOON BASE.*London: Herbert Jenkins*, [*1964*].
Boards. *First published . . . 1964* on copyright page.

THE MUTANTS REBEL.*London: Panther Books*, [*1953*].
Wrappers. No statement of printing on copyright page. *Panther Books 38* (1'6).

PLANET OF DREAD.*New York: DAW Books, Inc.*, [*1974*].
Wrappers. *First printing, July 1974/1 2 3 4 5 6 7 8 9* on copyright page. *DAW: sf Books UQ1123* (95¢). *Gregory Kern, pseudonym*.

PLANETFALL.*London: Printed in Great Britain and Published by Curtis Warren Limited*, [*1951*].
Wrappers. No statement of printing on copyright page. *Curtis Science Fiction* (1'6). *Gill Hunt, pseudonym*.

PLANETOID DISPOSALS LTD.*London: Milestone*, [*1953*].
Wrappers. *First published in Great Britain 1953* on copyright page. *Milestone Books No. 1019* (1'6). *Volsted Gridban, pseudonym*.

THE PRIMITIVE.*[London]: Futura Publications Limited*, [*1977*].
Wrappers. *First published . . . 1977* on copyright page. *An Orbit Book Science Fiction 0 8600 7974 0* (65p).

PRISON OF NIGHT.*New York: DAW Books, Inc.*, [*1977*].
Wrappers. *First printing, December 1977/1 2 3 4 5 6 7 8 9* on copyright page. *DAW: sf Books No. 271 UW1346* ($1.50).

*QUEST FOR QUANTRELL.*London: Spencer*, [*1956*].
Wrappers. *John Stevens, pseudonym*.

THE RESURRECTED MAN. *[London]: Dragon Press*, [*1954*].
Wrappers. *First published in Great Britain, 1954* on page [2]. *Scion Publication* (1'6).

REVERSE UNIVERSE.*London: Scion*, [*1952*].
Wrappers. *First Published in Great Britain 1952* on copyright page. *Scion Science Fiction No. 43699* (1'6). *Volsted Gridban, pseudonym*.

ROGUE PLANET.*New York: Published by Pocket Books*, [*1976*].
Wrappers. *September, 1976* on copyright page. *Pocket Books S/F 80710* ($1.50).

ALSO:*London: Arthur Barker Limited*, [*1977*]. Boards. No statement of printing on copyright page. First hardcover edition. Note: Despite the statement "Published in Great Britain simultaneously by Arthur Barker Ltd . . . and Futura Publications Ltd . . ." on copyright page, the Orbit edition was published in December 1976 while the Barker edition was published in March 1977. Both were preceded by the Pocket Books edition issued in September 1976.

*SANDS OF DESTINY.*London: Spencer*, [*1955*].
Wrappers. *Judy Cary, pseudonym*.

SATURN PATROL.*London: Printed in Great Britain and Published by Curtis Warren Limited*, [*1951*].
Wrappers. No statement of printing on copyright page. *Curtis Books* (1'6). *King Lang, pseudonym*.

A SCATTER OF STARDUST. *New York: Ace Books*, [*1972*].
Wrappers. No statement of printing on copyright page. *Ace Double 79975* (95¢). Bound with TECHNOS by Tubb.

ALSO: *London: Dennis Dobson*, [*1976*]. Boards. *First published in Great Britain in 1976* . . . on copyright page. First hardcover edition.

*SCOURGE OF THE SOUTH. *London: Spencer*, [*1956*].
Wrappers. *M. L. Powers, pseudonym*.

SEETEE ALERT! *New York: DAW Books, Inc.*, [*1974*].
Wrappers. *First printing, March 1974/1 2 3 4 5 6 7 8 9* on copyright page. *DAW: sf Books UQ1103* (95¢). *Gregory Kern, pseudonym*.

SLAVE SHIP FROM SERGAN. *New York: DAW Books, Inc.*, [*1973*].
Wrappers. *First printing, October 1973/1 2 3 4 5 6 7 8 9* on copyright page. *DAW: sf Books UT1078* (75¢). *Gregory Kern, pseudonym*.

THE SPACE-BORN. *New York: Ace Books*, [*1956*].
Wrappers. No statement of printing on copyright page. *Ace Double Novel Books D–193* (35¢). Bound with THE MAN WHO JAPED by Philip K. Dick.

SPACE HUNGER. *London: Milestone Publications, Ltd.*, [*1953*].
Wrappers. *First Published in Great Britain 1953* on copyright page. *A Milestone Science Fiction Novel* (1/6). *Charles Grey, pseudonym*.

SPAWN OF LABAN. *New York: DAW Books, Inc.*, [*1974*].
Wrappers. *First printing, September 1974/1 2 3 4 5 6 7 8 9* on copyright page. *DAW: sf Books UQ1133* (95¢). *Gregory Kern, pseudonym*.

SPECTRUM OF A FORGOTTEN SUN. *New York: DAW Books, Inc.*, [*1976*].
Wrappers. *First printing, November 1976/1 2 3 4 5 6 7 8 9* on copyright page. *DAW: sf Books No. 219 UY1265* ($1.25).

S.T.A.R. FLIGHT. *New York: Paperback Library*, [*1969*].
Wrappers. *First Printing: January, 1969* on copyright page. *Paperback Library Original Science Fiction 62–009* (50¢).

THE STELLAR LEGION. *London: Scion Distributors, Ltd.*, [*1954*].
Wrappers. *First published in Great Britain, 1954* on page 144.

TECHNOS. *New York: Ace Books*, [*1972*].
Wrappers. No statement of printing on copyright page. *Ace Double 79975* (95¢). Bound with A SCATTER OF STARDUST by Tubb.

TEN FROM TOMORROW. [*London*]: *Rupert Hart-Davis*, [*1966*].
Boards. *First published 1966* on copyright page.

TORMENTED CITY. *London: Milestone Publications Ltd.*, [*1953*].
Wrappers. *First published Gt. Britain 1953* on copyright page. *A Milestone Science Thriller* (1'6). *Charles Grey, pseudonym*.

TOUCH OF EVIL. [*London*]: *Fleetway Publications Ltd.*, [*1959*].
Wrappers. *First Printing, October 1959* on copyright page. *Sexton Blake Library No. 438*. *Arthur Maclean, pseudonym*.

TOYMAN.*New York: An Ace Book*, [*1969*].
Wrappers. No statement of printing on copyright page. *Ace Double 23140* (60¢). Bound with FEAR THAT MAN by Dean R. Koontz.

*TRAIL BLAZERS. *London: Spencer*, [*1956*].
Wrappers. *Chuck Adams, pseudonym.*

*VENGEANCE TRAIL.*London: Spencer*, [*1956*].
Wrappers. *James S. Farrow, pseudonym.*

VENUSIAN ADVENTURE.*London: Comyns (Publishers) Ltd.*, [*1953*].
Wrappers. No statement of printing.

VERUCHIA.*New York: Ace Books*, [*1973*].
Wrappers. *First Ace printing: June, 1973* on copyright page. *An Ace Book 86180* (95¢).

*WAGON TRAIL.*London: Spencer*, [*1957*].
Wrappers. *Charles S. Graham, pseudonym.*

THE WALL.*London: Milestone Publications Ltd.*, [*1953*].
Wrappers. *First published in Great Britain, 1953* on copyright page. *Milestone Book No. 1044* (1/6). *Charles Grey, pseudonym.*

THE WINDS OF GATH.*New York: Ace Books, Inc.*, [*1967*].
Wrappers. No statement of printing on copyright page. *Ace Double H–27* (60¢). Bound with CRISIS ON CHEIRON by Juanita Coulson. Issued later in Great Britain as GATH.

A WORLD AFLAME.*New York: DAW Books, Inc.*, [*1974*].
Wrappers. *First printing, November 1974/1 2 3 4 5 6 7 8 9* on copyright page. *DAW: sf Books UQ1144* (95¢). *Gregory Kern, pseudonym.*

WORLD AT BAY.*London: Panther Books*, [*1954*].
Two issues, no priority: (A) Cloth; (B) Wrappers. *Panther Books 110* (1'6). No statement of printing on copyright page.

ZENYA.*New York: DAW Books, Inc.*, [*1974*].
Wrappers. *First printing, August 1974/1 2 3 4 5 6 7 8 9* on copyright page. *DAW: sf Books No. 115 UQ1126* (95¢).

Arthur Wilson Tucker
(b. 1914)

THE CHINESE DOLL. *New York Toronto: Rinehart & Company, Inc.*, [*1946*].
First printing has Rinehart monogram on copyright page.

THE CITY IN THE SEA. *New York Toronto: Rinehart & Co., Incorporated*, [*1951*].
Boards. First printing has Rinehart monogram on copyright page.

THE DOVE. *New York Toronto: Rinehart & Company, Inc.*, [*1948*].
Boards. First printing has Rinehart monogram on copyright page.

THE HIRED TARGET. *New York: Ace Books*, [*1957*].
Wrappers. No statement of printing on copyright page. *Ace Double Novel Books D–241* (35¢). Bound with ONE DEADLY DAWN by Harry Whittington.

ICE AND IRON. *Garden City: Doubleday & Company, Inc., 1974*.
Boards. First edition so stated on copyright page.

ALSO: *New York: Ballantine Books*, [*1975*]. Wrappers. *First Printing: October, 1975* on copyright page. *Ballantine Books SF 24660* ($1.50). Final chapter is revised.

LAST STOP. *Garden City: Published for the Crime Club by Doubleday & Company, Inc., 1963*.
First edition so stated on copyright page.

THE LINCOLN HUNTERS. *New York Toronto: Rinehart & Company, Inc.*, [*1958*].
Boards. First printing has Rinehart monogram on copyright page.

THE LONG LOUD SILENCE. *New York Toronto: Rinehart & Co., Inc.*, [*1952*].
Boards. First printing has Rinehart monogram on copyright page.

ALSO: *New York: Lancer Books*, [*1970*]. Wrappers. *This edition specially revised and updated, published 1969* on copyright page. *Lancer Books 74–600* (75¢). Revised text. Note: Published in January 1970.

MAN FROM TOMORROW. *New York: Bantam Books*, [*1955*].
Wrappers. *Bantam edition published July, 1955* on copyright page. *Bantam Books 1343* (25¢). Reissue of WILD TALENT.

THE MAN IN MY GRAVE. *New York Toronto: Rinehart & Company, Inc.*, [*1956*].
Boards. First printing has Rinehart monogram on copyright page.

A PROCESSION OF THE DAMNED. *Garden City: Doubleday & Company, Inc., 1965*.
First edition so stated on copyright page.

RED HERRING. *New York Toronto: Rinehart & Company, Inc.*, [*1951*].
Boards. First printing has Rinehart monogram on copyright page.

THE SCIENCE-FICTION SUBTREASURY. *New York Toronto: Rinehart & Company, Inc.*, [*1954*].
Boards. First printing has Rinehart monogram on copyright page. Reissued as TIME: X.

THE STALKING MAN. *New York Toronto: Rinehart & Company, Inc., [1949]*.
  Boards. First printing has Rinehart monogram on copyright page.

THE WITCH. *Garden City: Doubleday & Company, Inc., 1971*.
  First edition so stated on copyright page.

TIME BOMB. *New York • Toronto: Rinehart & Company, Inc., [1955]*.
  Boards. First printing has Rinehart monogram on copyright page. Reissued as TOMORROW
  PLUS X.

THE TIME MASTERS. *New York Toronto: Rinehart & Co., Inc., [1953]*.
  Boards. First printing has Rinehart monogram on copyright page.

  ALSO: *Garden City: Nelson Doubleday, Inc., [1971]*. Boards. No statement of printing on
  copyright page. Two printings, priority as listed: (A) Code *B40* on page 185; (B) Code *C15*
  on page 185. Revised text. Note: First printing omitted the last four paragraphs of the final
  chapter. This chapter reset in the second printing to restore missing paragraphs.

TIME: X. *New York: Bantam Books, [1955]*.
  Wrappers. *Bantam edition published December 1955* on copyright page. *Bantam Books
  1400* (25¢). Reissue of the SCIENCE-FICTION SUBTREASURY.

TO KEEP OR KILL. *New York Toronto: Rinehart & Company, [1947]*.
  Boards. First printing has Rinehart monogram on copyright page.

TO THE TOMBAUGH STATION. *New York: Ace Books, Inc., [1960]*.
  Wrappers. No statement of printing on copyright page. *Ace Double Novel Books D–479*
  (35¢). Bound with EARTHMAN, GO HOME! by Poul Anderson.

TOMORROW PLUS X. *New York: Avon Publications, Inc., [1957]*.
  Wrappers. No statement of printing on copyright page. *Avon T 168* (35¢). Reissue of TIME
  BOMB.

THE WARLOCK. *Garden City: Doubleday & Company, Inc., 1967*.
  First edition so stated on copyright page.

WILD TALENT. *New York Toronto: Rinehart & Co., Inc., [1954]*.
  Boards. First printing has Rinehart monogram on copyright page. Reissued as MAN FROM
  TOMORROW.

THE YEAR OF THE QUIET SUN. *New York: Ace Publishing Corporation, [1970]*.
  Wrappers. No statement of printing on copyright page. *An Ace Science Fiction Special
  94200* (75¢).

  ALSO: *London: Robert Hale & Company, [1971]*. Boards. *First published in Great Britain
  1971* on copyright page. First hardcover edition.

Boyd Bradfield Upchurch
(b. 1919)

ANDROMEDA GUN. *New York: G. P. Putnam's Sons*, [*1974*].
No statement of printing on copyright page. *John Boyd, pseudonym.*

BARNARD'S PLANET. *New York: Published by Berkley Publishing Corporation*, [*1975*].
No statement of printing on copyright page. *John Boyd, pseudonym.*

THE DOOMSDAY GENE. *New York: Weybright and Talley*, [*1973*].
Boards. No statement of printing on copyright page. *John Boyd, pseudonym.*

THE GORGON FESTIVAL. *New York: Weybright and Talley, Inc.*, [*1972*].
No statement of printing on copyright page. *John Boyd, pseudonym.*

THE I.Q. MERCHANT. *New York: Weybright and Talley*, [*1972*].
No statement of printing on copyright page. *John Boyd, pseudonym.*

THE LAST STARSHIP FROM EARTH. *New York: Weybright and Talley*, [*1968*].
No statement of printing on copyright page. *John Boyd, pseudonym.*

THE ORGAN BANK FARM. *New York: Weybright and Talley*, [*1970*].
No statement of printing on copyright page. *John Boyd, pseudonym.*

THE POLLINATORS OF EDEN. *New York: Weybright and Talley*, [*1969*].
No statement of printing on copyright page. *John Boyd, pseudonym.*

THE RAKEHELLS OF HEAVEN. *New York: Weybright and Talley*, [*1969*].
No statement of printing on copyright page. *John Boyd, pseudonym.*

SCARBOROUGH HALL. [*New York*]: *Published by Berkley Publishing Corporation*, [*1976*].
Wrappers. *November, 1976* on copyright page. *A Berkley Medallion Book D3256* ($1.50).

SEX AND THE HIGH COMMAND. *New York: Weybright and Talley*, [*1970*].
No statement of printing on copyright page. *John Boyd, pseudonym.*

THE SLAVE STEALER. *New York: Weybright and Talley*, [*1968*].
No statement of printing on copyright page.

Alfred Elton van Vogt
(b. 1912)

THE ANARCHISTIC COLOSSUS.*New York: Ace Books*, [*1977*].
Wrappers. *First Ace printing: April, 1977* on copyright page. *Ace 02255–3* ($1.75).

AWAY AND BEYOND.*New York: Pellegrini & Cudahy*, [*1952*].
No statement of printing on copyright page.

ALSO: [*New York*]: *Published by Berkley Publishing Corp.*, [*1959*]. Wrappers. *February, 1959* on copyright page. *Berkley Books G–215* (35¢). Abridged reprint. Drops ''Vault of the Beast'' and ''Heir Unapparent.''

THE BATTLE OF FOREVER.*New York:Ace Books*, [*1971*].
Wrappers. No statement of printing on copyright page. *Ace Book 04860* (95¢).

ALSO:*London: Sidgwick & Jackson*, [*1972*]. Boards. *First published in Great Britain 1972* on copyright page. First hardcover edition.

THE BEAST.*Garden City: Doubleday & Company, Inc.*, *1963*.
First edition so stated on copyright page. Reissued as MOONBEAST. Later collected in A VAN VOGT OMNIBUS.

THE BEST OF A. E. VAN VOGT.*London: Sphere Books Limited*, [*1974*].
Wrappers. *First published in Great Britain . . . 1974* on copyright page. *Sphere 0 7221 8774 2* (60p).

ALSO:*London: Sidgwick & Jackson*, [*1974*]. Boards. *First published in Great Britain in 1974* on copyright page. First hardcover edition.

THE BEST OF A. E. VAN VOGT.*New York: Published by Pocket Books*, [*1976*].
Wrappers. *Published July, 1976* on copyright page. *Pocket 80546* ($1.95). Note: Contents differ from Sphere and Sidgwick & Jackson editions.

THE BLAL. [*New York*]: *Kensington Publishing Corp.*, [*1976*].
Wrappers. *First Printing: August, 1976* on copyright page. *Zebra Books 200* ($1.25). Reissue of MONSTERS.

THE BOOK OF PTATH.*Reading, Pennsylvania: Fantasy Press*, *1947*.
Two issues, no priority: (A) 500 copies with numbered leaf signed by author inserted; (B) Trade issue. First edition so stated on copyright page. Reissued as TWO HUNDRED MILLION A.D. Later collected in A VAN VOGT OMNIBUS.

THE BOOK OF VAN VOGT.*New York: DAW Books, Inc.*, [*1972*].
Wrappers. No statement of printing on copyright page. *DAW: sf Books No. 4 UQ1004* (95¢).

THE CHANGELING. [*New York*]: *A Macfadden-Bartell Book*, [*1967*].
Wrappers. *A Macfadden Book . . . . 1967* on copyright page. *Macfadden Books 50–335* (50¢). First separate edition. Originally collected in MASTERS OF TIME.

CHILDREN OF TOMORROW.*New York: Ace Books*, [*1970*].
Wrappers. No statement of printing on copyright page. *Ace Book 10410* (95¢).

ALSO:*London: Sidgwick & Jackson*, [*1972*]. Boards. *First published in Great Britain 1972* on copyright page. First hardcover edition.

THE DARKNESS ON DIAMONDIA. *New York: Ace Books*, [*1972*].
  Wrappers. No statement of printing on copyright page. *Ace Book 13798* (95¢).

  ALSO: *London: Sidgwick & Jackson*, [*1974*]. Boards. *Published in Great Britain in 1974* on copyright page. First hardcover edition.

DESTINATION: UNIVERSE! *New York: Pellegrini & Cudahy*, [*1952*].
  No statement of printing on copyright page.

EARTH FACTOR X. *New York: DAW Books, Inc.*, [*1976*].
  Wrappers. *First DAW printing, August 1976/1 2 3 4 5 6 7 8 9* on copyright page. *DAW: sf Books No. 206 UY1249* ($1.25). Reissue of THE SECRET GALACTICS.

EARTH'S LAST FORTRESS. *New York: Ace Books, Inc.*, [*1960*].
  Wrappers. No statement of printing on copyright page. *Ace Double Novel Books D–431* (35¢). Bound with LOST IN SPACE by George O. Smith. Reprint of MASTERS OF TIME. Also collected in TWO SCIENCE FICTION NOVELS.

EMPIRE OF THE ATOM. *Chicago: Shasta Publishers*, [*1957*].
  Boards. First edition so stated on copyright page.

THE FAR-OUT WORLDS OF A. E. VAN VOGT. *New York: Ace Books, Inc.*, [*1968*].
  Wrappers. No statement of printing on copyright page. *Ace Book H–92* (60¢). Later enlarged as THE WORLDS OF A. E. VAN VOGT.

  ALSO: *London: Sidgwick & Jackson*, [*1973*]. Boards. *First published in Great Britain in 1973* on copyright page. First hardcover edition.

FUTURE GLITTER. *New York: Ace Books*, [*1973*].
  Wrappers. *First Ace Printing: October 1973* on copyright page. *An Ace Book 25980* (95¢). Reissued as TYRANOPOLIS.

  ALSO: *London: Sidgwick & Jackson*, [*1976*]. Boards. *First published in Great Britain in 1976* on copyright page. First hardcover edition.

THE GRYB. [*New York*]: *Kensington Publishing Corp.*, [*1976*].
  Wrappers. *First Printing: May, 1976* on copyright page. *Zebra 182* ($1.25). Reprint collection. All stories collected from earlier books.

THE HOUSE THAT STOOD STILL. [*New York*]: *Greenberg: Publisher*, [*1950*].
  No statement of printing on copyright page. Revised as THE MATING CRY. Reissued as UNDERCOVER ALIENS.

M 33 IN ANDROMEDA. *New York: Paperback Library*, [*1971*].
  Wrappers. *First Printing: April, 1971* on copyright page. *A Paperback Library Science Fiction Original 65–584* (95¢).

THE MAN WITH A THOUSAND NAMES. *New York: DAW Books, Inc.*, [*1974*].
  Wrappers. *First Printing, August 1974/1 2 3 4 5 6 7 8 9* on copyright page. *DAW: sf Books No. 114 UQ1125* (95¢).

MASTERS OF TIME. *Reading, Pennsylvania: Fantasy Press, 1950.*
  Two bindings, priority as listed: (A) Dark red cloth, spine stamped in gold; (B) Tan cloth, spine stamped in black. Two issues, no priority: (A) 500 copies with numbered leaf signed by the author inserted; (B) Trade issue. First edition so stated on copyright page. Includes "The Changeling."

  ALSO: [*New York*]: *A Macfadden-Bartell Book*, [*1967*]. Wrappers. *A Macfadden Book . . . . 1967* on copyright page. *Macfadden Books 50–334* (50¢). Drops "The Changeling."

THE MATING CRY. [*New York*]: *Beacon Books*, [*1960*].
  Wrappers. No statement of printing on copyright page. *Beacon Book 289 (Galaxy Novel No. 44)* (35¢). Revision of THE HOUSE THAT STOOD STILL.

THE MIND CAGE. *New York: Simon and Schuster, 1957.*
  Boards with cloth shelf back. First printing so stated on copyright page. Later collected in VAN VOGT OMNIBUS (2).

MISSION: INTERPLANETARY. [*New York*]: *Published by the New American Library*, [*1952*].
  Wrappers. *First printing, January, 1952* on copyright page. *N.A.L. Signet Books 914* (25¢). Reissue of THE VOYAGE OF THE SPACE BEAGLE.

MISSION TO THE STARS. *New York: Berkley Publishing Corp.*, [*1955*].
  Wrappers. *December, 1955* on copyright page. *Berkley Books 344* (25¢). Reissue of THE MIXED MEN.

THE MIXED MEN. *New York: Gnome Press*, [*1952*].
  Two bindings, probable priority as listed: (A) Blue boards, spine lettered in red; (B) Blue cloth, spine lettered in red. First edition so stated on copyright page. Reissued as MISSION TO THE STARS.

MONSTERS. *New York: Paperback Library, Inc.*, [*1965*].
  Wrappers. *First Printing: February, 1965* on copyright page. *Paperback Library 52–515* (50¢). Note: Second printing issued in 1967 bears the cover title *SCIENCE FICTION MONSTERS*. Reissued as THE BLAL.

MOONBEAST. [*London*]: *Panther Science Fiction*, [*1969*].
  Wrappers. *Panther edition published 1969* on copyright page. *Panther 586 02937 0* (5/–). Reissue of THE BEAST.

MORE THAN SUPERHUMAN. [*New York*]: *A Dell Book*, [*1971*].
  Wrappers. *First printing—May 1971* on copyright page. *Dell 5818* (75¢). Note: Two stories are collaborations, one with Forrest J. Ackerman, the other with James H. Schmitz.

ONE AGAINST ETERNITY. *New York: Ace Books, Inc.*, [*1955*].
  Wrappers. No statement of printing on copyright page. *Ace Double Novel Books D–94* (35¢). Bound with THE OTHER SIDE OF HERE by Murray Leinster. Reissue of THE WEAPON MAKERS.

OUT OF THE UNKNOWN. *Los Angeles: Fantasy Publishing Company, Inc.*, [*1948*].
  Two bindings, priority as listed: (A) Light blue mesh weave cloth; (B) Dark blue pebbled grain cloth. First edition so stated on copyright page. With E. MAYNE HULL. Note: Collects three stories, ''The Sea Thing,'' ''The Witch,'' and ''The Ghost'' by van Vogt, with the remaining three by his wife, E. Mayne Hull.

  ALSO: [*Reseda, California: Powell Publications, Inc., 1969.*] Wrappers. No statement of printing on copyright page. *Powell Sci-Fi PP 128* (95¢). Adds introduction by van Vogt and story ''The Wellwisher'' by E. Mayne Hull. Issued later as THE SEA THING.

  ALSO: [*London*]: *New English Library*, [*1970*]. Wrappers. *First NEL abridged edition, October 1970* on copyright page. *New English Library Science Fiction 2793* (25p). Abridged reprint. Collects five of the six stories in the 1948 FPCI edition, deleting ''The Witch'' by van Vogt.

THE PAWNS OF NULL-A. *New York: Ace Books*, [*1956*].
  Wrappers. No statement of printing on copyright page. *Ace Double-Size Books D–187* (35¢). Reissued as THE PLAYERS OF NULL-A.

PLANETS FOR SALE.*New York: Frederick Fell, Inc., Publishers, [1954].*
   Boards. No statement of printing on copyright page. With E. MAYNE HULL. Note: A novelization of a series of five stories by E. Mayne Hull first published in *Astounding Science Fiction* in partial collaboration with van Vogt. It is probable that van Vogt is responsible for the novelization. Title page of the Fell edition credits E. Mayne Hull only. Novel was reissued in 1965 by the Book Company of America of Beverly Hills attributing the work to both authors. See van Vogt, *Reflections*, pp. 75–76. Later collected in A VAN VOGT OMNIBUS.

THE PLAYERS OF NULL-A. *[New York]: Published by Berkley Publishing Corporation, [1966].*
   Wrappers. *March, 1966* on copyright page. *Berkley Medallion F1195* (50¢). Minor textual revisions. Issued earlier as THE PAWNS OF NULL-A.

   ALSO: *London: Dennis Dobson, [1970].* Boards. *First published in Great Britain in 1970* on copyright page. Text follows 1966 Berkley edition. New introduction by van Vogt. First hardcover edition.

   ALSO: *Boston: Gregg Press, 1977. First Printing, June 1977* on copyright page. Text follows 1966 Berkley edition. Replaces van Vogt introduction with one by Charles Platt. Note: Not issued in dust jacket.

THE PROXY INTELLIGENCE AND OTHER MIND BENDERS. *New York: Paperback Library, [1971].*
   Wrappers. *First Printing: January, 1971* on copyright page. *A Paperback Library Science Fiction Original 64–512* (75¢). "The Proxy Intelligence" was later collected in THE UNIVERSE MAKER AND THE PROXY INTELLIGENCE.

QUEST FOR THE FUTURE. *New York: An Ace Book, [1970].*
   Wrappers. No statement of printing on copyright page. *Ace Book 69700* (95¢).

   ALSO: *New York: Ace Books, Inc., [1970].* Boards. No statement of printing on copyright page. Two printings, priority as listed: (A) Code *43L* on page 179; (B) Code *10 M* on page 179. First hardcover edition. Note: Issued by the Science Fiction Book Club.

ROGUE SHIP. *Garden City: Doubleday & Company, Inc., 1965.*
   First edition so stated on copyright page.

SCIENCE FICTION MONSTERS. See MONSTERS.

THE SEA THING AND OTHER STORIES. *London: Sidgwick & Jackson, [1970].*
   Boards. *First published in Great Britain 1970* on copyright page. With E. MAYNE HULL. Reissue of the 1969 Powell edition of OUT OF THE UNKNOWN.

THE SECRET GALACTICS. *Englewood Cliffs, New Jersey: Prentice-Hall, Inc., [1974].*
   Wrappers. No statement of printing on copyright page. *A Reward Book Science Fiction Original No. 1* ($2.45). Reissued as EARTH FACTOR X.

   ALSO: *London: Sidgwick & Jackson, [1975].* Boards. *First published in Great Britain in 1975* on copyright page. First hardcover edition.

SIEGE OF THE UNSEEN. *New York: Ace Books, Inc., [1959].*
   Wrappers. No statement of printing on copyright page. *Ace Double Novel Books D–391* (35¢). Bound with THE WORLD SWAPPERS by John Brunner. Issued later in Great Britain as THREE EYES OF EVIL (see TWO SCIENCE FICTION NOVELS).

THE SILKIE. *New York: Ace Books, Inc., [1969].*
   Wrappers. No statement of printing on copyright page. *Ace Book 76500* (60¢).

SLAN. *Sauk City: Arkham House, 1946.*
   No statement of printing on copyright page.

ALSO:*New York: Simon and Schuster, 1951*. Boards with cloth shelf back. First printing so stated on copyright page. Revised text. Later collected in TRIAD and VAN VOGT OMNIBUS (2).

SUPERMIND.*New York: DAW Books, Inc.*, [*1977*].
　　Wrappers. *First DAW printing, January 1977/1 2 3 4 5 6 7 8 9* on copyright page. *DAW: sf Books No. 224 UY1275* ($1.25).

THE THREE EYES OF EVIL AND EARTH'S LAST FORTRESS. See TWO SCIENCE FICTION NOVELS.

TRIAD. *New York: Simon and Schuster*, [*1959*].
　　Boards. Four printings, priority as listed: (A) Code *A13* on page [528]; (B) Code *A18* on page [528]; (C) Code *B-4* on page [528]; (D) Code *D45* on page [528]. No statement of printing on copyright page. Reprint. Collects THE WORLD OF Ā, THE VOYAGE OF THE SPACE BEAGLE, and SLAN. Note: Issued by the Science Fiction Book Club.

THE TWISTED MEN.*New York: Ace Books, Inc.*, [*1964*].
　　Wrappers. No statement of printing on copyright page. *Ace Double F–253* (40¢). Bound with ONE OF OUR ASTEROIDS IS MISSING by Calvin M. Knox.

TWO HUNDRED MILLION A.D.*New York: Paperback Library, Inc.*, [*1964*].
　　Wrappers. *First Printing: July, 1964* on copyright page. *Paperback Library Silver Edition 52–304* (50¢). Reissue of THE BOOK OF PTATH.

TWO SCIENCE FICTION NOVELS.*London: Sidgwick & Jackson*, [*1973*].
　　Boards. *This edition first published in 1973 . . .* on copyright page. Reprint. Collects THE THREE EYES OF EVIL (issued earlier in the U.S. as SIEGE OF THE UNSEEN) and EARTH'S LAST FORTRESS. First hardcover printing for both titles.

TYRANOPOLIS.*London: Sphere Books Limited*, [*1977*].
　　Wrappers. *First Sphere Books edition 1977* on copyright page. *Sphere SF 0 7221 8734 3* (85p). Reissue of FUTURE GLITTER.

UNDERCOVER ALIENS.[*London*]: *Panther*, [*1976*].
　　Wrappers. *Published in Great Britain in 1976 . . .* on copyright page. *Panther Science Fiction 586 043241* (50p). Reissue of THE HOUSE THAT STOOD STILL.

THE UNIVERSE MAKER.*New York: Ace Books, Inc.*, [*1953*].
　　Wrappers. No statement of printing on copyright page. *Ace Double Novel Books D–31* (35¢). Bound with THE WORLD OF NULL-A by van Vogt. Collected later in THE UNIVERSE MAKER AND THE PROXY INTELLIGENCE.

THE UNIVERSE MAKER AND THE PROXY INTELLIGENCE.*London: Sidgwick & Jackson*, [*1976*].
　　Boards. *First published in Great Britain in 1976 . . .* on copyright page. Reprint. Collects THE UNIVERSE MAKER and THE PROXY INTELLIGENCE. First hardcover printing for both titles.

A VAN VOGT OMNIBUS.*London: Sidgwick & Jackson*, [*1967*].
　　Boards. No statement of printing on copyright page. Reprint. Collects PLANETS FOR SALE (with E. Mayne Hull), THE BEAST, and THE BOOK OF PTATH.

VAN VOGT OMNIBUS (2).*London: Sidgwick & Jackson*, [*1971*].
　　Boards. No statement of printing on copyright page. Reprint. Collects THE MIND CAGE, THE WINGED MAN (with E. Mayne Hull), and SLAN.

THE VIOLENT MAN.*New York: Farrar, Straus and Cudahy*, [*1962*].
　　First printing so stated on copyright page.

THE VOYAGE OF THE SPACE BEAGLE. *New York: Simon and Schuster, 1950.*
Boards. No statement of printing on copyright page. Reissued as MISSION: INTERPLANET-
ARY. Later collected in TRIAD.

THE WAR AGAINST THE RULL. *New York: Simon and Schuster, 1959.*
Boards with cloth shelf back. First printing so stated on copyright page.

THE WEAPON MAKERS. *Providence, R.I.: Hadley Publishing Co., [1947].*
No statement of printing on copyright page.

ALSO: *New York: Greenberg: Publisher, [1952].* Boards. No statement of printing on
copyright page. Revised text. Reissued as ONE AGAINST ETERNITY.

THE WEAPON SHOPS OF ISHER. *New York: Greenberg: Publisher, [1951].*
No statement of printing on copyright page.

THE WINGED MAN. *Garden City: Doubleday & Company, Inc., 1966.*
First edition so stated on copyright page. With E. MAYNE HULL. Note: Short novel by Hull
rewritten and expanded by Van Vogt. Later collected in VAN VOGT OMNIBUS (2).

THE WIZARD OF LINN. *New York: Ace Books, Inc., [1962].*
Wrappers. No statement of printing on copyright page. *Ace Book F–154* (40¢).

ALSO: *[London]: New English Library, [1976].* Boards. *First published in hardcover in
Great Britain . . . in 1976* on copyright page. First hardcover edition.

THE WORLD OF Ā. *New York: Simon and Schuster, 1948.*
No statement of printing on copyright page. Later collected in TRIAD.

ALSO: THE WORLD OF NULL-A. *[New York]: Published by Berkley Publishing Corporation,
[1970].* Wrappers. *A Berkley Medallion Book S1802* (75¢). Revised text and new introduction.

THE WORLDS OF A. E. VAN VOGT. *New York: Ace Books, [1974].*
Wrappers. *First Ace printing: January 1974* on copyright page. *Ace 22812* ($1.25). Col-
lects contents of THE FAR-OUT WORLDS OF A. E. VAN VOGT and adds "The Storm," "The
Expendables," and "The Reflected Men."

Autobiography

Reflections of A. E. Van Vogt. *Lakemont, Georgia: Fictioneer Books Ltd., 1975.*
Wrappers. First edition so stated on copyright page. Includes a checklist of van Vogt's
writings. Note: Prepaid subscriber's copies bear an adhesive label affixed to the inside front
cover inscribed "Best wishes/ A E van Vogt."

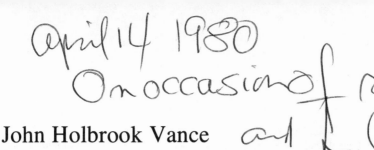

April 14 1980
On occasion of roast lamb and a jug of wine
Jack Vance

John Holbrook Vance

(b. 1920)

THE ANOME. *[New York]:A Dell Book, [1973]*.
Wrappers. *First printing—March 1973* on copyright page. *Dell 0441 (95¢). Jack Vance, pseudonym.*

THE ASUTRA. *[New York]: A Dell Book, [1974]*.
Wrappers. *First printing—May 1974* on copyright page. *Dell 3157 (95¢). Jack Vance, pseudonym.*

BAD RONALD. *New York: Ballantine Books, [1973]*.
Wrappers. *First Printing: September, 1973* on copyright page. *Ballantine Books 23477–4–125 ($1.25).*

THE BEST OF JACK VANCE. *New York: Published by Pocket Books, [1976]*.
Wrappers. *May, 1976* on copyright page. *Pocket Books Sci-Fi 80510 ($1.95). Jack Vance, pseudonym.*

BIG PLANET. *New York: Avalon Books, [1957]*.
No statement of printing on copyright page. *Jack Vance, pseudonym.*

THE BLUE WORLD. *New York: Ballantine Books, [1966]*.
Wrappers. *First edition: May, 1966* on copyright page. *A Ballantine Science Fiction Original U2169 (50¢). Jack Vance, pseudonym.*

THE BRAINS OF EARTH. *New York: Ace Books, Inc., [1966]*.
Wrappers. No statement of printing on copyright page. *Ace Double M–141 (45¢). Jack Vance, pseudonym.* Bound with THE MANY WORLDS OF MAGNUS RIDOLPH by Vance.

ALSO: *London: Dennis Dobson, [1975]*. Boards. *First published in Great Britain in 1975* on copyright page. First hardcover edition.

THE BRAVE FREE MEN. *[New York]: A Dell Book, [1973]*.
Wrappers. *First printing—August 1973* on copyright page. *Dell 1708 (95¢). Jack Vance, pseudonym.*

CITY OF THE CHASCH. *New York: Ace Books, Inc., [1968]*.
Wrappers. No statement of printing on copyright page. *An Ace Book G–688 (50¢). Jack Vance, pseudonym.*

ALSO: *London: Dennis Dobson, [1975]*. Boards. *First published in Great Britain in 1975* on copyright page. First hardcover edition.

THE DEADLY ISLES. *Indianapolis and New York: The Bobbs-Merrill Company, [1969]*.
First printing 1969 on copyright page.

THE DIRDIR. *New York: An Ace Book, [1969]*.
Wrappers. No statement of printing on copyright page. *Ace Book 66901 (60¢). Jack Vance, pseudonym.*

ALSO: *London: Dennis Dobson, [1975]*. Boards. *First published in Great Britain in 1975* on copyright page. First hardcover edition.

THE DRAGON MASTERS.*New York: Ace Books, Inc.*, [*1963*].
Wrappers. No statement of printing on copyright page. *Ace Double F–185* (40¢). *Jack Vance, pseudonym*. Bound with THE FIVE GOLD BANDS by Vance.

ALSO:*London: Dennis Dobson*, [*1965*]. Boards. *First published in Great Britain 1965* on copyright page. First hardcover edition.

THE DYING EARTH.*New York: Hillman Periodicals, Inc.*, [*1950*].
Wrappers. No statement of printing on copyright page. *HP No. 41* (25¢). *Jack Vance, pseudonym*.

ALSO:*San Francisco, California/Columbia, Pennsylvania: Underwood-Miller, 1976*. Three issues, no priority: (A) 11 copies lettered A–K signed by the author and illustrator George Barr; (B) 111 numbered copies signed by author and illustrator; (C) 1000 unnumbered copies. Trade issue. *First cloth edition–September, 1976* on copyright page. First hardcover edition.

EIGHT FANTASMS AND MAGICS.[*New York*]*: The Macmillan Company*, [*1969*].
First printing so stated on copyright page. *Jack Vance, pseudonym*.

EMPHYRIO.*Garden City: Doubleday & Company, Inc., 1969*.
First edition so stated on copyright page. *Jack Vance, pseudonym*.

THE EYES OF THE OVERWORLD.*New York: Ace Books, Inc.*, [*1966*].
Wrappers. No statement of printing on copyright page. *Ace Book M–149* (45¢). *Jack Vance, pseudonym*.

ALSO:*Boston: Gregg Press, 1977. First Printing, June 1977* on copyright page. First hardcover edition. Note: Not issued in dust jacket.

THE FIVE GOLD BANDS.*New York: Ace Books, Inc.*, [*1962*].
Wrappers. No statement of printing on copyright page. *Ace Double F–185* (40¢). *Jack Vance, pseudonym*. Bound with THE DRAGON MASTERS by Vance. Longer version issued earlier as THE SPACE PIRATE.

THE FOUR JOHNS.*New York: Published by Pocket Books, Inc.*, [*1964*].
Wrappers. *1st printing . . . March, 1964* on copyright page. *Pocket Books Edition 6229* (35¢). *Ellery Queen, pseudonym*. Notes: (1) A reprint identical in all particulars save for change of stock number to *4706* and price increase to *45*¢ has been observed. (2) Edited and rewritten by the publisher. Issued later in Great Britain as FOUR MEN CALLED JOHN.

FOUR MEN CALLED JOHN.*London: Victor Gollancz Ltd, 1976*.
Boards. No statement of printing on copyright page. *Ellery Queen, pseudonym*. Issued earlier in the U.S. as THE FOUR JOHNS.

THE FOX VALLEY MURDERS.*Indianapolis New York Kansas City: The Bobbs-Merrill Company, Inc.*, [*1966*].
First printing, 1966 on copyright page.

FUTURE TENSE.*New York: Ballantine Books*, [*1964*].
Wrappers. *First printing: June 1964* on copyright page. *A Ballantine Science Fiction Original U2214* (50¢). *Jack Vance, pseudonym*.

THE GRAY PRINCE.*Indianapolis/New York: The Bobbs-Merrill Company, Inc.*, [*1974*].
Boards. First printing so stated on copyright page. *Jack Vance, pseudonym*.

THE HOUSES OF ISZM.*New York: Ace Books, Inc.*, [*1964*].
Wrappers. No statement of printing on copyright page. *Ace Double F–265* (40¢). *Jack Vance, pseudonym*. Bound with SON OF THE TREE by Vance.

ISLE OF PERIL. *New York: Mystery House*, [*1957*].
No statement of printing on copyright page. *Alan Wade, pseudonym.*

THE KILLING MACHINE. [*New York*]: *Published by Berkley Publishing Corporation*, [*1964*].
Wrappers. *November, 1964* on copyright page. *Berkley Medallion F1003* (50¢). *Jack Vance, pseudonym.*

ALSO: *London: Dennis Dobson*, [*1967*]. Boards. *First published in Great Britain 1967* on copyright page. First hardcover edition.

THE LANGUAGES OF PAO. *New York: Avalon Books*, [*1958*].
No statement of printing on copyright page. *Jack Vance, pseudonym.*

THE LAST CASTLE. *New York: Ace Books, Inc.*, [*1967*].
Wrappers. No statement of printing on copyright page. *Ace Double H–21* (60¢). *Jack Vance, pseudonym.* Bound with WORLD OF THE SLEEPER by Tony Wayman.

THE MADMAN THEORY. *New York: Published by Pocket Books*, [*1966*].
Wrappers. *1st printing . . . August, 1966* on copyright page. *Pocket Books 50496* (50¢). *Ellery Queen, pseudonym.* Note: Edited and rewritten by the publisher.

THE MAN IN THE CAGE. *New York; Random House*, [*1960*].
Boards. First printing so stated on copyright page.

THE MANY WORLDS OF MAGNUS RIDOLPH. *New York: Ace Books, Inc.*, [*1966*].
Wrappers. No statement of printing on copyright page. *Ace Double M–141* (45¢). *Jack Vance, pseudonym.* Bound with THE BRAINS OF EARTH by Vance.

ALSO: *London: Dennis Dobson*, [*1977*]. Boards. *First published in Great Britain in 1977* on copyright page. First hardcover edition.

MARUNE: ALASTOR 933. *New York: Ballantine Books*, [*1975*].
Wrappers. *First Printing: September, 1975* on copyright page. *Ballantine Books SF 24518* ($1.50). *Jack Vance, pseudonym.*

MASKE: THAERY. *New York: Published by Berkley Publishing Corporation*, [*1976*].
No statement of printing on copyright page. *Jack Vance, pseudonym.*

MONSTERS IN ORBIT. *New York: Ace Books, Inc.*, [*1965*].
Wrappers. No statement of printing on copyright page. *Ace Double M–125* (45¢). *Jack Vance, pseudonym.* Bound with THE WORLD BETWEEN by Vance.

ALSO: *London: Dennis Dobson*, [*1977*]. Boards. *First published in Great Britain in 1977 . . .* on copyright page. First hardcover edition.

THE MOON MOTH AND OTHER STORIES. *London: Dennis Dobson*, [*1976*].
Boards. *First published in Great Britain in 1975* on copyright page. *Jack Vance, pseudonym.* Issued earlier in the U.S. as THE WORLD BETWEEN. Note: *Whitaker's Cumulative Book List* records month of publication as February 1976.

THE PALACE OF LOVE. [*New York*]: *Published by Berkley Publishing Corporation*, [*1967*].
Wrappers. *October, 1967* on copyright page. *Berkley X1454* (60¢). *Jack Vance, pseudonym.*

ALSO: *London: Dennis Dobson*, [*1968*]. Boards. *First published in Great Britain 1968* on copyright page. First hardcover edition.

THE PLEASANT GROVE MURDERS. *Indianapolis • Kansas City • New York: The Bobbs-Merrill Company, Inc.*, [*1967*].
First printing so stated on copyright page.

THE PNUME. *New York: An Ace Book,* [*1970*].
Wrappers. No statement of printing on copyright page. *Ace Book 66902* (60¢). *Jack Vance, pseudonym.*

ALSO: *London: Dennis Dobson,* [*1975*]. Boards. *First published in Great Britain in 1975* on copyright page. First hardcover edition.

A ROOM TO DIE IN. *New York: Published by Pocket Books, Inc.,* [*1965*].
Wrappers. *1st printing . . . July, 1965* on copyright page. *Pocket Books 35067* (35¢). *Ellery Queen, pseudonym.* Notes: (1) A reprint identical in all particulars save for change of stock number to *50492* and price increase to *50¢* has been observed. (2) Edited and rewritten by the publisher.

SERVANTS OF THE WANKH. *New York: Ace Books, Inc.,* [*1969*].
Wrappers. No statement of printing on copyright page. *Ace Book 66900* (50¢). *Jack Vance, pseudonym.*

ALSO: *London: Dennis Dobson,* [*1975*]. Boards. *First published in Great Britain in 1975* on copyright page. First hardcover edition.

SHOWBOAT WORLD. *New York: Pyramid,* [*1975*].
Wrappers. *March 1975* on copyright page. *Pyramid V3698* ($1.25). *Jack Vance, pseudonym.*

SLAVES OF THE KLAU. *New York: Ace Books, Inc.,* [*1958*].
Wrappers. No statement of printing on copyright page. *Ace Double Novel Books D–295* (35¢). *Jack Vance, pseudonym.* Bound with BIG PLANET by Vance.

SON OF THE TREE. *New York: Ace Books, Inc.,* [*1964*].
Wrappers. No statement of printing on copyright page. *Ace Double F–265* (40¢). *Jack Vance, pseudonym.* Bound with THE HOUSES OF ISZM by Vance.

SPACE OPERA. *New York: Pyramid Books,* [*1965*].
Wrappers. *First printing, February 1965* on copyright page. *Pyramid Books R–1140* (50¢). *Jack Vance, pseudonym.*

THE SPACE PIRATE. [*New York*]: *A Toby Press Book,* [*1953*].
Wrappers. No statement of printing on copyright page. *Jack Vance, pseudonym.* Shorter version issued later as THE FIVE GOLD BANDS.

THE STAR KING. [*New York*]: *Published by Berkley Publishing Corporation,* [*1964*].
Wrappers. *April, 1964* on copyright page. *Berkley Medallion F905* (50¢). *Jack Vance, pseudonym.*

ALSO: *London: Dennis Dobson,* [*1966*]. Boards. *First published in Great Britain 1966* on copyright page. First hardcover edition.

*TAKE MY FACE. *New York: Mystery House,* [*1957*].
No statement of printing on copyright page. *Peter Held, pseudonym.*

TO LIVE FOREVER. *New York: Ballantine Books,* [*1956*].
Two issues, no priority: (A) Cloth. Two variants, priority, if any, not established: (1) Dark blue cloth, spine lettered in dark red; (2) Light blue cloth, spine lettered in dark red.
(B) Wrappers. *Ballantine Books 167* (35¢). No statement of printing on copyright page. *Jack Vance, pseudonym.*

TRULLION: ALASTOR 2262. *New York: Ballantine Books,* [*1973*].
Wrappers. *First Printing: June, 1973* on copyright page. *Ballantine Books 03308–6–125* ($1.25). *Jack Vance, pseudonym.*

VANDALS OF THE VOID. *Philadelphia • Toronto: The John C. Winston Company, [1953].*
Two bindings, priority not established: (A) Cloth; (B) Boards. First edition so stated on
copyright page. *Jack Vance, pseudonym.*

THE WORLD BETWEEN AND OTHER STORIES. *New York: Ace Books, Inc., [1965].*
Wrappers. No statement of printing on copyright page. *Ace Double M–125* (45¢). *Jack
Vance, pseudonym.* Bound with MONSTERS IN ORBIT by Vance. Issued later in Great Britain
as THE MOON MOTH AND OTHER STORIES.

THE WORLDS OF JACK VANCE. *New York: Ace Books, [1973].*
Wrappers. *First Ace Printing: December 1973* on copyright page. *Ace 90955* ($1.25). *Jack
Vance, pseudonym.* All stories reprinted from earlier Vance collections.

Reference

Fantasms: a Bibliography of the Literature of Jack Vance, compiled by Daniel J.H. Levack
and Tim Underwood. *San Francisco, California/Columbia, Pennsylvania: Underwood/
Miller, 1978.*
1000 copies printed. Two bindings, no priority: (A) Blue cloth, lettered in red. 100 copies.
Note: Not issued with dust jacket. (B) Pictorial wrappers. 900 copies. First edition so stated
on copyright page.

Jack Vance: Science Fiction Stylist, by Richard Tiedman. [*Wabash, Indiana: Robert &
Juanita Coulson, 1965.*]
Self wrappers. First printing so stated on inside front wrapper. Mimeographed, stapled.
Cover title. 225 copies printed. Includes a bibliography of Vance's science fiction com-
piled by Robert Briney.

John Varley
(b. 1947)

THE OPHIUCHI HOTLINE. *New York: The Dial Press/James Wade, 1977.*
Boards. First printing so stated on copyright page.

Kurt Vonnegut, Jr.
(b. 1922)

BETWEEN TIME AND TIMBUKTU. *[New York]: Delacorte Press/Seymour Lawrence, [1972]*.
Boards with cloth shelf back. *First printing–1972* on copyright page.

BREAKFAST OF CHAMPIONS OR GOODBYE, BLUE MONDAY. *[New York]: Delacorte Press/Seymour Lawrence, [1973]*.
First printing–1973 on copyright page.

CANARY IN A CAT HOUSE. *Greenwich, Conn.: Fawcett Publications, Inc., [1961]*.
Wrappers. *First printing September 1961* on copyright page. *Gold Medal Book s1153* (35¢). Note: All but one of the stories in this collection, ''Hal Irwin's Magic Lamp,'' later collected in WELCOME TO THE MONKEY HOUSE.

CAT'S CRADLE. *New York Chicago San Francisco: Holt, Rinehart and Winston, [1963]*.
First edition so stated on copyright page.

GOD BLESS YOU, MR. ROSEWATER. *New York Chicago San Francisco: Holt, Rinehart and Winston, [1965]*.
Boards with cloth shelf back. First edition so stated on copyright page.

HAPPY BIRTHDAY, WANDA JUNE. *New York: Delacorte Press, [1971]*.
First printing so stated on copyright page.

ALSO: HAPPY BIRTHDAY, WANDA JUNE: A PLAY IN THREE ACTS. *New York Hollywood London Toronto: Samuel French, Inc., [1974]*. Wrappers. No statement of printing on copyright page. Drops author's note ''About This Play.''

MOTHER NIGHT. *Greenwich, Conn.: Fawcett Publications, Inc., [1962]*.
Wrappers. *First printing February 1962* on copyright page. *Gold Medal s1191* (35¢).

ALSO: *New York: Harper & Row, Publishers, [1966]*. Boards with cloth shelf back. First edition so stated on copyright page. First hardcover edition. Adds introduction by Vonnegut.

PLAYER PIANO. *New York: Charles Scribner's Sons, 1952*.
Boards. First printing has Scribner seal and *A* on copyright page. Reissued as UTOPIA 14.

THE SIRENS OF TITAN. *[New York]: A Dell First Edition, [1959]*.
Wrappers. *First printing—October, 1959* on copyright page. *Dell First Edition B138* (35¢).

ALSO: *Boston: Houghton Mifflin Company, 1961*. First printing so stated on copyright page. First hardcover edition.

SLAPSTICK OR LONESOME NO MORE! *[New York]: Delacorte Press/Seymour Lawrence, [1976]*.
Two printings, priority as listed: (A) Delacorte Press imprint as above. *First Delacorte printing* on copyright page. Two issues, priority as listed: (1) Trade issue. Issued in dust jacket; not slipcased. (2) 250 copies with numbered leaf signed by the author inserted. Issued in paper slipcase; no dust jacket. (B) Franklin Library. *Franklin Center, Pennsylvania: The Franklin Library, 1976*. Full leather. *This limited first edition/has been*

published/by special arrangement with/Delacorte Press/Seymour Lawrence on copyright page. Adds ''A special message to the members of The First Edition Society'' by Vonnegut. Note: Delacorte Press and Franklin Library settings differ. Delacorte trade issue was released a month prior to the limited issue and the Franklin Library edition.

SLAUGHTERHOUSE-FIVE. *[New York]: A Seymour Lawrence Book/Delacorte Press*, [*1969*]. First printing so stated on copyright page.

UTOPIA 14. *New York: Bantam Books*, [*1954*]. Wrappers. *1st Printing . . . October, 1954* on copyright page. *A Bantam Giant A 1262* (35¢). Reissue of PLAYER PIANO.

WELCOME TO THE MONKEY HOUSE. *[New York]: A Seymour Lawrence Book Delacorte Press*, [*1968*]. Boards with cloth shelf back. *First Delacorte printing* on copyright page.

Nonfiction

Wampeters Foma & Granfalloons (Opinions). *[New York]: Delacorte Press/Seymour Lawrence*, [*1974*]. First printing so stated on copyright page. Includes essays (with some mention of science fiction), addresses, and an interview.

Reference

Kurt Vonnegut, [by] James Lundquist. *New York: Frederick Ungar Publishing Co.*, [*1977*]. No statement of printing on copyright page.

Kurt Vonnegut Fantasist of Fire and Ice, [by] David H. Goldsmith. *Bowling Green: Bowling Green University Popular Press*, [*1972*]. Wrappers. No statement of printing on copyright page. *Popular Writers Series No. 2*.

Kurt Vonnegut, Jr., by Peter J. Reed. *New York: Warner Paperback Library*, [*1972*]. Wrappers. *First Printing: September, 1972* on copyright page. *Paperback Library 68-923* ($1.50).

ALSO: *New York: Thomas Y. Crowell Company*, [*1976*]. No statement of printing on copyright page. First hardcover edition.

Kurt Vonnegut, Jr., by Stanley Schatt. *Boston: Twayne Publishers*, [*1976*]. First printing so stated on copyright page.

Kurt Vonnegut, Jr. A Descriptive Bibliography and Annotated Secondary Checklist, by Asa B. Pieratt, Jr. and Jerome Klinkowitz. *[Hamden, Connecticut]: Archon Books, 1974*. Boards. *First published 1974 . . .* on copyright page.

Kurt Vonnegut: The Gospel from Outer Space (or, Yes We Have No Nirvanas), [by] Clark Mayo. *San Bernardino, California: R. Reginald The Borgo Press, MCMLXXVII*. Wrappers. *First Edition—October, 1977* on copyright page. *The Milford Series Popular Writers of Today Volume Seven* at head of title.

Vonnegut: A Preface to his Novels, [by] Richard Giannone. *Port Washington, N.Y.//London: Kennikat Press, 1977*. Boards. No statement of printing on copyright page.

Vonnegut in America: An Introduction to the Life and Work of Kurt Vonnegut. Original Essays, edited by Jerome Klinkowitz and Donald L. Lawler. [*New York*]: *Delacorte Press/Seymour Lawrence*, [*1977*].

    First Delacorte printing on copyright page.

The Vonnegut Statement, edited by Jerome Klinkowitz & John Somer. [*New York*]: *Delacorte Press/Seymour Lawrence*, [*1973*].

    First printing so stated on copyright page.

Herbert Russell Wakefield

(1888–1964)

BELT OF SUSPICION. *London: Published for the Crime Club by Collins*, [*1936*].
No statement of printing on copyright page.

THE CLOCK STRIKES TWELVE. *London: Herbert Jenkins Limited*, [*1940*].
First printing, 1940 on copyright page.

ALSO:*Sauk City: Arkham House, 1946*. No statement of printing on copyright page. Adds introduction and four stories. Abridged collection later issued as STORIES FROM THE CLOCK STRIKES 12.

GALLIMAUFRY. *London: Philip Allan & Co., Ltd.*, [*1928*].
First published in 1928 on copyright page. Issued later in the U.S. as HAPPY EVER AFTER.

GHOST STORIES. *London: Jonathan Cape*, [*1932*].
This collection first published in Florin Books 1932 on copyright page.

A GHOSTLY COMPANY. *London: Jonathan Cape*, [*1935*].
First published in Florin Books 1935 on copyright page.

HAPPY EVER AFTER. *New York: D. Appleton and Company, 1929*.
No statement of printing on copyright page. First printing has *(1)* on page [361]. Issued earlier in Great Britain as GALLIMAUFRY.

HEARKEN TO THE EVIDENCE. *London: Geoffrey Bles, 1933*.
No statement of printing on copyright page.

HOSTESS TO DEATH. *London: Published for The Crime Club*, [*1938*].
No statement of printing on copyright page.

IMAGINE A MAN IN A BOX. *London: Philip Allan & Co. Ltd.*, [*1931*].
First Published in 1931 on copyright page.

OLD MAN'S BEARD. *London: Geoffrey Bles*, [*1929*].
First published April 1929 on copyright page. Issued later the same year in the U.S. as OTHERS WHO RETURNED.

OTHERS WHO RETURNED. *New York: D. Appleton & Company, 1929*.
No statement of printing on copyright page. First printing has code *(I)* on page [275]. Issued earlier in Great Britain as OLD MAN'S BEARD.

STORIES FROM THE CLOCK STRIKES 12. *New York: Ballantine Books*, [*1961*].
Wrappers. *Ballantine Books edition published 1961* on copyright page. *Ballantine Books 531 (35¢)*. Abridged reprint. Twelve stories and introduction from THE CLOCK STRIKES TWELVE.

STRAYERS FROM SHEOL. *Sauk City: Arkham House: Publishers, 1961*.
No statement of printing on copyright page.

THEY RETURN AT EVENING. *London: Philip Allan & Co., Ltd.*, [*1928*].
First Edition – – – – – – – 1928 on copyright page.

Evangeline Walton (Ensley)

(b. 1907)

THE CHILDREN OF LLYR. *New York: Ballantine Books*, [*1971*].
Wrappers. *First Printing: August, 1971* on copyright page. *Ballantine Books 02332–3–095*
(95¢).

CROSS AND THE SWORD. *New York: Bouregy & Curl, Inc.*, [*1956*].
No statement of printing on copyright page. Issued later in Great Britain as SON OF DARK-
NESS.

THE ISLAND OF THE MIGHTY. *New York: Ballantine Books*, [*1970*].
Wrappers. *First Printing: July, 1970* on copyright page. *Ballantine Books 01959–8–095*
(95¢). Reissue of THE VIRGIN AND THE SWINE.

PRINCE OF ANNWN. *New York: Ballantine Books*, [*1974*].
Wrappers. *First Printing: November, 1974* on copyright page. *Ballantine/Fantasy 24233*
($1.50).

SON OF DARKNESS. *London: Hutchinson*, [*1957*].
Boards. *First published 1957* on copyright page. Issued earlier in the U.S. as CROSS AND
THE SWORD.

THE SONG OF RHIANNON. *New York: Ballantine Books*, [*1972*].
Wrappers. *First Printing: August, 1972* on copyright page. *Ballantine Books 02773–6–125*
($1.25).

THE VIRGIN AND THE SWINE. *Chicago New York: Willett, Clark & Company, 1936*.
No statement of printing on copyright page. Reissued as THE ISLAND OF THE MIGHTY.

WITCH HOUSE. *Sauk City: Arkham House, 1945*.
No statement of printing on copyright page.

Donald Wandrei
(b. 1908)

THE CHALLENGE FROM BEYOND. *N.p.: [A Weltschmerz Publication/Bill Evans/Franklin Kerkhof, Printer/The Pennsylvania Dutch Cheese Press/February 1954]*.
   Self wrappers. No statement of printing. Mimeographed, stapled. Cover title. With STANLEY G. WEINBAUM, EDWARD E. SMITH, HARL VINCENT, and MURRAY LEINSTER. Notes: (1) Published by William H. Evans for distribution through the Fantasy Amateur Press Association (FAPA). (2) Not to be confused with a booklet of identical title and format with a different round-robin story by C. L. Moore and others.

THE EYE AND THE FINGER. *[Sauk City]: Arkham House, 1944*.
   No statement of printing on copyright page.

STRANGE HARVEST. *Sauk City: Arkham House: Publishers, 1965*.
   No statement of printing on copyright page.

THE WEB OF EASTER ISLAND. *Sauk City: Arkham House, 1948*.
   No statement of printing on copyright page.

Edited Fiction

Beyond the Wall of Sleep, by H. P. Lovecraft. *Sauk City: Arkham House, 1943*.
   No statement of printing on copyright page. Collected, with introduction, by Wandrei with AUGUST DERLETH.

Marginalia, by H. P. Lovecraft. *Sauk City: Arkham House, 1944*.
   No statement of printing on copyright page. Edited by Wandrei with AUGUST DERLETH.

The Outsider and Others, by H. P. Lovecraft. *Sauk City: Arkham House, 1939*.
   No statement of printing on copyright page. Edited, with introduction, by Wandrei with AUGUST DERLETH.

Edited Nonfiction (Dealing with the Fantasy Genre only)

Selected Letters 1911–1924, by H. P. Lovecraft. *Sauk City: Arkham House: Publishers, 1965*.
   No statement of printing on copyright page. Edited, with preface, by Wandrei with AUGUST DERLETH.

Selected Letters 1925–1929, by H. P. Lovecraft. *Sauk City: Arkham House: Publishers, 1968*.
   No statement of printing on copyright page. Edited, with preface, by Wandrei with AUGUST DERLETH.

Selected Letters 1929–1931, by H. P. Lovecraft. *Sauk City: Arkham House: Publishers, 1971*.
   No statement of printing on copyright page. Edited, with preface, by Wandrei with AUGUST DERLETH.

Ian Watson
(b. 1943)

ALIEN EMBASSY. *London: Victor Gollancz Ltd, 1977.*
   Boards. No statement of printing on copyright page.

THE EMBEDDING. *London: Victor Gollancz Ltd, 1973.*
   Boards. No statement of printing on copyright page.

THE JONAH KIT. *London: Victor Gollancz Ltd, 1975.*
   Boards. No statement of printing on copyright page.

THE MARTIAN INCA. *London: Victor Gollancz Ltd, 1977.*
   Boards. No statement of printing on copyright page.

Stanley Grauman Weinbaum

(1902–1935)

THE BEST OF STANLEY G. WEINBAUM. *New York: Ballantine Books, [1974]*.
  Wrappers. *First Printing: April, 1974* on copyright page. *Ballantine 23890* ($1.65). All stories reprinted from earlier collections.

THE BLACK FLAME. *Reading, Pennsylvania: Fantasy Press, 1948*.
  Two issues, no priority: (A) 500 copies with numbered limitation leaf inserted; (B) Trade issue. First issue so stated on copyright page.

THE CHALLENGE FROM BEYOND. *N.p.: [A Weltschmerz Publication/BillEvans/Franklin Kerkhof, Printer/The Pennsylvania Dutch Cheese Press/February 1954]*.
  Self wrappers. No statement of printing. Mimeographed, stapled. Cover title. With DONALD WANDREI, EDWARD E. SMITH, HARL VINCENT, and MURRAY LEINSTER. Notes: (1) Published by William H. Evans for distribution through the Fantasy Amateur Press Association (FAPA). (2) Not to be confused with a booklet of identical title and format with a different round-robin story by C. L. Moore and others.

THE DARK OTHER. *Los Angeles: Fantasy Publishing Co., Inc., 1950*.
  Three bindings, priority as listed: (A) Blue cloth, spine lettered in black; (B) Black boards with Gnome Press imprint at base of spine; (C) Wrappers. No statement of printing on copyright page. Note: Sheets of this book were later combined with those of THE UNDESIRED PRINCESS by L. Sprague de Camp and issued in 1953 as [FANTASY TWIN]. According to Owings and Chalker in *The Index to the Science-Fantasy Publishers*, approximately 500 copies were so bound.

DAWN OF FLAME. *[Jamaica, N.Y.: Printed by Ruppert Printing Service, 1936.]*
  Fabrikoid. Two issues, probably simultaneous: (A) Unsigned introduction by Raymond A. Palmer. Five copies prepared for the sponsors of the volume: Conrad H. Ruppert, Julius Schwartz, Raymond A. Palmer, Lawrence A. Keating, and Margaret Weinbaum. (B) Foreword by Lawrence A. Keating replaces Palmer introduction. First edition so stated on copyright page. Notes: (1) 500 sets of sheets were printed but only 250 copies were bound. Based on apologies for delay appearing in *Fantasy Magazine*, the book was probably not bound until 1937. The remaining unbound sheets were destroyed by water in Palmer's basement. (2) Not issued in dust jacket. (3) Sam Moskowitz in *The Immortal Storm*, pp. 80–81 and in *Explorers of the Infinite*, pp. 309–10, and Owings and Chalker in *The Index to the Science-Fantasy Publishers*, p. 50 present conflicting accounts of the publishing history of this volume. Owings and Chalker state that the six-copy issue (Moskowitz states five copies) was a "deliberate variant" while Moskowitz in *The Immortal Storm* notes that the Palmer introduction was suppressed at the request of Weinbaum's wife Margaret, who characterized it as "too personal."

[FANTASY TWIN.] See THE DARK OTHER.

A MARTIAN ODYSSEY AND OTHER CLASSICS OF SCIENCE FICTION. *New York: Lancer Books, [1962]*.
  Wrappers. No statement of printing on copyright page. *The Lancer Science Fiction Library 74–808* (75¢). All stories reprinted from earlier collections.

A MARTIAN ODYSSEY AND OTHER SCIENCE FICTION TALES. *Westport, Connecticut: Hyperion Press, Inc., [1974]*.
  Hyperion edition 1974 on copyright page. "Graph" here first collected; other fiction collected from A MARTIAN ODYSSEY AND OTHERS and THE RED PERI. Also includes poem and autobiographical sketch by Weinbaum. Note: Not issued with dust jacket.

A MARTIAN ODYSSEY AND OTHERS. *Reading, Pennsylvania: Fantasy Press, 1949*.
  Two issues, no priority: (A) 500 copies with numbered limitation leaf inserted; (B) Trade issue. First edition so stated on copyright page.

THE NEW ADAM. *Chicago New York: Ziff-Davis Publishing Company, 1939*.
  No statement of printing on copyright page.

THE RED PERI. *Reading, Pennsylvania: Fantasy Press, 1952*.
  Four bindings, priority as listed: (A) Black cloth, spine stamped in gold; (B) Salmon cloth, spine stamped in black; (C) Brown cloth, spine stamped in gold; (D) Blue cloth, spine stamped in black. Two issues, no priority: (A) 300 copies with numbered limitation leaf inserted; (B) Trade issue. First edition so stated on copyright page.

Reference

After Ten Years: A Tribute to Stanley G. Weinbaum 1902–1935, collected by Gerry de la Ree, and Sam Moskowitz. *Westwood, N.J.: Published by Gerry de la Ree, November, 1945*.
  Wrappers. No statement of printing. Mimeographed, stapled. 100 copies printed. Includes autobiographical sketch by Weinbaum and extracts from letters to his agent, Julius Schwartz.

Manly Wade Wellman
(b. 1905)

APPOMATTOX ROAD FINAL ADVENTURES OF THE IRON SCOUTS. *New York: Ives Washburn, Inc., [1960].*
> No statement of printing on copyright page.

BATTLE AT BEAR PAW GAP. *New York: Ives Washburn, Inc., [1966].*
> No statement of printing on copyright page.

BATTLE FOR KING'S MOUNTAIN. *New York: Ives Washburn, Inc., [1962].*
> No statement of printing on copyright page.

THE BEASTS FROM BEYOND. *Manchester: World Distributors Manchester Ltd., [1950].*
> Wrappers. No statement of printing on copyright page. *A World Fantasy Classic* (1'6).

THE BEYONDERS. *[New York]: Warner Books, [1977].*
> Wrappers. *First Printing: April, 1977/10 9 8 7 6 5 4 3 2* on copyright page. *Warner Books 88–202* ($1.50).

BRAVE HORSE THE STORY OF JANUS. *Williamsburg, Virginia: Colonial Williamsburg . . . Distributed by Holt, Rinehart and Winston, Inc. New York, [1968].*
> Boards. No statement of printing on copyright page.

CANDLE OF THE WICKED. *New York: G. P. Putnam's Sons, [1960].*
> No statement of printing on copyright page.

CAROLINA PIRATE. *New York: Ives Washburn, Inc., [1968].*
> No statement of printing on copyright page.

CLASH ON THE CATAWBA. *New York: Ives Washburn Inc., [1962].*
> No statement of printing on copyright page.

THE DARK DESTROYERS. *New York: Avalon Books, [1959].*
> No statement of printing on copyright page.

> ALSO: *New York: Ace Books, Inc., [1960].* Wrappers. No statement of printing on copyright page. *Ace Double Novel Books D–443* (35¢). Abridged reprint. Bound with BOW DOWN TO NUL by Brian W. Aldiss.

DEVIL'S PLANET. *Manchester: Distributed by World Distributors Manchester Ltd . . . In collaboration with Sydney Pemberton Publisher, [1951].*
> Wrappers. No statement of printing on copyright page. *A World Fantasy Classic* (1'6). Note: Author's name misspelled ''Manley'' on front wrapper.

A DOUBLE LIFE. *Chicago: Century Publications, [1947].*
> Wrappers. No statement of printing on copyright page. Note: Novelization by Wellman of a screen play by Ruth Gordon and Garson Kanin.

FAST BREAK FIVE. *New York: Ives Washburn, Inc., [1971].*
> No statement of printing on copyright page.

FIND MY KILLER. *New York: Farrar, Straus and Company, 1947.*
  First printing has *ff* on copyright page.

FLAG ON THE LEVEE. *New York: Ives Washburn, Inc.*, [*1955*].
  No statement of printing on copyright page.

FORT SUN DANCE. [*New York: Published by Dell Publishing Company, Inc., 1955.*]
  Wrappers. No statement of printing on copyright page. *Dell First Edition 52* (25¢).

FRONTIER REPORTER. *New York: Ives Washburn, Inc.*, [*1969*].
  No statement of printing on copyright page.

THE GHOST BATTALION A STORY OF THE IRON SCOUTS. *New York: Ives Washburn, Inc.*,
[*1958*].
  No statement of printing on copyright page.

GIANTS FROM ETERNITY. *New York: Avalon Books*, [*1959*].
  No statement of printing on copyright page.

GRAY RIDERS JEB STUART AND HIS MEN. *New York: Aladdin Books, 1954.*
  First edition so stated on copyright page.

THE GREAT RIVERBOAT RACE A TALE OF THE NATCHEZ AND THE ROBERT E. LEE. *New York:
Ives Washburn, Inc.*, [*1965*].
  No statement of printing on copyright page.

THE HAUNTS OF DROWNING CREEK. [*New York*]: *Holiday House*, [*1951*].
  No statement of printing on copyright page.

THE INVADING ASTEROID. *New York: Stellar Publishing Corporation*, [*1932*].
  Wrappers. No statement of printing. Cover title. Issued as *Science Fiction Series No. 15.*

ISLAND IN THE SKY. *New York: Avalon Books*, [*1961*].
  No statement of printing on copyright page.

JAMESTOWN ADVENTURE. *New York: Ives Washburn, Inc.*, [*1967*].
  No statement of printing on copyright page.

THE LAST MAMMOTH. *New York: Holiday House*, [*1953*].
  No statement of printing on copyright page.

LIGHTS OVER SKELETON RIDGE. *New York: Ives Washburn, Inc.*, [*1957*].
  No statement of printing on copyright page.

MANY ARE THE HEARTS A PLAY IN ONE ACT. [*Raleigh*]: *The North Carolina Confederate
Centennial Commission*, [*1961*].
  Wrappers. No statement of printing on copyright page. Offset from typewritten copy.

THE MASTER OF SCARE HOLLOW. *New York: Ives Washburn, Inc.*, [*1964*].
  No statement of printing on copyright page.

MOUNTAIN FEUD. *New York: Ives Washburn, Inc.*, [*1969*].
  No statement of printing on copyright page.

MYSTERY AT BEAR PAW GAP. *New York: Ives Washburn, Inc.*, [*1965*].
  No statement of printing on copyright page.

THE MYSTERY OF LOST VALLEY. *Edinburgh New York Toronto: Thomas Nelson & Sons*, [*1948*].
No statement of printing on copyright page.

NAPOLEON OF THE WEST A STORY OF THE AARON BURR CONSPIRACY. *New York: Ives Washburn, Inc.*, [*1970*].
No statement of printing on copyright page.

NOT AT THESE HANDS. *New York: G. P. Putnam's Sons*, [*1962*].
Boards with cloth shelf back. No statement of printing on copyright page.

THE RAIDERS OF BEAVER LAKE. *Edinburgh New York Toronto: Thomas Nelson & Sons*, [*1950*].
No statement of printing on copyright page.

REBEL MAIL RUNNER. *New York: Holiday House*, [*1954*].
No statement of printing on copyright page.

RIDE, REBELS! ADVENTURES OF THE IRON SCOUTS. *New York: Ives Washburn, Inc.*, [*1959*].
No statement of printing on copyright page.

RIFLES AT RAMSOUR'S MILL A TALE OF THE REVOLUTIONARY WAR. *New York: Ives Washburn, Inc.*, [*1961*].
No statement of printing on copyright page.

THE RIVER PIRATES. *New York: Ives Washburn, Inc.*, [*1963*].
No statement of printing on copyright page.

ROMANCE IN BLACK. *London: Utopian Publications Ltd.*, *n.d.* [*ca. 1946*].
Wrappers. No statement of printing. *Gans T. Field, pseudonym.* Note: A pirated printing of "The Black Drama," a three-part serial first published in *Weird Tales* in 1938.

SETTLEMENT ON SHOCCO ADVENTURES IN COLONIAL CAROLINA. *Winston-Salem: John F. Blair, Publisher, 1963*.
No statement of printing on copyright page.

SHERLOCK HOLMES'S WAR OF THE WORLDS. [*New York*]: *Warner Books*, [*1975*].
Wrappers. *First Printing: September, 1975* on copyright page. *Warner Books 76–982* ($1.25). With WADE WELLMAN.

THE SLEUTH PATROL. *Edinburgh New York Toronto: Thomas Nelson & Sons*, [*1947*].
No statement of printing on copyright page.

SOJARR OF TITAN. *New York: Crestwood Publishing Co., Inc.*, [*1949*].
Wrappers. No statement of printing on copyright page. *Prize Science Fiction Novels No. 11* (25¢).

THE SOLAR INVASION. *New York: Popular Library*, [*1968*].
Wrappers. No statement of printing on copyright page. *Popular Library 60–2346* (60¢).

THE SOUTH FORK RANGERS. *New York: Ives Washburn*, [*1963*].
No statement of printing on copyright page.

THE SPECTER OF BEAR PAW GAP. *New York: Ives Washburn, Inc.*, [*1966*].
No statement of printing on copyright page.

THIRD STRING CENTER. *New York: Ives Washburn, Inc.*, *[1960]*.
No statement of printing on copyright page.

TO UNKNOWN LANDS. *New York: Holiday House*, *[1956]*.
No statement of printing on copyright page.

*A TRUE STORY OF THE REVOLTING & BLOODY CRIMES OF SERGEANT STANLAS, U.S.A. *Four Ducks Press, 1964*.
Wrappers.

TWICE IN TIME. *New York: Avalon Books*, *[1957]*.
No statement of printing on copyright page.

WHO FEARS THE DEVIL? *Sauk City: Arkham House: Publishers, 1963*.
No statement of printing on copyright page.

WILD DOGS OF DROWNING CREEK. *New York: Holiday House*, *[1952]*.
No statement of printing on copyright page.

WORSE THINGS WAITING. *Chapel Hill: Carcosa, 1973*.
First edition so stated on page [354]. Note: Paid subscribers' copies bear an illustrated sheet signed by author and illustrator Lee Brown Coye pasted to the front free endpaper.

YOUNG SQUIRE MORGAN. *New York: Ives Washburn, Inc.*, *[1956]*.
No statement of printing on copyright page.

Herbert George Wells
(1866–1946)

THE ADVENTURES OF TOMMY. *London: The Amalgamated Press, Ltd.*, [*1928*].
Wrappers. *No* [number inserted]/*Limited and Numbered*/*EDITION-DE-LUXE*/
Published/*for private circulation only* on title page.

ALSO:*London Bombay Sydney: George G. Harrap & Co. Ltd.*, [*1929*]. Boards with cloth
shelf back. *First published 1929* on copyright page. First hardcover edition.

ALL ABOARD FOR ARARAT. *London: Secker & Warburg, 1940.*
First Published 1940 on copyright page.

ANN VERONICA. *London: T. Fisher Unwin, MCMIX.*
No statement of printing on copyright page.

APROPOS OF DOLORES. *London: Jonathan Cape*, [*1938*].
First Published, 1938 on copyright page.

THE AUTOCRACY OF MR. PARHAM. *London: William Heinemann Ltd*, [*1930*].
First published 1930 on copyright page.

BABES IN THE DARKLING WOOD. *London: Secker & Warburg, 1940.*
First Published 1940 on copyright page.

BEALBY A HOLIDAY. *London: Methuen & Co. Ltd.*, [*1915*].
Two issues, priority as listed: (A) Blue cloth; pages [337–40] comprise publisher's advertisements dated *Spring, 1915* with an inserted 32-page catalogue dated *25/11/14* at rear;
(B) Violet cloth; four pages of advertisements dated *Spring, 1915* and an inserted 32-page
catalogue dated *8.5.15* at rear. *First Published in 1915* on copyright page.

ALSO:*London: Methuen & Co Ltd*, [*1958*]. Boards. *This abridged version first published
1958* on copyright page. Abridged text.

BEST SCIENCE FICTION STORIES OF H. G. WELLS. *New York: Dover Publications, Inc.*, [*1966*].
Wrappers. *This Dover edition, first published in 1966* . . . on copyright page. All stories
reprinted from earlier books.

BEST STORIES OF H. G. WELLS. *New York: Ballantine Books*, [*1960*].
Wrappers. No statement of printing on copyright page. *Ballantine Books S414K (75¢).* All
stories reprinted from earlier books.

BOON, THE MIND OF THE RACE, THE WILD ASSES OF THE DEVIL, AND THE LAST TRUMP.
London: T. Fisher Unwin, Ltd., [*1915*].
First published in 1915 on copyright page. *Reginald Bliss, pseudonym.* Second edition
issued in 1920 acknowledges Wells's authorship.

THE BROTHERS. *London: Chatto & Windus, 1938.*
No statement of printing on copyright page.

BRYNHILD. *London: Methuen and Company Limited, 1937.*
First published in 1937 on copyright page.

THE BULPINGTON OF BLUP. *London: Hutchinson & Co. (Publishers), Ltd., [1932].*
Two issues, probable priority as listed: (A) Pictorial endpapers. Occurs with and without inserted publisher's catalogue: (1) No inserted publisher's catalogue. Copy thus in the British Library received 12 January 1933. (2) 40-page publisher's catalogue dated *SPRING 1933/. . ./Spring List No. 1/(January)* inserted at rear. (B) Plain endpapers (not seen; reported by Eric Korn, London). No statement of printing on copyright page.

THE CAMFORD VISITATION. *London: Methuen & Co. Ltd., [1937].*
First Published in 1937 on copyright page.

CHRISTINA ALBERTA'S FATHER. *London: Jonathan Cape Ltd, [1925].*
First published in MCMXXV on copyright page.

THE CONE: ANOTHER COLLECTION OF HORROR STORIES. *[London]: Collins, [1965].*
Wrappers. *This selection first issued in Fontana Books 1965* on copyright page. *Fontana Books 1125* (3/6). All stories reprinted from earlier books.

THE COUNTRY OF THE BLIND AND OTHER STORIES. *London, Edinburgh, Dublin, Leeds, and New York . . . : Thomas Nelson and Sons, [1911].*
No statement of printing on copyright page. Five stories first collected in book form.

COUNTRY OF THE BLIND. *New York: Privately Printed Christmas 1915.*
Boards, paper label on front panel. No statement of printing on copyright page. First separate printing of this story. Collected earlier in THE COUNTRY OF THE BLIND AND OTHER STORIES.

ALSO: THE COUNTRY OF THE BLIND 1939. *[London]: The Golden Cockerel Press, [1939].*
280 copies printed. Two issues, no priority: (A) Full Orange Japan vellum. 30 copies numbered 1–30 signed by Wells and illustrator Clifford Webb. Signed issue. (B) Cloth with Japan vellum shelf back. 250 copies numbered 31–280, unsigned. Colophon reads *Printed and published . . . at the Golden Cockerel Press . . . finished on the sixth day of September, 1939 . . . . The edition is limited to 280 numbered copies. Numbers 1–30 are signed by the Author & Artist* [Clifford Webb]. *Number* [printed number inserted]. Includes new introduction by Wells, 1939 revised text, and original 1904 text.

THE COUNTRY OF THE BLIND. *Girard, Kansas: Haldeman-Julius Company, n.d.*
Wrappers. No statement of printing. *Little Blue Book no. 161.* Three stories reprinted from earlier books.

THE COUNTRY OF THE BLIND AND OTHER STORIES. *London • New York • Toronto: Longmans, Green & Co., [1947].*
Wrappers. *First published 1947* on copyright page. All stories collected from earlier books.

THE CROQUET PLAYER. *London: Chatto & Windus, 1936.*
No statement of printing on copyright page.

A CURE FOR LOVE. A STORY OF THE DAYS TO COME. (ANNO DOMINI 2090.) *[New York: Printed by the E. Scott Co., 1899.]*
Wrappers. No statement of printing. Caption title. Note: Probably prepared to protect U.S. copyright. Text comprises the first of five parts of Wells's novella "A Story of the Days to Come," collected later the same year in TALES OF SPACE AND TIME. Only recorded copy of this pamphlet is in the Library of Congress and was received by the library's Office of Register of Copyrights on 17 May 1899.

THE DESERT DAISY. *[Urbana, Illinois]: Published by Beta Phi Mu, 1957.*
No statement of printing on copyright page. 4413 copies printed of which 1413 are numbered.

THE DOOR IN THE WALL AND OTHER STORIES. *New York & London: Mitchell Kennerley, MCMXI*.

> 600 copies printed. Two issues, priority as listed: (A) Imprint as above. Boards with cloth shelf back. No statement of printing on copyright page. 540 copies. (B) Publisher's imprint on title page reads *London: Grant Richards Ltd. Publishers*. Boards. Publisher's statement in holograph on verso of first blank reads *This edition is limited to sixty copies/for the United Kingdom. January 1915./No . . .* [signatures of Wells and photographer Alvin Langdon Coburn]. All stories reprinted from earlier books.

THE DREAM. *London: Jonathan Cape*, [*1924*].

> Two issues, priority as listed: (A) Leaf [A]¹ is integral and verso carries advertisements for books by Wells with the statement at bottom, "All these are in print and on sale whatever a lazy bookseller may say to the contrary." (B) Leaf [A]¹ is a cancel and mounted on a stub. The "lazy bookseller" statement is removed. *First published 1924* on copyright page.
> Note: J. R. Hammond in *Herbert George Wells: An Annotated Bibliography of His Works* (New York & London: Garland Publishing, 1977), A18, notes proof copies with the "lazy bookseller" statement.

THE EMPIRE OF THE ANTS AND OTHER STORIES. *Girard, Kansas: Haldeman-Julius Company, n.d.*

> Wrappers. No statement of printing. *Little Blue Book no. 925*. All stories reprinted from earlier books.

THE FAMOUS SHORT STORIES OF H. G. WELLS. *Garden City: Doubleday, Doran & Company, Inc., 1937*.

> Flexible cloth. No statement of printing on copyright page. First printing has Doubleday, Doran device on copyright page. Reissue of THE SHORT STORIES OF H. G. WELLS. An abridgment of this collection was issued as THE FAVORITE SHORT STORIES OF H. G. WELLS.

THE FAVORITE SHORT STORIES OF H. G. WELLS. *Garden City: Doubleday, Doran & Company, Inc., 1937*.

> No statement of printing on copyright page. Abridged reprint. Collects the first thirty-one of sixty-three stories printed in THE FAMOUS SHORT STORIES OF H. G. WELLS.

THE FINAL MEN. *N.p., n.d.* [*Robert W. Lowndes, March 1940*].

> Front wrapper only. No statement of printing. Mimeographed, stapled. Cover title. Notes: (1) First separate printing of the episode from THE TIME MACHINE featuring the kangaroo-rat men and the giant insects included in the serialization in the *New Review*, January–May 1895, but omitted from all book editions save the 1960 text printed in THREE PROPHETIC NOVELS OF H. G. WELLS. (2) Bob Pavlat and Bill Evans in *Fanzine Index* (1965) credit preparation of this booklet to Lowndes and assign an issue date of March 1940.

THE FIRST MEN IN THE MOON. *Indianapolis: The Bowen-Merrill Company*, [*1901*].

> No statement of printing on copyright page. *PRESS OF/BRAUNWORTH & CO./ BOOKBINDERS AND PRINTERS/BROOKLYN, N.Y.* at base of copyright page. Title page printed in red and black. Notes: (1) Bowen-Merrill edition published 5 October 1901 preceding Newnes edition published in November 1901. Omits three pages of text (pp. 75–78 of Newnes edition); other minor textual differences. (2) Sheets of the first printing have been observed in a later binding of blue-gray vertically ribbed cloth stamped in gold and blind with *GROSSETT/AND/DUNLAP* at base of spine.

> ALSO: *London: George Newnes, Limited, 1901*. Four bindings, priority as listed: (A) Dark blue cloth stamped in gold; black endpapers; (B) Dark blue cloth stamped in gold; white endpapers; (C) Light blue cloth stamped in dark blue; white endpapers; (D) Blue-green cloth stamped in black; white endpapers. No statement of printing on copyright page. Textual differences.

ALSO: *London • New York • Toronto: Longmans, Green and Co, [1954]*. Wrappers. *First published 1954* on copyright page. Edited and abridged by Latif Doss.

THE FOOD OF THE GODS. *London: Macmillan and Co., Limited, 1904*.
Two bindings, priority as listed: (A) Green cloth, spine stamped in gold, front cover in gold and blind; integral title page, verso blank. Two variants: (1) Top edge gilt; [16]-page publisher's catalogue dated *20.7.04* inserted at rear; (2) Top edge plain; [16]-page publisher's catalogue dated *20.9.04* inserted at rear. (B) Green cloth, spine stamped in gold, front cover in blind; top edge plain; title page a cancel mounted on a stub, verso bears statement *COPYRIGHT;* inserted 32-page publisher's catalogue dated *20.3.13* at rear. No statement of printing. Pages [319–20] comprise publisher's advertisements.

H. G. WELLS: EARLY WRITINGS IN SCIENCE AND SCIENCE FICTION. *Berkeley • Los Angeles • London: University of California Press, [1975]*.
No statement of printing on copyright page. Edited, with critical commentary and notes, by Robert M. Philmus and David Y. Hughes.

THE HAPPY TURNING: A DREAM OF LIFE. *London • Toronto: William Heinemann Ltd, [1945]*.
Boards with cloth shelf back. *First Published 1945* on copyright page.

THE HISTORY OF MR. POLLY. *London, Edinburgh, Dublin . . and New York . . Leipzig . . . Paris . . . : Thomas Nelson and Sons*, [1910].
First Published 1910 on copyright page. Pages [375–84] comprise publisher's advertisements with page [375] headed "Notes on Nelson's New Novels."

THE HOLY TERROR. *London: Michael Joseph Ltd., [1939]*.
First published in 1939 on copyright page.

HOOPDRIVER'S HOLIDAY. *West Lafayette, Indiana: Department of English Purdue University, 1964*.
Wrappers. First edition so stated on title page. Offset from typewritten copy, stapled. 650 copies printed. Edited, with introduction and notes, by Michael Timko. Note: A dramatized version of THE WHEELS OF CHANCE written in 1904.

IN THE DAYS OF THE COMET. *London: Macmillan and Co., Limited, 1906*.
No statement of printing on copyright page. Three issues (printings?), priority as follows: (A) Integral title leaf, printer's imprint on verso reads *PRINTED BY/WILLIAM CLOWES AND SONS, LIMITED,/LONDON AND BECCLES.;* Sheets collate [A]^4, [B]–I, K–Q, [R]–U^8, X^2 + 4 leaves of ads. Signature X is a gathering of two leaves (four pages) as follows: Page 305, text; [306], printer's imprint; [307], blank; [308], blank. Eight pages of publisher's advertisements dated *C.5.5.'06* inserted between pages [306] and [307]. Note: Only located copy of this issue is the British Library copy deposited 8 July 1906, two months prior to publication. George Locke in *Science Fiction First Editions* (London: Ferret, 1978), pp. 94–96 speculates that the BL copy is a proof. (B) Sheets bulk 2.6 cm across top; Sheets collate [A]^4, [B]–I, K–Q, [R]–U^8, X^4 + 4 leaves of ads. Signature X is a gathering of four leaves (eight pages) as follows: Page 305, text; [306], printer's imprint; [307–12], publisher's ads. Eight-page publisher's catalogue dated *20.8.06* inserted at rear. Two variants: (1) Integral title leaf, Clowes imprint on verso. Note: Publisher's presentation copy noted thus. (2) Title leaf is a cancel mounted on a stub, verso is blank. (C) Sheets bulk 3 cm across top; Sheets collate as per issue (printing?) B, but printed on thicker, inferior-quality wove paper; Integral title leaf, Clowes imprint on verso. Eight-page publisher's catalogue dated *10.10.06* inserted at rear. Note: Colonial issue has title page headed *Macmillan's Colonial Library*. It is bound in dark blue cloth with spine and front cover stamped in gold and blind. Eight-page publisher's catalogue dated *10.2.06* inserted at rear. Further details lacking. Although examined by the compiler, the colonial issue was

recorded prior to the discovery of the bibliographical complexities of this book and no collation of sheets was made. It may represent the earliest issue (or printing) of the sheets. Present location of the examined copy is unknown.

THE INEXPERIENCED GHOST AND NINE OTHER STORIES. *New York/Toronto/London: Bantam Pathfinder Editions*, [*1965*].
> Wrappers. *Published February 1965* on copyright page. *A Bantam Pathfinder Edition FB81* (50¢). All stories reprinted from earlier books.

THE INEXPERIENCED GHOST AND THE NEW ACCELERATOR. *London: Vallancey Press Limited*, [*1944*].
> Wrappers. No statement of printing on copyright page. Both stories reprinted from earlier books.

THE INVISIBLE MAN. *London: C. Arthur Pearson Limited, 1897.*
> No statement of printing on copyright page. Pages [247–48] comprise publisher's advertisements.

> ALSO: *New York London: Edward Arnold, 1897.* No statement of printing on copyright page. Minor textual variations and first book appearance of ''The Epilogue.''

> *ALSO: *London: C. Arthur Pearson Limited, n.d.* [ca. 1903–1904?]. Wrappers. ''Cheap edition.'' Not seen but Eric Korn, London, reports textual changes incorporating material from the 1897 Pearson and 1897 Arnold editions.

THE ISLAND OF DOCTOR MOREAU. *London: William Heinemann, MDCCCXCVI.*
> Two bindings, priority as listed: (A) Publisher's monogram stamped in blind on rear cover. Publisher's catalogue inserted at rear occurs in two forms, priority not established: (1) 16 pages. Page 1 headed *THE MANXMAN;* page 16 headed *THE NAULAHKA.* Not seen. Recorded by Percy H. Muir, *Points 1874-1930* (London: Constable, 1931), p. 160. (2) 32 pages. Page [1] headed *THE MANXMAN*; page [32] headed *OUT OF DUE SEASON.* (B) No monogram on rear cover. Page [1] of inserted catalogue headed *THE NIGGER OF THE 'NARCISSUS.'* Copies in this binding were not issued prior to 1898. No statement of printing on copyright page. Note: British and U.S. editions have minor textual variations.

> ALSO: *New York: Stone & Kimball, MDCCCXCVI.* Three bindings, priority as listed: (A) Black cloth stamped in gold; *STONE &/KIMBALL/NEW YORK* at base of spine. (B) Blue cloth stamped in yellow: *STONE/CHICAGO* at base of spine. (C) Green cloth stamped in red and gold; *Stone/Chicago* at base of spine. *PRINTED BY JOHN WILSON AND SON AT/THE UNIVERSITY PRESS IN CAMBRIDGE/DURING MAY M DCCC XCVI. FOR/STONE AND KIMBALL/NEW YORK* on page [251].

JOAN AND PETER. *London, New York, Toronto and Melbourne: Cassell and Company, Ltd,* [*1918*].
> *First Published 1918* on copyright page. Printer's code *F.150.818* on page 748.

THE KING WHO WAS A KING. *London: Ernest Benn Limited,* [*1929*].
> Two bindings, priority as listed: (A) Brown cloth, spine lettered in gold; (B) Dark green cloth, spine lettered in light green. *First Published in 1929* on copyright page.

KIPPS A MONOGRAPH. *New York: Charles Scribner's Sons, 1905.*
> Wrappers. No statement of printing on copyright page. *J. F. TAPLEY CO./BOOK MANUFACTURERS/NEW YORK* at base of copyright page. Note: Printed for copyright purposes only. Received by Library of Congress 17 March 1905.

> ALSO: KIPPS THE STORY OF A SIMPLE SOUL. *New York: Charles Scribner's Sons, 1905. Published, 1905* on copyright page. Note: First published edition. Received by Library of Congress 25 September 1905. The Scribner edition was published 7 October 1905 preced-

ing the British edition by Macmillan between 21 and 28 October 1905. Macmillan edition received by British Library 7 November 1905.

LOVE AND MR. LEWISHAM: THE STORY OF A VERY YOUNG COUPLE. *New York: Frederick A. Stokes Company Publishers*, [*1900*].
   Wrappers. No statement of printing on copyright page. Title page printed in black. Note: Printed for copyright purposes only. Received by Library of Congress 3 January 1900.

   ALSO: *New York: Frederick A. Stokes Company Publishers*, [1900]. No statement of printing on copyright page. Title page printed in orange and black. First published U S. edition.

   ALSO: *London and New York: Harper & Brothers Publishers, 1900.* No statement of printing on copyright page. Pages [325–28] comprise publisher's advertisements. The Harper edition drops the subtitle from the title page. Note: Secondary sources indicate British edition published in June 1900 preceding published U S. edition issued in October 1900. Both are preceded by the U. S. copyright printing.

THE MAN WHO COULD WORK MIRACLES. *Girard, Kansas: Haldeman-Julius Publications*, [*1931*].
   Wrappers. No statement of printing on copyright page. *Little Blue Book no. 1661.* Reprint.

THE MAN WHO COULD WORK MIRACLES. *London: Todd Publishing Company*, [*1943*].
   Wrappers. *August 1943* on page 16. *Pollybooks* (sixpence). All stories collected from earlier books.

MAN WHO COULD WORK MIRACLES. . . . A FILM BASED ON THE MATERIAL CONTAINED IN HIS SHORT STORY. . . . *London: The Cresset Press, 1936.*
   No statement of printing on copyright page.

MARRIAGE. *London: Macmillan and Co., Limited, 1912.*
   No statement of printing on copyright page. Pages [553–60] comprise publisher's advertisements.

MEANWHILE. *London: Ernest Benn Limited, 1927.*
   No statement of printing on copyright page.

MEN LIKE GODS. *London, New York, Toronto and Melbourne: Cassell and Company, Ltd,* [*1923*].
   Two bindings, probable priority as listed: (A) *CASSELL* at base of spine stamped in gold; (B) *CASSELL* at base of spine stamped in blind. *First published 1923* on copyright page. Printer's code *F.200.123* on page 304.

A MODERN UTOPIA. *London: Chapman & Hall, Ld., 1905.*
   No statement of printing on copyright page.

MR. BLETTSWORTHY ON RAMPOLE ISLAND. *London: Ernest Benn Limited, 1928.*
   No statement of printing on copyright page.

MR. BRITLING SEES IT THROUGH. *London, New York, Toronto and Melbourne: Cassell And Company, Ltd*, [*1916*].
   First published 1916 on copyright page. Printer's code *F.100.716* on page [434].

THE NEW MACHIAVELLI. *New York: Duffield & Company, 1910.*
   Two issues, probable priority as listed: (A) No quotations by G. H. Lewes and William James on title page. Title leaf integral with [A⁷]. (B) Quotations by Lewes and James on title page. Cancel title leaf mounted on a stub. No statement of printing on copyright page. *THE PREMIER PRESS/NEW YORK* on copyright page.

THE OBLITERATED MAN AND OTHER STORIES. *Girard, Kansas: Haldeman-Julius Company, n.d.*
> Wrappers. No statement of printing on copyright page. *Little Blue Book no. 926.* All stories reprinted from earlier books.

THE PASSIONATE FRIENDS. *London: Macmillan and Co., Limited, 1913.*
> No statement of printing on copyright page. 12 pages of publisher's advertisements inserted at rear. Ads are paged 1–4, 1–[8] with page 1 of the second set dated *Autumn 1913.*

THE PLATTNER STORY AND OTHERS. *London: Methuen & Co., 1897.*
> No statement of printing on copyright page. 40-page publisher's catalogue dated *March 1897* inserted at rear.

A QUARTETTE OF COMEDIES. *London: Ernest Benn Limited, M.CM.XXVIII.*
> *First published 1928* on copyright page. Reprint. Collects KIPPS, THE HISTORY OF MR. POLLY, LOVE AND MR. LEWISHAM, and BEALBY.

THE RED ROOM. *Chicago: Stone & Kimball, MDCCCVCVI.*
> Self wrappers, sewn. No statement of printing on copyright page. Cover title. Notes: (1) 12 copies printed to establish U.S. copyright from type set for publication of the story in *The Chapbook,* February 15, 1896. None were for sale. (2) Misdated on cover *MDCCCVCVI.*

THE RESEARCH MAGNIFICENT. *London: Macmillan And Co., Limited, 1915.*
> No statement of printing on copyright page. Two numbered pages of advertisements for other books by Wells at rear, followed by inserted eight-page publisher's catalogue *New & Recent/Works Of Fiction* dated *C.15.8.15.*

THE SCIENTIFIC ROMANCES OF H. G. WELLS. *London: Victor Gollancz Ltd, 1933.*
> No statement of printing on copyright page. Reprint, save for new preface. Collects THE TIME MACHINE, THE ISLAND OF DR. MOREAU, THE INVISIBLE MAN, THE WAR OF THE WORLDS, THE FIRST MEN IN THE MOON, THE FOOD OF THE GODS, IN THE DAYS OF THE COMET, and MEN LIKE GODS. Issued later in the U.S. as SEVEN FAMOUS NOVELS BY H. G. WELLS with MEN LIKE GODS deleted.

THE SEA LADY. *London: Methuen & Co., 1902.*
> Two (three?) bindings, priority as listed: (A) Red cloth stamped in gold. Occurs with 40-page publisher's catalogue inserted at rear in three states: (1) dated *JULY 1902.* (2) dated *AUGUST 1902.* (3) dated *MARCH 1907* (not seen). (B) Green cloth, front and rear cover stamped in blind, spine stamped in gold. Note: 400 copies so bound issued in May 1907? (C) Binding not determined, inserted publisher's catalogue dated *February 1910.* Not seen. Recorded by Hammond in *Herbert George Wells: An Annotated Bibliography of His Works,* B8. No statement of printing on copyright page.

THE SECRET PLACES OF THE HEART. *London, New York, Toronto and Melbourne: Cassell and Company, Ltd, [1922].*
> Three issues, priority as listed: (A) Dark green cloth, front cover lettered in blind *The Secret Places/Of The Heart/H. G. Wells; Cassell* on spine measures 3.3 cm across; integral title page; *First published 1922* on copyright page. (B) Dark green cloth; front cover lettered in blind *The/Secret/Places/of the/Heart/H. G. Wells; Cassell* on spine measures 2.5 cm across; integral title page: *First published 1922* on copyright page. Remainder issue. (C) Pale green cloth; front cover unlettered; title page is a cancel pasted to contents page; *First Published May 1922/Printed in Great Britain* on copyright page. Remainder issue.

SELECT CONVERSATIONS WITH AN UNCLE. *London: John Lane-New York-The Merriam Company, 1895.*
> No statement of printing on copyright page. 16 pages of publisher's advertisements dated 1895 inserted at rear. Note: Contains twelve conversations and two short stories.

SELECTED SHORT STORIES. [*Harmondsworth, Middlesex*]: *Penguin Books*, [*1958*].
Wrappers. *Published in Penguin Books 1958* on copyright page. *Penguin Books 1310* (3/6).
Twenty-one stories reprinted from THE SHORT STORIES OF H. G. WELLS published by Ernest
Benn in 1927.

SELECTIONS FROM THE EARLY PROSE WORKS. . . .*London: University of London Press, Ltd.*,
1931.
No statement of printing on copyright page. Short stories and extracts from novels reprinted
from earlier books.

SEVEN FAMOUS NOVELS BY H. G. WELLS.*New York: Alfred A. Knopf, 1934*.
First Printing June 1, 1934 on copyright page. Basically a reprint of THE SCIENTIFIC
ROMANCES OF H. G. WELLS with some changes in preface and MEN LIKE GODS deleted.
Note: 1950 Dover edition drops preface.

THE SHAPE OF THINGS TO COME.*London: Hutchinson & Co. (Publishers), Ltd.*,
MCMXXXIII.
No statement of printing on copyright page.

SHORT STORIES . . . FIRST SERIES.*London Edinburgh and New York: Thomas Nelson and
Sons Ltd*, [*1940*].
First published, September 1940 on copyright page. All stories reprinted from earlier
books.

THE SHORT STORIES OF H. G. WELLS.*London: Ernest Benn Limited, M.CM.XXVII*.
No statement of printing on copyright page. Includes several short stories not previously
collected in book form. Issued in the U.S. under this title in 1929 and later as THE FAMOUS
SHORT STORIES OF H. G. WELLS.

*ALSO:*London: Odhams Press, n.d.* Abridged collection.

THE SLEEPER AWAKES. [*London*]: *Thomas Nelson and Sons*, [*1910*].
No statement of printing on copyright page. Revised text (comprising mostly deletion of
about 6000 words) and new introduction. Issued earlier as WHEN THE SLEEPER WAKES.

THE SOUL OF A BISHOP.*London, New York, Toronto and Melbourne: Cassell and Company,
Ltd*, [*1917*].
First Impression September 1917 on copyright page. Printer's code *F300. 717* on page
320.

STAR BEGOTTEN.*London: Chatto & Windus, 1937*.
No statement of printing on copyright page.

THE STOLEN BACILLUS AND OTHER INCIDENTS.*London: Methuen & Co., 1895*.
No statement of printing on copyright page. 32-page publisher's catalogue dated
SEPTEMBER 1895 inserted at rear.

THE STOLEN BACILLUS AND OTHER STORIES.*Girard, Kansas: Haldeman-Julius Company*,
n.d.
Wrappers. No statement of printing on copyright page. *Little Blue Book no. 927*. All
stories reprinted from earlier books.

THE STOLEN BODY AND OTHER TALES OF THE UNEXPECTED. [*London*]: *Published for Wm.
Collins Sons & Co., Ltd. by the London Book Co., Ltd.*, [*1931*].
Boards. No statement of printing on copyright page. All stories reprinted from earlier
books.

STORIES OF MEN AND WOMEN IN LOVE.*London: Hutchinson & Co. (Publishers), Ltd.,* [*1933*].
 No statement of printing on copyright page. Reprint, save for new preface. Collects LOVE AND MR. LEWISHAM, THE PASSIONATE FRIENDS, THE WIFE OF SIR ISAAC HARMAN, and THE SECRET PLACES OF THE HEART.

A STORY OF THE DAYS TO COME. [*London*]: *Corgi Books*, [*1976*].
 Wrappers. *Corgi edition published 1976* on copyright page. *Corgi Science Fiction 552 10185 0* (45p). Reprint. Collected earlier in TALES OF SPACE AND TIME.

TALES OF LIFE AND ADVENTURE.*London: W. Collins Sons & Co. Ltd., n.d.* [*ca. 1923?*].
 Boards. No statement of printing on copyright page. All stories reprinted from earlier books.

TALES OF SPACE AND TIME.*London and New York: Harper & Brothers Publishers, 1900* [*i.e., 1899*].
 No statement of printing on copyright page. Note: British Library copy received 21 November 1899.

TALES OF THE UNEXPECTED.*London: W. Collins Sons & Co. Ltd.,* [*1924*].
 Boards. No statement of printing on copyright page. Publisher's advertisements on page 1 dated *SPRING, 1924.* All stories reprinted from earlier books.

TALES OF WONDER.*London: W. Collins Sons & Co. Ltd., n.d.* [*ca. 1923?*]
 Boards. No statement of printing on copyright page. All stories reprinted from earlier books.

THINGS TO COME. . . . A FILM STORY. . . . *London: The Cresset Press, 1935.*
 No statement of printing on copyright page.

THIRTY STRANGE STORIES. *New York: Edward Arnold, 1897.*
 No statement of printing on copyright page. Three stories appear for the first time in book form.

THREE NOVELS.*London Melbourne Toronto: Heinemann,* [*1963*].
 Boards. *Re-issued in this Edition 1963* on copyright page. Reprint. Collects THE TIME MACHINE, THE WAR OF THE WORLDS, and THE ISLAND OF DOCTOR MOREAU.

THREE PROPHETIC NOVELS OF H. G. WELLS.*New York: Dover Publications, Inc.,* [*1960*].
 Wrappers. *This new Dover edition, first published in 1960* on copyright page. Reprint. Collects WHEN THE SLEEPER WAKES, "A Story of the Days to Come," and THE TIME MACHINE. Note: This edition of THE TIME MACHINE contains the episode featuring the kangaroo-rat men and the giant insects included in the serialization in *New Review,* January–May 1895 but omitted from all earlier book editions.

THE TIME MACHINE.*New York: Henry Holt and Company, 1895.*
 No statement of printing on copyright page. Two printings, priority as listed: (A) Tan buckram stamped in purple; Author's name misprinted *H. S. WELLS* on title page; six pages of publisher's advertisements inserted at rear. (B) Vertically ribbed red cloth, front cover and spine stamped in gold; *H. G. WELLS* on title page; no advertisements at rear. Note: Holt edition published prior to Heinemann edition. A deposit copy was received by the Library of Congress on 7 May 1895 and the book was announced in *Publishers Weekly* 18 May 1895. Text of the Holt edition differs significantly from the Heinemann edition and from the *New Review* serial. See Bernard Bergonzi, "The Publication of *The Time Machine,* 1894–1895" in *SF: The Other Side of Realism,* Thomas D. Clareson, ed. (Bowling Green, Ohio: Bowling Green University Popular Press, 1971), pp. 204–15.

ALSO:*London: William Heinemann, MDCCCXCV*. No statement of printing on copyright page. 10,000 copies printed. Published simultaneously in cloth and wrappers. In May 1895, 5000 copies were bound in wrappers and 1000 in cloth; In August 1895, 1000 copies were bound in wrappers and 500 in cloth. The remainder were bound as required, with many of the copies bound earlier in wrappers stripped and rebound in cloth. Rebound copies have all edges trimmed. The following bindings have been noted. Bindings A and B1 probably represent the earliest forms for wrappers and cloth copies, but the order as here presented for the remainder is all but arbitrary: (A) Light blue-gray wrappers printed in dark blue; inner front wrapper, inner back wrapper, and outer back wrapper imprinted with publisher's advertisements; all edges trimmed; no inserted publisher's catalogue. A copy thus received by the British Library 29 May 1895. (B) Gray cloth stamped in purple; binding measures 18.2 cm vertically; *HEINEMANN* at base of spine set in 12-point type; top edge untrimmed, bottom edge rough cut, fore edge untrimmed or rough cut; inserted publisher's catalogue at rear observed in three forms, priority as listed: (1) 16 pages. Page [1] headed: *THE MANXMAN*. (2) 32 pages. Includes reviews of THE WAR OF THE WORLDS. (3) 32 pages. Page [1] headed: *VOICES IN THE NIGHT*. This catalogue prepared circa 1900, as Stephen Crane's BOWERY TALES published in May or June 1900 is listed. (C) Gray cloth, front and rear cover stamped in dark gray, spine in blue; binding measures 18.2 cm vertically; *HEINEMANN* at base of spine set in 12-point type; top edge uncut, fore and bottom edges rough cut; 32-page publisher's catalogue inserted at rear with page [1] headed *THE OPEN QUESTION*. Not issued prior to 1899. (D) Brown wrappers printed in black on outer front wrapper and spine panel. *The/Time Machine/An Invention/H. G. Wells* is printed on outer front wrapper enclosed by a heavy ornate box. Inner front wrapper, inner back wrapper, and outer back wrapper are blank. (E) Gray cloth stamped in purple; binding measures 17.2 cm vertically; *HEINEMANN* at base of spine set in 14-point type; all edges trimmed; no inserted publisher's catalogue. (F) Gray cloth stamped in brown; no inserted publisher's catalogue. Three variants: (1) All edges trimmed. (2) Top and fore edges untrimmed, bottom edge rough cut. (3) Top and fore edges untrimmed, bottom edge trimmed. Note: Text differs from Holt edition above. Collected later with the kangaroo-rat men episode in THREE PROPHETIC NOVELS OF H. G. WELLS.

ALSO: *New York: Random House, 1931*. Boards with cloth shelf back. 1200 numbered copies. Adds new "Preface." Notes: (1) Issued in unprinted tissue paper dust jacket and paper slipcase. (2) Copies have been observed without the limitation statement on page [88].

THE TIME MACHINE: AN INVENTION AND OTHER STORIES. *Harmondsworth, Middlesex: Penguin Books, [1946]*.
   Wrappers. No statement of printing on copyright page. *Penguin Books 533* (one shilling). All material reprinted from earlier books.

THE TIME MACHINE AND OTHER STORIES. *New York: Scholastic Book Services, [1963]*.
   Wrappers. *1st printing . . . September 1963* on copyright page. *Scholastic Library Edition T 530* (45¢). All material reprinted from earlier books.

TONO-BUNGAY. *London: Macmillan and Co., Limited, 1909*.
   No statement of printing on copyright page. Two states of publisher's advertisements inserted at rear, priority as listed: (A) Dated *1.09;* (B) Dated *2.09.* Note: Publisher's imprint on title page of U.S. edition reads *New York: Duffield and Company, 1908*. May precede Macmillan edition published in January 1909. Publication date of Duffield not verified, but listed *Weekly Record* 23 January 1909.

THE TREASURE IN THE FOREST. [*New York: The Press of the Woolly Whale, June 1936.*]
   Boards. *The Treasure in the Forest by H. G. Wells,/here reprinted in an edition of 130 copies by/the Press of the Woolly Whale, New York,/finished in June, 1936* . . . on page [33]. Reprint. Collected earlier in THE STOLEN BACILLUS AND OTHER INCIDENTS.

THE TRUTH ABOUT PYECRAFT AND OTHER SHORT STORIES.*London: Todd Publishing Company*, [*1943*].

> Wrappers. *March 1943* on copyright page. *Pollybooks* (price sixpence). All stories reprinted from earlier books.

TWELVE STORIES AND A DREAM.*London: Macmillan and Co. , Limited New York: The Macmillan Company, 1903*.

> No statement of printing on copyright page. Pages [379–84] comprise publisher's advertisements. 16-page publisher's catalogue dated *20.9.03* inserted at rear.

28 SCIENCE FICTION STORIES OF H. G. WELLS. [*New York*]: *Dover Publications, Inc.*, [*1952*].

> No statement of printing on copyright page. All stories reprinted from earlier books.

TWO FILM STORIES THINGS TO COME MAN WHO COULD WORK MIRACLES.*London: The Cresset Press, 1940*.

> No statement of printing on copyright page. Reprint. Collects THINGS TO COME and MAN WHO COULD WORK MIRACLES.

THE UNDYING FIRE.*London, New York, Toronto and Melbourne: Cassell and Company, Ltd,* [*1919*].

> No statement of printing on copyright page. Printer's code *F.200419* on page [254].

*THE VACANT COUNTRY. [*New York: A. E. Kent?*], *n.d.* [*but 1899*].

> Page proofs, printed on rectos only and mounted on 18 leaves, plus title leaf not mounted. Probably prepared for U.S. copyright. Pulled from standing type prepared for U.S. magazine appearance? No copy located. Description from microfilm of the deposit copy discarded by the Library of Congress after filming. This copy was marked "second copy, 1899" and was received by the library's Office of Register of Copyrights on 10 June 1899. Text comprises the second of five parts of Wells's novella "A Story of the Days to Come," collected later the same year in TALES OF SPACE AND TIME.

THE VALLEY OF SPIDERS: A NEW COLLECTION OF SHORT STORIES. [*London*]: *Fontana Books*, [*1964*].

> Wrappers. *This selection first issued in Fontana Books 1964* on copyright page. *An Original Fontana 1035* (3'6). All stories reprinted from earlier books.

THE WAR IN THE AIR.*London: George Bell and Sons, 1908*.

> No statement of printing on copyright page. Five bindings, first and last as listed, sequence of others not established: (A) Blue cloth; all lettering and decoration on front cover and spine in gold; *GEORGE BELL & SONS* at base of spine. (B) Blue cloth; decorative title on front cover stamped in blind, otherwise as binding A. (C) Blue cloth; publisher's device and imprint *G. BELL & SONS* on spine stamped in blind; color reproduction of frontispiece mounted on front cover within a single rule box, otherwise as binding A. (D) Blue or red cloth; all spine stamping in gold; decorative title on front cover in black; color reproduction of frontispiece mounted on front cover within a single rule box; *G. BELL & SONS* at base of spine in a *sans serif* typeface. (E) Blue cloth; color reproduction of frontispiece mounted on front cover within a single rule box, otherwise as binding A. Cancel title page dated 1911. *Cheap reissue 1911* on verso.

THE WAR OF THE WORLDS.*London: William Heinemann, 1898*.

> No statement of printing on copyright page. Occurs with and without an inserted publisher's catalogue. Two states of inserted publisher's catalogue at rear, priority as listed: (A) 16 pages; dated *Autumn mdcccxcvii*. (B) 32 pages; page [1] headed *ILLUMINATION*.

> ALSO: *New York and London: Harper & Brothers Publishers, 1898*. No statement of printing on copyright page. Omits "The Epilogue;" other minor textual differences.

ALSO:*Melbourne :: London :: Toronto: William Heinemann Ltd*, *[1951]*. Boards. *Revised Edition 1951* on copyright page. Note: Bowdlerized rather than revised text. See David Y. Hughes, "McConnell's 'Critical Edition' of TM and WW," *Science-Fiction Studies* 4, no. 2 (July 1977), pp. 196–97.

THE WAR OF THE WORLDS AND THE TIME MACHINE. *New York: Globe Book Company, [1956]*.
No statement of printing on copyright page. Reprint. Collects THE WAR OF THE WORLDS and THE TIME MACHINE. Text adapted and edited by Lou P. Bunce.

THE WAR OF THE WORLDS, THE TIME MACHINE, AND SELECTED SHORT STORIES. *New York: Platt & Munk, Publishers, [1963]*.
Boards. No statement of printing on copyright page. Reprint. Collects THE WAR OF THE WORLDS, THE TIME MACHINE, and seven short stories from earlier collections.

THE WEALTH OF MR. WADDY. *Carbondale and Edwardsville: Southern Illinois University Press. London and Amsterdam: Feffer & Simons, Inc., [1969]*.
Crosscurrents/Modern Fiction edition, November, 1969 on copyright page. Note: Earliest surviving draft of KIPPS.

THE WHEELS OF CHANCE. *London: J. M. Dent and Co. New York: The Macmillan Co., 1896*.
Two issues, priority as listed: (A) Printer's imprint on page [314]; 10-page publisher's catalogue inserted at rear dated *October 1896*. (B) Page [314] is blank; no inserted advertisements. No statement of printing on copyright page.

WHEN THE SLEEPER WAKES. *London and New York: Harper & Brothers Publishers, 1899*.
No statement of printing on copyright page. Later abridged as THE SLEEPER AWAKES.

* ALSO:*London: W. Collins Sons & Co. Ltd., [1921]*. Boards. No statement of printing on copyright page. New preface.

THE WIFE OF SIR ISAAC HARMAN. *London: Macmillan and Co., Limited, 1914*.
No statement of printing on copyright page. Code *2 H* at base of page 465. 10 integral numbered pages of publisher's advertisements at rear.

THE WONDERFUL VISIT. *London: J. M. Dent & Co. , . . . New York: Macmillan & Co., 1895*.
Two bindings, probable priority as listed: (A) Red cloth, front cover blank. A copy so bound received by the British Library 26 September 1895. (B) Red cloth, title and figure of an angel stamped in gold on front cover. No statement of printing on copyright page.

THE WORLD OF WILLIAM CLISSOLD. *London: Ernest Benn Ltd., 1926*.
Three volumes. Two issues, no priority: (A) 218 sets signed by the author of which 198 were for sale and 20 for presentation; (B) Trade issue. No statement of printing on copyright pages.

THE WORLD SET FREE. *London: Macmillan And Co., Limited, 1914*.
No statement of printing on copyright page. 10 pages of publisher's advertisements at rear of which eight comprise an inserted catalogue with page 1 headed *Macmillan's/New Fiction*.

ALSO:*London: W. Collins Sons & Co. Ltd., [1921]*. Boards. No statement of printing on copyright page. New preface.

YOU CAN'T BE TOO CAREFUL. *London: Secker & Warburg, 1941*.
First Published . . . November 1941 on copyright page.

Collected Works

THE WORKS OF H. G. WELLS. *London: T. Fisher Unwin Ltd., MCMXXIV–MCMXXVII.*
[U.S. imprint reads: *New York: Charles Scribner's Sons, MCMXXIV–MCMXXVII.*]
  The Atlantic Edition. 28 volumes. Limited to 1670 sets. Two issues, no priority: (A) Unwin issue. 620 sets for Great Britain and Ireland of which 600 were for sale and 20 for presentation. (B) Scribner issue. 1050 sets for America of which 1000 were for sale and 50 for presentation. Numbered statement of limitation signed by Wells in volume one. Adds Wells's "A General Introduction To The Atlantic Edition." Note: Prospectus for the *Works* announced that all contents would be newly revised, but with respect to the fictions revisions are merely stylistic and quite trivial, with the exception of the use of the 1910 text of THE SLEEPER WAKES and deletion of two chapters from BOON. See R. D. Mullen, "An Annotated Survey of Books and Pamphlets by H. G. Wells" in *H. G. Wells and Modern Science Fiction,* Darko Suvin, ed. with Robert M. Philmus (Lewisburg: Bucknell University Press, 1977), pp. 264–68.

Autobiography and Letters

Arnold Bennett and H. G. Wells: A Record of a Personal and a Literary Friendship. *London: Rupert Hart-Davis, 1960.*
  No statement of printing on copyright page. Edited, with introduction, by Harris Wilson. Includes correspondence between Wells and Bennett, 1897–1931.

Experiment in Autobiography. *London: Victor Gollancz Ltd and The Cresset Press Ltd, 1934.*
  Two volumes. *First Published 1934* on copyright pages.

George Gissing and H. G. Wells: Their Friendship and Correspondence. *London: Rupert Hart-Davis, 1961.*
  No statement of printing on copyright page. Edited, with introduction, by Royal A. Gettmann. Includes correspondence between Wells and Gissing, 1896–1903.

Henry James and H. G. Wells: A Record of Their Friendship, Their Debate on the Art of Fiction, and Their Quarrel. *London: Rupert Hart-Davis, 1958.*
  No statement of printing on copyright page. Edited, with introduction, by Leon Edel and Gordon N. Ray. Includes correspondence between Wells and James, 1898–1915.

Associational

*Ann Veronica, [by] H. G. Wells Made Into a Comedy in Two Acts by Ronald Gow. *London: Samuel French, [1951].*
  Wrappers. *French Acting Edition No. 1824.*

Horrors of Doctor Moreau a Play in Four Scenes, by Joel Stone. Based on H. G. Wells's "The Island of Doctor Moreau." *New York Hollywood London Toronto: Samuel French, Inc., [1972].*
  Wrappers. No statement of printing on copyright page. *PRICE, $1.75* on front wrapper.

The War of the Worlds Dramatized by Brainerd Duffield From the Novel by H. G. Wells. *Chicago: The Dramatic Publishing Company, [1955].*
  Wrappers. No statement of printing on copyright page. *A Full-Length Play* at head of title.

Reference

For additional listings of secondary material see *New Cambridge Bibliography of English Literature*, IV, 424–28, and bibliographies by Watkins and the H. G. Wells Society listed below. An extended critical survey of recent Wells criticism is David Y. Hughes, "Bergonzi and After in the Criticism of Wells's SF," *Science-Fiction Studies* 3, no. 2 (July 1976), pp. 165–74.

A Bibliography of the Works of H. G. Wells 1893–1925 . . . by Geoffrey H. Wells. *London: George Routledge & Sons, Ltd., 1925.*
 Boards with cloth shelf back. No statement of printing on copyright page. 220 numbered copies.

 ALSO: The Works of H. G. Wells 1887–1925: A Bibliography, Dictionary and Subject-Index, by Geoffrey H. Wells. *London: George Routledge & Sons, Ltd., 1926.* No statement of printing on copyright page. Second edition, revised and enlarged.

Catalogue of the H. G. Wells Collection in the Bromley Public Libraries, edited by A. H. Watkins. *Bromley: London Borough of Bromley Public Libraries, 1974.*
 Boards. No statement of printing on copyright page. Errata slip laid in.

The Early H. G. Wells: A Study of the Scientific Romances, by Bernard Bergonzi. *Toronto: University of Toronto Press, 1961.*
 First published in Canada, 1961 on copyright page.

H. G. Wells, [by] Patrick Parrinder. *Edinburgh: Oliver and Boyd, [1970].*
 Two bindings, no priority: (A) Boards; (B) Wrappers. *First published 1970* on copyright page.

H. G. Wells: A Collection of Critical Essays, edited by Bernard Bergonzi. *Englewood Cliffs, N. J.: Prentice-Hall, Inc., [1976].*
 First printing has *10 9 8 7 6 5 4 3 2 1* on copyright page.

H. G. Wells: A Comprehensive Bibliography, compiled by The H. G. Wells Society. *Putney, London: H. G. Wells Society, 1966.*
 Boards. No statement of printing on copyright page. 500 copies printed.

 ALSO: *London: H. G. Wells Society, [1968].* Boards. *Second Edition (revised) . . . 1968* on copyright page.

 ALSO: *[Middlesex]: H. G. Wells Society, [1972].* Boards. *Third Edition . . . 1972* on copyright page. Adds new index.

H. G. Wells and Modern Science Fiction, edited by Darko Suvin with Robert M. Philmus. . . . *Lewisburg: Bucknell University Press London: Associated University Presses, [1977].*
 No statement of printing on copyright page. Includes selective bibliography of Wells's science journalism and annotated survey of his books and pamphlets.

H. G. Wells and the World State, by W. Warren Wagar. *New Haven: Yale University Press, 1961.*
 No statement of printing on copyright page.

H. G. Wells at Hofstra: A Catalog of the Comprehensive Collection of Books and Manuscripts by and about Herbert George Wells, 1866–1946. Held by the Department of Special

Collections Hofstra University Library . . . May, 1974, [compiled by J. Terry Bender and Sylvia Kaufman]. *Hempstead, Long Island: Hofstra University Library, Department of Special Collections, 1974.*
 Wrappers. No statement of printing.

H. G. Wells: Critic of Progress, by Jack Williamson. *Baltimore: The Mirage Press, 1973. First printing: February 1973* . . . on page [164]. Approximately 1500 copies printed.

H. G. Wells: His Turbulent Life and Times, [by] Lovat Dickson. [*London*]: *Macmillan,* [*1969*].
 Boards. *This edition first published 1969* . . . on copyright page.

H. G. Wells in the Cinema, [by] Alan Wykes. *London: Jupiter,* [*1977*].
 Boards. *First published in 1977* . . . on copyright page.

H. G. Wells: The Critical Heritage, edited by Patrick Parrinder. *London and Boston: Routledge & Kegan Paul,* [*1972*].
 First published 1972 . . . on copyright page.

Herbert George Wells: An Annotated Bibliography of His Works, [by] J. R. Hammond. *New York & London: Garland Publishing, Inc., 1977.*
 No statement of printing on copyright page.

Scientific Romances of H. G. Wells (A Critical Study), by Stephen Gill. *Cornwall, Ontario: Vesta Publications, 1975.*
 Wrappers. No statement of printing on copyright page.

The Time Traveller: The Life of H. G. Wells, by Norman and Jeanne Mackenzie. *London: Weidenfeld and Nicolson,* [*1973*].
 No statement of printing on copyright page.

Who's Who in H. G. Wells, [by] Brian Ash. *London: Elm Tree Books Hamish Hamilton,* [*1979*].
 Boards. *First published in Great Britain 1979* . . . on copyright page.

James White
(b. 1928)

THE ALIENS AMONG US. *New York: Ballantine Books*, [*1969*].
Wrappers. *First Printing: March, 1969* on copyright page. *A Ballantine Science Fiction 01545* (75¢).

ALL JUDGMENT FLED. *London: Rapp & Whiting*, [*1968*].
Boards. *First published in Great Britain in 1968* on copyright page.

DARK INFERNO. *London: Michael Joseph*, [*1972*].
Boards. *First published in Great Britain in 1972* . . . on copyright page. Issued later the same year in the U.S. as LIFEBOAT.

DEADLY LITTER. *New York: Ballantine Books*, [*1964*].
Wrappers. *First printing October 1964* on copyright page. *An Original Ballantine Science Fiction U2224* (50¢).

THE DREAM MILLENNIUM. *New York: Ballantine Books*, [*1974*].
Wrappers. *First Printing: June, 1974* on copyright page. *Ballantine 24012* ($1.25).

ALSO: *London: Michael Joseph*, [*1974*]. Boards. *First published in Great Britain in 1974* on copyright page. Note: According to White, although accidental, both editions were published simultaneously on 14 June 1974.

THE ESCAPE ORBIT. *New York: Ace Books, Inc.*, [*1965*].
Wrappers. No statement of printing on copyright page. *Ace Book F–317* (40¢). Issued later in Great Britain as OPEN PRISON.

HOSPITAL STATION. *New York: Ballantine Books*, [*1962*].
Wrappers. No statement of printing on copyright page. *A Ballantine Science Fiction Novel F 595* (50¢).

LIFEBOAT. *New York: Ballantine Books*, [*1972*].
Wrappers. *First Printing: September, 1972* on copyright page. *Ballantine Books Science Fiction 02797–3–125* ($1.25). Issued earlier the same year in Great Britain as DARK INFERNO.

MAJOR OPERATION. *New York: Ballantine Books*, [*1971*].
Wrappers. *First Printing: February, 1971* on copyright page. *Ballantine Books Science Fiction 02149–5–095* (95¢).

MONSTERS AND MEDICS. *New York: Ballantine Books*, [*1977*].
Wrappers. *First Edition: March 1977* on copyright page. *Ballantine 25623* ($1.50).

OPEN PRISON. [*London*]: *A Four Square Book*, [*1965*].
Wrappers. *First published, in Great Britain* . . . *in 1965* on copyright page. *A Four Square Book 1228* (3'6). Issued earlier in the U.S. as THE ESCAPE ORBIT.

SECOND ENDING. *New York: Ace Books, Inc.*, [*1962*].
Wrappers. No statement of printing on copyright page. *Ace Double F–173* (40¢). Bound with THE JEWELS OF APTOR by Samuel R. Delany.

THE SECRET VISITORS. *New York: Ace Books*, [*1957*].
   Wrappers. No statement of printing on copyright page. *Ace Double Novel Books D–237* (35¢). Bound with MASTER OF LIFE AND DEATH by Robert Silverberg.

   ALSO: *London and New York: White Lion Publishers*, [*1974*]. Boards. *First British hardcover edition by White Lion Publishers, 1974* on copyright page. First hardcover edition.

STAR SURGEON. *New York: Ballantine Books*, [*1963*].
   Wrappers. No statement of printing on copyright page. *An Original Ballantine Science Fiction Novel F 709* (50¢).

TOMORROW IS TOO FAR. *New York: Ballantine Books*, [*1971*].
   Wrappers. *First Printing: February, 1971* on copyright page. *Ballantine Science Fiction 02150–9–095* (95¢).

   ALSO: *London: Michael Joseph*, [*1971*]. Boards. *First published in Great Britain . . . 1971* on copyright page. First hardcover edition.

THE WATCH BELOW. *New York: Ballantine Books*, [*1966*].
   Wrappers. *First Printing February, 1966* on copyright page. *A Ballantine Book Science Fiction Original U2285* (50¢).

   ALSO: *London: Ronald Whiting & Wheaton*, [*1966*]. Boards. *First published in Great Britain 1966* on copyright page. First hardcover edition.

Terence Hanbury White
(1906–1964)

THE BOOK OF MERLYN. *Austin & London: University of Texas Press*, [*1977*].
No statement of printing on copyright page.

DARKNESS AT PEMBERLEY. *London: Victor Gollancz Ltd, 1932*.
No statement of printing on copyright page.

DEAD MR. NIXON. *London, Toronto, Melbourne and Sydney: Cassell and Company Ltd,*
[*1931*].
First published 1931 on copyright page. With R. McNAIR SCOTT.

EARTH STOPPED: OR MR MARX'S SPORTING TOUR. *London: Collins, 1934*.
No statement of printing on copyright page.

THE ELEPHANT AND THE KANGAROO. *New York: G. P. Putnam's Sons*, [*1947*].
No statement of printing on copyright page.

FAREWELL, VICTORIA. *London: Collins, 1933*.
Three bindings, sequence not established but probably as listed: (A) Light blue cloth, spine
lettered in dark blue; (B) Light green cloth, spine lettered in dark green; (C) Red boards,
spine lettered in black. No statement of printing on copyright page.

FIRST LESSON. *London: Chatto & Windus, 1932*.
No statement of printing on copyright page. *James Aston, pseudonym.*

GONE TO GROUND. *London: Collins, 1935*.
Four bindings, sequence not established but probably as listed: (A) Chocolate brown cloth,
spine lettered in gold; (B) Tan cloth, spine lettered in gold; (C) Red boards, spine lettered in
black; (D) Lime green boards, spine lettered in black. No statement of printing on
copyright page.

THE ILL-MADE KNIGHT. *New York: G. P. Putnam's Sons, 1940*.
No statement of printing on copyright page. Collected later with textual revisions in THE
ONCE AND FUTURE KING.

THE MASTER. *London: Jonathan Cape*, [*1957*].
Boards. *First published 1957* on copyright page.

MISTRESS MASHAM'S REPOSE. *New York: G. P. Putnam's Sons*, [*1946*].
No statement of printing on copyright page. Trade printing: Dark blue cloth, spine lettered
in gold; cream endpapers printed in brick red; *VAN REES PRESS* on copyright page. Note:
All book club printings have small dot stamped in lower right of rear cover.

THE ONCE AND FUTURE KING. *London: Collins, 1958*.
No statement of printing on copyright page. Dust jacket occurs in two states, priority as
listed: (1) Advertisement on rear panel headed *KING ARTHUR'S AVALON/by/JEFFREY
ASHE;* (2) Advertisement on rear panel headed *Leading reviews acclaim/THE ONCE
AND/FUTURE KING/by/T. H. WHITE.* Collects THE SWORD IN THE STONE (with two
new chapters), THE QUEEN OF AIR AND DARKNESS (revised and retitled version of THE
WITCH IN THE WOOD), THE ILL-MADE KNIGHT (revised), and THE CANDLE IN THE WIND
(first book appearance).

THE SWORD IN THE STONE. *London: Collins, 1938.*
No statement of printing on copyright page. Collected later with expanded text in THE ONCE AND FUTURE KING.

ALSO: *New York: Time Reading Program Special Edition/Time Incorporated, [1964].*
Wrappers. No statement of printing on copyright page. New "Introduction" by the author.

THEY WINTER ABROAD. *London: Chatto & Windus, 1932.*
No statement of printing on copyright page. *James Aston, pseudonym.*

THE WITCH IN THE WOOD. *New York: G. P. Putnam's Sons, 1939.*
No statement of printing on copyright page. Collected later with textual revisions as THE QUEEN OF AIR AND DARKNESS in THE ONCE AND FUTURE KING.

Letters

The White/Garnett Letters. *London: Jonathan Cape, [1968].*
First published 1968 on copyright page. Edited, with preface, by David Garnett.

Reference

T. H. White, by John K. Crane. *New York: Twayne Publishers, Inc., [1974].*
Two bindings, no priority: (A) Cloth; (B) Wrappers. No statement of printing on copyright page.

T. H. White: A Biography, by Sylvia Townsend Warner. *[London]: Jonathan Cape with Chatto & Windus, 1967.*
First published 1967 on copyright page.

Theodore Edward White

(b. 1938)

ANDROID AVENGER. *New York: Ace Books, Inc.,* [*1965*].
Wrappers. No statement of printing on copyright page. *Ace Double M-123* (45¢). Bound with THE ALTAR ON ASCONEL by John Brunner.

BY FURIES POSSESSED. [*New York*]: *New American Library,* [*1970*].
Wrappers. *First printing, June, 1970* on copyright page. *A Signet Science Fiction T4275* (75¢).

CAPTAIN AMERICA: THE GREAT GOLD STEAL. *Toronto New York London: Bantam Books,* [*1968*].
Wrappers. *July 1968* on copyright page. *A Bantam Book F3780* (50¢).

INVASION FROM 2500. *Derby, Connecticut: Monarch Books, Inc.,* [*1964*].
Wrappers. *Published in August, 1964* on copyright page. *Monarch Books 453* (40¢). With TERRY CARR. *Norman Edwards, pseudonym.*

THE JEWELS OF ELSEWHEN. *New York: Belmont Books,* [*1967*].
Wrappers. *April 1967* on copyright page. *Belmont Science Fiction B50-751* (50¢).

LOST IN SPACE. *New York: Pyramid Books,* [*1967*].
Wrappers. *First printing October, 1967* on copyright page. *Pyramid TV Special X-1679* (60¢). *Ron Archer, pseudonym.* With DAVE VAN ARNAM.

NO TIME LIKE TOMORROW. *New York: Crown Publishers, Inc.,* [*1969*].
No statement of printing on copyright page.

PHOENIX PRIME. *New York: Lancer Books,* [*1966*].
Wrappers. *A Lancer Book • 1966* on copyright page. *Lancer Books 73-476* (60¢).

SECRET OF THE MARAUDER SATELLITE. *Philadelphia: The Westminster Press,* [*1967*].
No statement of printing on copyright page.

SIDESLIP. *New York: Pyramid Books,* [*1968*].
Wrappers. *First printing April, 1968* on copyright page. *Pyramid Science Fiction X-1787* (60¢). With DAVE VAN ARNAM.

THE SORCERESS OF QAR. *New York: Lancer Books,* [*1966*].
Wrappers. *A Lancer Book • 1966* on copyright page. *Lancer Books 73-528* (60¢).

THE SPAWN OF THE DEATH MACHINE. *New York: Paperback Library, Inc.,* [*1968*].
Wrappers. *First Printing: July, 1968* on copyright page. *Paperback Library Original Science-Fantasy 53-680* (60¢).

STAR WOLF! *New York: Lancer Books,* [*1971*].
Wrappers. No statement of printing on copyright page. *Lancer Books 75252-095* (95¢).

TROUBLE ON PROJECT CERES. *Philadelphia: The Westminster Press,* [*1971*].
No statement of printing on copyright page.

Associational

[The Oz Encounter.] *New York: Pyramid Books,* [*1977*].
   Wrappers. *Published January, 1977* on copyright page. *Pyramid A4036* ($1.50). Note:
   Title page reads *Weird Heroes Volume 5: Phoenix. Created by Ted White. A Novel by
   Marv Wolfman* . . . . Novel written by Wolfman from idea, notes, and discussions with
   White.

Edited Fiction

The Best From Amazing Stories. [*New York*]: *Manor Books Inc.,* [*1973*].
   Wrappers. *A Manor Book* . . . *1973* on copyright page. *Manor Book 95–225* (95¢).
   Edited, with notes and short story ''Phoenix'' (a collaboration with Marion Zimmer Brad-
   ley), by White.

   ALSO:*London: Robert Hale,* [*1976*]. Boards. *This edition 1976* on copyright page. First
   hardcover edition.

The Best From Fantastic. [*New York*]: *Manor Books Inc.,* [*1973*].
   Wrappers. *A Manor Book* . . . *1973* on copyright page. *Manor Books 95242* (95¢).
   Edited, with foreword and notes, by White.

   ALSO:*London: Robert Hale & Company,* [*1976*]. Boards. *This edition 1976* on copyright
   page. First hardcover edition.

Henry St. Clair Whitehead
(1882–1932)

JUMBEE AND OTHER UNCANNY TALES. *[Sauk City]: Arkham House, 1944.*
   No statement of printing on copyright page.

WEST INDIA LIGHTS. *Sauk City: Arkham House, 1946.*
   No statement of printing on copyright page.

Kate Wilhelm (Knight)
(b. 1928)

ABYSS.*Garden City: Doubleday & Company, Inc., 1971.*
First edition so stated on copyright page.

ANDOVER AND THE ANDROID.*London: Dennis Dobson,* [*1966*].
Boards. *First published in Great Britain 1966* on copyright page. Issued earlier in the U.S. as THE MILE-LONG SPACESHIP.

CITY OF CAIN.*Boston—Toronto: Little, Brown and Company,* [*1974*].
Boards. First edition so stated on copyright page.

THE CLEWISTON TEST.*New York: Farrar Straus Giroux,* [*1976*].
First edition so stated on copyright page.

THE CLONE. [*New York*]: *Published by Berkley Publishing Corporation,* [*1965*].
Wrappers. *December, 1965* on copyright page. *Berkley Medallion F1169* (50¢). With THEODORE L. THOMAS.

ALSO:*London: Robert Hale,* [*1968*]. Boards. *First published in Great Britain 1968* on copyright page. First hardcover edition.

THE DOWNSTAIRS ROOM.*Garden City: Doubleday & Company, Inc., 1968.*
First edition so stated on copyright page.

FAULT LINES.*New York Hagerstown San Francisco London: Harper & Row, Publishers,* [*1977*].
Boards with cloth shelf back. First edition so stated on copyright page.

THE INFINITY BOX.*New York, Evanston San Francisco, London: Harper & Row Publishers,* [*1975*].
Boards with cloth shelf back. First edition so stated on copyright page.

THE KILLER THING.*Garden City: Doubleday & Company, Inc., 1967.*
First edition so stated on copyright page.

ALSO: THE KILLING THING.*London: Herbert Jenkins,* [*1967*]. Boards. *First published . . . 1967* on copyright page. Minor textual changes.

LET THE FIRE FALL.*Garden City: Doubleday & Company, Inc., 1969.*
First edition so stated on copyright page.

ALSO:[*London*]: *Panther,* [*1972*]. Wrappers. *Published in 1972 . . .* on copyright page. *Panther Science Fiction 586 03643 1* (30p). Corrections and cuts in the text.

MARGARET AND I.*Boston Toronto: Little, Brown and Company,* [*1971*].
Boards. First edition so stated on copyright page.

THE MILE-LONG SPACESHIP. [*New York*]: *Published by Berkley Publishing Corporation,* [*1963*].
Wrappers. *December, 1963* on copyright page. *Berkley Medallion F862* (50¢). Issued later in Great Britain as ANDOVER AND THE ANDROID.

MORE BITTER THAN DEATH. *New York: Simon and Schuster, 1963.*
  Boards. First printing so stated on copyright page.

THE NEVERMORE AFFAIR. *Garden City: Doubleday & Company, Inc., 1966.*
  First edition so stated on copyright page.

WHERE LATE THE SWEET BIRDS SANG. *New York, Evanston, San Francisco, London: Harper & Row, Publishers, [1976].*
  Boards with cloth shelf back. First edition so stated on copyright page.

YEAR OF THE CLOUD. *Garden City: Doubleday & Company, Inc., 1970.*
  First edition so stated on copyright page. With TED THOMAS.

Edited Fiction

Clarion SF. *[New York]: Published by Berkley Publishing Corporation, [1977].*
  Wrappers. *January, 1977* on copyright page. *A Berkley Medallion Book 0-425-03293-0* ($1.25). Edited, with introduction and notes, by Wilhelm.

Nebula Award Stories 9. *London: Victor Gollancz Limited, 1974.*
  Boards. No statement of printing on copyright page. Edited, with introduction, by Wilhelm.

Charles Walter Stansby Williams
(1886–1945)

ALL HALLOWS' EVE.*London: Faber & Faber Limited*, [*1945*].
  First published Mcmxlv on copyright page.

COLLECTED PLAYS.*London New York Toronto: Oxford University Press, 1963*.
  No statement of printing on copyright page. The only nonverse play collected here is ''Terror of Light.''

DESCENT INTO HELL.*London: Faber and Faber Limited*, [*1937*].
  First published in September Mcmxxxvii on copyright page.

THE GREATER TRUMPS.*London: Victor Gollancz Ltd, 1932*.
  No statement of printing on copyright page.

THE HOUSE OF THE OCTOPUS.*London: Edinburgh House Press, 1945*.
  First published 1945 on copyright page.

MANY DIMENSIONS.*London: Victor Gollancz Ltd, 1931*.
  No statement of printing on copyright page.

THE PLACE OF THE LION.[*London*]: *Mundanus Ltd/Victor Gollancz Publisher, 1931*.
  Two bindings, no priority: (A) Orange cloth, spine lettered in black; (B) Yellow wrappers lettered in orange and black. No statement of printing on copyright page.

SHADOWS OF ECSTASY.*London: Victor Gollancz Ltd, 1933*.
  No statement of printing on copyright page.

THREE PLAYS.*London: Oxford University Press, 1931*.
  Boards with cloth shelf back. No statement of printing on copyright page.

WAR IN HEAVEN.*London: Victor Gollancz Ltd, 1930*.
  No statement of printing on copyright page.

Prose Adaptations

The Ring and the Book, by Robert Browning. The Story Retold by . . . . [*London*]: *Oxford University Press, 1934*.
  Wrappers. No statement of printing on copyright page. Prose adaptation by Williams of the poem by Browning.

*The Story of the Aeneid. Retold by Charles Williams. *London: Oxford University Press, 1936*.
  Wrappers?

Reference

Charles W. S. Williams: A Checklist, [by] Lois Glenn. [*Kent, Ohio*]: *The Kent State University Press*, [*1975*].
  No statement of printing on copyright page.

Charles Williams, by John Heath-Stubbs. *London, New York, Toronto: Published for the British Council and the National Book League by Longmans, Green & Co., [1955].*
  Wrappers. *First published in 1955* on copyright page.

Charles Williams: A Critical Essay, by Mary McDermott Shideler. *[Grand Rapids, Michigan]: William B. Eerdmans/Publisher, [1966].*
  Wrappers. No statement of printing on copyright page. *Contemporary Writers in Christian Perspective/a Continuing Series Edited by Roderick Jellema* at head of title.

An Introduction to Charles Williams, by Alice Mary Hadfield. *London: Robert Hale Limited, [1959].*
  Boards. *First published in Great Britain 1959* on copyright page.

Shadows of Imagination: The Fantasies of C. S. Lewis, J. R. R. Tolkien, and Charles Williams, edited by Mark R. Hillegas. *Carbondale and Edwardsville: Southern Illinois University Press. London and Amsterdam: Feffer & Simons, Inc., [1969].*
  No statement of printing on copyright page.

  ALSO: *Carbondale and Edwardsville: Southern Illinois University Press/London and Amsterdam: Feffer & Simons, Inc., [1979].* No statement of printing on copyright page. "New edition." Adds afterword, "The Wonder of *The Silmarillion*," by Peter Kreeft.

The Theology of Romantic Love: A Study in the Writings of Charles Williams, [by] Mary McDermott Shideler. *[New York]: Harper & Brothers, [1962].*
  First edition so stated on copyright page.

Jack (John Stewart) Williamson
(b. 1908)

AFTER WORLD'S END. *London: Brown, Watson Limited,* [*1961*].
Wrappers. *First U.K. publication* on copyright page. *Digit R 538* (2'6). Reprint. Collected earlier in THE LEGION OF TIME.

BRIGHT NEW UNIVERSE. *New York: Ace Books, Inc.,* [*1967*].
Wrappers. No statement of printing on copyright page. *Ace Book G–641* (50¢).

ALSO:*London: Sidgwick & Jackson,* [*1969*]. Boards. *First published in Great Britain 1969* on copyright page. First hardcover edition.

THE COMETEERS. *Reading, Pennsylvania: Fantasy Press, 1950.*
Two bindings, priority as listed: (A) Dark green cloth, spine stamped in gold; (B) Blue cloth, spine stamped in gold with title only. Two issues, no priority: (A) 500 copies with numbered leaf signed by the author inserted; (B) Trade issue. First edition so stated on copyright page. Note: "One Against the Legion" was separately issued later with additional material.

ALSO:*New York: Pyramid Books,* [*1967*]. Wrappers. *First printing June, 1967* on copyright page. *Pyramid Science Fiction X–1634* (60¢). Abridged edition. Drops "One Against the Legion."

DARKER THAN YOU THINK. *Reading, Pennsylvania: Fantasy Press, 1948.*
Three bindings, priority as listed: (A) Dark green cloth, spine stamped in gold; (B) Brown cloth, spine stamped in black; (C) Gray cloth, spine stamped in black. Two issues, no priority: (A) 500 copies with numbered leaf signed by the author inserted; (B) Trade issue. First edition so stated on copyright page.

DOME AROUND AMERICA. *New York: Ace Books, Inc.,* [*1955*].
Wrappers. No statement of printing on copyright page. *Ace Double Novel Books D–118* (35¢). Bound with THE PARADOX MEN by Charles L. Harness.

DRAGON'S ISLAND. *New York: Simon and Schuster, 1951.*
Boards. No statement of printing on copyright page. Reissued as THE NOT-MEN.

DREADFUL SLEEP. [*Chicago: Published by Robert Weinberg, 1977.*]
Wrappers. No statement of printing on copyright page. Caption title. *Lost Fantasies #7.*

THE EARLY WILLIAMSON. *Garden City: Doubleday & Company, Inc., 1975.*
Boards. First edition so stated on copyright page.

FARTHEST STAR. *New York: Ballantine Books,* [*1975*].
Wrappers. *First Printing: February, 1975* on copyright page. *Ballantine Books SF 24330* ($1.50). With FREDERIK POHL.

THE GIRL FROM MARS. *New York: Stellar Publishing Corporation,* [*1929*].
Wrappers. No statement of printing. Cover title. *Science Fiction Series No. 1.* With DR. MILES J. BREUER. Collected later in THE EARLY WILLIAMSON.

GOLDEN BLOOD. *New York: Lancer Books,* [*1964*].
Wrappers. *Lancer Edition published July, 1964* on copyright page. *Lancer Science-Fiction Library 72–740* (50¢).

THE GREEN GIRL. *New York: Avon Publishing Co., Inc., [1950].*
Wrappers. No statement of printing on copyright page. *Avon Fantasy Novels 2* (25¢).

THE HUMANOIDS. *New York: Simon and Schuster, 1949.*
Boards. No statement of printing on copyright page.

LADY IN DANGER. *[London Utopian Publications Ltd.], n.d. [ca. 1945].*
Self wrappers. No statement of printing. Cover title. Two printings, priority as listed: (A) Printed on yellow paper; *Printed in Great Britain* at base of page 36. Note: In addition to the Williamson novelette this printing includes "The Spanish Vampire" by E. Hoffmann Price. (B) Printed on white paper; *Printed in Eire* at base of page 36. Note: In addition to the Williamson and Price contributions this printing includes "The Curse of the House" by Robert Bloch.

THE LEGION OF SPACE. *Reading, Pennsylvania: Fantasy Press, 1947.*
Two issues, no priority: (A) 500 copies with numbered leaf signed by the author inserted; (B) Trade issue. First edition so stated on copyright page.

THE LEGION OF TIME. *Reading, Pennsylvania: Fantasy Press, 1952.*
Two bindings, priority as listed: (A) Blue-green cloth, spine stamped in gold: [Double rule]/*THE/LEGION/OF/TIME* [set in 18-point capitals]/[dot]/*WILLIAMSON* ["W" set in 10-point, remainder in 8-point capitals]/[double rule]/[single rule]/*FANTASY/PRESS* [set in 10-point capitals]/[single rule]. (B) Details not available, apparently spine stamping differs from that of A. Not seen; recorded by George Locke in *Science Fiction First Editions* (London: Ferret, 1978), p. 61. Two issues, no priority: (A) 350 copies with numbered leaf signed by the author inserted; (B) Trade issue. First edition so stated on copyright page. Note: Includes "After World's End" which was later issued separately in Great Britain. Reissued as THE LEGION OF TIME/ AFTER WORLDS END.

ALSO: *London: Brown, Watson Limited, [1961].* Wrappers. *First U. K. publication* on copyright page. *Digit Books R522* (2'6). Abridged edition. Drops "After World's End."

THE LEGION OF TIME/AFTER WORLDS END. *[New York]: Published by Galaxy Publishing Co., [1963].*
Wrappers. No statement of printing on copyright page. *Magabook No. 2. Two Complete Novels* at head of title. Reprint of the 1952 Fantasy Press edition of THE LEGION OF TIME.

THE MOON CHILDREN. *New York: G. P. Putnam's Sons, [1972].*
Boards. No statement of printing on copyright page.

THE NOT-MEN. *[New York]: A Tower Book, [1968].*
Wrappers. *Second Tower Printing: 1968* on copyright page. *Tower 43–957* (60¢). Reissue of DRAGON'S ISLAND. Note: First printing under this title.

ONE AGAINST THE LEGION. *New York: Pyramid Books, [1967].*
Wrappers. *First printing, July 1967* on copyright page. *Pyramid Science Fiction X–1657* (60¢). "One Against the Legion" appeared earlier in THE COMETEERS. Includes first publication of novelette "Nowhere Near."

THE PANDORA EFFECT. *New York: An Ace Book, [1969].*
Wrappers. No statement of printing on copyright page. *Ace Book 65125* (60¢).

PEOPLE MACHINES. *New York: Ace Books, [1971].*
Wrappers. No statement of printing on copyright page. *Ace Book 65890* (75¢).

THE POWER OF BLACKNESS. *New York: Published by Berkley Publishing Corporation*, *[1976]*.
No statement of printing on copyright page.

THE REEFS OF SPACE. *New York: Ballantine Books*, *[1964]*.
Wrappers. *First Ballantine Printing September 1964* on copyright page. *Ballantine Books U2172* (50¢). With FREDERIK POHL. Collected later in THE STARCHILD TRILOGY.

ALSO: *London: Dennis Dobson*, *[1965]*. Boards. *First published in Great Britain in 1965* on copyright page. First hardcover edition.

THE REIGN OF WIZARDRY. *New York: Lancer books*, *[1964]*.
Wrappers. *A Lancer Book • 1964* on copyright page. *Lancer Books 72–761* (50¢).

ROGUE STAR. *New York: Ballantine Books*, *[1969]*.
Wrappers. *First Printing: December, 1969* on copyright page. *Ballantine Books Science Fiction 01797–075* (75¢). With FREDERIK POHL. Collected later in THE STARCHILD TRILOGY.

ALSO: *London: Dennis Dobson*, *[1972]*. Boards. *First published in Great Britain in 1972* on copyright page. First hardcover edition. Note: Coauthor's name misspelled *Frederick* on title page.

SEETEE SHIP. *New York: Gnome Press, Inc.*, *[1951]*.
First edition so stated on copyright page. *Will Stewart, pseudonym*. Collected later in SEETEE SHIP/SEETEE SHOCK.

SEETEE SHIP/SEETEE SHOCK. *New York: Lancer Books*, *[1971]*.
Wrappers. No statement of printing on copyright page. *Lancer Books 78706–125* ($1.25). Reprint. Collects SEETEE SHIP and SEETEE SHOCK.

SEETEE SHOCK. *New York: Simon and Schuster, 1950*.
Boards. No statement of printing on copyright page. *Will Stewart, pseudonym*. Collected later in SEETEE SHIP/SEETEE SHOCK.

STAR BRIDGE. *New York: Gnome Press, Inc.*, *[1955]*.
Boards with cloth shelf back. First edition so stated on copyright page. With JAMES E. GUNN.

STARCHILD. *New York: Ballantine Books*, *[1965]*.
Wrappers. *First printing: November, 1965* on copyright page. *A Ballantine Science Fiction Original U2176* (50¢). With FREDERIK POHL. Collected later in THE STARCHILD TRILOGY.

ALSO: *London: Dennis Dobson*, *[1966]*. Boards. *First published in Great Britain in 1966* on copyright page. First hardcover edition.

THE STARCHILD TRILOGY. *Garden City: Nelson Doubleday, Inc.*, *[1977]*.
Boards. No statement of printing on copyright page. Code *H 36* on page 435. Reprint. Collects THE REEFS OF SPACE, STARCHILD, and ROGUE STAR. With FREDERIK POHL. Note: Issued by the Science Fiction Book Club.

TRAPPED IN SPACE. *Garden City: Doubleday & Company, Inc.*, *[1968]*.
Boards. First edition so stated on copyright page.

THE TRIAL OF TERRA. *New York: Ace Books, Inc.*, *[1962]*.
Wrappers. No statement of printing on copyright page. *Ace Book D–555* (35¢).

TWO COMPLETE NOVELS. See THE LEGION OF TIME/AFTER WORLDS END.

UNDERSEA CITY. *Hicksville, N.Y.: The Gnome Press, Inc., Publishers, [1958]*.
  Two bindings, priority as listed: (A) Black boards lettered in red; (B) Gray cloth lettered in red. First edition so stated on copyright page. With FREDERIK POHL.

UNDERSEA FLEET. *New York: Gnome Press Inc., Publishers, [1956]*.
  Two bindings, probable sequence as listed: (A) Green cloth lettered in brown; (B) Gray boards lettered in red. First edition so stated on copyright page. With FREDERIK POHL.

UNDERSEA QUEST. *New York: Gnome Press Inc. Publishers, [1954]*.
  First edition so stated on copyright page. With FREDERIK POHL.

Nonfiction (Dealing with the Fantasy Genre only)

H. G. Wells: Critic of Progress. *Baltimore: The Mirage Press, 1973*.
  First printing: February 1973 . . . on page [164]. Approximately 1500 copies printed.

Gene Wolfe
(b. 1931)

THE DEVIL IN A FOREST. *Chicago: Follett Publishing Company*, [*1976*].
Two bindings, no priority: (A) Boards. Trade binding. (B) Washable cloth reproducing dust jacket design. Library binding. First printing has code *123456789/82818079787776* on copyright page.

THE FIFTH HEAD OF CERBERUS. *New York: Charles Scribner's Sons*, [*1972*].
Boards. First printing has code *A–4.72[c]* on copyright page.

OPERATION ARES. [*New York*]: *Published by Berkley Publishing Corporation*, [*1970*].
Wrappers. *July, 1970* on copyright page. *A Berkley Medallion Book S1858* (75¢).

ALSO: *London: Dennis Dobson*, [*1977*]. Boards. *First published in Great Britain in 1977* on copyright page. First hardcover edition.

PEACE. *New York/Evanston/San Francisco/London: Harper & Row, Publishers*, [*1975*].
Boards with cloth shelf back. First edition so stated on copyright page.

Donald Allen Wollheim
(b. 1914)

ACROSS TIME. *New York: Avalon Books*, [*1957*].
   No statement of printing on copyright page. *David Grinnell, pseudonym.*

DESTINATION: SATURN. *New York: Avalon Books*, [*1967*].
   No statement of printing on copyright page. *David Grinnell, pseudonym.*
   With LIN CARTER.

DESTINY'S ORBIT. *New York: Avalon Books*, [*1961*].
   No statement of printing on copyright page. *David Grinnell, pseudonym.*

EDGE OF TIME. *New York: Avalon Books*, [*1958*].
   No statement of printing on copyright page. *David Grinnell, pseudonym.*

THE MARTIAN MISSILE. *New York: Avalon Books*, [*1959*].
   No statement of printing on copyright page. *David Grinnell, pseudonym.*

MIKE MARS AND THE MYSTERY SATELLITE. *Garden City: Doubleday & Company, Inc.*,
[*1963*].
   Boards. First edition so stated on copyright page.

MIKE MARS AROUND THE MOON. *Garden City: Doubleday & Company, Inc.*, [*1964*].
   Boards. First edition so stated on copyright page.

MIKE MARS, ASTRONAUT. *Garden City: Doubleday & Company, Inc.*, *1961*.
   Boards. First edition so stated on copyright page.

MIKE MARS AT CAPE CANAVERAL. *Garden City: Doubleday & Company, Inc.*, *1961*.
   Boards. First edition so stated on copyright page. Note: A later printing is retitled MIKE
   MARS AT CAPE KENNEDY.

MIKE MARS FLIES THE DYNA-SOAR. *Garden City: Doubleday & Company, Inc.*, *1962*.
   Boards. First edition so stated on copyright page.

MIKE MARS FLIES THE X-15. *Garden City: Doubleday & Company, Inc.*, *1961*.
   Boards. First edition so stated on copyright page.

MIKE MARS IN ORBIT. *Garden City: Doubleday & Company, Inc.*, *1961*.
   Boards. First edition so stated on copyright page.

MIKE MARS, SOUTH POLE SPACEMAN. *Garden City: Doubleday & Company, Inc.*, [*1962*].
   Boards. First edition so stated on copyright page.

ONE AGAINST THE MOON. *Cleveland and New York: The World Publishing Company*, [*1956*].
   First edition so stated on copyright page.

THE SECRET OF SATURN'S RINGS. *Philadelphia Toronto: The John C. Winston Company*,
[*1954*].
   First edition so stated on copyright page.

THE SECRET OF THE MARTIAN MOONS. *Philadelphia Toronto: The John C. Winston Company*,
[*1955*].
    First edition so stated on copyright page.

THE SECRET OF THE NINTH PLANET. *Philadelphia Toronto: The John C. Winston Company*,
[*1959*].
    First edition so stated on copyright page.

TO VENUS! TO VENUS! *New York: An Ace Book*, [*1970*].
    Wrappers. No statement of printing on copyright page. *Ace Double 81610* (75¢). *David
    Grinnell, pseudonym*. Bound with THE JESTER AT SCAR by E. C. Tubb.

TWO DOZEN DRAGON EGGS. [*Reseda, California: Powell Publications, Inc.*, *1969.*]
    Wrappers. *First Printing September, 1969* on copyright page. *Powell Sci-Fi PP181* (95¢).

    ALSO: *London: Dennis Dobson*, [*1977*]. Boards. *First published in Great Britain 1977* . . .
    on copyright page. First hardcover edition.

Edited Fiction

Ace Science Fiction Reader. *New York: Ace Books*, [*1971*].
    Wrappers. No statement of printing on copyright page. *Ace Book 00275* (95¢). Edited,
    with introduction and notes, by Wollheim. Issued later in Great Britain as *Trilogy of the
    Future*.

Adventures in the Far Future. *New York: Ace Books, Inc.*, [*1954*].
    Wrappers. No statement of printing on copyright page. *Ace Double Books D–73* (35¢).
    Edited by Wollheim. Bound with *Tales of Outer Space*, edited by Wollheim.

Adventures on Other Planets. *New York: Ace Books, Inc.*, [*1955*].
    Wrappers. No statement of printing on copyright page. *Ace Books S–133* (25¢). Edited by
    Wollheim.

The Avon All-American Fiction Reader. *New York: Avon Publishing Co., Inc.*, *1951*.
    Wrappers. No statement of printing on copyright page. *Avon Double-Size Books 1002*
    (50¢). Anonymously edited by Wollheim.

Avon Bedside Companion: A Treasury of Tales for the Sophisticated. *New York: Avon Book
Company*, [*1947*].
    Wrappers. No statement of printing on copyright page. *Avon 109* (25¢). Anonymously
    edited by Wollheim.

Avon Book of New Stories of the Great Wild West. *New York: Avon Publishing Co., Inc.*,
[*1949*].
    Wrappers. No statement of printing on copyright page. *Avon 194* (25¢). Anonymously
    edited by Wollheim.

*Avon Detective Mysteries No. 3. *N[ew] Y[ork]: Avon Book Company*, [*1947*].
    Wrappers. Anonymously edited by Wollheim.

The Avon Fantasy Reader. [*New York*]: *An Avon Book*, [*1969*].
    Wrappers. *First Avon Printing, January, 1969* on copyright page. *Avon S384* (60¢). Edited
    by Wollheim with GEORGE ERNSBERGER.

Avon Fantasy Reader No. 1. *N[ew] Y[ork]: Avon Book Company,* [*1947*].
Wrappers. No statement of printing on copyright page. Edited, with notes, by Wollheim.

Avon Fantasy Reader . . . No. 2. *N[ew] Y[ork]: Avon Book Company,* [*1947*].
Wrappers. No statement of printing on copyright page. Edited, with notes, by Wollheim.

Avon Fantasy Reader No. 3. *N[ew] Y[ork]: Avon Book Company,* [*1947*].
Wrappers. No statement of printing on copyright page. Edited, with notes, by Wollheim.

Avon Fantasy Reader No. 4. *N[ew] Y[ork]: Avon Book Company,* [*1947*].
Wrappers. No statement of printing on copyright page. Edited, with notes, by Wollheim.

Avon Fantasy Reader No. 5. *N[ew] Y[ork]: Avon Book Company,* [*1947*].
Wrappers. No statement of printing on copyright page. Edited, with notes, by Wollheim.

Avon Fantasy Reader No. 6. *N[ew] Y[ork]: Avon Book Co., Inc.,* [*1948*].
Wrappers. No statement of printing on copyright page. Edited, with notes, by Wollheim.

Avon Fantasy Reader No. 7. *N[ew] Y[ork]: Avon Publishing Co., Inc.,* [*1948*].
Wrappers. No statement of printing on copyright page. Edited, with notes, by Wollheim.

Avon Fantasy Reader No. 8. *N[ew] Y[ork]: Avon Publishing Co., Inc.,* [*1948*].
Wrappers. No statement of printing on copyright page. Edited, with notes, by Wollheim.

Avon Fantasy Reader No. 9. *New York: Avon Publishing Co., Inc.,* [*1949*].
Wrappers. No statement of printing on copyright page. Edited, with notes, by Wollheim.

Avon Fantasy Reader No. 10. *N[ew] Y[ork]: Avon Novels Inc.,* [*1949*].
Wrappers. No statement of printing on copyright page. Edited, with notes, by Wollheim.

Avon Fantasy Reader No. 11. *N[ew] Y[ork]: Avon Novels Inc.,* [*1949*].
Wrappers. No statement of printing on copyright page. Edited, with notes, by Wollheim.

Avon Fantasy Reader No. 12. *N[ew] Y[ork]: Avon Novels, Inc.,* [*1950*].
Wrappers. No statement of printing on copyright page. Edited, with notes, by Wollheim.

Avon Fantasy Reader No. 13. *New York: Avon Novels, Inc.,* [*1950*].
Wrappers. No statement of printing on copyright page. Edited, with notes, by Wollheim.

Avon Fantasy Reader No. 14. *New York: Avon Novels, Inc.,* [*1950*].
Wrappers. No statement of printing on copyright page. Edited, with notes, by Wollheim.

Avon Fantasy Reader No. 15. *New York: Avon Novels, Inc.,* [*1951*].
Wrappers. No statement of printing on copyright page. Edited, with notes, by Wollheim.

Avon Fantasy Reader No. 16. *New York: Avon Novels, Inc.,* [*1951*].
Wrappers. No statement of printing on copyright page. Edited, with notes, by Wollheim.

Avon Fantasy Reader No. 17. *New York: Avon Novels, Inc.,* [*1951*].
Wrappers. No statement of printing on copyright page. Edited, with notes, by Wollheim.

Avon Fantasy Reader No. 18. *New York: Avon Novels, Inc.,* [*1952*].
Wrappers. No statement of printing on copyright page. Edited, with notes, by Wollheim.

Avon Science-Fiction Reader No. 1. *New York: Avon Novels Inc.,* [*1951*].
Wrappers. No statement of printing on copyright page. Edited by Wollheim.

Avon Science-Fiction Reader No. 2. *New York: Avon Novels, Inc., [1951]*.
Wrappers. No statement of printing on copyright page. Edited by Wollheim.

Avon Science-Fiction Reader No. 3. *New York: Avon Novels, Inc., [1952]*.
Wrappers. No statement of printing on copyright page. Edited by Wollheim.

*Avon Western Reader No. 3. *New York: Avon Publishing Co., Inc., [1947]*.
Wrappers. No statement of printing on copyright page. Edited by Wollheim.

*Avon Western Reader No. 4. *New York: Avon Publishing Co., Inc., [1947]*.
Wrappers. No statement of printing on copyright page. Edited by Wollheim.

The Best From the Rest of the World: European Science Fiction. *Garden City: Doubleday & Company, Inc., 1976*.
Boards. First edition so stated on copyright page. Edited, with introduction, by Wollheim.

The DAW Science Fiction Reader. *New York: DAW Books, Inc., [1976]*.
Wrappers. *First printing, July 1976/1 2 3 4 5 6 7 8 9* on copyright page. *DAW: sf Books No. 200 UW1242* ($1.50). Edited, with notes, by Wollheim.

The Earth in Peril. *New York: Ace Books, [1957]*.
Wrappers. No statement of printing on copyright page. *Ace Double Novel Books D–205* (35¢). Edited by Wollheim. Bound with WHO SPEAKS OF CONQUEST? by Lan Wright.

The End of the World. *New York: Ace Books, [1956]*.
Wrappers. No statement of printing on copyright page. *Ace Books S–183* (25¢). Edited by Wollheim.

Every Boy's Book of Science-Fiction. *New York: Frederick Fell, Inc., Publishers, [1951]*.
First printing so stated on copyright page. Edited, with introduction, by Wollheim.

Flight Into Space. *New York: Frederick Fell, Inc., [1950]*.
First printing so stated on copyright page. Compiled by Wollheim.

The Fox Woman & Other Stories, by A. Merritt. *New York: Avon Publishing Company, Inc., [1949]*.
Wrappers. No statement of printing on copyright page. *Avon 214* (25¢). Edited, with note, by Wollheim. Note: Wollheim is not credited on the title page as editor but his "Editor's Note" on page [3] is signed "D. A. W."

Giant Mystery Reader. *New York: Avon Publishing Co., Inc., [1951]*.
Wrappers. No statement of printing on copyright page. *Avon Double Size Books G–1004* (50¢). Anonymously edited by Wollheim.

The Girl With the Hungry Eyes and Other Stories. *New York: Avon Publishing Co., Inc., [1949]*.
Wrappers. No statement of printing on copyright page. *Avon 184* (35¢). Anonymously edited by Wollheim.

A Hell of a Good Time and Other Stories, by James T. Farrell. *New York: Avon Publishing Co., Inc., [1950]*.
Wrappers. No statement of printing on copyright page. *Avon Pocket-Size Books 252* (25¢). Anonymously edited by Wollheim. Note: A later printing of this collection issued in 1952 (Avon 468) provides the following printing history: *1st Printing. . .April, 1948. . ./2nd Printing. . .June, 1950. . ./3rd Printing. . .September, 1952. . .* on copyright page. The 1948 printing has not been located. The 1950 printing is the earliest listed by R. Reginald in *Cumulative Paperback Index 1939-1959* and cited by Wollheim. Avon book advertisements prior to 1950 do not list this title.

The Hidden Planet. *New York: Ace Books, Inc.*, [*1959*].
  Wrappers. No statement of printing on copyright page. *Ace Book D–354* (35¢). Edited, with introduction, by Wollheim.

Hollywood Bedside Reader. *New York: Avon Publishing Co., Inc.*, [*1951*].
  Wrappers. No statement of printing on copyright page. *Avon Pocket Size Books 338* (25¢). Anonymously edited by Wollheim.

*Let's Go Naked. *New York: Pyramid Books*, [*1952*].
  Wrappers. *Pyramid Books 62* (25¢). Edited by Wollheim.

The Macabre Reader, *New York: Ace Books, Inc.*, [*1959*].
  Wrappers. No statement of printing on copyright page. *Ace Book D–353* (35¢). Edited by Wollheim.

Men on the Moon. *New York: Ace Books, Inc.*, [*1958*].
  Wrappers. No statement of printing on copyright page. *Ace Double Novel Books D–277* (35¢). Edited, with introduction, by Wollheim. Bound with CITY ON THE MOON by Murray Leinster.

More Adventures on Other Planets. *New York: Ace Books, Inc.*, [*1963*].
  Wrappers. No statement of printing on copyright page. *Ace Book F–178* (40¢). Edited, with introduction, by Wollheim.

More Macabre. *New York: Ace Books, Inc.*, [*1961*].
  Wrappers. No statement of printing on copyright page. *Ace D–508* (35¢). Edited by Wollheim.

More Terror in the Modern Vein. *London: Brown, Watson Limited*, [*1961*].
  Wrappers. *First U.K. publication* on copyright page. *Digit Books R508* (2'6). Edited by Wollheim. Abridged reprint. Collects seven of the seventeen stories published in the U.S. edition of *Terror in the Modern Vein*.

The 1972 Annual World's Best SF. *New York: DAW Books, Inc.*, [*1972*].
  Wrappers. No statement of printing on copyright page. *DAW: sf Books No. 5 UQ1005–95* (95¢). Edited, with introduction and notes, by Wollheim. With ARTHUR W. SAHA. Note: A later printing bears the statement *First printing, May, 1972* on copyright page. DAW Books did not place printing statements on the copyright page prior to 1973. Reissued as *Wollheim's World's Best SF: Series One*.

  ALSO: *New York: DAW Books, Inc.*, [*1972*]. Boards. No statement of printing on copyright page. Code *45 N* on page [301]. First hardcover edition. Note: Issued by the Science Fiction Book Club.

The 1973 Annual World's Best SF. *New York: DAW Books, Inc.*, [*1973*].
  Wrappers. *First printing, May 1973/1 2 3 4 5 6 7 8 9* on copyright page. *DAW: sf Books No. 53 UQ1053* (95¢). Edited, with introduction and notes, by Wollheim. With ARTHUR W. SAHA.

  ALSO: *New York: DAW Books, Inc.*, [*1973*]. Boards. No statement of printing on copyright page. Code *O25* on page 273. First hardcover edition. Note: Issued by the Science Fiction Book Club.

The 1974 Annual World's Best SF. *New York: DAW Books, Inc.*, [*1974*].
  Wrappers. *First printing, May 1974/1 2 3 4 5 6 7 8 9* on copyright page. *DAW: sf Books No. 101 UY1109* ($1.25). Edited, with introduction and notes, by Wollheim. With ARTHUR W. SAHA. Issued later in Great Britain as *The World's Best SF Short Stories No. 1*.

552   Wollheim

ALSO: *New York: DAW Books, Inc.*, [*1974*]. Boards. Two printings, priority as listed: (A) Code *E 33* on page 244; (B) Code *37 R* on page 241. No statement of printing on copyright page. First hardcover edition. Note: Issued by the Science Fiction Book Club.

The 1975 Annual World's Best SF. *New York: DAW Books, Inc.*, [*1975*]. Wrappers. *First printing, May 1975/1 2 3 4 5 6 7 8 9* on copyright page. *DAW: sf Books No. 148 UW1170* ($1.50). Edited, with introduction, by Wollheim. With ARTHUR W. SAHA. Issued later in Great Britain as *The World's Best SF Short Stories No. 2*.

ALSO:*New York: DAW Books, Inc.*, [*1975*]. Boards. No statement of printing on copyright page. Code *Q30* on page 277. First hardcover edition. Note: Issued by the Science Fiction Book Club.

The 1976 Annual World's Best SF. *New York: DAW Books, Inc.*, [*1976*]. Wrappers. *First printing, May 1976/1 2 3 4 5 6 7 8 9* on copyright page. *DAW: sf Books No. 192 UW1232* ($1.50). Edited, with introduction, by Wollheim. With ARTHUR W. SAHA.

ALSO: *New York: DAW Books, Inc.*, [*1976*]. Boards. Two printings, priority as listed: (A) Code *R26* on page 276; (B) Code *R44* on page 276. No statement of printing on copyright page. First hardcover edition. Note: Issued by the Science Fiction Book Club.

The 1977 Annual World's Best SF. *New York: DAW Books, Inc.*, [*1977*]. Wrappers. *First printing, May 1977/1 2 3 4 5 6 7 8 9* on copyright page. *DAW: sf Books No. 240 UE1297* ($1.75). Edited, with introduction and notes, by Wollheim. With ARTHUR W. SAHA.

ALSO:*New York: DAW Books, Inc.*, [*1977*]. Boards. No statement of printing on copyright page. Code *H 44* on page 278. First hardcover edition. Note: Issued by the Science Fiction Book Club.

Operation Phantasy: The Best From The Phantagraph. *Rego Park, New York: The Phantagraph Press, 1967*. First edition so stated on copyright page. 420 numbered copies. Edited, with introduction, by Wollheim.

The Pocket Book of Science-Fiction. *New York: Pocket Books Inc.*, [*1943*]. Wrappers. *1st printing . . . March 1943* on copyright page. *Pocket Books 214* (25¢). Edited, wih introduction, by Wollheim.

The Portable Novels of Science. *New York: The Viking Press, 1945*. *September 1945* on copyright page. Compiled, with introduction and prefaces, by Wollheim.

Prize Science Fiction. *New York: The McBride Company*, [*1953*]. Boards. First edition so stated on copyright page. Edited, with introduction, by Wollheim. Issued later in Great Britain as *Prize Stories of Space and Time*.

Prize Stories of Space and Time. *London: Weidenfeld & Nicolson*, [*1953*]. Boards. *First published in Britain 1953* on copyright page. Edited, with introduction, by Wollheim. Issued earlier in the U.S. as *Prize Science Fiction*.

A Quintet of Sixes. *New York: Ace Publishing Corporation*, [*1969*]. Wrappers. No statement of printing on copyright page. *Ace Book 70000* (60¢). Edited, with introduction, by Wollheim.

The 2nd Avon Fantasy Reader. [*New York*]: *An Avon Book*, [*1969*]. Wrappers. *First Avon Printing, February, 1969* on copyright page. *Avon S385* (60¢). Edited by Wollheim with GEORGE ERNSBERGER.

Swordsmen in the Sky. *New York: Ace Books, Inc.*, [*1964*].
  Wrappers. No statement of printing on copyright page. *Ace Book F–311* (40¢). Edited by
  Wollheim.

Tales of Outer Space. *New York: Ace Books, Inc.*, [*1954*].
  Wrappers. No statement of printing on copyright page. *Ace Double Books D–73* (35¢).
  Edited by Wollheim. Bound with *Adventures in the Far Future*, edited by Wollheim.

Terror in the Modern Vein. *Garden City: Hanover House*, [*1955*].
  First edition so stated on copyright page. Edited, with introduction and notes, by
  Wollheim.

  ALSO:*London: Brown, Watson Limited*, [*1961*]. Wrappers. *First U.K. publication* on
  copyright page. *Digit Books R460* (2'6). Abridged collection. Eight of the seventeen
  stories collected in the U.S. edition.

Trilogy of the Future. *London: Sidgwick & Jackson*, [*1972*].
  Boards. *First published in Great Britain 1972* on copyright page. Edited, with introduction
  and notes, by Wollheim. Issued earlier in the U.S. as *Ace Science Fiction Reader*.

The Ultimate Invader and Other Science-Fiction. *New York: Ace Books, Inc.*, [*1954*].
  Wrappers. No statement of printing on copyright page. *Ace Double Novel Books D–44*
  (35¢). Edited by Wollheim. Bound with SENTINELS OF SPACE by Eric Frank Russell.

Where the Girls Were Different and Other Stories, by Erskine Caldwell. *New York: Avon
Book Co., Inc.*, [*1948*].
  Wrappers. No statement of printing on copyright page. *Avon 151* (25¢). Anonymously
  edited by Wollheim.

Wollheim's World's Best SF: Series One. *New York: DAW Books, Inc.*, [*1977*].
  Wrappers. *First Printing, May, 1972/4 5 6 7 8 9 10 11 12* [i.e., fourth printing, December
  1977] on copyright page. *DAW: sf Books UE1349* ($1.75). Edited, with introduction and
  notes, by Wollheim. With ARTHUR W. SAHA. Note: Originally issued as *The 1972 Annual
  World's Best SF*, the fourth printing is the first to bear the new title.

World's Best Science Fiction 1965. *New York: Ace Books, Inc.*, [*1965*].
  Wrappers. No statement of printing on copyright page. *Ace Books G–551* (50¢). Edited,
  with introduction, by Wollheim. With TERRY CARR.

World's Best Science Fiction 1966. *New York: Ace Books, Inc.*, [*1966*].
  Wrappers. No statement of printing on copyright page. *Ace Book H–15* (60¢). Edited, with
  introduction, by Wollheim. With TERRY CARR.

World's Best Science Fiction: 1967. *New York: Ace Books Inc.*, [*1967*].
  Wrappers. No statement of printing on copyright page. *Ace Book A–10* (75¢). Edited, with
  introduction, by Wollheim. With TERRY CARR.

World's Best Science Fiction 1968. *New York: Ace Books Inc.*, [*1968*].
  Wrappers. No statement of printing on copyright page. *An Ace Book A–15* (75¢). Edited,
  with introduction, by Wollheim. With TERRY CARR.

  ALSO:*London: Victor Gollancz Ltd, 1969*. Boards. No statement of printing on copyright
  page. First hardcover edition.

World's Best Science Fiction 1969. *New York: An Ace Book*, [*1969*].
  Wrappers. No statement of printing on copyright page. *Ace Book 91352* (95¢). Edited,
  with introduction and notes, by Wollheim. With TERRY CARR.

ALSO:*New York: An Ace Book*, [*1969*]. Boards. No statement of printing on copyright page. Code *28 K* on page 379. First hardcover edition. Note: Issued by the Science Fiction Book Club.

World's Best Science Fiction 1970. *New York: An Ace Book* [*1970*].
Wrappers. No statement of printing on copyright page. *Ace Book 91357* (95¢). Edited, with introduction and notes, by Wollheim. With TERRY CARR.

ALSO:*New York: An Ace Book*, [*1970*]. Boards. No statement of printing on copyright page. Code *31 L* on page 337. First hardcover edition. Note: Issued by the Science Fiction Book Club.

World's Best Science Fiction 1971. *New York: Ace Books*, [*1971*].
Wrappers. No statement of printing on copyright page. *Ace Book 91358* (95¢). Edited, with introduction and notes, by Wollheim. With TERRY CARR.

ALSO:*New York: An Ace Book*, [*1971*]. Boards. No statement of printing on copyright page. Code *31 M* on page 367. First hardcover edition. Note: Issued by the Science Fiction Book Club.

The World's Best SF Short Stories No. 1. [*Morley*]: *The Elmfield Press*, [*1975*].
Boards. *Published 1975 . . .* on copyright page. Edited, with introduction and notes, by Wollheim. With ARTHUR W. SAHA. Issued earlier in the U.S. as *The 1974 Annual World's Best SF*.

The World's Best SF Short Stories No. 2. [*Morley*]: *The Elmfield Press*, [*1976*].
Boards. *Published 1976 . . .* on copyright page. Edited, with introduction, by Wollheim. With ARTHUR W. SAHA. Issued earlier in the U.S. as *The 1975 Annual World's Best SF*.

Yesterday's Love and Eleven Other Stories, by James T. Farrell. *New York: Avon Book Co., Inc.*, [*1948*].
Wrappers. No statement of printing on copyright page. *Avon 157* (25¢). Anonymously edited by Wollheim.

Yvette and Other Stories, by Guy de Maupassant. *New York: Avon Publishing Co., Inc.*, [*1949*].
Wrappers. *Avon Reprint Edition* on copyright page. *Avon 198* (25¢). Anonymously compiled and edited by Wollheim.

Nonfiction (Dealing with the Fantasy Genre only)

The Universe Makers. *New York, Evanston, and London: Harper & Row, Publishers*, [*1971*].
Boards with Cloth shelf back. First edition so stated on copyright page.

Wayne Woodard
(1914–1964)

BEYOND THE GOLDEN STAIR.*New York: Ballantine Books*, [*1970*].
Wrappers. *First Printing: November, 1970* on copyright page. *Ballantine Books 02093–6–095* (95¢). *Hannes Bok, pseudonym*.

THE BLACK WHEEL.*New York: New Collectors' Group, 1947.*
Two bindings, priority as listed: (A) Title set in three lines on front cover *THE/BLACK/WHEEL*. Issued in plain white paper dust jacket. (B) Title set in one line. Issued in a printed yellow paper dust jacket. Note: This state comprises sheets bound by fantasy collector/dealer Julius Unger. First edition so stated on copyright page. Limited to 1000 numbered copies. This fantasy by A. Merritt was completed by Woodard. *Hannes Bok, pseudonym*. Notes: (1) Observed with and without cancel copyright notice on copyright page. (2) Although stated limitation was 1000 copies, more were printed. Unnumbered copies have been observed.

THE FOX WOMAN/THE BLUE PAGODA.*New York: New Collectors Group, 1946.*
Two bindings, priority as listed: (A) Tight weave mesh (nearly smooth) black cloth. Issued in plain paper dust jacket. (B) Glossy pebbled black cloth. Issued without dust jacket. Two states, simultaneous issue: (A) Illustration on page [19] depicting nude woman; (B) Illustration on page [19] depicting nude man. First edition so stated on copyright page. Contains ''The Fox Woman,'' a fantasy by A. Merritt completed by Woodard, and Woodard's short story ''The Blue Pagoda.'' *Hannes Bok, pseudonym*. Notes: (1) Although stated limitation was 1000 copies, more were printed. Unnumbered copies have been observed and in some cases booksellers numbered them. (2) It is possible that part of the edition was never bound. A number of sets of gathered and padded sheets lacking cloth casing have been observed.

THE SORCERER'S SHIP.*New York: Ballantine Books*, [*1969*].
Wrappers. *First Ballantine Books edition: December, 1969* on copyright page. *Ballantine Books 01795* (95¢). *Hannes Bok, pseudonym*.

Reference

And Flights of Angels: The Life and Legend of Hannes Bok, by Emil Petaja and Others. *San Francisco: Published by The Bokanalia Memorial Foundation*. [*1968*].
Wrappers with spiral plastic spine. No statement of printing on copyright page. Includes a biography by Petaja, memoirs by friends and associates, and checklists of his published art and writings. Note: 10 copies were later bound in black cloth and issued without dust jacket. These were signed on the title page by Petaja.

Bok A Tribute . . . , by Gerry de la Ree and Others. *Saddle River, N.J.: Published by Gerry de la Ree, 1974.*
Two bindings, no priority: (A) Cloth. 75 numbered copies. (B) Wrappers. 500 numbered copies. First edition so stated on copyright page.

A Hannes Bok Sketchbook, edited by Gerry de la Ree and Gene Nigra. *Saddle River, N.J.: Published by Gerry de la Ree, 1976.*
Wrappers. No statement of printing on copyright page. 1000 copies printed. Includes memoir ''Remembering Hannes'' by de la Ree.

Interim Hannes Bok Illustration Index, by Ned Brooks. *Newport News, Virginia: A Purple Mouth Press Publication, Summer, 1967.*
    Wrappers. No statement of printing. Spirit duplication, stapled. Cover title.

Hannes Bok Illustration Index, compiled by Ned Brooks and Don Martin for the Collectors Bureau of the National Fantasy Fan Federation. *Newport News, Virginia: National Fantasy Fan Federation, cop. 1970.*
    Wrappers. No statement of printing. Offset, stapled. Cover title.

Revised Hannes Bok Checklist, [edited by C. W. Brooks]. *[Baltimore: T–K Graphics, 1973.]*
    Wrappers. *This second edition was completed in December, 1973* on page [2]. A revision of *Hannes Bok Illustration Index.* Note: This source should be consulted for listings of art portfolios and books by others containing Woodard's illustrations.

Austin Tappan Wright
(1883–1931)

ISLANDIA. *New York • Toronto: Farrar & Rinehart • Inc, [1942]*.
  First printing has F&R monogram on copyright page.

Reference

An Introduction to Islandia its History, Customs, Laws, Language, and Geography as
Prepared by Basil Davenport. . . . *Toronto • New York: Farrar & Rinehart, Inc., [1942]*.
  Boards. No statement of printing. Cover title. Note: This promotional book was not issued
  with title page.

The Islandian World of Austin Wright, [by] Lawrence Clark Powell. [*Los Angeles: Printed
. . . under the direction of Horace F. Turner, 1957.*]
  Self wrappers. No statement of printing. Cover title.

Sydney Fowler Wright
(1874–1965)

THE ADVENTURE OF THE BLUE ROOM.*London: New York: Melbourne: Sydney: Rich & Cowan, [1945].*
No statement of printing on copyright page. *Sydney Fowler, pseudonym.*

THE ADVENTURE OF WYNDHAM SMITH.*London: Herbert Jenkins Limited, [1938].*
First printing 1938 on copyright page.

THE AMPHIBIANS.*London: The Merton Press, Ltd., [1925].*
No statement of printing on copyright page. Errata slip laid in. Comprises book I of THE WORLD BELOW. Note: Second edition issued in March 1926 has a preface by the author not printed in first edition.

ARRESTING DELIA.*London: Jarrolds Publishers, [1933].*
First published in Great Britain January 1933 on copyright page. *Sydney Fowler, pseudonym.*

THE ATTIC MURDER.*London: Thornton Butterworth Ltd, [1936].*
First published . . . 1936 on copyright page. *Sydney Fowler, pseudonym.*

THE BELL STREET MURDERS.*London Bombay Sydney: George G. Harrap & Co. Ltd., [1931].*
First published 1931 on copyright page. *Sydney Fowler, pseudonym.*

BEYOND THE RIM.*London: Jarrolds Publishers, [1932].*
First published in Great Britain July 1932 on copyright page.

A BOUT WITH THE MILDEW GANG.*London: Eyre and Spottiswoode, 1941.*
No statement of printing on copyright page. *Sydney Fowler, pseudonym.*

BY SATURDAY.*London: John Lane The Bodley Head Ltd., [1931].*
First Published in 1931 on copyright page. *Sydney Fowler, pseudonym.*

THE CASE OF ANNE BICKERTON. *[New York]: Albert & Charles Boni, 1930.*
No statement of printing on copyright page. Boni device (Pan with pipes) on copyright page. Issued earlier in Great Britain under the Sydney Fowler pseudonym as THE KING AGAINST ANNE BICKERTON and later as REX V. ANNE BICKERTON.

CRIME & CO.*New York: The Macaulay Company, [1931].*
No statement of printing on copyright page. Published later in Great Britain under the Sydney Fowler pseudonym as THE HAND-PRINT MYSTERY.

DAVID.*London: Thornton Butterworth, Ltd., [1934].*
First Published – – – –1934 on copyright page.

DAWN.*New York: Cosmopolitan Book Corporation, MCMXXIX.*
First edition so stated on copyright page.

DELUGE.*London: Fowler Wright Ltd, 1927.*
No statement of printing on copyright page.

DINNER IN NEW YORK. *London: Eyre and Spottiswoode, 1943.*
No statement of printing on copyright page. *Sydney Fowler, pseudonym.*

DREAM OR THE SIMIAN MAID. *London Bombay Sydney: George G. Harrap & Co. Ltd.,*
[1931].
First published 1931 on copyright page.

ELFWIN. *London Bombay Sydney: George G. Harrap & Co. Ltd., [1930].*
First published in 1930 on copyright page.

*THE END OF THE MILDEW GANG. *London: Eyre and Spottiswoode, 1944.*
Sydney Fowler, pseudonym.

FOUR CALLERS IN RAZOR STREET. *London: Herbert Jenkins Limited, [1937].*
First printing 1937 on copyright page. *Sydney Fowler, pseudonym.*

FOUR DAYS WAR. *London: Robert Hale & Company, [1936].*
First published 1936 on copyright page.

THE HAND-PRINT MYSTERY. *London: Jarrolds Publishers, [1932].*
No statement of printing on copyright page. *Sydney Fowler, pseudonym.* Issued earlier in
the U.S. as CRIME & CO.

THE HANGING OF CONSTANCE HILLIER. *London: Jarrolds Publishers, [1931].*
No statement of printing on copyright page. *Sydney Fowler, pseudonym.*

THE HIDDEN TRIBE. *London: Robert Hale & Company, [1938].*
Two bindings, priority as listed: (A) Black cloth, spine lettered in yellow; (B) Green cloth
lettered in black (not seen). No statement of printing on copyright page.

THE ISLAND OF CAPTAIN SPARROW. *London: Victor Gollancz, Ltd, 1928.*
No statement of printing on copyright page.

THE JORDANS MURDER. *London: Herbert Jenkins Limited, [1938].*
First printing 1938 on copyright page. *Sydney Fowler, pseudonym.*

ALSO:*London and Manchester: Withy Grove Press Limited, [1941].*
Wrappers. No statement of printing on copyright page. *Cherry Tree Book No. 153.*
Abridged text.

JUSTICE & THE RAT. *London: Published by Books of Today Ltd., n.d. [ca. 1945?]*
Wrappers. No statement of printing. *Two Famous Stories* at head of title. Reprint. Both
stories appeared earlier in THE NEW GODS LEAD.

THE KING AGAINST ANNE BICKERTON. *London Bombay Sydney: George G. Harrap & Co.*
Ltd., [1930].
First published 1930 on copyright page. *Sydney Fowler, pseudonym.* Published later
in the U.S. as THE CASE OF ANNE BICKERTON and later in Great Britain as REX V. ANNE
BICKERTON.

LORD'S RIGHT IN LANGUEDOC. *London: Jarrolds Publishers, [1933].*
First published in Great Britain, May 1933 on copyright page.

MEGIDDO'S RIDGE. *London: Robert Hale Limited, [1937].*
First published in Great Britain, 1937 on copyright page.

THE MURDER IN BETHNAL SQUARE. *London: Herbert Jenkins Limited, [1938].*
First printing 1938 on copyright page. *Sydney Fowler, pseudonym.*

THE NEW GODS LEAD.*London: Jarrolds Publishers*, [*1932*].
First Published—*April 1932* on copyright page. Enlarged edition issued later in the U.S. as
THE THRONE OF SATURN.

ORDEAL OF BARATA.*London: Herbert Jenkins Limited*, [*1939*].
First printing 1939 on copyright page.

POST-MORTEM EVIDENCE.*London: Thornton Butterworth Ltd.*, [*1936*].
First Published . . . 1936 on copyright page. *Sydney Fowler, pseudonym*.

POWER.*London: Jarrolds Publishers*, [*1933*].
No statement of printing on copyright page.

ALSO:*London and Manchester: Withy Grove Press Limited*, [*1939*]. Wrappers. No statement of printing on copyright page. *A Bay Tree Book No. 2*. Abridged text.

PRELUDE IN PRAGUE A STORY OF THE WAR OF 1938.*London: George Newnes, Limited*,
[*1935*].
No statement of printing on copyright page. Issued later in the U.S. as THE WAR OF 1938.

RED IKE.*London: Hutchinson & Co. (Publishers) Ltd.*, [*1931*].
No statement of printing on copyright page. With J. M. DENWOOD. Issued later in the U.S.
as UNDER THE BRUTCHSTONE.

REX V. ANNE BICKERTON.*Harmondsworth, Middlesex: Penguin Books*, [*1947*].
Wrappers. *Published in Penguin Books 1947* on copyright page. *Penguin 585* (1/–). Issued
earlier in Great Britain as THE KING AGAINST ANNE BICKERTON and in the U.S. as THE
CASE OF ANNE BICKERTON.

THE RISSOLE MYSTERY.*London: Rich & Cowan, Ltd.*, [*1941*].
No statement of printing on copyright page. *Sydney Fowler, pseudonym*.

THE SCREAMING LAKE. *London: Robert Hale & Company*, [*1939*].
Two bindings, priority as listed: (A) Black cloth, spine lettered in yellow (not seen).
(B) Green cloth, spine lettered in black. No statement of printing on copyright page.

SECOND BOUT WITH THE MILDEW GANG.*London: Eyre and Spottiswoode, 1942*.
No statement of printing on copyright page. *Sydney Fowler, pseudonym*.

THE SECRET OF THE SCREEN.*London: Jarrolds Publishers*, [*1933*].
First published in Great Britain, July 1933 on copyright page. *Sydney Fowler, pseudonym*.

SEVEN THOUSAND IN ISRAEL.*London: Jarrolds Publishers*, [*1931*].
No statement of printing on copyright page.

THE SIEGE OF MALTA.*London: Frederick Muller Ltd.*, [*1942*].
Two volumes. *First published . . . in 1942* on copyright pages.

SPIDERS' WAR.*New York: Abelard Press*, [*1954*].
Boards. No statement of printing on copyright page.

THREE WITNESSES.*London: Thornton Butterworth, Ltd.*, [*1935*].
First Published – – – –1935 on copyright page. *Sydney Fowler, pseudonym*.

THE THRONE OF SATURN.*Sauk City: Arkham House: Publishers, 1949*.
No statement of printing on copyright page. Includes the contents of THE NEW GODS LEAD
plus two stories, ''The Temperature of Gehenna Sue'' and ''Original Sin,'' first collected
here.

TOO MUCH FOR MR. JELLIPOT. *London: Eyre & Spottiswoode, 1945.*
First published in 1945 on copyright page. *Sydney Fowler, pseudonym.*

TWO FAMOUS STORIES. See JUSTICE & THE RAT.

UNDER THE BRUTCHSTONE. *New York: Published . . . by Coward-McCann, Inc., 1931.*
No statement of printing on copyright page. With J. M. DENWOOD. Issued earlier in Great
Britain as RED IKE.

VENGEANCE OF GWA. *London: Thornton Butterworth, Ltd, [1935].*
First published 1935 on copyright page. *Anthony Wingrave, pseudonym.*

THE WAR OF 1938. *New York: G. P. Putnam's Sons, [1936].*
No statement of printing on copyright page. Issued earlier in Great Britain as PRELUDE IN
PRAGUE A STORY OF THE WAR OF 1938.

WAS MURDER DONE? *London: Thornton Butterworth Ltd, [1936].*
First published . . . 1936 on copyright page. *Sydney Fowler, pseudonym.*

WHO ELSE BUT SHE? *London: Jarrolds Publishers, [1934].*
First published in Great Britain September, 1934 on copyright page. *Sydney Fowler,
pseudonym.*

WHO MURDERED REYNARD? *London :: New York :: Melbourne :: Sydney :: Cape Town:
Rich & Cowan, [1947].*
No statement of printing on copyright page. *Sydney Fowler, pseudonym.*

THE WILLS OF JANE KANWHISTLE. *London: Herbert Jenkins Limited, [1939].*
First printing 1939 on copyright page. *Sydney Fowler, pseudonym.*

THE WITCHFINDER. *London: Books of Today Limited, [1945].*
No statement of printing on copyright page.

WITH CAUSE ENOUGH? *London: The Harvill Press, [1954].*
Boards. *Published . . . 1954* on copyright page. *Sydney Fowler, pseudonym.*

THE WORLD BELOW. *London Glasgow Sydney Auckland: W. Collins Sons & Co Ltd, [1929].*
No statement of printing on copyright page. Note: Book I issued in 1925 as THE AMPHIB-
IANS. Book II appears for the first time.

ALSO: *New York: Longmans, Green and Co., 1930.* First edition so stated on copyright
page. Adds preface dated "New York, January 15, 1930" which did not appear in the
British edition.

Adaptation

The Last Days of Pompeii, by Lord Lytton. A Redaction by S. Fowler Wright. *[London]:
Vision, [1948].*
No statement of printing on copyright page. Adapted by Wright.

Translation

Marguerite de Valois Newly Rendered from Alexander Dumas, by S. Fowler Wright.
London: C. & J. Temple, Ltd., [1947].
Boards. No statement of printing on copyright page. Translated and adapted by Wright.

Philip Gordon Wylie

(1902–1971)

AFTER WORLDS COLLIDE. *New York: Frederick A. Stokes Company, MCMXXXIV.*
No statement of printing on copyright page. With EDWIN BALMER.

THE ANSWER. *New York Toronto: Rinehart & Company, Inc., [1955].*
Boards. First printing has Rinehart monogram on copyright page.

AN APRIL AFTERNOON. *New York Toronto: Farrar & Rinehart Incorporated, [1938].*
First printing has F&R monogram on copyright page.

AS THEY REVELED. *New York: Farrar & Rinehart Incorporated, [1936].*
First printing has F&R monogram on copyright page.

AUTUMN ROMANCE. *New York: Lancer Books, [1965].*
Wrappers. *A Lancer Book • 1965* on copyright page. *Lancer Books 72–981* (50¢). All
stories reprinted from earlier books.

BABES AND SUCKLINGS. *New York & London: Alfred A. Knopf, 1929.*
No statement of printing on copyright page. Reissued as THE PARTY (publisher and date of
publication unknown).

THE BEST OF CRUNCH AND DES. *New York Toronto: Rinehart & Company, Inc., [1954].*
Boards with cloth shelf back. First printing has Rinehart monogram on copyright page.
Stories reprinted from earlier books.

ALSO: *Greenwich, Conn.: Fawcett Publications, Inc., [1958].*
Wrappers. *First CREST printing, September 1958* on copyright page. *Crest Book s240*
(35¢). Abridged reprint.

THE BIG ONES GET AWAY! *New York Toronto: Farrar & Rinehart, Inc., [1940].*
First printing has F&R monogram on copyright page.

BLONDY'S BOY FRIEND. *New York: Chelsea House, [1930].*
No statement of printing on copyright page. *Leatrice Homesley, pseudonym.*

CORPSES AT INDIAN STONES. *New York Toronto: Farrar & Rinehart, Inc., [1943].*
First printing has F&R monogram on copyright page.

CRUNCH AND DES STORIES OF FLORIDA FISHING. *New York Toronto: Rinehart & Company,
Incorporated, [1948].*
First printing has Rinehart monogram on copyright page.

*DANGER MANSION. *Los Angeles: Bantam Publications, [1941].*
Wrappers. *BPLA 27* (10¢).

THE DISAPPEARANCE. *New York: Rinehart & Co., Inc., [1951].*
Boards with cloth shelf back. First printing has Rinehart monogram on copyright page.

THE END OF THE DREAM. *Garden City: Doubleday & Company, Inc., 1972.*
First edition so stated on copyright page.

EXPERIMENT IN CRIME. *New York: Avon Publications Inc.*, [*1956*].
Wrappers. No statement of printing on copyright page. *Avon 711* (25¢). Reprint. Collected earlier in THREE TO BE READ.

FINNLEY WREN. *New York: Farrar & Rinehart, 1934.*
First printing has F&R monogram on copyright page.

FISH AND TIN FISH CRUNCH AND DES STRIKE BACK. *Toronto • New York: Farrar & Rinehart, Inc.*, [*1944*].
First printing has F&R monogram on copyright page.

FIVE FATAL WORDS. *New York: Ray Long & Richard R. Smith, Inc., 1932.*
No statement of printing on copyright page. With EDWIN BALMER.

FOOTPRINT OF CINDERELLA. *New York: Farrar & Rinehart Incorporated*, [*1931*].
First printing has F&R monogram on copyright page. Reissued as 9 RITTENHOUSE SQUARE.

GLADIATOR. *New York: Alfred A. Knopf, 1930.*
No statement of printing on copyright page.

THE GOLDEN HOARD. *New York: Frederick A. Stokes Company, MCMXXXIV.*
No statement of printing on copyright page. With EDWIN BALMER.

HEAVY LADEN. *New York: Alfred A. Knopf, 1928.*
No statement of printing on copyright page.

LOS ANGELES: A. D. 2017. *New York: Popular Library*, [*1971*].
Wrappers. No statement of printing on copyright page. *Popular Library 445-00272-095* (95¢).

THE MURDERER INVISIBLE. *New York: Farrar & Rinehart Incorporated Publishers*, [*1931*].
First printing has F&R monogram on copyright page.

NIGHT UNTO NIGHT. *New York Toronto: Farrar & Rinehart, Inc.*, [*1944*].
First printing has F&R monogram on copyright page.

9 RITTENHOUSE SQUARE. *New York: Popular Library*, [*1964?*].
Wrappers. No statement of printing on copyright page. *Popular Library 60-2138* (60¢). Reissue of THE FOOTPRINT OF CINDERELLA.

OPUS 21. *New York and Toronto: Rinehart & Company, Inc.*, [*1949*].
First printing has Rinehart monogram on copyright page.

THE OTHER HORSEMAN. *New York Toronto: Farrar & Rinehart, Inc.*, [*1942*].
First printing has F&R monogram on copyright page.

THE PARTY. See BABES AND SUCKLINGS.

*A RESOURCEFUL LADY. *New York: Popular Library*, [*1966*].
Wrappers.

SALT WATER DAFFY. *New York Toronto: Farrar and Rinehart, Inc.*, [*1941*].
First printing has F&R monogram on copyright page.

*THE SAVAGE GENTLEMAN. *New York: Farrar and Rinehart, 1932.*

SELECTED SHORT STORIES OF PHILIP WYLIE. *New York: Editions for the Armed Services, Inc.*, [*1946*].
>Wrappers. No statement of printing. *Armed Services Edition S–8*. Stories reprinted from earlier books.

THE SHIELD OF SILENCE. *New York: Frederick A. Stokes Company, MCMXXXVI*.
>No statement of printing on copyright page. With EDWIN BALMER.

THE SMUGGLED ATOM BOMB. *New York: Avon Publications*, [*1956*].
>Wrappers. No statement of printing on copyright page. *Avon 727* (25¢). Reprint. Collected earlier in THREE TO BE READ.

THE SPY WHO SPOKE PORPOISE. *Garden City: Doubleday & Company, Inc.*, *1969*.
>First edition so stated on copyright page.

THEY WERE BOTH NAKED. *Garden City: Doubleday & Company, Inc.*, *1965*.
>First edition so stated on copyright page.

THREE TO BE READ. *New York Toronto: Rinehart & Co., Inc.*, [*1952*].
>First printing has Rinehart monogram on copyright page.

TOMORROW! *New York Toronto: Rinehart & Company, Inc.*, [*1954*].
>Boards with cloth shelf back. First printing has Rinehart monogram on copyright page.

TOO MUCH OF EVERYTHING. *New York: Farrar & Rinehart Incorporated Publishers*, [*1936*].
>First printing has F&R monogram on copyright page.

TREASURE CRUISE AND OTHER CRUNCH AND DES STORIES. *New York ★ Toronto: Rinehart & Company, Inc.*, [*1956*].
>Boards with cloth shelf back. First printing has Rinehart monogram on copyright page.

TRIUMPH. *Garden City: Doubleday & Company, Inc.*, *1963*.
>First edition so stated on copyright page.

WHEN WORLDS COLLIDE. *New York: Frederick A. Stokes Company, 1933*.
>No statement of printing on copyright page. With EDWIN BALMER. Note: First printing bound in red cloth with pale blue stamping. Later printing statements do not appear on copyright pages of subsequent printings but do appear on dust jacket flaps.

Reference

Philip Wyle, by Truman Frederick Keefer. *Boston: Twayne Publishers*, [*1977*].
>First printing so stated on copyright page. Note: Issued without dust jacket.

Christopher Samuel Youd

(b. 1922)

BABEL ITSELF.*London: Cassell and Company Limited*, [*1951*].
  First published 1951 on copyright page. *Samuel Youd* on title page.

BELLA ON THE ROOF. [*London*]: *Longmans*, [*1965*].
  Boards. *First published 1965* on copyright page. *Hilary Ford, pseudonym*.

BEYOND THE BURNING LANDS.*London: Hamish Hamilton*, [*1971*].
  Boards. *First published in Great Britain 1971* on copyright page. *John Christopher, pseudonym*.

BRAVE CONQUERORS.*London: Cassell & Company Ltd*, [*1952*].
  Boards. *First published 1952* on copyright page. *Samuel Youd* on title page.

A BRIDE FOR BEDIVERE.*London: Hamish Hamilton*, [*1976*].
  Boards. *First published in Great Britain 1976* on copyright page. *Hilary Ford, pseudonym*.

THE BURNING BIRD. [*London*]: *Longmans*, [*1964*].
  Boards. *This edition first published 1964* on copyright page. *Samuel Youd* on title page.
  Issued earlier in the U.S. as THE CHOICE.

CASTLE MALINDINE.*London: Hamish Hamilton*, [*1975*].
  Boards. *First published in Great Britain 1975 . . .* on copyright page. *Hilary Ford, pseudonym*.

THE CAVES OF NIGHT.*New York: Simon and Schuster*, *1958*.
  Half cloth and boards. First printing so stated on copyright page. *John Christopher, pseudonym*.

THE CHOICE.*New York: Simon and Schuster*, *1961*.
  Boards. First printing so stated on copyright page. *Samuel Youd* on title page. Issued later in Great Britain as THE BURNING BIRD.

THE CITY OF GOLD AND LEAD. [*London*]: *Hamish Hamilton*, [*1967*].
  Boards. *First published in Great Britain 1967* on copyright page. *John Christopher, pseudonym*.

  *ALSO: [*London*]: *Longman*, [*1974*]. Wrappers. *This edition first published 1974* on copyright page. *Longman Structural Readers: Fiction/Stage 5* at head of title. Text abridged and simplified by A. G. Eyre.

CLOUD ON SILVER. [*London*]: *Hodder and Stoughton*, [*1964*].
  Boards. *First printed 1964* on copyright page. *John Christopher, pseudonym*. Issued earlier in the U.S. as SWEENEY'S ISLAND.

CROWN AND ANCHOR.*London: Cassell & Company Ltd*, [*1953*].
  Boards. *First published 1953* on copyright page. *Samuel Youd* on title page.

DAUGHTER FAIR.*London: Michael Joseph*, [*1958*].
  Boards. *First published . . . 1958* on copyright page. *Peter Graaf, pseudonym*.

THE DEATH OF GRASS. *London: Michael Joseph,* [*1956*].
  Boards. *First published . . . 1956* on copyright page. *John Christopher, pseudonym.* Issued later in the U.S. as NO BLADE OF GRASS.

DOM AND VA. *London: Hamish Hamilton,* [*1973*].
  Boards. *First published in Great Britain 1973* on copyright page. *John Christopher, pseudonym.* Rewritten from IN THE BEGINNING.

DUST AND THE CURIOUS BOY. *London: Michael Joseph,* [*1957*].
  Boards. *First published . . . 1957* on copyright page. *Peter Graaf, pseudonym.* Issued later the same year in the U.S. as GIVE THE DEVIL HIS DUE.

EMPTY WORLD. *London: Hamish Hamilton,* [*1977*].
  Boards. *First published in 1977 . . .* on copyright page. *John Christopher, pseudonym.*

FELIX RUNNING. *London: Eyre & Spottiswoode Ltd, 1959.*
  Boards. *First published 1959* on copyright page. *Hilary Ford, pseudonym.*

FELIX WALKING. *London: Eyre & Spottiswoode Ltd, 1958.*
  Boards. *First published 1958* on copyright page. *Hilary Ford, pseudonym.*

*FIGURE IN GREY. *Kingswood: The World's Work, Ltd, 1973.*
  Hilary Ford, pseudonym.

THE FRIENDLY GAME. *London: Michael Joseph,* [*1957*].
  Boards. *First published . . . 1957* on copyright page. *William Godfrey, pseudonym.*

GIANT'S ARROW. *London: Victor Gollancz Ltd, 1956.*
  Boards. No statement of printing on copyright page. *Anthony Rye, pseudonym.* Note: Published in the U.S. in 1960 by Simon and Schuster as by Samuel Youd.

GIVE THE DEVIL HIS DUE. *New York: M.S. Mill Co. and William Morrow & Co., 1957.*
  Boards. No statement of printing on copyright page. *Peter Graaf, pseudonym.* Issued earlier in Great Britain as DUST AND THE CURIOUS BOY.

THE GUARDIANS. [*London*]: *Hamish Hamilton,* [*1970*].
  Boards. *First published in Great Britain 1970* on copyright page. *John Christopher, pseudonym.*

THE GULL'S KISS. *London: Peter Davies,* [*1962*].
  Boards. *First published 1962* on copyright page. *Peter Graaf, pseudonym.*

HOLLY ASH. *London: Cassell & Company Ltd,* [*1955*].
  Boards. *First published 1955* on copyright page. *Samuel Youd* on title page. Issued later in the U.S. as THE OPPORTUNIST.

*IN THE BEGINNING. [*London*]: *Longman,* [*1972*].
  Wrappers. *First published 1972* on copyright page. *Longman Structural Readers: Fiction/Stage 2* at head of title. *John Christopher, pseudonym.* Note: This 2000-word fiction rewritten as DOM AND VA.

THE LITTLE PEOPLE. *New York: Simon and Schuster,* [*1966*].
  First printing so stated on copyright page. *John Christopher, pseudonym.*

THE LONG VOYAGE. *London: Eyre & Spottiswoode,* [*1960*].
  Boards. *First published 1960 . . .* on copyright page. *John Christopher, pseudonym.* Issued later in the U.S. as THE WHITE VOYAGE.

THE LONG WINTER. *New York: Simon and Schuster, 1962.*
Boards with cloth shelf back. First printing so stated on copyright page. *John Christopher, pseudonym.* Issued earlier (?) in Great Britain as THE WORLD IN WINTER.

THE LOTUS CAVES. *[London]: Hamish Hamilton, [1969].*
Boards. *First published in Great Britain 1969* on copyright page. *John Christopher, pseudonym.*

MALLESON AT MELBOURNE. *London: Museum Press, [1956].*
Boards. *First published in Great Britain . . . 1956* on copyright page. *William Godfrey, pseudonym.*

MESSAGES OF LOVE. *New York: Simon and Schuster, 1961.*
First printing so stated on copyright page. *Samuel Youd* on title page.

NO BLADE OF GRASS. *New York: Simon and Schuster, [1957].*
Boards with cloth shelf back. First printing so stated on copyright page. *John Christopher, pseudonym.* Issued earlier in Great Britain as THE DEATH OF GRASS.

THE OPPORTUNIST. *New York: Harper & Brothers Publishers, [1957].*
Boards with cloth shelf back. First edition so stated on copyright page. *Samuel Youd* on title page. Issued earlier in Great Britain as HOLLY ASH.

PALACE OF STRANGERS. *London: Cassell & Company Ltd, [1954].*
Boards. *First published 1954* on copyright page. *Samuel Youd* on title page.

*PATCHWORK OF DEATH. *New York, Chicago, San Francisco: Holt, Rinehart and Winston, [1965].*
Peter Nichols, pseudonym.

PENDULUM. *New York: Simon and Schuster, [1968].*
First printing so stated on copyright page. *John Christopher, pseudonym.*

PLANET IN PERIL. *New York: Avon Book Division, [1959].*
Wrappers. No statement of printing on copyright page. *Avon T371* (35¢). *John Christopher, pseudonym.* Issued earlier in Great Britain as THE YEAR OF THE COMET.

THE POOL OF FIRE. *[London]: Hamish Hamilton, [1968].*
Boards. *First published in Great Britain 1968 . . .* on copyright page. *John Christopher, pseudonym.*

ALSO: *[London]: Longman, [1974].* Wrappers. *This edition first published 1974* on copyright page. *Longman Structural Readers: Fiction/Stage 6* at head of title. Text abridged and simplified by A. G. Eyre.

THE POSSESSORS. *New York: Simon and Schuster, [1964].*
First printing so stated on copyright page. *John Christopher, pseudonym.*

THE PRINCE IN WAITING. *London: Hamish Hamilton, [1970].*
Boards. *First published in Great Britain 1970* on copyright page. *John Christopher, pseudonym.*

THE RAGGED EDGE. *New York: Simon and Schuster, [1966].*
First printing so stated on copyright page. *John Christopher, pseudonym.* Issued earlier in Great Britain as A WRINKLE IN THE SKIN.

SAPPHIRE CONFERENCE. *London: Michael Joseph, [1959].*
Boards. *First published . . . 1959* on copyright page. *Peter Graaf, pseudonym.*

SARNIA.*London: Hamish Hamilton*, [*1974*].
Boards. *First published in Great Britain 1974* on copyright page. *Hilary Ford, pseudonym.*

A SCENT OF WHITE POPPIES.*New York: Simon and Schuster, 1959*.
Boards. First printing so stated on copyright page.*John Christopher, pseudonym.*

THE SUMMERS AT ACCORN. [*London*]: *Longmans*, [*1963*].
Boards. *First published 1963* on copyright page. *Samuel Youd* on title page.

SWEENEY'S ISLAND.*New York: Simon and Schuster, 1964*.
Boards with cloth shelf back. First printing so stated on copyright page.*John Christopher, pseudonym.* Issued later in Great Britain as CLOUD ON SILVER.

THE SWORD OF THE SPIRITS.*London: Hamish Hamilton*, [*1972*].
Boards. *First published in Great Britain 1972* on copyright page. *John Christopher, pseudonym.*

THE TWENTY-SECOND CENTURY. [*London*]: *Grayson & Grayson Ltd.*, [*1954*].
Boards. *First published in volume form, 1954* on copyright page. *John Christopher, pseudonym.*

THE WHITE MOUNTAINS. [*London*]: *Hamish Hamilton*, [*1967*].
Boards. *First published in Great Britain 1967* on copyright page. *John Christopher, pseudonym.*

*ALSO: [*London*]: *Longman*, [*1974*]. Wrappers. *This edition first published 1974* on copyright page. *Longman Structural Readers: Fiction/Stage 4* at head of title. Text simplified and abridged by A. G. Eyre.

THE WHITE VOYAGE. [*New York*]: *Simon and Schuster, 1961*.
Boards with cloth shelf back. First printing so stated on copyright page.*John Christopher, pseudonym.* Issued earlier in Great Britain as THE LONG VOYAGE.

WILD JACK.*New York: Macmillan Publishing Co., Inc.*, [*1974*].
First printing has code *1 2 3 4 5 6 7 8 9 10* on copyright page.*John Christopher, pseudonym.*

*ALSO: [*London*]: *Longman*, [*1974*]. Wrappers. *This edition first published 1974* on copyright page. *Longman Structural Readers: Fiction/Stage 5* at head of title. Note: Although published later, this novelette was the earlier version, later expanded to novel length.

THE WINTER SWAN.*London: Dennis Dobson Ltd*, [*1949*].
First published in Great Britain in MCMXLIX . . . on copyright page. *Christopher Youd* on title page.

THE WORLD IN WINTER.*London: Eyre & Spottiswoode, 1962*.
Boards. *First published in 1962* on copyright page. *John Christopher, pseudonym.* Issued later (?) in the U.S. as THE LONG WINTER.

A WRINKLE IN THE SKIN. [*London*]: *Hodder and Stoughton*, [*1965*].
Boards. *First printed 1965* on copyright page.*John Christopher, pseudonym.* Issued later in the U.S. as THE RAGGED EDGE.

THE YEAR OF THE COMET.*London: Michael Joseph*, [*1955*].
Boards. *First published . . . 1955* on copyright page.*John Christopher, pseudonym.* Issued later in the U.S. as PLANET IN PERIL.

Robert Franklin Young

(b. 1915)

A GLASS OF STARS. *Jacksonville, Illinois: Harris-Wolfe & Co., Publishers, [1968]*.
No statement of printing on copyright page.

THE WORLDS OF ROBERT F. YOUNG. *New York: Simon and Schuster, [1965]*.
Boards with cloth shelf back. First printing so stated on copyright page.

Roger Joseph Zelazny
(b. 1937)

BRIDGE OF ASHES. [*New York*]: *New American Library*, [*1976*].
Wrappers. *First Signet Printing, July, 1976/1 2 3 4 5 6 7 8 9* on copyright page. *Signet Y7080* ($1.25).

CREATURES OF LIGHT AND DARKNESS. *Garden City: Doubleday & Company, Inc., 1969*.
First edition so stated on copyright page.

DAMNATION ALLEY. *New York: G. P. Putnam's Sons,* [*1969*].
Boards. No statement of printing on copyright page.

DEUS IRAE. *Garden City: Doubleday & Company, Inc., 1976*.
Boards. First edition so stated on copyright page. With PHILIP K. DICK.

THE DOORS OF HIS FACE, THE LAMPS OF HIS MOUTH. *Garden City: Doubleday & Company, Inc., 1971*.
First edition so stated on copyright page.

DOORWAYS IN THE SAND. *New York Hagerstown San Francisco London: Harper & Row, Publishers,* [*1976*].
Boards with cloth shelf back. First edition so stated on copyright page.

THE DREAM MASTER. *New York: Ace Books, Inc:,* [*1966*].
Wrappers. No statement of printing on copyright page. *Ace Book F–403* (40¢).

ALSO: *London: Rupert Hart-Davis, 1968*. Boards. *First published in Great Britain 1968* on copyright page. First hardcover edition.

FOUR FOR TOMORROW. *New York: Ace Books, Inc.,* [*1967*].
Wrappers. No statement of printing on copyright page. *Ace Book M–155* (45¢). Issued later in Great Britain as A ROSE FOR ECCLESIASTES.

ALSO: [*New York & London: Garland Publishing, Inc., 1975.*] First U.S. hardcover edition. Notes: (1) Photo-offset from 1973 Ace Books second printing. (2) Not issued in dust jacket.

THE GUNS OF AVALON. *Garden City: Doubleday & Company, Inc., 1972*.
First edition so stated on copyright page.

THE HAND OF OBERON. *Garden City: Doubleday & Company, Inc., 1976*.
Boards. First edition so stated on copyright page.

ISLE OF THE DEAD. *New York: Ace Books, Inc.,* [*1969*].
Wrappers. No statement of printing on copyright page. *An Ace Science Fiction Special 37465* (60¢).

ALSO: [*London*]: *A Rapp and Whiting Book, Andre Deutsch,* [*1970*]. Boards. *First published 1970* on copyright page. First hardcover edition.

JACK OF SHADOWS. *New York: Walker and Company,* [*1971*].
Boards. *First published in the United States of America in 1971* on copyright page.

LORD OF LIGHT. *Garden City: Doubleday & Company, Inc., 1967.*
First edition so stated on copyright page.

MY NAME IS LEGION. *New York: Ballantine Books,* [*1976*].
Wrappers. *First edition: April, 1976* on copyright page. *Ballantine Books SF 24867* ($1.50).

NINE PRINCES IN AMBER. *Garden City: Doubleday & Company, Inc., 1970.*
First edition so stated on copyright page.

A ROSE FOR ECCLESIASTES. *London: Rupert Hart-Davis, 1969.*
Boards. *First published in Great Britain 1969* on copyright page. Issued earlier in the U.S. as FOUR FOR TOMORROW.

SIGN OF THE UNICORN. *Garden City: Doubleday & Company, Inc., 1975.*
Boards. First edition so stated on copyright page.

THIS IMMORTAL. *New York: Ace Books, Inc.,* [*1966*].
Wrappers. No statement of printing on copyright page. *Ace Book F–393* (40¢).

ALSO: *London: Rupert Hart-Davis, 1967.* Boards. *First published in Great Britain 1967* on copyright page. First hardcover edition.

TO DIE IN ITALBAR. *Garden City: Doubleday & Company, Inc., 1973.*
First edition so stated on copyright page.

TODAY WE CHOOSE FACES. [*New York*]: *New American Library,* [*1973*].
Wrappers. *First printing, April, 1973* on copyright page. Below the statement *All rights reserved* appears *First Printing* [through] *Tenth Printing* set on ten lines. *Signet 451–Q5435* (95¢).

ALSO: [*London*]: *Millington,* [*1974*]. Boards. *First published 1974 . . .* on copyright page. First hardcover edition.

Edited Fiction

Nebula Award Stories Three. *Garden City: Doubleday & Company, Inc., 1968.*
First edition so stated on copyright page. Edited, with introduction and afterword by Zelazny.